Global Land Grabbing and Political Reactions 'from Below'

When the 2007–2008 food and financial crises triggered a global wave of land grabbing, scholars, activists and policy practitioners assumed that this would be met with massive peasant resistance. As empirical evidence accumulated, however, it became clear that political reactions 'from below' to land grabbing were quite varied and complex. Violent resistance, outright expulsions, everyday 'weapons of the weak' and demands for better terms of incorporation into land deals were among the outcomes that emerged. Readers of this collection will encounter a multinational group of scholars who use the tools of social movements theory and critical agrarian studies to examine cases from Argentina, Mexico, Guatemala, Nicaragua, Colombia, Ethiopia, Madagascar, Mozambique, Uganda, Mali, Ukraine, India, and Laos, as well as the Rio +20 Sustainable Development Conference. Initiatives 'from below' in response to land deals have involved local and transnational alliances and the use of legal and extra-legal methods, and have brought victories and defeats. This book was first published as a special issue of *The Journal of Peasant Studies*.

Marc Edelman is professor of anthropology at Hunter College, USA, and the Graduate Center of the City University of New York, USA. His books include *The logic of the latifundio* (1992), *Peasants against globalization* (1999), *The anthropology of development and globalization* (co-edited 2005), *Social democracy in the global periphery* (co-authored 2007), *Transnational agrarian movements confronting globalization* (co-edited 2008), *Global land grabs: history, theory and method* (co-edited 2015), *and Political Dynamics of Transnational Agrarian Movements* (co-authored 2016).

Ruth Hall is an associate professor at the Institute for Poverty, Land and Agrarian Studies (PLAAS) at the University of the Western Cape, South Africa, and holds a DPhil in politics from the University of Oxford, UK. Her research focuses on land and agrarian reform in South Africa, and she also does research on land rights, agricultural commercialization and 'land grabbing' in Africa. She is a founding member and co-convenor of the Land Deal Politics Initiative and the BRICS Initiative in Critical Agrarian Studies, and is the coordinator of the Future Agricultures Consortium's work on land in Africa and coordinator of its regional hub for Southern Africa.

Saturnino M. Borras Jr. is a professor of agrarian studies at the International Institute of Social Studies (ISS) in The Hague, the Netherlands, an adjunct professor at China Agricultural University in Beijing, and a fellow of the Amsterdam-based Transnational Institute (TNI) and of the California-based Institute for Food and Development Policy (Food First). He is a founding member and co-convenor of the Land Deal Politics Initiative.

Ian Scoones is a professorial fellow at the Institute of Development Studies at the University of Sussex, UK, and Director of the ESRC STEPS Centre, UK. He works on land, agricultural and agrarian and environmental change in Africa. He is a founding member and co-convenor of the Land Deal Politics Initiative.

Ben White is an emeritus professor of rural sociology at the International Institute of Social Studies (ISS) in The Hague, the Netherlands. His research has focused mainly on processes of agrarian change and the anthropology and history of childhood and youth. He has been engaged in research on these issues in Indonesia since the early 1970s.

Wendy Wolford is Polson Professor of Development Sociology at Cornell University, USA. Her research interests include the political economy of development, social movements, land distribution, agricultural knowledge and the politics of land management. She is a founding member and co-convenor of the Land Deal Politics Initiative and a member of the editorial collective of the Journal of Peasant Studies.

Critical Agrarian Studies

Series Editor: *Saturnino M. Borras Jr.*

Critical Agrarian Studies is the new accompanying book series to *The Journal of Peasant Studies*. It publishes selected special issues of the journal and, occasionally, books that offer major contributions in the field of critical agrarian studies. The book series builds on the long and rich history of the journal and its former accompanying book series, the Library of Peasant Studies (1973–2008) which had published several important monographs and special-issues-as-books.

For a full list of books in this series please visit https://www.routledge.com/Critical-Agrarian-Studies/book-series/CAG.

Recent titles in this series include:

An Endogenous Theory of Property Rights
Edited by Peter Ho

Global Land Grabbing and Political Reactions 'from Below'
Edited by Marc Edelman, Ruth Hall, by Saturnino M. Borras Jr, Ian Scoones and Wendy Wolford

Critical Perspectives in Rural Development Studies
Edited by Saturnino M. Borras Jr.

The Politics of Biofuels, Land and Agrarian Change
Edited by Saturnino M. Borras Jr., Philip McMichael and Ian Scoones

New Frontiers of Land Control
Edited by Nancy Lee Peluso and Christian Lund

Outcomes of Post-2000 Fast Track Land Reform in Zimbabwe
Edited by Lionel Cliffe, Jocelyn Alexander, Ben Cousins and Rudo Gaidzanwa

Green Grabbing: A New Appropriation of Nature
Edited by James Fairhead, Melissa Leach and Ian Scoones

The New Enclosures: Critical Perspectives on Corporate Land Deals
Edited by Ben White, Saturnino M. Borras Jnr., Ruth Hall, Ian Scoones and Wendy Wolford

Rural Politics in Contemporary China
Edited by Emily T. Yeh, Kevin O'Brien and Jingzhong Ye

Global Land Grabbing and Political Reactions 'from Below'

Edited by
Marc Edelman, Ruth Hall, Saturnino M. Borras Jr., Ian Scoones, Ben White and Wendy Wolford

Routledge
Taylor & Francis Group
LONDON AND NEW YORK

First published 2018
by Routledge

2 Park Square, Milton Park, Abingdon, Oxfordshire OX14 4RN
52 Vanderbilt Avenue, New York, NY 10017

Routledge is an imprint of the Taylor & Francis Group, an informa business

First issued in paperback 2019

British Library Cataloguing in Publication Data
A catalogue record for this book is available from the British Library

ISBN 13: 978-1-138-08237-3 (hbk)
ISBN 13: 978-0-367-23492-8 (pbk)

Typeset in Times New Roman
by RefineCatch Limited, Bungay, Suffolk

Publisher's Note
The publisher accepts responsibility for any inconsistencies that may have arisen during the conversion of this book from journal articles to book chapters, namely the possible inclusion of journal terminology.

Contents

Citation Information

The chapters in this book were originally published in *The Journal of Peasant Studies*, volume 42, issue 3–4 (May – July 2015). When citing this material, please use the original page numbering for each article, as follows:

Chapter 1

Resistance, acquiescence or incorporation? An introduction to land grabbing and political reactions 'from below'
Ruth Hall, Marc Edelman, Saturnino M. Borras Jr., Ian Scoones, Ben White and Wendy Wolford
The Journal of Peasant Studies, volume 42, issue 3–4 (May – July 2015) pp. 467–488

Chapter 2

Anything but a story foretold: multiple politics of resistance to the agrarian extractivist project in Guatemala
Alberto Alonso-Fradejas
The Journal of Peasant Studies, volume 42, issue 3–4 (May – July 2015) pp. 489–516

Chapter 3

Listening to their silence? The political reaction of affected communities to large-scale land acquisitions: insights from Ethiopia
Tsegaye Moreda
The Journal of Peasant Studies, volume 42, issue 3–4 (May – July 2015) pp. 517–540

Chapter 4

Land grabbing, legal contention and institutional change in Colombia
Jacobo Grajales
The Journal of Peasant Studies, volume 42, issue 3–4 (May – July 2015) pp. 541–560

Chapter 5

Resistance or participation? Fighting against corporate land access amid political uncertainty in Madagascar
Mathilde Gingembre
The Journal of Peasant Studies, volume 42, issue 3–4 (May – July 2015) pp. 561–584

Chapter 6
Policy processes of a land grab: at the interface of politics 'in the air' and politics 'on the ground' in Massingir, Mozambique
Jessica Milgroom
The Journal of Peasant Studies, volume 42, issue 3–4 (May – July 2015) pp. 585–606

Chapter 7
Resistance or adaptation? Ukrainian peasants' responses to large-scale land acquisitions
Natalia Mamonova
The Journal of Peasant Studies, volume 42, issue 3–4 (May – July 2015) pp. 607–634

Chapter 8
Politics from below? Small-, mid- and large-scale land dispossession in Teso, Uganda, and the relevance of scale
Matt Kandel
The Journal of Peasant Studies, volume 42, issue 3–4 (May – July 2015) pp. 635–652

Chapter 9
Social struggles in Uganda's Acholiland: understanding responses and resistance to Amuru sugar works
Giuliano Martiniello
The Journal of Peasant Studies, volume 42, issue 3–4 (May – July 2015) pp. 653–670

Chapter 10
Territorial restructuring and resistance in Argentina
Zoe W. Brent
The Journal of Peasant Studies, volume 42, issue 3–4 (May – July 2015) pp. 671–694

Chapter 11
Networked, rooted and territorial: green grabbing and resistance in Chiapas
Dianne E. Rocheleau
The Journal of Peasant Studies, volume 42, issue 3–4 (May – July 2015) pp. 695–724

Chapter 12
Guerrilla agriculture? A biopolitical guide to illicit cultivation within an IUCN Category II protected area
Connor Joseph Cavanagh and Tor A. Benjaminsen
The Journal of Peasant Studies, volume 42, issue 3–4 (May – July 2015) pp. 725–746

Chapter 13
Reclaiming the worker's property: control grabbing, farmworkers and the Las Tunas Accords in Nicaragua
Bradley R. Wilson
The Journal of Peasant Studies, volume 42, issue 3–4 (May – July 2015) pp. 747–764

Chapter 14

The 'Goan Impasse': land rights and resistance to SEZs in Goa, India
Preeti Sampat
The Journal of Peasant Studies, volume 42, issue 3–4 (May – July 2015) pp. 765–790

Chapter 15

Oil palm expansion without enclosure: smallholders and environmental narratives
Antonio Castellanos-Navarrete and Kees Jansen
The Journal of Peasant Studies, volume 42, issue 3–4 (May – July 2015) pp. 791–816

Chapter 16

Rubber, rights and resistance: the evolution of local struggles against a Chinese rubber concession in Northern Laos
Karen E. McAllister
The Journal of Peasant Studies, volume 42, issue 3–4 (May – July 2015) pp. 817–838

Chapter 17

Space for pluralism? Examining the Malibya land grab
Nicolette Larder
The Journal of Peasant Studies, volume 42, issue 3–4 (May – July 2015) pp. 839–858

Chapter 18

The right to resist: disciplining civil society at Rio+20
Catherine Corson, Bridget Brady, Ahdi Zuber, Julianna Lord and Angela Kim
The Journal of Peasant Studies, volume 42, issue 3–4 (May – July 2015) pp. 859–878

Notes on Contributors

Alberto Alonso-Fradejas is a PhD candidate at the International Institute of Social Studies (ISS) in the Netherlands.

Tor A. Benjaminsen is a human geographer and Professor in the Department of International Environment and Development Studies (Noragric), Norwegian University of Life Sciences.

Saturnino M. Borras Jr. is a professor of agrarian studies at the International Institute of Social Studies (ISS) in The Hague, the Netherlands.

Bridget Brady is recent graduate of Mount Holyoke College, USA, where she majored in environmental studies and sustainable development.

Zoe W. Brent is a PhD student at the Institute of Social Studies (ISS) in The Hague, the Netherlands, and a fellow at Food First, Institute of Food & Development Policy in Oakland, California, USA.

Antonio Castellanos-Navarrete is a researcher in the Knowledge, Technology and Innovation (KTI) Group at Wageningen University, the Netherlands.

Connor Joseph Cavanagh is a PhD Fellow in the Department of International Environment and Development Studies (Noragric), Norwegian University of Life Sciences.

Catherine Corson is an assistant professor of environmental studies at Mount Holyoke College, USA.

Marc Edelman is professor of anthropology at Hunter College, USA, and the Graduate Center of the City University of New York, USA.

Mathilde Gingembre is a PhD researcher at the Institute of Development Studies, University of Sussex, UK.

Jacobo Grajales is a junior lecturer (ATER) at Sciences Po Rennes, France, and an associate researcher at the Center for International Studies and Research (CERI), France.

Ruth Hall is an associate professor at the Institute for Poverty, Land and Agrarian Studies (PLAAS) at the University of the Western Cape, South Africa.

Kees Jansen is Associate Professor at KTI, Wageningen University, the Netherlands.

Matt Kandel is a British Academy Newton International Fellow in Development Studies at SOAS University of London.

Angela Kim is an analyst for business intelligence software at a healthcare consulting and technology firm based in Washington, DC, USA.

Nicolette Larder recently completed a PhD in the School of Social Sciences at the University of Queensland, Australia.

Julianna Lord currently works in clean technology at Next Step Living in Boston, USA.

Natalia Mamonova completed a PhD at the International Institute of Social Studies (ISS) of Erasmus University Rotterdam, the Netherlands in 2016.

Giuliano Martiniello is a research fellow at the Makerere Institute of Social Research, Makerere University, Uganda.

Karen E. McAllister is completing a doctorate in anthropology at McGill University in Montreal, Canada.

Jessica Milgroom completed an interdisciplinary PhD from Wageningen University, the Netherlands, in 2012.

Tsegaye Moreda is a PhD candidate at the International Institute of Social Studies (ISS) of Erasmus University Rotterdam in the Netherlands.

Dianne E. Rocheleau is a professor of geography and global environmental studies at Clark University, USA.

Preeti Sampat currently teaches in the Department of Sociology at Ambedkar University Delhi, India.

Ian Scoones is a professorial fellow at the Institute of Development Studies at the University of Sussex, UK, and Director of the ESRC STEPS Centre, UK.

Ben White is an emeritus professor of rural sociology at the International Institute of Social Studies (ISS) in The Hague, the Netherlands.

Bradley R. Wilson is an assistant professor of geography at West Virginia University, USA.

Wendy Wolford is Polson Professor of Development Sociology at Cornell University, USA.

Ahdi Zuber works with the United Nations Environment Programme Regional Office for North America.

Resistance, acquiescence or incorporation? An introduction to land grabbing and political reactions 'from below'

Ruth Hall, Marc Edelman, Saturnino M. Borras Jr., Ian Scoones, Ben White and Wendy Wolford

Political reactions 'from below' to global land grabbing have been vastly more varied and complex than is usually assumed. This essay introduces a collection of ground-breaking studies that discuss responses that range from various types of organized and everyday resistance to demands for incorporation or for better terms of incorporation into land deals. Initiatives 'from below' in response to land deals have involved local and transnational alliances and the use of legal and extra-legal methods, and have brought victories and defeats. The relevance of political reactions to land grabbing is discussed in light of theories of social movements and critical agrarian studies. Future research on reactions 'from below' to land grabbing must include greater attention to gender and generational differences in both impacts and political agency.

Introduction

Critical scholarly analysis of processes of agrarian change has long emphasized peasant agency and aimed to uncover forms of resistance, even in the midst of dispossession, oppression and processes of social differentiation. This collection draws on the rich base of existing scholarship to ask: in the midst of the 'global land grab', what are the political reactions 'from below'? While some reactions from people directly affected may involve resistance, the essays in this collection suggest that understanding the diversity of reactions from below requires critical empirical investigations of responses in specific situations. We thus frame 'political reactions from below' in a wider way, to refer to responses that extend far beyond 'resistance' in its many manifestations, and range from mobilizations seeking to improve the compensation for people's expulsion from their land to demands to be inserted into land deals as workers or contract farmers to counter-mobilizations against land deal resisters. Beyond the local level, highly varied responses by societies and states at national levels and in international multilateral fora and transnational movements also call for more detailed and critical assessment by social scientists.

In the midst of enclosures and commercialization of land and other natural resources across the global South, tensions and synergies mark political reactions 'from below' to global land grabbing. A fuller understanding of the politics from below around land grabs brings us to some classic concepts in critical agrarian studies, including the dual front of 'struggle against dispossession' and 'struggle against exploitation', as well as the question of the state. Yet even this classic political economy-based framing of people's struggles may not fully capture the range and complexity of the politics around contemporary enclosures where the ecological dimension has become increasingly prominent. But an important starting point is to draw on concepts and analytical tools in critical agrarian studies, such as *agrarian class politics* and *everyday forms of peasant resistance*. Analytical tools from *identity politics* will also be relevant in understanding politics from below around global land grabbing.

When land deals gain momentum, they trigger complex political dynamics – expected and unexpected, intended and unintended – within the state and in society. Early media reports, as well as activist and academic discussions, often assumed that land deals expel people from the land and that those expelled – typically referred to as 'local people' or 'local communities' – engage in 'resistance'. Recent research, however, indicates that what happens on the ground is more varied and complex (e.g. White et al. 2012; Wolford et al. 2013; Edelman, Oya, and Borras 2013). When land deals hit the ground, they interact with social groups within the state and in society that are differentiated along lines of class, gender, generation, ethnicity and nationality, and that have historically specific expectations, aspirations and traditions of struggle. These reshape, limit or make possible different kinds of land deals. As the contributions to this collection show, political debates and academic research have increasingly picked up *differentiated impacts* and *variegated political reactions* to land deals.

This collection addresses these questions and builds on a series of *Journal of Peasant Studies* (*JPS*) editions over the past five years that have interrogated the phenomenon of global land grabbing through the lens of critical agrarian studies. It brings together papers originally presented at the Global Land Grab II International Conference[1] organized by the Land Deal Politics Initiative (LDPI[2]). This follows a *JPS* Forum on Global Land Grabbing II which dealt with methodologies and the limits to existing approaches to enumerating, explaining and assessing the impacts of land deals (Scoones et al. 2013), and a *JPS* collection on *The New Enclosures: Critical Perspectives on Corporate Land Deals* (White et al. 2012) which drew together a broad spectrum of papers outlining the contours of the phenomenon, and which drew from the Global Land Grab I International Conference,[3] also organized by the LDPI. These in turn followed the first *JPS* Forum on Global Land Grabbing (Borras et al. 2011) which, ahead of the Global Land Grab I conference, outlined a research agenda for understanding the current land grab. This initial *JPS* collection of papers drew attention to the ways in which questions and approaches from within critical agrarian studies could help to systematize our knowledge and make sense both of the drivers of land grabbing and of the changes in agrarian economies and societies that land deals set in motion. The current collection aims to build on these contributions and to challenge dominant framings of rural and peasant communities across the global South as either passive victims or unified resisters of land grabs.

[1]The Global Land Grab II International Conference was held at Cornell University, 17–19 October 2012 (see http://www.cornell-landproject.org/program/).
[2]See the Land Deal Politics Initiative website (www.iss.nl/ldpi).
[3]The Global Land Grab I International Conference was held at the Institute for Development Studies at the University of Sussex, 4–6 April 2011 (http://www.future-agricultures.org/events/global-land-grabbing).

Explaining resistance and its absence

Three broad models for explaining resistance and its absence dominate the scholarly literature: classical collective action paradigms, Marxism and heterodox theories of social movements. First, in classical collective action paradigms, resistance is viewed as an exception, and inaction as the norm. The 'logic' of this position derives from premises central to neoclassical economics and rational choice theory, namely that individuals strategically weigh potential benefits and risks of particular courses of action and then proceed in their own self-interest. Because risks of collective resistance tend to be high – lost time, arrests, beatings and assassinations – the calculating individual will likely sit on the sidelines as a 'free rider', hoping to reap the gains of others' risk-taking and sacrifices. As Mancur Olson, the foundational theorist of this approach, argued, 'When the class-oriented action Marx predicted does not materialize, it does *not* indicate that the economic motivation is not predominant, as some of his critics imply, but rather than there are *no* individual economic *incentives* for class action' (Olson 1965, 108, original emphasis).

Second, Marxists (unlike Olson) have generally supposed that there is a direct line from shared grievances to collective action. While they acknowledge that some forms of resistance are individual, they tend to assume that common oppression gives rise to class politics and common political projects (Barker 2014). The Marxist canon is not, of course, entirely consistent on this issue, but its numerous lamentations about 'false consciousness', 'hegemony' or failure to recognize the collective's 'true' – i.e. proletarian – interests are suggestive of lingering Hegelian teleological influences in Marxism.

Third, heterodox social movement scholars have taken issue with both the figure of the rational, calculating *Homo economicus* in collective action theories and the Marxist presumption of oppression inexorably producing proletarian consciousness and collective struggle. Some have pointed out, for example, that the notion of 'free riders', and the 'collective action problems' that these supposedly produce, is based on a vision of the isolated individual, lacking in kin, class, ethnic, religious, national or group identities and loyalties. When scholars belatedly began to analyze the role of emotion in social movements, they naturally found that affective ties and allegiances to other movement participants were an essential ingredient in mobilization and frequently accounted for why people unite and struggle in the face of daunting risks and unfavourable odds (Goodwin, Jasper, and Polletta 2001). The Marxists' bemoaning of 'false consciousness', similarly, gets turned on its head by the more perspicacious social movements theorists. Burdick (1995, 367), for example, argues that as soon as analysts' gaze shifts from the 'individual toward collective patterns', it permits posing a 'highly constructive political question: not why do people fail to come to the movement, but why is the movement failing to reach more people?'.

Critical agrarian studies and particularly research on struggles around land have made important – albeit frequently implicit – contributions to this theoretical discussion. Both Marxists (e.g. Hobsbawm 1959) and social movements theorists (e.g. Tilly 1986) posited a historical periodization of protest that distinguished 'primitive', 'defensive' and 'pre-political' mobilizations from those in the nineteenth century and after that aimed at seizing or at least influencing the state. Peasants' 'failure' (for many Marxists) to manifest a proletarian consciousness in contention over land, or to transcend 'defensive' local struggles (for social movements theorists), became just one more indication of their atavistic politics and culture. When struggles for land are seen in their own terms, however, it is obvious that claiming land or defending the land one has often reflects clear class consciousness, albeit of a smallholding peasant rather than a proletarian character.

Of the papers in this collection, Natalia Mamonova's makes the most significant and original contribution to the discussion around the absence of resistance to land grabbing. In her analysis of contemporary Ukraine, now home to some of the largest farms in the world, Mamonova critiques the premises that resistance is the only or most likely response of rural people to large-scale land acquisitions, that peasants are incapable of adapting to or coexisting alongside large-scale industrial farms, and that 'ideological concerns about the "peasant way of life", food and land sovereignty dominate in peasant struggles'. As an alternative to these bedrock *a priori* assumptions of so much agrarian scholarship, she advocates analyzing the terms of inclusion in land deals (see also Borras and Franco 2013), distinguishing between 'illusive inclusion' (where peasants, many of them elderly, receive land from the state and then rent it to commercial farmers), 'subordinate inclusion' (where peasants rent or lose land and then go to work on large holdings) and 'competitive exclusion' (where peasant farms are outcompeted by subsidized agroindustrial enterprises). In all three cases, collectively patterned individual choices lead in directions other than oppositional mobilization.

The outcomes Mamonova describes do not fit easily in any of the three broad explanatory frameworks outlined above. Ukrainian peasants are not eschewing collective action because they hope, à la Olson, to free ride on others' coattails. They are hardly a Marxian class 'for itself' in any meaningful sense. They have not remained unorganized because existing movements have failed to reach them. Mamonova intentionally shuns explanations for the lack of mobilization against land grabbing that rely on the negative legacies of 70 years of socialism (e.g. memories of the collectivization of agriculture, which was especially brutal in Ukraine, or ongoing fears of political repression). Nonetheless, her argument relies on a historically-informed reading of the current moment. Rural people in Ukraine, she says, perceive today's large farms as a continuation of Soviet collective and state farms – and refer to them as '*kolkhozy*' and '*sovkhozy*', respectively. The weight of pre-existing class relations still looms large. Employment on large farms, with their relatively high salaries and social wage, combined with income from tiny intensively-cultivated private plots, appears to be a congenial alternative, familiar from Soviet times and preferable to unequal and quixotic struggles with uncertain outcomes.

Class and identity politics, mobilizations and alliances

Borras and Franco (2013) suggest that understanding political reactions 'from below' to land deals requires both locating the dynamics in broader agrarian transformation processes and analyzing a main axis of political conflict. Let us look at the first question. When the land is needed but labour is not, the most likely outcome is the expulsion of people from the land (Li 2011). Those expelled may find jobs in other sectors of the economy. When they do not, land grabs are implicated in the creation of a 'relative surplus population'. On occasions when investors need the land and the labour, peasants and villagers are not expelled, but may be subsumed into corporate enterprises as workers (perhaps even leasing their land to their employer) or as contracted small-scale farmers.

The second question involves the axis of political conflict. There are three main types: poor people versus corporate/landed elites, poor people versus the state and poor people versus poor people (Borras and Franco 2013; Borras, Franco, and Wang 2013). There are many high-profile instances where poor people confronted corporate and landed elites, such as the infamous case of Kampong Sugar in Cambodia (IDI 2014). Relatively more common is a confrontation between affected villagers and the state, which can take the form of organized national mobilizations by agrarian movements, such as occurred in the Philippines in 2006–2007 over the allocation of 1.4 million hectares of land to Chinese investors. The mobilizations in this case resulted in the cancellation of the investment agreements. Villager–state conflict may also take the form of 'everyday forms of peasant politics' or individual protests directed at the local state bureaucracy (Scott 1976); indeed, this is the most common form of land conflict in contemporary China (O'Brien and Li 2006). Probably the most frequent type of conflict is one that combines the first two: poor people versus corporate/landed elites and the state. This is not surprising, because the state is almost always implicated in the current land rush (Wolford et al. 2013). There is, however, the third axis: poor-on-poor conflict. From one land deal site to the next, we see social groups divided, not fully united, and with varied takes on engaging with land deals. While some may invoke the principle of free, prior and informed consent (FPIC) to justify opposition to a land deal, another group may use FPIC to justify their acceptance of and incorporation into it – a conflict usually instigated and fanned by those behind land deals (see Franco 2014). Poor-on-poor conflict is probably one of the most complex and sensitive dimensions of land deal-related conflict to research, especially for outsiders. The papers in this collection aim to redress this lacuna in the literature.

The two perspectives discussed above – the location of land deals in broader agrarian transformations and the axis of political conflicts – provide a clearer picture of what is actually happening on the ground, as several contributions to this collection illustrate. This framework also facilitates a critical examination of class and identity politics and of mobilizations and alliances for or against land deals. Such alliances – tactical or strategic – may link groups with a common objective that nonetheless have different or even competing class or other interests and ideological leanings. They may be alliances *against*, alliances *for* or alliances in the *struggles within* land deals. Typically, the boundaries between these three ideal types are porous and flexible, with individuals and groups changing positions all the time.

Social groups that were expelled or threatened with expulsion by land deals, or whose livelihoods are threatened more generally, do not automatically get organized and mount resistance. We know from classic literature on agrarian politics that there are triggers of and conditions for the emergence of these kinds of politics, and that the presence or absence of allies may be key to the kind of reaction that emerges 'from below'.[4] Probably most of those who suffer from 'unjust land deals' do not openly resist. Mamonova (2015) has demonstrated this in the case in contemporary Ukraine (see also Visser et al. 2012). More commonly, adversely-affected groups engage in 'everyday politics' – individual covert and unstructured forms of contention, as in the case of Ethiopia (see Moreda 2015). The 'rightful resistance' type of defiance characteristic of most recent Chinese land conflicts – i.e. individual, unorganized but noisy and overt protest (O'Brien and Li 2006) – may be gaining ground in places outside China, such as Vietnam (Kerkvliet 2014). Gingembre (2015), for example, analyzing local resistance to a land deal in Madagascar, highlights the role of an alliance that involved key state and non-state actors from local to international levels in the issue-analysis and demand-making processes among affected social groups. External allies often are elites themselves, such as legal experts who know both national and international laws and how these can be employed to reinforce subaltern claims, as in the Colombian case examined by Grajales (2015). In confronting the global land rush, local agrarian groups frequently find allies among the ranks of other social

[4]For competing explanations, see Popkin (1979) and Scott (1976), as well as Wolf (1966), Paige (1975) and Fox (1993).

justice movements, such as the labour, women's, environmental, food and human rights movements.

But not all mobilizations and alliances are against land deals. Sometimes social groups in local communities mobilize, seek allies and demand to be inserted *into* land deals. Larder (2015) shows that in the iconic case of the Malibya land deal in Mali, which involved at least 100,000 hectares, sectors of the local rice-farming population sought integration into the project. Similarly, in the case of the Ecofuel sugarcane investment in northern Philippines, which involves 11,000 hectares, a significant number of those affected have mobilized and forged alliances with local and national government agencies to participate in the enterprise by renting out their land or engaging in contract growing schemes, or as plantation workers (Franco, Carranza, and Fernandez 2011; Alano forthcoming).

Long histories of government neglect and a lack of alternative livelihood possibilities suggest institutional and structural bases for these efforts at incorporation. Typically, local communities that see no state support forthcoming are told that corporate investment is the only option for their livelihoods, whether this is explicit, as in the Philippines case, or not, as in the case of Mali. The subtle forms of coercion also have a clear class basis. The Philippine case involves poor peasants who do not have other livelihood alternatives and who welcomed the investment (Franco, Carranza, and Fernandez 2011) in direct opposition to other members of their community and their outside allies, who are opposed to the investment project (Alano, forthcoming). This is a classic poor-on-poor conflict around land deals, and it is not an isolated case. In many conflicts, smallholders whose subsistence is threatened by a land deal, absentee plot holders who gladly agree to lease land to investors, and landless and migrant workers rejoice at the entry of corporations that promise to provide employment. Obviously, class interest does not automatically translate into class politics.[5]

Moreover, class is not the only factor that shapes political contention from below. Other intersecting identities are equally important: gender, generation, ethnicity, race, caste, religion and nationality (Edelman 1999). Additional fissures may separate those with or without formal claims and those potentially entitled to land or not under particular laws (see Grajales 2015). This intersection brings both synergies (as we see alliances forged between peasants and indigenous peoples) and tension (as when divisions arise within and between peasant and indigenous communities) (see Brent 2015; Alonso-Fradejas 2015, and Fontana 2014).

Struggles around land deals are not just either for or against land deals. Important struggles by the working class are fought *within* land deals – to (re)negotiate the *terms of their incorporation* into the emerging enterprises, whether as workers (through labour justice demands) or as contracted small farmers (through agrarian justice or environmental justice demands). Few systematic studies have addressed this theme. Pye (2010), however, has noted the diversity among civil society groups working on the issue of palm oil, based on their distinct ideological and political locations within and between labour, agrarian and environmental justice movements. The Chikweti forestry project in the northern province of Niassa in Mozambique is an important case illustrating a complex response by local people to investments, which is neither for nor against land deals, but rather squarely in the category of struggles *within* land deals. Here, social groups in local communities are demanding more jobs within the enterprise alongside continued access to their plots for subsistence production (FIAN 2012). These situations raise difficult political dilemmas: when a

[5]For a general discussion with reference to India in the context of Green Revolution, see Byres (1981).

situation is acceptable in terms of labour justice, but not in terms of agrarian justice; when it is acceptable in terms of agrarian justice, but not in environmental justice terms, and so on (Borras and Franco 2012, 56–57). These dilemmas are partly manifestations of the intersection of class and identity, a theme central to this collection and addressed to varying extents by the different contributors.

Transnationalization and diffusion: responses from the local to global

Mobilizations around land deals are animated by a range of state and societal actors at different levels: local/subnational, national and international. At times, political contention arises from local social groups and their efforts to find international and national allies – whether against, for, or within land deals (see Gingembre 2015 on Madagascar). At other times, political campaigns originate among international groups and diffuse to local–national levels, as Corson et al. (2015) show in relation to alliances on climate justice. The *origin* of political contention is important because it tells us about the dominant framing of the issues and demands, while the *trajectory* is important as it may reveal the strategies and objectives of campaigns. Real-life politics, of course, are not as neat as we suggest here; real situations are probably more about the convergences and unique configurations of various actors seeking allies than assumptions about one-way internationalization or diffusion (see Edelman and Borras forthcoming).

Larder (2015) demonstrates how the difficult dilemmas outlined above can manifest in conflicting narratives and claims among civil society groups working on land grabbing issues. Concretely, she identifies a group of poor rice farmers mobilizing to be incorporated into the Malibya project who would never think about it as a 'land grab', while international social movement organizations claim it is an iconic land grabbing case and seek to stop and roll it back. These local and international groups described by Larder are both likely on solid moral ground – which is why such cases raise troubling political dilemmas and why there are competing interpretations of the same or similar cases. These interpretations frame divergent responses. International civil society organizations tend to demand land reform as the most appropriate response to land grabbing. While this overarching frame will gain political traction in societies marked by highly unequal distribution of access to and ownership of land, the same does not occur in communities with customary tenure or in pastoralist societies, as in much of Africa (Kandel 2015; see Borras, Franco, and Monsalve Suarez 2015 for a broader context).

Not all urgent land issues today are about 'land grabbing'. Pre-existing concentration is just as pervasive and compelling as the post-2007 enclosures. Some civil society groups mobilize around land issues, but not necessarily around current land grabs. The coming together of key civil society actors in a common campaign may not be as easy as activists might wish. One key centre of gravity in international agrarian justice campaigns today is the 'Peasants' Rights' process within the United Nations (UN) Human Rights Council (HRC). It is framed broadly and strategically, and not on the urgent and narrow issue of land grabs. The subjective forces behind the process are not all engaged in the anti-land grabbing campaigns, and vice versa – despite the fact that their campaigns are closely related (Edelman and James 2011).

Enclosures versus integration: dilemmas of adverse incorporation

The global land grab has been widely represented as an enclosure dispossessing local people – often peasant or family farmers – and privatizing and commodifying common property resources such as rangelands, water and forests. Yet land grabs are not all about displacement and expulsion. Since the term 'land grab' became mainstream shorthand denoting the corporate scramble for land and water, it has become apparent that much of what has been included under this rubric does not involve corporations taking direct control of land. Rather, as this collection shows, more complex processes are underway, with new value chains emerging, often as family farmers are induced to take up cash-crop production on contract for processing companies.

Discussing the centrality of labour in understanding land grabs and their effects, Li (2011) asked, 'What happens when the land is needed and the labour is not?' Here we need to invert the question: What happens when the land is needed *and* the labour is needed? In such contexts, capital tends to incorporate rather than exclude. Some have questioned the term 'land grab' in cases where farmers have been incorporated into corporate agribusiness, not only because accumulation proceeds without dispossession but also because peasants actively seek incorporation into new corporate value chains. Such processes may not involve 'enclosure' or 'accumulation by dispossession' (Harvey 2005). Yet, even in the absence of dispossession, the penetration of corporate capital into rural economies may nonetheless have profound impacts on class formation and commodity relations.

Why does dispossession not always occur? Reasons may include the existing tenure regime, state restrictions on the terms of corporate penetration, and the interests of companies seeking flexible investments and risk-sharing. In Chiapas, Mexico, as Castellanos-Navarrete and Jansen (2015) point out, the *ejido* system provided secure tenure for farmers and limited the expansion of oil palm companies, forcing them to engage with peasant farmers. Mamonova (2015) argues similarly that 'the way land tenure systems and informal markets work, the type of land investments, and the implementation of smallholder development schemes in villages are critical factors that influence the exclusion or inclusion of local people in land deals'.

The 'land grab' thus involves not only displacement of populations, but also the extension of value chains and corporate control over production and territories. The extension of domestic and global capital in controlling land and its uses might, drawing on Peluso and Lund (2011), be more accurately termed 'land control grabbing' rather than 'land grabbing' *per se*. The terms of inclusion are, as a result, crucial, and may be on more or less adverse terms. Peasant attitudes to land grabs, then, may be conditioned by the 'terms of inclusion' (McCarthy 2010). Central to understanding these processes is the concept of 'adverse incorporation' (Hickey and du Toit 2007) – in other words, the manner in which people may be incorporated into corporate agribusiness and even global value chains while simultaneously being excluded from processes of capital accumulation. The term 'adverse incorporation' itself draws attention to the exploitative character of such relations even where people seek inclusion in them, and so redirects attention to the structural transformations underway and their relationships to reactions and responses from below.

Such distinctions between enclosure and incorporation, specifically through contract farming, have been extensively documented and analyzed even outside and prior to the current land rush. In much of Africa, a long history of failed attempts at establishing large-scale commercial farming – through coercion as well as direct or indirect subsidies – has seen contract farming and outgrower schemes emerging as a key way in which peasants have been incorporated in circuits of capital accumulation (Little and Watts 1994; Oya 2012; Baglioni and Gibbon 2013). Contract farming is one solution to the problems of sourcing and disciplining labour while extending the territorial reach of corporate capital. Even in the absence of dispossession, such incorporation may produce social differentiation processes similar to those arising from enclosure and dispossession, as families with more resources and larger landholdings may be better able to reap the benefits of contract farming and emerge as medium- or large-scale producers, while others may enter into debt, may experience land loss and may or may not be incorporated as wage labour (Smalley 2013).

Land deals that start out as enclosures can also be transformed, sometimes in response to resistance, to incorporate rather than exclude local farmers. This is evident in the Malibya project, where resistance and bad publicity prompted state authorities to make some of the irrigated land in the new canal system available to local rice farmers (Larder 2015). Such efforts underscore the ways in which 'reformist' positions by farmers' associations and social movements may preserve or promote production by family farmers even while locating this within corporate agriculture (see Holt Giменéz and Shattuck 2011). Incorporation, even on less-than-adverse terms, does not challenge the overarching direction of agrarian change or the wider structures of capital within which it may be located. As Castellanos-Navarrete and Jansen (2015) emphasize, the 'overemphasis on enclosure limits our understanding of the ways capitalism impacts rural livelihoods and environments'. To deepen our understanding of the agrarian transformations underway, more analysis is needed about 'how and why rural people engage with capitalism'. Addressing the ways in which land deals incorporate local people – who, how, why and on what terms – can help us to understand what conditions responses, including resistance of various kinds as well as the absence of resistance, and so deepen our critical inquiry into the global land grab.

Engagements with the state

Scholarly and activist work on land grabbing initially had a Manichean perspective on the state. Nation-states were either 'target countries', too weak to defend their borders from the threat of foreign investment, or 'host countries', either directly sponsoring land grabs through state-owned enterprises or indirectly sponsoring them by providing infrastructure for accumulation. As scholars and activists alike grappled with the dynamic phenomenon of land grabbing across regions and historical periods, their research has proven the Manichean perspective to be problematic. Land grabbing has provided an impetus and opportunity for an increasingly sophisticated body of research on relationships between states, governance and authority over land (Margulis, McKeon, and Borras 2013; Wolford et al. 2013). The papers in this collection make several contributions to this discussion.

States are not coherent, unified entities that consistently act with premeditation, competence or consensus. They contain multiple actors, factions and interests, many of which are in direct competition for political influence. As Milgroom's paper (2015) on Mozambique demonstrates, policies may be crafted at a high level but their effects depend on how they are implemented or, as she says, how they are 'enacted'. In Mozambique, government officials deploy sophisticated technologies, such as remote sensing and global positioning systems (GPS), to gather and present data, but they often do so in an 'ad hoc fashion' so that the seemingly scientific results suit their particular interests. Competing forces within the state are not always easy to see, since official discourses tend to project an artificial coherence. Corson et al.'s paper on the Rio+20 meetings suggests that the most effective sites for seeing and enacting governance – at the national and international levels – are informal, everyday spaces rather than official texts or meeting halls. Corson et al. (2015) quote a participant at Rio+20 as saying, 'A lot of the UN negotiation never really happens on the floor; it always happens in the corridors .... So we sit one on one ... catch them when they're going to the toilet, or when they're walking to coffee'.

A common division within the state, highlighted by several of the papers, occurs between officials at local, regional and national levels. Competition between these actors sometimes provides opportunities for land deals to move forward but may also create the political space or opportunity for resistance. Moreda's paper (2015) on land deals in lowland Ethiopia indicates that contemporary investment needs to be situated in a long history of domination in the lowlands by national (highlander) and foreign (Sudanese) elites. Partly to remedy this history of subordination, the 1995 Ethiopian constitution devolved considerable power to states to administer their own land. With the recent rise in land values, however, the national government has again become involved in local land affairs, not least through a highly disruptive programme of villagization. In a paper on Colombia, Grajales (2015) makes a different but related point, suggesting that while the national government has devolved power to local regions and elites, this has given rise to 'subnational authoritarianism' and made it more difficult for villagers to fight dispossession.

At times, differences between levels of the state are exacerbated by transnational commitments. In the papers in this collection, the importance of notions of universal human rights, identity and land use are especially salient. In Argentina, Brent's paper (2015) suggests, provincial governments privilege the sanctity of private property while the national government privileges territorial, cultural or ethnic claims to land. As a result, indigenous land titles are promised by the national government and undermined by the provincial government. Differences between local- and national-level officials do not necessarily preclude collaboration. Moreda (2015) highlights, in Ethiopia, ongoing partnerships between local chiefs and central authorities, where the chiefs maintain their positions by exploiting their own communities and kin. In some cases, the central state appears absent altogether, leaving local authorities considerable space to govern, as in Mamonova's account (2015) of land deals in post-socialist Ukraine.

States also change their orientations, as Wilson's study of the *Las Tunas* movement in Nicaragua suggests. In the 1980s, the revolutionary Sandinista state distributed over 2.5 million hectares of land to farming collectives, individual peasant farmers and state-owned enterprises, but after the *Frente Sandinista de Liberación Nacional* (FSLN) – the Sandinistas – lost the 1990 presidential elections, many aspects of these reforms were reversed. In a paper on Special Economic Zones in the Indian state of Goa, Sampat (2015) similarly indicates that states need to be seen as contested sites in which 'land grabbers don't always win'. In Goa, mobilization by a cross-class, cross-society coalition led to the cancellation of 15 approved SEZs, some of which had already begun to develop the land.

Working with rather than directly confronting state authority may also be effective for those too remote and marginal to mount direct resistance to threatened dispossession. In Laos, an ethnic-minority Khmu community invoked state development discourses to challenge a concession to a Chinese company that intended to plant rubber trees on over half their territory (McAllister 2015). This state attempt to allocate community land for commercial purposes was justified with arguments that the land was degraded and formed part of 'state forests'. The reactions 'from below' ranged from 'anonymous acts of sabotage, refusal to work for the company, identification of powerful allies in the government and civil society, and recourse to law and state institutions'. Informed by perceptions of risk and opportunity, this Khmu community was able to stall the planned plantation by working with state structures in a process that underlines the degree to which forms of resistance are often unrecognized as such, occurring as they often do in remote locations far from public view.

Understanding reactions to land deals in geographically remote locations is a theme also highlighted by Martiniello (2015). He locates community reactions to an impending land deal in northern Uganda within a long history of resistance to central state control and efforts to establish commercial agriculture, from colonial times to the present, in a region that is economically and geographically peripheral to the Ugandan state. He shows how the Ugandan government's attempt to provide land for a sugar plantation to the Madhvani Group provoked a range of social struggles that echo and are locally understood as building on this history of resistance to state authority and violence. Here, too, responses 'manifested in both everyday, hidden, practices of resistance and moments of open, militant, contestation [that] are aimed at (re)establishing and securing access to means of social reproduction'. Cumulatively, these diverse forms of resistance represent both opposition to an imminent dispossession and claims to land sovereignty and autonomy.

As a collection, the papers also highlight the importance of seeing states as relationships rather than discrete institutions. States are grounded in particular places and times and are constituted through relationships with society. And just as there are multiple perspectives within the state, there are multiple relationships between state and society. The border between the two is dynamic and porous; state actors are often civil society actors and vice versa in different times or spaces. Protestors or actors who work closely with the state sometimes have more influence over land deals than those who work 'outside'. As Castellanos-Navarrete and Jansen (2015) point out for Chiapas, 'Environmentalists within the state were able to make a concrete difference while radical organizations outside the state were never able to build alliances'. At the same time, both Castellanos-Navarrete and Jansen as well as Corson et al. show how state–society collaboration can discipline the latter, such that civil society is always just that – 'civil' – and playing by existing rules of the game.

In democracies, a key component of state–society relationships is the electoral process and, in most of the cases analyzed in the papers, elected politicians manifest responsiveness to popular discontent. Gingembre's contribution (2015) on Madagascar shows this, albeit in a very particular way:

> Political uncertainty in the wake of the coup against the Ravolmanana government provided more space for civil society, which organized quickly because of empowerment and a sense of having 'missed the boat' during the [2009] Dae Woo [anti-land grab] protests.

Gingembre indicates that the timing of parliamentary elections made 'officials even more sensitive to the whiff of protest' but, ironically, this sensitivity was so influenced by memories of the 2009 coup that local leaders disregarded those people who would have liked to be involved in the Lalifuel land deal. Wilson (2015) argues that in Nicaragua, elected leaders were forced to cede to mobilization once the images of protest focused more on the daily trials of survival than on military or guerrilla war: 'The material reality of hungry children and hungry women struggling to feed them established some credibility of the movement within the media outlets and created a powerful symbol with which to shame the government'. Sampat's (2015) research in Goa similarly suggests that successful negotiations with the state hinged on the electoral – and physical – power of the people.

Rights and legal repertoires

Can contesting land grabs through invoking 'rights' and legal repertoires stop or reverse them? Several of the papers in this collection explore how people in diverse situations have used the language of rights and legal institutions to advance their struggles. Many states do not adequately protect customary and informal land tenure in their statutes, so land deals that dispossess people of such rights can be legal under national law, even while violating human rights principles (Wily 2012). Efforts led by states and elites to reform, formalize, individualize and register land and property can legalize theft of poor people's land. While neoliberal institutions and theorists (e.g., de Soto 1989) frequently hail property deeds as protection for the very poor, in historical perspective formal titles are also a central tool in land rushes (Wily 2012). Several assertions used in prior rushes are again evident in the past decade, including the notion that unfarmed lands are vacant 'wastelands', that customary and informal occupation does not confer rights, and that mass individualization and titling programmes should be at the centre of state land policy. The result is that land deals often proceed in 'legally binding' ways that protect the rights of investors and elites, but not those of the rural poor. In the face of these threats, social movements have adopted diverse positions, either contesting the legal terrain or rejecting state power as anathema to their interests.

The move towards legalizing land titles has been used to ambiguous effect in different contexts. Alonso-Fradejas' paper on Guatemala after the mid-2000s argues that national land titling programmes, originally seen as a 'good governance fix', were increasingly used to provide factors of production for 'well-capitalized outsiders'. The illegal appropriation of titles, he indicates, paved the way for elite resource accumulation and concentration. Grajales (2015), however, describes a Colombian case in the Lower Atrato where collective organization allowed a community to resist displacement and win meaningful collective land rights. Gingembre (2015) raises a complementary point and suggests that in Madagascar formal legal norms were less important than the content of claims to land based on 'customary, local discourses and identities'. Brent (2015) suggests, similarly, for Argentina, that legal ownership may be less important than control. The Argentinean state has made media headlines for restricting foreign land ownership in the wake of concerns over land appropriation, but the focus on ownership obscures the more important aspect of who actually controls the land and its production. This extinguishes grassroots voices and livelihoods even more effectively than outright ownership in a context where power derives from force rather than consent.

In many countries, the absence of democratic local land governance institutions constitutes a major stumbling block. There are exceptions, however, as in Tanzania, where village councils established through Nyerere's Ujamaa policy administer land at the local level. The 'rights' approach and the use of formal legal institutions are perhaps most effective in collective resistance to large land deals, rather than smaller and more localized ones. Nonetheless, local elites and politically-connected national businesses often grab significantly more land – at least cumulatively – than transnational actors do (Jayne, Chamberlin, and Headey 2014; Kandel 2015).

Critiques of the global land grab initially focused largely on rights violations: land dispossession and displacement of people from land they considered they owned. Concern with rights violations prompted a proliferation of regulatory initiatives to complement and shape national laws. At the global level, the UN Committee on World Food Security (CFS) *Voluntary Guidelines on Responsible Governance of Land, Fisheries and Forests in the Context of National Food Security* ('Voluntary Guidelines') are the most comprehensive, and are the outcome of several years of intense negotiation between states, civil society and development agencies (FAO 2012). While 'voluntary', the Guidelines reference existing binding international law and human rights norms, and so constitute the most definitive global framework regarding land and related natural resource rights. The seven

Principles for Responsible Agricultural Investment (RAI), endorsed by the World Bank, the International Fund for Agricultural Development and the UN Council on Trade and Development, on the other hand, are a framework for self-regulation by investors. Following the adoption of the Voluntary Guidelines, the CFS initiated consultations that gave rise to *Principles for Responsible Investment in Agriculture and the Agro-food System* (FAO 2014 – the 'CFS–RAI') as an alternative to the World Bank-sponsored RAI.

The political and ideological bases of alliances and campaigns both unite and divide the ranks of actors working around land deals, giving rise to three main approaches to regulating land grabbing: regulate to facilitate, regulate to mitigate negative impacts and maximize opportunities, and regulate to block and roll back land grabs (Borras, Franco, and Wang 2013). Agrarian social movements such as La Vía Campesina and critical agrarian scholars have debated how to respond to this 'land governance rush' and whether these frameworks can gain traction. Controversies centre primarily on three issues. First, were the guidelines premised on human rights and property rights (as in the Voluntary Guidelines) or self-regulation by corporate investors (as in the RAI)? Second, what were the roles of civil society, farmer associations and social movements in the process of developing these frameworks, and how legitimate and inclusive are the results? While civil society and farmers' groups were integrally involved in drafting the Voluntary Guidelines, the RAI were the product of the development agencies themselves, led by the World Bank. The third question was the extent to which these frameworks address only procedural questions of governance and transparency – to make land grabbing 'responsible' – or whether they provide a basis for more substantive forms of agrarian change (Holt Gimenéz and Shattuck 2011).

What partly explains the momentum that the CFS has gained among progressive and radical social movements, such as the International Planning Committee (IPC) for Food Sovereignty and La Vía Campesina, is that the Voluntary Guidelines cut across broad 'resource control' issues and invoke a variety of international laws and treaties. They are an international governance instrument that can be flexibly used by those confronted by corporate land grabs (White et al. 2012), green grabs (Fairhead, Leach, and Scoones 2012) and water grabs (Mehta, Veldwisch, and Franco 2012) – as well as by those who are outside the ambit of the global land rush (Seufert 2013; McKeon 2013; Monsalve 2013). How and within what framework to bring together all social forces confronting a variety of land questions, and not just those directly provoked by the current land rush, is an urgent political question for all those who work around social justice issues, and an urgent agenda for inquiry by 'engaged researchers'.

Do human rights frameworks serve as an effective tool in local struggles? Very few of the contributions in this collection suggest that transnational governance has had any real influence. It is too early to tell if the Voluntary Guidelines or other international instruments will have any effect, or if the transnational scale is one better suited to framing issues than to adjudicating conflicts. Franco's discussion of FPIC demonstrates both the potential and pitfalls of depending on a regulatory tool with limited authority (Franco 2014).

Rights frameworks in international law often coexist with national laws as well as local practices that contradict them. Alonso-Fradejas (2015) draws attention to how, in Guatemala, the 'repertoire of contention' included strategic litigation as a form of 'politico-juridical advocacy "from above"' alongside 'grounded practices of resistance "from below"'. Despite obvious limitations, he argues, as long as the state remains an arena of contention, legal repertoires can be put to work. Invoking human rights frameworks, peasants in Colombia have simultaneously recognized the institutionalized violence of the state and taken their struggles to state institutions and the judiciary (Grajales 2015). Here, both investors and rural people resisting them have engaged in 'legal contention'. The

Colombian experience represents a paradox where widespread lawlessness and violence either inflicted or condoned by the state and corporations exists alongside legal institutions that, while constrained by this wider political economy, offer some opportunities for legal remedy.

This 'judicialization' of politics may not necessarily entail the displacement of political struggles into legal institutions, but rather a more complex navigation of multiple avenues of struggle. In Colombia, the association of corporate interests with paramilitaries, drug traffickers, money laundering and extra-judicial killings has led rural populations to respond with direct resistance and with legal strategies aimed at establishing land grabbing not only as a property infringement issue but as a human rights one (Grajales 2015). In such situations, international human rights instruments, such as the CFS Voluntary Guidelines, may provide important leverage for resistance. Human rights-based responses to global land grabbing can gain traction only through a concerted effort by state and non-state actors operating at international, national and local levels (Golay and Biglino 2013). For effective use of legal repertoires, whether in national courts or multilateral fora, mass mobilization and pressure from below are essential.

Green politics from below

Linked to wider concerns over 'land grabbing' are forms of resistance around environmental issues. The 'financialization' of nature and resources – widespread in contemporary neoliberal capitalism (Büscher et al. 2012) – involves imposing 'environmental' agendas around such labels as 'green economy', 'low-carbon transitions' or 'sustainable intensification'. The expansion of quasi-privatized national parks, tourist zones and other 'protected areas' is part of this, as are 'payment for ecosystem services', biodiversity offsets or the promotion of biofuels or carbon forestry schemes in the name of climate change mitigation (Matondi, Havnevik, and Beyene 2011; McAfee 2012; Dietz et al. 2014; Leach and Scoones 2015). Collectively, these phenomena have often been described as 'green grabbing' – 'the appropriation of land and nature for environmental ends' (Fairhead, Leach, and Scoones 2012, 238). But just as with 'land grabbing', 'green grabs' take multiple forms and result in diverse politics from below, as several papers in this collection point out.

The expansion of oil palm plantations for biofuels in Guatemala (Alonso-Fradejas 2015) represents a classic 'agrarian extractivist project', like those in much of the land and green grab literature. The 'repertoires of contention' range from the everyday to the more structured. Long histories of agrarian politics give rise to these patterns of resistance and the contests between different actors as a result of the intervention. Resistance has emerged across diverse axes as Q'eqchi lowlanders articulate a discourse around 'the defence of territory'. This promotes indigenous identity and a sense of community, and also generates support for local land use and agricultural practices. This language facilitates alliances with human rights non-governmental organizations (NGOs), the Catholic Church and others, in turn nurturing multiple forms of politics from below.

Yet oil palm development does not always result in confrontational politics when embedded in smallholder settings. Castellanos-Navarrete and Jansen (2015) offer a contrasting case from Chiapas, Mexico, where a state-supported oil palm programme has involved smallholders and indigenous peoples. In this instance, peasant engagement with capital accumulation has undermined environmentalists' efforts to restrict the spread of oil palm. Castellanos-Navarrete and Jansen argue that 'a green agrarian question solely focusing on enclosure is unable to explain agrarian environmental processes'. Large-scale land grabs may involve the willing co-optation of peasant producers, who are then able to improve their livelihoods. In this case, radical environmental organizations that used global green narratives around climate change, biodiversity and land-use change were unable to forge coalitions at the local level to resist oil palm. Instead, actors within the state forged alliances that adopted environmental arguments, but linked these to the oil palm project and the interests of local producers and indigenous peoples. By reconfiguring old forms of clientelist politics, the oil palm programme created a new network of support, involving actors within and outside the state. No classic oppositional politics emerged, but rather one rooted in much more complex engagements with the state and capital that would be obscured by a simplistic focus on enclosure and 'grabbing'.

Similarly, Cavanagh and Benjaminsen (2015) explore the 'biopolitics' of protected areas and the dispossessions these provoke. Focusing on the case of conservation initiatives at Mount Elgon in Uganda, they identify responses that include nonviolent, militant, discursive and formal-legal tactics. In this case, and more broadly, they argue, rural populations faced with enclosure of farmlands and rangelands respond not only with overt resistance but through illicit cultivation in territories earmarked for conservation – a kind of 'guerrilla agriculture'. These reactions do not merely represent survival strategies by supposedly passive victims of land enclosure but form a part of struggles in the face of direct and indirect violence to establish spheres of existence autonomous of both conservation authorities and the national state. In these ways, they 'circumvent policies that bolster the global public good of biodiversity at the expense of local and traditional livelihoods' and challenge the 'naturalization of dispossession'.

Rocheleau (2015), in a paper on Chiapas, analyzes the use of 'networked, distributed, rooted and territorial power' – by investors and by resistance movements – around a number of 'green' investments, including a major tourism project. Again, compared to classic 'land grabbing', there is a 'fog of greening', involving networked assemblages spread across a wide territory. The network of actors promoting such investments links tourism to reserves, and connects the state, security forces and corporate investors. State agents regularly foment rural violence, and the process of 'restoring order' provides a pretext for evictions that make an area 'safe' for investment. Rocheleau maintains that 'Disneyland in the forest and Cancún in the forest are a prelude to pipelines in the forest, plantations in the forest, highways in the forest, paradise for sale in the forest' and more.

'Politics from below' and resistance to green discourses and practices may not always occur, however. In a 'collaborative event ethnography' of the Rio+20 conference in 2012, Corson et al. (2015) show how opponents of the 'green economy' discourse mobilized in an international setting. NGOs, mostly from the global South, energized a movement inside and outside the UN process, labelled 'rights at risk', and deployed multiple forms of mobilization, such as 'side-events, morning meetings, thematic clusters, letters, petitions and protests'. The 'green economy' became the key signifier in debates at Rio and many viewed it as 'selling nature to save the economy', invoking crisis and scarcity to create new forms of privatization of nature, and thus conditions for 'green grabbing'. The 'rights-at-risk' movement made some headway, though Corson et al. (2015) observe that 'it is not always through the official structures of participation or orchestrated resistance that progressive action takes place'. Instead, it may be that change happens through 'unforeseen moments of opportunity'.

These papers show how so-called 'green grabs' involve enclosure and expropriation of land and resources, but the politics of contestation around environmental questions may also operate in more complex and subtle ways, through networked forms of resistance and via discursive battles operating across scales over the meaning of environment and sustainability. The 'politics from below' around environmental issues are perhaps especially varied, as agrarian and environmental movements have distinct – sometimes converging and at over times diverging – agendas.

Silences: gender and generation

Two important dimensions of 'political responses from below' – their gendered and generational dynamics – are largely missing from this collection. Although the Land Deal Politics Initiative (LDPI) explicitly included gender (and, more recently, generational) dynamics in its calls for research proposals and conference papers, the response has been rather modest. This, we feel, reflects the general state of the art. The importance of analyzing the gendered dimensions of large-scale land deals was rightly flagged some years ago (Behrman, Meinzen-Dick, and Quisumbing 2012), and a few articles and chapters on this have appeared in recent years (e.g., Doss, Summerfield, and Tsikata 2014; Julia and White 2012; Tsikata and Yaro 2014; White, Park, and Julia 2014). However, work in this area has been slow to emerge, and also the balance of its focus has been on gendered impacts and vulnerabilities resulting from land deals rather than gendered agency, responses and resistance (but see Edelman and León 2013).

Gender relations also structure both the varied experiences of land deals and responses to them, as shown in the case of oil palm in Indonesia (Morgan 2013). Loss of common property resources may dispossess women of resource rights on which they depend, while simultaneously incorporating men in commodity relations (Tsikata and Yaro 2014). Incorporation is virtually always a gendered process, shaped by historical and existing gender relations and divisions of labour, and in turn entrenching or ameliorating gendered inequalities. Reactions too are gendered, with women and men responding, both individually and collectively, in diverse ways to the promises and threats of land deals. In the case of a sugar plantation in Amuru District in northern Uganda, described by Martiniello (2015), women were at the forefront of community opposition. To prevent state surveyors and company representatives from demarcating land for the plantation, women protestors stripped naked, in a confrontational act of resistance that mobilized the cultural symbolism of women's bodies and reproductive roles, and which proved effective – along with several legal challenges – in stalling the land deals for several years.

Researchers have given even less attention to generational differences and tensions in local people's engagement with corporate land deals and agribusiness. This neglect is surprising. Intergenerational relationships and tensions have been a recurring theme in studies of agrarian change, especially in Africa, but they consistently receive less notice than class and gender relations (Sumberg et al. 2012). A youth and generational perspective adds another powerful reason to De Schutter's arguments that large-scale land deals (whether for purchase or long lease) should be seen as the 'last and least desirable option' (De Schutter 2011) because they close off the smallholder option, not only for today's farmers but also for members of the next generation, who face permanent alienation from land on which they, or their children, might want to farm, and in the absence of livelihood opportunities elsewhere (White 2012).

While smallholder dispossession for plantation agriculture or contract farming schemes may make some provision for existing smallholders in terms of (reduced) land allocation, generally there is no provision for the next generation. Following the Scottish Highland Clearances of the eighteenth and early nineteenth centuries, dispossession often left the older generation of crofters and cottars 'hanging on', despite the onslaught on their land and livelihoods, but still reluctant to leave. The next generation, however, was less willing to acquiesce to these straitened circumstances, often made trouble, and was encouraged and sometimes forced to migrate to the south, or to North America. No land at all was made available for young couples wanting to marry (Napier Commission 1884). Young people may have different interests in land deals (pro or con), and different ways of promoting their interests and engaging with state and corporate power. We hope to see work on these generational issues in the next few years.

Conclusion

This collection draws attention to a spectrum of reactions to land deals which extend far beyond resistance *per se*, and collectively constitute the 'politics from below' of the global land grab. What explains successful resistance, and what does resistance produce? Some of the papers show how cross-class, identity-based and even transnational alliances mounted effective resistance to land deals, while others focus on engagement with the state and private capital rather than direct confrontation. Reactions are shaped by and in turn shape social differentiation, shifting the contours of and possibilities for political alliances. Less clear are the alternatives that emerge, and that are proposed. While some of the papers depict rural communities mounting powerful counter-narratives to land enclosures, commodification and commercialization, and seeking land sovereignty and autonomy from the state and markets, others point to demands from below for incorporation, or changed terms of incorporation, in land deals and the tenure arrangements, production systems and value chains that they produce.

We emphasize how the framing of research on land deals is enriched by explicit connection to the scholarship on the peasantry and to critical agrarian studies. Conceptual and analytical frames from the agrarian literature are helpful in illuminating the range of reactions to land deals. Key concepts include repertoires of contention, exclusion versus incorporation, disciplining, defensive versus propositional practices, Polanyian counter-movements and governance fixes, among others. Methods and disciplinary approaches from various traditions and schools of thought – ranging from political ecology to geography, rural sociology and anthropology – shape the questions we ask about the politics of land deals, the methods we use and the understandings we derive. The papers we present here also highlight differences in terms of spatial dimensions and the scale at which land deals and reactions to them are analyzed – from transnational, to national, regional, local, community, kinship, household and individual levels, with the latter requiring further disaggregation to account for gender and generational differences.

What does this current state of research on the 'politics from below' in response to land grabbing imply for future research agendas? This collection suggests that the 'politics from below' is not just the reactions of local communities to the expansion of corporate and state control over community land and territory in the global South. Importantly, 'politics from below' is also constitutive of trajectories of agrarian change. To deepen our understanding and to sharpen analysis in critical agrarian studies, we need signposts for future research. First is the urgent need to address the near-total absence of critical analysis of gendered differences. While there is a growing literature on gendered impacts of land deals, there is little empirical work and even less analytical and theoretical treatment of gendered responses to land deals. Second is the continued silence on the intergenerational dynamics of land deals and the responses to them, including inter-generational conflict, and implications for future generations and the possibilities for agrarian livelihoods.

Acknowledgements

The authors wish to acknowledge the generous support provided to the Land Deal Politics Initiative and its convenors' institutions, both during and after the Global Land Grab II conference at Cornell University in 2012, from the Ford Foundation, Future Agricultures Consortium, UK Department for International Development, Transnational Institute, Misereor, Austrian Development Cooperation, Interchurch Organization for Development Cooperation, Institute for the Social Sciences at Cornell, Atkinson Center for a Sustainable Future at Cornell and Department of Development Sociology at Cornell, and especially from the faculty, staff and graduate students who put in so much time.

Disclosure statement

No potential conflict of interest was reported by the authors.

References

Alano, L. Forthcoming. The political economy of large-scale land investments: Lessons from the Ecofuel sugarcane plantation, northern Philippines. Draft PhD diss., University of Amsterdam, The Netherlands.

Alonso-Fradejas, A. 2015. Anything but a story foretold: Multiple politics of resistance to the agrarian extractivist project in Guatemala. This collection.

Baglioni, E., and P. Gibbon. 2013. Land grabbing, large- and small-scale farming: What can evidence and policy from 20th century Africa contribute to the debate? *Third World Quarterly* 34, no. 9: 1558–81.

Barker, C. 2014. Class struggle and social movements. In *Marxism and social movements*, ed. C. Barker, L. Cox, J. Krinsky, and A.G. Nilsen, 41–61. Chicago: Haymarket Books.

Behrman, J., R. Meinzen-Dick, and A. Quisumbing. 2012. The gender implications of large-scale land deals. *Journal of Peasant Studies* 39, no. 1: 49–79.

Borras, S.M. Jr., and J.C. Franco. 2012. Global land grabbing and trajectories of agrarian change: A preliminary analysis. *Journal of Agrarian Change* 12, no. 1: 34–59.

Borras, S.M. Jr., and J.C. Franco. 2013. Global land grabbing and political reactions 'from below'. *Third World Quarterly* 34, no. 9: 1723–47.

Borras, S.M. Jr., J.C. Franco, and S. Monsalve Suarez. 2015. Land and food sovereignty. *Third World Quarterly* 36, no. 3: 600–617.

Borras, S.M. Jr., J.C. Franco, and C. Wang. 2013. The challenge of global governance of land grabbing: Changing international agricultural context and competing political views and strategies. *Globalizations* 10, no. 1: 161–79.

Borras, S.M. Jr., R. Hall, I. Scoones, B. White, and W. Wolford. 2011. Towards a better understanding of global land grabbing: an editorial introduction. *Journal of Peasant Studies* 28, no. 2: 209–216.

Brent, Z. 2015. Territorial restructuring and resistance in Argentina. This collection.

Burdick, J. 1995. Uniting theory and practice in the ethnography of social movements: Notes toward a hopeful realism. *Dialectical Anthropology* 20, no. 3: 361–85.

Büscher, B., S. Sullivan, K. Neves, J. Igoe and D. Brockington. 2012. Towards a synthesized critique of neoliberal biodiversity conservation. *Capitalism Nature Socialism* 23, no. 2: 4–30.

Byres, T.J. 1981. The new technology, class formation and class action in the Indian countryside. *Journal of Peasant Studies* 8, no. 4: 405–54.

Castellanos-Navarrete, A., and K. Jansen. 2015. Oil Palm expansions without enclosure: Accumulation and environmentalisms in Mexico. This collection.

Cavanagh, C., and T. Benjaminsen. 2015. Guerrilla agriculture? A biopolitical guide to illicit cultivation within an IUCN Category II protected area. This collection.

Corson, C. et al. 2015. The right to resist: Disciplining civil society at Rio+20. This collection.

De Schutter, O. 2011. How not to think of land-grabbing: Three critiques of large-scale investments in farmland. *Journal of Peasant Studies* 38, no. 2: 249–79.

De Soto, H. 1989. *The other path: The invisible revolution in the Third World*. New York: Harper & Row.

Dietz, K., B. Engels, O. Pye, and A. Brunnengräber, eds. 2014. *The political ecology of agrofuels*. London: Routledge.
Doss, C., G. Summerfield, and D. Tsikata, eds. 2014. *Land, gender, and food security*. Special Issue, *Feminist Economics* 20, no. 1.
Edelman, M. 1999. *Peasants against globalization: Rural social movements in Costa Rica*. Stanford: Stanford University Press.
Edelman, M., and S.M. Borras Jr. Forthcoming. *Political dynamics of transnational agrarian movements*. Halifax: Fernwood.
Edelman, M., and C. James. 2011. Peasants' rights and the UN system: Quixotic struggle? Or emancipatory idea whose time has come? *Journal of Peasant Studies* 38, no. 1: 81–108.
Edelman, M., and A. León. 2013. Cycles of land grabbing in Central America: An argument for history and a case study in the Bajo Aguán, Honduras. *Third World Quarterly* 34, no. 9: 1697–722.
Edelman, M., C. Oya, and S.M. Borras Jr. 2013. Global land grabs: Historical processes, theoretical and methodological implications and current trajectories. *Third World Quarterly* 34, no. 9: 1517–31.
Fairhead, J., M. Leach, and I. Scoones. 2012. Green Grabbing: A new appropriation of nature? *Journal of Peasant Studies* 39, no. 2: 237–61.
FAO (Food and Agricultural Organization of the United Nations). 2012. *Voluntary guidelines on the responsible governance of tenure of land, fisheries and forests in the context of national food security*. Rome: FAO.
FAO (Food and Agricultural Organization of the United Nations). 2014. *Principles for responsible investment in agriculture and food systems*. Rome: Committee on World Food Security, FAO.
FIAN (Food First Information and Action Network). 2012. The human rights impacts of tree plantations in Niassa Province, Mozambique: A report, Heidelberg: Foodfirst Information and Action Network.
Fontana, L.B. 2014. Indigenous peoples vs peasant unions: Land conflicts and rural movements in plurinational Bolivia. *Journal of Peasant Studies* 41, no. 3: 297–319.
Fox, J. 1993. *The politics of food in Mexico: State power and social mobilizations*. Ithaca: Cornell University Press.
Franco, J.C. 2014. *Reclaiming free prior and informed consent (FPIC) in the context of global land grabs*. Amsterdam: Transnational Institute (TNI).
Franco, J.C., D. Carranza, and J. Fernandez. 2011. *New biofuel project in Isabela, Philippines: Boon or bane for local people?* Amsterdam: Transnational Institute.
Gingembre, M. 2015. Resistance or participation? Reclaiming land sovereignty amid political uncertainty in Madagascar. This collection.
Golay, C., and I. Biglino. 2013. Human rights responses to land grabbing: A right to food perspective. *Third World Quarterly* 34, no. 9: 1630–50.
Goodwin, J., J.M. Jasper, and F. Polletta, eds. 2001. *Passionate politics: Emotions and social movements*. Chicago: University of Chicago Press.
Grajales, J. 2015. Land grabbing, legal contention and institutional change in Colombia. This collection.
Harvey, D. 2005. *A brief history of neoliberalism*. Oxford: Oxford University Press.
Hickey, S., and A. du Toit. 2007. Adverse incorporation, social exclusion and chronic poverty. Chronic Poverty Research Centre Working Paper 81. Manchester and Cape Town: Institute for Development Policy Management and Institute for Poverty, Land and Agrarian Studies.
Hobsbawm, E.J. 1959. *Primitive rebels: Studies in archaic forms of social movement in the 19th and 20th centuries*. Manchester: Manchester University Press.
Holt Gimenéz, E., and A. Shattuck. 2011. Food crises, food regimes and food movements: Rumblings of reform or tides of transformation? *Journal of Peasant Studies* 38, no. 1: 109–44.
IDI. 2014. ANZ bankrolls massive land grab in Cambodia. http://www.inclusivedevelopment.net/anz-bankrolls-massive-land-grab-in-cambodia/ (accessed March 26, 2015.
Jayne, T.S., J. Chamberlin, and D.D. Headey. 2014. Land pressures, the evolution of farming systems, and development strategies in Africa: A synthesis. *Food Policy* 48: 1–17.
Julia, with B. White. 2012. Gendered experiences of dispossession: Oil palm expansion in a Dayak Hibun community in West Kalimantan. *The Journal of Peasant Studies* 39, no. 3–4: 995–1016.
Kandel, M. 2015. Politics from below? Small-, mid-, and large-scale land dispossession in Teso, Uganda and the relevance of scale. This collection.

Kerkvliet, B. 2014. Protests over land in Vietnam: Rightful resistance and more. *Journal of Vietnamese Studies* 9, no. 3: 19–54.
Larder, N. 2015. Disrupting the land grabbing narrative through a study of responses to the Malibya project. This collection.
Leach, M., and I. Scoones, eds. 2015. *Carbon conflicts and forest landscapes in Africa*. London: Routledge.
Li, T.M. 2011. Centering labor in the land grab debate. *Journal of Peasant Studies* 38, no. 2: 281–98.
Little, P.D., and M.J. Watts, eds. 1994. *Living under contract: Contract farming and agrarian transformation in sub-Saharan Africa*. Madison: University of Wisconsin Press.
Mamonova, N. 2015. Resistance or adaptation? Ukrainian peasants' responses to large-scale land acquisitions. This collection.
Margulis, M.E., N. McKeon, and S.M. Borras Jr. 2013. Land grabbing and global governance: Critical perspectives. *Globalizations* 10, no. 1: 1–23.
Martiniello, G. 2015. Social struggles in Uganda's Acholiland: Understanding responses and resistance to Amuru sugar works. This collection.
Matondi, P.B., K. Havnevik, and A. Beyene, eds. 2011. *Biofuels, land grabbing and food security in Africa*. London: Zed Books.
McAfee, K. 2012. The contradictory logic of global ecosystem-services markets. *Development and Change* 43, no. 1: 105–31.
McAllister, K. 2015. Rubber, rights and resistance: The evolution of local struggles against a Chinese rubber concession in Northern Laos. This collection.
McCarthy, J.F. 2010. Processes of inclusion and adverse incorporation: Oil palm and agrarian change in Sumatra, Indonesia. *Journal of Peasant Studies* 37, no. 4: 821–50.
McKeon, N. 2013. 'One does not sell the land upon which the people walk': Land grabbing, transnational rural social movements, and global governance. *Globalizations* 10, no. 1: 105–22.
Mehta, L., G.J. Veldwisch, and J. Franco. 2012. Introduction to the special issue: Water grabbing? Focus on the (re) appropriation of finite water resources. *Water Alternatives*: 193–207.
Milgroom, J. 2015. Policy processes of a land grab: At the interface of politics 'in the air' and politics 'on the ground' in Massingir, Mozambique. This collection.
Monsalve Suárez, S. 2013. The human rights framework in contemporary agrarian struggles. *Journal of Peasant Studies* 40, no. 1: 239–90.
Moreda, T.S. 2015. Listening to their silence? The political reaction of affected communities to large-scale land acquisitions: insights from Ethiopia. This collection.
Morgan, M. 2013. Women, gender and protest emergence: Contesting oil palm expansion in Sambas District, Indonesia, LDPI Working Paper 49. The Hague: Land Deal Politics Initiative. http://www.iss.nl/fileadmin/ASSETS/iss/Research_and_projects/Research_networks/LDPI/LDPI_WP_49.pdf
Napier Commission. 1884. *Evidence taken by her Majesty's commission of enquiry into the conditions of the crofters and cottars in the Highlands and Islands of Scotland*. Digitised by Lochaber Collage Mallaig, 2007 http://www.whc.uhi.ac.uk/napier-commission/highlands-and-islands-commission
O'Brien, K.J., and L.J. Li. 2006. *Rightful resistance in rural China*. Cambridge: Cambridge University Press.
Olson, M. 1965. *The logic of collective action: Public goods and the theory of groups*. Cambridge: Harvard University Press.
Oya, C. 2012. Contract farming in sub-Saharan Africa: A survey of approaches, debates and issues. *Journal of Agrarian Change* 12, no. 1: 1–33.
Paige, J. 1975. *Agrarian revolution: Social movements and export agriculture in the underdeveloped world*. New York: Free Press.
Peluso, N.L., and C. Lund. 2011. New frontiers of land control: Introduction. *Journal of Peasant Studies* 38, no. 4: 667–81.
Popkin, S. 1979. *The rational peasant: The political economy of rural society in Vietnam*. Berkeley: University of California Press.
Pye, O. 2010. The biofuel connection–transnational activism and the palm oil boom. *Journal of Peasant Studies* 37, no. 4: 851–74.
Rocheleau, D. 2015. Networked, rooted and territorial: Green grabbing and resistance in Chiapas. This collection.

Sampat, P. 2015. The 'Goan Impasse': Land rights and resistance to SEZs in Goa, India. This collection.
Scoones, I., R. Hall, S.M. Borras Jr, B. White, and W. Wolford. 2013. The politics of evidence: Methodologies for understanding the global land rush. *Journal of Peasant Studies* 40, no. 3: 469–83.
Scott, J.C. 1976. *The moral economy of the peasant*. New Haven: Yale University Press.
Seufert, P. 2013. The FAO voluntary guidelines on the responsible governance of tenure of land, fisheries and forests. *Globalizations* 10, no. 1: 181–86.
Smalley, R. 2013. Plantations, contract farming and commercial farming areas in Africa: A comparative review. Working Paper 55. Brighton and Nairobi: Future Agricultures Consortium.
Sumberg, J., N.A. Anyidoho, J. Leavy, D.J.H. te Lintelo, and K. Wellard. 2012. Introduction: The young people and agriculture 'Problem' in Africa. *IDS Bulletin*. Special Issue: Young People and Agriculture in Africa 43, no. 6: 1–8.
Tilly, C. 1986. *The contentious French*. Cambridge: Harvard University Press.
Tsikata, D., and J.A. Yaro. 2014. When a good business model is not enough: Land transactions and gendered livelihood prospects in rural Ghana. *Feminist Economics* 20, no. 1: 202–26.
Visser, O., N. Mamonova, and M. Spoor. 2012. Oligarchs, megafarms and land reserves: Understanding land grabbing in Russia. *Journal of Peasant Studies* 39, no. 3–4: 899–931.
White, B. 2012. Agriculture and the generation problem: Rural youth, employment and the future of farming. *IDS Bulletin* 43, no. 6: 9–19.
White, B., Saturnino M. Borras Jr., Ruth Hall, Ian Scoones, and Wendy Wolford. 2012. The new enclosures: Critical perspectives on corporate land deals. *Journal of Peasant Studies* 39, no. 3–4: 619–47.
White, B., C.M. Park, and Julia. 2014. The gendered political ecology of agrofuels expansion. In *The political ecology of agrofuels*, ed. K. Dietz, B. Engels, O. Pye, and A. Brunnengräber, 53–69. London: Routledge.
Wilson, B. 2015. Reclaiming the worker's property: Control grabbing, farmworkers and the *Las Tunas* Accords in Nicaragua. This collection.
Wily, L.A. 2012. Looking back to see forward: The legal niceties of land theft in land rushes. *Journal of Peasant Studies* 39, no. 3–4: 751–75.
Wolford, W., Saturnino M. Borras, Ruth Hall, Ian Scoones, Ben White. 2013. Governing global land deals: The role of the state in the rush for land. *Development and Change* 44, no. 2: 189–210.

Anything but a story foretold: multiple politics of resistance to the agrarian extractivist project in Guatemala

Alberto Alonso-Fradejas

Sugarcane and oil palm agribusinesses are in the vanguard of an emergent project of agrarian capitalism in Guatemala, which is defined here as a financialized and flexible type of agrarian extractivism. Meanwhile, Maya-Q´eqchi´ residents of the northern lowlands believe that the changes in the labor regime, land relations and the agro-ecosystem that the expansion of these agribusinesses has brought threaten their subsistence in multiple and unfamiliar ways. Indeed, growing difficulties in dealing with (vital) grievances is leading many, even those who initially welcomed the corporate sugarcane and oil palm plantations, to transform their unrest into a practice of resistance. Elaborating on what is presented here as a multiple politics perspective, this contribution discusses the nature and character of such contemporary political dynamics of agrarian change. The forms, strategies and practices of the two main and most antagonistic repertoires of contention are explored here: the one in 'defense of territory' and the one in the promotion of the 'agrarian extractivist project'. The tensions across and within multiple corporate, state and social actors who are pushing for, resisting, complying with or operating at the most violent margins of the agrarian extractivist project are also examined. By assessing continuities and ruptures between current and previous cycles of contention around the control of land, water and other natural resources, this paper stresses the often forgotten lesson about trajectories of agrarian change not being a story foretold, but the product of multiple and dynamic politics.

Introduction

Questions around the political dynamics of agrarian change regained momentum from the mid-2000s onwards, with the growing financialization of the economy (Fine 2012) and nature (Lander 2011) in general, and of agriculture (Isakson 2014) and land (Fairbairn 2014) in particular. Financialization shapes, and is shaped by, convergent economic, energy, environmental and food crises in a world historic juncture in which rapidly growing economies like the BRICS countries (Brazil, Russia, India, China and South Africa) and middle-income countries (MICs) display a high demand for large amounts of raw materials and food. In short, favorable politico economic conditions have been at play to (re)invigorate international accumulation projects based on the control of land, water and related natural resources (hereinafter land resources).

In the context of the many land resource-based accumulation projects spreading all over the country,[1] in 2008, the government of Guatemala considered the spectacular figure of 1,101,604 hectares, or 37 percent of the country's total farmland, to be suitable for sugarcane and oil palm cultivation (Alonso-Fradejas, Caal Hub, and Chinchilla 2011). These are not just any kind of tropical cash crops but two important 'flex crops'. That is, they have 'multiple uses (food, feed, fuel, industrial material) that can be, or are thought to be, flexibly inter-changed' (Borras et al. 2014, 2). According to Borras et al., flex crops and commodities are highly valued these days because they

> seem to deal with [the challenge of increasing price volatility in world markets] by reducing uncertainty in a single crop sector through diversification of the product portfolio, thereby enabling investors to better anticipate and more nimbly react to changing prices in either direction – e.g., to better exploit price spikes or to better withstand price shocks [in short] their multifunctionality helps to negate the purported trade-off between risk and yield on investments. (2014, 2, 7)

Moreover, flex crops and commodities are better equipped to navigate regulatory constraints, and circumvent social opposition, thanks to their 'flex policy narratives' (Borras et al. 2014, 16), especially when displayed in a 'discursive flexibility' fashion. That is through 'the ability to strategically switch among multiple legitimating discourses which construe the necessary meanings and representations to achieve an objective' (Hunsberger and Alonso-Fradejas forthcoming). Indeed, legitimating narratives of the sugarcane and the oil palm agribusinesses spin around food and energy security, and green energy generation and climate change mitigation, as well as economic development and even (rural) democratization.

A few years before the government's announcement, a group of agrarian, financial and industrial firms in the hands of a small-but-almighty post-colonial oligarchy (which occasionally allies with transnational investors and financiers) had already started taking *control* of large swaths of land for sugarcane and oil palm plantations. I stress the question of land control building on Borras et al.'s understanding of current land grabs as 'grabbing the power to control land and other associated resources such as water in order to derive benefit from such control of resources [...] control grabbing is inherently relational and political; it involves political power relations' (2012, 851). Indeed, as Holt-Giménez (2008) argues in the case of open-pit gold mining in the Guatemalan western highlands, the expansion of corporate sugarcane and oil palm plantations is restructuring rural *territories*[2] in a deep and comprehensive way. I suggest the means for such territorial restructuring has to do with the two complementing strategies of expansion of the oil palm and the sugarcane agribusinesses. One is what Harvey (2003) named the 'temporal deferment' of their investment. Current high revenues pay for costly and long-term investments including land and (flexible) oil palm and sugarcane mills. The other strategy is the making of governable spaces to fit their investment. That is, influencing not only formal regulatory frameworks and institutions, but especially, ideas, discourses and practices of multiple state, corporate

[1]Such as mining, oil extraction, commercial tree plantations, carbon trading, hydro-power generation, cattle ranching, high-end tourism and narco-traffic money laundering. All these accumulation projects shape, and are shaped by, increasing economic and logistical corridors, and mushrooming environmental enclosures (Alonso-Fradejas 2012).

[2]Understood as 'spatial assemblages of power relations and identity strategies [signifying] the "bottom-up" spatial contexts for identity and cultural difference (or place) more than the "top-down" connections between state and territory' (Gregory et al. 2009, 745–46).

and social actors, across different scales[3] and places,[4] to accommodate their accumulation interests. This, in turn, entails at least two distinct and major fixes. On the one hand, there is a labor regime fix to reshape the 'specific methods of mobilizing labor and organizing it in [capitalist agriculture] production, and their particular social, economic and political conditions' (Bernstein 1988, 31–32 in White et al. 2012, 622). This contribution discusses the ways in which flex crop agribusinesses are reducing local wage work opportunities, while enforcing a community-detached, flexible and hyper-commodified labor regime which does not allow workers to make ends meet. There is, on the other hand, a land 'good governance' fix performing 'as a persuasive ethical power that allows for self-regulation, making it possible for governments to intervene less intrusively and more efficiently' (O'Laughlin 2008, 946). This implies the production of a durable consensus around a particular rationality of governing land resources, which not only meets the agribusinesses' interests, but is also perceived as desirable by concerned state and social actors. This land good governance fix is rooted in the freehold land tenure imperative, which has been spread since the early 1990s through The International Fund for Agricultural Development (IFAD) and World Bank-promoted market-led agrarian reform. As we shall see, the workings towards the labor regime and land good governance fixes involve not just the use of physical force and violence, but also, and increasingly, that of different means of enticement and of economic and legal coercion which are 'involved in the governance of conduct and, a fortiori, in the production of hegemony' (Jessop 2010, 342).

Current sugarcane and oil palm agribusiness accumulation and governmental projects are the main vectors and expressions of what I consider to be an emergent but major transformation in agrarian capitalism in Guatemala and, arguably, in other similar national contexts in Latin America and elsewhere. Clearly, capitalist social relations of production were already dominant long before the beginning of the twenty-first century, though unevenly internalized across traditional landed upper classes, peasant classes and rural laborers (see the seminal works of Martínez Peláez 1976; Figueroa Ibarra 1980; Handy 1984; Hurtado 2008, among others). Nonetheless, I suggest that from the mid-2000s onwards, a distinctive project of agrarian capitalism has been emerging in Guatemala, which could be aptly described as a financialized and flexible type of *agrarian extractivism.*

In short, there are three main and convergent dynamics at play in the Guatemalan countryside informing this work-in-progress analysis.[5] Firstly, agricultural production in commercial sugarcane and oil palm plantations is being reshaped by the increasing use of

[3]Comprising 'the nested (and sometimes not so nested) hierarchy of bounded spaces of differing size' (Jessop 2007, 104–05).

[4]Broadly understood as a 'unit of space that has discrete boundaries, shared internal characteristics, and that changes over time and interacts with other similar units' (Gregory et al. 2009, 539).

[5]This preliminary argument for, and understanding of, an emergent agrarian extractivist project is inspired by the reflection on my empirical research in the Guatemalan countryside since 2003, in the light of two main analytical threads. On one side is the classic agrarian question posed by Marx (1974[1867]) and further developed by Engels (1951[1894]), Kautsky (1988[1899]) and Lenin (1964[1899]), and, particularly, the later discussion by Byres (1991, 1996) and Bernstein (2004, 2006) about the need revisit the classic agrarian question(s) in the socially diverse contexts of the South today. On the other side is the vivid debate on the politics of 'neo-extractivism', around mining and hydrocarbon extraction projects in Latin American states with progressive governments (Gudynas 2009; Veltmeyer and Petras 2014; Acosta 2013; Bebbington 2007; Leff 2006; Martínez-Alier 2002, among others). Especially important is the need to contextualize this debate: (1) in contemporary accumulation projects in the realms of biomass in general, and agriculture in particular; and (2) in non-progressive government Latin American states, like Guatemala.

new farming techniques, such as precision agriculture, and especially of highly versatile biotechnologies. Contrary to their promised outcomes, these technologies are increasing the already heavy dependency of modern agricultural production on petrochemicals and other costly inputs. In this search for ever-growing yields to maximize profit: (1) the knowledge rift between traditional ways of farming and those relying on biotechnologies and information technologies is severed, excluding those producers unable to meet the required capital intensity, or reducing them to little more than lessors of landed-property and occasional labor (i.e., most contract farmers; see Goodman, Sorj, and Wilkinson 1987; Netting 1993; Altieri and Toledo 2011, among others); and (2) the metabolic rift between agricultural production and the ecosystem is pushed beyond the limit allowing for the biophysical reproduction of soil nutrients, underground fresh water sources and agro-biodiversity (see Foster 2000; Akram-Lodhi and Kay 2009; IAASTD 2009; Moore 2011; Mingorría et al. 2014, among others).

Secondly, as mentioned earlier, the labor regime brought about by oil palm and sugarcane agribusinesses limits wage work opportunities without accommodating a living wage to most plantation workers (Alonso-Fradejas, Caal Hub, and Chinchilla 2011; Hurtado and Sánchez 2011). While labor and labor arrangements are flexibly organized to maximize surplus extraction, the working conditions are damaging workers' physical and mental health in severe and even deadly ways (Alonso-Fradejas, Caal Hub, and Chinchilla 2011; Hurtado and Sánchez 2011). Indeed, somehow differently from the classic formulation of agricultural commodity production 'freeing' labor from landed property towards a nascent industrialization, the flex-crop labor regime is freeing agricultural labor, but this is not being absorbed in any other productive realm of the economy. This 'free' labor turns into a sort of expendable 'relative surplus population' (Marx 1974[1867]) with no, or few, prospects for either (self-)employment or state support (Li 2011).

And, thirdly, as advanced by Bernstein in his review of the classic agrarian question in times of globalization, 'the range of non-agrarian, non-indigenous sources of agrarian capital is likely to expand and diversify, and their significance to increase, over the history of capitalism' (2006, 10). In today's oil palm and sugarcane plantations, the surplus value and the land rent generated are no longer appropriated by local landed upper classes, nor subsidizing an industrialization project. They are, instead, increasingly appropriated by financialized capitals exerting an increasing control throughout the flex commodity value chain(s), from production to transformation, fractionation for multiple uses, industrialization, shipping and retailing (see Goodman, Sorj, and Wilkinson 1987; Solano 2009; Fairbairn 2014; Isakson 2014, among others).

I suggest, then, that engaging with the politics of the making of governable spaces to accommodate the agrarian extractivist *project*[6] is a meaningful means to assess the political dynamics of contemporary agrarian change in Guatemala. Elaborating on research since 2006[7] on the politics of sugarcane, and especially oil palm agribusinesses' expansion in the Guatemalan northern lowlands (see Figure 1 below), I will describe the broad contours of major economic, political and ideological distribution conflicts fuelling what could be

[6]So far, I have approached agrarian extractivism as an accumulation and governmental *project*, which might or might not coalesce in a distinctive *regime* of accumulation within capitalism.

[7]Research methods include geographic information system analysis, interviews, participatory observation and a gender-differentiated household survey carried out in October 2010. The survey's sample was stratified by village (significance level 5 percent) and included 294 randomly selected households (586 surveys) in 20 villages of six municipalities within the northern lowlands (see Figure 1).

well considered a new 'cycle of contention'[8] in the Guatemalan countryside. In so doing, I will elaborate on what I call a *multiple politics* perspective. This methodological approach is considered to be helpful in circumventing aprioristic and/or reductionist assessments of usually complex, dynamic and erratic politics of contention around land and natural resources control, in socially diverse, geographically and historically situated agroecological settings. Analytical attention is given to multiple state, corporate and social actors, and to their fluid ideological and political positioning in time. This allows for an assessment of the nature and character of multiple and dynamic relations among such actors or, in other words, of the *politics within the politics* of contention.

Nonetheless, the main interest in this collection is to focus on what Borras and Franco framed as the differentiated 'political reactions "from below" – e.g. among groups of poor, vulnerable and marginalised people and peoples who are affected by large-scale land deals' (2013, 1724). I will, therefore, attempt to put forward an initial discussion on *why*, *how* and *whose* dissent turns into a practice of resistance to changing labor and land control relations in the Guatemalan countryside. In doing so, I will discuss some of the politics *between* historically antagonistic forms of organizing agrarian production and of governing land resources (i.e. agrarian extractivism vs. indigenous-peasant farming), the politics *across* multiple actors resisting agrarian extractivism (e.g. grassroots groups and organizations vs. national militant peasant movements) and the politics *within* particular groups of actors in resistance (e.g. the indigenous 'peasantry').

Beyond a series of conclusions regarding ruptures and continuities between current and previous cycles of contention, my main point here is one over which I claim no novelty, but believe to be worth stressing nonetheless: that trajectories of agrarian change are not a story foretold, but the product of multiple and dynamic politics.

Q´eqchi´ lowlanders' grievances about expanding oil palm and sugarcane agribusinesses

The Guatemalan northern lowlands encompass almost half of the national territory and are mainly inhabited by the Maya-Q´eqchi´ peoples[9] (hereinafter Q´eqchi´). It is in this agrarian frontier that the (1.6-million-hectare) Mayan Biosphere Reserve coexists with tens of thousands of indigenous cultivators supplying Guatemalan and Central American food markets, traditional coffee estates and cattle ranches, and, more recently, sugarcane and oil palm agribusinesses. As mentioned, this paper builds on research since 2006 in various villages from six municipalities within three distinct sub-regions of the northern lowlands depicted in Figure 1 below.

The three sub-regions share a tropical climate, and an altitude of less than 500 meters above sea level, but show significant differences in their historical constitution. As Edelman and León (2013) remind us, putting changing social relations around land and agricultural production into a historical perspective is a sine qua non condition to assessing their character, and discussing their possible trajectories. At the risk of over-simplification, since a fully-fledged historization of the three sub-regions goes beyond the scope of this essay, I suggest two distinct processes of territorialization that characterize the social construction

[8]Understood by Tarrow as 'less momentous than revolutions, more connected than contingent chains of events' (2012, 215).

[9]The Q´eqchi´, with an estimated population of more than two million people, is probably (since the last official population census dates back to 2002) the largest of the 22 Mayan peoples in Guatemala.

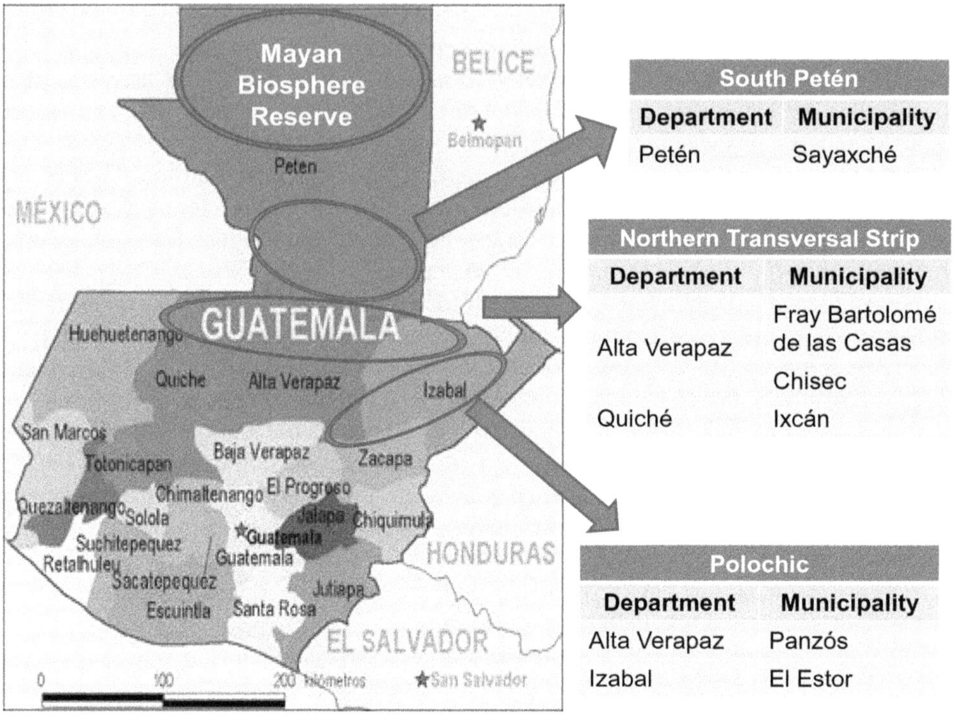

Figure 1. Research sub-regions, departments and municipalities in the Guatemalan northern lowlands region.
Source: Author's elaboration based on Government of Guatemala (2009). Scale: 1:3,000,000.

of the Polochic (see Wagner (2001), Grandin (2004), and Hurtado (2008)), on the one hand, and South Petén and the Northern Transversal Strip on the other (see Schwartz (1990), McCreery (1994), Castellanos Cambranes (1996 [1985]), and Grandia (2012), among other relevant background sources). On the one hand, and South Petén and the Northern Transversal Strip on the other. The Polochic river valley fertile lands were first granted to German settlers, 'white' Guatemalan oligarchs and government cronies by the national state in the 1870s, and they set about establishing large coffee estates. Q´eqchi´ families living in the area were incorporated into the estates under the *colonato*[10] labor regime. As an in-between tenancy and bonded-labor arrangement, this relation of production has many variants that evolved through time and place in Guatemala, and elsewhere in Latin America. It generally combined wage labor with in-kind or labor payments to the landlord (patron) in exchange for the colono family's right to live and farm (only) self-sufficient crops in the patron's hacienda. Families expelled from, or fleeing, the haciendas settled in the hilly lands surrounding the valley during the twentieth century. Others remained as *colonos* in the haciendas up until very recently. Farther north, the agrarian colonization of Petén and the Northern Transversal Strip rainforests was sponsored by military regimes in compliance with the counter-revolutionary land policies following the 1961 Alliance for Progress Initiative. Since then, thousands of families (especially Q´eqchi´) fleeing the colonato labor regime (e.g. in the Polochic) and/or the violence associated with the genocidal

[10]For a fresh review of the *colonato* regime in Guatemala, see Hurtado (2008).

war[11] arrived in these two sub-regions in search of farmland. Alongside this majority of landless and indigenous populations, 'white' traditional large-scale landlords, small- and medium-sized 'ladino'[12] cattle ranchers, and government and military officials also arrived in South Petén and the Northern Transversal Strip during the second half of the twentieth century.

It is within these milieus, where traditional haciendas and ranches coexist with capitalist agriculture and peasant farming, that the sugarcane and oil palm agribusinesses are harnessing control over land resources. That is, according to Ribot and Peluso, they are controlling 'the ability to mediate others' access' (2003, 158). Control over access is just one amongst the three dynamics 'constitutive of relations among actors in relation to resource appropriation, management or use' (Ribot and Peluso 2003, 158); these are *gaining*, *maintaining* and *controlling* access to resources (Ribot and Peluso 2003). There were active land and labor markets in the northern lowlands long before the mid-2000s. But it is since then, and in the context of renewed interests in land resource control for accumulation purposes as mentioned above, that the Market-Led Agrarian Reform (MLAR) and land titling programs implemented by the state land fund (FONTIERRAS) rendered local land resources commodities of interest to capitalized 'outsiders'. Crucially, this set the conditions for major changes in the social relations around land and around capitalist agricultural production, which ultimately became major sources of unrest among Q´eqchi´ lowlanders. These sources of unrest are intimately linked to a series of historically constituted and interrelated grievances of an agrarian, socio-ecological and ideologico-political nature, as well as to grievances related to the 'terms of incorporation'[13] into the emergent agrarian extractivist project.

Agrarian grievances are related to directions of change in land control relations. Broadly speaking, there are two categories of landless people in the northern lowlands. The first, and larger, one is that of second- and third-generation descendants of the 1960s' settlers. The second group comprises those who became landless in the context of expanding sugarcane and oil palm plantations. Eleven percent of the families from the studied areas in the northern lowlands lost their land tenure rights between 2000 and 2010, mostly in order to give way to oil palm and sugarcane plantations (Alonso-Fradejas 2012, 518). Indeed, the land use change analysis between 2005 and 2010, depicted in Figure 2 below, shows that 23 percent of the lands used for oil palm in 2010 were previously used by small-scale cultivators to grow staples.

The land currently under the control of oil palm and sugarcane agribusinesses was privately titled by the state, with the result that corporate acquisitions could be considered perfectly 'legal'. As the manager of a leading oil palm company argues, 'land acquisitions, at least by us, have always been *legal*. If the transaction is *legal* I do not see any problem. We have the *right* to buy [...] When buying land, we must be sure there is not a single problem with the title' (quoted in Hernández 2012, emphasis added). However, almost half of the surveyed male heads-of-household who lost their land, and were not working for an oil palm or a sugarcane company when surveyed, said they were *compelled* to sell their

[11]During the 36 years of war, and especially under the early 1980s military-led scorched earth policy, there were also 160 massacres in these sub-regions. The 1996 Peace Agreements led to the official end of a conflict which left 200,000 people killed or disappeared. Over 80 percent of the victims were civilian, rural, Maya indigenous people (Comisión para el Esclarecimiento Histórico 1999).

[12]This is akin to the *mestizo* racialized identity elsewhere in Latin America.

[13]Ranging from advantageous to adverse terms and conditions of people's incorporation into an accumulation project (Du Toit 2004, 1003).

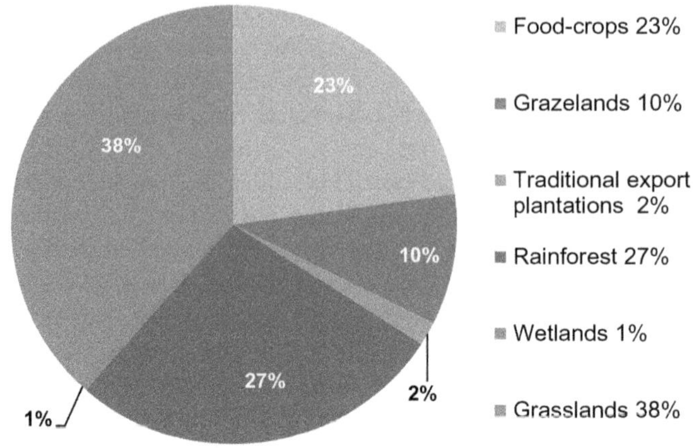

Figure 2. Land uses in 2005 of the land under oil palm cultivation in 2010. Guatemalan northern lowlands.
Source: Alonso-Fradejas, Caal Hub, and Chinchilla (2011).

land. A third of them said they sold it because it was *useless for farming*, and the rest because they were *highly indebted*. Meanwhile, the meager payment most Q´eqchi´ peasant families received for their land did not allow them to develop alternative non-farming livelihoods, nor to regain access to farmland (Alonso-Fradejas 2012, 519).

Socio-ecological grievances are associated with changing land- and water-scapes. Figure 2 above shows that 27 percent of the lands used for oil palm in 2010 were rainforests in 2005, whilst one percent were wetlands and 38 percent grasslands. Rivers are usually diverted to irrigate plantations and, together with other fresh water sources, have become contaminated with sugarcane mill vinasses, oil palm mill effluents and different petro-chemicals (Alonso-Fradejas, Caal Hub, and Chinchilla 2011). The expansion of flex crops is redrawing the land- and water-scapes of fragile socio-ecological systems and having a detrimental impact on these.

There are also far-reaching ideologico-political grievances. As expressed by a middle-aged Q´eqchi´ peasant man from the Sayaxché municipality,

> we, the Q´eqchi´, are facing a major problem. Our thinking is being dominated as well as our beliefs. This is the result of the way the powerful and rich people think. Of those who want to dispossess us from our lands once again. (group meeting, March 2010)

Indeed, many Q´eqchi´ lowlanders feel outraged at the fact that they are losing the land and autonomy they fought so hard for as swidden cultivators who settled as far as possible from estate patrons and state officials.

Finally, the expansion of oil palm and sugarcane over lands previously dedicated to peasant and small-scale capitalist farming is eroding local wage labor opportunities because it is much less labor-intensive. As depicted in Figure 3, oil palm and sugarcane require 52 and 36 working days per ha per year respectively, while, for instance, the two annual maize harvests require 112 and chili cultivation 184 working days.

Besides, many of those incorporated into the agrarian extractivist project as plantation workers or small-scale outgrowers feel they were adversely so. Firstly, piece-meal wages are common in plantation work, and do not cover even the basic food basket cost (Alonso-Fradejas, Caal Hub, and Chinchilla 2011). Working arrangements and conditions

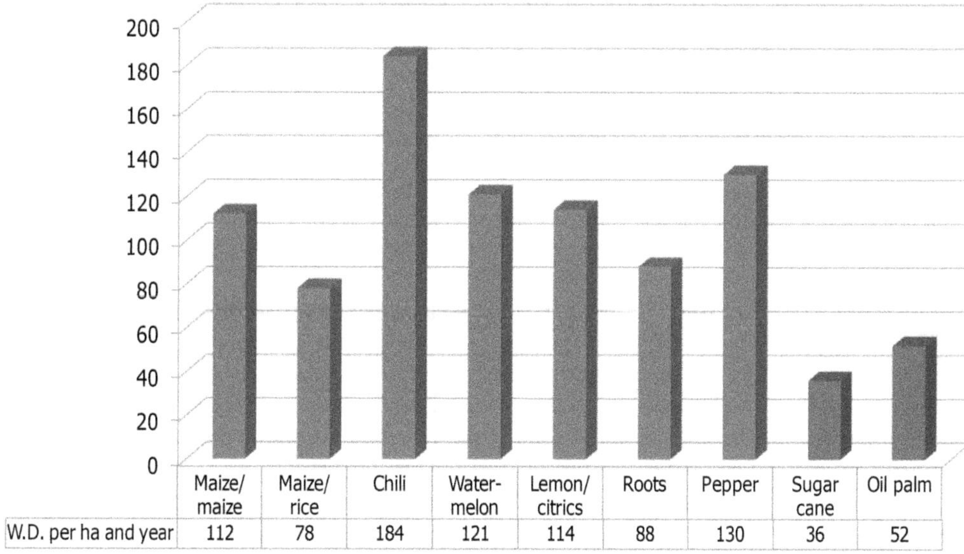

Figure 3. Working days (WD) per ha per year in peasant farming, petty commodity production, sugarcane and oil palm (2009).
Source: Dürr (2011). 'Maize/maize' refers to the two annual harvests of maize on that hectare of land.

are flexible in time and space and outsourced via subcontracted crews, and thus lack labor liability (Alonso-Fradejas, Caal Hub, and Chinchilla 2011). Furthermore, workers and people living near the plantations claim they are suffering from a series of accidents and maladies related to the forms of oil palm and sugarcane production. Machete cuts, sunstroke, dehydration, snake bites, gastrointestinal problems from polluted drinking-water, back, shoulder and wrist injuries due to lifting heavy oil palm fresh fruit bunches, and breathing problems due to the smoke from pre-harvest sugarcane field burning, amongst others, have been reported (Alonso-Fradejas, Caal Hub, and Chinchilla 2011). Most distinctively, a rare kidney disease is killing thousands of sugarcane cutters all over Central America (Sanders and Riordan Seville 2012). In addition, fetal malformations are related to aerial agrochemical spraying (interview with the doctor in charge of Teleman [Panzós] public health posts, June 2009) and increasing rates of venereal diseases to mushrooming brothels (interviews with representatives from *AQT*, Q´eqchi´ women organization, in Chisec, February 2010, and from *Mamá Maquín*, in Fray, November 2013). Secondly, lack of technical assistance and access to sufficient credit, together with variable pricing and high quality and uniformity standards for the oil palm fresh fruit bunches delivered by small-scale outgrowers, are forcing many out of contract-farming, and even into landlessness. Within the emergent labor regime, Bernstein's 'agrarian question of labor' becomes a central one: 'what if the forms of capitalism, including industrialization [...] in the South today are incapable of generating sufficient, and sufficiently secure, employment to provide "a living wage" to the great majority?' (2006, 13).

Overall, these grievances are related to concrete issues that make it harder for many to make ends meet. Different groups of Q´eqchi´ lowlanders feel their 'subsistence minimum' (Scott 1976) is being violated. This feeling is enhanced by narrowing (or breaking) moral economic arrangements of inter-class reciprocity (Thompson 1971; Scott 1976). The moral economy relations which allowed for the continuous (re)negotiation of survival standards between (non-indigenous) traditional landed upper classes, capitalist farmers, and what are becoming fully-fledged Q´eqchi´ rural 'classes of labor',[14] are fading away. As argued by an elder Q´eqchi´ man and former landless movement organizer:

> Sometimes I wonder if we have advanced at all. As *colonos* in the estate the patron forced us to work for almost nothing. Still, we had a patch of land to grow our maize. If anything went wrong with the harvest he would never let us starve. He looked after us because he needed us. Now we are free labor, they say. Free to starve, I say. The rich people do not need us and so do not care about us anymore. (interview in Panzós municipality, November 2007)

The previous statement is very telling of historically constituted subsistence levels among Q´eqchi´ lowlanders across different agricultural labor regimes. Elders often argue that even though patron–client relations under the *colonato* labor regime were exploitative and humiliating, they still allowed for the continuous renegotiation of the minimum requirements for the reproduction of the family. Even during the outbreak of neoliberalism in Guatemala (arguably from the mid-1980s on) and throughout the phase of agrarian capitalism under neoliberal globalization, wage and working conditions of seasonal and/or occasional laborers were still based on similar (if not celebrated, at least tolerated) moral economy arrangements. Things have changed from the mid-2000s on under the impersonal, hyper-commodified and precarious flexible labor regime enforced by oil palm and sugarcane agribusinesses. Wages, labor arrangements and conditions are standardized by absentee owners and inaccessible managers, so it has become far more difficult to negotiate subsistence minimums, compared with the past. In addition, multiple attributes in terms of class, gender, age and their manifold intersections lead to multiple interpretations of what subsistence means, and where its minimum threshold lies. For instance, Q´eqchi´ food cultivators (landed or not, occasional laborers or otherwise) show not only higher expectations, but also higher satisfaction levels, regarding their reproduction needs in comparison to non-farming Q´eqchi´ laborers (Alonso-Fradejas, Caal Hub, and Chinchilla 2011). Poorer Q´eqchi´ women tend to include access to drinking water, firewood, housing materials and medicinal plants as minimum requirements for subsistence more often than less-poor women and men in general (Alonso-Fradejas, Caal Hub, and Chinchilla 2011). Q´eqchi´ elders consider access to, and respect for, sacred places a must, while youngsters across genders and classes generally hold urban living standards in higher regard, and claim that access to information technologies is important for them. Despite the fact that grievances are experienced in different ways, growing difficulties in dealing with them are leading many to transform their unrest into a practice of resistance.

Q´eqchi´ lowlanders' resistance to expansion of sugarcane and oil palm agribusinesses

Resistance can be approached as a complex and non-linear process of defiance, which often combines a messy group of practices of a material and ideational nature. Its capacity to sustain itself is contingent on multiple interventions and tensions between, across and within contenders in different scales and places. In engaging with situated practices of

[14]According to Bernstein, these include all those who 'have to pursue their reproduction through insecure, oppressive and increasingly "informalised" wage employment and/or a range of likewise precarious small-scale and insecure "informal sector" ("survival") activity, including farming; in effect, various and complex combinations of employment and self-employment' (2010, 73).

resistance of the Q´eqchi´ lowlanders, I will discuss the way they *frame* their unrest within and across communities and social groups, through 'shared understandings and identities that justify, dignify and animate collective action' (Tarrow 1998, 21). I will go on to describe the different forms and particular strategies of resistance to agribusiness expansion informing the Q´eqchi´ *repertoire of contention* – that is, 'the ways people act together in pursuit of shared interests' (Tarrow 1998, 30).

Resistance framed as defense of territory

A synthetic review of the recent history of master frames of contention in rural Guatemala is useful to understand the way Q´eqchi´ lowlanders frame their struggles today. During the war (1962–1996), revolutionary uprising relied upon urban and (mainly) rural poor working classes-in-and-for-themselves. Indigenous peoples' demands were contingent upon the triumph of the revolution. National peasant organizations related in different but militant ways to guerilla groups and/or to Catholic Liberation Theologians, and framed their contention for a land-to-the-tiller land reform as part of the broader revolutionary struggle. Some of these organizations disappeared, but others remain active and will be addressed here as 'militant' organizations, often with (inter)national scope.

Neoliberalism was forged and enforced in Guatemala a decade before the Peace Agreements were fully signed in 1996. By then, outcomes of the Washington Consensus' deregulation, liberalization and privatization imperatives were already a major cause of grievances across (rural) classes of labor. The 1992 National Peasant Congress echoed the problems related to unfavorable terms of (agricultural) trade and the dumping of cheap, subsidized corn from the USA. Nonetheless, after the bloodiest scorched-earth massacres were inflicted by the military during the 1980s,[15] and popular expectations for the revolution's success languished, militant peasant organizations and others framed their contention as a *struggle for life* (lucha por la vida) prioritizing the state's respect for politico-civil rights. It was only after 1996, and in the context of deepening neoliberal globalization, that militant peasant organizations embraced *food sovereignty*[16] as their master frame of contention against the Transnational Companies (TNCs)-captured world agri-food system characteristic of the dominant food regime (Friedmann and McMichael 1989).

On top of the exclusion of the (indigenous) peasantry from food, labor and credit markets, and the drastic reduction of public support for their forms of farming during agrarian capitalism under the orthodox neoliberal globalization period, from the mid-2000s onwards they became also excluded from controlling the most productive land resources, as previously discussed. It is in this context that resistance to the emergent project of agrarian capitalism, which I am branding as agrarian extractivism, came to be framed as *defense of territory*. In essence, this is not a novel concept. The right of native peoples to territory was already enshrined in the International Labor Organization (ILO) Convention 169 in 1989. It was further developed in the United Nations (UN) Declaration on the Rights of Indigenous Peoples in 2007. Notwithstanding its formal

[15]Rios Montt, one of the most influential generals at the time, was convicted by a Guatemalan Court of genocide and crimes against humanity on 10 May 2013. Ten days later, the Constitutional Court reversed the verdict. The case was still open during the writing of this article.

[16]See The Declaration of Nyéléni for a definition: http://www.nyeleni.org/IMG/pdf/DeclNyeleni-en.pdf. For a critical discussion on the food sovereignty vision see the three special issues in the *Journal of Peasant Studies* (41:6 2014), *Globalizations* (forthcoming 2015) and *Third World Quarterly* (forthcoming 2015).

regulatory history, I suggest that it is only within the current cycle of contention in the Guatemalan countryside that a discourse on 'territory' has been (1) appropriated by *larger* (other than the leaders of the national indigenous movement) and *wider* (other than Mayan indigenous peoples) grassroots constituencies. Indeed, a historically distinctive feature of defense of territory today has to do with its development and enactment from below. There are, of course, charismatic leaders and ideologues elaborating on the concept. But it is from the grassroots that such actors in particular, and (national) militant peasant organizations more generally, adopt this master frame of contention; and (2) politicized via a strategically essentialized discourse on (collective) rights. As argued by an influential Q´eqchi´ ideologue (lawyer and Member of Congress), the ultimate goal of this frame of contention is to 'move from practices of cultural resistance to the full exercise of collective rights in the territory'.[17]

As we will see below, and contrary to what the etymology of 'defense' may suggest, defense of territory entails defensive and oppositional practices as well as propositional ones, regarding strengthening 'peoples' sovereignty' over their life territories. Among other things, it could be argued that defense of territory aims to bring together two distinct, but intimately related, visions: one is a vision for a self-determined government of social relations of access, control and use of land resources. Accordingly, 'a government agency, an oil palm company or a conservation NGO [non-governmental organization] needs to deal not with individuals but with a collective rights subject that is the *indigenous community*, via its particular institutions of government'.[18] The other is a territorialized vision of food sovereignty, to inform social relations around food production and distribution. Indeed, defense of territory for Q´eqchi´ lowlanders is rooted in their self-representation as *R'al Ch'och* (Sons and Daughters of the Earth). This shared ethnic identity intertwines with one of a traditional sort of (self-sufficient) peasant class for itself (even if often no longer 'in itself') to dignify, encourage and justify Q´eqchi´ collective action in defense of territory.

Q´eqchi´ lowlanders' repertoire of contention in defense of territory

Tilly understood the repertoire of contention as 'the whole set of means that a group has for making claims of different kinds on different individuals or groups' (1986, 4, in Tarrow 2012, 222). Q´eqchi´ lowlanders' repertoire of contention in defense of territory is informed by corporate agents, government officials, national militant organizations and other allies of the indigenous–peasant *movement*. For Tarrow, social movements are 'those sequences of contentious politics that are based on underlying social networks and resonant collective action frames, and which develop the capacity to maintain sustained challenges against powerful opponents' (1998, 2). But, as Tilly remarks, 'social movements are a particular, historically discrete form of organizing contention and not the be-all and end-all of contentious politics' (2004, in Tarrow 2012, 222). Evidence from the northern lowlands suggests struggles in defense of territory are organized in both these ways, namely via more structured social movements and other relatively less structured forms. Hence, I will discuss now a constellation of resistance practices involving both overt-but-occasional structured forms, and surreptitious-but-ubiquitous everyday forms, as summarized in Figure 4 below.

[17]In Asociación Pro Bienestar en Acción Saaq Aach'ool Nimla K'aleba'al (APROBASANK) workshop in Guatemala City, 26 June 2013.
[18]In APROBASANK's workshop in Guatemala City, 26 June 2013, emphasis in original.

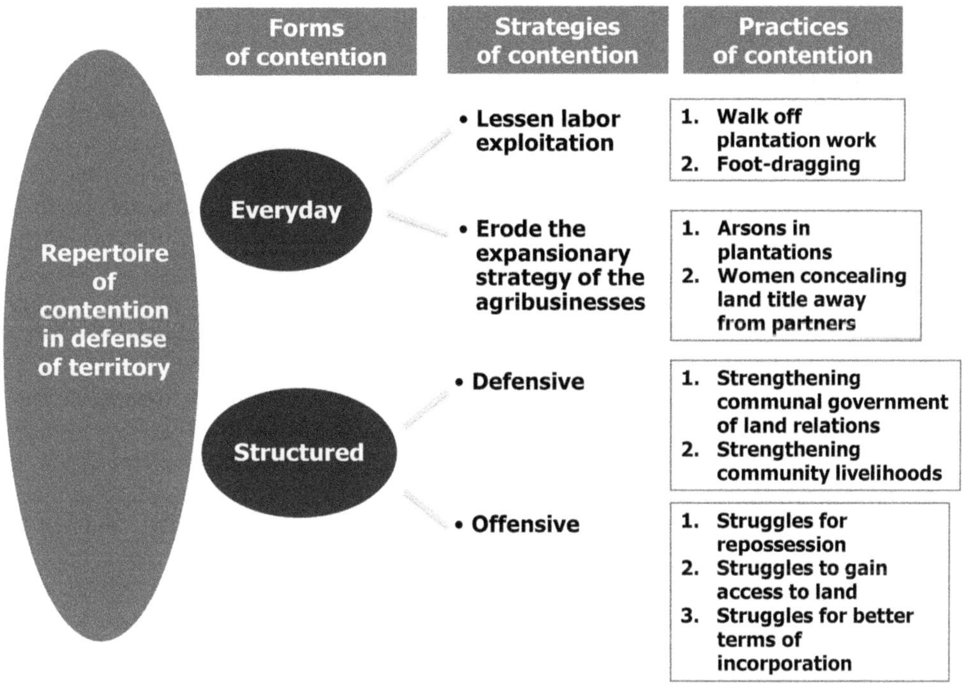

Figure 4. Forms, strategies and practices of the repertoire of contention in defense of territory.
Source: Author's elaboration.

Scott defined everyday forms of resistance as 'the nearly permanent, continuous, daily strategies of subordinate rural classes under difficult conditions' (1986, 22). In addition to frequent gossiping and grieving in trust networks, there are at least four other recurrent practices of everyday resistance to flex crop agribusinesses by Q´cqchi´ lowlanders. I have clustered them in two couples here. The first couple is particular to landless or occasional wage laborers. It is aimed at reducing exploitation in plantation work. One resistance practice here is walking off plantation work without prior notice or subsequent justification. Sometimes this becomes a group response either to unfulfilled promises by the agribusinesses (e.g. to support the community school) or to offences by foremen. There are, in fact, several cases where a community agreement stipulates not to work for a sugarcane/oil palm agribusiness. The other resistance practice is foot-dragging and reporting more work than actually performed. In the municipalities of Ixcán and Chisec, though, foot-dragging turned into defiant sabotage during 2011 and 2012. Full sacks of agro-chemical were buried instead of applied to oil palms. Drain canals were dug, but only next to the roads on which supervisors drove by, and not alongside the plantation. This almost led the main oil palm company in the area to face bankruptcy (interview with a small-scale oil palm outgrower, Chisec, July 2013). However, the company was refloated with new funding, and, in retaliation, local laborers are no longer hired.

The other couple of everyday practices of resistance are particular to the peasantry, and part of a strategy aimed at eroding the expansionary strategy of the agribusinesses. One resistance practice has to do with a wave of arson. In 2007, dozens of oil palms caught fire in South Petén when cultivators burnt their fields in preparation for farming. When questioned by private security or the police, village members would associate such incidents with 'unintended negligence'. Nonetheless, oil palm companies sued the owners of the plots from which the fire spread out, and asked for USD 1875 per burned oil palm.[19] This was considered to be terribly unfair by the peasants, who, in many cases, found no other option than to sell or give their land as in-kind payment to the company. Similar events took place in 2007 and 2008 in the Polochic Valley. The differences were that the maize cultivators were simply leasing the land; that both sugarcane and oil palm plantations were partially burnt; and payment to the agribusinesses was not in kind, but as free labor. The other practice of resistance is carried out by Q´eqchi´ peasant women, and it involves them concealing land titles so their partners find it more difficult to sell the family plot. Indeed, 86 percent of female heads-of-household within those households who sold their land between 2000 and 2010 were openly opposed to the sale (Alonso-Fradejas 2012, 519).

Despite the fact that everyday forms of resistance by the rural poor are ubiquitous, Scott also argued how 'at times of *crisis* or *momentous political change* [they] may be complemented by other forms of struggle which are more opportune. [Everyday forms] are the stubborn bedrock upon which *other forms of resistance may grow*' (1986, 22, emphasis added). Everyday forms of resistance in the northern lowlands are increasingly complemented by, or scaled up towards, more structured forms of defiance. As of July 2012, the Guatemalan Secretariat of Agrarian Affairs reported '1,214 cases of unresolved conflicts in the countryside (involving) 1,000,055 peasants claiming rights over 338,935 hectares of land' (Prensa Libre, 4 September 2012). Figure 5 below shows how 76.4 percent of the different land conflicts reported by the Secretariat (not limited to those related to oil palm and sugarcane expansion) were concentrated in the northern lowlands region.

Negative experiences with FONTIERRAS' MLAR and land titling programs motivated many Q´eqchi´ lowlanders to move away from a 'freehold land property route' towards securing private property rights over particular land plots, to a 'defense of territory route' towards achieving juridico-political status as subjects of collective rights in their territory. Accordingly, Q´eqchi´ overt and structured struggles around land are no longer so much about securing land property *rights*, but about developing and strengthening their own abilities to *control* and *use* land as a means of production, and as territory. Structured forms of contention in defense of territory by Q´eqchi´ lowlanders include both *defensive* and *offensive* strategies. The former are aimed at developing and strengthening their abilities to maintain and control access to land resources. The latter seek to (re)gain access to land, and to improve the terms of incorporation into the agrarian extractivist project.

Regarding the defensive, structured forms of contention, Q´eqchi´ ideologues and grassroots organizations alike suggest that forcing the state to formally recognize communities as subjects of collective rights is a relatively simple 'juridical juggling'.[20] Aware of the fact that law is neither self-interpreting nor self-implementing (Franco 2008), they argue that the state's recognition is of little use if not underpinned by strong grassroots organization and vibrant livelihoods. Hence, defensive strategies to maintain and control access to land resources revolve around community self-determination in the ideologico-political and economic realms. There are ongoing initiatives to strengthen community-led systems of governing village politics in general, and the social relations around land, water and other natural resources in particular. One common practice of contention in this regard is the refusal to

[19]The official monthly minimum wage in Guatemala was USD 190 in 2007 (Alonso-Fradejas et al. 2011, 45).
[20]In APROBASANK's workshop in Guatemala City, 26 June 2013.

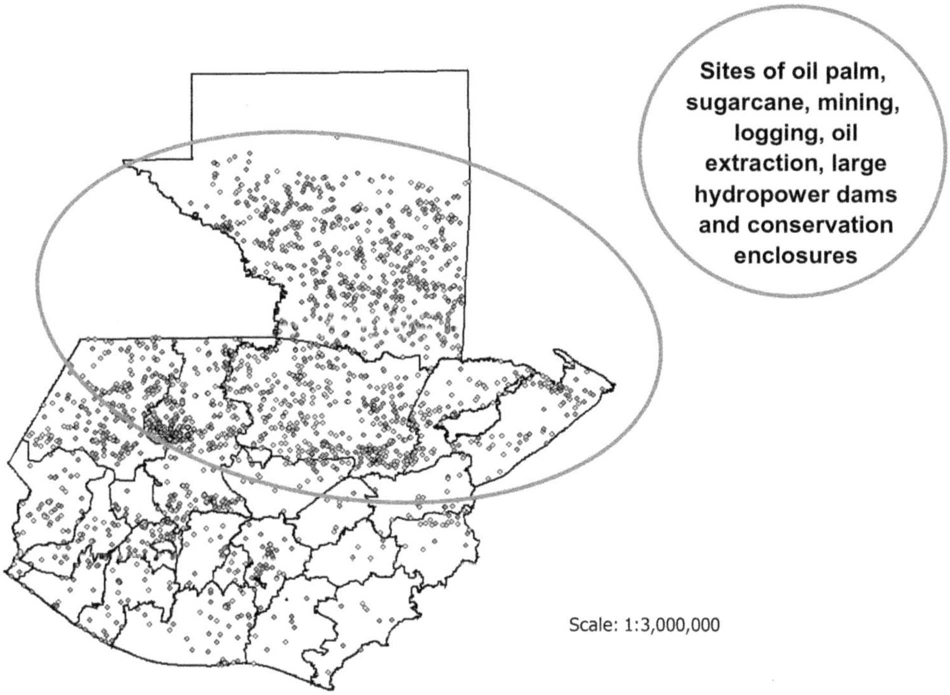

Figure 5. Geographical location of the 1214 agrarian and environmental conflicts registered by the Government of Guatemala in 2012.
Source: Based on Government of Guatemala (http://portal.saa.gob.gt/ accessed on 25 July 2012).

give right of way through village lands to trucks, machinery or workers from sugarcane or oil palm agribusinesses. Many a time this is done in retaliation for similar practices carried out by the companies. Another recurrent practice to resist dispossession is that of counter-ruling freehold land tenure. For example, a communal deed from a Sayaxché village states: 'In the villages where companies are settled, people's freedom is not respected…they privatize all that is indigenous people's patrimony […] so we agree none of us will engage in any land deals with them' (community deed number 19–2007). Other times, community members are prevented from leasing or lending farmland to those who had sold their land before to a rancher or to an agribusiness without a community-sanctioned reason, or without offering it first to other members. Similar practices include that of not accepting as a new community member anyone known to have voluntarily sold his/her land before, and that of expelling from the village anyone who challenges these rulings.

Notwithstanding, counter-ruling freehold land tenure is rarely effective if the reasons for villagers with individual land titles to engage in land deals are not comprehensively addressed. Thus, there are, in addition, initiatives to strength community livelihoods. Most often, available livelihood options for rural Q´eqchi´ lowlanders revolve around farming. Freehold land tenure has contributed to the shift from a communal system of yearly allocation of farmland according to every family's reproductive needs, to one in which the village lands became privately owned and 'fixed' in time and space. As many as eight out of 10 Q´eqchi´ families from the northern lowlands had to abandon an agro-ecologically, culturally and socially sound swidden farming system (see Schwartz (1990), Grandia (2012) and Grünberg et al. (2012), among others) for a more intensive one, suitable to the freehold land tenure regime. Agricultural intensification has usually been akin to increasing dependence on petro-chemical inputs. Evidence from socio-ecological metabolism analysis of Q´eqchi´ peasant households (Mingorría et al. 2014) and from sustained low external input agricultural practices (AVSF and APROBASANK 2011) show, however, that the means to higher yields in the karstic soils of the northern lowlands has little to do with a new Green Revolution miracle. Successful agricultural intensification has more to do with the ability of the family to divert higher amounts of labor towards a low external input-dependent intensification strategy. Becoming aware of this, and lacking support from decimated government extension agencies, groups of Q´eqchi´ lowlanders are being supported by their grassroots organizations, and a few committed (inter)national NGOs, to develop '*Campesino a Campesino*'[21] agroecological knowledge exchanges, on the one hand, and 'peasant markets'[22] in search of more favorable terms of exchange and increased control over local food distribution and sales, on the other hand. Whilst both 'Campesino a Campesino' exchanges and 'Peasant Markets' are not necessarily 'new', they have been re-signified within this cycle of contention as means of struggle against the expansion of oil palm and sugarcane agribusinesses. This represents one of the multiple ways in which the food sovereignty frame informs, and contributes to, defense of territory (and vice versa).

The *offensive* strategies within more structured forms of contention in defense of territory include struggles for repossession, for access to land resources, and for better terms of incorporation into the agrarian extractivist project. These are often confrontational struggles involving a wide range of Q´eqchi´ rural working classes. Two cases of struggles for *repossession* are worth describing here because of their particular character of 'access without control'. The first one is that of a community from Fray municipality, which had its land officially titled in 1981, long before the FONTIERRAS MLAR. Around 20 hectares of community land were seized by a large cattle rancher in the late 1990s, and since then community representatives have been complaining to FONTIERRAS about it. FONTIERRAS officials reassured them there was no need for concern because the land was titled in their name. In 2008, the cattle rancher became an out-grower for an oil palm company and planted the contested 20 hectares with oil palm. Discouraged by government inaction, the community decided to occupy the plantation, chop off the branches from the oil palms, and plant maize among them. In an interview in October 2009, in Coban municipality area, company representatives claimed 'the problem is between the community and the out-grower; we have nothing to do with it'. The conflict was not yet resolved by May 2014. The second case involves another oil palm company and a Q´eqchi´ village from Raxruhá municipality. In June 2012, the community council filed a petition to FONTIERRAS because 2.5 hectares of community land were seized by the company to establish an oil palm nursery. A freshwater creek supplying the village flows through the contested land, and villagers maintain that the company polluted it with agrochemicals. In November 2012, the villagers decided to put pressure on FONTIERRAS and blocked the nearby national road. They allowed drivers to bypass the blockage only after they had carried two baby oil palms from the nursery and into the middle of the road. The company was forced to withdraw from the 2.5 hectares of land, but up until May 2014, villagers were still being harassed by the company's private security when fetching water from the creek.

[21]See Holt-Giménez 2006 for a compelling historicization of this movement in Central America.

[22]Ongoing successful examples include the weekly 'peasant markets' in Chisec and Raxruhá, where only direct producers can sell their produce.

Notwithstanding other practices,[23] land occupations remain the most common way of *gaining access* to land resources beyond FONTIERRAS' market mechanism. The most striking example in Guatemala's recent history is the 2010 occupation of sugarcane plantations by around 800 landless Q´eqchi´ families in the Polochic Valley. It was here that, from 2005 onwards, an agribusiness purchased 5400 hectares of land from traditional estates to move its sugar mill from the southern Pacific region to the Polochic. As mentioned, the Polochic Valley was basically inhabited by Q´eqchi´ families living under long-term *colonato* relations. Since 2002, most of these families were already negotiating with their patron the purchase of the estate's land through FONTIERRAS. Negotiations dragged on due to FONTIERRAS' bureaucratic procedures, and suddenly came to an end when the sugar mill arrived in the Polochic Valley. The offer of a higher price and immediate payment by the sugarcane agribusiness quickly convinced traditional estate owners to call an end to negotiations with their *colonos*. In retaliation, hundreds of landless Q´eqchi´ families from the valley and the surrounding hilly areas occupied 14 estates in November 2010. Five months later, 1500 soldiers and policemen, together with the company's private security staff, evicted all families from the estates.

> Crops and houses were burned down and one Q´eqchi´ squatter was killed by the police. Two more would be assassinated later on by hitmen. In June 2011 the Inter-American Human Rights Commission called on the Guatemalan state to secure the life and food security of the evicted families. (Franco et al. 2012, 9)

In October 2013, the President of Guatemala announced the allocation of a 3.5-hectare plot to every family. As of May 2014, less than 10 percent of the evicted families have been granted such land, and two of the estates were occupied once again. Nevertheless, the sugarcane mill was in full production.

The third and last category of the offensive type of structured forms in defense of territory entails struggles for better terms of incorporation into the agrarian extractivist project, either as plantation workers, or as out-growers. On the one hand, and particularly in Sayaxché, where most farmland is under oil palm cultivation, Q´eqchi´ plantation workers have been struggling for increased wages and de-flexibilized labor arrangements and conditions. Following a major strike during 2012, a negotiating table was promoted by government representatives. Whenever negotiations became stuck, or the companies hired workers from other regions to put pressure on them, local workers would ban any truck with fresh oil palm fruit from accessing the mills. Some consider it to be a great success that every worker is now paid the official minimum wage, and carried to work in a bus instead of in cattle trucks (interview with the workers' representative on the government negotiating table, November 2013). For others, mainly casual landed laborers, but also landless ones, these are not achievements, but just the minimal observance of basic labor rights (group meeting with village representatives from Sayaxché, November 2013). On the other hand, half of the 300 small-scale oil palm outgrowers in Guatemala claimed, in a letter sent on December 2013 to their contractor, that 'the company promised oil palm cultivation was the way out of poverty. However, after four years of meager financial and technical support, together with increasingly unfavorable conditions of exchange, oil palm is rather leading us to bankruptcy and landlessness'.

---

[23]Such as being granted access to communal land resources by the community council, or claiming land legally as an in-kind payment for unobserved wages and labor liabilities as former estate *colonos*.

All these forms, strategies and practices informing the repertoire of contention in defense of territory are relatively well known among contending actors. Yet a distinctive feature from previous cycles of contention lies in the way this repertoire is activated nowadays. In fact, these practices of struggle are increasingly conceived not so much as an end, but as a means for *strategic litigation* processes. Strategic litigation involves grounded practices of resistance exerting pressure 'from below', together with politico-juridical advocacy 'from above', and support from research and social communication 'from the sides'. This is why many Q´eqchi´ grassroots organizations and village representatives are working on alliance building with different actors within and beyond the local/territorial scales.

Scaling up contention: the politics of alliance-building in defense of territory

Becoming aware of the structural nature of their grievances, many Q´eqchi´ grassroots organizations, and entire communities, are willing to get involved in strategic litigation processes as a means to amplify their struggle in defense of territory. This requires forging tactical and strategic alliances. Q´eqchi´ lowlanders have found not many, but definitely diverse, allies. These include (inter)national militant rural social movement organizations, (inter)national development and human rights NGOs, alternative media networks, engaged researchers, some representatives of the Catholic Church and even some progressive state actors. Among the latter, the 'two doors policy' group of government officials stands out. Led by the Rural Development Bureau Secretariat, this group advocates for differentiated policy responses to peasant farming, and agrarian extractivism. They believe there are 'intersections and possible complementarities among these agricultural development models' (Minister of Food, Livestock and Agriculture 2011). Advocates of this current are critical of both radical rural social movements and ultra-conservative oligarchs – a convenient positioning for those promoting an 'extractivism committed to the rule of law and the green economy principles, with corporate social and environmental responsibility' (Director of Strategic Policy, Ministry of Natural Resources and Environment 2013).

An ally more committed to strategic litigation, though less influential within the state, is the mayor of Raxruhá municipality. He was sued in the Constitutional Court by the oligarchic Guatemalan Agricultural Chamber (*Cámara del Agro*) after trying to tax oil palm companies in order to 'recover part of the huge expenses we have to pay to restore what they destroy and pollute' (interview with Raxruhá mayor, August 2013). This move by the Agricultural Chamber, and the negative court verdict in May 2014, radicalized the mayor and the other 56 auxiliary community mayors, who now demand that oil palm companies leave (assembly of Raxruhá village authorities, May 2014).

Notwithstanding, Q´eqchi´ lowlanders are linking more systematically with national militant peasant, indigenous, rural women and youth movement organizations,[24] and their allies. This is not an easy endeavor. Changing class configurations intersect with age, gender and kinship attributes, resulting in an increasingly complex range of positionings within and across Q´eqchi´ communities. This is not always read properly by militant peasant organizations, which can approach Q´eqchi´ villages as a *tabula rasa* of peasants struggling for autonomy (van der Ploeg 2010). This is part of the story, but definitely

[24]With few exceptions from the environmental justice side, alliances with environmental organizations have been difficult and rare, not to mention those with big international conservation NGOs. On the latter, see Ybarra (2011) and Grandia (2012).

not the whole story. Militant cadres complain about 'how hard it is to organize people to struggle for land reform' (interview with a community organizer from a major militant peasant organization, October 2009), while village representatives claim sometimes that national organizations do not pay enough attention to local politics and the pace of struggle (group meeting with authorities from different villages, November 2013). Some grassroots organizations complain that national militant peasant organizations are still very much influenced by Socialist imaginaries, and do not take on board their particular claims as indigenous peoples (interview with a representative from an influential grassroots organization, October 2013). Indeed, Q´eqchi´ lowlanders' demands in defense of territory are too 'indigenist' for some peasant organizations, while their food sovereignty vision is too 'peasantist' for some Pan-Mayan indigenous organizations.

Nonetheless, Q´eqchi´ grassroots groups are engaging more and more actively with, and many times even becoming part of, militant rural social movements (often linked to transnational activist networks) to scale up their struggles in defense of territory. Conversely, Q´eqchi´ lowlanders' place-based practices of resistance allow for the relocalization of national militant rural social movements. These were somehow detached from territorial practices of resistance from the mid-1990s to the mid-2000s, during their commitment to energy-consuming contention in the national and international arenas.[25] Place-based practices of resistance by the Q´eqchi´ (and others) in defense of territory are, indeed, reshaping from below the frames and repertoires of contention of national rural social movements. The 'land-to-the-tiller' and 'food sovereignty' frames are resignified within defense of territory. One example of this is 'The Popular, Peasant, Women and Indigenous March' (*La Marcha Indígena, Campesina, Popular y de Mujeres*). Originally planned by evicted families in the Polochic Valley and a major national militant peasant organization as a nine-day march from Cobán to Guatemala City, it became a major political event. Some 15,000 people walked into the capital city on 27 March 2012, and handed petitions to the President and the Congress. The government agreed upon four points related to agrarian conflict resolution and stricter controls over private armed groups. President Pérez Molina stated that other demands like 'cancelling the debt of hundreds of peasant groups with FONTIERRAS, a moratorium on development projects led by private investors, and the withdrawal of new military detachments were signed with many reservations' (Prensa Libre 28 March 2012). As for Congress, a deed was signed where representatives from most parties agreed on the fast-track approval of Initiative 4084 on the 'Comprehensive Rural Development System Law'. Mostly unfulfilled so far, 'The March' petitions illustrate a coordinated response to the strategies deployed by multiple actors working on the making of governable spaces to accommodate agrarian extractivism.

Repertoire of contention in the promotion of the agrarian extractivist project

Frames and repertoires of contention are critical arenas of struggle in themselves, which serve 'just as easily for social control as for insurgency' (Tarrow 1998, 202). In their making of governable spaces to advance agrarian extractivism, while at the same time countering struggles in defense of territory, corporate, state and social actors employ a repertoire of contention based in three mutually reinforcing strategies. One could be

[25] In other words, they were struggling against the makings of the neoliberal food system at the World Trade Organization and around the negotiations of free trade agreements.

described as the *Trojan horse*[26] strategy. Its aim is to divide and rule through enticement in the local/territorial scales, and its fundamental form of contention is of a discursive and symbolic nature. The second one is the *pretty up* strategy. This is intended to make the agribusinesses' accumulation project seem to be one of socially responsible solutions to pressing ecological problems, across geographical scales. The pretty up strategy also relies on enticement, and its fundamental forms of contention are of a discursive and private regulatory nature. The third strategy is that of *ruling by fiat*. It involves ensuring an openly biased interpretation and implementation of statutory regulation towards particular (corporate) interests be the only one that complies with the 'rule of law' in everybody's interests. This strategy has the double intention of securing what was accomplished through enticement, and achieving through legal coercion and/or the use of physical force what enticement could not. Its fundamental forms of contention are of a statutory regulatory and repressive nature. The character of these three strategies is schematically depicted in Figure 6 below.

Actors pushing for agrarian extractivism are aware of the fact that consent and legitimation in the local/territorial scales today are at least as important as in national and international ones. They are also clear that 'beliefs, ideological controls and discursive practices, as well as negotiated systems of meaning, shape all forms of access [to resources]' (Ribot and Peluso 2003, 168). That is why oil palm and sugarcane agribusi-

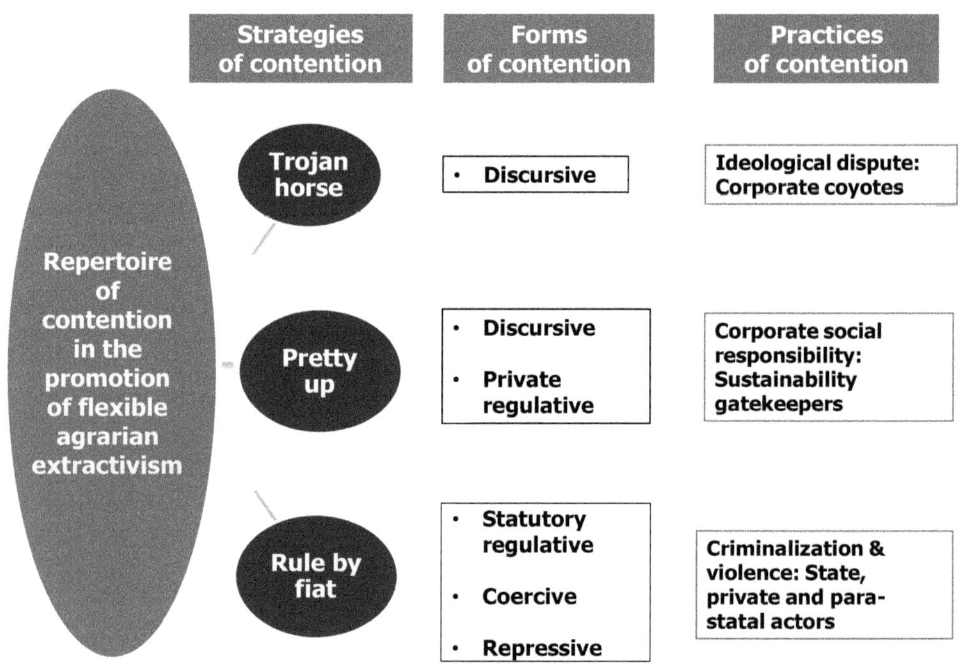

Figure 6. Strategies, forms and practices of the repertoire of contention in the promotion of the agrarian extractivist project.
Source: Author's elaboration.

[26]I am thankful to SiuSue Mark for suggesting this naming.

nesses use the Trojan horse strategy to influence the ideological dispute around the symbolic power (Bourdieu 1989) underpinning dominant knowledge, beliefs and practices in Q´eqchi´ villages and communities. The agribusinesses' Trojan horse is full of what people call 'corporate coyotes'. These are locally recognized and charismatic subjects,[27] who are either hired occasionally or directly employed by the companies. As argued by a group of dispossessed families from Sayaxché:

> They came to cheat us. 'You better sell your land before it is flooded by the Puebla to Panama Plan hydroelectric mega-dams', they said. 'The companies will provide employment and welfare that the state cannot', they also told us. And they were not people from faraway places, not even company lawyers or engineers. They were our brothers from neighboring villages! (group meeting in March 2010)

Corporate coyotes can therefore pervade communal institutions to counter dominant knowledge and imaginaries in the community, like those informing social relations around land, water and other natural resources. They elaborate on class, gender, generational or any other power cleavage available, to erode and reframe the community consensus. The coyotes understand that socially differentiated subsistence minimums lead to multiple positionings within and across communities. Broadly speaking, it is mainly Q´eqchi´ young, landless men who are often more enticed by the 'fast monies' offered by sugarcane and oil palm agribusinesses. There are also youngsters who would rather farm or look for another type of wage work, and those who changed their mind after realizing that 'money goes as fast as it comes and you have to work yourself into the ground in the plantation for it; it is just not a good deal' (group interview with young Q´eqchi´ men from Sayaxché, June 2013). Conversely, Q´eqchi´ women across age groups and peasant and working classes are often the first to act against their partners' or fathers' will to engage in deals with the agribusinesses. As discussed before, women usually act individually and covertly, though they can also join forces to push through gendered hierarchies in community government bodies, and challenge corporate coyotes' narratives.

However, building a favorable consensus is just a part of the coyotes' job. There is a need to 'mobilize' the new consensus (Tarrow 1998, 175) within and across community groups, so that social opposition is pre-empted, and people *willingly*[28] engage in land, labor or out-growing deals with the agribusinesses. Furthermore, for this consensus to become fully hegemonic at the local/territorial scales, it is necessary to go beyond peasant and rural working classes to include other relevant actors, such as local government officials, traditional landed upper classes, grassroots organizations and even different churches. For example, together with the small-scale oil palm outgrowers mentioned before, there are medium and large sugarcane and oil palm outgrowers who are anything but happy with their long-term contract-farming arrangements (interview with a large oil palm out-grower in Fray, December 2013). Some feel the agribusinesses are not supportive enough when problems arise, like the outgrower who was abandoned by the oil palm company in his 20-hectare land conflict with a 'bordering' community in Fray municipality.

[27]They include preachers, teachers, doctors, NGO representatives, community leaders, local radio station announcers, traditional landlords/patrons, ranchers, village mayors, corn traders, civil servants, etc.

[28]Indeed, the ideological dispute played out by corporate coyotes shapes all kind of decision-making processes, including free prior and informed consent (FPIC) by 'the community'.

Or, many owners of traditional large estates and ranches who refused to (or could not) join the flex crops bandwagon feel socially displaced and negatively impacted by expanding plantations. Medium and large cattle ranchers complain their cattle get sick, often after drinking the water running through or by plantations under intense agrochemical inputs, or become stressed by the plague of flies around the mills (interviews with ranchers from the northern lowlands, 2013/2014).

The Trojan horse strategy is informed by, and an expression of, the *pretty up* strategy. The sugarcane and especially the oil palm industries are reframing their social image from simply another accumulation project to the 'answer' to food and energy insecurity, climate change, rural poverty and un-governability, just as was defended by industry representatives from Guatemala, Honduras, Colombia and Ecuador during the First Latin American Congress of Oil Palm Growers (17–18 October 2013, Antigua Guatemala). In fact, the oil palm industry wants to project itself as a 'sustainable' and 'responsible' type of answer to these problems. In prettying up agrarian extractivism as a socially responsible and ecologically sustainable project, what I call 'sustainability gatekeepers' are of outstanding relevance. No matter whether intentionally or not, they play a major role in resignifying oil palm from a hazard to the best option for rural working classes and the environment. Sustainability gatekeepers are championed by big development and conservation (inter)national NGOs, but can also include universities and consultancy firms, which are part and parcel of corporate social responsibility (CSR) initiatives such as the Roundtable on Sustainable Palm Oil (RSPO), Better Sugarcane Initiative (BONSUCRO), or the Roundtable on Sustainable Biomaterials (RSB). First, they bargain over the set of social and ecological standards particular to each initiative with the corporate actors involved. And, then, these sustainability gatekeepers are hired by the very same companies to evaluate whether they comply or not with those standards in order to be granted the 'sustainability seal'. Both corporate coyotes and sustainability gatekeepers 'coincide with the greater political power and have a hegemonic advantage [hence] a pre-eminent position in crafting emergent dominant traditions' (Sivaramakrishnan 2005, 350). Indeed, via the 'Guatemalan Sugar Producers Association' (ASAZGUA) and the 'Oil Palm Growers Guild' (GREPALMA), these agribusinesses are well represented on the powerful 'Guatemalan Agricultural Chamber' and, from there, on the almighty 'Coordinating Committee of Agricultural, Commercial, Industrial, and Financial Associations' (CACIF). Whilst there are various others, CACIF is the main ideologue prettying up agrarian extractivism as *the* socially responsible and environmentally sustainable 'national development' project.

Yet, when enticement and CSR strategies fall short, there is always the possibility to *rule by fiat*. As argued by Li, 'more authoritarian forms of government are often reserved for sections of a population deemed especially deficient and unable to exercise the responsibility of freedom' (2005, 387). The owners of the Polochic sugarcane mill, for instance, called on the state to secure the rule of law when violently evicting hundreds of Q´eqchi´ families: 'We bring employment and wealth; how are they going to progress with those little maize plants [*maicitos*]? Who else would be willing to invest US$ 50 million in this petty valley [*vallecito de pipiripau*]? Rule of law to protect investors is what is needed here' (Guatevisión 29 May 2011). And rule of law was also what the CACIF called for when suing the mayor of Raxruha in court. However, even though the Constitution acknowledges a constitutional hierarchy to international human rights treaties, such as the ILO convention number 169, or the International Covenant on Economic, Social and Cultural Rights, the Constitutional Court does not recognize the outcomes of 61 'community consultations held in good faith' between May 2005 and March 2012.[29]

Ruling by fiat also meant the fast-track approval by the Congress of eight new laws on investment protection and labor flexibility, as promoted by the CACIF in February 2013, while freezing the legal initiative on rural development agreed with 'The March'. Furthermore, the government is using the 1965 counter-insurgent 'Decree 7 on Preventive States of Emergency' to deploy the military in villages where there are land control grab-related conflicts. National attorneys, for their part, deal with disruptive collective action through the Anti-terrorist Bill, and treat land occupations, for instance, as penal offenses of 'aggravated usurpation of property'. This is leading to dozens of peasant leaders and organizers being put in jail (interview with a member of the Maya Lawyers Association, Guatemala City, June 2013). This particular interpretation and enforcement of the law speaks for itself regarding whose interests prevail within core institutions of the Guatemalan state.

In addition to state violence, private and parastatal violence is also part of the game. Public tracks are closed by the gates built by sugarcane and oil palm agribusinesses. It is common for the plots belonging to peasants and even to medium-scale ranchers, who refuse to sell or grow oil palm on their land, to end up being enclosed by plantations. Men refusing to sell their land are threatened by the companies' private security staff who use ultimatums such as: 'either you sell at the price we offer, or we will have to bargain with the widow instead' (group meeting in a South Petén village, March 2008). Threats are sometimes carried out, and many have been assassinated or disappeared after refusing to sell their land, or when mobilizing in defense of territory.[30] What is more, if resistance is one side of the survival coin, and compliance is the other, joining criminal gangs, private security forces or becoming a narco hit man are the survival coin's edge of growing despair in the northern lowlands. Scott argued how 'certain combinations of atomisation, terror, repression, and pressing material needs can, indeed, achieve the ultimate dream of domination: to have the dominated exploit each other' (1986, 30). Or attack each other. This is the case when groups of generally poor, landless Q´eqchi´ men are hired to assault and/or evict their fellow resisters.

Conclusion

The current cycle of contention around the agrarian extractivist project in the Guatemalan countryside resembles previous cycles in many ways. For instance, the state persists as both a relevant means for, and an arena of, contestation. And many of the strategies, forms and practices of contention in defense of territory, and in the promotion of the agrarian extractivist project, have been adapted from previous cycles of contention.

Nonetheless, there are important ruptures with the past too, many of which have to do with the discussed dynamics around the labor regime fix, and the land good governance fix at play. Subsistence minimums are pushed to unprecedented thresholds. There are also new actors, such as the financialized flex crop agribusinesses, small-scale oil palm outgrowers, new fragmented classes of rural labor, global land (good) governance institutions and NGOs, multi-stakeholder CSR certification schemes, radicalized grassroots organizations and so on, with a sharpened accumulation and governmental project on one side, and

[29]In all of them, communitarians unanimously rejected different accumulation and development projects ongoing or planned in what they consider their territories.
[30]It is difficult to give an exact figure because many resisters are attacked in moments and places other than those of direct confrontation. The Social Pastoral of Petén estimated in 'dozens' the number of resisters killed in Petén only between 2004 and 2009 (workshop in Petén, November 2009).

with historically refined practices of resistance on the other. There are, in short, analytical and political challenges ahead, in and around the emergent agrarian extractivist project.

Framing resistance to agrarian extractivism as defense of territory offers the possibility to bridge 'the best of both worlds' informing collective identities in the Guatemalan countryside – that is, community-accountable forms of governing land resources, as indigenous peoples, and low external input farming practices, as peasants. It also allows for grounding the vision of food sovereignty, while making of it both a fundamental means of struggle against the agrarian extractivist project and a vision informing a transformative life project. However, the defense of territory master frame also brings new challenges with regards to Borras' and Franco's differentiated political reactions 'from below' to land grabbing. First, a representational challenge: the unified bearer of collective rights enshrined within defense of territory – that is, the (indigenous-peasant) 'community' – is subject to major social differentiation dynamics. Second, a targeting challenge: strengthening farming livelihoods and community command over land relations may provide the necessary means and meanings for resistance. But whether, and how, to engage with the state regulatory powers remains so far unresolved questions, if such self-determined practices aim to have a future as part of a transformative project. And lastly, an alliance-building challenge: in scaling up resistance towards strategic litigation processes, there remains the hurdle of the knowledge dialogue between, across and within village authorities, grassroots collectivities, national militant peasant, indigenous and women movements' organizations, and other allies in the academia, the media, the (International)NGO community, and the state.

Efforts to assess the political dynamics of contemporary agrarian change in socio-agroecological settings like the ones discussed here will benefit, thus, from engaging with the politics of the making of governable spaces to accommodate the agrarian extractivist project. In doing so, it is critical to examine the changing practices of, and relations between, across and within multiple corporate, state and social actors who are pushing for, resisting, complying with or operating at the most violent margins of the agrarian extractivist project. Following this multiple politics perspective, then, it is worth stressing again that trajectories of agrarian change are not a story foretold, but the product of multiple and dynamic politics.

Acknowledgements

The author is most grateful to the editors of this collection and to the two anonymous reviewers for their meaningful comments. He is also very thankful to Jun Borras, Mindi Schneider, Max Spoor, SiuSue Mark, Ben Mckay, Zoe Brent, María Banos Smith, Tsegaye Moreda Shegro, Daniela Andrade, and Natalia Mamonova for their very helpful comments on earlier versions and/or copy-editing support. Any remaining errors are his own.

References

Acosta. 2013. Extractivism and neoextractism: Two sides of the same curse. In *Beyond development: Alternative visions from Latin America*, ed. M. Lang and D. Mokrani, 61–86. Quito/Amsterdam: Transnational Institute / Rosa Luxemburg Foundation.

Akram-Lodhi, A.H., and C. Kay. 2009. The agrarian question: Peasants and rural change. In *Peasants and globalization: Political economy, rural transformation and the agrarian question*, ed. A.H. Akram-Lodhi and C. Kay, 3–34. London: Routledge.

Altieri, M.A., and V.M. Toledo. 2011. The agroecological revolution in Latin America: Rescuing nature, ensuring food sovereignty and empowering peasants. *Journal of Peasant Studies* 38, no. 3: 587–612.

Alonso-Fradejas, A. 2012. Land control-grabbing in Guatemala: The political economy of contemporary Agrarian change. *Canadian Journal of Development Studies/Revue canadienne d'études du développement* 33, no. 4: 509–28.
Alonso-Fradejas, A., J.L. Caal Hub, and T. Miranda Chinchilla. 2011. *Plantaciones Agroindustriales, Dominación y Despojo Indígena-Campesino en la Guatemala del Siglo XXI*. Guatemala: IDEAR and Magna Terra Editores.
AVSF and APROBASANK. 2011. *Agriculturas Campesinas En Zona De Frontera Agrícola, Estudio De Casos*. Chisec, Guatemala: Unpublished.
Bebbington, A. 2007. *Minería, Movimientos Sociales y Respuestas Campesinas: Una Ecología Política De Transformaciones Territoriales*. Vol. 2. Lima: Instituto de Estudios Peruanos.
Bernstein, H. 1998. Labour regimes and social change under colonialism. In: Ben Crow, Mary Thorpe et al., eds. *Survival and change in the third world*. Cambdridge: Polity Press, pp. 30–49.
Bernstein, H. 2004. Changing before our very eyes': Agrarian questions and the politics of land in capitalism today. In Redistributive land reform today, ed. T.J. Byres. *Journal of Agrarian Change* 4, no. 1–2: 190–225.
Bernstein, H. 2006. From transition to globalization: Agrarian questions of capital and labour, International Conference on Land, Poverty, Social Justice and Development, 9–14 January 2006, Institute of Social Studies pp.1–22.
Bourdieu, P. 1989. Social space and symbolic power. *Sociological Theory* 7, no. 1: 14–25.
Borras, S.M., and J.C. Franco. 2013. Global land grabbing and political reactions 'from below. *Third World Quarterly* 34, no. 9: 1723–747.
Borras, S.M., J.C. Franco, R. Isakson, L. Levidow, and P. Vervest. 2014. Towards understanding the politics of flex crops and commodities: Implications for research and policy advocacy. Think Piece Series on Flex Crops and Commodities No.1, Amsterdam, Transnational Institute (TNI).
Borras, S.M., J.C. Franco, S. Gómez, C. Kay, and M. Spoor. 2012. Land grabbing in Latin America and the Caribbean. *Journal of Peasant Studies* 39, no. 3–4: 845–72.
Byres, T.J. 1991. The agrarian question and differing forms of capitalist transition: An essay with reference to Asia. In *Rural transformation in Asia*, ed. J. Breman and S. Mundle, 3–76. Delhi: Oxford University Press.
Byres, T.J. 1996. *Capitalism from above and capitalism from below. An essay in comparative political economy*. London: Macmillan.
Castellanos Cambranes, J.C. 1996 [1985]. *Café y campesinos. Los orígenes de la economía de plantación moderna en Guatemala, 1853–1897*. Madrid: Catriel.
Comisión para el Esclarecimiento Histórico. 1999. *Conclusiones Y Recomendaciones Del Infrome De La Comisión Para El Esclarecimiento Histórico. Guatemala Memoria del Silencio Tz'inil Na'tab'al*. Guatemala: United Nations.
Declaration of Nyéléni. 27 February 2007. http://www.nyeleni.org/IMG/pdf/DeclNyeleni-en.pdf (accessed September 22, 2014).
Director of Strategic Policy, Ministry of Natural Resources and Environment. 2013. In Government of Guatemala's 'I National Congress on Racism and Discrimination', 7–9 August 2013, Guatemala.
Du Toit, A. 2004. Social exclusion discourse and chronic poverty: A South African case study. *Development and Change* 35, no. 5: 987–1010.
Dürr, J. 2011. *Diez mitos y realidades sobre las cadenas agroalimentarias en Guatemala, y una cuenta nacional de base agraria. Documento de Trabajo para Discusión*. Guatemala: GIZ/IDEAR.
Edelman, M., and A. León. 2013. Cycles of land grabbing in central America: An argument for history and a case study in the Bajo Aguán, Honduras. *Third World Quarterly* 34, no. 9: 1697–722.
Engels, F. 1951[1894]. The peasant question in France and Germany. In: K. Marx and F. Engels, ed. *Selected works*, Vol. 2. pp. 381–99. Moscow: Foreign Languages Publishing House.
Fairbairn, M. 2014. Like Gold with Yield': Evolving intersections between Farmland and finance. *Journal of Peasant Studies* 41, no. 5: 777–95.
Figueroa Ibarra, C. 1980. *El Proletariado Rural En El Agro Guatemalteco*. Guatemala: Editorial Universitaria USAC.
Fine, B. 2012. La financiarisation en perspective. *Actuel Marx* 51: 73–85.
Foster, J.B. 2000. *Marx's ecology: Materialism and nature*. New York: Monthly Review Press.
Franco, J.C. 2008. Making land rights accessible: Social movement innovation and political-legal strategies in the Philippines. *Journal of Development Studies* 44, no. 7: 991–1022.

Franco, J.C., S.M. Borras, A. Alonso-Fradejas, N. Buxton, R. Herre, S. Kay, and T. Feodoroff. 2012. *The global land grab: A primer*. Amsterdam: Transnational Institute.

Friedmann, H., and P. McMichael. 1989. Agriculture and the state system: The rise and decline of national agricultures, 1870 to the present. *Sociologia Ruralis* 29, no. 2: 93–117.

Government of Guatemala http://portal.saa.gob.gt/ accessed on 25 July 2012

Goodman, D., B. Sorj, and J. Wilkinson. 1987. *From farming to biotechnology. A theory of Agro-industrial Development*. Oxford and New York: Basil Blackwell.

Grandin, G. 2004. *The last colonial massacre: Latin America in the cold war*. Chicago: University of Chicago Press.

Grandia, L. 2012. *Enclosed: Conservation, cattle, and commerce among the Q'Eqchi' Maya Lowlanders*. Seattle: University of Washington Press.

Gregory, D., R. Johnston, G. Pratt, M. Watts, and S. Whatmore. 2009. *The dictionary of human geography*. Oxford, UK: Wiley-Blackwell.

Grünberg, G., L. Grandia, A. Alonso-Fradejas, B. Milián, L. Hurtado, R. Euler, and E. Cotom. 2012. *Tierra y Desigualdad en Petén, Guatemala. Informe de Evaluación del Programa de Administración de tierras en Petén*. Washington D.C.: The World Bank.

Guatevisión 29 May 2011. 30 minutos. Guatemala

Gudynas, E. 2009. Diez tesis urgentes sobre el nuevo extractivismo. Contextos y demandas bajo el progresismo sudamericano actual. In Centro Andino de Acción Popular (CAAP)/Centro Latinoamericano de Ecología Social (CLAES) (ed.): Extractivismo, Política y Sociedad. Quito: CAAP/ CLAES, 187–225.

Handy, J. 1984. *Gift of the devil: A history of Guatemala*. Vol. 2. Toronto: Between the Lines.

Harvey, D. 2003. *The new imperialism*. New York: Oxford University Press.

Hernández, O.J. 2012. Desplazar Para no Ser Desplazados. *Plaza Pública*, 30 September.

Holt-Giménez, E. 2006. *Campesino a Campesino: Voices from Latin America's Farmer to Farmer Movement for Sustainable Agriculture*. Oakland: Food First Books.

Holt-Giménez, E. 2008. Territorial Restructuring and the Grounding of Agrarian Reform: Indigenous Communities, Gold Mining and the World Bank TNI Land Policy Series 2, Amsterdam: Transnational Institute.

Hunsberger, C. and A. Alonso-Fradejas. 2015. The discursive flexibility of 'flex crops': comparing oil palm and jatropha (forthcoming).

Hurtado, L. 2008. *Dinámicas Agrarias Y Reproducción Campesina En La Globalización. El Caso De La Alta Verapaz*. Guatemala: F&G Editores.

Hurtado, L., and G. Sánchez. 2011. *Qué Tipo de Empleo Ofrecen las Empresas Palmeras en el Municipio de Sayaxché, Petén?* pp. 1–60. Guatemala: Action Aid.

IAASTD International Assessment of Agricultural Knowledge, Science and Technology for Development. 2009. *Agriculture at a crossroads. Global Report*. Washington: UNDP, FAO, UNEP, UNESCO, World Bank, WHO, Global Environment Facility.

Isakson, R. 2014. Food and finance: The financial transformation of agro-food supply chains. *Journal of Peasant Studies* 41, no. 5: 749–75.

Jessop, B. 2010. Cultural political economy and critical policy studies. *Critical Policy Studies* 3, no. 3–4: 336–56.

Jessop, B. 2007. *State power*. Cambridge: Polity Press.

Kautsky, K. 1988[1899]. *The Agrarian question*. Vol. 2. London: Zwan.

Lander, E. 2011. The green economy: The Wolf in Sheep's clothing. TNI Working Paper. Amsterdam: Transnational Institute.

Leff, E. 2006. La Ecología Política en América Latina. Un campo en construcción. In *Los tormentos de la materia. Aportes para una ecología política latinoamericana*, ed. H. Alimonda, 21–39. Buenos Aires: CLACSO.

Lenin, V.I. 1964[1899]. *The development of capitalism in Russia: The process of formation of a home market for large-scale industry* (2nd edn). Moscow: Progress Publisher.

Li, T.M. 2005. Beyond 'the state' and failed schemes. *American Anthropologist* 107, no. 3: 383–94.

Li, T.M. 2011. Centering Labor in the Land Grab Debate. *Journal of Peasant Studies* 38(2): 281–298

Martínez-Alier, J. 2002. *El ecologismo de los pobres: conflictos ambientales y lenguajes de valoración*. Barcelona: Icaria.

Martínez Peláez, S. 1976. *La Patria Del Criollo: Ensayo De Interpretación De La Realidad Colonial Guatemalteca*. San Jose: Editorial Universitaria Centroamericana.

Marx, K. 1974[1867]. *Capital: A critique of political economy*. Vol. I. London: Lawrence and Wishart.
McCreery, D. 1994. *Rural Guatemala, 1760–1940*. Stanford: Stanford University Press.
Mingorría, S., G. Gamboa, B. Martín-López, and E. Corbera. 2014. The oil palm boom: Human well-being implications for Q'eqchi' communities in the Polochic valley, Guatemala' Environment. *Development and Sustainability* 16: 841–71.
Minister of Food, Livestock and Agriculture. 2011. Una nueva propuesta de USAC y URL (en construcción) para el abordaje del Desarrollo Rural Integral. In 'Conference on Agrarian and Rural Dynamics in 21st Century Guatemala', 11 October 2011, Rafael Landivar University, Guatemala
Moore, J. 2011. Transcending the metabolic rift: A theory of crises in the capitalist world-ecology. *Journal of Peasant Studies* 38, no. 1: 1–46.
Netting, R.M. 1993. *Smallholders, householders: Farm families and the ecology of intensive, sustain able agriculture*. California: Stanford University Press.
O'Laughlin, B. 2008. Governing capital?. Corporate social responsibility and the limits of regulation. *Development and Change* 39, no. 6: 945–57.
Prensa Libre 28 March 2012, printed edition
Prensa Libre, 4 September 2012, printed edition. Guatemala
Ribot, J.C., and N.L. Peluso. 2003. A theory of access. *Rural Sociology* 68, no. 2: 153–81.
Sanders, K., and L. Riordan Seville. 2012. Mystery kidney disease decimates Central America sugar-cane workers, October 16, NBC News. http://investigations.nbcnews.com/_news/2012/10/16/13866856-mystery-kidney-disease-decimates-central-america-sugarcane-workers (accessed September 22, 2014).
Schwartz, N.B. 1990. *Forest society: A social history of Petén, Guatemala*. Philadelphia: University of Pennsylvania Press.
Scott, J. 1986. Everyday forms of peasant resistance. *Journal of Peasant Studies* 13, no. 2: 5–35.
Scott, J.C. 1976. *The moral economy of the peasant: Rebellion and subsistence in Southeast Asia*. New Haven and London: Yale University Press.
Sivaramakrishnan, K. 2005. Some intellectual genealogies for the concept of everyday resistance. *American Anthropologist* 107, no. 3: 346–55.
Solano, L. 2009. Estudio Del Destino De La Producción De Caña De Azúcar Y Palma Africana Y La Situación De La Producción Y El Mercado De Agrocombustibles En Guatemala, pp. 1–74. Guatemala: Action Aid.
Tarrow, S.G. 1998. *Power in movement: Social movements and contentious politics*, (2nd edn). Cambridge: Cambridge University Press.
Tarrow, S.G. 2012. *Strangers at the gates: Movements and states in contentious politics*. New York: Cambridge University Press.
Thompson, E.P. 1971. The moral economy of the English crowd in the eighteenth century. *Past & Present* 50: 76–136.
Tilly, C. 1986. *The Contentious French*. Cambridge, MA: Harvard University Press.
Tilly, C. 2004. *Social Movements 1768-2004*. Boulder: Paradigm Publishers.
Van der Ploeg, J.D. 2010. 'The peasantries of the twenty-first century: the commoditisation debate revisited. *Journal of Peasant Studies* 37, no. 1: 1–30.
Veltmeyer, H., and J. Petras. 2014. *The new extractivism in Latin America*. London: Zed.
Wagner, R. 2001. *Historia del café de Guatemala*. Bogotá: Villegas Editores.
White, B., S.M. Borras Jr., R. Hall, I. Scoones, and W. Wolford. 2012. The new enclosures: Critical perspectives on corporate land deals. *Journal of Peasant Studies* 39, no. 3–4: 619–47.
Ybarra, M. 2011. Privatizing the Tzuultaq'a?. Private property and spiritual reproduction in post-war Guatemalaj. *Journal of Peasant Studies* 38, no. 4: 793–810.

Listening to their silence? The political reaction of affected communities to large-scale land acquisitions: insights from Ethiopia

Tsegaye Moreda

In Ethiopia, large-scale land acquisitions have been growing ever larger over the last few years, mainly in the lowland parts of the country. A substantial amount of land has already been acquired by both domestic and foreign investors in the Benishangul-Gumuz region. The land acquisitions pose apparent threats to the economic, cultural and ecological survival of local indigenous communities. In particular, Gumuz ethnic groups, who depend on customary forms of land access and control, and whose livelihoods are based heavily on access to natural resources, are being differentially affected. Through a case study in some selected administrative districts of the Benishangul-Gumuz region, this paper uses empirical evidence to examine how local indigenous communities are engaging with or challenging the recent land acquisitions. By doing so, the paper shows how the apparent silence of the Gumuz people regarding the land acquisitions is misleading. It shows how local communities, although not organized either politically or economically, express their discontent in differentiated ways against the state and social forces – particularly over land and access to employment, and around state politics. As I show in this paper, local reactions range from covert to more open forms of resistance.

1. Introduction

This paper sets out to examine how local indigenous communities perceive ongoing large-scale land acquisitions in Ethiopia, and how these communities, with a particular focus on the Gumuz people in the Benishangul-Gumuz region, have been reacting to them.

Ethiopia could be cited as one example of a country in which large-scale agricultural investments are growing ever larger. Clearly upward trends in land acquisitions, by both domestic and foreign investors, have been observed over the last few years, mainly in the lowland parts of the country. As the land acquisitions have proceeded, civil society and human rights groups, opposition political parties, academics and researchers have increasingly expressed their concerns, emphasizing that these land acquisitions are threatening local livelihoods and the environment. In this regard, emerging but limited empirical studies focusing particularly on questions of local land rights have demonstrated the implication of land deals on local communities (Rahmato 2011; Lavers 2012a; Shete 2011). As is the case of Ethiopia, where the state formally owns land and at the same time is sympathetic to large investments in land, it is rather common for local communities to lose out in the process, since they cannot effectively negotiate under a situation of wider inequalities in bargaining power (e.g., Von Braun and Meinzen-Dick 2009, 2). This is exacerbated in areas where customary land rights are not respected or where clearly defined property rights and effective judicial systems to protect such rights do not exist or are weak.[1] Historical experiences suggest that land rights often define or are a reflection of the dynamics of power relationships that exist between peasants and the state. Control over land resources has always been the main source of political power, and the basis for state hegemony in which the state assumes a decisive role over rights of access to and disposal of land resources (Rahmato 2009, 283).

It should be noted that land-based political power is of particular concern today as pressure and competition for land resources are alarmingly high. In light of this, there is no doubt that land acquisitions are disrupting local land-based social relations, as the land rights of local communities are pushed aside when powerful interest groups, including the state, need the land (Borras, Fig and Suarez 2011; Li 2011; HLPE 2011; Toulmin 2008; Visser and Spoor 2011). Practically, the land acquisitions taking place in many developing countries are not based on a consideration of 'the complex and messy actually existing land-based social relations' (Borras and Franco 2010a, 34), but rather rely predominantly on simplified categorizations by the state (Scott 1998).[2] For instance, indigenous ethnic groups in the Benishangul-Gumuz region that have distinct and longstanding local land-based social relations and territorial claims are now under renewed pressure because of current trends of land acquisitions by more powerful interests. This is because the land acquisition processes are largely carried out on the perception of abundant 'unoccupied' land availability in the region, in which existing traditional land-use practices and social relations that are rooted in the traditions of indigenous communities have been or are being deliberately overlooked. Studies conducted so far in the country related to the issue, though limited, show that adverse implications have already occurred for these indigenous communities and their environment, and contend that these will likely worsen in the future (e.g., Rahmato 2011; Kelbessa, Aklilu and Woldemariam 2009; Shete 2011; Fisseha 2011; Lavers 2012b). For example, Rahmato (2011), through a case study in Bako Tibee *woreda* (Oromiya region) and Gambella region, demonstrated how the land acquisitions caused land displacement and damage to the livelihoods of local communities by depriving them from accessing 'vital resources from what until now was their common property'.[3] Beyond looking at the impact of land investments, recent papers by Lavers (2012a, 2012b) make a useful analysis of the role of domestic political economy and the state in influencing emerging patterns of agrarian transformation in the country. Yet these existing studies make only passing reference to, or say nothing at all about, local reactions (responses) to these growing land acquisitions. Nor do they help us understand how local communities are trying to engage with or challenged the land acquisitions. This is, of course, not to say that the implications of the land acquisitions for local communities are well researched, but it is to draw attention to the need to also examine how local

[1]In analyzing large-scale land acquisitions, the notion of property rights is here conceived not just as 'a bundle of rights' over land but as 'a bundle of powers' that focuses on ability, and this brings attention to relationships that enable or constrain the ability to access resources (Ribot and Peluso 2003).

[2]As a counter to this 'state simplification', emphasizing the notion of 'land sovereignty' is crucial for grounding analysis from actually 'existing local land-based social relations' in order to ensure that local people are consulted appropriately and their priorities addressed in the process (Borras and Franco 2010a). What lies at the core of the 'land sovereignty' concept is 'the rural poor people's right to land' (Borras and Franco 2010a, 35).

[3]There are five tiers of government administration in the country, which include (from the highest to lowest administrative unit): federal, region, zone, *woreda* and *kebele*. *Woreda* is roughly equivalent to district, while *kebele*, especially in rural areas, corresponds to a group of villages.

communities are engaging with or challenging them. Therefore, it is essential to empirically demonstrate how affected indigenous communities perceive and react to the land acquisitions and why.

As generally argued in the emerging body of literature on 'land grabbing', large-scale land acquisitions do not always result in people losing their land, although in many instances they have led to the dispossession and displacement of peasants and indigenous people. Those people affected by such acquisitions may not necessarily engage in outright resistance, as this depends on the particular economic, political, social and cultural contexts in which they are situated (Borras and Franco 2013). When resistance does occur, it occurs in a differentiated way depending on the economic and political agencies involved. Likewise, the choice of which strategies of resistance to use tends to vary depending largely on the specific social structures, strengths and defensive capacities of the resisters (Scott 1987, 422). Although the indigenous communities in Ethiopia, particularly the Gumuz, appear to be 'silent' about the land acquisitions, both covert and overt forms of resistance are taking place. The reasons for the resistance of the Gumuz people are not just because they have been displaced from their lands or are being threatened with displacement, but also because they feel marginalized from emerging (but limited) employment opportunities available because of the 'land investments', and because of the lack of fulfilment of other promises that such investments were purported to bring. As will be demonstrated in this paper, the Gumuz have been challenging the land acquisitions in various ways, challenging the state and social forces particularly over land and access to jobs, and around state politics.

This paper is thus an attempt to use empirical evidence in order to demonstrate the type and nature of reactions by local communities towards land acquisitions, through a case study in Benishangul-Gumuz region. By doing so, the paper tries to show how local communities, although not organized either politically or economically, express their discontent in various ways. Information for this study comes from a combination of various data collection methods carried out during intensive fieldwork from April to June 2012. It includes semi-structured, in-depth interviews with key informants, focus group discussions (FGDs), direct field observation and secondary literature review. The in-depth interviews were conducted with 17 key Gumuz informants and 14 selected government officials and experts at various hierarchical levels. In addition, in the selected case study villages, a total of seven focus group discussions were conducted with the communities affected by the land acquisitions. Interviews were also conducted with five managers of investment projects operating in the study areas.

This paper is structured in such a way that the next section provides an overview of the context of the study area. This is followed by a brief outline of the conceptualization of local resistance. The fourth section presents the empirical discussion and analysis. Finally, section five draws a short conclusion.

2. Introducing the socioecological, historical and political economic context

The Benishangul-Gumuz region, on which this study focuses, is one of the nine administrative regions of Ethiopia. This region, which is one of the areas where many of the current land acquisitions are focused, is located in the northwestern part of the country, sharing an international border with Sudan and South Sudan in the west. In a national setting, the region shares borders with the Amhara and Oromiya regional states (Figure 1). It occupies an estimated total area of 50,380 km^2 (BGRS 2004), and has a total population of 670,847 (CSA 2008). The population consists of indigenous ethnic minority groups of Berta, Gumuz, Shinasha, Mao and Komo. It is also inhabited by settlers from

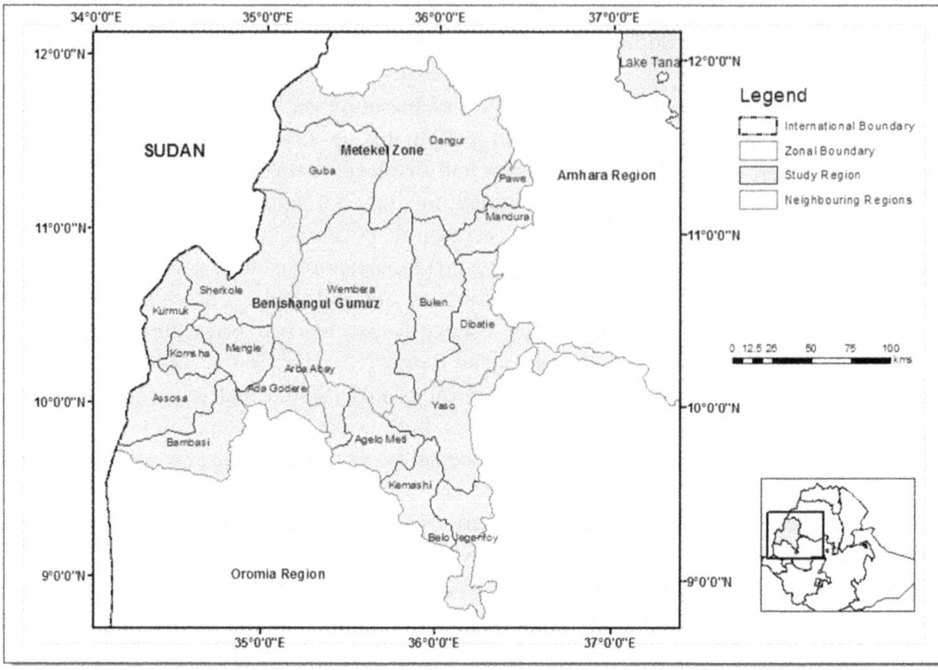

Figure 1. Map of Benishangul-Gumuz regional state, Ethiopia (showing location of study *woredas*). Note: This map was made by Abel Markos, a colleague in the Department of Geography and Environmental Studies, University of Gondar (Ethiopia).

other regions, with a diverse ethnic background. Starting in the 1950s, these settlers moved into the area because of 'distress push' migration, mainly from drought-affected areas of the northern part of the country, and later through state-sponsored forced resettlement schemes by the Derg regime.

The region is perceived to have extensive and untapped land resources with a great potential for agricultural development, and has a vast vegetation cover of natural forests, bushes and shrubs.[4] In terms of its land-use pattern, over three quarters (77.4%) of the region's land mass is covered in bushes and shrubs, while forestlands constitute about 11.4% (MoFA 2010). In addition, cultivated land and grazing lands constitute about 5.3 and 3.2%, respectively. Marginal land is estimated at about 2.3% of the total landmass of the region. The region is endowed with streams and rivers that flow throughout the year, with a great potential for irrigation: the Dabus, Dedessa, Beles and Abay (Blue Nile) are the major rivers that flow through it. About 1 million hectares of land in the region are estimated to be potentially irrigable. Agro-ecologically, about 75% of the region is classified as lowland (*kolla*) while 24% and the remaining 1% of the region's area are classified as midland (*Woina dega*) and highlands (*Dega*), respectively (MoFA 2010).

The Gumuz ethnic group, the focus of this study, largely inhabits Metekel and Kemashi administrative zones, constituting the most numerous ethnic group of these zones

[4]This perception by the federal state and local political elites appears to have shaped the current policy of leasing vast tracts of the region's land to investors.

(Figure 1). The Gumuz people, who are recognized as the original inhabitants of these areas, depend on a customary land-tenure system of communal ownership.[5] Gumuz people are traditionally shifting cultivators who practice slash-and-burn agriculture. The practice of shifting cultivation by the Gumuz has often been confused with pastoralism. However, the Gumuz are not actually pastoralists. They rely on shifting cultivation for their livelihood, which is supplemented with other subsidiary activities such as hunting, gathering, fishing and honey production and collection. They also keep some livestock. Unlike the highlanders, the Gumuz people do not cultivate their fields intensively. Rather, they cultivate a given plot of land for about 3 to 5 years, then leave it to lie fallow when a decline in yield is perceived. Within their clan territory, new land is then cleared and cultivated in the same way until the yield is again seen to deplete. In the process, the whole village or part of the village may also be abandoned if the newly acquired lands are located too far from current villages. However, the Gumuz do not in fact move to new places all the time but rather move around and return to their abandoned lands that were left to regenerate. This shifting cultivation system is practiced according to their customary practice of land access and control.

Individual Gumuz associate themselves to a group that is basically identified in terms of its spatial location/territory. Within Metekel administrative zone, for instance, there have been main groups into which individual Gumuz have associated themselves; for example, the Gumuz of Mandura, the Gumuz of Manbouk (Dangur), the Gumuz of Dibati, the Gumuz of Guba and the Gumuz of Wombera. These groups are differentiated on the basis of their territorial attachments and are separated by natural features such as rivers. For example, Beles River separates the Gumuz of Mandura from those of Manbouk. Each of these groups is then divided into several clans. Accordingly, each clan owns all the resources inside its territory marked by land features such as rivers, hills, big trees, roads and footpaths. To the Gumuz, land resources are communal property and rights to these resources are derived from the clan. Individual members thus have usufruct rights enabling them to clear and cultivate the land within the boundary of their clan. In this way, they enjoy possession rights over the land they are cultivating until they leave it fallow. Once they leave the land unused, other members of the clan can use it. Generally, the real owner of the land is the clan, not individuals (see also Rahmato 1988; Abbute 2002). It is this fluid and complex customary land-based social relationship that has been at stake because of the large-scale land acquisitions underway in many parts of the region.

Situating the recent large-scale land acquisitions taking place in the region within a historical, political-economic and socioecological context is vital for understanding the nature of the relationship that exists between the region's indigenous ethnic groups, the central state and territory. Historically, the indigenous ethnic groups of the region have suffered for centuries the encroachment and exploitation by Ethiopian highlanders and Sudanese

[5]Unlike other regions, for instance the Amhara region, land registration and certification has not been undertaken in the Benishangul-Gumuz regional state and, thus, traditional land-tenure systems are still widely practiced. Note that the difference in the de facto tenure system between highland regions and the lowlands, including the Benishangul-Gumuz region, cannot be attributed to the absence of land registration in the latter, as land registration is a recent phenomenon that took place in most highland areas only from 2003 onwards. Despite the Derg's 1975 land reform proclamation that abolished differences in land tenure over the whole country by distributing usufruct rights only, tenure in the highlands has long been based on individual holdings, while customary forms of tenure have been largely practiced in the lowland regions.

states.[6] As a sizable body of literature illustrates, this region, which is now referred to as the Benishangul-Gumuz, currently one of the nine regional states under the federal political system based on ethnic regional administrations, was annexed and incorporated into the Ethiopian empire towards the end of the nineteenth century during the reign of emperor Menelik II (Ahmad 1999; Zewdie 1991, 83; Pankhurst 1977). After this incorporation, its people were made to pay tribute in 'slaves, ivory and gold' to the central state as well as to local chiefs (Ahmad 1999, 433). Historical accounts even show that in the mid-nineteenth century, Kassa Hailu (later Emperor Tewodros II) is said to have raided these north-western borderlands for slaves (Crummey 1986, 139). Nonetheless, as far back as the fourteeth century, the Gumuz people were already paying tribute to the central state of the then-emperor Yeshaq (Pankhurst 1977; Huntingford 1989, 93). In the following periods, they faced continuous acts of domination and subordination by the Ethiopian highlanders on one side and the Sudanese Arabs on the other side of the border. The people of the area were not only enslaved by outsiders but local power elites were also actively involved in slave raiding and trading. Notably, ruling chiefs such as Sheikh Khojele of Asossa and Hamdan Abu Shok of Gubba (Metekel) were powerful local rulers who had historically raided and traded their own subjects (Donham 2002; Ahmad 1999, Gonzalez-Ruibal and Fernandez 2007). In so doing, these local rulers collaborated with central state authorities in subduing their own kin. As Markakis explains, past exploitations and oppressions 'tore the fabric of indigenous communities, fragmenting and dispersing the people to find refuge in inaccessible malaria-ridden [lowland areas], from where they emerged only recently to confront a perplexing world' (Markakis 2011, 84).

Traditionally, population growth and distribution trends in Ethiopia tended to concentrate in the highland areas, whereas lowland regions remained sparsely inhabited by indigenous people and underdeveloped in terms of basic infrastructure as compared to their neighbouring highland areas. Since the second half of the twentieth century, the indigenous Gumuz communities have come under increasing pressure from migrants from drought-affected and environmentally degraded parts of the country, and from the gradual encroachments by their neighbouring highlander plow cultivators who were expanding into the area slowly in search of cultivable land (Abbute 2002). The effort of the land-hungry highlanders' search for land was later reinforced by the resettlement programme of the Derg regime that has moved a large number of them to the lowlands. This consequently brought them into direct confrontation with indigenous communities, with predictably troubling consequences (Markakis 2011). In the 1980s, for example, tens of thousands of impoverished people from other areas were resettled on land that belonged to the Gumuz. These patterns added extra pressures on indigenous lowland communities, separate from the longstanding subordination and subjugations. It is worth noting that the highlanders had deeply entrenched racist attitudes, which have not completely vanished today, towards the Gumuz, whom they often described as inferior and hostile and called what is now a derogatory name – 'shanqila', meaning 'slave' (Ahmad 1999; Markakis 2011). Such stereotypical prejudice is still evident to this day in the interaction of the highlanders with the Gumuz and other indigenous communities (see Section 4.2).

Starting in the early 1990s, the Gumuz people of the Metekel area experienced another form of land alienation caused by the introduction of private rain-fed agricultural investment schemes. A number of private investors, commonly from the highlands, leased

[6]Historically, a large part of the Benishangul-Gumuz region was 'a buffer zone and a trade entrepôt' between Ethiopia and Sudan (Markakis 2011, 84).

around 38,250 hectares of land from the regional government for commercial farming and natural gum and incense harvesting (Abbute 2002, 123). More recently, large-scale land acquisitions that involve both domestic and foreign investors are underway in the region, pushing the local communities farther away: these communities are finding that they have no place left to retreat. For the Gumuz communities, 'easy retreat, mobility and inaccessibility through dispersion and bad communications have been the means of self-preservation' (James 1986, 35) when they faced intense pressure. In this regard, considerable land acquisitions have occurred at a significant scale throughout the region, particularly in Metekel, while the land rights and natural resource-based livelihoods of indigenous local communities appear to have been subverted in the process. During fieldwork, I gathered data from various government sources (including the Regional Investment Bureau and the Environmental Protection, Land Use and Administration Bureau) to estimate the amount of land that has been granted to investors in the region. The amount of land already transferred to investors has now reached about 390,590 hectares and recent trends suggest that the transfer will most likely increase in the future, as much additional land has been already earmarked for this purpose (see Moreda 2013).

A recent trend of implementing a villagization programme in the region, particularly in the areas that are the focus of land acquisitions, is instructive of the efforts being made by the government to clear more land for investors. For example, in 2011/2012, it envisaged settling 19,763 households from their scattered settlements to designated villages across most of the *woredas* within the region (BGRS 2011). Although the government presented this villagization programme as a major strategy through which the deprived indigenous communities of the region could be transformed, especially through the provision of services such as water, health care clinics, schools, transportation and agricultural extension services, the very fact that villagization is currently occurring in the same areas as the land acquisitions makes plausible the claim that such a strategy may be used to clear the land for investors. For example, Gumuz informants interviewed in Dangur *woreda*, who were recently relocated to newly designated villages, were quite explicit in indicating that most of their previous lands have already been transferred to investors and the remainder will also inevitably be given away soon as well (Interview, Qotta *kebele*, May 2012).

No one else, particularly the local communities, researchers and independent observers, denies the immense damage and pressure brought to the Gumuz communities and their local environment by all these processes, both past and present, although the government clearly does. It should be noted here that the current government claims that since it is leasing out 'unused' or 'underutilized' lands to investors, it is unlikely that the ongoing land investments will have an adverse impact on the lives of local communities. But critical questions have already been posed regarding the land that is described as 'unused' or 'underutilized', suggesting such a view is the outcome of the undervaluing of existing local land uses and different categories of users. In the present study areas, given the fact that most of the indigenous ethnic groups mainly depend on shifting cultivation, rising land acquisitions have been causing adverse impacts on local land-use practices and land resources, including land displacements, declining access to resources and environmental destruction. Although land scarcity is not a problem, at least for the moment, the Gumuz interviewed in all study *kebeles* unvaryingly sense that this will soon become a reality due to the enclosure of the large land resources they had access to under their traditional system of tenure. The Gumuz generally view the land acquisitions as threats that create additional challenges by exerting intensified pressures on their local land rights and on access to their traditional source of livelihood (see also Moreda 2013).

In spite of the various types of pressures, the Gumuz traditionally attempted to defend their customary land from 'outsiders' using various forms of resistance. And, when the pressures become too much, the Gumuz simply fled to inaccessible, remote areas so that they could continue to pursue their traditional way of life. Finally, however, even these remote areas appear to have been reached by the current large-scale land acquisitions underway throughout the region. This is the situation that the Gumuz and other indigenous local communities of the region are stuck with today. It is to this issue that the next section turns and attempts to examine the reactions of those affected local communities to ongoing land acquisitions. First, however, I would like to make a few points from the literature, both theoretical and empirical, regarding the conceptualization of local resistance.

3. Conceptualizing local resistance

If we are to examine the reactions of local communities against the large-scale land acquisitions today, then *a priori* understanding of the concept of resistance is critical. Although there is the risk of oversimplification, this section tries to achieve its goal through consulting the dominant literature about the conceptualization of local resistance. For almost the past four decades, a number of scholars have been engaged in the study of peasant resistance, heavily influencing current debates about its conceptualization (e.g. Scott 1976; 1985; 1987; Kerkvliet 1986; 1993; 2005; 2009; Isaacman 1990; Moore 1998).

In the context of contemporary land grabs, local communities who have faced land alienation or are being threatened by displacement as a result of current land acquisitions engage in different forms of resistance in order to maintain their socio-cultural identities and moral economies (Scott 1976; Walker 2008; Malseed 2008). From 'a moral economy discourse', when the actions of the state and other actors threaten or cause damage to the local livelihoods of rural communities that are often characterized by distinct cultural identities, then the morality of 'the subsistence ethic' is disrupted and will likely lead to rebellion (Scott 1976, 3). Here, the subsistence aspect of peasant households forms the central tenet of Scott's argument. He understands peasants as moral and political actors who can defend their values as well as their individual security.

Viewed in this light, local rural communities engage in various forms of resistance to counteract the processes that threaten their livelihoods (Scott 1985; Walker 2008; Malseed 2008; Schneider 2011). Differences in the strategy of peasant resistance emanate from multiplicities in their political behaviour and relative strengths that in turn depend on their particular context (Isaacman 1990, 21), the forms of appropriation and appropriating class they are facing (Scott 1985) and their own historical experience as well as their cultural background (Gonzalez-Ruibal 2012). As local rural communities can be politically fractured and socially differentiated in more complex ways than is often assumed, the impact of land grabs on and within even small communities can be differentiated, and consequently their reaction to it will likewise be differentiated depending on their particular economic, political, social and cultural contexts (Borras and Franco 2013).

Much of the debate has been related to the definition of resistance and what actions actually qualify as resistance. Scott (1985, 290) asserts that

> class resistance includes any act (s) by a member (s) of a subordinate class that is or are intended either to mitigate or deny claims made on that class by superordinate classes (for example, landlords, large farmers, the state) or to advance its own claims (for example, work, land, charity, respect) vis-à-vis those superordinate classes.

Kerkvliet (2009, 233) defined resistance as 'what people do that shows disgust, anger, indignation or opposition to what they regard as unjust, unfair, illegal claims on them by people in higher, more powerful class and status positions or institutions'. What stands out clearly in these definitions is that resistance comprises thoughts as well as actions. In his most influential work on the *Weapons of the weak*, based on the case of a Malaysian village, Scott (1985, xvi) identifies diverse forms of everyday resistance that include verbal characterization of superiors, dissimulation, pilfering, foot dragging, sabotage, false compliance, feigned ignorance, slander, arson, desertion and so on. In this work, he demonstrated that while engaging in these various forms of resistance, 'subaltern' people belittled dominance and hence were not mere victims of hegemony.

However, other scholars have argued that such actions do not actually qualify to be considered as resistance since they do not have revolutionary potential: they do not directly challenge the underlying political system and hence are not politically effective. Drawing from Marx's discussion, Das (2007, 363) pointed out that

> as long as grassroots agency is confined to and aimed at a power structure within its own immediate vicinity, it is necessarily self-defeating. Class power is concentrated in the state at the national level, and those who proclaim the efficacy of everyday forms of resistance tend to forget this.

For this reason, it has been argued that resistance needs to be organized via the collective action of many people that directly threatens and challenges the system of oppression.

Moral economists such as Scott and Kerkvliet, however, note that the reactions of peasants against exploitation and subordination often tend to be individualized, unorganized and localized forms of insurgency that do not often make headlines. For Scott particularly, excluding these forms of peasant actions from the category of 'real resistance' would 'fundamentally misconstrue[s] the very basis of the economic and political struggle conducted daily by subordinate classes in repressive settings' (Scott 1985, 292), and he warns that those who hold these views will 'miss the very wellsprings of peasant politics' (Scott 1985, 295). The goal of most everyday peasant resistances is not, after all, 'to overthrow or transform a system of domination but rather to survive ... within it' (Scott 1987, 424). Following Scott, Isaacman (1990, 33) also underscores the significance of everyday forms of resistance, in which 'to ignore the weapons of the weak is to ignore the peasants' principal arsenal'. Indeed, Scott strongly argues that formal political activity involving co-ordination among many people is generally exercised by the elites, the intelligentsia and the middle classes, since they are in a better position to gain easy access to the institutions of the state and other targeted actors to contest with. Peasants are likely to have limited access to these institutions and thus 'it would be naïve to expect that peasant resistance can or will normally take the same form' (Scott 1985, 299). Empirically, Kerkvliet (2005) has shown the power of everyday politics in transforming national policies, for example in the case of Vietnam. Nevertheless, as Borras and Franco (2010b, 23) argue, the ground for exercising everyday politics is not smooth and is played out under various constraining structures that make such activities difficult political endeavours. These constraints undermine the capacity of peasants to pursue their agendas further and, hence, such resistance generally does not have far-reaching consequences.

A crucial issue that emerged from these debates therefore relates to 'what really counts as resistance'. In this regard, Scott demonstrates that such forms of peasant politics need not necessarily be effective to be considered resistance: for him, what is important is the intention of the actions more than the outcome, although it is sometimes difficult to understand the intentions behind some actions. This conception is essential because the very presence of resistance is often an indicator of the existence of discontent among the resisters towards the rules of the 'development' endeavour pursued by the state and other elite groups.

The following empirical section scrutinizes the ways in which local communities have been reacting to the recent large-scale land acquisitions. As touched upon in the previous section, in spite of their long history of exposure to exploitative practices and subjugation, the Gumuz communities did not in fact fall passive victim to 'false consciousness', dominant highlanders' ideology and the state's hegemonic representations.[7] They were able, to a certain extent, to resist the subjugation and hegemonic ideologies of the highlanders and the state in order to maintain their material as well as their cultural space. As will be discussed in what follows, the reactions of the Gumuz target those individuals and groups, including the state, that have participated and facilitated the land acquisitions in one way or another. In their reactions, the Gumuz try to make their actions and thoughts felt by the targets, although they are very careful in maintaining the anonymity of the individuals involved. This bears a resemblance to how Kerkvliet characterized the features of everyday resistance: '[to] the extent that the target is rather specific, those who resist imagine that their actions would not be condoned by the target' (Kerkvliet 1986, 108).

4. Local reactions

4.1. *Reaction against investors*

As was indicated earlier, the threat to rural livelihoods of increasing trends in land acquisitions appears to be on the rise. Although the land rights and natural resources-based livelihoods of local communities have been under pressure from encroachments by highlanders, state-sponsored resettlement schemes and state farms over the past several decades (Abbute 2002; Gebre 2003), the pressure is now increasing as more and more land resources are given out by the state to commercial agricultural investments, particularly in the last few years. This in turn is resulting in land disputes and contestations between local communities, the state and investors. Despite these contestations, because of the weak bargaining power of local communities, the interests of those who have the power to manipulate institutional and administrative frameworks are prevailing. Specifically, the Gumuz are the overlooked losers in the process.

Interviews and discussions with local individuals and groups in the study areas made it clear that there have been increased disputes over the dispossession of cultivated lands and access to water associated with land investment projects. However, the informants underscored how powerless they are in defending their rights due to the strong politicization of the land investment undertakings, which now also involve the federal government. In this regard, the federal government was viewed as an entity against which it is impossible to

[7]As Gramsci (1971) argued, the dominant classes normally control not only the material means of production but also the symbolic means of production. Through creating discourses as well as through coercion, the dominant groups try to install or solicit 'consent' for their hegemonic rule by defining what is beneficial and legitimate and, as a result, the subordinate groups accept such hegemonic ideologies and exploitations as normal and justified. Nonetheless, Scott (1976, 1977) demonstrated that peasants were capable of opposing and struggling against exploitative practices and dominant ideologies that threatened their moral economies in ways that did not conform to the assumptions articulated in Gramsci's formulation and, hence, he contended that peasants were not in fact victims of 'false consciousness'. According to Scott (1977, 280), 'there can be no question of hegemony when vital needs are ignored or violated by elites, for these needs are an integral part of peasant consciousness and values'.

dispute, something that has made the Gumuz fearful. As one Gumuz man (Guba *woreda*) concisely puts it: 'We cannot wrestle with these rich investors … we know that they have a link with and support from the government. If we wrestle with them, it is obvious that we will lose' (Interview, Ayicid *kebele*, 6 June 2012). A similar view was found among local and regional authorities, though in a muted form, over their reduced influence in relation to land allocations.

Nevertheless, several scattered forms of resistance took place through which the Gumuz people expressed their discontent towards the ongoing land acquisitions. The local reactions targeted all of the actors involved in the land acquisitions in one way or another. One of the main actors targeted by the local communities were the investors. The local communities generally reflected negative attitudes towards investors operating in their surroundings, and several instances of covert expressions of resistance against them have occurred. Within Dangur *woreda*, for example, informants indicated that local communities sabotaged one of the investment projects that acquired land in their *kebele* (Interviews, Gimtiya *kebele*, May 2012). According to informants, a farm machinery warehouse belonging to the Jaba Agro-industry Private Limited Company (PLC) was set on fire during the night by individuals who still remain anonymous. The manager of the project told me that as a result of the sabotage, machinery such as tractors, threshers and spare parts as well as many other valuable goods were destroyed (Interview, Gimtiya *kebele*, 17 May 2012). He believes that this was sabotage carried out by the local community. As the warehouse was the main target, he suspects that the action was mainly orchestrated by former guards working in the warehouse who knew the whereabouts of key machinery. Because of threats of more action, the company was reluctant to make further investments, speculating that more damage might be inflicted. Actually, the manager was well aware of the risks in the area, mentioning that this was not the first incident that had happened in that specific area. He explained that the land which now belongs to Jaba Agro-industry PLC used to be farmed by another domestic company which left the area some years ago because of the attacks it had faced. The brother of the investor who used to work as the manager on the project was killed on the land by a Gumuz arrow. Soon after that, the investor stopped the project and left the area. Bows and arrows are the main traditional weapon used by the Gumuz for self-defense and hunting. As the case above demonstrates, such sporadic and anonymous actions by local people cannot be overlooked and could in fact have the potential to have a major impact on projects.

During focus group discussions on the above arson incident, the Gumuz noted that indeed Jaba-Agro Industry PLC had suffered huge losses because of it, but they preferred to be silent on the issue and they did not want to speculate on who may have been behind it (FGD, Gimtiya *kebele*, 20 May 2012). Rather, they emphasized the damage the project had caused them. They were even angry about the name of the project itself: Jaba is the name of a village in another area, though within the same *woreda*. The local communities of Gimtiya *kebele* considered this an insult and contended 'how embarrassing it is to hear the name of another place being given to our land while we have our local name'. Some of the informants among the Gumuz during individual interviews indicated that they wanted these people to leave the land as nothing good has happened since their arrival (Interview, Gimtiya *kebele*, May 2012).

Damaging field crops is another act of resistance that has been undertaken by the Gumuz people in Belojiganfoy *woreda*. In this *woreda*, for example, an estimated 700 hectares of land covered by maize ready for harvest was destroyed by fire. The investor accused the local community of deliberately causing the fire. Here again, local communities remained quiet when asked for the possible cause of the damage. Their silence cannot necessarily be taken as a sign of their ignorance. Here, it is fairly obvious that, as Scott (1985, 290) asserted, 'the actor is unlikely to admit to the action itself, let alone explain what he had in mind'. From an interview with an official in the regional capital, Assosa, it is clear that the regional government is aware of the hostile attitudes of local communities towards the investors, and thus speculates that the crop damage might have been one of their strategies to chase out investors from the land they were allotted by the government (Interview, Assosa, 18 April 2012).

The Gumuz were not only involved in covert forms of reaction; there were also incidents of overt actions taken against the investors. Local people took part in outright conflicts with the investors in villages that were relatively far from zonal and *woreda* towns so that government forces could not easily intervene. Disregarding the claims made by investors, several Gumuz people occupied and cultivated the land already allocated to the investment projects. This was especially the case in Yaso and Belojiganfoy *woreda*, where local people occupied the land, disregarding the investors, in order to counteract them. In Dangur *woreda*, villagers of Gimtiya *kebele* also insisted on cultivating the land that was already cleared by investors in their villages. A key informant from Gimtiya *kebele* administration described it as follows:

> One of the investors who acquired about 3000 hectares of land in our *Kebele*, for example, tried to clear [a] large part of it. However, this investment project is actually unable to secure this whole land it is trying to develop, as some people in this village defy the land boundaries claimed by the project. In every direction, the villagers encroach upon the investor's land when the planting season comes in order to take advantage of the already cleared land. We tried to tell them in various community meetings not to encroach on the land already cleared by the investors but they just ignore us. And instead claim that the land originally belonged to them. We even tried to warn the villagers that they must stop this or they will be jailed. (Interview, Gimtiya, 16 May 2012)

In interviews, one of the project managers of investment sites in the area complained that it is harder to chase these people from the land without the help of local government authorities, something which might stir even more animosity (Interview, Gublak town, 18 May 2012). He indicated that once they sow crop seeds on the field then it is unthinkable to touch it because their revenge or reaction to that would be so serious. The investors generally refrained from taking measures in such situations for fear of inflaming and provoking violent confrontations. The solution was to compromise; that is, let them cultivate unless they push further and, of course, until permanent mechanisms to force the local people to stop such acts were devised. Despite this, there were times in which investors brought in the federal police forces stationed in the nearby town of Gublak to threaten the local people from advancing further into the investment lands already cleared. The villagers, however, claimed that they were cultivating their ancestral land and rejected claims of any wrongdoing. One elderly Gumuz stated that 'it is them who came to us, not us who went to them. We were here, always' (Interview, Gimtiya *kebele*, 19 May 2012).

Here it is worth emphasizing that the shift in the resistance strategies from covert to overt by the Gumuz people as described is thus related to the state's inability to exert authority over remote locations, implying that the state's presence and ability to enforce control over territory and people is the defining feature in this instance.

4.2. *Reactions against seasonal immigrant labourers*

As a strategy to undermine the land acquisitions, local communities attempt to resist the immigration of seasonal agricultural wage labourers migrating from the central highlands of the Amhara region. In this regard, it is interesting to note that investment projects almost totally depend on agricultural labourers recruited from other regions of the country, particularly neighbouring regions. Following the ongoing land acquisitions, there has been a growing influx of highland seasonal migrant labourers coming to the area for wage employment in areas such as weeding and mowing.[8]

Not only do these migrant workers work as seasonal agricultural labourers, they also introduce a new form of encroachment on the available land resources. As the jobs are mostly seasonal in nature, many of the labourers stay in the area after the completion of their contracts. They tend to encroach into the forest to acquire land so that after a year or so of cultivating it they can bring their families, and hence establish new settlements.

The creation of such 'illegal' settlements has generated additional challenges for local communities, intensifying the pressure on available land resources. This has been the case mainly in Dangur and Guba *woredas*, where the *woreda* authorities now consider it to be a major challenge to the peace and security of the area, likely to fuel land conflicts (Interviews, Manbouk and Mankush towns, June 2012). The Gumuz people are well aware of this kind of encroachment on their land and its implications for them. One informant from the Agriculture Office of Dangur *woreda* illustrates that the people who encroach and establish new settlements tend to over-exploit the local land resources as their continued existence on the land is highly uncertain (Interview, Manbouk town, 29 May 2012), and that sooner or later they will be forced to leave. Due to this uncertainty, they resort to using the land and other natural resources more intensively, in contrast to the land-use practices of local Gumuz communities.[9] Notwithstanding his earlier argument, this same informant also concedes that these 'illegal settlers' hope that they might claim permanent control of the land they occupy once they have occupied and farmed it for a few years. This did not, however, seem to stop them from exploiting the resources to the greatest extent possible.

Local communities have been reacting against the influx of migrant workers, not just in order to prevent their encroachment on local land resources but also to undermine the land investment projects by denying the investors access to labour. Several migrant agricultural workers interviewed in Gimtiya and Gublak *kebeles* within Dangur *woreda* stressed that they were 'scared' of the Gumuz people (Interview, May 2012). They emphasized that they are fearful to the extent that they felt unable to go on foot from the places where the investment projects are located to nearby towns. According to these informants (seasonal labourers), many migrant workers had been killed by the local communities while they were trying to go back to their home areas on foot. Reacting to these allegations, the Gumuz people contended that the incidents had nothing to do with them. Rather, they explained how migrant workers face challenges when they come to the area (Interview, Gimtiya *Kebele*, 21 May 2012). The labourers migrate to these destinations from various areas such as Gojjam, Gondar and Siemen Shewa, and not knowing their way around is one of the challenges they face. The lowlands are covered in vast expanses of woodlands and forested areas and the migrants, unfamiliar to the area, get lost in these vast areas, unclear of the direction they need to take. Once they are lost, many do not manage to find their way out. The Gumuz complain that when something happens to these workers everybody puts the blame on them.

[8]Most of these seasonal wage labourers, migrating mainly from the central highlands of the Amhara region, are landless young men or those with small landholdings who are unable to provide for their families from such holdings. For many of these labourers, seasonal migration is the only available source of income.

[9]For a detailed analysis of more or less similar cases in Metekel, see Abbute (2002).

But migrant workers insist that they face intimidation from the local communities every day. Similar attitudes towards the Gumuz were reflected during FGDs I held in some selected villages of Tach Gayint *woreda* of the Amhara region, among the main areas of origin of seasonal labour migrants (FGDs, July 2012). The participants stressed that threats from the Gumuz are the major risk factor that they consider when deciding whether to move to the Metekel area, with malaria and harsh climatic condition forming other risk factors. Many labourers, particularly inexperienced young workers, could not withstand the harsh daily labour and long working hours expected on the investment projects, and found the harsh climate and cultural shocks they face difficult to cope with. As a result, some decide to return to their home areas, partly on foot in order to save some money. According to the participants, there were cases in which these people were attacked and killed by the Gumuz while they were travelling. However, it should be noted here that such allegations could also be related to the stereotypical views prevalent in the highlands which characterize the Gumuz as hostile. Nevertheless, one local official from Dangur *woreda* administration council admitted that there were a number of such incidents in the *woreda* but they did not know who was behind them. Whoever is to blame, and whichever group – the Gumuz or the migrants – is right, it is evident from both individual interviews and group discussions with the Gumuz that they have explicit, negative attitudes towards both the migrant workers and the investment projects.

A closer look into the issue reveals that the hostilities of the Gumuz towards the land acquisitions are not only because they face threats of dispossession and displacement from their ancestral lands, but also because they feel marginalized from the employment opportunities brought by the projects. As already pointed out, with the exception of a few guard positions, almost all the seasonal wage employment opportunities are filled by labourers from the highland areas. Since I was curious to know the reasons why the projects make use of outside labour coming from as far away as Siemen Shewa, the manager of one of the farm projects located in Gimitiya *kebele* (Dangur *woreda*) explained that they have been forced to bring labourers from other regions because of the lack of interest among the local communities to engage in seasonal labour activities (Interview, Gublak town, 18 May 2012). Implicit in his argument is the clear inference that local indigenous people are 'lazy' and have a culture that does not encourage hard work. A highlander himself, his views were no different from those hegemonic ideologies of highlanders in general that considered the Gumuz people 'as little better than animals – unintelligent, ugly, heathen and evil' (Gonzalez-Ruibal 2012, 69). In contrast to this, however, in my own interviews and discussions, most of the Gumuz expressed their interest in making use of the employment opportunities. This is what the following FGD account demonstrates:

> We wanted to work and get some money. … But these investors don't like us. They don't want to employ our people. They say this community [Gumuz] is not capable of doing daily wage work and they even went to the extent of calling our people lazy. This is their common response when we approach them for employment. They don't even see us as human beings. … That is why they prefer to employ migrant workers. These same investors first promised that they would employ our people and that they would only employ people from other places if there were not enough workers from our communities. But this is not what is happening here. We always ask them for work. Except for a few guard positions in which our people are employed, the available job opportunities are almost all filled by migrant people coming from the Amhara region … . That is what we see here in connection with these investors. (Gimtiya, Dangur *woreda*, 20 May 2012)

Similarly, one young Gumuz man, who once worked as a guard and for almost 3 months was in charge of looking after some daily labourers in an investment project located in

Dangur *woreda*, expressed the view that the Gumuz people are very hardworking and that they can accomplish their tasks (such as weeding and mowing) in a very short time when given the opportunity (Interview, Gublak town, 26 May 2012).

Women in particular stressed that when they approached the investment projects for employment, they were treated suspiciously by the employers and even seen as thieves who went there not to work but to steal (Interview, Gimtiya *kebele*, 21 May 2012). Generally, the Gumuz informants stressed that this is why they wanted to make the investment projects leave. So, although the investors argued that they were forced to employ highland migrants for the available seasonal work because of the lack of local labour, which they attributed to a lack of motivation among the Gumuz,[10] the fact that local people seeking the work were not even offered the chance or were less preferred suggests that the project leaders gave preference to highlanders. In terms of employment opportunities, therefore, the experience with existing investment projects is that they appear to have benefited highland migrants rather than the local communities, at least in the present study areas. This discussion reminds us of an earlier observation made by Tania Li (2011, 286) in Southeast Asia, in which she cogently described the situation of the local population in such a way that 'their land is needed, but their labor is not'.

4.3. *Reaction against the state*

Generally, the Gumuz reflected negative attitudes and hostilities not only towards investors and migrant labourers but also towards the government, which they perceived as facilitating the land acquisitions that were threatening their traditional land-use practices and the natural environment. The Gumuz contend that even before the current displacements due to land acquisitions, the state had been at the forefront of their subordination and subjugation, and that what they are now facing is nothing but the continuation of their long history of exploitation and marginalization.[11] Looking back to the establishment of state farms and state-sponsored resettlement schemes in the 1970s and 1980s, and the introduction of private commercial farms in Metekel in the 1990s, some scholars have argued that these initiatives exemplified the central state's desire to consolidate its control over people and territory. Contesting the motive of the 1980s resettlement schemes, Gebre (2003, 54), for example, argues that

> although the resettlement was portrayed as a response to the famine [that affected the country in the 1980s], the overall decision to establish resettlement in remote locations may have been partly driven by perceived collateral advantages, such as controlling outpost regions.

In the context of the current ongoing process of land acquisitions, state categorization of land as 'unused' or 'underutilized' in order to lease it out to investors is based primarily on expected short-term economic benefits. It does not take into account the social and cultural dimensions of existing local land uses, despite the fact that these are critical for indigenous communities (Scott 1998; Borras and Franco 2010a). It is important to note that current government perceptions and discourses favour the highland plough cultivators and commercial farmers, while undervaluing the land use of the lowlander peripheral

[10]Interview with managers of two investment projects in Dangur *woreda*, May 2012.

[11]For further reading as regards the history of centre/periphery relationships, which was characterized by a long history of inequality, exploitation and marginalization, see Ahmad (1999), Gebre (2003), Abbute (2002), Pankhurst (1977, 2001), Zewdie (1991), Donham (2002), Markakis (2011) and Makki (2012).

communities such as the Gumuz.[12] It was such a discourse that shaped the recent state policy of making lowland areas major sites for large-scale production of commercial crops and biofuels. As Makki (2014, 89) puts it, 'instead of the alliance between smallholders and the state envisioned in the highlands, the strategic alignment in the lowlands involves a pact between the state and large-scale investors'.

Land transfers to investors across the region have been undertaken by the federal government on the one hand, and regional and local government authorities on the other hand. At the federal level, increasing levels of land transfers in the region have been carried out by the Agricultural Investment Support Directorate (AISD), which was established in 2009 to identify potential investment lands in the regional states. It has been argued that this trend of land administration by the federal government is justified due to the prevailing limited capacity of the regional government to manage substantial land investments. Strikingly, information collected during fieldwork for this paper revealed that neither local communities nor respective regional authorities have been involved in most of the land deals carried out so far by the federal government. Land transfers negotiated with the federal government were easily able to bypass legitimate rural land administration authorities at the regional government. The regional government was simply notified about the land transfer deals carried out between the federal government and the investor.

This apparently contradicts the clearly stipulated desire by both federal and regional governments to enhance decentralized political power and decision-making in rural land administrations. Due to the inherent power asymmetries in the relationship between the regional state and the federal government, the latter has undisputed sway: local and regional authorities seem to have exerted no or very little influence over substantial land deals administered by the federal government, despite the fact that these could have considerable impact on local land use and biodiversity. While the central state has always maintained its key concern for the 'peripheral' areas in the borderlands in relation to the control of territory and people, recent decisions around land investments have direct consequences for contestations over authority between state actors at federal and regional levels. This serves to illustrate not only how contests over land and authority are played out in federal and regional state contexts, but also their salience as sites for the reproduction of the history of marginalization reflected in the pre-1991 subordinated power relations. Although the federal government may have reasserted its authority over territory and people in this way, the implications of undermining the authority of local and regional state actors over the allocation, use and regulation of land resources within their jurisdictions may become a focal point of resistance.

At the regional level, before the present regional land administration proclamation 85/2010 that provided the mandate for administering rural lands to the Bureau of Environmental Protection, Land Use and Administration, land investment processes in the region involved different regional government offices. This created overlaps and ambiguities in land acquisition processes and procedures.[13] For example, although the *woreda* authorities

[12]The use of land by pastoralists and shifting cultivators in the lowlands is contested by the state as such existing land uses are perceived to be unsustainable or inefficient (Lavers 2012b). This image of existing land uses in the lowlands has been very formative in the design of state policy that focuses on leasing vast tracts of land to investors in those areas.

[13]Above all, recentralizing the facilitation and administration of investment lands as observed in recent land deals in fact undermines the political process that was intended to promote and implement a decentralized land administration system, as was stipulated in regional land administration proclamation 85/2010 (BGRS 2010).

were in charge of identifying and facilitating the land acquisition process, there were also cases in which the investors themselves identified the desired investment land and approached local authorities for approval. As these land acquisition processes appear to have lacked consistency and coordination, individuals (investors and representatives of the state acting in their own private interests) were able to manipulate them, exploiting the existing confusions and overlaps in the land administration process.

As a strategy of resistance and to undermine its legitimacy, focus group participants in Gimitiya and Qotta *kebeles* in particular expressed their anger at the government, suggesting that they had been deceived by local officials and had their ancestral land taken out of their hands. Thus they threatened not to pay taxes, although they were aware that this would bring them into direct confrontation with the government. More than anything else, the Gumuz were highly irritated by the muteness and, at times, the role of local authorities in the land acquisitions. This is particularly so because, in contrast to previous regimes, most of the local administrative offices are now filled by people from the indigenous communities themselves. One elderly informant in Ayicid *kebele* (Guba *woreda*) expressed his sentiment by remarking:

> How come a person who is born from us lets their ancestral marks be destroyed by outsiders, or worse, by those people who enslaved our fathers and us for generations? We thought a new day has come for us in which our voices will be heard when our children assumed government positions and kids started going to school. But these local officials of ours did not stand on our side when our lands were grabbed. They deceived us instead. We don't trust them anymore, I swear! Had it not been for our fierce resistance, we would have disappeared from this area long ago. (Interview, 7 June 2012)

This comment highlights how important had been their own agency in defending their territory. Indeed, during group discussions, local communities emphasized that they appealed to local authorities almost every single day. For example, the administrator of Qotta *kebele* particularly stressed that all the grievances of the community are directed at him and that he faces intimidations every day, forcing him in turn to talk to *woreda* and zonal authorities in various instances.

Almost all Gumuz informants interviewed held the view that an effort to relocate many of their villages is a strategy of the government to expropriate their land. Some people who were already relocated to new villages refused to stay and returned to their previous villages, although in some places, for example Qotta *kebele*, their lands had already been taken by investors. Informants contended that they would not leave their current villages entirely for fear that if they did, they would lose their land and would not be able to come back again (Interview, Qotta *kebele*, May 2012). As a result, they comply with local authorities by accepting relocation to new villages as a strategy in order to avoid confrontation, but in practice they also insist on maintaining their previous villages. This is an act of resistance without directly challenging the government's villagization programme. Other people resisted the villagization efforts outright and refused to comply with them.

Historically, the Gumuz have been able to resist pressures from the state at various conjunctures. Gonzalez-Ruibal (2012, 70) describes their resistance as follows:

> It is not only strange that the Gumuz have not vanished as a people or their numbers drastically reduced after centuries of enslaving and exploitation. It is equally surprising the degree to which their culture has resisted the pressures of dominant groups, avoiding disappearance or mixture to a large extent.

Although it seems ambiguous, at least for some scholars, to consider flight as a form of resistance, the Gumuz have been able to maintain their moral economies and cultural identities because of their continuous flight to remote areas when the forces they had to fight, including the state, were too strong. The current widespread land acquisitions that have been claiming large tracts of land from the Gumuz appear, however, to have greatly reduced the number of areas to which the Gumuz might flee. It was through flight that the Gumuz resisted and refused to live side by side with other groups in the past. And this resonates with what Adas (1986, 64) once called 'avoidance protest', referring to cases in which peasants used flight as an act of social protest and a means of defending themselves from what they perceived to be exploitative conditions. Indeed, violent forms of resistance against the ongoing land acquisitions have been rare among the Gumuz. This sharply resonates with Scott's argument based on the case of rural Malaysia in which he argued that the lack of more violent forms of resistance among the peasantry is largely 'the result of a prudent, calculated, and historically tested choice favoring other strategies more attuned to [their] particular social structure, strengths, and defensive capacities' (Scott 1987, 422).

4.3.1. *Official politics*[14]

The agitations and discontents of local communities related to land acquisitions, as expressed in various forms as discussed above, appear to be shared by some local and regional officials. As indicated earlier, in contrast to earlier regimes, local political power in the region is now in the hands of officials that belong to the indigenous ethnic groups. Some of the officials interviewed admitted their discontent over the land acquisition process, although they were very cautious in voicing opinions that would identify them as being explicitly against the system of which they are a part. For example, two regional government officials interviewed in Assosa and Gilgel Beles, who requested anonymity, expressed their concerns regarding the involvement of the federal government in the administration of investment lands in the region, with particular concerns over the processes and relations of power this implied (Interview, April 2012).[15] The officials contended that this current trend of direct federal government intervention undermines the regional government's authority to challenge and negotiate land transfers that may potentially affect local land rights, and to promote investments based on distinct regional socioeconomic and ecological contexts. For example, as the fieldwork for this particular study was underway, there was a widely circulating rumour among both experts and *woreda* and zonal authorities related to the transfer of an area which is known for its rich woodland, water and wildlife resources. This area covers large tracts of land in both Dangur and Guba *woredas*, and is bordered by Alatish Park in Quara of the Amhara regional state, the boundary being marked by Ayima River. Local and regional authorities contended that they would resist such an acquisition by investors if the federal government actually went ahead with it.

This example indicates that local and regional authorities seem to have reacted to some of the land deals that threaten the natural environment. However, their resistance does not seem to have changed or contributed to the rethinking of policies related to the ongoing

[14]See Kerkvliet (2009) for a discussion of this.

[15]During the interviews, especially with one of the higher officials in the zonal capital, Gilgel Beles, before starting the interview formally, I was asked by the official not to record any of the discussions that we would have on the issue, and for that, I had to remove the batteries from my voice recorder and hand it over together with my cellphone until we finished the discussions.

practices of land acquisitions. It is also not in the open, as most local officials do not wish to openly speak out and oppose the political system of which they are part, but choose, rather, to be silent in order to maintain their position in office. Thus, while engaged in a form of official politics (resistance) backstage, local regional authorities have also been working alongside the federal government in the process of land acquisition despite professing that they do not support many of its aspects.

Although it seems clear that some internal dissension has been occurring among local authorities regarding land acquisitions, in practice, such tensions have not been linked to the hostilities of local communities in order to reduce the latter's political and economic marginality. Of course, regional authorities, though they are recruited from local communities, are in fact ‘creations’ of the federal government to serve its interests. As Markakis (2011, 8) argues, although there are fundamental changes in the ‘social composition’ of ‘political space’ in the peripheral regions, the trend of soliciting the collaboration of a ‘subordinate elite’ in the longstanding centre/periphery relationship that could help the administration of the peripheries has not changed to this day. This is further explained in the following quote:

> The imperial regime was able to secure the collaboration of traditional authorities in the conquered lands and compensated them accordingly. This class was dispossessed by the 1974 Revolution along with the entire imperial establishment, and the military rulers produced an alternative peripheral elite in the form of a ‘Marxist’ cadre corps to staff the state apparatus. The cadre corps in turn was ousted by the Ethiopian People's Revolutionary Democratic Front (EPRDF), which then produced its own auxiliary elite in the form of a class of ‘regional intellectuals’ to administer the periphery. In no instance was the hegemony of the centre diminished. (Markakis 2011, 11–12)

In the context of the recent large-scale land acquisitions, while the federal constitution in principle granted the regional state the authority to administer its land resources, the reality on the ground reveals that the federal government has already reasserted/recentralized its authority in administering investment lands.[16] That is why the regional authorities were unable to contest the land deals committed to by the federal government, irrespective of whether the deals had adverse implications for local communities or not. In short, the ‘Central rulers devolved authority and prerogative to localities, but local leaders often found that what they had been handed was an “empty envelope”’ (Boone 2003, 317, quoted in Markakis 2011, 12).

[16]The Constitution of Ethiopia adopted in 1995 gives regional states the power to administer all land and other natural resources. However, recent rises in land values have seen the federal government recentralize the administration of land resources (e.g., investment lands), taking the power from regional states, in a move which is, in fact, contrary to the constitution. While the federal system has restored some of the autonomy of lowland areas in terms of self-administration, in practice, these regions have nominal authority to administer their land resources, especially when it comes to much of the potentially cultivable and valuable land that can be brought under large-scale commercial agriculture. This is particularly interesting, as the exploitation of land resources in lowland regions was perceived on a grand scale. As Markakis (2011, 260) rightly pointed out, the recent ‘process of leasing land touched the very core of the federal arrangement, since the main advantage of decentralization from the viewpoint of the periphery was to give its communities a measure of control over their land, and to prevent it being taken over by [the centre] as in the past’. Similar remarks were also made by Lavers (2012b, 814): ‘Despite the creation of an ethnic federal system, which is intended to protect the rights of minority ethnic groups, recent processes of agricultural investment seem likely to continue past patterns of exploitation of the resources of minority ethnic groups for the benefit of the centre’.

5. Conclusion

In this paper, I have tried to demonstrate that the Gumuz people, who are now under mounting threats from current large-scale land acquisitions, are hostile to such acquisitions and have reacted in various ways to threats of dispossession and displacement that have already occurred or will certainly occur. Although the Gumuz seem silent, resistance is occurring. The emerging discontent of the Gumuz people, expressed in various ways, is not, however, in the form of organized and structured large-scale reactions. Likewise, the Gumuz are not supported by local authorities or civil society organizations in defending their local land rights effectively.[17] Despite this, the overall intention of the reactions is to challenge the land acquisitions taking place on their ancestral lands. As has been demonstrated, their reactions are not only against investors and migrant seasonal agricultural labours, but also against the state, challenging its definition of 'development'. Such local reactions, which range from covert forms (such as destroying field crops and machineries, and attacking/killings) to more open forms (such as intimidation, refusal to comply with villagization, threats to not pay taxes and encroachment onto land already acquired by investors), are in fact illustrations of how the Gumuz have not been entirely helpless (though they do not often want to speak about their actions). These reactions are efforts to challenge the recent large-scale land acquisitions, not just because of their implications for possible displacement, dislocation and disruptions to local livelihoods, but also because of the absence of economic benefits from the land acquisitions both in the present and in the future. It seems unlikely, however, that the Gumuz will be able to effectively defend their land this time from the current widespread land acquisitions that involve both domestic and foreign companies with a strong connection to and support from the state. In the current context of the ongoing strong politicization of land investment undertakings involving the federal state, the disadvantages to the Gumuz and other indigenous communities stand out more clearly.

As shown in this paper, local resistance strategies and investors' capacity to enforce their claims to land vary depending on the state's presence and level of authority. This implies that future expansion of investment (and the threat to the Gumuz) is dependent on the state's continued protection of investors. Nevertheless, the state's willingness to protect and support investors certainly depends on the latter's ability to deliver on their promises to the government in terms of actually developing the land leased, raising productivity and producing goods for export. If investors' performance is perceived as poor, it will likely affect the state's willingness to intervene on their behalf. In light of this paper's findings, the resistance of local communities through the types of actions described is therefore a potentially important factor that will affect the economic viability of these projects.

Acknowledgements

Special thanks to Jun Borras, Max Spoor and Ian Scoones for their assistance, constructive comments and suggestions. A draft of this paper was first presented in a seminar on 'The Politics of Land

[17]Given the country's civil society law, enacted in 2009, that appeared to severely weaken the work of civil society organizations, particularly those of human rights defenders and advocates of democratic governance, it seems very unlikely that local indigenous communities who are threatened by the land acquisitions will be supported by such organizations in defending their local land rights against the combined weight of the state and private capital (domestic and foreign). The Charities and Societies Proclamation No. 621/2009 prohibits all foreign nongovernmental organizations (NGOs) as well as those local NGOs that receive more than 10 percent of their funding from foreign sources from engaging in activities pertaining to human rights and conflict.

Grabbing; Strategies of Resistance' at the University of Limerick, Ireland on 4–5 June 2013, and a revised version was later presented at the FLACSO-ISA Joint Conference on the panel 'Land, Land Grabbing, Resistance and Agrarian Struggles' at the University of Buenos Aires, Argentina from 23–25 July 2014. I thank the participants in these fora for their constructive comments, particularly Rachel Ibreck, Tom Lodge and Matias Margulis. Also, I am very grateful to this journal's two anonymous reviewers for their helpful comments and suggestions.

Funding

I would like to thank the Netherlands Fellowship Programme (NFP) and the Land Deal Politics Initiative (LDPI) for providing financial support to conduct the fieldwork.

References

Abbute, W. 2002. Gumuz and highland resettlers: Differing strategies of livelihood and ethnic relations in Metekel, northwestern Ethiopia. PhD diss. Gottingn: Gottinger Studien Zur Ethnologie.

Adas, M. 1986. From footdragging to flight: The evasive history of peasant avoidance protest in south and south-east Asia. *Journal of Peasant Studies* 13, no. 2: 64–86.

Ahmad, A.H. 1999. Trading in slaves in Bela-Shangul and Gumuz, Ethiopia: Border enclaves in history 1897–1938. *Journal of African History* 40, no. 3: 433–46.

BGRS. 2004. Benishangul-Gumuz regional state food security strategy. October 2004, Asossa.

BGRS. 2010. Benishagul-Gumuz regional state land administration and use proclamation. Proclamation no, 85/2010, Assosa.

BGRS. 2011. Benishangul-Gumuz regional state villagization plan for 2011/2012. Regional Bureau of Agriculture and Rural Development. Assosa.

Boone, C. 2003. *Political topographies of the African state: Territorial authority and institutional choice*. Cambridge: Cambridge University Press.

Borras, S.M., D. Fig and S.M. Suarez. 2011. The Politics of agrofuels and mega-land and water deals: Insights from the ProCana case, Mozambique. *Review of African Political Economy* 38, no. 128: 215–34.

Borras, S.M., and J.C. Franco. 2010a. Towards a broader view of the politics of global land grabs: rethinking land issues, reframing resistance. ICAS Working Paper Series No, 001.

Borras, S.M. and J.C. Franco. 2010b. Contemporary discourses and contestations around pro-poor land policies and land governance. *Journal of Agrarian Change* 10, no. 1: 1–32.

Borras, S.M. and J.C. Franco. 2013. Global land grabbing and political reactions 'from below'. *Third World Quarterly* 34, no. 9: 1723–47.

Crummey, D. 1986. Banditry and resistance: Noble and peasant in nineteenth century Ethiopia. In *Banditry, rebellion and social protest in Africa*, ed. D. Crummey, 133–150. London: James Currey.

CSA. 2008. *Central statistical agency (CSA) – Summary and statistical report of the 2007 population and housing census: Population size by age and sex*. Addis Ababa: Federal Democratic Republic of Ethiopia Population Census Commission. http://www.csa.gov.et/pdf/Cen2007_firstdraft.pdf (accessed June 19, 2011).

Das, R.J. 2007. Introduction: Peasant, state and class. *Journal of Peasant Studies* 34, no. 3–4: 351–70.

Donham, D.L. 2002. Old abyssinia and the new Ethiopian empire: Themes in social history. In *The southern marches of imperial Ethiopia*, ed. D.L. Donham and W. James, 3–50. London: James Currey.

Fisseha, M. 2011. *Commercial pressures on land in Ethiopia: A case study of the Bechera agricultural development project*. Rome: International Land Coalition.

Gebre, Y. 2003. Resettlement and the unnoticed losers: Impoverishment disasters among the Gumuz in Ethiopia. *Human organization* 62, no. 1: 51–61.

Gonzalez-Ruibal, A. and V. M. Fernandez. 2007. Exhibiting cultures of contact: A museum for Benishangul-Gumuz, Ethiopia. *Stanford Journal of Archaeology* 5: 61–90.

Gonzalez-Ruibal, A. 2012. Generations of free men: Resistance and material culture in western Ethiopia.

Gramsci, A. 1971. *Selections from the prison notebooks of Antonio Gramsci*, edited and translated by Q. Hoare and G.N. Smith. London: Lawrence and Wishart.
HLPE. 2011. Land tenure and international investments in agriculture. A report by the high level panel of experts on food security and nutrition of the Committee on World Food Security, Rome.
Huntingford, G.B. 1989. *The historical geography of Ethiopia: From the first century AD to 1704*. Oxford: Oxford University Press.
Isaacman, A. 1990. Peasants and rural social protest in Africa. *African Studies Review* 33, no. 2: 1–120.
James, W. 1986. Lifelines: Exchange marriage among the Gumuz. In *The southern marches of imperial Ethiopia*, ed. D.L. Donham and W. James, 119–47. Cambridge: Cambridge University Press.
Kelbessa, E., N. Aklilu and T. Woldemariam. 2009. *Agrofuel development in Ethiopia: Findings of an assessment*. Addis Ababa: Forum for Environment.
Kerkvliet, B.T. 1986. Everyday resistance to injustice in Philippine village. *Journal of Peasant Studies* 13, no. 2: 107–23.
Kerkvliet, B.T. 1993. Claiming the land: Take-overs by villagers in the Philippines with comparisons to Indonesia, Peru, Portugal, and Russia. *Journal of Peasant Studies* 20, no. 3: 459–93.
Kerkvliet, B.T. 2005. *The power of everyday politics: How vietnamese peasants transformed national policy*. Ithaca, NY: Cornell University Press.
Kerkvliet, B.T. 2009. Everyday politics in peasant societies (and ours). *Journal of Peasant Studies* 36, no. 1: 227–43.
Lavers, T. 2012a. Land grab' as development strategy?. The political economy of agricultural investment in Ethiopia. *Journal of Peasant Studies* 39, no. 1: 105–32.
Lavers, T. 2012b. Patterns of agrarian transformation in Ethiopia: State-mediated commercialization and the 'land grab'. *Journal of Peasant Studies* 39, no. 3–4: 795–822.
Li, T.M. 2011. Centering labor in the land grab debate. *Journal of Peasant Studies* 38, no. 2: 281–98.
Makki, F. 2012. Power and property: Commercialization, enclosures, and the transformation of agrarian relations in Ethiopia. *Journal of Peasant Studies* 39, no. 1: 81–104.
Makki, F. 2014. Development by dispossession: Terra nullius and the social-ecology of new enclosures in Ethiopia. *Rural Sociology* 79, no. 1: 79–103.
Malseed, K. 2008. Where there is no movement: Local resistance and the potential for solidarity. *Journal of Agrarian Change 8, no. 2 and* 3: 489–514.
Markakis, J. 2011. *Ethiopia: The last two frontiers*. London: James Currey.
MoFA. 2010. Benishangul-Gumuz regional state development gap assessment report, 2010. Ministry of Federal Affairs in collaboration with Benishangul-Gumuz regional state and Department for International Development (DFID).
Moore, D. 1998. Subaltern struggles and the politics of place: Remapping resistance in zimbabwe's Eastern highlands. *Cultural Anthropology* 13, no. 3: 344–81.
Moreda, T. 2013. Postponed local concerns?. Implications of land acquisitions for indigenous local communities in Benishangul-Gumuz regional state, Ethiopia. Land Deal Politics Initiative (LDPI) Working Paper No 13.
Pankhurst, R. 1977. The history of the Bareya, Shanqella, and other Ethiopian slaves from the borderlands of the Sudan. *Sudan Notes and Records* 59: 1–43.
Pankhurst, R. 2001. *The Ethiopian borderlands. Essays in regional history from ancient times to the end of the 18th century*. Lawrenceville, NJ, Asmara: Red Sea Press.
Rahmato, D. 1988. Settlement and resettlement in Metekel, western Ethiopia. *Africa: Rivista trimestrale di studi e documentazione dell'Istituto italiano per l'Africa e l'Oriente, Anno* 43, no. 1: 14–34.
Rahmato, D. 2009. *The Peasant and the state: Studies in agrarian change in Ethiopia 1950s-2000s*. Addis Ababa: Addis Ababa University Press.
Rahmato, D. 2011. *Land to investors: Large-scale land transfers in Ethiopia. FSS Policy Debates Series No, 1*. Addis Ababa: Forum for Social Studies.
Ribot, J. and N. L. Peluso. 2003. A theory of access. *Rural Sociology* 68, no. 2: 153–81.
Schneider, A.E. 2011. What shall we do without our land?. Land grabs and resistance in rural Cambodia. Paper presented at the International Conference on Global Land Grabbing, 6–8 April 2011, University of Sussex.
Scott, J.C. 1976. *The moral economy of the peasant: Subsistence and rebellion in southeast Asia*. New Haven, CT: Yale University Press.
Scott, J.C. 1977. Hegemony and the peasantry. *Politics and society* 7, no. 3: 267–96.

Scott, J.C. 1985. *Weapons of the weak: everyday forms of peasant resistance*. New Haven, CT: Yale University Press.
Scott, J.C. 1987. Resistance without protest and without organization: Peasant opposition to the Islamic Zakat and the Christian Tithe. *Comparative Studies in Society and History* 29, no. 3: 417–52.
Scott, J.C. 1998. *Seeing like a state: How certain schemes to improve the human condition have failed*. New Haven: Yale University Press.
Shete, M. 2011. Implications of land deals to livelihood security and natural resource management in Benishangul-Gumuz Regional State, Ethiopia. Paper presented at the International Conference on Global Land Grabbing 6–8 April 2011. Institute of Development Studies, University of Sussex: Land Deal Politics Initiative (LDPI).
Toulmin, C. 2008. Securing land and property rights in sub-Saharan Africa: The role of local institutions. *Land Use Policy*, 26: 10–9.
Visser, O. and M. Spoor. 2011. Land grabbing in post-Soviet Eurasia: the world's largest agricultural land reserves at stake. *Journal of Peasant Studies* 38, no. 2: 299–323.
Von Braun, J., and R. Meinzen-Dick. 2009. Land grabbing by foreign investors in developing countries: Risks and opportunities. *IFPRI Policy Brief* 13.
Walker, K. 2008. From covert to overt: Everyday peasant politics in China and the implications for transnational agrarian movements. *Journal of Agrarian Change* 8, no. 2 & 3: 462–88.
Zewdie, B. 1991. *A History of modern Ethiopia 1855–1974*. London: James Currey.

Land grabbing, legal contention and institutional change in Colombia

Jacobo Grajales

The entanglement of violence and legal institutions in Colombia has led some scholars to argue that this country is characterized by a 'law without state', or that the law has a mere 'symbolic function'. This would explain an apparent paradox: high-intensity violence has been accompanied by the preservation of legal institutions and a common belief in their social importance. Yet the mobilization of the legal repertoire against violent land grabbing by peasant movements shows their belief in the legitimacy of legal institutions. Instead of measuring the efficiency of these actions, this paper will analyse the interaction between local orders and national legal institutions. This study argues that legal arenas have served to address land conflict, in a context of egregious violence. With their own dynamics and rules, they have not completely disrupted the logics of violent dispossession, yet they have defined land not only as an object of business transactions but also as an issue of human rights and collective identities.

Introduction

Colombia is a particularly interesting case for land grabbing analysts, as it combines political and economic incentives to develop agribusiness with a development discourse centred on global markets, while involving criminal actors who are able to use physical violence and bureaucratic connections in order to seize and accumulate land.

Yet Colombia is also a highly judicialized polity, with a strong tradition of legal contention and cause lawyering. Moreover, a certain number of formal rights run in favour of the dispossessed peasant population; there is a relatively strong recognition of land rights, which has been reinforced by the recently enacted 'Land and Victims Law'. Yet these formal rights suffer from prosaic, underground and violent forms of reaction on the part of the new land owners, often linked to paramilitary militias.

In Colombia, land grabbing has been seized as an opportunity for large investors and armed actors to launder illegal assets and to transform the power of violence into legitimate capital. The complexity of the legal field has been both an opportunity for land grabbers and a potential vector of resistance for local communities. The international visibility of the Colombian conflict and the commitment of international human rights organizations have given extra resources to domestic actors, and have transformed land grabbing into a public problem in Colombia. Yet in the lack of a real peace-building process and an effective enforcement of the rule of law, land ownership might remain an issue of violent contention for years to come.

The assessment of the linkages between political contention and the legal arena in Colombia will show the potentialities and obstacles for the use of this strategy in land grabbing issues. Contrary to Blanquer (2002), who considers that in Colombia there is 'law without state', I will argue that this country's situation is characterized by a combination of legal and illegal strategies presiding at the distribution of power and resources. Despite the magnitude of violence, legal institutions are not a mere 'veil', which hides the cruelty of dispossession and repression. Neither are they intrinsically progressive arenas, essentially opposed to the ruling of violence. Judicial institutions are a central locus of political conflict, governed by specific rules, but as dependent on the global distribution of power as the rest of society.

The next section of the paper will present the theoretical framework and the empirical case that will allow us to deal with the apparent paradox underlying this story: high-intensity violence has been accompanied by the preservation of legal institutions and the common belief in their social importance. The subsequent section of the paper will examine the specific case of judicialization of land grabbing. We will show that, despite the egregious violence that has affected the country for decades, legal institutions have not only been kept alive but also strengthened. Colombian judges – specifically, the Constitutional Court – have recognized the rights of forcibly displaced communities to recover grabbed land. More broadly, the judicialization of these issues has been accompanied by its internationalization, with the intervention of the Interamerican Human Rights Court on behalf of the communities.

Land grabbing and judicialization of politics

Colombia: the paradox of law and order

The concept of 'judicialization of politics' points at a historical process where courts and judges have gained influence in political processes and where widespread popular demand is addressed to these actors in a great variety of topics (Angell, Sieder, and Schjolden 2005). Cepeda (2005) points at a Colombian paradox, with a strong tradition of judicial review coexisting with high levels of violence and human rights violation. Judicialization of politics is defined, in the Colombian situation, as a 'twofold process by which, first, legal arguments are raised in the course of the political process, as a consequence of relevant judicial decisions ... second, constitutional judges end up substantially contributing to the orientation of the public policy' (Cepeda 2005, 68).

Yet Colombia also presents a fragmented political order, with a high degree of autonomy for local powers, and an entanglement of legal political actors and criminal networks in the periphery (Ballvé 2013; Duncan 2005; Grajales 2013; Romero 2007, 2011). Historically, the Colombian state has been characterized by the weight of peripheral elites in the formation and maintenance of local orders (Bushnell 1993). The authority of the centre has not been built over the direct control of local institutions, but on a strategy of discharge, leaving the responsibility of peripheral control – including on security issues – with local elites associated to the state. The weakness of the centre has been partially compensated by the distribution of resources through the national parties, tying the destiny of local leaders to their alliances with the central partisan elites;[1] these local orders are not entirely based on violence, but also on the distribution of resources and services; such domination dynamics have been

[1]This process of discharge is remarkably well described by López-Alves (2003) and Roldan (2002).

described by Fox (1994), in the Mexican context, as 'authoritarian clientelism'. This system was disturbed by the rise of a new group of professional politicians linked to drug smugglers and paramilitary militias. Thanks to their shadowy allies, these 'nouveaux riches' were less dependent on national leaders (Leal Buitrago and Dávila 1990; Gutierrez Sanín 2007). In consequence, they intended – and sometimes managed – to create peripheral orders relatively autonomous from the centre. This process can be described as an instance of 'subnational authoritarianism', defined by Gibson as

> The existence of a democratic national government alongside a provincial authoritarian government within the nation-state .... Two levels of government with jurisdiction over the same territory operate under different regimes, understood as the set of norms, rules, and practices that govern the selection and behavior of state leaders. (Gibson 2005, 103)

The establishment of these authoritarian enclaves transcends the private/public division; it is not only a matter of official institutions and formal legal mechanisms, but more broadly it engages a formal and informal 'bundle of powers' (Lund 2011; Lund and Peluso 2011) exercised by different actors gathered by common economic interests. The establishment of these enclaves does not lead to the isolation of local power arenas. On the contrary, they are characterized by the overlapping of legal and informal orders (Franco 2008; Gibson 2005).

How can we interpret this coexistence of judicial institutionalization and violent fragmentation of the polity? Through a study of strategies of land grabbing, as well as resistance to land grabbing, this contribution argues that law and violence are not antithetical elements, but participate in diverse ways to the historical process of state formation (Briquet and Favarel-Garrigues 2010). This analysis is comparable to Gayer's approach to the city of Karachi in terms of 'ordered disorder' as a situation where 'endemic forms of collective ... violence' do not lead to a situation of Hobbesian chaos and 'do not preclude the existence of a democratic order and a thriving economy' (Gayer 2014, 12). According to Gayer, social order does not necessarily equate with the control and monopolization of violence, but can be defined as the existence of

> underlying principles (the rules of the game) of a historical *figuration*, in Elias' sense of a 'game structure' organised around interdependent actors and reproducing itself through a 'fluctuating, tensile equilibrium' (Elias), which may accommodate a significant level of competition over the means of coercion. [Emphasis in the original]. (Gayer 2014, 13)

This is convergent with Comaroff and Comaroff's arguments that, following Derrida and Agamben, point out empiric situations where the 'violence and the law, the legal and the lethal are constitutive of one another' (Comaroff and Comaroff 2008, x). According to these scholars:

> Both the anxiety and the fascination point to a very general preoccupation in the postcolonial world with 'the law' and the citizen as legal subject, a preoccupation growing in counterpoint to, and deeply entailed in, the rise of the felonious state, private indirect government, and endemic cultures of illegality. (Comaroff and Comaroff 2008, 20)

In consequence, contemporary politics in the post-colony are characterized by a displacement of the political into the legal, and by the belief that courts and legal provisions offer a 'repertoire of more or less standardized terms and practices that permit the negotiation of values, beliefs, ideals and interests across otherwise-impermeable lines of cleavage' (Comaroff and Comarof 2008, 32).

Land grabbing cases are relevant points of observation for the study of problems of law, order and violence. As stressed by Lucia Goldfarb (2012) in the case of Argentina, the judicialization of conflicts for land control and property engage both the companies seeking to secure their investments and social movements opposed to the commoditization of land and the expansion of certain crops (genetically modified crops, for instance). In the Colombian case, violent land grabbing needs to be legalized in order to integrate the land into the agribusiness market; legalization is possible thanks to the association of local politicians, business actors and paramilitary groups (Ballvé 2013; Goebertus Estrada 2008; Grajales 2011, 2013). This recognition is particularly relevant for criminal actors, as the sustainability of their operations depends on their capacity to convert criminal profits into legal capital, to 'launder' those assets, i.e. to integrate them into the legal market. Therefore, it does not suffice to occupy a plot; the profitability of land grabbing requires the institutional recognition of property rights over those spurious holdings.

Furthermore, I will also argue that an approach that embraces law and violence, the legal and the lethal, is rich for the study of land grabbing. Such a large conception of the legal field encompasses strategies of resistance, denunciation and protection, but also land accumulation and violent dispossession. Consequently, following Borras and Franco (2013), this paper aims to problematize the reaction to land grabbing; these two authors show how the impact of land deals, state-sponsored land grabbing and/or violent dispossession is not uniform. In consequence, political actors' reactions must be addressed with a sociological lens, in order to show which are the institutional, historical and sociological conditions that determine reactions to land grabbing. In this contribution, the role of the state will be characterized as ambiguous and diverse, as it facilitates land grabbing but also shapes the structure of political opportunities that determines collective action. Such an ambiguity can only be addressed through the idea that state formation is inseparable from processes of territorialization, integration to the market and resource commoditization.

Paramilitary violence and land grabbing

According to a study of the Magdalena University, two thirds of internally displaced persons (IDPs) in the Colombian Caribbean lowlands were peasants (Barbosa, Renán, and Suárez 2007). Whether they had an individual legal title deed over their land or any other form of right (especially rights of occupancy), their forced migration addressed the question of land ownership and land grabbing. The minority of those who tried to return to the countryside, challenging the lethal threat represented by armed groups (guerrilla and paramilitaries), found that forced displacement had given way to land grabbing. In some cases, paramilitary militias had repopulated the vacated zones with loyal individuals – friends or family members of their rank-and-file. But, in most cases, grabbed land had been integrated into existing farms, frequently contributing to the expansion of the country's flourishing agribusiness. High-value crops – oil palm in the first place – started to be produced in those plots forcibly abandoned by small peasants. The perpetrators of this massive land grab were corporations linked to the paramilitary commanders, directed by their families or front-men. Other companies and businessmen, attracted by agribusiness, were willing to pay an informal tax to these paramilitary entrepreneurs, and profit from this new 'agrarian frontier'.

This section will analyse a specific case of land grabbing and further legal mobilization. Between 1996 and 1998, 17,000 people were forced to leave the region of the Lower Atrato valley, in the Chocó province (northwest); they were fleeing from the violence of a massive counter-insurgent campaign deployed by the military and paramilitary militias.

In 2005, after the communities’ long-standing mobilization, supported by national non-governmental organizations (NGOs), the case was taken to the Inter-American Human Rights Commission, and a series of official inquiries confirmed the link between forced displacement and land grabbing. While the Lower Atrato people enjoyed specific rights as ‘Afro-Colombians’, the force of weapons was, at least initially, stronger than the force of law. Such a conclusion is consistent with Li’s findings (2011); this author considers that the existence of formal rights is dependent on the structure of the society and the unequal distribution of power. Indeed, land rights recognition is not a sufficient asset for communities to protect their access to land (Vermeulen and Cotula 2010). The Lower Atrato case exemplifies the fact that while ‘legal empowerment’ has a positive effect on these communities, bargaining capacity is mostly determined by the economic order and its underlying power relations (Cousins 2009).

This case is one of the best-documented instances of violent land grabbing and has been abundantly studied (Ballvé 2013; Grajales 2013; Restrepo and Franco 2011; Rolland 2007). The abundance of information is mainly due to the intervention of the Inter-American Commission for Human Rights and the Colombian Constitutional Court, both of which called for a variety of official surveys on this issue, mainly from Colombian institutions such as the General Controller (*Contraloría General*) or the General Inspector (*Procuraduría General*).

The Lower Atrato is an extremely marginal region, populated by the descendants of African slaves and located under the scope of influence of different regional poles.[2] In the absence of regional elite, the paramilitary control of the region was not, as elsewhere in Colombia, the result of an alliance between powerful local actors. On the contrary, it was a sort of ‘armed colonization’, where violent white/*mestizo* entrepreneurs got rid of the local black population, whose land was considered ‘vacant’ (Oslender 2007). In consequence, the constitution of an authoritarian enclave is not only the result of the local power holders’ strategy. It is also – and mostly – the consequence of a situation of geographical, political and ethnic marginality.

The paramilitary advance came from the northern region of Urabá, one of the country’s most important agribusiness poles. This armed strategy was crafted as a response to the Revolutionary armed forces of Colombia, (Fuerzas armadas revolucionarias de Colombia) (FARC) guerrillas’ threat – historically present in the region – as well as the need for vacant land to expand the agribusiness economy of Urabá. Paramilitary harassment was joined and accompanied by official counter-insurgency operations. From early 1997, military forces from the 17th Brigade deployed intense bombing against presumed guerrilla positions.[3] This bombing was indiscriminate, and forced the population to leave their houses and hide in the jungle. After the bombing, the army troops were brought in by helicopters and entered the villages. They gathered the locals and warned them about the obligation to cooperate with them and provide them with information about the guerrillas.

[2]The Colombian Pacific Lowlands region has been studied by Escobar (2008); he apprehends the Colombian government policies in this region as determined by both the neoliberal agenda, that led to the development of agribusiness, and the multicultural paradigm that allowed the emergence of black and indigenous social movements.

[3]The collaboration between paramilitary groups and the military in the Urabá region was included in a criminal investigation against General Rito Alejo del Río, convicted in 2012 for the murder of a peasant during these joint operations. The description of the 1996–1997 armed operations is based on the Del Río trial.

According to the confessions of the former chief of the AUC[4] in the region, Fredy Rendón, 12 of his men participated in these military operations. They had precise knowledge of the region, and acted as 'guides'. In the aftermath of bombings and harassments, more than 4000 people left the region and sought refuge in neighbouring towns, as well as beyond the Panamanian border.

Shortly after the eviction of the Lower Atrato inhabitants, oil palm crops were planted; they were part of a violent territorial appropriation project. According to some testimonies, one of the paramilitary leaders' motivations was to colonize this region with demobilized militiamen, while simultaneously making good use of the investment in land for money-laundering operations.[5] One of the key men of this strategy was Vicente Castaño, the AUC's head of finance. His business strategy vision was not opposed to that of state institutions; on the contrary, it was intertwined with official statements on economic development:

> We have palm crops in Urabá. I found the businessmen myself to invest in those projects that are durable and productive. The idea is to bring the rich to invest in such projects in different parts of the country. By bringing rich people to these areas, state institutions will come. Unfortunately, the state institutions only come when you are rich. We must bring those rich businessmen all over the country; that is one of our commanders' missions. (Semana 2005)

The creation of the first Lower Atrato palm firm, Urapalma, by Vicente Castaño, took place in 1999. Urapalma's board of directors was controlled by his friends and relatives (El Espectador 2010). Asoprobeba, another palm firm in the region, was controlled by Sor Teresa Gómez, a Castaño relative and an active member of the AUC. Asoprobeba was supposed to be a non-profit foundation, formed by more than 100 peasant families. The beginnings of palm business also attracted entrepreneurs engaged in agribusiness in other zones of the Caribbean lowlands.

Legal strategies played a key role in the process of violent land grabbing. The profitability of the land grab depended on the regularization of title deeds, or at least on the legalization of the commercial exploitation of land. Property rights were transferred through clear-cut criminal means – falsifying title deeds, for instance. Such practices implied the collaboration of notaries and public officials, and illustrate the entanglement of local institutions and paramilitary groups (Restrepo and Franco 2011). Other methods took advantage of the issue of overlapping title deeds and loose boundaries. For example, a number of plots were purchased from people claiming de facto right of tenure, determined by the mere occupancy of land.

Even more complex strategies were equally used. Some agribusiness companies obtained effective land control without purchasing the plots. Land transfer was operated through usufruct contracts or 'strategic alliances'. Usufruct contracts transfer the effective control over land and land-based profits, and were signed by people who claimed title deeds over land or who enjoyed a representative mandate in the community councils. In most

[4]The United Self-Defence Forces of Colombia (*Autodefensas Unidas de Colombia*) was a confederation of paramilitary militias, strongly linked to large landowners, narcotraffickers and local politicians. Negotiations held between the government and the AUC representatives between 2003 and 2005 led to the formal demobilization of these groups. Most of its leaders were extradited to the United States for drug traffic charges. An undetermined share of the medium-level commanders and the rank-and-file created new armed groups or joined existent militias linked to drug smuggling.

[5]Author interviews, Bogota, January and February 2011.

cases, the community councils denied that they had granted this mandate to the contractors; some cases might be simple impersonation, while others could indicate divisions among the community councils.

The creation of the legal framework for 'strategic alliances' was among the first responses of the national government to the issues of land grabbing. It permitted the association of local communities and palm oil firms in order to use former collective territories in agribusiness projects. Strategic alliances were initially presented as a remedy to land grabbing issues, thus making the interests of community councils and those of agribusiness firms compatible. One of the consequences of such alliances was the availability of subsidies reserved for projects launched within strategic alliances, which made them even more attractive to agribusiness companies.

As a consequence of the economic importance of the palm oil market, the Colombian government adopted a program of subsidies for the palm industry during the 2000s. These subsidies were abundantly allocated to the Lower Atrato firms, even after severe criticism had been expressed by the Inter-American Commission and the Ombudsman Bureau (*Defensor del Pueblo*). Lower Atrato firms received millions in public subsidies for several years. Urapalma, for instance, received substantial credit from Finagro (public fund for agricultural development), for more than 2.5 million US dollars. A 2009 Controller Bureau (CGN 2009) report found that Finagro had approved credit for more than 7.5 million US dollars. Urapalma received 89 percent of all the Rural Credit Incentives distributed in the Lower Atrato. Urapalma even got funds through USAID (the US Agency for International Development); thanks to its participation in a program of illegal crop substitution, the firm received more than 6 million US dollars from this American agency.[6]

The brief account of the Lower Atrato case shows that the convergence of state action and violent land grabbing in Colombia is not the result of a lawless situation, but the outcome of the convergence between legal strategies, violent coercion and criminal networks. Unlike the situations of Sierra Leone and Belize, respectively described by Reno (2008) and Duffy (2008), private violent accumulation does not engage the whole state apparatus (described as a 'shadow state' by these authors) but is a central element of intra-state conflicts. The following pages will show that if legal arenas can be a locus of the legalization of dispossession, they also can supply the resources for mobilization. The translation of land grabbing issues into the human rights frame will exemplify this point.

Violence, justice and human rights

The case of the Lower Atrato, but more broadly the paramilitary problem, could lead us to conclude that Colombia experienced during those years a process of 'partial state failure',[7] or that Colombia has become a 'felon state', as Avilés (2007) seems to believe when he argues that the privatization of violence and the implementation of neoliberal reforms participate in the domination of a globalized technocratic elite.

Yet the enormous difficulties experienced by the legal system when dealing with political and prosaic violence do not mean that courts and judges have lost their legitimacy

[6] Ballvé (2013) and Restrepo and Franco (2011) abundantly explore the issue of the links between criminal and corporate actors.

[7] As stated by *Foreign Affairs* (2005), that placed Colombia at the 14th position of its 'Failed States Index' in 2005.

to interpret and enforce the law (Uprimny 2007). On the contrary, violence has been accompanied in Colombia by the continuous belief in the social role of the legal system, reaffirmed by common citizens as well as by political actors. For some scholars, like Julieta Lemaitre Ripoll (2009), the reliance of social movements on the law is not only a matter of strategy and repertoires, but of social representations as well. For Lemaitre Ripoll, in a context of intense violence, the usage of law by social movements helps to give a meaning to violent experiences and to build collective identities. More specifically, the dominant narrative used by these organizations to describe the Colombian situation is international humanitarian law. According to Winifred Tate (2007), the usage of the category of 'human rights violations' to describe a particular situation comes down to a categorization of violence and generates specific kinds of social obligations, namely urging the state to protect the population.

The usage of international law as a social narrative has not led to a marginalization of national law. On the contrary, domestic jurisdictions have integrated the international treaties and jurisprudence into their legal reasoning (Cepeda 2005). Colombian judges see themselves as not only recipients, but also creators of an international doctrine on human rights (Lecombe 2009). In short, even if the Colombian legal jurisdictions have been unable to prosecute a considerable number of human rights violations, they have succeeded in remaining a central political arena for addressing these issues.

Land grabbing has not been an exception to this rule. The issue of violent land grabbing has been initially problematized through the specific rights of IDPs. Furthermore, the intervention of international legal actors (the Interamerican Human Rights Commission and Court), but also domestic actors, provoked the Colombian Constitutional Court's intervention in the case of the Lower Atrato. The special attention paid to this case is also a result of the mobilization of a legal repertoire by local organizations and national NGOs. Yet interventions were not limited to this single case. The interest of the Constitutional Court in land grabbing also led this institution to intervene on the broader subject of 'rural development'. The following pages will subsequently deal with the introduction of the human rights framework in Colombian politics, the definition of internal displacement as a political issue and the establishment of a link between armed violence and land grabbing.

Human rights: subversive or conservative?

This section will tackle an apparent paradox, the fact that the judicialization of politics has been parallel with the aggravation of armed conflict. The mobilization of the human rights framework in order to problematize and politicize violence in Colombia has been a political strategy used both by social movements and the state. While the latter saw human rights as a source of legitimacy, the implementation of reforms, even if they were initially instrumentalized, led to the opening of new contentious arenas. In order to understand this interaction, it is necessary to address the complex entanglement of contentious politics, diplomacy and public policies.

Since the early 1980s, the government, as well as the social movements, have asked for judicial responses to violence (Daviaud 2006). The emergence of human rights as a conflict arena has not been the automatic consequence of international pressure, but the result of a joint construction, involving international actors as well as domestic movements (Gallón 1997). The language of human rights was adopted by social organizations from the 1980s. It seemed particularly attractive, as it was a gate to international arenas, such as the United Nations (UN) Committee for Human Rights or the Interamerican Commission of Human Rights (Tate 2007).

In Colombia, human rights organizations are heirs of the 1960s' cause lawyers, who represented the presumed members of guerrilla organizations prosecuted by military justice. At the time, even if the country was governed by civilians, the military had a monopoly on security issues. Prosecuted individuals charged with 'terrorism' or 'subversion' were under the scope of martial law.

These legal networks constituted the basis of the first human rights organizations. They stayed focused on the defence of 'political prisoners', as well as on the denunciation of police and military brutality, and forced disappearance. The strategy of these pioneer organizations was initially focused on domestic courts (Daviaud 2006; Tate 2007). At the time, Colombia was seen by foreign countries as a stable democracy on a continent governed by military dictators (Gallón 1997; Pardo and Tokatlian 1989; Garibay and Guerrero 2007). Consequently, it was difficult to obtain the attention of international advocacy organizations.

Yet from the end of the 1980s, the development of links between Colombian activists and foreign NGOs became one of the main vectors of professionalization in the human rights arena. For instance, contacts between Colombian lawyers and members of the Geneva-based International Commission of Jurists led to the creation of a Colombian branch of this organization (Tate 2007, 119). Such links were the necessary condition for the success of international advocacy campaigns. From the beginning of the 1990s, Colombian NGOs lobbied at international forums, such as the UN Committee, and met American Congress members. They also took cases to the Interamerican Human Rights Courts, seeking to provoke a 'boomerang effect' (Sikkink and Keck 1998), so that international pressure materializes into domestic decisions.

From the end of the 1980s, international NGOs and networks of lawyers have pointed out the responsibility of the state in the exactions committed by the military and paramilitary groups. In 1988, a judicial observation commission was set up. That same year, four international NGOs – Americas Watch, Amnesty International, International Commission on Jurists and Pax Christi – reported on the human rights situation in Colombia. Amnesty International highlighted specific cases, mentioning the names of the military members suspected of murder and torture, arguing that 'the Colombian military forces have adopted a terror policy in order to intimidate and eliminate opposition' (Amnesty International 1989).

Under this pressure, the government changed its discourse. The new strategy was aimed at recognizing the gravity of the situation and the commitment of the state in favour of peace and the rule of law (Daviaud 2006). From then on, the human rights frame was progressively incorporated by the establishment, in spite of its contentious origins.

Yet the appropriation of the human rights narrative was not limited to discourse. In the middle of a democratization process which led to the establishment of a new constitution in 1991, a new institutional arrangement was promoted. Human rights started to be considered as the axis of the new democracy and a basis for peace-building. In consequence, new institutions, such as the People's Ombudsman (*Defensor del Pueblo*), were charged with the implementation of an undefined human rights policy (Ungar 2004).

At first sight, the appropriation of the human rights discourse by the state could be interpreted as a propaganda strategy, aimed at the re-legitimization of the ruling elites through an institutional disruption. This is a common discourse mobilized by NGOs and activists, who denounce the fact that most of the policies intended to guarantee the rights of vulnerable populations are no more than empty shells, without any power or budget, used to enhance the international image of the Colombian government.

Yet, while lacking any coercive power, these new institutions change the conditions and resources for mobilization. The case of the first Ombudsman illustrates the ambivalence of human rights institutions. Jaime Córdoba Triviño, a criminal attorney, started his career as an Inspector General's Office assistant. He represented his office at the Supreme Court, and was in charge of the human rights division. After being nominated as the People's Ombudsman, Córdoba Triviño was extremely active. He organized a series of investigative commissions charged with determining the responsibility of the military in several murder cases. The most important of these commissions, in charge of the 'Trujillo Massacre', resulted in the recognition by the president of the state's responsibility in the torture and murder of more than 300 civilians by members of the army and paramilitary groups. Yet the Ombudsman suffered from the gap between his political visibility and legitimacy and a complete lack of coercive power. His mission was to investigate and report about the human rights situation. The Ombudsman had no judicial function, as denunciations were transmitted to the Attorney General's office, the only jurisdiction competent to press charges. Yet Córdoba Triviño was generally recognized as a human rights advocate inside the state, and his legitimacy as a jurist was recognized by his election as a Constitutional Court justice.

The Constitutional Court and the issue of internal displacement

The current section will briefly trace the intervention of the Constitutional Court in matters of forced displacement. The importance of this description is linked to the fact that the definition of forced displacement as a human and constitutional rights violation paved the way to the judicialization of land grabbing. As the end of the section will show, legal mobilization against land grabbing has not been entirely focused on the legal rights over land, but more broadly on the link between the individual, the community and the territory, in a context of massive forced displacement.

Among the institutional reforms introduced by the 1991 Constitution, one of the most outstanding has been the creation of the Constitutional Court. This organization, placed at the very summit of the legal pyramid, is defined as the watchdog of the Chart's integrity. It has interpreted civil and human rights in an extensive manner, in order to influence public policies in an extremely progressive direction. According to Blanquer (2002, 56), the Constitutional Court has become a policy maker, compensating the legislator's unwillingness to assume the defence of the rule of law. One of the specific points where the Court's influence has been pivotal is internal displacement. Its decisions have led to the recognition of the specific rights of IDPs. One of those specific rights – doubtlessly the most conflictive one – has been the right to recover violently grabbed land.

According to the Geneva based Internal Displacement Monitoring Center (IDMC), the internal conflict in Colombia has led to the displacement of 4.9 to 5.5 million people,[8] which makes it the country with the second largest IDP population, after Sudan. Yet, partially as a consequence of the fragmentation of the political order, internal displacement was considered for years as a marginal phenomenon. It concerned the poor population from the countryside, generally peasants from segregated peripheries, who migrated to the large cities. According to Lucas Gómez (2012), until the early 1990s, decision makers and journalists had not perceived the link between armed conflict and internal displacement. It was generally thought that IDPs were just the most recent wave of rural migration, something

[8]Since the late 1990s, there has been continuous debate over the figures of internal displacement in Colombia. IDMC's different figures correspond to the Colombian government (the lowest assessment) and to the Colombian NGO CODHES (the highest).

natural in a country marked by an extremely quick urbanization process during the second half of the century.

At the beginning of the 1990s, the growth of internal displacement became undeniable. Standing at every street-corner, peasant families were the living proof of its magnitude. The political reaction to internal displacement was long to come and rather chaotic. Initially, the problem was perceived as the inevitable consequence of the armed conflict. IDPs had the same rights as the victims of natural catastrophes, and there was no specific definition of their situation. Internal displacement was defined as the product of an accidental cause, thus closing the door to the establishment of particular responsibilities and/or the procurement of specific rights (Gómez 2012; Rodriguez Garavito and Rodriguez Franco 2010).

As shown by the sociology of public problems, the definition of an issue determines responses and subsequent institutional arrangements, or as Gusfield puts it: 'To give a name to a problem is to recognize or suggest a structure developed to deal with it' (1989, 432). The constructionist view on social problems invites us to be attentive to the impact of the definitional activities of social actors. In that respect, the Constitutional Court's first intervention was to name the problem of internal displacement, to define it as a human rights' violation; in so doing, judges established the state's responsibility and the specific rights of IDPs (Rodriguez Garavito and Rodriguez Franco 2010).

The definition of IDPs as human rights violation victims was, in the first place, a claim made by NGOs and social organizations. The qualification of IDPs as a special population, protected by international law, was introduced around 1994, when the UN's special rapporteur for IDPs visited the country. Such international visibility gave a window of opportunity to domestic NGOs to increase the public and policy makers' awareness of the IDPs' lot. Despite large mobilization and despite the number of organizations advocating for the rights of this population, public policies remained innocuous, and did not address the issue of specific IDPs' rights.

The breaking point was a decision of the Constitutional Court; responding to a writ for protection of fundamental rights (*acción de tutela*), the Court stated that internal displacement was a massive and permanent violation of human rights. The judges established that the state was failing in its fundamental duties towards a particularly vulnerable population. They considered that the state had the obligation of elaborating a public policy specifically aimed at the protection of IDPs.

In the aftermath of its decision, the Court established a monitoring process, in order to enforce the rights it intended to protect. Public audiences organized to monitor the situation of IDPs became an institutional arena leading to the mobilization of social organizations and other political actors. The Court defined internal displacement as intrinsically linked to constitutional rights and to the maintenance of the rule of law; from that point, besides being a political controversy, it became a legal issue.

Legal action

The legal mobilization in the case of the Lower Atrato aimed at establishing a clear-cut relation between forced displacement and land dispossession in order to problematize land grabbing, not as a conflict over land property and control, but as an issue of human and constitutional rights. This idea was advanced by NGOs under the form of a 'correlation between forced displacement and land usurpation' and a 'debate on land grabbed in blood and fire to more than 3 million displaced persons' (Comisión Colombiana de Juristas 2006, 7–10).

In compliance with some of the provisions of the new 1991 constitution, the Colombian congress passed Law 70 in 1993, establishing a new legal framework for the protection of collective property and ethnic identity of the black communities of the Pacific coast. The law defined 'black communities' as collective recipients of multicultural rights, thus contributing to create a specific 'black' identity (Cárdenas 2012). Among the possibilities opened by Law 70 was the recognition of property rights over land under the form of collective titles. This provision involved the organization of 'community councils', a local government form aimed at representing the interests of the community as a collective subject. Collective titles have a particularly solid legal protection; they are unalienable and indivisible.

Law 70, apparently securing community property rights over land, was expected to reverse the land grabbing. Predictably, it provoked harsh opposition among the most conservative sectors of landholders, who even claimed that the law had a 'subversive origin', as stated by a businessman:

> We are deeply concerned ... for the more than 6 million hectares of the Colombian Pacific lowlands that had been conquered with dark purposes by Law 70 and its famous community councils, imposed by the law of the subversive rifle (Justicia y Paz 2007).

Using the legal possibilities offered by Law 70, the inhabitants of the Lower Atrato created the Great Community Council of Jiguamiandó and Curvaradó, coordinating minor councils and paving the way for the procurement of collective rights over their land. A collective title deed was issued in December 2000, apparently securing these communities' rights to land. This achievement, intended to secure the population's rights over the land, was not the automatic result of the provisions of the law. It was also the consequence of a process of collective organization, specially forged in the aftermath of their experience of forced displacement. Moreover, their cause attracted NGOs interested in supporting collective action, and taking the case to legal jurisdictions. The shared trauma created solidarity links among the local inhabitants and led to their identification as a collective actor. According to Rolland (2007), collective action is intrinsically linked to territorial identity, as it is primarily aimed at the delimitation of a protected territory, under the form of 'humanitarian zones' or 'peace communities'. Social movements built a discourse based on legal national and international provisions that stresses the neutrality of the civil population and the specific rights of ethnic minorities. At the same time, they adopted an attitude of autonomy and opposition to the state, considering that its representatives were intimately linked to paramilitary groups. The ambiguity of this mobilization follows the fact that it aims to transform individuals and communities into legal subjects, yet the state is still perceived as an illegitimate actor.

Indeed, the procurement of the collective title deeds did not mark the end of the mobilization, but only the beginning of a new contentious cycle. A few months after the signature of the agreements, a new paramilitary offensive caused waves of forced displacement, reducing the recently acquired property right to an abstract claim. Most of those who were already mobilized around the collective titles refused to seek refuge in the surrounding towns, and preferred to stay in the refugee camps, not far from their land. The same pattern was repeated several times between 2003 and 2007, while palm crops were profusely cultivated. Altogether, from 1996 to 2007, 13 cases of massive forced displacement were reported, and 115 civilians were murdered in this zone (Justicia y Paz 2007).

The community councils and their legal advisor, the Colombian NGO *Justicia y Paz*, required the intervention of competent authorities. They initiated a criminal complaint against members of the 17th Brigade of the army, and most notably its commander at the time of the first bombings, General Rito Alejo del Río. They also asked for the immediate protection of the lives and lands of the forcibly displaced communities. An action for protection was referred to the People's Ombudsman. Its response – issued in 2002 – was the first intervention of a public authority on behalf of the Lower Atrato communities. The Ombudsman recognized the violations presumably committed by members of the army and paramilitary militias against the local inhabitants. Most importantly, the Ombudsman recognized the link between the forced displacement and the development of palm crops. Its report stated that: 'palm crops have been illegally developed, by individuals and firms unconnected to the communities ... thus violating the basic rights of the Black communities' (DP 2002).

This link rapidly became one of the central issues of the controversy around forced displacement and land grabbing. The government was willing to acknowledge its duties concerning the protection of the displaced families – although without taking concrete measures – but was fiercely opposed to establishing any link between armed violence and land grabbing.

Despite the recognition by the Ombudsman of the egregious violence the Lower Atrato people had suffered, its report did not trigger off any official intervention. Moreover, the criminal case against the military was at a dead end. In 2001, the chief of the human rights unit at the Attorney General's office obtained the indictment of General Del Río. Following the demand of the victims' representative – *Justicia y Paz*, the already-mentioned NGO – the act of indictment mentioned the crime of 'paramilitary conspiracy' as well as the forced disappearance of more than 150 people. Yet the recently nominated Attorney General, Luis Camilo Osorio, withdrew the indictment, took the case and started a disciplinary investigation against the former prosecutor. Osorio, a jurist known for his conservative positions, had already declared to the press that he considered that the Attorney General's Office had a pro-guerrilla bias, and expected to 'redress the balance'. The Del Río case remained at a dead point for 3 years, and Osorio finally dismissed it in 2004.[9]

The lack of protective measures covering the Lower Atrato people, as well as the manipulation of the criminal inquiries, led the representatives of the communities to bring a complaint before the Interamerican Commission for Human Rights. Following the complaints, the Commission organized an official visit in December 2001, a few months after a violent campaign of harassment against the Lower Atrato communities, perpetrated by paramilitary militias and the military. For 2 years, the Commission accumulated an important amount of data about human rights violations, and especially about the link between violence and land-grabbing. The Commission documented the existence of palm crops illegally planted by the firm Urapalma. The firm, connected to the paramilitary militias, occupied the land that had already been allocated to the communities; its facilities were protected – according to the Commission – by both paramilitary militias and men of the 17th Brigade of the army.

In March 2003, after 2 years of inquiry and monitoring by the Commission, the Interamerican Court issued provisional protection measures covering the communities of the Lower Atrato. This legal act engaged the Colombian state to protect the beneficiaries, under the terms of the American Convention on Human Rights. Considering the fact that the prevention measures adopted by the Commission had not produced any effect, the

[9]Author interview with the attorney in charge of the first indictment against Del Río. Bogota, February 2011.

Court summoned the Colombian state to provide effective protection to the Lower Atrato People, and to investigate the criminal facts that had been denounced by the Commission (CIDH 2003).

The Commission required the recognition of the link between armed violence and land grabbing, and declared that the paramilitary violence and the army operations were both aimed at facilitating the occupation of the land for purposes of oil palm production:

> Since the year 2001, Urapalma corporation has promoted oil palm crops in approximately 1500 hectares of land belonging to the collective territory of the communities .... The operations and armed incursions into this territory have pursued the objective of intimidating the members of the communities, in order to force them to associate to palm production or to leave the region (CIDH 2003).

The most controversial issue raised by the Interamerican Court's intervention was the link between forced displacement and land grabbing. The Commission's memorandum specifically pointed to land exploitation as the underlying motivation behind the armed operations. Yet the Court did not mention this issue in its 2003 conclusions. In the aftermath of the first resolution, the Court received diverse monitoring reports from the Commission, as well as the communities' representatives. These reports stressed the fact that land grabbing had continued, and was part and parcel of the multiple human rights violations endured by the Lower Atrato people. In the meantime, the Colombian government had the obligation of reporting to the Court on the measures taken to protect the communities. The documents produced by the government representatives stated that the monitoring of palm crops was not required by the Court's decision. In addition, these reports affirmed that palm entrepreneurs had respected the limits of the collective lands, and denied any link between palm business and armed violence.

Yet the Interamerican Court and Commission's intervention progressively led to a series of public inquiries, which shed light onto the mechanisms of violent land grabbing. This intervention created a new advocacy and bureaucratic field, and enhanced the legitimacy of the issue as a public policy problem. In 2005, the General Inspector's Office[10] issued an official report recognizing the responsibility of the state as it failed to protect the Lower Atrato communities from paramilitary and military violence. It was the first official conclusion that gave credit to the community representatives' claims. Yet the link between violence and land grabbing was only marginally addressed, and did not lead to specific conclusions or procedures.

This recognition came from a different public agency. In 2005, the Colombian Institute for Agricultural Development (INCODER) reported the land grab of almost 4000 hectares in the Lower Atrato. The agribusiness investors were depicted as opportunistic actors, who profited from forced displacement to develop palm crops in the collective land (Incoder 2005). By this time, no reliable information was available on the collusive links between business actors and paramilitary militias, even if the hypothesis was already evoked.

Yet the immediate impact of this action was reduced; a few months after the publication of the report, a second INCODER document stated that most of the investors' title deeds were legal, and had been legitimately purchased. A subsequent Ombudsman report severely criticized this revocation and confirmed the initial information (DP 2006).

[10]The General Inspector's Office is in charge of controlling the public servants' compliance to the law.

The turning point of the land grabbing controversy was the recognition by the Interamerican Court of the link between land grabbing and forced displacement. In its March 2005 resolution, the tribunal established that palm crops were the main cause of forced displacement, and a severe obstacle to the local families' return. The Court's intervention accorded a high level of recognition to the NGOs' claims, and denounced the government's official discourse that had refused to link land grabbing and forced displacement.

The Interamerican Court's provisions were assumed by several domestic institutions. In 2006, the General Inspector's Office issued a report recognizing land grabbing as one of the main causes of forced displacement. According to this data, 76 percent of IDPs in Colombia were peasants at the moment of their forced displacement: 'Land grabbing, dispossession and plundering' are considered to be a part of a 'counter agrarian reform' mostly perpetrated by paramilitary groups in alliance with corporate actors (PGN 2006). Moreover, 'indigenous peoples' and 'Afro-Colombian communities' are considered to be particularly vulnerable to violent land grabbing. The General Inspector's Office then analyzed what is called a 'political ecology of war' and considered the cases of the Lower Atrato, where 'those who came back to their lands, in the aftermath of forced displacement, found them covered with oil palm crops' (PGN 2006). Based on those observations, the report pleads for an integration of issues of land control and land grabbing into the public policy of IDPs' assistance.

The interaction between national and international institutions contributed to the creation of a contentious arena for NGOs as well as domestic jurisdictions. In 2009, the Constitutional Court pointed to the noncompliance of the Interamerican Court's provisions by the Colombian government. In one of the internal displacement monitoring acts, the Court stated that the government had failed to protect the rights of the Lower Atrato people. Based on data provided by the Ombudsman and the General Inspector's offices, the Court dictated the parameters of a specific plan that would address the necessities of the Lower Atrato people. It ordered the relevant ministries and agencies to determine the threats to the collective title deeds (CC 2009a).

The judicialization of land grabbing was not limited to the case of the Lower Atrato, which I have used here to illustrate the interaction between national and international legal arenas, as well as the link between land control issues and internal displacement. The intervention of the Constitutional Court in the case of the 'rural development statute' (Law 1152 of 2007) is also a relevant case of judicialization of land grabbing. The law had a clear-cut business approach to land, considering that rural development in a context of globalization 'requires a new impetus to business development and a key role reserved to the private sector'. The stress was put on 'improvements in the profitability and competitiveness of (agricultural) products'.[11] The law was harshly criticized by NGOs and representatives of peasant organizations and IDPs. The provisions aiming to 'rationalize' and 'clarify' land property were interpreted by these organizations as a threat to small peasants and ethnic communities. Moreover, several mechanisms that were intended to facilitate the issuing of title deeds were also seen as a legalization of violent land grabbing. The law intended to redistribute land that was considered to be abandoned or unexploited. However, the causes of abandonment were not addressed; in consequence, the law might lead to massive land grabs in the zones affected by internal displacement.

[11]Source : Ley 030 de 2006-Senado, por la cual se dicta el estatuto de desarrollo rural, se reforma el Instituto Colombiano de Desarrollo Rural (INCODER), y se dictan otras disposiciones.

In 2009, the Constitutional Court ruled that the 'rural development statute' was unconstitutional. The case against the law had been brought by the Colombian commission of jurists, an NGO associated with the International Commission of Jurists (ICJ). The NGO's arguments concerned the violation by the Colombian government of the Indigenous and Tribal Peoples Convention, an International Labour Organisation Convention that was ratified by the Colombian parliament in 1991. According to the Colombian Constitution and to the Court's jurisprudence, the text is a part of the 'constitutional block'. Yet one of its key provisions (article 6) concerns the necessity to 'consult the peoples concerned, through appropriate procedures and in particular through their representative institutions, whenever consideration is being given to legislative or administrative measures which may affect them directly'. According to the Court, 'the rural development statute constitutes a comprehensive regulation on use, distribution, and use of agricultural property'. Therefore, it affects directly the indigenous and Afro-Colombian communities, as 'the vast majority of them live in rural areas' and they 'have a special bond with the land, derived from their traditions and customs that are constitutive of their identity' (CC 2009b).

Conclusion

This contribution has argued that the Colombian case can be heuristic for the study of the co-construction of legal institution in charge of the enforcement of the rule of law and the protection of property rights. As shown by the Lower Atrato case, these institutions are the product of interactions between international law, institutional changes affecting the centre and grassroots mobilization. Moreover, the response of the Colombian state to land grabbing, and more broadly to forced displacement, cannot be interpreted as merely a result of international pressure. Power balances inside the state apparatus but also mobilization from below are necessary factors for institutional change.

Some scholars argue that the direct impact of judicial decisions on social change in Colombia is reduced. According to Sandoval Rojas (2013), legal provisions only concern specific cases of individuals (as in the Lower Atrato communities) or are focused on judicial review (as in the 'rural development statute'). The Constitutional Court's decisions do not challenge the economic model and the political ecology of agribusiness. However, this same author argues (Sandoval Rojas 2013, 212) legal decisions constitute a basis for further mobilisations; they impell the emergence of public problems (as in the case of internal displacements analysed by Gómez 2012) and enrich the movements' repertoire with new legal and political skills. Other scholars, such as Lemaitre Ripoll (2009), stress the fact that legal struggles are key moments for the formation of collective identities and the constitution of individuals and groups as legal subjects.

This contribution has argued that, in Colombia, legal decisions and institutional reforms have been extremely ambivalent, as the action of judicial courts and human rights institutions cannot be reduced to a strategy for legitimizing the regime, nor has it sufficed to enforce the rights of peasant communities. This converges with the work of David Recondo (2007), who has studied the implementation of multiculturalism in Mexico. No actor – he argues – even those who implement reforms, has full control over the course of events. Reforms, even those which are instrumentalized by the government, cannot be confined to one single group of decision makers. They involve a variety of actors who will try to direct them for personal benefits. Reforms often result from the convergence of antagonistic interests; as such, their outcome is rather unclear. In a context of democratization, new institutions, initially created to moderate social mobilization, can become fuel for new conflicts, redistributing resources and redefining demands.

The outcome of the current debates about land grabbing and land control in Colombia might be useful to enrich our understanding of these issues. By the 2010 presidential election, the issue of land grabbing and land-related violence had become a legitimate public problem. Following his election, the new president Juan Manuel Santos announced his commitment to the enactment of an ambitious 'Land and Victims Law'. The bill would benefit the several million people who suffered personal or material damage from the action of organized armed actors, including those whose land was extorted by violent entrepreneurs.

The enactment of the Land and Victims Law opened a window of opportunity for peasant and IDP organizations. It gave visibility to their cause, and it permitted them to point to specific cases of violent dispossession and to obtain media attention. Yet this visibility also exposed collective and individual actors to violence; according to the Ombudsman bureau, at least 71 leaders of peasant organizations were murdered between 2006 and 2011. In June 2012, more than 15,000 people had addressed formal complaints for land restitution. Several hundred have asked for special police protection following murder threats linked to their demands.

Land grabbing and land reform have been integrated into the agenda of the peace process currently held between the Colombian government and the FARC guerrillas.[12] While the issue of the peace negotiations is still unknown, the implementation of new policies of rural development that will take into account the necessities of peasants, indigenous and afro-descendants has been defined by the government as a necessary step in the process of peace building. As such, our retrospective analysis has shown that the judicialization of land grabbing in Colombia has been a key step in the process of defining land not only as an object of business transactions but also as an issue of human rights and collective identities.

Acknowledgements

I wish to thank the anonymous reviewers, as well as Jun Borras and Yves-Pol Hémonin, for their valuable comments and for the time and patience they devoted to the early versions of this manuscript. I also owe much gratitude to the Land Deal Politics Initiative (LDPI) network, which provided me with extremely helpful support within the Small Grants Programme.

Funding

This work was supported by the Land Deal Politics Initiative Small Grants Programme.

References

Angell, A., Schjolden, L., and Sieder, R., eds. 2005. *The judiciarization of politics in Latin America.* New York: Palgrave Macmillan.

Amnesty International. 1989. *Colombia: El panorama de los derechos humanos.* London.

[12] *Fuerzas Armadas Revolucionarias de Colombia* – Revolutionary armed forces of Colombia.

Avilés, W. 2007. *Global capitalism, democracy, and civil-military relations in Colombia*. Albany: SUNY Press.
Ballvé, T. 2013. Grassroots masquerades: development, paramilitaries, and land laundering in Colombia. *Geoforum* 50: 62–75.
Barbosa, J., Renán, W., and Suárez, W. 2007. *La propiedad rural en el Magdalena 1970–2004 y algunas relaciones con el desplazamiento forzado*. Santa Marta: DTCH. Universidad del Magdalena, Vicerrectoría de Investigación, Fonciencias, Sección II, informe final convocatoria 2004.
Blanquer, J.-M. 2002. Colombie: les droits sans Etat. *Problèmes d'Amérique Latine* 44: 49–62.
Borras, S., and Franco, J. 2013. Global land grabbing and political reactions 'from below'. *Third World Quarterly* 34, no. 9: 1723–47.
Briquet, J.-L., and G. Favarel-Garrigues. 2010. *Organized crime and states: The hidden face of politics*. London: Palgrave Macmillan
Bushnell, D. 1993. *The making of the modern Colombia: A nation in spite of itself*. Berkeley: University of California Press.
Cárdenas, R. 2012. Green multiculturalism: Articulations of ethnic and environmental politics in a Colombian 'black community'. *Journal of Peasant Studies* 39, no. 2: 309–33.
CC. 2009a. Auto 005/09. MP. José Manuel Cepeda Espinosa. Corte Constitucional. January 26.
CC. 2009b. Decision C-175/09. March 18.
Cepeda, M.J. 2005. Judicialization of politics in Colombia: The old and the new. In *The judiciarization of politics in Latin America*, ed. A. Angell, L. Schjolden, and R. Sieder, 67–104. New York: Palgrave Macmillan.
CGN (Contraloria general de la nacion). 2009. Auditoria gubernamental con enfoque integral, modalidad regular, al fondo para el financiamiento para el sector agropecuario, FINAGRO, vigencia fiscal 2005–2006. Bogota.
CIDH. 2003. Resolucion. Asunto comunidades del Jiguamiando y del Curbarado. Corte Interamericana de derechos humanos. March 6.
Comaroff, J., and Comaroff, J.L. 2008. Law and disorder in the postcolony: An introduction. In *Law and disorder in the postcolony*. Chicago: University of Chicago Press.
Comisión Colombiana de Juristas. 2006. *Revertir el destierro forzado: protección y restitución de los territorios usurpados. Obstáculos y desafíos para garantizar el derecho al patrimonio de la población desplazada en Colombia*. Bogotá.
Cousins, B. 2009. Capitalism obscured: The limits of law and rights-based approaches to poverty reduction and development. *Journal of Peasant Studies* 36, no. 4: 893–908.
Daviaud, S. 2006. *Droits de l'homme et politique. L'enjeu des droits fondamentaux dans le conflit colombien*. Paris: EHESS.
DP. 2002. Violaciones masivas de derechos humanos y desplazamiento forzado en la region del Bajo Atrato Chocoano. Defensoria del Pueblo. Resolucion defensorial no. 25. October.
DP. 2006. Informe de seguimiento a al resolucion defensorial no. 39 del 2 de junio de 2005. Defensoria del Pueblo.
DP. 2012. Comunicado de prensa. Defensoria del pueblo. March 28.
Duffy, R. 2008. «Shadow state» : mondialisation, criminalisation et changements environnementaux au Belize. In *Milieux criminels et pouvoir politique. Les ressorts illicites de l'Etat*, ed. J.-L. Briquet and G. Favarel-Garrigues, 129–48. Paris: Karthala.
Duncan, G. 2005. *Los señores de la guerra*. Bogota: Planeta.
El Espectador. 2010. 'El emisario de Castano en Uraba', *El Espectador*, 14 October.
Escobar, A. 2008. *Territories of difference: Place, movements, ilfe, redes*. Duke: Duke University Press.
Foreign Affairs. 2005. The failed states index. *Foreign Affairs*, no. 149.
Fox, J. 1994. The difficult transition from clientelism to citizenship: Lessons from Mexico. *World Politics* 46, no. 2: 151–84.
Franco, J. 2008. Making land rights accessible: Social movements and political-legal innovation in the rural Philippines. *Journal of Peasant Studies* 44, no. 7: 991–1022.
Gallón, G. 1997. Diplomacia y derechos humanos: Entre la inserción y el aislamiento. In *Colombia entre la inserción y el aislamiento. La política exterior colombiana en los años noventa*, ed. S. Ramírez and L. Restrepo, 202–31. Bogotá: IEPRI-Siglo del Hombre.

Garibay, D., and J.-C. Guerrero. 2007. Identifier et interpréter une « crise extrême ». La « communauté internationale » face au conflit armé en Colombie. In *Crises extremes*, ed. Le Pape and Vidal Siméant, 136–50. Paris: La Découverte.

Gayer, L. 2014. *Karachi: Ordered disorder and the struggle for the city*. London, New York: Hurst, Oxford University Press.

Gibson, E. 2005. Boundary control subnational authoritarianism in democratic countries. *World Politics* 58: 101–32.

Goebertus Estrada, J. 2008. Palma de aceite y desplazamiento forzado en Zona Bananera:« trayectorias » entre recursos naturales y conflicto. *Colombia internacional*, no. 67: 152–75.

Goldfarb, L. 2012. The frontiers of genetically modified soya in Argentina. Possession Rights and New Forms of Land Control and Governance. In *International conference on global land grabbing*. Ithaca, Cornell University.

Gómez, L. 2012. *Le déplacement forcé par la violence en Colombie: émergence, réinscription et transformations d'une nouvelle catégorie de l'action publique*. Paris: Sciences Po.

Grajales, J. 2011. The rifle and the title: Paramilitary violence, land grab and land control in Colombia. *Journal of Peasant Studies* 38, no. 4: 771–92.

Grajales, J. 2013. State involvement, land grabbing and counter-insurgency in Colombia. *Development and Change* 44, no. 2: 211–32.

Gusfield, J. 1989. Constructing the ownership of social problems: Fun and profit in the welfare state. *Social Problems* 36, no. 5: 431–41.

Gutierrez Sanín, F. 2007. *Lo Que El Viento Se Llevo?: Los Partidos Politicos y La Democracia En Colombia, 1958–2002*. Bogotá: Norma.

Incoder. 2005. Los cultivos de palma de aceite en los territorios colectivos de las comunidades negras de los rios Curvarado y Jiguamiando.

Justicia y Paz. 2007. Informe 64. Deforestacion ilegal hacia el Jiguamiando. Comision intereclesial justicia y paz. December 15.

Leal Buitrago, F., and Dávila, A. 1990. *Clientelismo. El sistema político y su expresión regional*. Bogotá: Tercer Mundo – IEPRI.

Lecombe, D. 2009. Trust and distrust about the diffusion of transitional justice in Colombia. International Political Science Association Congress, Santiago de Chile.

Lemaitre Ripoll, J. 2009. *El derecho como conjuro. Fetichismo legal, violencia y movimientos sociales*. Bogotá: Siglo del Hombre (Derecho y Sociedad).

Li, T.M. 2011. Centering labor in the land grab debate. *Journal of Peasant Studies* 38, no. 2: 281–298.

López-Alves, F. 2003. *La Formación del Estado y la Democracia en América Latina: 1810–1900*. Bogotá: Norma.

Lund, C. 2011. Fragmented sovereignty: Land reform and dispossession in Laos. *Journal of Peasant Studies* 38, no, 4: 885–905.

Lund, C., and Peluso, N. 2011. New frontiers of land control: Introduction. *Journal of Peasant Studies* 38, no. 4: 885–904.

Monsalve, S. 2012. The human rights framework in contemporary Agrarian struggles. *Journal of Peasant Studies* 40, no. 1: 239–90.

Oslender, U. 2007. Violence in development: The logic of forced displacement on Colombia's Pacific coast. *Development in Practice* 17, no. 6: 752–64.

Pardo, R., and Tokatlian, J.G. 1989. *Política exterior colombiana: de la subordinación a la autonomía ?* (Colección Uniandes 40 años).

PGN. 2006. Proyecto control preventivo y seguimiento a las political publicas en materia de reinsercion y desmovilizacion. Procuraduria general de la nacion.

Romero, M., ed. 2007. *Parapolítica. La ruta de la expansión paramilitar y los acuerdos políticos*. Bogotá: Corporacion Nuevo Arco Iris.

Romero, M., ed. 2011. *La economía de los paramilitares*. Bogotá: Random House Mondatori.

Recondo, D. 2007. *La Política del Gatopardo: Multiculturalismo y Democracia en Oaxaca*. México DF: CIESAS.

Reno, W. 2008. *Corruption and State Politics in Sierra Leone*. Cambridge: Cambridge University Press.

Restrepo Echeverri, J., and V. Franco Restrepo. 2011. La toma de la tierra: lógicas de guerra y acumulación en el Bajo Atrato. In *La economía de los paramilitares*, ed. M. Romero. Bogotá: Random House Mondatori.

Rodriguez Garavito, C., and D. Rodriguez Franco. 2010. *Cortes y cambio social. Como la Corte Constitucional transformó el desplazamiento forzado en Colombia*. Bogotá: Dejusticia-Antropos.
Roldan, M. 2002. *Blood and fire: la Violencia in Antioquia, Colombia, 1946–1953*. Duke: Duke University Press.
Rolland, S. 2007. De l'individuel au collectif : Des stratégies de survie des déplacés colombiens aux regroupements communautaires. *Asylon(s)*, no. 2.
Sandoval Rojas, N. 2013. La movilización social en tiempos de la Constitución: feministas, indígenas y víctimas de crímenes de Estado ante la Corte Constitucional colombiana. *Colombia Internacional*, no. 79: 191–217.
Semana. 2005. 'Habla Vicente Castano', Semana, 4 June.
Sikkink, K., and M. Keck. 1998. *Activists beyond borders*. Ithaca: Cornell University Press.
Tate, W. 2007. *Counting the dead: the culture and politics of human rights activism in Colombia*. Berkeley: University of California Press.
Ungar, M. 2004. Human rights in the Andes. The Defensoría del Pueblo. In *Politics in the Andes*, ed. J.-M. Burt and P. Mauceri, 164–86. Pittsburgh: University of Pittsburgh Press.
Uprimny, R. 2007. La justice au cœur du politique: potentialités et risques d'une judiciarisation en Colombie. In *La fonction politique de la justice*, ed. J. Commaille and M. Kaluszynski, 229–50. Paris: La Découverte.
Vermeulen, S., and L. Cotula. 2010. Over the heads of local people: Consultation, consent, and recompense in large-scale land deals for biofuels projects in Africa. *Journal of Peasant Studies* 37, no. 4: 899. doi:10.1080/03066150.2010.512463

Resistance or participation? Fighting against corporate land access amid political uncertainty in Madagascar

Mathilde Gingembre

Drawing on a micro-level ethnography, this paper explores the process by which a rural municipality managed to pressure the state into temporarily halting the land extension of a large-scale biofuel project in an agropastoral area of southern Madagascar. It documents how the coalition of local leaders and wealthy cattle owners behind the protest resisted threats to their land access and local domination by finding spaces of expression outside the control of local consultation, and creating alliances with influential activists. In a moral economy veering between rationales of autochthony and extraversion, the transnationalisation of the protest sent shock waves through a state apparatus divided and focused on the prospects of coming elections. By analysing the environmental, cognitive and relational mechanisms behind the emergence and repercussions of this bottom-up struggle, this paper points to the varied bargaining endowments that exist within agrarian communities as well as to the issues of authority at stake within corporate enclosure of land. In states where the rural poor have been historically marginalised from decision-making, consultation processes generally offer little space for participation. This paper demonstrates that contexts of political uncertainty open up new spaces for them to claim their rights but that gains made in such circumstances are fragile and contested.

Introduction

Mr Herizo was trying to remain calm but his bitterness overwhelmed him. There was no doubt in his mind that the Lalifuel agribusiness project was offering much-needed opportunities of national and local development. In exchange, however, the project had been greeted by a smear campaign:

> You know all they said on the internet, nothing is true. We never moved out tombs, we never displaced people, nothing like that. Well you've seen haven't you? But the mayor of Benala went so far as going onto TV and in full screen, like that, he said we were profaning tombs, taking people's land and all of these things. But listen, we don't even work in Benala so come on, cut that! (Mr Herizo, Antananarivo, 13 May 2013)

At the time, the Lalifuel project was facing serious difficulties. A subsidiary of a European holding working in the energy sector, Lalifuel's original plans were to develop a biofuel (*Jatropha curcas*) and biomass (*Moringa* and vetiver) plantation on 100,000 ha in an agro-pastoral area of southern Madagascar. But after four years of activity, the project had generated very low economic returns due to agronomic failures, and the parent company had called for an audit following suspicions of embezzlement. In the meantime, the concern expressed by villagers from the municipality of Benala had attracted the attention of the very activists who had contributed to publicising the now-infamous Daewoo land deal and had, as such, indirectly contributed to the fall of the Ravalomanana regime in 2009.[1] Amidst this turmoil, the *Vice-Primature en charge du Développement et de l'Aménagement du Territoire* (VPDAT), the ministry responsible for development and country planning, ordered the suspension of all additional land transfers to Lalifuel (VPDAT 2012).

In this chain of events, the accusations made by the municipality of Benala were both pivotal and following Mr Herizo's logic, arguably unjustified: the 30-year renewable lease Lalifuel had obtained on 6558 ha in 2012 concerned the municipalities of Arivony and Antafoka. On paper, the territory of neighbouring Benala was not even affected.

Nevertheless, it is crucial to indicate that the municipality had originally been targeted by the company. For Lalifuel staff, this is further proof of the inadmissibility of the accusations made against them and of the company's respect for the local population. The refusal by the residents of Benala to host the jatropha plantations and the project's subsequent decision to divert its land requests to others areas indicate, in their mind, that the consultation process had offered local villagers genuine opportunities of participation in the decision-making process. The careful consideration of the negotiation process by which Lalifuel secured this first land access reveals the fallacy of this simplification. First this claim implies that consultation processes happen in neutral spaces in which opinions can be freely expressed by communities who know their rights and do not fear to uphold them. By scrutinising the discursive and relational mechanisms at work within these spaces, this paper demonstrates instead that the possibility of refusing land dispossession was less *offered* to Benala villagers than it was *seized* by them. Second the causal connection made between the villagers' will and the company's respect for it obscures the power of the host state in allowing or precluding the company's land access. This paper reintroduces these two sets of heterogeneous actors to shed light on the essential role played by Benala elites and to outline the unusual, albeit non-linear, way in which the state responded to their mobilisation.

What must be appreciated is that in Madagascar as in many other places, it is rare for rural communities to withhold consent during consultation processes (Burnod et al. 2011; Evers et al. 2011). Disagreements, when they are expressed, usually come in reaction to, rather than in anticipation of, land dispossession (Borras and Franco 2013; German, Mwangi, and Schoneveld 2013). There is a lack of effective mechanisms for land users to either reject or shape land deals. Even when local consultations take place, agrarian communities' bargaining power is limited by a lack of access to economic and institutional alternatives (Ferguson et al. 2014; Vermeulen and Cotula 2010). In Madagascar, fears of the state combined with entrenched misconceptions that all untitled land is state-owned (Teyssier et al. 2009) generally transform local consultations into rubberstamping procedures instead of spaces of participatory decision-making (Burnod, Gingembre, and Andrianirina Ratsialonana 2013; Ferguson et al. 2014). In Benala, however, people not only withheld consent, they simultaneously engaged in a lobbying and communication campaign in a bid to publicise their opposition and to gain support. Through letters to

[1]In November 2008, the *Financial Times* broke the story that secret negotiations were taking place between the Malagasy government and Daewoo corporation for the long-term leasing of 1.3 million ha of arable land. The news caused great outrage and was used by Andry Rajoelina and the opposition as a key argument to legitimise its overthrow of the Ravalomanana regime (2009).

government officials and public interventions supported by civil society, they spoke out in favour of the same development model as the one defended by the 'land sovereignty alternative', that is, one in which the right to access and control land belongs to those who work and live on it.[2] With the mobilisation of brokers of different nature, the grassroots mobilisation spread into cyber spaces of transnational activism, leading to noticeable realignments within the spheres of local and national decision-making, culminating in the decision to order the suspension of all additional land transfers in favour of the project. This rather unusual chain of events – a proactive grassroots-led resistance gathering support from the state – raises two questions. First, how did the rural municipality of Benala succeed in appropriating rights that, despite protective laws and the process of local consultation, have remained very theoretical in the other municipalities? Second, how and why did this isolated grassroots struggle gather such momentum? In seeking to answer these questions, this paper demonstrates that the exclusion of Benala's territory from the first lease granted to the Lalifuel project is the result of a complex, power-laden interplay of conflicting multi-scalar agencies in a context of political uncertainty.

The political ecology approach adopted in this paper will be complemented by insights from the literature on contentious politics. The conceptual tools of 'mobilising structures', 'collective action frames' and 'repertoires of contention' that have been developed by social movement scholars to study protest over the past 40 years could all be relevant to the analysis. However, instead of using these as a checklist of necessary variables, this paper adopts the dynamic, interactive approach formalised by McAdam, Tarrow and Tilly in their book *Dynamics of contention* (2004; first published in 2001). This approach consists in exploring the 'environmental, cognitive and relational mechanisms' at work in episodes of contentious politics (McAdam, Tarrow, and Tilly 2004, 25) and in understanding how their sequencing shaped the outcome of the movement.

In this model, McAdam, Tarrow, and Tilly stress the importance of scrutinising individual action but argue that causal efficacy lies within relational processes (2004, 23). This paper follows them in proposing that in order to grasp the complexity and fluidity of a mobilisation, one needs to examine the 'interpersonal networks, interpersonal communication, and various forms of continuous negotiation including the negotiation of identities' that are being activated throughout the course of this episode of contentious politics (McAdam, Tarrow, and Tilly 2004, 22). In the same vein, other scholars have argued that closer attention must be paid to the interactions between resisters, targets and third parties (Hollander and Einwohner 2004) to gain a better understanding of the recursive constitution of resistance and power (Foucault 1979). While heeding this recommendation, the present contribution stresses that this episode of contention is driven as much, if not more, by the relations and dynamics *internal* to each of these groups. In particular, it highlights the contestations fuelled by the foreign project in local communities divided by competing land claims, different needs and strong socio-economic inequalities, as these tensions were found to have both accelerated and shaped the modalities of the protest.

[2]Arguing that alternative food systems cannot be achieved without a simultaneous move towards democratic land control, some engaged researchers have recently launched a discussion over 'land sovereignty' as a potential land framework for the food sovereignty campaign (Borras and Franco 2013; Borras, Franco, and Monsalve, forthcoming). Land sovereignty is presented as both an alternative analytical framework (going beyond calls for land reform) and a political project whose core principle lies in 'the right of the working people to have effective access to, control over and use of land, and live on it as a resource, space and territory' (Borras, Franco, and Monsalve, forthcoming, 11).

As far as environmental mechanisms are concerned, the paper examines what social movement scholarship has called 'political opportunity structures' (Eisinger 1973; McAdam 1982; Tilly 1978). Different meanings have been given across the literature to this concept (Tarrow 1996). The purpose of this contribution is not to assess the global opportunities that the Malagasy state offers in terms of protest, opposition, dissent etc. – that is, the static opportunity structures. Instead, the analysis highlights the fluidity of the political context or what McAdam et al. call 'changing political environments' (McAdam, Tarrow, and Tilly 2004, 14). During the five-year 'transition' that Madagascar underwent after the coup organised by Andry Rajoelina in March 2009, national politics was pervaded by a heightened sense of uncertainty, with a regime under international sanctions repeatedly postponing elections (Galibert 2011). This paper outlines the divisions and opportunistic realignments that this sense of uncertainty fuelled in the course of one contentious episode around the Lalifuel project. In that respect, the case study reasserts the need to look at states as complex, heterogeneous, divided entities when analysing their role in land deals (Wolford et al. 2013).

These tensions and contradictions will be related to the 'moral economy' of the particular time and place. Moral economy, as constructed by Edward Thompson (1971), 'highlights the relationship between people and leaders (political or economic) to material sustenance in times of economic turmoils' (Siméant 2011, 8), and looks at how protests are informed by implicit theories of legitimate wealth and legitimate economic transactions. Interested in the expectations that tie people to their rulers, the concept of moral economy also conveys a sense of relational legitimacy. This paper explores the authorities' quests for legitimacy and authority, and highlights the tensions state agents face as they try to navigate between the rationale of autochthony and the rationale of extraversion (Galibert 2009). This focus on legitimacy and authority will help to understand the 'critical albeit contradictory role of the state in securing land for investors' (Borras and Franco 2013, 1742), with the original facilitators of the land deal ending up being the main force obstructing it.

The paper starts by exploring the emergence of the grassroots resistance, the repertoires it mobilised and the process of transnationalisation it went through. Contrasting the reactions in Benala to those in the other two municipalities, it then explores the internal and relational dynamics that have allowed disgruntled agrarian communities to move beyond the 'ordinary weapons of relatively powerless groups' (Scott 1986) in order to formalise and publicise their protest. The study of the mechanisms of 'collective attribution of opportunity and threat' (McAdam, Tarrow, and Tilly 2004) sheds light on the constructed rationale that guided Benala mobilisers in taking pre-emptive action to defend their territory from corporate enclosure. This section also documents how mechanisms of 'social appropriation' (McAdam, Tarrow, and Tilly 2004) fostered a mix of consent and coercion that contributed to the formalisation and to the imposition of their position onto the rest of the community. The paper then looks at 'how politics shaped the development and outcomes of movements' (McAdam et al. 1996) by examining the reaction of state officials to these initiatives. Finally, while acknowledging its successes so far, the paper highlights the fragility of this resistance.

This study is the product of three field visits carried out in 2011, 2013 and 2014. It draws on a search and review of documents produced during the deal-making process as well as on repeated semi-structured interviews and informal discussions with a wide range of actors involved in the deal making: from regional and local state officials to customary leaders through brokers, elected village representatives, managers and staff from the agribusiness company, activists and villagers from different age, gender, class and ethnic groups. A total of 26 villages were visited across the three municipalities, and, during the last period of fieldwork, three in-depth village case studies were carried out. To protect the confidentiality of the interviewees, the names of the project, of the localities and of individuals have been changed.

Refusing the manufacture of consent

Non-violent, active and outspoken, Benala's resistance contrasts with more common forms of peasant struggle. In Madagascar, a few instances of local protest were recently seen against large-scale agribusiness projects but these struggles either used violence as a means of expression (ITO investment project) or were initiated by local officials (N-Fuel and NewProd) rather than by the affected communities themselves (Burnod, Gingembre, and Andrianirina Ratsialonana 2013; Medernach and Burnod 2013).

Benala's mobilisation also stands out with regards to the official reactions of the other municipalities targeted by the Lalifuel project. As such, the Lalifuel case study provides a vivid illustration of the variety of local responses that are brought to large-scale land deals (Borras and Franco 2013). In the municipalities of Arivony and Antafoka, both state and local leaders participated in the consultation process and formally agreed to transfer land to Lalifuel. The first tracts were obtained in Arivony, where Lalifuel set up its base and developed a tree nursery. A year later, the company started negotiating with villages in the municipality of Antafoka where the remainder of the first 6558 ha were obtained.

This outward compliance should not be mistaken for consensual or genuine approval, any more than the strong determination displayed in Benala means that all villagers were opposed to the project. What these different municipal positions do, however, show is that there is room for manoeuvre at the local level. In all three municipalities, different sets of dominant actors used a mix of coercion and consent to impose, with more or less success, their position onto the rest of the municipality. Before exploring the process by which this was achieved, the paper describes the procedure by which Lalifuel obtained the first lease.

The first lease

As mentioned above, out of the 100,000 ha originally envisaged, so far 6558 have been formally leased to Lalifuel, and these are spread on 15 non-contiguous plots. This portion-by-portion land access is the co-product of the company's approach and of political acts taken after the fall of the Ravalomanana regime.

Legally, in Madagascar, land cannot be transferred without the local population being consulted. Since the 2005 land reform, untitled land can no longer be leased or sold immediately by the state as local uses are protected under the presumption of 'untitled private property'[3] (Teyssier et al. 2009). Before it can be transferred, untitled land first needs to be titled in the name of the state, and part of this titling procedure involves sending a 'commission' to the site to check whether the land is available or already under productive use (*mise en valeur*).[4] The commission includes the mayor, the head of *fokontany* (the elected representative of the village cluster) and members of the regional land services, and is responsible for summoning the land seeker(s), the neighbours and the *fokonolona* (local community). Should the neighbours or others disagree with the titling, their views are recorded in the

[3]Law 2005-019 of 17 October 2005 fixing the principles governing land statutes (free translation).
[4]Article 18, law 2008-014 of 5 January 2009 on the private property of the state.

proceedings of the commission, which is also responsible for reconciling the different parties.[5] Some local consultation must also be held during the Environmental Impact Assessment (EIA) which is required for all agricultural projects over 1000 ha.[6] However, the rights of the population during this consultation are loosely laid out and meagre in practice (Andriamanalina and Burnod 2014; Ferguson et al. 2014).

Lalifuel conducted an EIA in 2011 but, in this context, the consultation of the population seems to have been restricted to one collective meeting where the presence of senior local and regional authorities can be thought to have acted as a deterrent for anyone who would have liked to express concern. Moreover, Lalifuel's current managers show little, if any, knowledge of the findings or recommendations of this document.[7] Nevertheless, before the land access application was passed on from the regional land services to the relevant ministry, village-level consultations were organised as is required by law: out of the 26 villages interviewed in Arivony and Antafoka, nearly all confirmed having received some kind of visit from the company. A majority reported having been allowed to choose which tract(s) would be given to the project and in most cases (but not all), this choice had so far been respected. However, the analysis of these villages' experiences betrays inconsistencies in terms of the promises made, the communication of fragmented information and at times recourse to false pretences to accelerate consent. As a result, while villagers commonly insisted that 'Lalifuel was not forcing people'[8], very few of those consulted actually understood they had a right to refuse giving land altogether since, for them, the project had already been approved at higher levels. The consultation was therefore understood at best as a chance to choose which tract(s) to give and to express their wishes in terms of compensation. Finally, it was extremely rare to have a full representation of all of those holding claims on the land. By favouring one hamlet over the others – in this area, each village is generally made up of a minimum of three or four hamlets – and overlooking the importance of holding discussions *between* villages – neighbouring villages frequently share use rights over rangeland – the consultation ended up fuelling tensions between and within villages.

In Benala, the project's approach was not rejected straight away. In September 2011, the mayor welcomed the EIA team and the regional official who accompanied them. In the minutes of the meeting, the mayor is reported to have expressed doubts as to the desire of the population 'to change', and some concern over the reduction of local cattle wealth the project could lead to.[9] He is also reported to have attempted to negotiate the incorporation of the local population through an out-grower agreement. A few months later, the mayor's cousin and right-hand man agreed to take one of Lalifuel's local managers around some villages. The company gained nothing other than a polite refusal on the part of both villagers and local leaders. This experience proved that, as long as they were channelled (as in this example, with the mayor's cousin showing the company

[5]Article 28 and 29 of decree 2010-233 laying down the procedures for applying law 2008-014.
[6]Decree no. 99-954 of 15 December 1999 modified by decree no. 2004-167.
[7]The EIA has not been validated by the ONE (National Office for the Environment) who require that a new EIA is conducted for the area affected by the first lease instead of the whole 100,000 ha. The Lalifuel project therefore operates without the required environmental licence.
[8]The local expression that recurred was: 'Tsy nanao forcé i Lalifuel'.
[9]'Tatitry ny fivoriana. Tetik'asa voly savoa region X Lalifuel. Fanadihadihana ny amin'ny fiantraika (EIE) amin'ny tontolo iaiana ny mponina' [Minutes of the meeting-Lalifuel project Jatropha plantation. Assessing the consequences on the people and the environment (EIA)], hand-written document, 16 September 2011, 1 page.

around), consultation could help to build an image of unanimous hostility without having to adopt a confrontational attitude.

However, the problems caused by the extension of Lalifuel in neighbouring municipalities combined with attempts by individuals within Benala to collaborate with the project forced the anti-Lalifuel contingent to move beyond the ordinary weapons of the weak (Scott 1986) and to publicly declare their outright refusal of all land transfers.

Grassroots opposition

Benala first broke its silence following signs that Lalifuel was close to encroaching on land that some of its villages considered as theirs. On 25 August 2011, six villages from the *fokontany* of Analaroa wrote a letter to the regional and local authorities after they spotted one of Lalifuel’s vehicles on their village land. Interestingly, it was not the company who was blamed for this but a villager from the neighbouring municipality of Arivony, who had ‘fooled’ the developers and brought them to a tract that ‘belonged’ to villagers from Benala. A couple of months later, another village sent a letter to the regional authorities: there were rumours that a neighbouring village from the municipality of Antafoka had ‘sold’ some of their village land to Lalifuel although they had previously made it clear that they were not willing to part with this land. Shortly after the first of these two complaints, the municipal authorities organised a meeting in Benala’s town hall. The minutes of the meeting were typed and sent to state officials: this document formalised the resistance to the project and presented it as a ‘collective stance adopted by the majority’.[10] The meeting also instigated a ‘collective duty’ to ‘check over any further extension of territory by the investor’. The letter was accompanied by 493 signatures, collected from a total of nine *fokontany* and more than 25 villages. Another four villages wrote to state officials in the following two years, each expressing opposition in principle to Lalifuel activities on their land. Simultaneously, the municipality engaged in the process of creating an association ‘to keep an eye on the potential extensions of Lalifuel’s plantations’.[11]

Gaining allies

In November 2012, over a year after the first letters were sent, a dozen of the main local mobilisers went to Antananarivo to participate in a press conference. Organised by the SIF (*Sehatra Iombonana ho an’ny Fananan-tany*), a platform of Malagasy associations working on land rights, this event allowed them to publicly express, for the first time, their concern over the Lalifuel project, which was then accused of serious land and human rights violations. Few newspapers reported on the press conference, but it was transmitted on radio Don Bosco, one of the few stations with national coverage, as well as on TV. For most of the villagers, it was their first visit to the capital and their first contact with any civil society organisation. A grouping of non-governmental organisations (NGOs) and of national, regional and municipal farmers’ associations, the SIF works for the promotion of ‘land access for human development’ through lobbying, advocacy and sensitisation (SIF website n.d.). Funded by international solidarity associations such as

[10]Source: Document entitled ‘Minutes of meeting. Object: opposition to the project requiring large tracts of land in the municipality of Benala’, 18 November 2011.

[11]Discussion, village of Ambalava, municipality of Benala, 4 May 2013. By mid-2014, the association was still not registered with the state, though.

the International Land Coalition (ILC), the Catholic Committee against Hunger and for Development (CCFD) and Swiss Intercooperation, it has taken on an ever-increasing role in the defence of local land rights in the context of large-scale corporate projects, organising meetings and workshops with local associations in affected areas.

The initiatives of Benala's villagers were brought to the SIF's attention by M. Tovolahy, a catholic friar who had implemented development projects in the municipalities of Arivony and Antafoka for more than 20 years. Literate and well-travelled, M.Tovolahy is well connected both inside Madagascar and abroad. He currently lives in the capital and has not been seen by the villagers for a few years now. As such, he may not be as closely linked to domestic networks and opportunities as those 'rooted cosmopolitans' Tarrow describes in *The New Transnational Activism* (Tarrow 2005, xiii). However, M. Tovolahy has remained in touch with local people and events, which is critical in Madagascar where national civil society still struggles to reach the grassroots level (Burnod, Gingembre, and Andrianirina Ratsialonana 2013), and the SIF, despite efforts at decentralisation, is not spared from this problem.[12] Besides his role as a broker between a remote civil society and isolated grassroots protesters, M. Tovolahy ran an active communication campaign on social media against the expansion of Lalifuel.

Investigations revealed that Benala's opposition was also helped by some people within the regional state apparatus. In 2011, the head of the district endorsed Analaroa's letter with a small note saying that 'it was unacceptable to seize cattle-nurturing earth by force and that the population needed to be confronted for harmony to be preserved'.[13] With regards to the enthusiastic support Lalifuel had received from other state officials, this was a rather bold and unusual act. While no other evidence of regional state officials giving open support to Benala's struggle has been found, there are signs that some have been helping in more discreet ways. Villagers and the activists supporting them were indeed found to possess pieces of information that only those actors involved to some degree in the deal making could have possessed. The former confirmed having allies within the regional state apparatus while taking extra care to keep their identities secret.

Linking outwards

In parallel, a vocal transnational mobilisation was launched in support of the villagers. Shortly after the press conference, the *Collectif Tany*, the diaspora advocacy group that had contributed to publicising the Daewoo land scandal in 2008–2009, published a press release to relay Benala's call of distress and invite support 'against the land grab of vast tracts of land by the company Lalifuel in Madagascar' (Collectif Tany 2012). The accusations of encroachment of land rights that the villagers had made during the press conference were confirmed by 'private testimonies' and the picture was completed by allusions to the national politics that were being played out around the land deal. The Collectif Tany also pointed to the active involvement of Hajo Andrianainarivelo, the Minister responsible for development and country planning and Vice Premier Minister (VPM). He had recently delivered, on behalf of Lalifuel, a 4 × 4 vehicle and two laptops to the regional government of the affected area (La Gazette de la Grande Ile 2012). *Collectif Tany*'s note was quickly reproduced on a number of websites and blogs, including those of established networks of international NGOs such as the ILC and of activist organisations such as Grain and Oxfam.

[12]Interview with a member of the SIF, Antananarivo, 22 January 2014.
[13]Free translation.

Informed through these fora and other networks of trust and activism, Malagasy citizens in Antananarivo and abroad took up the struggle. Using the internet and social media, they launched a campaign against both the company and the VPM, whom they later accused of having traded his support to Lalifuel for funding of his electoral campaign.[14]

This international interest contrasted with the low level of coverage that was given of the protest in national media. While Lalifuel was being transformed into the new land grab scandal on Malagasy cyberspaces, it had little national profile and only one small opposition party referred to the affair during the 2013 electoral campaign. Nevertheless, as in the Daewoo case, the transnational mobilisation ended up reverberating in the national space and affecting national politics (Coordination Sud 2010). This process will be closely examined in the third section of this paper.

Through this series of non-violent initiatives, people from Benala therefore found spaces of expression outside the control of local consultation and in the process gained wider leverage and support.

Legitimising and imposing resistance

Most contentious episodes are premised on the construction of a shared understanding of the potential consequences of action (opportunity) or failure to act (threat) (McAdam, Tarrow, and Tilly 2004, 95). In the Lalifuel case, the 'collective attribution of opportunity and threat' (McAdam, Tarrow, and Tilly 2004, 95) acted as a central mechanism in the diffusion of the protest. To impose the pre-eminence of land access and control over perceived advantages of collaborating with the agribusiness project, and to discourage alternative voices, the anti-Lalifuel contingent also mobilised identities and customary institutions.

Collective attribution of opportunity and threat

The construction of Lalifuel as an imminent, irredeemable threat played a major role in triggering and feeding the grassroots mobilisation. The argument was that no middle-ground solution was possible. First, food security was at risk, despite the commitment of Lalifuel managers to leave farmed land untouched. In the context of a growing population and depleting natural resources, unfarmed uplands were necessary to middle- and even short-term survival:

> The state thinks that there are wide free tracts of land here, that's why they decide to give the *tazoa* (uplands). But here there isn't any farmland left. All the lowlands are farmed and so we now need the use the *tazoa* to grow rice as well. Even if we have to wait for the rain there, it's this or nothing. We need the *tazoa*. (municipal councillor, *fokontany* of Anjorobe, municipality of Benala, 8 May 2013)

While this argument on the importance of land reserves came up regularly, the real anxiety concerned cattle herding: in a system of extensive pastoralism, any loss of land would imply a loss of cattle. As their letters explicitly highlighted, Lalifuel's large-scale project was therefore threatening the two inseparable elements in which the economy but also their social organisation, identities, histories and belief systems were embedded. Insisting on the importance of cattle and land in mediating their relations with the ancestors and

[14]M. Andrianainarivelo officially announced his candidature in April 2013 but he was accused of having started his campaign well before (Madagascar Tribune online 2013).

regulating behaviour with one another, they were drawing a compelling explanation of the all-encompassing function of land as both tangible and intangible resource.

The project's business model and, more precisely, the decision not to use a contract-farming model (despite announcements to the contrary[15]) further reinforced their fears. M. Toniaina, Benala's current mayor, actually proposed that the jatropha could be farmed by the local population; only, he reported, for the company to come back with an insultingly low offer.[16] Whether these calls for an alternative model of incorporation in the business project were actually made or not, this account signals clear-sightedness as to the lack of bargaining power that illiterate, agrarian communities have over these high-return land allocation processes (Vermeulen and Cotula 2010). 'It's not that we are against Lalifuel', another villager explained. 'If we knew how to read and write then we would have accepted'.[17] When the only option left would be to work for the company, being a wage-worker is seen as 'a form of slavery'.[18] Again, this vision is embedded in the Malagasy cosmogony where the severing of connections with the ancestors entailed by land loss implies losing one's history and thereby becoming a slave.[19] The fear of renouncing identity and control is reinforced by the crop chosen by the investor. The risk is not only to lose control over the land but also to lose control over its output: 'I remember the day where I went to Arivony with Lalifuel's managers, people were saying "this thing [the jatropha] is useless. You can't even do coffins with it and the leaves can't even be used as fodder either"' (senior regional official, 13 May 2013).

In comparison with these losses, the social services offered by Lalifuel did not impress, and neither did discussions about alternative economic activities:

> They talk about schools and other advantages the project can bring. But out of 1000 kids who go to school, only 10 maybe can become bureaucrats! And so what will the others do then if their land is taken away from them? (mayor of Benala, provincial capital, 5 May 2013)

The sense of threat is also spread through the accounts of the ordeals faced by the villages from the other two municipalities already affected by the project. Reproduced by media and activists, their stories talk of severe violations of rights, such as evictions under the threat of armed force, the display of power through the use of security services, and the encroachment of burial sites.[20] Although consultations did not fulfil the conditions of free, prior and informed consent, and concern over lost land is significantly increasing, none of these more serious accusations has so far been confirmed by villagers from Arivony and Antafoka. In sum, the lobbying campaign of anti-Lalifuel protesters has been underpinned by the manufacture of rumours as much as by descriptions of the perceived threats.

As far as professional activists were concerned, this rare expression of opposition on behalf of rural populations presented a timely opportunity to advance their claims.

[15]The business plan announced that 25 percent of the surface would be farmed following a model of contract farming.
[16]Interview, mayor of Benala, provincial capital, 5 May 2013.
[17]Interview, son of *lonaky*, Itaosy village, 9 May 2013.
[18]Minutes of meeting, municipality of Ambatolahy, 18 November 2013. The same expression was used by the head of *fokontany* of Analaroa (interview, 4 May 2013, Benala village, municipality of Benala).
[19]On the connection between landlessness and the status of *andevo* (slave), cf. Evers (2006).
[20]Interview, deputy head of *fokontany*, Ambalava village, municipality of Benala, 10 May 2013, and quotations from the press conference.

McAdam et al. note that 'sensing an opportunity to strengthen or revitalize their organisation through the facilitation of grassroots activity, members of established organisations commonly serve as brokers for emergent movements' (McAdam, Tarrow, and Tilly 2004, 104). For the SIF, time had come to make up for their noted silence during the Daewoo affair. 'We were determined not to miss the boat this time', explained one of its members.[21] As for the *Collectif Tany* who had been actively campaigning against land grabbing in Madagascar over the previous three years, this grassroots resistance offered a powerful justification of their calls for transparency and accountability. The moment to speak out could not have been better chosen: while general elections were approaching, and with them the opportunity to increase pressure on government officials, Lalifuel itself was experiencing internal strife as suspicions of embezzlement had led the company's headquarters to call for an audit and to replace the management team.

This sense of opportunity was partially passed on to the grassroots protesters, who gained some crucial, albeit fragile, confidence in the legitimacy and potential of the struggle. Thanks to their allies within civil society and the administration, villagers of Benala were able to access information and decisions taken in closed, official spaces. When the *Vice-Primature en charge du Développement et de l'Aménagement du Territoire* (VPDAT) ordered the regional land services to suspend all additional land transfers to Lalifuel, they were amongst the first to know. They were given a copy of the official memorandum accompanied by its translation (from French to Malagasy).[22] This access to information gave them optimism as to the power of collective action, as evidenced by the pride with which this note was brandished by the protesters when asked whether they thought their initiatives had made a difference.

Generally speaking, the intervention of civil society is seen as instrumental in ensuring that agrarian communities fully understand the ins and outs of projects, know their rights and therefore express an informed opinion when consulted (Andriamanalina and Burnod 2014; Evers et al. 2011). In the Lalifuel case, it certainly allowed villagers to access an alternative point of view to that conveyed by most officials.

> Yes I think the press conference was useful. It was good to hear that the jatropha plantation was not favourable for us Malagasies. And also it was good to be able to share our concerns and express our problems. Each one of us had a chance to talk and explain. Personally I explained why it was so important to have a lot of land free for our cattle. […] We were all able to talk one after the other. (*komity* [village secretary], village of Amboanjobe, municipality of Antafoka, 18 February 2014)

This feedback makes it clear that, besides finding justification for their struggle, participants felt empowered by a rare opportunity to express their opinions freely and publicly. Nevertheless, it is surprising that local land claims were never backed up with reference to the 2005 land reform. As pointed out by scholars and activists, cattle herders' rights are insufficiently protected as 'very large-scale pastures' are explicitly excluded from law 2006–031 on untitled private property (Andriamanalina and Burnod 2014). Untitled private property does however include 'traditional family pastures'.[23] This provision has nevertheless never been referred to (nor have any others).

---

[21]Interview, M. Tsihory, Antananarivo, 25 Jan 2014.

[22]Note de service, Direction Générale des Services Fonciers, no. 392/12/VPMDAT/SG/DGSF, 1 December 2012.

[23]Law no. 2006-031 of 24 November 2006 determining the legal regime of untitled private land property.

Social appropriation through consent and coercion

Although concerns over land loss exist in the other municipalities, only in Benala were they voiced openly and did they lead to a determined, coordinated action. What allowed this emancipation from the expected and internalised patterns of action? McAdam et al. note that however transgressive a collective action may be, it usually thrives thanks to the appropriation of existing social space and collective identities (2004, 102). Although action used against Lalifuel borrowed from the state-legal repertoires (letters, petitions, press conference), resistance was premised on local experiences, customary institutions and discursive constructions of autochthony. Local structures and collective identities were also mobilised on a more coercive basis.

In 2006, only a few years before Lalifuel arrived in Benala, Sedeti Limited, an Asian agribusiness investor, had sought to develop a large-scale corn plantation in the area. The project forced its way into the municipality against the wishes of non-state local authorities. Supported by the central government and facilitated by both the former regional head (*chef de région*) and by the former mayor of Benala, procedures for a first lease of 6500 ha were started, and 600 ha of rangeland were ploughed along the national road. Operations were stopped rather quickly, however, because of agronomic and financial problems. This experience provided the villagers with useful skills and insights. First, it contributed to a certain degree of legal empowerment: 'Since Sedeti, we know that investors have to do a lease. Because we were victims of Sedeti, we opposed Lalifuel. That's why there is no lease here' (deputy head of *fokontany*, Analaroa village, municipality of Benala, 4 May 2013).

This understanding is crucial when contrasted with the widespread perception that deals have already been concluded when the local consultation takes place. The encounter with the Asian investor was also instrumental in gaining a first experience of resistance and developing certain repertoires of action. At the time, the struggle was led by a retired policeman originating from one of the local wealthy cattle owning families. Following the accidental discovery of the land deal that was secretly being negotiated between the state and the company, he began to lobby regional state officials and, with the support of a local religious association, organise group discussions to sensitise village leaders and authorities. The threats he received from the state, he explains, encouraged people to start writing letters. Collective action was used as a way to confront the repressive mechanisms of the state.

The repercussions of the Sedeti experience on the local political sphere are also key to understanding the posture chosen by M. Toniaina, the current mayor, regarding Lalifuel. When villagers heard that the previous mayor had agreed to give land to Sedeti without having consulted the *lonaky* (heads of sub-lineage governing at the village level), a *dina* (tenet of customary law) was written, condemning him to exile. The sanction was ultimately dropped but the mayor lost his seat and is still despised for this action. The strong force of opposition demonstrated in this context by local figures of authority is worth noting in a country where mayors have gained significant political leverage since the reforms of decentralisation in the 1990s and the development of the ideology of 'local is beautiful' among international donors (Bidou, Droy, and Fauroux 2008). It also helps to contextualise the determination shown by M. Toniaina in prohibiting the project from operating in his municipality. The son of a rich cattle owner and the descendant of a powerful lineage himself, he stands at a crucial intersection of state and non-state politics.

Although he insists on the grassroots nature of a mobilisation for which he was only a spokesperson, the mayor talks with pride of the role he played at different moments in this contentious episode. He is undoubtedly considered essential to the resistance, if only because villagers know that land transfers cannot be made without his approval. A dozen other local elites have shown signs of active engagement in the struggle, drawing authority from lineage descent (*lonaky*), cattle wealth, administrative skills (heads of *fokontany, komity* etc.) or a combination of these attributes. Some attempts were made by regional officials to soften their position but pressure seems to have been moderate and no threats were reported.

It is important to say that the municipality has substantial cattle wealth with a reported total of 34,000 head of cattle (against 20,000 and 10,000 for Arivony and Antafoka respectively) for a population of 12,000 inhabitants. This wealth is quite strongly concentrated with several cattle owners owning more than 5000 head each.[24] It supports large patronage networks through the practice of *confiage*, whereby rich cattle owners lend cattle to poor villagers within and outside their village (and often beyond their municipality). This position of wealth and local power presumably underpins the relative autonomy and immunity that the leaders of Benala's resistance have shown to enjoy in relation to the state. Another factor that has certainly facilitated their opposition to the foreign project is the presence within these families of people who are educated and know how the state administration works. Formerly headmaster of Benala's primary school, the mayor, for instance, spends most of his time in the provincial capital and regularly travels to Antananarivo, where he is said to have high connections.[25]

Several incidents nevertheless suggest that this elite-led mobilisation against Lalifuel is not unanimously appreciated within Benala's villages. Circumventing their control by going directly to the villagers, Lalifuel staff managed, on several occasions, to secure some type of agreement to transfer land. These initiatives were met by firm, swift reactions on the part of Benala's authority figures, which convinced the project to back down. These episodes nevertheless stressed the need for the elites to tighten their control. The next section outlines how resistance was imposed as the official, and only acceptable, stance.

Imposing unity

The arrival of Lalifuel undoubtedly activated a sense of community solidarity within the population of Benala. Threats to the ancestral land and actions taken to counter them reinforced a sense of community revolving around the critical notion of autochthony and of belonging to the land. M. Toniaina's strong opposition to Lalifuel is systematically related to his origins:

> It's easy to understand why our mayor opposed Lalifuel and the other mayors collaborated: our mayor is a *zana-tany* [native] and a *topontany* [literally a master of the land] whereas the mayor of Arivony is a *mpivahiny* [guest or non-native]. (*Lonaky*, village of Vadilongo, municipality of Benala, 6 May 2013)

In establishing this causal connection, villagers are quick to forget that their previous mayor, a *zana-tany* as well, yielded to previous corporate pressures. While providing easy answers to complex questions, the referral to origins is instrumental in reinforcing a

---

[24]Source: INSTAT (National Institute of Statistics), provincial capital and village interviews.

[25]Both the mayor and his cousin mentioned on several occasions having 'high connections in Antananarivo'. The same information was given by the uncle of Benala's mayor, who refused to reveal the identities of these contacts but explained: 'These are very powerful people. If Lalifuel acts badly, I can tell you that they will regret it' (Mr Ritra, *lonaky* of Talata, municipality of Arivony, 2 April 2013).

sense of belonging and unity. When questioned on the reasons why villagers from other municipalities were not standing up to Lalifuel in the same way, most interviewees referred to a 'problem of division' which they contrasted to their own sense of cohesion.

However performative, these discourses of consensual cohesion do not stand up to scrutiny. The disagreements and lack of communication that actually divide Benala were made explicit on several occasions. One day, for instance, villagers from the village of Raketra (municipality of Benala) woke up to Lalifuel tractors ploughing their land. As they walked angrily to them to ask for an explanation, the company's employees told them they had received authorisation from the village. The head of *fokontany* rushed to the mayor who confirmed he had never given his consent to this operation and sent a message to the village. Lalifuel stopped its work immediately. The identity of those who had invited Lalifuel did not evade anyone in the village. These people had previously tried to obtain an official approval to transfer land but both the head of *fokontany* and the mayor had refused to endorse their letter. The failure of both their open and secret endeavours to invite the project to develop in their village highlights the power of the mayor in terms of 'access control' (Peluso and Ribot 2003). According to local rules, alienation rights are owned by the *lonaky*. In this case, not only did the *lonaky* fail to prevent other villagers from appropriating these rights, but had to request an intervention from the mayor to address that usurpation.

Following this event, more direct mechanisms of censorship were set up. During the meeting held at Benala town hall in November 2011, a message was sent that 'the *fokonolona* [the local community] will take measures against those who would want to counter the ideas of the majority. These will be punished by the *dinam-pokonolona* [village justice]'.[26] The threat was specified and toughened with the association of cattle herders whose statutes stipulate that anyone who gives land to private projects shall be evicted from the municipality. The *lonaky* also engaged their authority as mediators between the living and the ancestors, threatening to deprive those who attempted to give land of their rights to the *tsipirano*, the ritual ceremony of blessing held at different life stages and in cases of sickness or misfortune. With regards to the centrality of the *tsipirano* on issues of identity, social integration and ancestral blessing, this is a risk few may be willing to take.

The determination with which Benala's elites reacted to this isolated attempt to collaborate with Lalifuel points to the fact that this struggle against corporate enclosure is directly related to stakes of local domination and social stratification. The village-by-village type of consultation conducted by Lalifuel confronted Benala's elites with two different types of exclusion mechanisms. Firstly, they were excluded from decisions about land on which they used to enjoy use rights (and sometimes claimed alienation rights) on the grounds that this land did not belong to the municipality in which their village was located. These are the land transfers that were contested in their letters. These situations stress the difficulty of accommodating the fluidity and complexity of local land tenure within consultation processes as well as the problematic discrepancies between administrative and local borders. Secondly, the project bypassed local channels of decision-making by dealing directly with non-elite villagers, thereby showing its potential to undermine local structures of power. In this context, refusing all collaboration with the project has been a means to defend their territory as much as to address threats to their authority.

By scrutinising the mechanisms of collective attribution and social appropriation, the previous paragraphs documented how the protest emerged, spread and evolved across

[26]Minutes of the meeting, municipality of Benala, 18 November 2011.

scales. Here the paper turns to the state's reactions, exposing how, faced with this externally supported expression of popular discontent, some senior decision-makers moved from being active supporters of the Lalifuel project to threatening to cancel contracts.

The state under pressure: divisions, electoral strategies and realignments

Under the 'transitional regime' that followed the overthrow of president Ravalomanana (2009–2014), Madagascar sank into economic recession, political turmoil and international isolation (Razafindrakoto, Roubaud, and Wachsberger 2014). In reaction to Andry Rajoelina's seizure of power (Randrianja 2012), bilateral and multilateral donors suspended budget assistance and all 'non-essential' aid funding. These measures dealt a hard blow to an economy in which foreign aid represented approximately 40 percent of the government's budget and 75 percent of public spending (Ploch and Cook 2012). The political tensions and climate of insecurity that followed the coup adversely affected key sectors such as tourism, textile and construction, and led to a sharp drop in the level of private investments (International Crisis Group 2014). According to the World Bank, economic growth in Madagascar collapsed to just 0.6 percent in 2009, from 7 percent in 2008 (IRIN 2010).

In this context, projects related to the extraction and exploitation of the country's natural resources were one of the few sources of official and unofficial funding remaining. In the mining sector, some highly lucrative deals were negotiated with new partners such as the 100 million American dollars making-available right paid by the company WISCO to access the iron-rich zone of Soalala. A total of 10 new mining projects are estimated to have started under Rajoelina's regime, three of which are huge investments concerning areas of over 500,000 ha,[27] all adding to the concern over social and environmental damage already raised by major projects such as Madagascar Oil Tsy Miroro, Ambatovy and QMM/Rio Tinto (Seagle 2012). Negotiation over large-scale land transfers were also conducted in the forestry sector as part of carbon-offsetting schemes.[28] The agribusiness sector for its part suffered from a sharp drop in investment (from 82 projects announced between 2005 and 2014 to roughly 10 projects still active in 2014), as concern for Madagascar's political instability was compounded by a general lack of expertise in the agricultural sector and difficulties in securing land access, making it difficult for entrepreneurs to secure funding (Andrianirina et al. 2011; Burnod, Andriamanalina, and Andrianirina Ratsialonana 2014).

This context of political instability and financial scarcity fuelled intense competition over the Lalifuel project. In Madagascar, responsibility for land governance is spread across a wide number of state agencies (Burnod, Gingembre, and Andrianirina Ratsialonana 2013). However, it is not always clear where one authority begins and another ends, especially in a context where formal decentralisation is hampered by legal confusions and political obstructions (Bidou, Droy, and Fauroux 2008; Rochegude and Plançon 2009).

[27]Petrochina (688,400 ha), Pan African Mining (1 million ha) and Mainland Mining (more than 2 million ha). These figures, as well as the other ones mentioned in this paragraph, are based on cross-referenced information from media articles, expert reports (Andrianirina et al. 2011; Burnod et al. 2014; Raharinirina 2013) and civil society accounts (Andrew Lee Trust 2009; Franchi et al. 2013; SIF 2013, and newsletters from the Collectif Tany). However, they cannot be considered to be definitive, in view of the opacity that surrounds these projects.

[28]An area of 40,000 ha was bought by Madawoodlands in the Sofia region (Re:Common 2013). In Makira protected forest in the northeast, carbon credits were allegedly sold to Microsoft and the zoo of Zurich on an area of 320,000 ha (Collectif Tany, newsletter no. 31, 31 March 2014).

This lack of clarity allowed different levels to try and manoeuvre in order to capture rent and control the company's land access. As the resistance against the project became more vocal, however, engagement with the foreign company turned into a sensitive issue.

The next paragraphs draw on the concepts of extraversion (Bayart 2000) and moral economy (Thompson 1971) to explore the rationales behind the contradictory, shifting positions adopted by state agents. Focus is on their attempts to negotiate authority and legitimacy in a highly fluid political environment where control of the outside world is a crucial resource for both political action and social struggles.

From committed support to requests of suspension

The central government initially showed enthusiasm and support towards the Lalifuel project. In compliance with *circulaire* 321–10/MATD/SG/DGSF (2010) on large-scale land acquisitions, an inter-ministerial commission convened to examine its business plan. In this document, the agribusiness investment was clearly framed as a project that would favour local and national development. Besides bringing tax revenues to the state, the biofuel and biomass project would strengthen local capacities in the energy sector and further the country's energetic independence, and was 'highly relevant' with regards to the country's large 'reserves of unused or insufficiently used arable land' (Lalifuel 2011, 2). Moreover, a strong commitment was made not to affect 'private land, villages, land used by peasants for crop farming and land already legally attributed to other projects or companies' (Lalifuel 2011, 14). The local population would also benefit from the project through jobs,[29] knowledge transfer and capacity building, and the company was pledging to help them on issues of human and cattle health, local food security, water infrastructure and rural electrification.[30] In Madagascar, such tropes of sustainability and green capitalism are regularly mobilised by investing companies in alliance with the state and some environmental NGOs to provide an enabling environment for corporate land access and the extraction of surplus value on previously uncommodified resources (Corson 2011; Neimark 2012; Seagle 2012). In the case of Lalifuel, these win–win narratives were indeed quickly reproduced by decision-makers at all levels.

Following approval from the inter-ministerial commission, an authorisation of prospection was delivered (May 2011). As the procedure moved down to the regional and local levels, the minister responsible for development and country planning and Vice Premier Minister (VPM) put his political weight behind the project, carrying out field visits and mediating the company's socio-economic compensation (see above).

[29]Depending on the stages of the project, the business plan projected the creation of 40 to 500 permanent and 250 to 5000 seasonal jobs per year between 2009 and 2019.

[30]By April 2014, the Lalifuel project had invested in most of the areas mentioned above. They had constructed a dam, a secondary school and a new town hall, made borings and water pumps, set up an affordable local health centre whose staff they pay and rehabilitated a few other public buildings. They had also invested in public electricity (but this help had been short-lived) and, at the time of the last fieldwork (January–April 2014), were carrying out daily street cleaning. Although functioning projects like the health centre and the water pumps were highly appreciated, the socio-economic commitment of the company was also creating a lot of frustration: most of these projects were indeed concentrated in Arivony's main village while very few of the promises made to the other villages who had given land had been fulfilled.

Local and regional authorities also provided key support, especially by helping Lalifuel to secure land access at the ground level. The mayors of Arivony and Antafoka contributed to the effort by offering tracts from their own family possessions (or that of their in-laws). Together with the regional officials, they also helped the project with what is referred to as 'the social approach'. On 20 July 2011, a meeting was organised in Arivony in order to 'sensitise and present the Lalifuel project to the population'. No less than 22 local and regional officials attended, from the head of district and the regional directors of various ministries through the mayors and the cabinet director of the regional government. A few days later, a 'regional commission responsible for the sensitisation, information and monitoring of Lalifuel project' was created and regional authorities started accompanying Lalifuel's visits to the villages, accelerating feelings, within the consulted population, that the deal was already made. In Benala, the regional head himself made the trip.[31]

This positive collaboration was short lived, however. Just over a year later, in August 2012, the commission was disolved on the grounds that the '*circulaire* 321–10 had been violated'.[32]

Soon thereafter, in December 2012, the regional land services (CIRDOMA, *Circonscription Domaniale et de la Propriété Foncière*, and CIRTOPO, *Circonscription Topographique*) received the afore-mentioned memorandum from the VPDAT. Insinuating that the regional land services had proceeded with a second lease without prior approval, the *vice-primature's* 'call to order' recalled that 'all requests for large-scale land acquisitions had to be approved by the superior authorities first' and asked for the 'immediate suspension of all ground operations related to the extension of Lalifuel project'. The company was also notified of this decision. In the letter they were sent, they were accused of having breached procedures, since no request of extensions could be made before the government had verified that the land already allocated had been duly developed.[33]

Any secret dealings between the regional land services and Lalifuel are beyond the scope of this research. What matters is to highlight the rationale behind two decisions – the dissolution of the regional commission and the memorandum – that indicate a shift in position of both the regional and the central state. Discourse and documents analysis suggest that they are less acts of regulation than the outcome of local politics driven by competition for 'access control' (Peluso and Ribot 2003) on the one hand, and related struggle for authority (Sikor and Lund 2009) on the other.

Competition and divisions

When questioned about the nature of the 'violations' that had caused the dissolution of the regional commission, members of the *Région* (regional government) explained that the *services déconcentrés* (regional representation of the ministries) were 'playing it alone' and acting 'secretly' with the Lalifuel company, thereby excluding the rest of the commission.[34] Even prior to the land deal there were tensions between these two bodies of the regional state. Interviews with personnel from both agencies painted a picture of mutual suspicion, fed by a lack of dialogue, unclear institutional statutes and overlapping

[31]Interview, head of *fokontany* Kibanivato, Ambatolahy, 6 May 2013.
[32]Décision no. 216/12-RIH portant abrogation de la décision no. 33/11-RIH du 23 Juillet 2011. Signed in Ihosy on 1 August 2012 by the regional head.
[33]Letter from the General Direction of the VPDAT to Lalifuel, 21 December 2012.
[34]Interview, senior member of the regional government, Antananarivo, 13 May 2013.

jurisdictions.[35] However, the mutual accusations of prevarication over Lalifuel indicated that these tensions had been exacerbated by the project. The regional head is reported to have complained of an unfair distribution of benefits after Lalifuel equipped the regional land services (one of the *services déconcentrés)* with laptops and 4/4 vehicles.[36] A short while later, the VPDAT was asked, by the *Région*, 'to withhold, immediately, the boundary marking operations […] as well as all the land procedures that were engaged for the Lalifuel project' (VPDAT 2013, 3). According to Lalifuel staff, the attitude of the regional head shifted after the company refused to yield in to his pressures for material benefits.[37]

The reaction of the VPDAT to alleged negotiations between the regional land services and the company highlights the competition that also exists between different scales of decision-making. After the 2005–2010 period where most emerging agribusiness projects negotiated their land access at the local level with little, if any, involvement of the central authorities (Andrianirina et al. 2011), several administrative initiatives were taken by the Rajoelina regime to recentralise control over large-scale transfers of farmland in the country. In his first two years in power, two administrative notes – the ministerial note no. 621/09/MATD (2009) and the *circulaire* 321–10/MATD/SG/DGSF (2010) – reminded regional and local agents that no large land requests could be processed without the prior authorisation of the superior authorities.[38]

Research on other land deals in Madagascar has revealed that divisions and competition between state agencies frequently end up delaying investors' land access (Burnod, Gingembre, and Andrianirina Ratsialonana 2013), as opposing the land deal is seen as a means to regain authority by those who have felt unduly side-lined during the negotiation process. As far as the Lalifuel land deal was concerned, the intervention of central state officials was certainly driven by ambitions to reclaim control over a negotiation process that threatened to escape them. In this case, however, the challenge to their authority that they sought to address was the consequence not of having been excluded from the decision-making process but, conversely, of having been known to have played a major role in it.

Quest for legitimacy in a context of elections

The anti-Lalifuel protest may not have succeeded in shaking the mainstream narrative that portrayed the project as a win–win but it did generate anxiety within the state:

> In 2012, Lalifuel wanted to extend its perimeters but the villagers were against it, explained a regional official. You know there are things that people really can't understand: for them, it's foreigners coming to take their land, they even talked of tombs being profaned. And so they went up to Antananarivo and then they talked in private radios, wrote in newspapers etc. That's how things started degenerating and the regional head said: "I'm not the one who signed the authorisation. It's the general direction of the Land Ministry and even sometimes the Vice Prime-Minister who signs emphyteutic leases for tracts over 50 ha.[39] They are the ones who should be approached. (senior regional official, 13 May 2013)

[35]Law 2004-001 of 17 June 2004 defines the *Régions* as 'both decentralised territorial entities and administrative circumscriptions' (art. 4).
[36]Interview, Mr Herizo, Antananarivo, 13 May 2013.
[37]Interview, Mr Herizo, Antananarivo, 13 May 2013.
[38]A provision already set out in law 2007-036 of 14 January 2008 on investments in Madagascar.
[39]Law 2008-014 stipulates indeed that all cession of land above 50ha in a rural municipality needs to be approved and signed by the Minister responsible for state land (art. 27).

The need to deflect responsibility must have felt all the more pressing as the regional head was planning to stand in the parliamentary elections. Like the presidential elections, these were held in October–December 2013, but had been announced as far back as 2010 (Galibert 2011). The fear of an electoral sanction can explain why the parliamentary candidate requested a postponement of the highly sensitive boundary marking operations.[40] The close relations he had with M. Andrianainarivelo, the Vice Prime Minister, were certainly of help here. However, M. Andrianainarivelo's decision to suspend land extensions was more than a gesture of support for his *protégé*. The memorandum was sent on 1 December 2012, only two weeks after the Benala contingent had held its press conference, as the attacks on the Minister were in full swing. With the potent rhetorical tools that 'land grabs' could offer the opposition – as demonstrated by the Daewoo case – the Minister may have been worried about potential backlash from the affair on his own electoral campaign.

Going a step further, his successor at the VPDAT went with a delegation of officials to visit the Lalifuel project (September 2013). Their mission report pointed to the change of farmed crops[41] as non-compliant with the *cahier des charges* (technical agreements) and to a number of 'local land disputes occasioned by the fact that the marking made for the company included tracts that were already occupied and farmed traditionally or that were used as rangeland or as places of worship' (VPDAT 2013, 4). Following these observations, they proposed the partial cancellation of the lease contract (VPDAT 2013, 4). Indicating a major shift in official discourses, these criticisms and threats could be seen as a success for those who had actively lobbied for the protection of local land rights.

Regulation or short-term calculation?

However, the outcome of this mission was not advertised, nor was the VPDAT's order to suspend land extensions. As noted above, it was discreetly communicated to the regional authorities by memorandum, an internal administrative document, and to Lalifuel by letter. It was circulated through social media but this can be assumed to be the result of a leak by the invisible brokers mentioned above. Had the ministry wanted to communicate it widely, they would certainly have called the media or organised a press conference.

It is also telling that no one wished to claim responsibility for this change. On the one hand the regional government and regional land services insisted the decision came from the top,[42] and on the other the national government, in its official report, explained that it was made following warnings sent by the *Région* (VPDAT 2013, 3). This lack of publicity and the absence of follow-up make it clear that these two ministerial interventions were pre-emptive moves in anticipation of political attacks rather than genuine attempts to pressure the company into following the rules and respecting local land rights.

In a country where a large portion of government spending relies on external funds, few state power-holders actually wish to see foreign investors withdraw, especially in the context in which Madagascar was at the time. Arguing that dominant actors of African

[40]The boundary marking operations were finally held in July–August 2013, more than a year after the lease was issued.

[41]The document mentions geranium but Lalifuel is actually growing quite a few other crops, with corn and sunflower representing roughly half of the total area farmed (1500 ha at the time of the last fieldwork), and jatropha only a fifth of it (interview, local manager Lalifuel, Satrokala , 5 April 2014).

[42]Interview with officials from the regional land services, Ihosy, 25 March 2013; interview with officials from the regional ministry, Ihosy, 12 April 2013 and Antananarivo, 13 May 2013.

states have historically gained from the insertion of their country as unequal partners in the world economy, Jean-François Bayart explains that 'the people who manage this unequal relationship with the international economic system are able to derive from it the resources necessary for their domestic overlordship' (Bayart 2000, 231). In this case, foreign agribusiness projects may represent threats to subsistence economies; they also represent opportunities for power-holders to deliver on their promises of developing infrastructure and social services, gain access to official and unofficial rent to support their patronage networks and, ultimately, strengthen their authority.

These 'strategies of extraversion' (Bayart 2000) require skill and caution, though. The upheaval that preceded the military coup in 2009, with its violent lootings, arsons and acts of vandalism, sent a strong message to the Malagasy political class. In its targeting of president Ravalomanana's agro-industrial and media empire, this unusual outburst of popular violence may have been orchestrated; it was also an expression of frustration and anger at a broken contract: the providential, self-made man of 2001 who was priding himself on his 'Malagasy-made' (*vita gasy*) social ascension had turned into an extraverted predator, ready to sell an immense share of the country's farmland to foreign investors (Galibert 2009; Pellerin 2009). In Madagascar's current moral economy, dealing with foreign investors is a complex balancing act. Eloquent reminders of the sensitivity of these issues were sent by Benala elites and their allies, forcing decision-makers to slow down the process of private land appropriation.

However, the latest developments guard local land rights activists against excessive enthusiasm. As mentioned above, threats with no follow-up action are a far cry from acts of regulation aimed at negotiating a greater participation of local populations in the deal making or a fairer distribution of potential benefits. On the contrary, in affected villages, concern is growing with the increasing mechanisation and extension of the Lalifuel project which is under pressure from the parent company to accelerate yields and 'stop acting like an NGO'.[44] So far, Benala's land has mostly been left untouched but the project's recent undertakings suggest that this situation may not last. In April 2014, there were signs of unofficial boundary marking (tractor-made furrows) in several *fokontany* in western Benala. Among those concerned was the village of Ansatra, one of the few villages within the municipal territory of Benala to already be affected because its village land extends onto the municipality of Arivony. In their case, the demarcations were discreetly discussed with the two poorest hamlets of the village, against the will of the village leaders and cattle owners. This targeting of Benala signals a shift towards a less consensual approach on the part of the company. It also shows a certain softening of the resistance. Those opposed to the implementation of the project appear to be losing hope as contacts with both civil society and their mayor are diminishing. Moreover, with the elections now over, lobbyists may find it more difficult to pressure the government.

Conclusion

Benala's resistance to the Lalifuel project emerged around an alliance of local elites, and built on the skills and knowledge acquired during a previous encounter with a foreign investor interested in accessing land. A number of strategies were used to mobilise the rest of the community, through the creation of a sense of solidarity, but also through the use of threats. The struggle was discursively legitimised through a variety of mechanisms and galvanised

[44]M. Patrick, Senior field manager Lalifuel, Arivony village, municipality of Arivony, 2 April 2013.

through the creation of wider alliances and networks. The mobilisation of transnational activists in a context of elections was critical to a successful outcome. The prospect of being involved in a scandal around land at such a juncture prodded influential state officials into ordering the temporary suspension of land extensions, but these successes are precarious. Several insights emerge from this case nonetheless.

On the issue of participation, it has been demonstrated that the formal protection of local land rights does not automatically translate into better chances for local populations to express their views and defend their livelihoods (Burnod, Gingembre, and Andrianirina Ratsialonana 2013; Vermeulen and Cotula 2010). Even when local consultations are held, genuine participation in the decision-making generally implies overcoming fears of the state and resisting pressures to give silent consent. The case of Benala reveals that bargaining power can be gained through alliances with influential allies and the use of new spaces of expression where voice can be expressed outside the control of the official consultation process. It is obvious, however, that some groups start with more 'bargaining endowments' than others (Cotula 2008, 16). In Benala, the local power of rich cattle owners and of the mayor were crucial assets to overcome widespread feelings of disenfranchisement and pressure from superior regional officials. Their networks, combined with a certain familiarity with state-legal procedures, favoured the use of formal action over more common forms of everyday resistance. However, their initiatives also contributed to censoring those who wanted to be incorporated into the project.

This paper also sheds light on the contradictory role of states like Madagascar in facilitating corporate enclosure. Previous studies have established that, in this state characterised by a strong instability and a high degree of factionalism (Randrianja 1997), competition between state entities frequently ends up hampering private land acquisitions without necessarily promoting a better enforcement of those laws meant to protect local land rights (Burnod, Gingembre, and Andrianirina Ratsialonana 2013). This study highlighted how these contradictions are embedded within a moral economy veering between rationales of autochthony and extraversion (Galibert 2009). According to their individual trajectories, political identities and networks of belonging, incumbent power-holders (and their challengers) follow different pathways to legitimacy in relation to the penetration of private capital: some focus on negotiating social infrastructure and services for their communities, some on conducting resistance and others, as shown here, move from one pathway to the other depending on flexible political opportunities. Laurent Berger's ethnography of the implementation of a shrimp aquaculture project in northern Madagascar gives a vivid illustration of the intricacies of these dynamics in societies characterised by complex social stratification with strategies towards the private project shown to be shaped by local rivalries, multi-level interpersonal relations and heterogeneous interests (Berger 2006).

The case of Benala stresses how the externalisation of a protest can substantially amplify the echo of local voices. As Bayart notes, in 'extraverted governmentalities, the external environment is a major resource not only for dominant actors but also for social struggles' (Bayart 2000, 219). In a state haunted by the spectre of a previous land scandal, the mobilisation of transnational activists transformed a local counter-enclosure campaign into a significant threat to the legitimacy of senior state agents.

To conclude, in states where the rural poor have been historically marginalised from decision-making, consultation processes generally offer little space for participation, unless they promote genuine free, prior and informed consent and take into account both the heterogeneity of agrarian societies and the complexity of local land tenure. This paper demonstrates that contexts of political uncertainty open up new spaces for them to claim their rights, but that gains made in such circumstances are fragile and contested.

Acknowledgements

My gratitude goes to all of those who took part in this study and, through their time and hospitality, made this research possible. I would also like to thank my research assistant who has been working on this case study with me since 2011, as well as Jun Saturnino M. Borras, James Sumberg, Ian Scoones, Perrine Burnod, Antoine Bouhey and the three anonymous reviewers for the insightful comments made on earlier versions of the paper. This paper draws on research funded by the Economic and Social Research Council (ESRC) and the Institute of Development Studies, UK.

References

Andrews Lee Trust. 2009. *Voices of change: oral testimony of the Antanosy people*. London: Andrew Lees Trust and Panos. http://www.andrewleestrust.org/hepa.htm (accessed January 14 2015).

Andriamanalina, B., and P. Burnod. 2014. *Existing and potential tools to regulate land access for investors in Madagascar*. Paper presented at the Annual World Bank Conference on Land and Poverty, Washington DC, March 24–27.

Andrianirina Ratsialonana, R., L. Ramarojohn, P. Burnod, and A. Teyssier. 2011. *After Daewoo? Analysis and perspectives on large-scale land acquisitions in Madagascar*. Antananarivo/Montpellier/Rome: Observatoire du Foncier à Madagascar – Cirad – ILC.

Bayart, J.F. 2000. Africa in the world: a history of extraversion. *African Affairs* 99: 217–67.

Berger, L. 2006. Les voix des ancêtres et les voies du développement. Les populations de l'Ankarana en butte à la mondialisation. *Etudes Rurales* 178: 129–60.

Bidou, J.E., I. Droy, and E. Fauroux. 2008. Communes et régions à Madagascar. De nouveaux acteurs dans la gestion locale de l'environnement. *Mondes en Développement* 141, no. 1: 29–46.

Borras, S.M. Jr., and J. Franco. 2013. Global land grabbing and political reactions 'from below'. *Third World Quarterly* 34, no. 9: 1723–47.

Borras, S.M. Jr., J. Franco, and S. Monsalve Suarez. forthcoming. Land and food sovereignty. *Third World Quaterly*.

Burnod, P., H. Papazian, A. Adamczewski, P.M. Bosc, J.P. Tonneau, and J.Y. Jamin. 2011. Régulation des investissements agricoles à grande échelle. Etudes de Madagascar et du Mali. *Afrique Contemporaine* 237: 111–29.

Burnod, P., M. Gingembre, and R. Andrianirina Ratsialonana. 2013. Competition over authority and access: International land deals in Madagascar. *Development and Change* 43, no. 5: 190–209.

Burnod, P., B. Andriamanalina, and R. Andrianirina Ratsialonana. 2014. De la crise politique aux échecs des projets d'investissements agricoles à grande échelle. *Afrique Contemporaine* 251: 152–54.

Collectif Tany. 2012. Newsletter n°20, Paris, 27 November 2012.

Coordination Sud. 2010. La résistance à l'accaparement des terres à Madagascar. Le cas Daewoo. In *Agricultures familiales et sociétés civiles face aux investissements massifs dans les terres*, ed. Coordination Sud, 67–78. Paris: Coordination Sud.

Corson, C. 2011. Territorialization, enclosure and neoliberalism: non-state influence in struggles over Madagascar's forests. *The Journal of Peasant Studies* 38, no. 4: 703–26.

Cotula, L. 2008. Legal empowerment to secure land rights-defining the concept. In *Legal empowerment in practice: using legal tools to secure land rights in Africa*, eds. L. Cotula. and P. Mathieu, 7–19. London: International Institute for Environment and Development.

Eisinger, P. 1973. The conditions of protest behavior in American cities. *American Political Science Review* 67, no. 1: 11–28.

Evers, S. 2006. Expropriated from the hereafter: the fate of the landless in the southern highlands of Madagascar. *Journal of Peasant Studies* 33, no. 3: 413–44.

Evers, S., P. Burnod, A. Teyssier, and R. Andrianirina Ratsialonana. 2011. Foreign Land Acquisitions in Madagascar. Competing Jurisdictions of Access Claims. In *African engagements. Africa negotiating an emerging multi-polar world*, eds. T. Dietz, K. Havnevik, M. Kaag, and T. Oestigaard, 110–133. Leiden and Boston: Brill.

Ferguson, B., C. Gardner, M. Andriamarovolonona, T. Healy, F. Muttenzer, S. Smith, N. Hockley, and M. Gingembre. 2014. Governing ancestral land in Madagascar: have policy reforms contributed to social justice? In *Governance for justice and environmental sustainability: lessons across natural resource sectors in Sub-Saharan Africa*, eds. M. Sowman and R. Wynberg, 63–94. Oxford: Earthscan.

Foucault, M. 1979. *Discipline and punish: the birth of a prison*. New-York: Knopf Doubleday Publishing group.
Franchi, G., M. Rakotondrainibe, E. Hermann Raparison, and P. Randrianarimanana. 2013. *Les accaparements de terres à Madagascar - Echos et témoignages du terrain* - 2013, Rome/Antananarivo/Paris: Re:Common, SIF and Collectif Tany. http://terresmalgaches.info/IMG/pdf/Rapport_Accaparements_de_terres_Madagascar_2013.pdf (accessed February 3, 2014).
Galibert, D. 2009. Mobilisation populaire et répression à Madagascar. Les transgressions de la cité cultuelle. *Politique Africaine* 113: 139–51.
Galibert, D. 2011. Rigidités et "glocalisation": un regard anthropologique sur la crise malgache (2009–2011). *Les Cahiers d'Outre-Mer* 255: 413–26.
German, L., E. Mwangi, and G. Schoneveld. 2013. Contemporary processes of large-scale land acquisition in Sub-Saharan Africa: Legal deficiency or elite capture of the rule of law? *World Development* 48: 1–18.
Hollander, J., and R. Einwohner. 2004. Conceptualizing resistance. *Sociological Forum* 19, no. 4: 533–54.
International Crisis Group. 2014. A cosmetic end to Madagascar's crisis? Africa Report, 218. 19 May. http://www.crisisgroup.org/~/media/Files/africa/southern-africa/madagascar/218-a-cosmetic-end-to-madagascar-s-crisis.pdf (accessed May 22, 2014).
IRIN. 2010. Analysis: Madagascar's year of crisis. http://www.irinnews.org/report.aspx?ReportId=88447 (accessed March 20, 2010).
La Gazette de la Grande Ile. 2012. VPDAT en déplacement, 03 Oct. (accessed October 04, 2012).
Lalifuel. 2011. Projet biocarburant et biomasse – Descriptif du projet et business plan, Business Plan, 100 pages.
Madagascar Tribune online. 2013. 'Hajo Andrianainarivelo. "Quand on fait de la politique, on fait de la propagande"', 27 March 2013. (accessed January 30, 2014).
McAdam, D. 1982. *Political process and the development of black insurgency*. Chicago: University Chicago Press.
McAdam, D., J. McCarthy, and M.N. Zald. 1996. *Comparative perspective on social movements. Political opportunities, mobilizing structures and cultural framings*. Cambridge: Cambridge University Press.
McAdam, D., S. Tarrow, and C. Tilly. 2004 (first published 2001). *Dynamics of contention*. Cambridge: Cambridge University Press.
Medernach, K., and P. Burnod. 2013. Recompositions inattendues d'un système agraire malgache par l'agrobusiness. *Etudes Rurales* 191: 63–76.
Neimark, B.D. 2012. Green grabbing at the 'pharm' gate: rosy periwinkle production in southern Madagascar. *The Journal of Peasant Studies* 39, no. 2: 423–45.
Pellerin, M. 2009. Madagascar: un conflit d'entrepreneurs. Figures de la réussite économique et rivalités politiques. *Politique Africaine* 113: 152–65.
Peluso, N., and J. Ribot, 2003. A theory of access. *Rural Sociology* 68, no. 2: 153–81.
Ploch, L., and N. Cook. 2012. Madagascar's political crisis. Congressional Research Service 22.
Raharinirina, V. 2013. Madagascar: conflits "glocaux" autour des projets extractifs et agraires, in Etats des résistances dans le Sud: les mouvements paysans. *Alternatives Sud*, Belgique 20, no. 4: 55–66.
Randrianja, S. 1997. Madagascar entre restauration autoritaire et réseaux mafieux. In *L'Afrique politique. Revendications populaires et recompositions politiques*, 21–38. Paris: Karthala.
Randrianja, S. (dir) 2012. *Le coup d'Etat de mars 2009 à Madagascar*. Paris: Karthala.
Razafindrakoto, M., F. Roubaud, and J.M. Wachsberger, (dir.). 2014. Madagascar : anatomie d'un état de crise. *Afrique contemporaine* 251: 193p.
Rochegude, A., and C. Plançon. 2010. *Décentralisation, acteurs locaux et foncier*. Rapport Comité Technique Foncier and Développement.
Scott, J. 1986. Everyday forms of peasant resistance. *The Journal of Peasant Studies* 13, no. 2: 5–35.
Seagle, C. 2012. Inverting the impacts: mining, conservation and sustainability claims near the Rio Tinto/QMM ilmenite mine in Southeast Madagascar. *The Journal of Peasant Studies* 39, no. 2: 447–477.
SIF website. http://sif-mada.mg/ (accessed August 26, 2014).
SIF. 2013. Quelques cas illustrant l'accaparement des terres à Madagascar selon la Solidarite des Intervenants pour le Foncier, Antananarivo. http://sif-mada.mg/communique-sif-2/quelques-cas-de-landgrabbing_version-francaise_24072013/ (accessed January 15, 2015).

Sikor, T., and C. Lund. 2009. Access and property: a question of power and authority. *Development and Change* 40, no. 1: 1–22.

Siméant, J. 2011. The concept of moral economy applied to riots and protest in poor countries: how it helps and why it should be used with caution-the example of Mali. Paper presented at the ECPR conference, Reykjavik, 24–27 August.

Tarrow, S. 1996. States and opportunities : the political structuring of social movements. In *Comparative perspective on social movements. Political opportunities, mobilizing structures, and cultural framings*, eds. D. McAdam, J. McCarthy, M. Zald, 41–61. Cambridge: Cambridge University Press.

Tarrow, S. 2005. *The new transnational activism*. Cambridge: Cambridge University Press.

Teyssier, A., R. Andrianiriana Ratsialonana, R. Razafindralambo, and Y. Razafindrakoto. 2009. Décentralisation des terres à Madagascar : processus, enjeux et perspectives d'une nouvelle politique foncière. In *Les politiques de reconnaissance des droits fonciers. Du cadre légal aux pratiques locales*, eds. J.P. Colin et al., 273–97. Paris : IRD Karthala.

Thompson, E. 1971. The moral economy of the English crowd in the eighteenth century. *Past and Present* 50: 76–136.

Tilly, C. 1978. *From mobilisation to revolution*. Michigan: University of Michigan.

Vermeulen, S., and L. Cotula. 2010. Over the heads of local people: consultation, consent and recompense in large-scale land deals for biofuels projects in Africa. *Journal of Peasant Studies* 37, no. 4: 899–916.

VPDAT 2012. Note de service no 392/12/VPMDAT/SG/DGSF. 1 December.

VPDAT 2013. Rapport de mission dans la région X, du 19 au 21 septembre 2013. Unpublished mission report, 41 pages.

Wolford, W., S.M. Borras Jr., R. Hall, I. Scoones, and B. White. 2013. Governing global land deals: the role of the state in the rush for land. *Development and Change* 44, no. 2: 189–210.

Policy processes of a land grab: at the interface of politics 'in the air' and politics 'on the ground' in Massingir, Mozambique

Jessica Milgroom

The creation and enforcement of policies have been proposed as necessary to protect rural dwellers from dispossession by land grabs. Failing to consider the influence of the micro-politics of the policy implementation phase, these policies are insufficient. Based on an in-depth case study from southern Mozambique of a collision between a green grab and a land grab, this paper describes how two policies were used, first to facilitate a land grab and then to rescind the land concession. At a shifting intersection between politics 'in the air' and politics 'on the ground', convergence and later divergence among powerful groups shaped the space for policy enactment.

> They come in and want to invest 510 million dollars, but I have to tell them that the law says they have to consult with the communities?? They don't want to have to do that! They just want to know if they can invest or not, and if they can't they'll go elsewhere.
>
> –Anonymous government official, September 2007

Introduction

Government officials negotiating large-scale private land acquisitions find themselves in a complicated situation. They can be stuck between adhering to policies designed to protect citizens, and demands placed on them by foreign investors, other governmental bodies or their own personal interests to bend or reinterpret policies. National policy meant to protect people's rights to their land exists in many countries, but has proven to be minimally effective (Cotula and Vermeulen 2011). Despite this, debates about how to protect the people most vulnerable to loss of livelihoods from the threats that large-scale foreign land acquisitions pose focus on international policy that national governments would be responsible for enforcing (Seufert 2013; von Braun and Meinzen-Dick 2009). While improved national laws and international guidelines may provide a resource for peasant resistance against dispossession of land, they also provide a resource for government officials and private companies to legitimate land grabs (Borras and Franco 2010; De Schutter 2011; Li 2011). The micro-politics of how these policies get enacted in practice is ultimately what determines whether they will help or hinder the defense of rural dwellers' rights to their land and resources, yet there is little research available that documents this process.

Policy analysts have long been troubled by the topic of how to narrow the gap between policy intention, such as the protection of land tenure, and policy in practice. Insights from policy analysis reveal that policy is rarely implemented in the way that was intended (DeLeon and DeLeon 2002). Policy is in fact not implemented, implying a linear process, but *enacted*. Policy enactment is the 'creative processes of interpretation and translation, that is, the recontextualisation through reading, writing and talking, of the abstractions of policy ideas into contextualised practices' (Braun et al. 2011, 586). The way that a policy process plays out in practice depends on the interpretation of the policy by the range of actors involved. Different actors may interpret the same policy to have contradictory practical implications, and search for other groups that have similar interests to strengthen their case (Wagenaar 2011). This paper explores the convergence and divergence of networks of people and how this influenced the trajectory of three simultaneous land claims in southern Mozambique. The three land claims studied were: a large-scale foreign land acquisition of a company called ProCana, considered to be a land grab for the production of sugar and ethanol (Borras, Fig, and Suárez 2011); the Limpopo National Park (LNP), established in 2001, considered to be a green grab because of the way in which the establishment of the park has affected the residents of the area (Lunstrum Forthcoming); and a community-based nature conservancy funded and facilitated by the African Wildlife Foundation (AWF). The way in which two policies, the Mozambican National Land Law and the World Bank Operational Procedure for Involuntary Resettlement, were first enacted to favor the land acquisition by ProCana and subsequently to terminate it is analyzed. This research was carried out primarily at the local level and provides the kinds of details that are necessary to understand the micro-politics of how large-scale land acquisition policy processes play out on the ground. This paper uses the notion of policy enactment to explore the potential for international policy to contribute to protecting the land tenure of the rural dwellers threatened by land grabs, and what happens when a green grab intersects with a land grab.

I first introduce land grabbing and policy enactment, then outline methods used in data collection and analysis and the background of the case study before presenting the case material.

Land grabbing and green grabbing

Land grabs are considered to be major land acquisitions made by transnational corporations or foreign governments in another country through long-term leases, concessions, purchases and even theft (Rosset 2011). Land has been acquired through land grabbing for a number of purposes, such as for growing biofuel and food crops, mining concessions, large infrastructure projects, carbon-credit plantations and tourism (Zoomers 2010). Green grabbing is a form of land grabbing for conservation or environmental purposes. This includes protected areas such as national parks established and owned by the state, often linked also to private interests and the commodification of nature (Fairhead, Leach, and Scoones 2012; Ojeda 2012). While green grabbing has been a less obvious form of land grabbing, it legitimizes land appropriation that restructures the rules of access and use of resources, negatively impacting the livelihoods of local people (Fairhead, Leach, and Scoones 2012). To date, there has been little empirical evidence of what happens when a land grab and a green grab compete for the same land and political resources (Lunstrum Forthcoming).

These land deals, including the case presented in this paper, involve close alignment between national governments and foreign investors (Alden Wily 2011a; Borras and Franco 2010), and can leave the resident population landless or without access to the natural resources that form the basis of their livelihood activities (Zoomers 2010). Loss of access to resources for productive purposes, as well as loss of heritage and of important cultural resources, is one way that land grabs are causing dispossession for local people (Vermeulen and Cotula 2010). Loss of self-determination, autonomy and control over resources is another way in which people are being dispossessed – this is being done through administrative and procedural mechanisms that systematically exclude residents and resource users (Vermeulen and Cotula 2010). Alden Wiley demonstrates how most of the dispossession is occurring through legal means, by national governments, within the terms of domestic property laws (Alden Wily 2012), and that the laws that govern land tenure are actually enablers of the dispossession (Alden Wily 2011a).

The general international response to this wave of land grabbing has been to propose improved governance in the host countries to minimize unjust dispossession of land and resources through, for example, improved demarcation of land and international guidelines (Deininger and Byerlee 2011). Two sets of voluntary guidelines have been developed to regulate land grabbing: one by the African Union (AU) (African Union 2009) and the other by the Food and Agricultural Organization (FAO) (FAO 2012; Seufert 2013). There has been little reported about the implementation of these guidelines, but considerable debate on the potential for them to protect people from dispossession.

Cernea (1993) argues that new guidelines that set higher standards than the existing ones, if there are any at all, provides something for affected people to lean on and mobilizes political and economic resources in support of the cause. Some cases illustrate the ways in which resistance of local populations can and do shape land deals (Neville and Dauvergne 2012; Smalley and Corbera 2012). The role of mobilization of people and resources including knowledge is fundamental in negotiating and challenging land grabs (White et al. 2012). A policy or a code of conduct can become a resource in this process of mobilization (Fortina and Richardson 2013). As Vermeulen and Cotula (2010, 915) suggest, the struggle to maintain control of land and resources may well open new space for political organization among marginalized groups.

Some authors think, however, that guidelines will do little to curb the processes of land grabbing (Zoomers 2010). Others argue that the idea of guidelines does not sufficiently question the underlying causes of land grabbing, accepts that land grabbing is inevitable and embraces the assumption that transparent and participatory land acquisitions are better than non-participatory ones (Borras and Franco 2012). De Schutter (2011) argues that attempts to regulate foreign land acquisition presuppose that investments can lead to a desirable situation if properly managed, and goes on to describe why this is not the case. Borras and Franco (2010) describe how any effort to regulate a land deal is unlikely to produce positive outcomes for local people, barring the local elite, if the main aim of the land acquisition is not primarily to protect and advance the interests of the residents. These guidelines could also become enablers of dispossession in the way that Alden Wily (2011a) describes that national laws have become. Borras and Franco (2010, 521) suggest that a human rights-based approach should be taken to prevent land grabbing rather than accepting a second-best response to an inevitable advancement of capitalist interests. Cotula and Vermeulen (2011) suggest focusing efforts on legal empowerment, collective action and improvement of national policies and procedures rather than on the development of international guidelines. Borras and Franco (2013) explore how reactions from 'below' are under-researched.

International policy assumes that governments have an interest and the capacity to improve practices and protect the rights of rural dwellers, but it has been argued that this is not necessarily the case (Cotula and Vermeulen 2011; Hall and Paradza 2012; Wisborg 2013a). The 'state' as a player in land grabs is often portrayed as a single, unified institution, whereas in practice it often consists of multiple, contradictory and ambiguous perspectives (Hall and Paradza 2012). Many states are in fact active partners in land deals (Wolford et al. 2013) in which individuals in government stand to benefit significantly from the deals (Fairbairn 2013). The governments of countries where land grabbing is an important phenomenon tend to also be those most interested in foreign investment, as well as those that can be considered to be 'weak states' (FAO et al. 2010). However, the conclusion that 'improved' governance is the answer to the problems of land-grabbing fails to take into consideration the micro-politics at hand (Li 2011). In order to understand the potential of a policy to protect the rights of rural dwellers, or to make space for their resistance, it is crucial to analyze the micro-politics that shape the policy process. In this paper, I explore the interface between politics 'in the air', referring to the networks formed around a large-scale land acquisition at the level of the state, donors and foreign private company when they are functioning far from the land itself, and politics 'on the ground', involving the residents of the land and local actors affected by the project in practice, including the private foreign company itself when it begins to implement activities in the terrain. The use of these terms is intended to highlight the way in which local people do not react to or resist land claims in isolation, but rather they are embedded in networks and influenced by events and development narratives. It is also a fluid categorization in which actors shift from being 'in the air' to 'on the ground' and vice versa.

Policy enactment

Despite the fact that it is widely recognized that policies are not implemented in a linear fashion, the policy process continues to be conceptualized linearly, from policy formulation to some sort of practical improvement of the problem at hand (Keeley and Scoones 2003). This is evident in international debates about environmental and social problems, such as land grabbing, that end in a call for new policies, guidelines or treaties, or better enforcement of existing ones. Many earlier explanations for the 'gap' between policy intention and policy in practice identified technical practicalities, such as the wording of the policy text, miscommunication, lack of incentives or lack of capacity, to be major causal factors (DeLeon and DeLeon 2002; Yanow 1996). This kind of explanation is based on the assumption that the problems are concrete and fixable, and the 'correct solution' can be found (Hofmann 1995; Yanow 1996).

This perspective ignores the inherently political nature of policy (Keeley and Scoones 2003). Policies are written and implemented giving primacy to a specific kind of knowledge, such as scientific knowledge, and often ignore other types of knowledge, such as local or traditional knowledge (McGee 2004). Furthermore, studies have shown how the same policy artifact can give rise to different events, outcomes and practices in different contexts (DeLeon and DeLeon 2002). People come to understand policy messages based on their own agency, pre-existing knowledge, practices and perceptions of the world, their social context and the nature of their connections to the policy (Coburn 2001; Spillane, Reiser, and Reimer 2002; Yanow and Schwartz-Shea 2006). The actual text of policy documents is rarely read, and policy ideas are transmitted by other people through networks, already embodying considerable interpretation (Van Bommel et al. 2010) even before the policy in practice is consolidated as a set of practices.

In this paper, I use the concept of 'enactment' to refer to the process of interpretation and reinterpretation of policy ideas into contextualized practices (Braun et al. 2011). Conceptualizing policy implementation as enactment shifts the focus away from the policy intentions and gives primacy to the process of co-creation of the contextualized practices that ultimately determine policy in practice. At the collective level, the contextualized practices resulting from policy enactment are influenced by a combination of factors including political, historical and social contexts, as well as power struggles and socially constructed meanings of the policy ideas (Yanow 1995). The way that networks converge to actively create, maintain and change the meanings of policy ideas is an important factor that influences the course of the policy process (Wagenaar 2011). The case in this paper is presented in a chronological fashion in order to illustrate how, through convergence and divergence of networks, the same policy ideas are consolidated as one set of practices and later altered to entail another, very distinct set of practices.

Data collection and analysis

This paper is based on ethnographic research carried out during a total of 40 months between December 2006 and June 2010, and a follow-up visit during the month of July 2014 in the district of Massingir. Research was focused on the process of resettlement of people from the LNP, specifically the enactment of the World Bank Operational Policy for Involuntary Resettlement (WB OP 4.12). However, when the conflicts between the resettlement project and ProCana became a central part of the resettlement process in 2007, I also turned to focus on the 1997 Mozambican Land Law. Participant observation and interviews were the main methods employed while living in the first village resettled from the LNP over a period of 2 years during the preparation for resettlement (December 2006 to November 2008), and for 18 months in the post-resettlement location (November 2008 to June 2010). Deliberations between village residents, park officials and representatives of the company ProCana, as well as between donor representatives and government officials, were documented. More than 200 open and semi-structured interviews with residents in eight villages, district, provincial and national government officials (including park staff), donor representatives, private consultants, and nongovernmental organization (NGO) staff were conducted. In addition, I attended and recorded the proceedings of 11 park and two internal village meetings in which resettlement was discussed. Meetings and interviews were transcribed and translated, as were unpublished park documents, consultancy reports and meeting minutes.

Background: a rush for land and the policies in place

Overview of the case

In 2001, the LNP was established in the province of Gaza in Southern Mozambique as part of the Great Limpopo Transfrontier Conservation Area (GLTFCA). The GLTFCA connects the Kruger National Park in South Africa with Gonarezhou National Park in Zimbabwe and Zinhave, and Banhine and Limpopo National Parks in Mozambique. Inside the boundaries of the park, there were 27,000 people who claimed the land as their home. Park managers decided in 2003, after the establishment of the park, that approximately 7000 of these people, those living in the center of the park, would be resettled outside the park's boundaries, mostly to the south of the park, in the district of Massingir (Milgroom and Spierenburg 2008) (Figure 1). Major funding for the creation of the LNP and for resettlement was

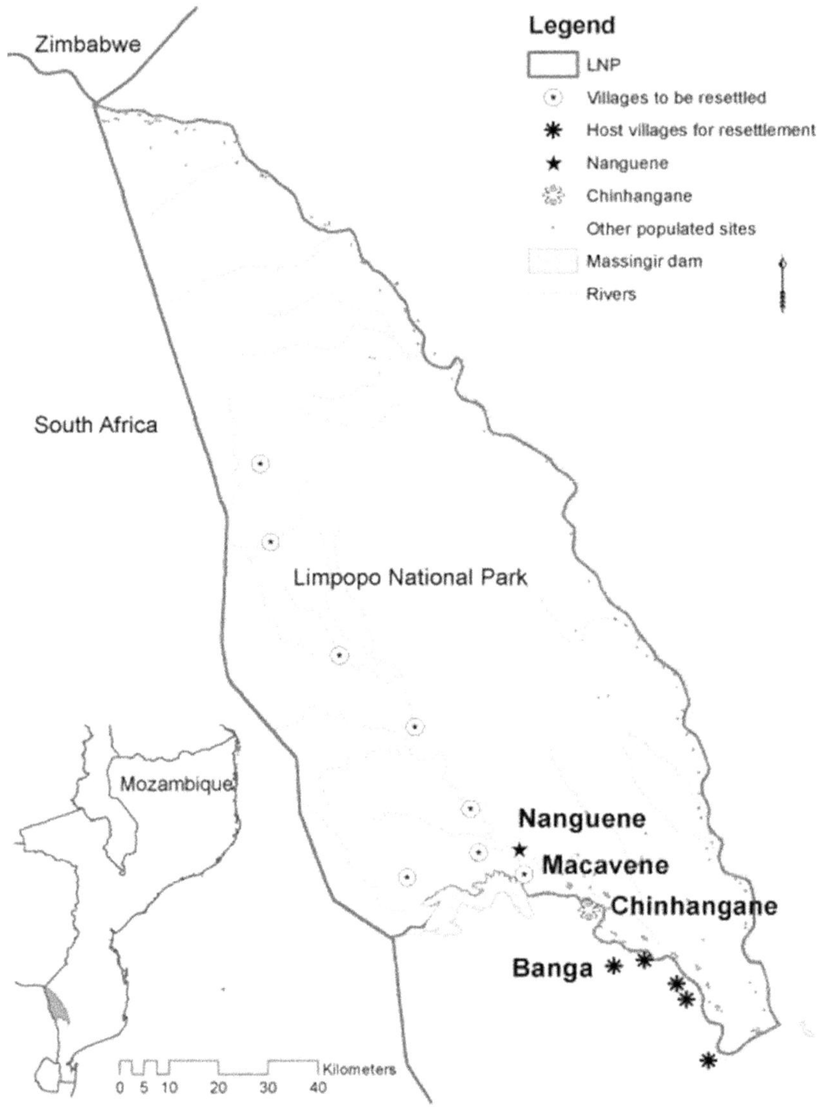

Figure 1. The location of the Limpopo National Park in Mozambique, the first two villages to be resettled – Nanguene and Macavene – and their respective host villages (post-resettlement locations) – Chinhangane and Banga.
Source: J. Milgroom.

provided by the German development bank that was then called Kreditanstalt für Wiederaufbau (KfW)[1] (Duffy 2006; Milgroom and Spierenburg 2008; Spierenburg and Wels 2006; Wolmer 2003), but KfW made an agreement that the World Bank (WB), which was also funding a different part of the Transfrontier Park project, would oversee the resettlement process because of the WB's experience with resettlement (Milgroom 2012). The World Bank Operational Policy for Involuntary Resettlement was adopted by the Ministry

[1]KfW is now merged into the KfW Bankengruppe.

of Tourism (MiTur), the ministry in charge of the national parks, as the guiding framework for the resettlement initiative. The LNP is considered a green grab because of the way in which the establishment of the park has negatively affected the livelihoods of residents (Lunstrum Forthcoming).

The land that was planned for resettlement, but not officially registered through the national cadaster, was granted in 2007 by the Ministry of Agriculture (MinAg) to a company called ProCana, a subsidiary of the Central African Mining Company. Widely recognized as a land grab, ProCana proposed to invest USD 510 million to grow sugarcane for ethanol production and create 7000 seasonal jobs. A global hype about the potential for biofuels to become a lucrative business swept Mozambique between approximately 2004 and 2010, peaking in 2008 (Schut, Slingerland, and Lock 2010). Fueled by discourses of a widespread economic, fuel and food crisis, governments across Africa began to map their so-called 'marginal' and 'empty' lands in an effort to identify areas for the production of crops suitable for biofuel production (Benjaminsen and Bryceson 2012; Borras, Fig, and Suárez 2011).[2] Strategically located next to the Massingir dam and along the Elephants River, the area conceded to ProCana offered ample land – although by no means 'marginal' or 'empty' – proximity to South Africa, and a source of reliable water, bringing into question, but not analyzed in this paper, the largely overlooked and understudied problem of water grabbing (Borras, Fig, and Suárez 2011; Franco, Mehta, and Veldwisch October 2013).

A compromise was reached between MinAg, supporting the ProCana project, and MiTur, in charge of the national parks and the resettlement project. This plan included creating an 'improved' grazing area to compensate resettling and existing villages for land lost to the sugar cane plantation on the other side of the road (Figure 2). This area was already occupied by a project facilitated by the AWF to create a community-based nature conservancy covering approximately 41,000 ha (Contour Project Managers 2006) on land belonging to three communities. The AWF project is not considered a land grab because of the community-based, participatory and transparent nature of the initiative in its early stages.[3] The details of the case, how decisions were made, local participation in these decisions and the role of the two main policies enacted will be presented below.

Two guiding policies

The two main policies that came into play in this case were the Mozambican National Land Law and the World Bank Operational Policy 4.12. Both are described briefly here.

The Mozambican National Land law

The Frelimo party (Liberation Front of Mozambique) has been the governing party in Mozambique since independence from Portugal in 1975. Originally harboring a Marxist–Leninist orientation, the end of the Mozambican civil war in 1992 marked a gradual shift to market capitalism, democracy and an administrative decentralization that attempted to promote local-level autonomy (Abrahamsson and Nilsson 1995). The Mozambican land

[2]In Mozambique, by 2008, MinAg had purportedly received 17 proposals from companies wanting to invest in biofuel projects (Schut, Slingerland, and Lock 2010). These projects requested a total of 245,404 ha of land and implied an investment of USD 1.301 billion (Schut, Slingerland, and Lock 2010).

[3]The AWF project never came to fruition; therefore whether or not elements of green grabbing may have emerged in practice is impossible to know.

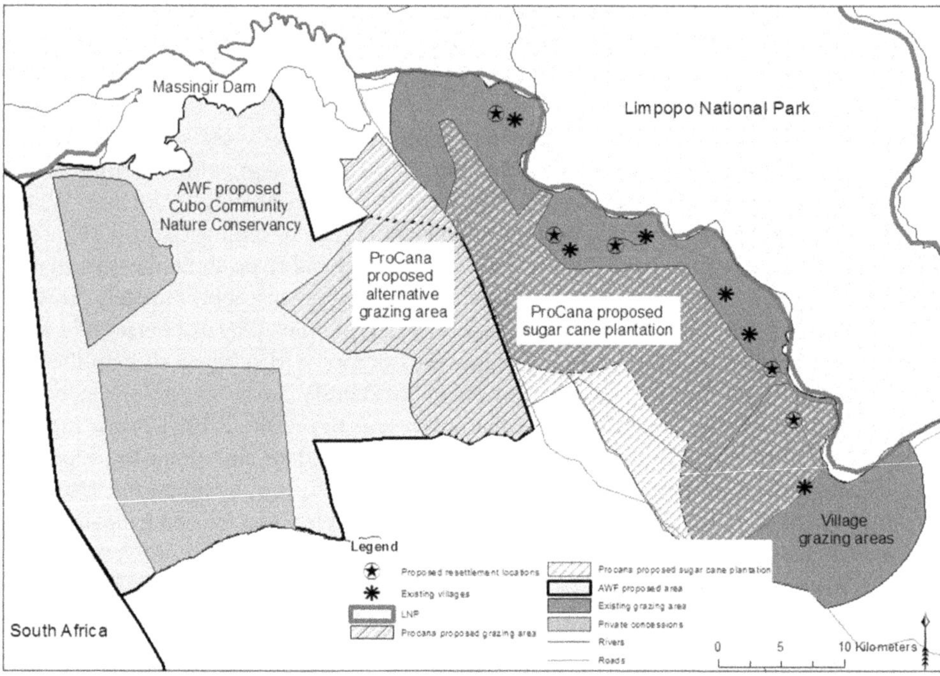

Figure 2. Overlapping land claims in Massingir district, Mozambique. The land secured for the African Wildlife Foundation (AWF) community nature conservancy overlapped with two existing private concessions. The concession given to ProCana overlapped with grazing areas for existing villages and the areas designated for resettlement of villages from the Limpopo National Park (LNP). To compensate villages for lost grazing area, alternative land was identified in AWF's project site causing the community nature conservancy project to stop and AWF to leave Massingir in 2008. ProCana withdrew in 2010.
Source: J. Milgroom.

law, passed in 1997, is a reflection of the political history of the country (Tanner 2010). This law was considered one of the most progressive land laws in the world at the time, and continues to be considered one of the most progressive in Africa, having been drafted through a participatory process, and recognizing customary land tenure (Nhantumbo and Salomão 2010). Under the land ownership of the state, individuals and communities can request that their land be delimited so that they can hold a certificate of occupancy that secures the rights to the use and benefit of the land (*direito de uso e aproveitamento da terra* – DUAT), with which the holder can choose to sell, rent or lease their rights to use the resources on that land. This provides a mechanism to facilitate private investment and at the same time provides communities with the right to be consulted about private use of their land (Tanner 2010). The law requires investors to engage in consultation with communities in order to negotiate use of their land, relegating the state to the role of mediator or regulator (Lunstrum 2008; Norfolk 2004). The ways in which this law is implemented in practice are still intricately tied up in politics (Fairbairn 2013).

The World Bank Operational Policy for Involuntary Resettlement

Aware of how politically complex resettlement is, and having decided to resettle people from the LNP, the German Development Bank, KfW, depended on the World Bank to support them in this aspect of their project. The World Bank Operational Policy for Involuntary Resettlement was therefore adopted as the guiding policy for the resettlement project. Adherence to this policy was a condition for the continued funding of the LNP project (Milgroom 2012).

In 1980, the WB developed the first international policy for resettlement (Cernea and McDowell 2000). After a thorough review of resettlement projects funded by the WB (World Bank 1994), the Bank's in-house sociologist, Michael Cernea, developed the Impoverishment Risk and Reconstruction model (Cernea 1997). The model defines the risks commonly associated with resettlement, including economic (landlessness, joblessness and loss of access to common property), socio-cultural (social disarticulation, marginalization) and social welfare risks (homelessness, food insecurity, and morbidity and mortality). This model became the basis for the current World Bank Operational Policy on Involuntary Resettlement.

WB OP 4.12 is one of the most commonly used policies in a wide range of resettlement schemes in both WB and non-WB funded projects around the world (Scudder 2012). It has been adopted as the foundation for many national policies on resettlement (Cernea and Schmidt-Soltau 2006). One of the WB principles of the policy particularly relevant to this case is that it refuses to fund or support projects on disputed lands. Therefore, a fundamental prerequisite for WB approval of projects that involve resettlement is to prove that there are no overlapping land claims. Whether this principle is requested and enforced or not is case-specific.

Interpreting policy in favor of the land acquisition (2007–2008)

ProCana managed to secure a DUAT in less than a year, while it took the AWF community-based project 5 years to do the same following the procedure in the 1997 land law (see also Lunstrum 2008). According to the project reports, it took more than 3 years for the three communities to get their own land delimited and to secure the certificates of occupancy (Stalmans 2004; Contour Project Managers 2006).

The land granted to ProCana overlapped with land needed for resettlement (Figure 2), which had been identified in 2005 (Massango and Chaúque 2005), but not officially registered with the national cadastre.[4] When the WB, responsible for overseeing the resettlement project, found out about the ProCana project on a visit in July of 2007, the representative responsible for the project evoked the principle in the WB OP 4.12, stating that there must not be overlapping land claims on land reserved for resettlement.[5]

Despite conflicts over the overlapping land claim between MinAg (supporting ProCana) and MiTur (supporting the LNP resettlement project), representatives from these ministries aimed to find a rapid solution to the problem so that both of their projects could continue. The potential creation of jobs that the ProCana project promised was also of benefit to the LNP resettlement initiative (and therefore to KfW and WB, who wanted to see resettlement occur as quickly as possible) because it would provide an alternative source of livelihoods for resettled people. This alignment of interests and subsequent convergence of networks allowed the two policies to be enacted in such a way as to favor the land acquisition of ProCana.

[4]Interview, LNP park staff member, Massingir, 22 January 2008.
[5]Interview, External consultant to the LNP resettlement project, Massingir, 30 March 2008.

Convergence between ProCana and the Ministry of Agriculture

MinAg granted the 50-year lease of 30,000 ha of land belonging to villages and overlapping other private land concessions. ProCana guaranteed that they adhered to the requirements of the land law, but residents of the villages did not agree with this statement. In the political context of a heavy-handed national government, many residents and village leaders thought they had no choice but to agree to the project. The representatives of ProCana were accompanied by district government officials on their community consultation visits. While community consultation about use of land is supposed to consist of thorough negotiation, these meetings were carried out with a number of villages in a short time period (between October 2006 and early 2007). District officials reportedly instructed the leaders of the villages to find land for ProCana (Manuel and Salomao 2009). As one village leader described the situation,

> ProCana just came here and met with the leaders of the communities and in the first meeting leaders had to sign. Some of them just wanted to drink so they took their 300 meticais because they thought it was a government project and that they had no choice at all. But then when the community found out, they were very unhappy. They were upset with the leaders for signing before being informed and they were upset with the project because they would be left with very little space for their cattle.[6]

Widespread rumors of bribery at many different levels pervaded discussions about ProCana. It was claimed that ProCana offered money to the district government officials, to national-level officials from MinAg and to the leaders of the villages.

While the LNP was entirely inside of Gaza Province, it was a national park, and therefore governed primarily at the national level by MiTur, often overstepping district and provincial governments. With decentralization efforts in full swing, the governor of the province often disregarded park efforts[7] because the provincial level of governance was regularly bypassed regarding park issues.[8] Resenting this, the governor supported ProCana, also because it was seen to be a more economically lucrative project than a national park, as did the national-, provincial- and initially the district-level branch of MinAg, a more powerful ministry than MiTur. The investment of USD 510 million represented a significant amount for the province, which was at the time one of the least developed provinces of the country. ProCana claimed that conservation would never be able to bring economic development to the area, but that their project would.[9] Rumors spread about the actions that the provincial government was taking to create support for the project at the district level. An anonymous government official reported,

> It is also clear that various district level agriculture directors and district authorities have been taken from their posts and moved to other places in Massingir for not being in agreement with the ProCana plan. The previous district level official in the department of agriculture saw clearly all the confusion of the plan proposed by ProCana and stated in a report, which was commented on by the LNP, some of the potential negative consequences of ProCana's plan. Apparently that report was modified and those parts cut out before they got to the national level government and he got moved because of it.[10]

---

[6]Interview, Leader of a village in the area claimed by ProCana, 28 March 2008.
[7]The dynamics of the governors's role in resettlement changed considerably after 2010, when the provincial and district government began to take a more active role in resettlement (interviews, 2014).
[8]Interview, External consultant, Massingir, 31 July 2007.
[9]Interview, ProCana representative, Massingir, 10 May 2007.
[10]Interview, Anonymous, Massingir, 31 July 2007.

These kinds of actions left little room for voices of resistance against the project by those who feared dispossession. Expectations 'on the ground' were also high about what opportunities the company would actually bring to the region.

Convergence among the World Bank, the Ministry of Agriculture, the Ministry of Tourism and ProCana

The WB was responsible for monitoring the resettlement project and its adherence to WB OP 4.12. In January 2008, KfW halted all funding to the resettlement project, at the recommendation of the WB.[11] The WB had three fundamental concerns: first, the security of the land tenure in the resettlement location due to overlapping land claims; second, the lack of consultation with village residents about ProCana; and, third, a lack of technical information about the quantity and quality of grazing resources for the resettling and existing villages in the first phase of both resettlement and ProCana.

With respect to the first concern, in September 2007, the Economic Council of Ministries called a meeting to address the case of the contested land. In this meeting, according to the revised contract signed between MinAg and ProCana, ProCana agreed to compensate the resettled communities for the grazing land they would occupy by providing alternative land for grazing. However, the alternative area identified by ProCana was land on which AFW was planning their project (Figure 2). ProCana promised to improve the grazing potential in the alternative area and to establish an intensive grazing system, complete with boreholes, fences and new varieties of cattle (Contrato Final Procana-LNP, September 2007). AFW was offered a significantly less desirable piece of land, a long strip that measured 4 km × 22 km and was not feasible for developing a conservancy. Having been forced to abandon their investment of around USD 100,000 and more than 5 years of work, AWF closed their office in Massingir in late 2007. As an AWF employee described it,

> It is a long strip of land that is half outside of our community land. What can we do with this? We are interested in conservation; what can we conserve in a space like that? The vegetation is homogeneous, there is no water and it is surrounded by private game concessions. [...] We couldn't even put up a lodge there because there is nothing attractive about the place .... There is not even room for a campsite there! What are we doing? We can't go ahead with a project that is not sustainable and will never be valid![12]

The resolution of this conflict was ironic in the sense that it highlights the insecurity of the land tenure established through the national land law. As one government official described it,

> AWF helped to delimit land and get land titles for the villages, and went through a process of consultation with the villages, who then agreed to the AWF project. But even still, that land is being taken away and used for something else, therefore they say that the resettlement land could also be taken away, therefore the resettlement land is not secure. The problem is that this is the only instrument that we have in Mozambique right now and I don't know what kind of instrument they want to use to make it more secure.[13]

Yet the option to provide grazing for the resettled villages on AWF's land satisfied the WB's concerns that there were competing land claims, despite the fact that it implied

[11]Interview, Jean Michel Pavy, Programme Director at the World Bank, Massingir, 17 April 2008.
[12]Interview, AWF employee, Massingir, 17 September 2007.
[13]Interview, Government official, Maputo, 31 January 2008.

that AWF had to leave the region after 5 years of work,[14] and that the proposed plan was likely to be culturally inviable. The concept of keeping cattle far from the homestead was not acceptable for most residents, and changing management practices including the varieties of cattle, maintaining the fences and boreholes and ensuring the security of the cattle far away from any villages were elements of the proposal seen to be likely practical obstacles to the success of the initiative.[15]

To address the second concern of the WB, ProCana and the LNP organized a meeting on 23 August 2007 to formally document the consultation with villages. ProCana, government officials, park staff, NGO representatives and the leaders of the villages affected by the ProCana project were present. After this meeting, an agreement was drafted stating that:

> All of the leaders were unanimous in affirming that they were waiting to see the ProCana project advance, they had enough land for all of the communities, they had already accepted the proposed grazing areas because these were going to help with the control of the livestock and contribute that their sons would go to school instead of to herd cattle, and that the project was taking too long to start.[16]

It is unclear exactly what happened in this meeting, but according to many of the leaders, they were not, in fact, in agreement with these statements and many others on the signed agreement. A similar agreement was reported, in a document written for the WB, to have been reached with the village that has a DUAT for the land on which the alternative grazing was to be developed, the land previously set aside for the AFW project. The document states that more than 100 village residents present in the meeting agreed to cede their land to the livestock of the resettling villages (Limpopo National Park 2007). Although details could not be confirmed, interviews revealed considerable frustration with the government on the part of the residents involved in the AFW project for its termination, and therefore it is unlikely that this agreement was reached willingly. Attaining signatures on documents despite disagreement with the content is a strategy observed when park staff and government officials from MiTur asked the leaders of the villages slated for resettlement to sign a document saying that they agreed to the meeting minutes, but in actual fact the document was used by MiTur to prove to KfW and the WB that residents had participated in the design of the resettlement houses and agreed to be resettled (Milgroom 2012).

To resolve the third concern of the WB, LNP staff and government officials from MiTur contracted consultants to carry out a carrying capacity study to determine if there were enough grazing resources for the villages affected by the first stage of the ProCana project, and including the alternative grazing area.[17] The hired consultant produced three versions of the first consultancy report, in which the area of land estimated to be available differed significantly (Table 1). The conclusion of the first version was that there was enough land to support the cattle belonging to the existing and resettlement villages of the first two villages resettled – in other words, Nanguene which was to be resettled to Chinhangane, and Macavene resettled to Banga (Escrivão 2007). This version calculated the area of available land to be 20,000 ha. The second version gave a significantly reduced

[14]Interview, Jean Michel Pavy, Programme Director at the World Bank, Massingir, 17 April 2008.
[15]Interviews with residents, park staff and consultants, January to July 2008.
[16]Agreement signed on 23 August 2007 by the village leaders present. Copies were made and circulated amongst them.
[17]Interview, Jean Michel Pavy, Programme Director at the World Bank, Massingir, 17 April 2008.

Table 1. Two consultancies were carried out to determine available land for grazing post-resettlement, one in December 2007 before funds were stopped due to overlapping land claims, and one in May 2008 after the project had already been allowed to continue.

Date	Consultancy report version	Village	Grazing land available (ha)	Carrying capacity (AU)	Total AU requirement after resettlement	Calculated balance (AU)	Final conclusion
December 2007	1	Chinhangane + Banga	20,000	2875	2427	+448	The current grazing area is enough to support resettlement, but after 1 year there will be a deficit of land because of growth of herds
	2	Chinhangane + Banga	8000	1375	2426	−1051	There is not enough land to support the existing livestock before resettlement
	3	Chinhangane	7300	1137	1015	+122	There is enough land to support livestock from Chinhangane and Nanguene
		Banga	3000	637.5	1412	−774	There is not enough land for the livestock of Banga and Macavene, but alternative land will be made available (20,000 ha)
May 2008	1	Chinhangane	1621	565	1131	−566	Area available for grazing only covers 50% of the needs of the livestock in Chinhangane with Nanguene
		Banga	2630	1106	1568	−462	Area available for grazing only covers 60% in Banga with Macavene

Notes: Conclusions about available land differed between versions of the same consultancy and between the two consultancies. The third version of the first consultancy (shaded in grey) was the one the Ministry of Tourism presented to the World Bank to obtain approval for the project to continue.

figure for the total area available (8000 ha) and concluded that there was insufficient land even for the existing livestock (Escrivão 2007). The third version concluded that there was enough land at the time of resettlement and for the future for the villages of Nanguene and Chinhangane, but that there would not be enough for Macavene and Banga, and therefore the additional alternative land where AWF had its project would be needed (Escrivão 2007). This last version was the one presented to the WB representatives, who gave their approval to continue the project. A WB representative explained his perspective about the situation in the following way:

> We demanded a carrying capacity study and when we got it, it said that indeed even with ProCana there was enough space for all the cattle in both Chinhangane and Nanguene. What worries me is that there was *just* enough room for the existing animals but not for growth of the herds. But then I was told that they don't even use all of the grazing area – they sometimes send their cattle far away to graze from where they live.[18]

This statement highlights the way in which the WB values the technical knowledge about grazing potential without knowing either how the calculations were made, or about the local grazing practices. Residents send their cattle farther away if there is no longer anything for cattle to eat close by. Having access to less area will only exacerbate this problem – it does not make the issue irrelevant, as this WB representative implies. The use of different figures to calculate carrying capacity, and the initial value for available land, were described by an external observer to comprise a process akin to trial and error:

> They hired a consultant from the university to do a quick carrying capacity study of Chinhangane and it showed that given the figure of 20,000 available ha, at a use rate of 7–8 ha per animal unit, this was initially enough land. I asked him where he got the figure of 20,000. He said that it was a government official that told him. The consultant checks this figure using maps and found that there was only 3500 ha of available land. Given this area, there was no way that it could support even the existing cattle in Chinhangane after ProCana. Officials from MiTur consulted the cadastre and found a new figure of 7000 ha by borrowing land from Banga. Using 7000 ha and 5 ha per animal unit the animals of Chinhangane and Nanguene can just squeeze in. This information was submitted to the World Bank and they approved the Resettlement Action Plan again.[19]

After the resettlement project was underway again in 2008, a second study was carried out to determine carrying capacity based on more thorough research and measurements of land (Rural Consult 2008). The report's authors measured the land available for grazing based on global positioning system (GPS) points, excluding the land proposed to be used by ProCana, and concluded, embedded in a paragraph in the final chapter of the report, which was only in Portuguese, that there were only 1,621 ha available for Chinhangane and Nanguene and that this could satisfy only 50 percent of their current livestock's needs (Table 1).

Reinterpreting policy to rescind the land acquisition agreement (2008–2009)

Tensions between local residents, the district government and ProCana began to mount during 2008, when ProCana began to engage in activities on the ground. Until the first

[18]Interview, Jean Michel Pavy, Programme Director at the World Bank, Massingir, 17 April 2008.
[19]Interview, External observer, Massingir, 30 March 2008. The Resettlement Action Plans were submitted to KfW, who depended on the World Bank for support in the resettlement process.

village was resettled from the LNP in November of 2008, MiTur's interests were still aligned with MinAg's interests: to allow peaceful continuation of both projects. In December 2009, however, the government of Mozambique called on the national land law to rescind ProCana's contract. The land law decrees that long-term leases can be retracted if the holder of the lease does not comply with commitments outlined in the contract. The official reason for the termination of the government's contract with ProCana was that the company had not complied with commitments, only having plowed 800 of the 30,000 ha granted to them, and had not been able to begin to produce sugar cane, much less ethanol, despite investments. However, the primary reason for the termination of the lease was reported to be economic; due to international economic changes and global reduced interest in non-carbon fuel sources, the main investor suspended further investment in the project (Borras, Fig, and Suárez 2011; Schut, Slingerland, and Lock 2010). NGOs applauded the government's actions in a public letter to the government reminding us that the contract was rescinded in a moment of elevated conflict between residents and the company, and requesting that future projects take care not to jeopardize the rights and interests of the local communities (Centro Da Terra Viva 2010).

Distrust between ProCana and residents

The relationship between ProCana and village residents was characterized by distrust from the beginning of the project in late 2006 and early 2007, when ProCana only held meetings with leaders and important elders of the villages to establish consent to use the land. This distrust and lack of transparency was augmented by the suspicions of corruption on the part of some government officials. Then, in September of 2007, when the private interests of the company prevailed over the community-based AWF project, a project that was generally seen as genuinely for the benefit of and run by the villages involved, resentment began to grow. Later, in late 2008 and 2009, ProCana was felt to have disrespected agreements about the boundaries of the land (see also Manuel and Salomao 2009). Leaders of the villages went with ProCana managers to decide on the boundaries they could use and were found later to be cutting trees along another boundary, one closer to the villages, in some cases leaving very little land for grazing and charcoal making. When LNP staff inquired about this, ProCana apparently responded that it was a mistake,[20] yet when village residents complained, ProCana responded that they were marking the line that the airplane told them to mark (referring to GPS points).[21] One village, Marenguele, allowed ProCana to temporarily use a plot of land for a demonstration of a drip irrigation system for 1 year, but it was not returned to the village until 2 and a half years later when ProCana withdrew from the region (CTV 2010). The frustrated residents responded to this by stealing vegetables, sugar cane and other property belonging to ProCana. In a context of conflict and divergence, as described further below, as well as mounting discontent with ProCana on the ground after an initial period of high expectations, there was more space for residents' voices to be heard. This space, as well as the importance given to the voices coming through, contributed to residents having more influence in policy enactment.

[20]Interview, LNP staff member, Massingir, 22 January 2009.
[21]Interview, Chinhangane leader, Chinhangane, 25 January 2009.

NGO support of residents against ProCana

NGOs also supported the villages in their resistance against ProCana, by giving publicity to the cause, organizing meetings and providing the residents with information. However, the role that NGOs could play in the first phase was hampered by pressure from both government and ProCana not to make 'noise'.[22] One NGO, ORAM (Organização Rural para Ajuda Mútua, translated as Rural Association for Mutual Help) was publically reprimanded by the governor of the province in a speech in which he stated that ORAM was working against the government that was trying to do everything possible to promote the development of the area.[23] This was a common discourse among ProCana and government officials in an attempt to discredit NGO activity. A ProCana manager said,

> These NGOs are getting in the way of development. They don't want these people to come out of poverty. No NGO has ever lifted a country out of poverty. We are trying to and they are just trying to stop us. You should know that rich countries get rich through business, not through small-scale agriculture.[24]

This pressure was so strong that when AWF was forced to leave the area and abandon their project, they decided not to question the decision made by the Council of Ministries, but to accept it out of fear of being discriminated against by the government if they wanted to continue to work in other places in Mozambique. They were well aware of the injustice of the decision for the residents of the area who had invested time and effort into establishing the community-based nature conservancy, and that the decision went directly against the national land law. Not wanting to jeopardize their work in Bahnine National Park, an AWF employee said,

> We thought about making a case of this and bringing it to court, but we have to ask ourselves some things: Are we prepared to take this case to court? Would we take it on? Or would the community take it to court and we pay for the lawyer? Are we able to win this case? We decided that we didn't want to be seen as making more conflicts and we didn't want to get involved with land conflicts here in Mozambique.[25]

Later in the process, in 2009, once the resettlement of the first village was completed (November 2008) and as ProCana began to progress with their activities, other NGOs including Centro da Terra Viva (CTV) organized meetings and debates to provide a forum for discussion between the local residents and ProCana.

Divergence between the district government and ProCana

Increasingly, the district-level government was also called in to resolve problems caused by ProCana that put them in uncomfortable positions, stuck between their allegiances to the project and their need to be supported by the local population. Interviews with district-level government officials were marked by a drastic withdrawal of enthusiasm and support of the ProCana project over time, without which ProCana's conflicts with local

[22] As a researcher inquiring about the activities of ProCana, I was verbally accosted by ProCana managers who thought that I was working for an NGO.
[23] Interview, External observer, 31 July 2008.
[24] Interview, ProCana employee, Massingir, 10 May 2007.
[25] Interview, AWF employee, Massingir, 17 September 2007.

residents became more and more difficult to manage. Many people speculated that perhaps ProCana was no longer offering financial reward to the district government, but this could not be confirmed.

Unlikely bedfellows: LNP, residents and the WB OP 4.12

Increasing conflict between ProCana and local residents as well as between ProCana and the LNP also created a situation of unlikely alliance between the LNP and local residents. At the beginning of the conflict about the overlapping land claims (early 2007), it was unclear where the park stood with respect to ProCana. As one Nanguene resident described the negotiations, 'The park says, "we are in the process of delimiting land with ProCana" and we said, "they are stealing our land"'.[26] But as time went on and tensions rose, park meetings with resettling residents became increasingly focused on ProCana because of the uncertainly and delay the ProCana plans created for the resettlement process. LNP staff responsible for resettlement facilitated discussions within the meetings organized to plan resettlement actions about the pros and cons of ProCana (employment, future development, a better future for their children, etc.). These discussions were an attempt to prepare leaders of resettling villages and host villages to confront ProCana. LNP staff attempted to equip them with a united response about their position towards the ProCana project. Commissions were even set up in these meetings to spearhead actions against ProCana, and a park staff member offered to set up a meeting between residents and the district administration about their concerns regarding ProCana.[27] The LNP staff were interested in the residents confronting ProCana and allying with the district government because they were concerned with the success of the resettlement project and felt that if residents were empowered to act for themselves to get what they needed, the resettlement would more likely to be a success. Also, at the time, the resettlement process was totally halted. If the land for resettlement could be secured faster, resettlement could progress.

The LNP staff first used the land law and the WB guidelines as resources in displacing residents from the park. In the period 2006–2010, the WB guidelines were seen by certain members of government to be a limitation for rapid resettlement and an externally imposed model that they had to comply with to be eligible for donor funding.[28] In this later phase, the principles of WB OP 4.12 were evoked regularly as park staff informed residents about their rights to compensation for the grazing land. Although follow-through was not as promising as the original discussions about potential actions, it was the beginning of an alliance between the LNP and local residents that strengthened as conflicts with ProCana escalated.

Divergence between the Ministry of Agriculture and ProCana

ProCana's contract was rescinded primarily because of economic reasons, but fault lines in the support for ProCana, between MiTur and MinAg, and between the national and the district and provincial governments, created space for voices of resistance to be heard and for alternative interpretations of policy. ProCana confronted many challenges on the ground, partially because of the resistance by residents, the LNP (MiTur), NGOs and, later, the district-level government.

---

[26]Interview, Nanguene resident, Nanguene, 23 June 2007.
[27]Park meeting, 22 May 2007.
[28]Park meeting, 15 August 2008.

In 2011, the land that had been previously granted to ProCana was granted to Massingir Agro-Industrial (MAI) (Hall and Paradza 2012). With many of the same Mozambican partners, the company has begun to re-launch the failed ProCana project as what will be known as the Massingir Project for Biofuel Development, this time with a different international partner: TSB, formerly Transvaal Suiker Beperk, from South Africa (Esi-Africa 2011; Hall and Paradza 2012). However, at the time of publication of this paper, the MAI project had still not begun to plant sugar cane. This points to another inconsistency in the enactment of the land law – it has been more than 2 years and MAI has not advanced further than ProCana, yet their contract has not been rescinded.

Conclusions

The relationship between policy ideas and policy in practice is not easily predictable. Policies such as WB OP 4.12 or the Mozambican national land law in this case, and the Voluntary Guidelines in other cases, of land grabbing quickly become a contested resource (Borras, Franco, and Wang 2013). The mere adoption of these policies is insufficient to protect rural dwellers from dispossession (Fortina and Richardson 2013; Wisborg 2013b). Therefore, the task at hand is to identify patterns that help us to understand policy enactment in the context of land grabbing. This case points to three conclusions. First, convergence among powerful groups was a key factor in shaping the policy process, creating a challenge for ensuring informed consent and hearing voices of resistance. Second, space for enactment of policy is shaped at the interface of politics from 'in the air' and politics from 'on the ground'. Third, when a land grab and a green grab collided, more actors and their corresponding policies and development narratives were brought into the policy enactment environment, making it even more complex.

When three land claims collided, the resolution agreed upon by government at the national level excluded the longstanding AWF project and disregarded the consequences that the compromise would have on local residents. These two issues were not a concern for the council of ministries when the agreement was made, or to the WB when the plan was approved. When powerful groups aligned with each other, policy was enacted to dispossess residents of their land (see also Alden Wily 2011b; Vermeulen and Cotula 2010). The notion of a 'weak' state lacking in capacity is again refuted here (Hall and Paradza 2012). The means used by the state, under the observation of international donors, to exclude local people and silence voices of resistance point to the challenge of attaining truly informed consent or participation of residents in negotiating land deals (Seufert 2013). At a later phase, divergence between powerful groups did allow space for local residents to defend their rights to land and express their discontent with the actions of ProCana.

Second, this case highlights the way policy enactment was a co-creation at the interface of politics 'in the air', and politics 'on the ground'. As Borras and Franco (2013) discuss the false dichotomy of the reactions of local people to large-scale land acquisitions, this case shows that not only were there multiple reactions and forms of resistance from the far-from-powerless, heterogeneous local residents, but that they changed over time. When ProCana was still 'in the air', some residents were hopeful that the project would bring economic and other benefits. Residents both welcomed the land acquisition and actively mobilized against the company when promises did not materialize into reality. When the work in the terrain began and ProCana began to actively engage in politics 'on the ground', bringing the district-level government with them, local residents in Massingir had considerable power to exert their sovereignty over their territory (Hall and Paradza 2012). NGOs were also increasingly permitted to participate, as government officials saw benefit in aligning themselves with the resistance movement in order to gain the support of the local residents. This analytical lens highlights how policy was enacted during the phase in which the land was being secured for the land grab, when ProCana was engaged in politics 'in the air', and how the policy process shifted when activities began on the land itself and the company engaged in politics 'on the ground'.

The collision between a land grab for sugar cane production and a green grab for nature conservation brought together a wider range of actors, policies and narratives than in the case of a single or even multiple land grabs of the same nature. This created a complex environment for the process of policy enactment in which alliances shifted and outcomes were surprising. Networks converged, joined by certain development narratives, supported by specific types of knowledge, to sway policy enactment. The network supporting ProCana represented a narrative about the potential of agro-industry to bring development, while the network supporting the LNP represented a narrative about the global value of conservation and the potential of tourism to bring development, and therefore the need to resettle people. The compromise found to allow both projects to co-exist prioritized first the interests of the land grab (ProCana), then the green grab (LNP). The agreement was based on a development narrative of more intensive and efficient grazing, backed by 'scientific' knowledge and approved by the WB. These narratives have the power to mobilize people and money, which can result in displacement and pressure on local people's livelihoods (Lunstrum Forthcoming).

In conclusion, at the interface of politics 'in the air' and politics 'on the ground', there is a sphere of micro-politics in which policy is translated into action. If we are to better understand the potential for policy to protect rural dwellers from dispossession, we must not ignore what goes on in this complex space.

Acknowledgements

I would like to thank Cees Leeuwis, Janice Jiggins and Ken Giller for their support, and Ruth Hall, Elizabeth Lunstrum and three anonymous reviewers for constructive comments on earlier drafts. I thank Elisa Francisco Mate, Reginaldo Soto and the residents of Nanguene and Chinhangane as well as the LNP staff for their participation and assistance with my research.

Funding

I acknowledge the United States National Science Foundation Graduate Fellowship Program, the Great Limpopo Transfrontier Conservation Area working group of the Animal and Human Health for the Environment And Development (AHEAD-GLTFCA) and the Interdisciplinary Research and Education Fund (INREF) research programme 'Competing claims on natural resources: overcoming mismatches in resource use through a multi-scale perspective', Wageningen University, the Netherlands, for funding of the field research. I also give thanks to The Land Deal Politics Initiative (LDPI) for funding for the writing of this paper.

References

Abrahamsson, H., and A. Nilsson. 1995. *Mozambique: The troubled transition – From socialist construction to free market capitalism*. Atlantic Highlands, NJ: Zed Books.

African Union. 2009. *Framework and guidelines on land policy in Africa. Land policy in Africa: A framework to strengthen land rights, enhance productivity and secure livelihoods*. Addis Ababa: AU.

Alden Wily, L. 2011a. 'The law is to blame': The vulnerable status of common property rights in sub-Saharan Africa. *Development and Change* 42, no. 3: 733–57.

Alden Wily, L. 2011b. 'The law is to blame': The vulnerable status of common property rights in sub-Saharan Africa. *Development and Change* 42, no. 3: 733–57.
Alden Wily, L. 2012. Looking back to see forward: The legal niceties of land theft in land rushes. *Journal of Peasant Studies* 39, no. 3–4: 751–75.
Benjaminsen, T.A. and I. Bryceson. 2012. Conservation, green/blue grabbing and accumulation by dispossession in Tanzania. *The Journal of Peasant Studies* 39, no. 2: 335–55.
Borras Jr, S.M., D. Fig, and S.M. Suárez. 2011. The politics of agrofuels and mega-land and water deals: Insights from the ProCana case, Mozambique. *Review of African Political Economy* 38, no. 128: 215–34.
Borras Jr, S.M., and J.C. Franco. 2010. From threat to opportunity? Problems with the idea of a "code of conduct" for land grabbing. *Yale Human Rights & Development Law Journal* 13: 507–23.
Borras Jr, S.M., and J.C. Franco. 2012. Global land grabbing and trajectories of Agrarian change: A preliminary analysis. *Journal of Agrarian Change* 12, no. 1: 34–59.
Borras, S.M., and J.C. Franco. 2013. Global land grabbing and political reactions 'from below'. *Third World Quarterly* 34, no. 9: 1723–47.
Borras, S.M., J.C. Franco, and C. Wang. 2013. The challenge of global governance of land grabbing: Changing International agricultural context and competing political views and strategies. *Globalizations* 10, no. 1: 161–79.
Braun, A., S.J. Ball, M. Maguire, and K. Hoskins. 2011. Taking context seriously: Towards explaining policy enactments in the secondary school. *Discourse* 32, no. 4: 585–96.
Centro Da Terra Viva. 2010. Carta aberta ao governo de Mocambique. http://www.ctv.org.mz/index.php?option=com_content&view=article&id=1229%3Acarta-aberta-ao-governo-mocambicano-&catid=101%3Atodas-noticias&Itemid=554&lang=en
Cernea, M. 1993. Social science research and the crafting of policy on population resettlement. *Knowledge, Technology & Policy* 6, no. 3: 176–200.
Cernea, M.M. 1997. The risks and reconstruction model for resettling displaced populations. *World Development* 25, no. 10: 1569–87.
Cernea, M.M., and C. Mcdowell, eds. 2000. *Risks and reconstruction: Experiences of resettlers and refugees*. Washington, DC: The World Bank.
Cernea, M.M., and K. Schmidt-Soltau. 2006. Poverty risks and national parks: Policy issues in conservation and resettlement. *World Development* 34, no. 10: 1808–30.
Coburn, C.E. 2001. Collective sensemaking about reading: How teachers mediate reading policy in their professional communities. *Educational Evaluation and Policy Analysis* 23, no. 2: 145–70.
Contour Project Managers. 2006. Management & business plan for the Cubo community nature conservancy in Massingir district, Mozambique: Situational Analysis Report: African Wildlife Foundation.
Cotula, L. and S. Vermeulen. 2011. Contexts and procedures for farmland acquisitions in Africa: What outcomes for local people. *Development* 54, no. 1: 40–48.
De Schutter, O. 2011. How not to think of land-grabbing: Three critiques of large-scale investments in farmland. *Journal of Peasant Studies* 38, no. 2: 249–79.
Deininger, K., and D. Byerlee. 2012. The rise of large farms in land abundant countries. Do they have a future? *World Development* 40, no. 4: 701–14.
Deleon, P. and L. Deleon. 2002. What ever happened to policy implementation? An alternative approach. *Journal of Public Administration Research and Theory* 12, no. 4: 467–92.
Duffy, R. 2006. The potential and pitfalls of global environmental governance: The politics of transfrontier conservation areas in southern Africa. *Political Geography* 25: 89–112.
Escrivão, R.J.A. 2007. *Avaliação da Capacidade de Carga animal das Aldeias de Chinhangane e Banga, Distrito de Massingir*. Maputo, Mozambique: University of Eduardo Mondlane, Vetrerinary Faculty.
Esi-Africa. 2011. Procana bio-fuel project to be re-launched [online] URL: http://www.esi-africa.com/node/13887.
Fairbairn, M. 2013. Indirect dispossession: Domestic power imbalances and foreign access to land in Mozambique. *Development and Change* 44, no. 2: 335–56.
Fairhead, J., M. Leach, and I. Scoones. 2012. Green grabbing: A new appropriation of nature? *The Journal of Peasant Studies* 39, no. 2: 237–61.
Fao, Ifad, Unctad and The World Bank Group. 2010. Principles for responsible agricultural investment that respects rights, livelihoods and resources. In http://siteresources.worldbank.org/INTARD/214574-1111138388661/22453321/Principles_Extended.pdf

Food and Agriculture Organization of the United Nations. 2012. *Voluntary guidelines on the responsible governance of tenure of land, fisheries and forests in the context of national food security*. Rome, 11 May 2012: Committee on Food Security, FAO.

Fortina, E., and B. Richardson. 2013. Certification schemes and the governance of land: Enforcing standards or enabling scrutiny? *Globalizations* 10, no. 1: 141–59.

Franco, J., L. Mehta, and G.J. Veldwisch. October 2013. The global politics of water grabbing. *Third World Quarterly* 34, no. 9: 1651–75(25).

Hall, R., and G. Paradza. 2012. Foxes guarding the Hen-house: The fragmentation of 'The State' in negotiations over land deals in Congo and Mozambique. Paper presentat at the International Academic Conference on Global Land Grabbing, in Cornell University, Ithaca NY, USA.

Hofmann, J. 1995. Implicit theories in policy discourse: An inquiry into the interpretations of reality in German technology policy. *Policy Sciences* 28, no. 2: 127–48.

Keeley, J., and I. Scoones. 2003. *Understanding environmental policy processes: Cases from Africa*. London: Earthscan.

Li, T.M. 2011. Centering labor in the land grab debate. *Journal of Peasant Studies* 38, no. 2: 281–98.

Limpopo National Park. 10 December 2007. Resettlement of 144 families from nanguene and macavene villages – the current situation regarding the availability of replacement communal grazing land.

Lunstrum, E. 2008. Mozambique, neoliberal land reform and the Limpopo National Park. *Geographical Review* 98, no. 3: 339–55.

Lunstrum, E. Forthcoming. Green grabs, land grabs, and the spatiality of displacement: Eviction from Mozambique's Limpopo National Park. *AREA*.

Manuel, L., and A. Salomao. 2009. Biofuels and land rights in Mozambique – the ProCana case. *Haramata* 54: 16–18.

Massango, H.A., and T.M. Chaúque. 2005. Areas potencias de reassentamento para as comunidades de Shingwedzi; critérios de selecção.

Mcgee, R. 2004. Unpacking policy: Actors, knowledge and spaces. In *Unpacking policy: Knowledge, actors and spaces in poverty reduction in Uganda and Nigeria*, ed. K. Brock, R. Mcgee, and J. Gaventa, 1–26. Kampala: Fountain Publishers.

Milgroom, J. 2012. Elephants of democracy: Enacting participatory resettlement policy. In *Elephants of democracy: An unfolding process of resettlement in the Limpopo National Park*, 1–322. Wageningen: Wageningen University.

Milgroom, J., and M. Spierenburg. 2008. Induced volition: Resettlement from the Limpopo National Park, Mozambique. *Journal of Contemporary African Studies* 26, no. 4: 435–48.

Neville, K.J., and P. Dauvergne. 2012. Biofuels and the politics of mapmaking. *Political Geography* 31, no. 5: 279–89.

Nhantumbo, I., and A. Salomão. 2010. *Biofuels, land access and rural livelihoods in Mozambique*. ed. L. Cotula. London: International Institute for Environment and Development.

Norfolk, S. 2004. Examining access to natural resources and linkages to sustainable livelihoods: A case stude of Mozambique. Livelihood Support Programme Working Paper 17, 1–70, in Rome, Food and Agriculture Organization of the United Nations.

Ojeda, D. 2012. Green pretexts: Ecotourism, neoliberal conservation and land grabbing in Tayrona National Natural Park, Colombia. *The Journal of Peasant Studies* 39, no. 2: 357–75.

Rosset, P. 2011. Food sovereignty and alternative paradigms to confront land grabbing and the food and climate crises. *Development* 54, no. 1: 21–30.

Rural Consult. 2008. *Estudo pedológico e de avaliação de capacidade de carga da região entre aldeias de chinhangane e banga, vale do rio dos elefantes*. Maputo: Ministry of Tourism.

Schut, M., M. Slingerland, and A. Lock. 2010. Biofuel developments in Mozambique. Update and analysis of policy, potential and reality. *Energy Policy* 38: 5151–65.

Scudder, T. 2012. Resettlement outcomes of large dams. In *Impacts of large dams: A global assessment*, 37–67. Berlin, Heidelberg: Springer.

Seufert, P. 2013. The FAO voluntary guidelines on the responsible governance of tenure of land, fisheries and forests. *Globalizations* 10, no. 1: 181–86.

Smalley, R., and E. Corbera. 2012. Large-scale land deals from the inside out: Findings from Kenya's Tana Delta. *Journal of Peasant Studies* 39, no. 3–4: 1039–75.

Spierenburg, M., and H. Wels. 2006. Securing space: Mapping and fencing in transfrontier conservation in southern Africa. *Space & Culture* 6, no. 3: 294–312.

Spillane, J.P., B.J. Reiser, and T. Reimer. 2002. Policy implementation and cognition: Reframing and refocusing implementation research. *Review of Educational Research* 72, no. 3: 387–431.

Stalmans, M., W.P.D. Gertenbach, and F. Carvalho-Serfontein. 2004. Plant communities and landscapes of the Parque Nacional do Limpopo, Moçambique. *Koedoe* 47, no. 2: 61–81.

Tanner, C. 2010. Land rights and enclosures: Implementing the Mozambican land law in practice. In *The struggle over land in Africa. Conflicts politics and change*, ed. W. Anseeuw, and C. Alden, 105–30. Cape Town, South Africa: HSRC Press.

Van Bommel, S., E. Turnhout, S. Vellema, and R. Zeiss. 2010. Travelling standards: Enactment, friction and alignment in the case of the forest stewardship council certification scheme. In *unpublished paper*: Wageningen University.

Vermeulen, S., and L. Cotula. 2010. Over the heads of local people: Consultation, consent, and recompense in large-scale land deals for biofuels projects in Africa. *Journal of Peasant Studies* 37, no. 4: 899–916.

Von Braun, J., and R. Meinzen-Dick. 2009. "Land grabbing" by foreign investors in developing countries: Risks and opportunities. *IFPRI policy brief* 13: 1–3.

Wagenaar, H. 2011. *Meaning in action: Interpretation and dialogue in policy analysis*. New York: M.E. Sharpe.

White, B., S.M. Borras Jr, R. Hall, I. Scoones, and W. Wolford. 2012. The new enclosures: Critical perspectives on corporate land deals. *Journal of Peasant Studies* 39, no. 3–4: 619–47.

Wisborg, P. 2013a. Human rights against land grabbing? A reflection on norms, policies, and power. *Journal of Agricultural and Environmental Ethics*: 1–24.

Wisborg, P. 2013b. Human rights against land grabbing? A reflection on norms, policies, and power. *Journal of Agricultural and Environmental Ethics* 26, no. 6: 1199–222.

Wolford, W., S.M. Borras, R. Hall, I. Scoones, and B. White. 2013. Governing global land deals: The role of the state in the rush for land. *Development and Change* 44, no. 2: 189–210.

Wolmer, W. 2003. Transboundary conservation: The politics of ecological integrity in the Great Limpopo Transfrontier Park. *Journal of Southern African Studies* 29, no. 1: 261–78.

World Bank. 1994. Resettlement and development: The bank-wide review of projects involving involuntary resettlement 1986–1993. Washington, DC: The World Bank, Environment.

Yanow, D. 1995. Practices of policy interpretation. *Policy Sciences* 28, no. 2: 111–26.

Yanow, D. 1996. *How does a policy mean? Interpreting policy and organizational actions*. Washington, DC: Georgetown University Press.

Yanow, D., and P. Schwartz-Shea, eds. 2006. *Interpretation and method: Empirical research methods and the interpretive turn*. New York: M.E. Sharpe.

Zoomers, A. 2010. Globalisation and the foreignisation of space: Seven processes driving the current global land grab. *Journal of Peasant Studies* 37, no. 2: 429–47.

Resistance or adaptation? Ukrainian peasants' responses to large-scale land acquisitions[†]

Natalia Mamonova

While globally it is reported that peasants are fighting against land grabbing, Ukrainian rural dwellers show tolerance and peaceful acceptance of land grab-related changes. This paper analyses the 'exceptional' case of non-resistance of Ukrainian peasants and argues that it is not as exceptional as it seems at first glance. By studying various rural responses to the large-scale agricultural development in Ukraine and the resulting socio-economic transformations within rural communities, this research demonstrates that: the politics of dispossessed groups depend on the terms of inclusion in land deals; adaptive response strategies are common and can be advantageous for rural people; and peasants are more concerned with personal gains from land grabs than with benefits for the whole community, which often leads to their acceptance of large-scale land acquisitions. This research challenges the dominant assumptions about rural resistance to land grabbing and calls for rethinking the nature of the contemporary peasants' politics worldwide.

1. Introduction

The assumption that resistance is an indispensable response of the rural poor to land grabbing is ingrained in the politics of many social movements, nongovernmental organisations and rural development groups (i.e. La Via Campesina, MST). A number of academic and non-academic studies have been launched to find ways of helping rural dwellers all over the world in their struggles against the development of large-scale industrial agriculture and for redefinition of their 'way of life' (Quan 2000; Adnan 2011; Schneider 2011). However this focus on resistance suffers from simplification. Land grabs affect different rural groups in different ways, which creates a variety of reactions to them, from outright resistance to reckless enthusiasm or cautious acceptance.

This research challenges three major assumptions about peasant responses to land grabbing, namely: (1) resistance is the only response of rural dwellers toward large-scale land acquisitions; (2) peasants are unable to adapt and coexist with large-scale industrial agriculture; and (3) ideological concerns about the 'peasant way of life', food and land sovereignty

[†]An earlier version of this paper was presented at the international conference 'Global Land Grabbing II', Cornell University, Ithaca, 17–19 October 2012 under the title "Challenging the dominant assumptions about peasant responses to land grabbing", and later it appeared as a Land Deals Politics Initiative (LDPI) Working Paper.

dominate in peasant struggles. The paper exposes these assumptions based on an empirical study of peasant response strategies to land grabbing[1] and the development of large-scale agriculture in Ukraine.

Ukraine was recently included by the World Bank in the list of resource-rich and finance-poor countries that became targets for land grabbing. The country possesses more than 25 percent of the world's richest and most fertile soil, so-called Black Earth, and was the Soviet Union's Bread Basket. After the collapse of the USSR in 1991, Ukraine launched a land reform aimed at breaking down *kolkhozy* and *sovkhozy* (collective and state farms) and distributing their lands to rural dwellers for private farming development. However, as all the necessary factors complementary to land (capital, know-how, upstream and downstream markets, the rule of law) disappeared with the breakdown of the collectives, rural dwellers could not make use of their new resource. Instead, land became concentrated: first in the hands of rural elites, and later accumulated by large domestic and foreign investors that were motivated by the upswing in world food markets and the global land rush of the early 2000s (Visser and Spoor 2011; Plank 2013). To date, 60 percent of Ukrainian farmland is controlled by large farm enterprises (LFEs), whose size and scale are comparable with the largest latifundia in Brazil and Argentina (Visser and Mamonova 2011; Lapa, Lissitsa, and Tovstopyat 2008). Similar to many other countries affected by land grabs, the large-scale land acquisitions in Ukraine are often carried out in 'shadow' schemes, which deprive the local population of their rights (Visser and Spoor 2011).

The distinguishing feature of Ukraine lies in the near-absent overt protests[2] of rural dwellers against large-scale land acquisitions (Visser and Mamonova 2011). Even the recent political crisis and the 2014 Ukrainian Revolution, which created 'open moments'[3] for contestations, did not stimulate rural dwellers to mobilise and resist the LFEs' domination. The lack of open resistance among post-Soviet peasants is usually

[1]It should be noted that there are ongoing debates on how to interpret the current process of large-scale land acquisitions in Ukraine (and in the former Soviet Union at large). Some authors argue that it is a land grabbing process, that might jeopardise the subsistence of small-scale farmers and lead to irresponsible land use (Visser and Spoor 2011; Plank 2013). Others are convinced that it is a development opportunity, in which more efficient large-scale agricultural producers substitute for less efficient former collectives and small- and medium-scale farming (Lapa et al. 2008; Petrick et al. 2013). The latter position is often supported by the fact that large-scale land acquisitions are predominantly taking place on former collective lands; although distributed to rural dwellers during the land reform, these lands were not used for private farming and were abandoned for a decade. This latter position sees land deals as investments, not grabs. Although in this paper I analyse the ongoing land acquisitions within a land grabbing framework, I do acknowledge the less dramatic character of this process in the case of Ukraine (and in the former Soviet Union at large); therefore, I generally refer to 'large-scale land acquisitions', and only use the 'land grabbing' term in the most extreme situations, when land deals were done with violation of peasants' rights and jeopardised their subsistence.
[2]This research purposely overlooks covert forms of rural politics toward land grabbing. According to Scott (1985), peasant resistance acts often remain hidden in social settings where open rural protest is restricted by political and economic factors. There is an ongoing debate on whether gossiping, stealing and foot-dragging should be classified as the post-Soviet peasants' covert resistance, a 'parasitic symbiosis' between households and large farm enterprises, or just hooliganism (see e.g. Mamonova and Visser 2014). That being said, hidden politics do not represent a significant force of change in the current post-Soviet countryside, no matter what they are referred to as (Spoor and Visser 2004).
[3]Political crises can open the political system to new challenges and alternative policies, creating what Gourevitch (1986) terms 'open moments' for contestations. State failure can politicise the citizenry and fragment elite unity, potentially prompting the re-examination of both government policy and political alliances.

explained by 70 years of socialism (a time when expressions of disagreement were prosecuted), the ageing of the rural population (24.1 percent of rural residents are older than 60), peasant traditional dependency on large-scale farming, and a 'culture of repression' that limits the political consciousness of the rural population (see Mamonova and Visser 2014). That being said, although historical legacies and socio-political contextual factors are important variables in explaining the passivity of the post-Soviet peasantry, they make up only one side of the coin.

This paper explains the Ukrainian peasant tolerance and peaceful acceptance of land grab-related changes by analysing terms upon which rural population is incorporated in land deals. The analysis distinguishes between illusive inclusion, subordinate inclusion and competitive exclusion, and reveals the reactive behaviour of rural households to each of these terms. The paper also analyses the peasants' most and least adaptive response strategies and the subsequent socio-economic transformations in rural communities. It indicates that the adaptive response strategies often lead to more advantageous positions in the rural society, and as frequent as non-adaptive strategies. Finally, the paper shows that peasants are more concerned with personal gains from land grabs than with benefits for the whole community, which often leads to their acceptance of large-scale land acquisitions. This analysis aims to challenge our assumptions about rural resistance in the post-Soviet countryside, and calls for rethinking the nature of the contemporary peasants' politics worldwide.

This research is largely based on fieldwork conducted by the author during the summer of 2012 in two regions of Ukraine: the Letichevsk district (the Khmelnitsk region, Western Ukraine) and the Pereyaslav-Khmelnitskiy district (the Kiev region, Central Ukraine). These two regions are characterised by high soil fertility and a large number of LFEs operating there. The analysis of peasant responses to land grabbing is drawn from 52 semi-structured in-depth interviews with inhabitants from the analysed districts (44 small-scale farmers and rural workers, three chief managers of LFEs, and five representatives of local authorities). The small-scale farmers and rural workers also participated in a household survey that was developed and conducted by the author. The survey findings were supplemented by a number of all-Ukrainian surveys: the 'Socio-economic situation in the contemporary Ukrainian village' survey, conducted by the Gorshenin Institute in 2011, the 'Land relations in Ukraine: sociological portrait of the situation' survey, conducted by the Centre of Social Expertise of the Institute of Sociology of the National Academy of Sciences (NAS) of Ukraine in 2013, and the FAO Farm Survey conducted in 2005 (NAS survey 2013; Gorshenin survey 2011; FAO Farm Survey 2005). Furthermore, various sources of academic literature, mass media publications, and statistical sources such as the State Committee of Ukraine for Statistics (UkrStat), and World Bank reports informed the analysis.

The paper is structured as follows. The next section discusses three major assumptions about peasant responses to land grabbing in academic and non-academic literature. I then provide a historical analysis of the Ukrainian peasantry, in order to characterise the level of socio-economic stratification within rural communities at the moment land grabbing occurred. In the fourth section, I analyse the different processes of peasant exclusion and inclusion in modern agricultural development that shape rural attitudes toward land deals. The fifth section demonstrates the pros and cons of the Ukrainian villagers' adaptive and resisting response strategies to large-scale agribusinesses. The sixth section examines peasants' attitudes to land grabbing using the attitude to land sales as an indicator. The final section of this paper discusses the generalisability of the findings and their application in wider rural communities.

2. Three major assumptions about peasant responses to land grabs

In recent literature on land grabbing, rural dwellers are considered victims of large-scale land acquisitions whose traditional subsistence schemas are threatened by limiting their access to land and other natural resources (Quan 2000; Adnan 2011; Schneider 2011). Adnan (2011, 4) writes: 'the political responses of the dispossessed groups have involved resistance to land grabbing and dispossession as well as struggles for gaining possession or repossession of land'. The common assumption that *peasants inherently oppose large-scale land acquisitions* is applied by many anti-land grab social movements, such as La Via Campesina and MST (McMichael 2006). 'Farmers and civil society groups have strongly opposed land grabbing everywhere … ', stated La Via Campesina in its call for mobilisation at the International Day of the Peasant's Struggle (viacampesina.org 2013).

Meanwhile, according to the World Bank Group, large-scale land acquisitions can be, to some extent, beneficial to the local population. Indeed, there are many people being included or incorporated into the emerging enclaves of land-based investments, through a variety of schemes: contract farming, plantation workers, etc. (Borras and Franco 2013). The critics of this 'win–win' scenario argue that this inclusion of rural dwellers is an 'adverse incorporation', i.e. the exploitation and subordination of incorporated groups in highly unequal power relations. According to Hickey and du Toit (2007, 21), this leads to the marginalisation of subordinated groups, and their chronic poverty.

However, different academic studies show that even under adverse incorporation, rural dwellers manage to find advantages. Thus, peasants benefit from the recent large-scale agricultural development in Kazakhstan by taking the jobs it creates. Rural Kazakhs, according to Petrick, Wandel, and Karsten (2013, 164), 'due to the socialist tradition of industrialised farming operations […] regard themselves primarily as workers and not as land owners', and therefore do not struggle for autonomy, and accept work at the new latifundia. Smalley and Corbera (2012, 1050) found that the attitude to land investments varies across different rural groups in Kenya. Their interviews with farmers indicated the 'vision of development through jobs' and the 'desire for agricultural development projects' as the reasons behind the support of land deals; in contrast, the majority of the interviewed pastoralists opposed land acquisitions, referring to 'fear of eviction or lost access'. Consequently, for some rural groups and sectors, land grabbing does not necessarily bring negative changes.

The peasants' attitude to land grabbing critically depends on the 'terms of inclusion' of local population in land deals (McCarthy 2010). According to Witcher (2003, 7) 'terms of inclusion' are derived from 'societal relationships and criteria for access prioritised by whichever dominates'. Therefore, understanding the political economy of the new social structures and the labour regimes that emerge from them is highly important for analysing various rural responses to land grabbing.

The second popular assumption is that *peasants are unable to adapt to and coexist with large-scale industrial agriculture*. This revitalises the long-standing debate on the persistence and disappearance of the peasantry (see Araghi 1995; Boltvinik 2012). Populist social movements redefine the 'peasant way'[4] in opposition to a globalised neo-liberal corporate-driven model of agricultural production in order to mobilise peasants against land grabbing (Desmarais 2002; McMichael 2006). Class-based theorists, on the other hand, observe how the peasantry disappears under the competitive pressures of modern corporate agriculture, and see the ongoing rural unrest as a class struggle (Bernstein 2004; Adnan 2011).

[4]The concept of the 'peasant way' is characterised as 'involving a subsistence family economy, stem family arrangements and a highly localised cultural and co-operative system' (Síocháin 2003, 864).

These positions largely overlook the ability of peasants to adapt to and coexist with industrial agriculture, and become an active participant, not a protesting victim. The possibility of combining large-scale agriculture with small-scale peasant farming is advocated by the World Bank. The Bank suggests that, at low levels of population density, large-scale investments in land are appropriate, and 'voluntary land transfers that make everybody better off are possible' (World Bank 2010, 55). Olivier de Schutter (2011, 259–61), a former United Nations Special Reporter on the Right to Food, criticised the Bank's position for 'simplification'. However, he acknowledged that the 'coexistence' scenario is possible, if the existing rights of land users are clearly defined, and the markets where peasants and large agriculturalists operate can remain highly segmented – for instance, when all the production of large-scale agriculture is shipped abroad, while the food security in the home country is guaranteed by small-scale producers.

Analysing market niches where peasants and large-scale agribusiness operate, as well as the structural changes in peasants' modes of production, is highly important for understanding rural response strategies to land grabbing.

The third assumption about peasant struggles is that *peasants are concerned with the 'peasant way', food and land sovereignty, and economic and ecological justice, when they adopt strategies to respond to land grabbing*. This position is centre-stage in the works of many academics (Rosset et al. 2011; Kay 2012), and grounds the programmes of rural social movements defending peasants' rights for food and land sovereignty (McMichael 2006).

Meanwhile, Pye (2010) identifies the frequent mismatch between the global campaigns of civil society and rural social movements, and the local concerns of villagers, in the context of Indonesia. For example, while biofuel debates are globally framed in terms of biodiversity conservation and climate justice, local concerns focus on land rights and employment conditions. As Pye argues, the complaints of palm oil smallholders and plantation workers are conspicuously absent at the international level of civil society and social movement campaigns (Borras, McMichael, and Scoones 2010). Boyer (2010) studied the failure of the global food sovereignty campaign of La Via Campesina in post-war Honduras, and came to the conclusion that the transnational agrarian movement ignores local peasant understandings, needs and organisations. According to the author, La Via Campesina's food sovereignty programme was associated by Honduran peasants with the powers of nation states, while the concept of food security resonated with deeply held peasant understandings of security for their continued social reproduction in insecure social and natural conditions. Edelman and León (2013), in their analysis of land grabbing cycles, noticed that, contrary to the fact that palm oil plantations are often linked with land grabbing, the rural population in Honduras is very positive about this crop and is willing to engage in contract farming agreements[5] with large private investors despite heavy criticism from Honduran civil activists. Mamonova (2013) analysed the mismatch between the demands of the 'Defenders' social movement in the Moscow region (who clamoured against the grabbing of historical land in Radonezh) and the local rural population (who

[5]The contract farming model was proposed by large private palm oil investors in Honduras. According to this model, peasant households produce raw African palm fruit and assume all production risks, while the large private plants process and market the palm oil, and, therefore, accrue the value added in processing. Although this model is not beneficial to small-scale palm fruit producers, it transcends simple economics and engages with the cultural meaning of African palm oil plantations, which evoke images of a better life and success.

were more concerned with access to the forest and river, which were blocked by the land grabbers).

Placing the land and food sovereignty concepts in the centre of peasant struggles and romanticizing peasants’ motives for land grab resistance might bring us to the wrong conclusions, and, consequently, to the development of wrong policies and programmes for the protection of peasant rights.

The following analysis of the contemporary peasants’ politics in Ukraine is an attempt to look beyond the common assumptions about rural resistance toward land grabs.

3. Development of Ukrainian peasant agriculture before land grabs

In order to understand the nature of rural responses to land grabbing and transformations within rural communities, I will first address the pattern of agrarian evolution and the level of socio-economic stratification in Ukraine at the moment land grabbing occurred.

Traditionally, Ukrainian peasants, like many peasants in the Russian Empire,[6] belonged to communes, which were responsible for collective decision making, tax payments and the periodic redistribution of land among peasants.[7] The Stolypin land reform (1905–1915) aimed to break down the commune system and create private land ownership. The emerging system of private agriculture caused an increase of agricultural yields and sown area in Ukrainian provinces; however, it only lasted a short period (Malienko 2010). The socialist revolution of 1917 and the establishment of the Ukrainian Soviet Socialist Republic in 1919 ended the prospects for private property. Leninist ideologies consider private property as the basis of class exploitation and the dependency of employed workers on a privileged group of owners. The Soviet goal was to abolish ‘immoral’ capitalist private property and to create a class of rural labourers who would share the socialist values of common ownership and equality between people (Zemstov 1991).

The socialist agrarian reforms of 1919–1921 revitalised the commune system and launched *podroskladka* (a campaign of confiscating grain and other agricultural produce from the peasants for a fixed price). The socialisation of agriculture and the subtractive policy of the Soviet state caused mass peasant revolts in Ukraine. These uprisings, along with other threats to Bolshevik dictatorship, forced Lenin to reconsider his economic policy. The New Economic Policy (NEP) was implemented in 1921–1927 and was primarily a new agricultural policy (Cohen 1980). It established a mixed socialist market economy, which allowed private landholdings, and substituted *podroskladka* with *prodpodatok* (a tax on the peasants, payable in the form of raw agricultural product). This allowed small-scale producers to keep their surplus, which positively affected their productivity and caused an increase in gross agricultural production.

Stalin, who became the USSR leader in 1928, saw the NEP as a return to capitalism and launched the Collectivisation campaign (1929–1933), which aimed to consolidate individual land, property and labour into kolkhozy and sovkhozy – and therefore eliminate independent small-scale agricultural producers. The Soviet leadership was convinced that these measurements would increase agricultural productivity and create the grain reserves needed

[6]The majority of Ukraine was incorporated into the Russian Empire after the second partition of Poland in 1793, while the remaining section (the principality of Galicia) remained part of the Austro-Hungarian Empire until World War I.

[7]Households mostly did not have fixed entitlement to the land they cultivated. Land was frequently redistributed anew among the villagers’ households according to the needs (and capacity) of the households (e.g. depending on changes in household size).

for the country's industrialisation. Although the increase of agricultural productivity was rather unfeasible and accomplished predominantly by violent measures like harvest expropriation and dekulakisation[8] (leading to famines in 1931–1932 in Ukraine), the relative equalisation of rural dwellers was indeed achieved by the collectivisation (Humphrey 2002). Throughout the Soviet period, the state exercised total control over the stratification of rural communities by regulating household incomes and equalising the size of household plots (Wegren 2005).

The 'Soviet peasant'[9] lost the peasant-like features of 'autonomous, property-conscious economising', but retained 'corporatism' and 'egalitarianism' (Humphrey 2002). Despite the proclaimed proletarianisation of society, Soviet villagers did not completely become rural labourers. Even though nearly all Ukrainian peasants had official jobs at kolkhozy and sovkhozy, they also conducted subsistence farming on their household plots of 0.4 ha on average, which peasants had been allowed to have since the late 1930s. This highly productive small-scale peasant agriculture was 'outside the state planning and procurement system' (Wegren 2005, 8). Even the 'state war against personal subsidiary farming'[10] launched by Khrushchev in 1958–1959 did not eradicate this form of production (although it minimised the amount of livestock held by the rural population). The Brezhnev government (1966–1982), instead, stimulated peasants' self-food provisioning due to the failure of the centrally planned economy to provide enough food for the population. Therefore, despite the Soviet anti-peasantry policy, Ukrainian peasants preserved important elements of a peasant mode of production, i.e. family-based subsistence agriculture and land possession.

After the collapse of the Soviet Union in 1991, Ukraine launched a land reform aimed at revitalising peasant agriculture. During the first stage of land reform (1990–1999), former collective lands were distributed to rural dwellers by means of land-share certificates for private farming. Consequently, in addition to household plots, rural dwellers gained the right to use land plots (average 4 ha), which were located usually at a distance from villages. Ownership of the distributed lands could occur if the certificate holder underwent the process of land registration and privatisation, or devoted his or her share to the authorised capital of the reorganised collective farm. Contrary to the expectations of the reform developers, land recipients did not show much interest in leaving the collectives to establish individual farms. Only 3 percent of certificate holders registered their land rights by 1995 (Lerman et al. 2007).

A common explanation for the failure of this stage of the land reform has been that exit costs for individual workers were too high (in terms of finance and equipment), and emerging markets were still largely geared toward large collective successor farms (Mathijs and Swinnen 1998). Some authors refer to the rural population's possession of household plots as a reason for the unsuccessful collective land distribution. Wegren (2005, 19) indicated that

[8]Dekulakisation (in Ukrainian: *Rozkurkulennya*) was the Soviet campaign of political repression, including arrests, deportations and executions of millions of the better-off peasants and their families in 1929–1932. The richer peasants were labeled *kulaks* and considered class enemies.

[9]The 'Soviet peasant' terminology was used as an official social category, evolving through the 1930s–1940s and the 1950s–1960s, and peaking in the Brezhnev period of the 1970s–1980s (Humphrey 2002).

[10]Nikita Khrushchev believed that the low agricultural production at kolkhozy and sovkhozy was caused by the population's personal subsidiary farming. In 1958, he initiated a policy directed against private households. After that, it was forbidden to keep livestock at rural households. The state offered rural dwellers the option to sell their livestock to kolkhozy and sovkhozy at a fixed price. However, this caused a mass slaughtering and led to a significant reduction in livestock and poultry in the country (Taubman 2004).

> at the onset of market reforms some 97% of rural households already had [household] land plots, and most households had limited human capital. Therefore, the expansion of landholdings through privatization would be attractive or feasible to a relatively small percentage of rural households.

Lerman, Csaki, and Feder (2004, 149) argue that farm managers, who were seen as 'omniscient community leaders', were interested in the preservation of large-scale organisation as a way to keep their power and perquisites – and, therefore, used their authority to manipulate information about the land reform. A 1997 World Bank survey shows that only a few Ukrainian peasants knew about the possibilities of establishing private farming on the distributed lands, while the majority of the rural population (80 percent) was informed that they could 'invest' their land shares back to farm enterprises (Csaki and Lerman 1997). This concentrated the collective lands in the hands of the rural elites, who 'gained de facto ownership of land and with it, the autonomy and economic incentive to persist in their new roles as leaders in a quasi-feudal system' (Allina-Pisano 2002, 314). Those few private farmers that emerged in the post-1991 period were almost always either former Party-connected functionaries or rural elite, who had known how to organise business under the Soviet rule. The majority of post-Soviet peasants had lost the historical memory and cultural tradition of entrepreneurship due to a 70-year reign of socialist principles and socialist ideology (Petrick and Carter 2009; Visser 2010).

The first stage of the land reform was accompanied by a sharp reduction of state subsidies in agriculture and the price liberalisation of agricultural products. This led to the bankruptcy of many collective farms and the abandonment of collective farmlands (Visser and Spoor 2011). This in turn induced a rapid growth of rural unemployment, a drastic decline in the livelihood conditions and living standards of many peasant families, a lack of social security and a rising psycho-social tension caused by little hope for the future (Borodina 2009). In order to guarantee their subsistence, many Ukrainian villagers became largely dependent on subsistence farming on their household plots. Von Braun and Lohlein (2003) observed a significant increase in the share of agricultural land devoted to subsistence production and the number of rural dwellers engaged in subsistence farming during the period of 1990–1999. At the time, in-kind income from subsidiary plots accounted for 44.4 percent of the total rural household income, while wages and social transfers made up 16.3 percent and 13.4 percent, respectively (Moroz 2010).

The first stage of the land reform had, indeed, revitalised peasant agriculture in Ukraine; however, it created a large group of small traditional subsistence cultivators, instead of individual family farmers. On the eve of massive land grabbing in Ukraine, the stratification within rural communities was minimal: a first, very small group was that of the rural elites (5 percent of the population, according to Wegren 2005), who had maintained their ruling positions since the Soviet Union; the second group (in fact, the main rural population) was represented by impoverished peasants – who did have some small income from wage work but were largely dependent on subsistence farming on their household plots.

4. Large-scale land acquisitions and 'terms of inclusion' of rural population in land deals

Large-scale land acquisitions by domestic and foreign investors started in Ukraine with the beginning of the second stage of the land reform (1999 to present; Borodina 2009; Plank 2013). The 1999 Presidential Decree forced the collective agricultural enterprises to distribute the land shares in kind to rural dwellers. Since then, nearly 7 million rural residents have become official owners of physical land plots (not just paper-based certificates), and about 65 percent of the arable land is physically owned by rural individuals (Lerman et al. 2006). In 2001, the Land Code came into force, which legally guaranteed land titles and imposed a moratorium on land sales until 2005. The moratorium has already been extended several times (until 2008, 2012, 2013 and 2016), and was shelved indefinitely after the 2014 Ukrainian Revolution.[11] Although the moratorium aims to protect peasant ownership, in practice, it only serves as a formal prevention of land deals (Visser and Spoor 2011; Plank 2013).

The rise of global food prices and the relative stabilisation of the investment climate in Ukraine brought new players to the Ukrainian land market. Many domestic and foreign investors gained control over Ukrainian farmlands through various leasing schemes and, in some cases, through fraudulent purchases, despite the land sale moratorium (Visser and Mamonova 2011). As a result, export-oriented LFEs emerged in Ukraine. Their size and scale are comparable with the largest latifundia in Brazil and Argentina. To date, the 18 largest LFEs control 1.7 million ha of agricultural land, which constitutes approximately 11 percent of all farmland controlled by large- and middle-sized private farms of Ukraine (Lapa, Lissitsa, and Tovstopyat 2008). The leading position is held by 'agroholdings' (vertically and horizontally integrated groups of affiliated and associated agroenterprises), which has become a customary term to characterise the Ukrainian agricultural development. Agroholdings contribute up to 20 percent in total agricultural production (Kobuta, Sikachyna, and Zhygadlo 2012). These operators expand much faster than the average farm producers and are often associated with land grabbing (Rylko 2009).

The rapid development of large-scale industrial soil-intensive agriculture put Ukraine on the list of the major agricultural exporters in the world. In 2008–2009, Ukraine was the third largest exporter of grain worldwide. Even the 2014 Ukrainian Revolution and consequent civil war did not affect the country's leading position in food exports. In 2014, Ukraine ranked second among exporters of sunflower seed, fifth for barley, sixth for rapeseed and corn (maize), and ninth for wheat (IndexMundi 2014).

But what has happened to Ukrainian peasants? One might expect a rise of rural resistance to large-scale agricultural development, as occurred in many other countries affected by land grabs (McMichael 2006). Instead, Visser and Mamonova (2011) reported incredibly weak rural opposition to large-scale land acquisitions in Ukraine. Even the open moments for contestations, which occurred during the 2014 Ukrainian Revolution, did not trigger peasants' rebellion against the system of LFE's domination.[12]

---

[11]'Ukraine's Ministry of Agrarian Policy and Food, which is responsible for land policy, is currently controlled by the political party Freedom. Although declaring itself to be the right-wing political force, this party proclaims the establishment of a complete ban on the alienation of agricultural lands in its political programme. In the near future, the party plans to create a draft law which would ban the land sales completely (but which would allow the right to sell the lease rights). However, this law is unlikely to be supported by the new Ukrainian parliament. The European Commission, the World Bank, and the IMF [The International Monetary Fund] do not demand that Ukraine should open agricultural land market. They believe that this is our internal affair. The liberalisation of the land market is therefore not expected in the near future' (interview with Andrey Martyn, head of the Department of Land Use Planning of the National University of Bioresources and Nature Management of Ukraine, conducted by email, 18 June 2014).

[12]'During the revolutionary events, the rural population participated in the protests very little, because it is initially more passive and elderly. The typical active participants in the protests are relatively young city dwellers with higher education. In general, the revolution had no impact on the activities

According to McCarthy (2010), the peasants' attitude to land grabbing depends on the 'terms of inclusion' of the local population in land deals. He argues that the way land tenure systems and informal land markets work, the type of land investments and the implementation of smallholder development schemes in villages are critical factors that influence the exclusion or inclusion of local people in land deals.

Below, I distinguish three different terms upon which Ukrainian peasants are incorporated in land deals, which define their attitudes to land grabbing.

4.1. *Illusive inclusion*

The term 'illusive inclusion' is borrowed from poverty and inequality studies. The illusive inclusion occurs in social settings when 'inclusion is ensured but the outcome is not different from that of being excluded' (Joseph 2012, 6). The illusive inclusion of Ukrainian peasants in land deals started with the titling programme in 2001. Although rural dwellers received titles on the distributed land plots, they were hardly able to derive substantial benefits from them. At the time, 95 percent of the title recipients were of retirement and pre-retirement age, and were unable to cultivate the given lands (Koteneva 2010). According to Bondarchuk (2011, 1), 'this process was just a farce, aimed at showing the "fairness" of land distribution and led to the concentration of Ukrainian black soil in the hands of rich rogues'.

Nevertheless, the land titles allow their holders to lease the distributed land plots to LFEs and receive a '*pai*' (from the Ukrainian word for 'share', a word used by the local population to name annual monetary or in-kind compensation for leased land plots). The current average size of the pai, reported by agricultural enterprises, is 500 UAH (equal to 47 Euros) per land parcel of 4 ha (NAS survey 2013). In practice, many enterprises pay the pai in-kind in shares of 5 percent from the crop harvested on the leased lands, which is less than the declared average price (estimations derived from the fieldwork interviews). Many peasants are dissatisfied with the low price they get for their land shares. The pai accounts for up to 4.2 percent of the average household income (Lerman et al. 2006). In cases when peasant families hold livestock, the in-kind pai becomes an additional feed source.

The pai system is, in fact, the continuation of the former kolkhozy and sovkhozy support of households. In the Soviet times,

> households were allowed to use a whole array of collective facilities, from obtaining young livestock from the collective to letting private cattle graze on collective pastures, using kolkhoz machinery, and selling their produce through the sales networks of the collectives. (Visser 2010, 289)

Furthermore, collective farms regularly supplied their production to their workers as a compensation for meagre wages. Previously, this support was informal. It has currently become formalised through contractual transfers, but has also shrunk to only crop sharing. Nevertheless, the formalisation of support has made rural dwellers feel included in the distribution of benefits from land use. Maria (65), an inhabitant of the village Rysanivtsy, said:

---

of rural households. They keep doing the same things they used to do. The new government has not made any significant changes in agricultural policy until this moment' (interview with Andrey Martyn, head of the Department of Land Use Planning of the National University of Bioresources and Nature Management of Ukraine, conducted by email, 18 June 2014).

> Formerly, kolkhoz brought grain to our road with a truck – take as much as you want ... Now they [agroenterprise] pay us the pais. I receive 800 kilograms of wheat for my land plot of 3 hectares. It is not as good as in the Soviet Union, but it is at least something. [...] I feed my chickens with it[13].

Most of the elderly rural population welcomes large-scale land investments in Ukraine. LFEs are seen as successors of Soviet collective farms. Elderly peasants still call them 'kolkhozy' and 'sovkhozy'. The persistence of old terms not only expresses the habits of colloquial speech, but also demonstrates the actual and perceived continuity of the dual system of agricultural production: large-scale (collective) agriculture versus small-scale peasant subsistent farming. Visser, Spoor, and Mamonova (2014), based on the example of Russian agriculture (which underwent a transformation roughly similar to the one in Ukraine), argued that there was no significant redistribution of farmland during the post-socialist land reform: kolkhozy and sovkhozy have been transferred into LFEs, while the rural population continues subsistence farming at their household plots. Nikulin (2011) even applies the term 'post-kolkhoz' to contemporary LFEs to stress the continuity of collective farming. This continuity impacts peasants' emotional expectations of their relationships with LFEs. Furthermore, the use of Soviet language in contemporary speeches demonstrates the rural population's strong nostalgia for the Soviet past. Heady and Gambold-Miller (2006), for instance, demonstrate in one of their case studies how peasants welcome the revitalisation of an abandoned kolkhoz by a new investor, hoping to return to the 'good old times'.

Therefore, the continuation and formalisation of some Soviet practices meets the emotional expectations of elderly peasants and creates a positive attitude towards the ongoing large-scale land acquisitions in Ukraine. These pai recipients feel included in the land deals, although on a smaller scale than they wish to be. Furthermore, the elderly people do not have sufficient labour resources to cultivate the distributed lands, which results in a lack of competition for lands between these peasants and LFEs.

4.2. *Subordinate inclusion*

The fieldwork data indicate that the majority of working-age peasants see large-scale land acquisitions as an opportunity for wage work. The use of the distributed land plots for family farm business is highly constrained by a number of factors: the pro-large-scale agricultural policy of the Ukrainian state, the LFEs' control over the agri-food value-chain, the erosion of peasant entrepreneurial features during the Soviet period, and rural poverty. According to the 2005 FAO Farm Survey, 96 percent of the Ukrainian rural population did not want to start individual farming (Lerman et al. 2006). In the meantime, 24 percent of rural respondents to the 2011 Gorshenin survey indicated a strong desire for a job at an LFE.

The post-Soviet legacy of industrial farming largely defines the rural demand for wage work (Petrick, Wandel, and Karsten 2013). However, the peasants prefer the work at agroholdings to employment at individual farms or kolkhoz-style LFEs. This might be explained by peasants' rational cost-benefit calculations from the subordinate inclusion in the new form of farming. Agroholdings, as a rule, provide decent wages to their employees and offer higher labour standards (Lapa, Lissitsa, and Tovstopyat 2008). To date, the

[13]The interview was conducted in the Rusanivtsy village of the Letichevsk district, Khmelnitsk region, Ukraine, 29 July 2012.

average monthly salary in agriculture is about 1960 UAH (equal to 187 Euros) (UkrStat 2014). The field research for this paper indicates that the workers of agroholdings receive 2–3 times more.

This causes a struggle for incorporation into large-scale agriculture in subordinate positions (subordinate inclusion) among rural dwellers. According to Viktor Prikazhnuk, the director of the 'Obry' agrocompany (a subsidiary of a large American agroholding), more than 30 people are on a waiting list for the position of a combine driver. However, agroholdings require skilled workers without 'bad habits' (i.e. drinking, unreliability), which is often missing in Ukraine (Lerman et al. 2007). According to the FAO Farm Survey (2005), 40 percent of agrocompanies complain of a rural labour shortage, despite high rural unemployment.

The last decade of large-scale agricultural development in the Ukrainian countryside is characterised by the reduction of overall rural poverty. The share of rural households with average per capita monthly expenses below the living wage decreased from 82.6 percent in 2000 to 63.9 percent in 2006[14] (Moroz 2010). Furthermore, there is an increase in the wage work share in household income: from 16.3 percent in 1999 to 23 percent in 2012 (NAS survey 2013; UkrStat 2014). At the same time, however, the rise of salaries in agriculture is accompanied by declining employment rates. The rapidly expanding agroholdings strive to achieve economies of scale and apply labour-saving technologies. This caused the decrease in the rural labour force from 8.9 million people in 1999 to 8.3 million people in 2005, a 6.7 percent decrease (Moroz 2010).

4.3. *Competitive exclusion*

A negative attitude to LFEs is inherent among private family farmers. However, it is difficult to define how peasant-like these farmers are. Many of these farmers are the former Soviet rural *intelligentsia* and elite (agronomists, accountants, chairmen of reorganised kolkhozy and sovkhozy), who managed to detach their land plots during the land reform and accumulated additional lands by leasing them from their neighbours. The average size of the lands cultivated by these farmers is 175 ha (NAS survey 2013). Currently, these farmers account for 5 percent of the gross agricultural product of the country (UkrStat 2014).

Farmers have to compete with LFEs for leased lands and are forced to pay a pai sum equal to the share paid by regional agroenterprises, which is usually beyond farmers' financial capacities.

Furthermore, LFEs, especially agroholdings, are major recipients of indirect and direct state subsidies, such as cash transfers, grants, tax credits and low-interest loans. According to Volodymyr Lapa,[15] the general director of the Ukrainian Agribusiness Club, 60 percent of the total national agricultural subsidies in 2012 were obtained by LFEs. Moreover, the vertical integration of the agroholdings allows them to control the value chain and exclude other agricultural operators from it (Plank 2013). These factors create the competitive exclusion (i.e. exclusion through competition) of farmers from agribusiness and, consequently, from land markets in Ukraine. Private farmer Nikolay (45) described the unequal competition with agroholdings:

[14]In rural areas near cities, rising income might partly be caused by the rural dwellers' increased employment in the cities, or by their engaging in non-agricultural activities.
[15]The interview was conducted in Kiev, Ukraine, 22 July 2012.

> Agroholdings! Who are they? They are bandits! They evade taxes. They do not pay taxes at all! [...] Moreover, they receive millions in state subsidies. No farmer, no *odnoosibnik* [independent peasant] has received any *kopeyka* [cent] from the state. Furthermore, they export the grain. They have access to foreign markets. They export it at a good price. Meanwhile, the resellers grab my grain at the lowest price .... [16]

Due to such unfair competition, many private farmers go bankrupt. The Ukranian State Committee for Statistics declared a slight decrease in the number of private farmers: from 43,000 in 2006 to 40,800 in 2013 (UkrStat 2014). The Committee explains this through farm consolidations and the global financial crisis. However, Kropivko (2012) suggests that, in reality, this decrease is much larger. The fieldwork for this research identified that many farmers are bankrupt or on the brink of bankruptcy, but remain registered in the State Register of Legal Entities. In fact, they are subsistence farmers – producing just enough to guarantee the subsistence of their families, or being hired by LFEs to work the field with their private machinery.

The three above-mentioned terms upon which Ukrainian peasants are incorporated in land deals refute the assumption of peasants' outright opposition to large-scale agricultural development. The land tenure system in Ukraine allows the large group of elderly pai recipients to benefit from the activities of LFEs by engaging in land leasing relationships with them. The absence of smallholder development schemes in Ukrainian villages, as well as the absence of entrepreneurial features among many working-age peasants, prevents them from establishing individual family farms, which leads to their desire for wage work at LFEs. Only when the rural dwellers and LFEs operate on the same markets and compete for the same land (as in the case of private farmers) is the resistance to large-scale agribusiness unavoidable.

5. Household response strategies and socio-economic differentiation of the peasantry

As shown in section 3, the stratification of the peasantry on the eve of land grabbing was minimal. Therefore, I accept the relative homogeneity of the peasant society as the starting point of analysis, and do not disaggregate different rural strata in advance. However, I agree that demographic characteristics, occupation, and slightly different access to production resources in Ukrainian villages in the late 1990s influenced the peasants' choice of one response strategy or another.

Table 1 summarises the arguments presented in the paper about peasants' attitudes to land grabbing, terms of their incorporation in land deals ('terms of inclusion'), different response strategies and consequential stratification within rural communities.

This table is based on the household survey developed and conducted for the purposes of this analysis. The rural households were sampled through a random process, except for the category of family farmers, which was selected based on purposive sampling in order to increase the observations-to-variables ratio for this category. The sample size met the requirements of the 'Rule of 5' (the number of observations is no lower than five per variable); therefore, this sample size is large enough to define the differences between the five groups.

[16]The interview was conducted in the Hreblya village of the Pereyaslav-Khmelnitsky district, Kiev region, Ukraine, 1 August 2012.

Table 1. Household response strategies to land grabs and their outcomes in Ukraine.

N	Household response strategies	Terms of inclusion	Outcome	Consequential rural stratification	Attitude to land sales	Number of respondents
S1	Competition with large farm enterprises	Competitive exclusion	Bankruptcy	Farmers, peasant-workers, subsistence farmers	Negative	5
S2	Taking a free market niche	Illusive inclusion	Coexistence, semi-independence	Odnoosibniks	Negative	13
S3	Employment	Subordinate inclusion	Semi-proletarisation	Peasant-workers	Positive	6
S4	Rural out-migration	Illusive inclusion	Social exclusion	Jobless	Positive	7
S5	Indifference	Illusive inclusion	Dependence on social transfers (pension)	Pensioners-subsistence farmers	Negative	7
			Social exclusion	Marginals	Positive	5

The 'household response strategies' were defined by analysing the daily activities and the main income source of households. The various 'terms of inclusion' were distinguished based on how the rural dwellers managed the distributed land shares and gained access to the products of their own labour. The category 'outcomes' was derived from the analysis of changes in income, occupation and relations to the means of production (land, labour and capital). The agrarian transformation theories were used to construct the 'consequential rural stratification' category. 'Attitude to land sales' refers to the peasants' views on the moratorium. The last column presents the number of respondents per category.

5.1. *S1: Competition with LFEs*

The 'competition with LFEs' strategy conducted by Ukrainian farmers was partly discussed earlier, in the subsection on 'competitive exclusion'. In the present section, I focus on the farmers' efficiency and resilience, as well as prospects for private farming.

Private farmers constitute less than 1 percent of the rural population. The core business of Ukrainian farmers was (and is) grain production, which is threatened by agroholdings that became dominant in this market segment (Kobuta, Sikachyna, and Zhygadlo 2012). In comparison with large-scale agribusiness, small farmers in the fieldwork area have lower yields per hectare. Thus, farmers from the Pereyaslav-Khmelnitskiy district harvest 20 *centners*[17] of wheat per hectare, while the Ukrainian–British agroholding 'Niva Pereyaslavschiny' operating in the same region harvests twice as much, because of its intensive use of fertilisers. The board chairman of this holding, Olexander Yaroschuk, said about the farmers' choice for competition with large-scale agriculture:

> I do not understand what they [private farmers] are doing in this business! They do not know how to be efficient; they do not know the technologies. They cannot compete with us. I do not

[17] 1 centner = 0.1 ton (the centner is a unit of weight often used in Ukraine).

understand why they keep on growing wheat and reject the idea of planting ... strawberries, for example, which is much more labour intensive and does not require economies of scale![18]

Repositioning to another market niche requires significant financial investments, which are often unavailable to farmers. Commercial farmers are less flexible and adaptive (than peasants) to changing environments as they do not control their resource base (more than 50 percent of their lands are leased), often use hired labour and have fixed obligations to suppliers and counterparts (e.g. leasing storage facilities). Furthermore, the labour-intensive farming sector is occupied by peasants, who manage to produce these products at lower costs (see the next subsection).

Unequal competition and farmers' reluctance (and inability) to adapt to large-scale agricultural development, as well the absence of state programmes supporting private farmers, lead to the disappearance of individual commercial farming in Ukraine. Lapa, Lissitsa, and Tovstopyat (2008) expect that, in the coming years, large agroholdings will squeeze the majority of private farmers out from the agriculture sector, and that those who remain will only hold single niches in agroproduction.

5.2. *S2: Taking a free market niche*

The majority of agroholdings in Ukraine specialise in export-oriented intensive monocrop production that brings quick profits. Meanwhile, less profitable, more time-consuming and more labour-intensive farming (such as the production of potatoes, vegetables, fruits, and milk) were left outside the focus of large agribusiness (Prokopa and Borodina 2012). The adaptation strategy of the majority of Ukrainian households consisted of abandoning the grain production sector (where they had been present before the year 2000), and specialising fully in labour-intensive farming.

Table 2 outlines such changes in the production of three major farm products: wheat, potatoes and milk (so chosen because they characterise the division of market niches between the peasantry and large agribusiness). The period before the year 2000 is characterised by a drastic decline in the production and share of agricultural enterprise in total agricultural output, and a rise in peasant farming. With the expansion of LFEs after the year 2000, the market division occurred.

LFEs became specialised in wheat production, producing more than 80 percent of the total wheat harvested. According to official statistics, the share of households has not changed. However, the fieldwork observations showed a drastic decline of wheat production in peasant households compared to previous years. This mismatch between the official data and the actual situation can be explained by calculating the household production based on household consumption, which in the case of wheat is supplemented by the in-kind pai received from LFEs (which is not reflected in official statistics).

The reverse is observed in the milk production sector. The share of dairy farm enterprises has decreased by 30 percent from the year 2000 to now; in contrast, peasants continued increasing milk production and have become dominant in this market segment. Currently, peasant households contribute up to 81 percent of the milk produced and up to 67 percent of the milk marketed in Ukraine (Tarassevych 2005). Potato production is less indicative, as households were always the major potato producers, and, since the

[18]The interview was conducted in the Pereyaslavskoye village of the Pereyaslav-Khmelnitskiy district, Kiev region, 1 August 2012.

Table 2. Production (and share in total production) of wheat, potatoes and milk per agricultural producer (million tons).

	1990	1995	2000	2001	2002	2004	2007	2009	2012
Wheat									
Agricultural enterprises[a]	30.2 (100%)	15.7 (97%)	9.2 (90%)	18.7 (88%)	17.1 (83%)	14.6 (83%)	11.5 (83%)	17 (83%)	12.7 (82%)
Households	0.1 (0%)	0.5 (3%)	1 (10%)	2.6 (12%)	3.5 (17%)	2.9 (17%)	2.4 (17%)	3.8 (17%)	3.1 (18%)
Total	30.3 (100%)	16.2 (100%)	10.2 (100%)	21.3 (100%)	20.6 (100%)	17.5 (100%)	13.9 (100%)	20.9 (100%)	15.8 (100%)
Potatoes									
Agricultural enterprises	4.9 (29%)	0.6 (4%)	0.2 (1%)	0.3 (2%)	0.2 (1%)	0.3 (1%)	0.4 (2%)	0.4 (2%)	0.7 (2%)
Households	11.9 (71%)	14.1 (96%)	19.6 (99%)	17 (98%)	16.4 (99%)	20.5 (99%)	18.7 (98%)	19.2 (98%)	22.5 (98%)
Total	16.8 (100%)	14.7 (100%)	19.8 (100%)	17.3 (100%)	16.6 (100%)	20.8 (100%)	19.1 (100%)	19.6 (100%)	23.2 (100%)
Milk									
Agricultural enterprises	18.6 (76%)	9.4 (54%)	3.7 (29%)	3.6 (27%)	3.5 (24%)	2.5 (19%)	2.2 (18%)	2.2 (18%)	2.4 (20%)
Households	5.9 (24%)	7.8 (45%)	9 (71%)	9.8 (73%)	10.7 (76%)	11.2 (81%)	10.1 (82%)	9.4 (82%)	8.9 (80%)
Total	24.5 (100%)	17.3 (100%)	12.7 (100%)	13.4 (100%)	14.1 (100%)	13.4 (100%)	12.3 (100%)	11.6 (100%)	11.3 (100%)

Source: UkrStat (1990–2013).

[a]The State Committee of Ukraine for Statistics (UkrStat) does not distinguish large farm enterprises (LFEs) from private farmers in its reports, and calculates 'agricultural enterprises' production as a sum total of the LFEs and private farmers' production.

collapse of the Soviet Union, their share in potato yields has been increasing. LFEs are not interested in potato production, even though domestic demand for this farm product is high. This demand is met by potatoes from peasant households. Peasants contribute up to 98 percent of the total harvest of potatoes in the country. Furthermore, they produce 86 percent of the vegetables and 85 percent of fruits and berries. In total, 52.7 percent of the gross agricultural output is produced by rural households (UkrStat 2014).

In their study of the post-Soviet peasantry's adaptation, O'Brien, Patsiorkovski, and Wegren (2004, 474) argued that 'those household that have made a more successful adaptation to a developing market economy by growing and selling more food would also receive a higher proportion of income from that source'. Indeed, the Ukrainian peasants who took the free market niches became relatively independent (the largest income share comes from subsistence farming and selling their products at local markets). These rural dwellers are called '*odnoosibniks*' (independent peasants).

Odnoosibniks are largely reminiscent of the middle peasants, who have a self-controlled resource base, derive their income wholly or mainly from their own labour and exhibit a degree of self-sufficiency (Deere and de Janvry 1979). According to the fieldwork observations, every small village of 40 households has at least 1–3 odnoosibnik families. The southern regions of Ukraine feature even larger concentrations of these independent peasants. Typical odnoosibniks are middle-aged and older married couples who hold livestock, cultivate household plots and engage in local market relations, but produce just enough to meet the pressures of simple reproduction. Although not every subsistence farmer is called 'odnoosibnik' by their fellow villagers (due to their being of retirement age, or the death of one of the spouses), this study distinguishes 13 peasant households (out of the 43 participants) which adopted the 'taking a free market niche' strategy. These small-scale agricultural producers outcompete commercial farmers due to their capacity for 'self-exploitation'[19] (increasing labour inputs at the expense of leisure) that allows them to produce at lower costs and adjust to market changes. Odnoosibnik Luba (54) describes the impact of market price fluctuation on her family's labour:

> We are like slaves, working from sunrise till late at night. What did my children see? No vacation, nothing. We have to pay for everything: for milk certification, for feed, for a place at a local market .... And then they [buyers] say: 'your milk is too expensive,[20] it costs 8 hryvnias in a supermarket, and you sell it for 10'. We have to sell for 8, what else can we do ... ?[21]

The labour-intensive type of niche farming operated by rural dwellers and the lack of productive resources to expand their households at the expense of former-collective land plots prevent any competition between peasants and LFEs at this stage of agricultural development. Peasants' occupation of market niches free from large agribusiness guarantees their subsistence and makes the coexistence scenario possible. However, for how long? Olivier de Schutter (2011, 261) argued:

[19]The concept of 'self-exploitation' was developed by Chayanov in *The theory of peasant economy* (1925).

[20]Meanwhile, the milk prices in Ukraine are very low, especially according to international standards, which allows resellers to make a profit on it (see Van Der Ploeg [2009] about the Parmalat corporation's imports of Ukrainian milk to Italy).

[21]The interview was conducted in the Hreblya village of the Pereyaslav-Khmelnitsky district, Kiev region, Ukraine, 2 August 2012.

the coexistence scenario will likely be short-lived: it will simply be a slow motion path to the transition towards a rural economy dominated by large production units, in which small-scale farming will be marginalized and subordinated to the large production units and in which further rural migration will be encouraged.

5.4. *S3: Looking for employment opportunities*

The struggle for incorporation into large-scale agriculture on terms of employment was already mentioned as one of the rural strategies. Below I discuss means of subsistence and persistence of this rural stratum. Wage work accounted for 41 percent of the rural family income, with at least one family member employed by an agroenterprise (FAO Farm Survey 2005); subsistence farming on household plots remains the second source of subsistence for such families. The combination of wage work with subsistence farming created the basis for the 'peasant-worker' label. This rural stratum of semi-peasants, semi-workers is not unique. In the American colonies, slaves were forced to grow some part of their own subsistence (Mintz and Price 1973), in Zanzibar rural dwellers received small food plots in exchange for a rent in labour (Cooper 1980) and in colonial Sumatra plantation coolies were assigned unused estate fields to cultivate consumption crops in their 'spare time' (Stoler 1986).

The Ukrainian case might be seen differently, as the peasant-workers are often landholders who lease their lands to LFEs. Farmer Olexander (41) calls this situation 'the Ukrainian land paradox', under which 'the bourgeoisie leases lands from its proletariat'.[22] Indeed, many farm workers are owners of land shares cultivated by the enterprises that employ them. However, the shareholders' engagement in corporate decision making is rather nominal, and these relations remain characterised as 'illusive inclusion' in land deals.

According to class-based theory, the 'peasant-worker' is a temporary formation: the capitalist class would tend to subordinate small landowners by reducing them to dependent labourers (Paige 1975). In contrast, Stoler (1986, 43) argued that the combination of wage work and subsistence farming is a stable mode, and represents 'a state of "flux equilibrium" advantageous to management and labour alike'. LFEs in Ukraine make no efforts to have the lands in ownership and are satisfied with a long-term lease, as it does not require huge capital investments. For rural dwellers, the employment at LFEs increases the family monetary income, while also allowing land ownership and a peasant mode of production. As a result, this rural stratum has the lowest poverty risk, according to Vlasenko's (2008) estimations.

5.5. *S4: Rural out-migration*

During the economic recession that came after the collapse of the Soviet Union, many people moved to rural areas as it was easier to survive by relying on private subsistence economies. During 1990–1999, Ukrainian villages gained more than 350,000 people[23]

[22]The interview was conducted in the Yerkivtsi village of the Pereyaslav-Khmelnitsky district, Kiev region, Ukraine,1 August 2012.

[23]It should be noted that migration is not the major component of the rural population change in Ukraine. The natural decrease has been (and remains) very high in Ukraine, which is the major reason for depopulation in the countryside. During 1991–2011, the mortality rate exceeded the natality rate and produced a natural decrease of 2 million people, which accounted for 14 percent of the rural population.

(2 percent increase of rural population) due to the in-migration of former rural residents. These in-migrants had moved to the cities prior to the economic crisis of the 1990s, but were now forced to come back due to limited employment opportunities in urban areas (Skryzhevska and Karacsonyi 2012).

The direction of the migration flow reversed with the emergence of large-scale land investments. Since 2002, rural out-migration has outpaced in-migration. During 2002–2011, more than 2 million people (15 percent of the rural population) left the countryside (UkrStat 2014). The incomers did not compensate for this decrease, and the net migration was –265,000 people (or –1.6 percent of the rural population) during the last decade. The escape from villages can be seen as a population response to large-scale land acquisitions. The reluctance to adapt to capitalist agriculture made some rural dwellers move to the cities (or abroad). The out-migration was stimulated by the short-term possibility to sell land shares (through various exchange schemes that were not forbidden by the moratorium at that time[24]), which gave peasants the money to leave the countryside.

However, the out-migrated rural dwellers are not able to compete with urban residents for well-paid jobs due to the low quality of rural education. As a result, rural dwellers accept low-paid and often informal work in the cities, or join the ranks of the urban unemployed (Skryzhevska and Karacsonyi 2012).

Since 2005, the rural net migration outflow has been slowing down: the out-migration remains the same, while the in-migration has increased. The return of many rural dwellers to villages was caused by urban 'push factors' (i.e. high costs of living, demand for qualified labour, urban unemployment). Contrary to the population return in the transition period when the land rights were still secured, current in-migration does not guarantee the subsistence of those who are coming back to the villages. The absence of household and land plots made these people bound for miserable living conditions. The fieldwork data shows that many of the returning peasants experience social exclusion, and later find employment in a (non-)agricultural sector or join their parents (or relatives) in household farming.

5.6. *S5: Indifference*

The rural residents who showed no changes in response to land grabbing were elderly widows and working-age villagers who are not able/willing to adapt to socio-economic changes. While the indifference of elderly widows can be explained by the guaranteed income from social transfers (pensions) and the lack of labour resources for taking free market niches, the second group depicts the inability of a few people to adapt to market conditions, which often leads to their social exclusion[25] and marginalisation.

The elderly widows represent about 12 percent of the rural population (NAS survey 2013). They continue household cultivation at the scale they used to do before the collapse of the Soviet Union. It is difficult to distinguish this group from those who have chosen the 'taking a free market niche' strategy, because elderly widows also produce labour-intensive farm products, which are included in the total agricultural output of peasant households in

[24]During 2002–2004, the option existed to exchange land plots for other properties, which did not contradict the moratorium on land sales. In such a way, many rural dwellers 'sold' their lands. Later, these exchange operations were forbidden by the new version of the moratorium (Yurchenko and Miroshnichenko 2006).

[25]Social exclusion is a process in which individuals or entire communities of people are systematically blocked from rights, opportunities and resources, which are normally available to members of society and which are key to social integration (Silver 1994).

statistics. However, their agriculture-derived income is much lower than that of *odnoosibniks*, and the major source of their living is their pension, which provides a small but stable income (Vlasenko 2008).

The above-mentioned rural household strategies demonstrate that the least adaptive strategies (i.e. competition, migration and indifference) are more likely to lead to poverty. The resilience to changes often results in lower income, social exclusion and socio-economic dependency. Meanwhile, the adaptive strategies (i.e. taking a free market niche, and searching for employment) are less risky and practiced by nearly half of the survey respondents.[26] This demonstrates the ability of many peasants to adapt to and coexist with the capitalist agriculture. Thus, under the present conditions, the development of large-scale industrial agriculture in Ukraine does not lead to the disappearance of peasants or the creation of landless rural labour. Instead, it stimulates the appearance of self-provisioning small-scale rural households and creates peasant-workers (reminiscent of the 'Soviet peasant'), who, although they have wage work, remain dependent on subsistence agriculture.

6. Peasants' personal gains from land grabbing versus community benefits

The peasants' choice between pursuing self-interests and the interests of the whole community, and their concerns over material rather than immaterial benefits from land deals, became demonstrable in their talks about the cancellation of the land moratorium.[27] Although the opening of land markets will only formally legalise the ownership of LFEs, which are already *de facto* landholders in Ukraine, peasants express a negative attitude toward land sales. According to the 2011 Gorshenin survey, 70 percent of villagers are convinced that farmland should not be sold as a commodity. Petro (76), from the village Trebukhovtsy, forecasts negative consequences for rural communities from land sales: 'As soon the moratorium is eliminated, bandits will grab all the lands. People will not get the pai anymore, nobody would care about villagers, nobody would need them. The Ukrainian village will disappear, it will die'.[28] Despite these negative predictions, Petro plans to sell his land plot and move to a city. The personal benefits seem to outweigh community interests.

The 2013 NAS survey indicates the desire to sell land among 23 percent of the rural population; 12 percent have not decided yet. The share of those who would not sell the land after the moratorium's cancellation has been decreasing. In 2010, the share of rural dwellers who wanted to continue leasing their land plots to LFEs after the moratorium's cancellation was 84 percent, in 2011 they accounted for 80 percent and in 2013 their number has dropped to 65 percent (NAS survey 2013). This could be explained by an ageing rural population (24.1 percent of rural residents are older than 60), and

[26]The least adaptive strategies (competition, migration and indifference) are practiced by 24 households out of the participating 43, while the adaptive strategies (taking a free market niche, and searching for employment) are practiced by 19 respondents. Taking into account the fact that the sample for private farmers was chosen according to the purposive selection method, the proportion of those who adapt and those who do not adapt might be approximately the same at the population scale.

[27]The fieldwork interviews were conducted in the summer of 2012. At that time, the moratorium on land sales was expected to be cancelled in January 2013. It was a very important topic for the rural population, and they actively discussed the pros and cons of the coming changes.

[28]The interview was conducted in the Trebukhovtsy village of the Letichevsk district, Khmelnitsk region, Ukraine, 28 July 2012.

their unwillingness to see their offspring working on these lands and/or living in the countryside (40 percent of the respondents of the 2011 Gorshenin survey answered that they want their children to live in urban areas). Therefore, a number of elderly peasants are intending to sell their lands in order to improve their material standing or help their children in cities. Maria (69) from the village Rusanivtsy explains her choice in favour of land sales:

> I will sell my land plot. Why do I need it? I am already an old woman. I will not farm it. If they give me at least a *kopeyka* [cent] for this land .... I need to help my children. One of my sons lives in poverty. I will sell my land and give the money to him. Maybe he will get out of his troubles ....[29]

The peasants' preferences for personal benefits despite the negative consequences for the whole community can also be inferred from their reaction to the soil degradation caused by large-scale agricultural development. In the in-depth interviews for this research, peasants criticised the LFEs' monocrop agriculture and fertiliser usage; however, no one was intending to withdraw his or her shares from their tenants, even though they violate environmental standards. The rent price was the factor that made a difference, while environmental sustainability played a minor role. Only 5 percent of rural dwellers are concerned about ecological problems in their villages (Gorshenin survey 2011). In fact, LFEs often entice peasants from more eco-friendly private farmers by offering larger pais for leasing their lands.

When choosing between possible tenants for their land plots, peasants are also guided by the prospects of social support from LFEs. Apart from the formalised support (pai payments), LFEs frequently pursue corporate citizenship programmes, which allow them to gain the sympathies of the local population; this, in turn, ensures their control over farmlands. Viktor Prikazhnuk, the director of the 'Obry' agrocompany, describes his idea of corporate social responsibility:

> Formerly, kolkhozy helped rural dwellers a lot. People expect the same from us. We have to help, otherwise they could lease their lands to someone else .... People ask us to buy equipment for the local hospital, or to repair the roads. We allocate money for this .... There was a case of fire in one rural house. The inhabitant asked us to help. We gave him some money and cipher to repair the roof.[30]

Furthermore, peasants get some assistance with household plot cultivation and seeds from LFEs (FAO Farm Survey 2005). According to the fieldwork, this support is the major peasant argument against land sales; concerns over land sovereignty or land ownership do not play a part. Tamara (55) from Hreblya village is convinced: 'If we will sell our lands, the new owners will do nothing for rural dwellers. The renting gives us a possibility to control them, to ask for assistance'.[31]

These arguments contradict the assumption of many rural civil society organisations, which believe that peasants' resistance to land sales comes in protest to the ecological

[29]The interview was conducted in the Rusanivtsy village of the Letichevsk district, Khmelnitsk region, Ukraine, 29 July 2012.
[30]The interview was conducted in the Trebukhotsy village of the Letichevsk district, Khmelnitsk region, Ukraine, 28 July 2012.
[31]The interview was conducted in the Hreblya village of the Pereyaslav-Khmelnitsky district, Kiev region, Ukraine, 2 August 2012.

unsustainability of large-scale industrial agriculture, the destruction of the 'peasant way' of life and the deprivation of rural community interests. The Ukrainian case demonstrates that the rural attitude to land deals and large-scale agriculture largely depends on the personal gains peasants receive from land leases versus sales (which outmatch community interests), and that material benefits (such as social support and pai size) take precedence over more ideological concerns (i.e. about environmental sustainability and land sovereignty).

7. Discussion of the research findings' generalisability

This research examines various rural response strategies toward large-scale land acquisitions and industrial farm development in Ukraine, and investigates socio-economic transformations within rural communities as a consequence of peasants' adaptation to these processes (as opposed to resistance). The study goes beyond the common assumption of peasants' outright opposition to land grabbing. It critically looks at peasants' attitudes to land deals, ongoing changes in rural household activities, and rural arguments for or against land sales.

The paper provides an empirical confirmation of McCarthy's (2010) argument that the peasants' attitude to land grabbing critically depends on the local population's 'terms of inclusion' in land deals. The 'illusive inclusion' of the Ukrainian rural population in land deals is done through the formalisation of LFEs' support to households (pai payments and corporate social responsibility programmes), which, together with the continuity of the dual system of agriculture (large-scale versus small-scale), creates a positive attitude among many original landholders. Some peasants' sympathy toward large-scale land acquisitions is achieved through the option of 'subordinate inclusion' by employment at LFEs. In a context of high rural unemployment, low salaries in agriculture and a lack of material and cultural stimuli for creating independent family farming, subordinate inclusion is seen as a desired option and leads to the peasants' struggle for incorporation in large agribusiness. Only when the villagers and large agrocompanies operate in the same markets and compete for the same land is the rural resistance to land grabbing unavoidable.

This research has shown that peasants' response strategies toward large-scale agricultural development influence the socio-economic stratification of rural dwellers. The more adaptive peasant responses lead to more advantageous positions of their households in rural communities, while the least adaptive strategies cause peasants' social exclusion and increase their poverty risk.

The paper demonstrates that the coexistence of small- and large-scale farming became possible due to the market segmentation and rural households' ability to adjust their production in order to avoid competition with LFEs. However, the persistency of this 'coexistence scenario' depends on trends in the world food market, which currently keeps Ukrainian LFEs in the crop export niche, and the dependency of land investors on renting agreements with peasants, who *de jure* remain the owners of Ukrainian farmland, and, thereby, may 'discipline' the investors.

Furthermore, this research questions the idealisation of the peasantry. The empirical data demonstrates that Ukrainian peasants respond to land sales based on their estimation of possible material benefits derived from the lease, sale or cultivation of their lands, while concerns with land sovereignty, the 'peasant way' of life and environmental sustainability are largely absent in the countryside. Moreover, despite the peasants' collectivist features, their self-interest in land deals often outweighs the importance of community interests.

However, how generalisable are these findings?

Because of high land availability and low rural population density in Ukraine, land grabbing is pursued without the physical displacement of the local population. This factor might be seen as a point of difference in comparison with many 'typical' cases of land grabbing. However, recent scholars have noted a shift from land grabbing to *land control* grabbing, which is not always accompanied by land purchases and peasants' relocations (White et al. 2012). The various forms of acquiring control over land and related resources include purchase, lease, contract farming, forest conservation and so on. In his analysis of expansion of sugarcane and oil palm plantations in Guatemala, Alonso-Fradejas (2012) gives an example of lease schemes and contract farming agreements which resulted in the disenfranchisement and impoverishment of the local population. Wilkinson, Reydon, and Di Sabbato (2012) analyse land grabs for soy cultivation in Brazil where some agricompanies apply models that are based on land leases and complete responsibility for the management of agricultural production, turning the landowner into a mere 'rentier'. Thus, the Ukrainian example does not seem to be an exceptional case.

Another fact which could influence the general application of the findings is the Ukrainian peasants' exclusion from the distributive land reform in its early stages. The land distribution process did not make the official landowners dependent on their lands, and, therefore, the loss of control over their property does not endanger the peasants' subsistence. However, voluntary transfers of land ownership are common even in countries where peasants had a chance to farm their lands before land grabbing. Thus, in Chile, lack of access to loans for land reform beneficiaries and the existence of agrarian debts prevented them from investing in the emerging fruit and vegetable activities. As a consequence, most peasants sold their lands to entrepreneurs, who could invest in these profitable activities (de Janvry and Sadoulet 2002).

Certainly, there are a lot of country-specific factors that influence rural responses to land grabbing. The moratorium on land sales and the preservation of the peasants' official ownership of farmland is not a common practice in the countries affected by land grabbing. However, the prohibition of open land sales is just a formal ban for agroholdings, who are *de facto* land holders in Ukraine (Spoor and Visser 2011). Furthermore, the degree of population ageing is very high in Ukraine and is significantly higher than in other counties affected by land grabs: 24.1 percent of Ukrainian rural dwellers are older than 60 (Skryzhevska and Karacsonyi 2012). As a comparison, the number of rural inhabitants in this age group constitutes 7 percent of the rural population in Ghana (which is among the highest in Africa), and 7.5 percent in rural India (Chuks 2004, CensusIndia 2010). Among the other country-specific factors are: the Soviet history of collective agriculture, the erosion of peasant-like features such as 'individualism' and 'property consciousness economizing', and the abandonment of farmlands previous to land grabs. However, how significant is the influence of these factors on rural responses to large-scale land acquisitions?

With this paper, I argue that the common assumptions about peasant politics in large-scale agricultural development should be reconsidered. The rural propensity to adapt and find benefits even in land grabbing can play an important role in shaping policies of rural social movements and developing recommendations to governments and investors in regard to large-scale land acquisitions. Moreover, taking into account the specificity of the Ukrainian case,[32] the new insights on peasants' arguments and response strategies to

[32]The ongoing Russification of parts of Ukraine (especially the annexation of Crimea by the Russian Federation in 2014) is less likely to affect the dynamics described in the paper. The agricultural systems in Russia and Ukraine have strong similarities. Land reforms in both countries were

land grabbing should be integrated in the land grab academic debates. This work indicates the need for further research on rural communities' responses and differentiation in the context of large-scale land acquisitions.

Acknowledgements

The research for this paper benefited from a grant provided by the Land Deal Politics Initiative (LDPI), which enabled the fieldwork in Ukraine. I would like to express my gratitude to a rural community in the Pereyaslav-Khmelnitskiy district for cooperation and logistical support, a Ukrainian-American agroholding (which preferred to remain anonymous) for disclosure of information and providing access to its farms, and my colleague and companion on this trip, Simone Donati, a photojournalist from Italy. I would like to thank Dr. Oane Visser, Dr. Jun Borras and Dr. Martin Petrick for their valuable inputs for this paper, and all other colleagues who provided comments and feedback on earlier versions.

Funding

This work was supported by a Land Deal Politics Initiative (LDPI) 2012 Small Grant to carry out research on land grabbing.

References

Adnan, S. 2011. Resistance to accumulation by dispossession in the context of neoliberal capitalism and globalization. Paper presented at the International Conference on Global Land Grabbing, Ithaca.

Allina-Pisano, J. 2002. Reorganization and its discontents: A case study in Voronezh oblast. In *Rural reform in post-Soviet Russia*, eds. D. O'Brien and S. Wegren, 298–324. Washington: Woodrow Wilson Center Press.

Alonso-Fradejas, A. 2012. Land control-grabbing in Guatemala: The political economy of contemporary agrarian change. *Canadian Journal of Development Studies* 33, no. 4: 509–28.

Araghi, F. 1995. Global depeasantization, 1945–1990. *Sociological Quarterly* 36, no. 2: 337–68.

Bernstein, H. 2004. Changing before our very eyes: Agrarian questions and the politics of land in capitalism today. *Journal of Agrarian Change* 4, no. 1–2: 190–225.

Boltvinik, J. 2012. Poverty and persistence of the peasantry, http://www.crop.org/viewfile.aspx?id=261 (accessed May 25, 2013).

Bondarchuk, A.V. 2011. Analysis of land reform results in Ukraine, http://rk.org.ua/rk/582/1.html (accessed August 21, 2012).

---

implemented by similar schemes: after the collapse of the Soviet Union, land parcels were distributed by means of land share certificates to former workers of reorganised kolkhozy and sovkhozy. To date, the dual system of agricultural production has developed in both countries: a dominance of LFEs (including vertically and horizontally integrated agroholdings) and the small-scale subsistence agriculture of rural households. Allina-Pisano, in her book *The post-Soviet Potemkin village* (2007), studies the Black Earth regions of Russia and Ukraine, and describes how, despite different formal reform policies in the regions on both sides of the border, the resulting farm structure was much alike. Furthermore, Visser and Spoor (2011), in their study of land grabbing in the former Soviet Union, reveal many similarities between the processes of large-scale land acquisitions in Russia and Ukraine. The main difference between these countries concerning land tenure is that Russia lifted the moratorium on land sales in 2001, while Ukraine has not yet done so. However, the Ukrainian farmlands in Crimea, which are currently controlled by Russia, will remain under moratorium until Russia develops a plan of Crimean Territorial Development. Moreover, due to its gas and oil revenues, the Russian state has more resources to invest in agricultural projects. In Ukraine, the state has very few resources.

Borodina, O. 2009. Food security and socioeconomic aspects of sustainable rural development in Ukraine. IIASA Interim Report, IR-09-053, Laxenburg, http://webarchive.iiasa.ac.at/Admin/PUB/Documents/IR-09–053.pdf (accessed September 29, 2014).

Borras, S.M. Jr., and J.C. Franco. 2013. Global land grabbing and political reactions 'from below'. *Third World Quarterly* 34, no. 9: 1723–47.

Borras, S.M. Jr., P. McMichael, and I. Scoones, 2010. The politics of biofuels, land and agrarian change: Editors' introduction. *Journal of Peasant Studies* 37, no. 4: 575–92.

Boyer, J. 2010. Food security, food sovereignty, and local challenges for transnational agrarian movements: The Honduras case. *Journal of Peasant Studies* 37, no. 2: 319–51.

CensusIndia. 2010. Population composition, http://www.censusindia.gov.in/vital_statistics/srs/Chap_2_-_2010.pdf (accessed May 29, 2013).

Chayanov, A.V. 1925. Peasant farm organisation. Published in English in 1966 in A.V.Chayanov, The theory of peasant economy. Homewood: American Economic Association.

Chuks, J.M. 2004. Population ageing and poverty in rural Ghana. http://www.wikieducator.org/images/2/26/AGRIC_chuksmba.pdf (accessed May 20, 2013).

Cohen, S.F. 1980. *Bukharin and the Bolshevik revolution: A political biography, 1888–1938*. Oxford: Oxford University Press.

Cooper, F. 1980. Peasants, capitalists and historians. *Journal of Southern African Studies* 7, no. 2: 284–314.

Csaki, C., and Z. Lerman. 1997. Land reform and farm restructuring in East Central Europe and CIS in the 1990s: Expectations and achievements after the first five years. *European Review of Agricultural Economics* 24: 428–52. doi:10.1093/erae/24.3-4.428

Deere, C.D., and A. de Janvry. 1979. A conceptual framework for the empirical analysis of peasants. *American Journal of Agricultural Economics*, 61, no. 4: 601–11.

De Janvry, A., and E. Sadoulet. 2002. World poverty and the role of agricultural technology: Direct and indirect effects. *Journal of Development Studies* 38, no. 4: 1–26.

De Schutter, O. 2011. How not to think of land-grabbing: Three critiques of large-scale investments in farmland. *Journal of Peasant Studies* 38, no. 2: 249–79.

Desmarais, A.A. 2002. Peasants speak - the Vía Campesina: Consolidating an international peasant and farm movement. *Journal of Peasant Studies* 29, no. 2: 91–124.

Edelman, M. and A. León. 2013. Cycles of land grabbing in Central America: An argument for history and a case study in the Bajo Aguán, Honduras. *Third World Quarterly* 34, no. 9: 1697–1722.

FAO Farm Survey. 2005. Results are presented in Lerman *et al.* (2006).

Gorshenin survey. 2011. Socio-economic situation in the contemporary Ukrainian village [in Ukrainian]. http://institute.gorshenin.ua/researches/81_Sotsialnoekonomichne_stanovishche_.html (accessed multiple times 2013–2014).

Gourevitch, P. 1986. *Politics in Hard Times*. Ithaca: Cornell University Press.

Heady, P., and L. Gambold-Miller. 2006. Nostalgia and the emotional economy: A comparative look at rural Russia. In *Postsocialism: Politics and emotions in central and Eastern Europe*, ed. M. Svašek, 34–52.

Hickey, S., and A. du Toit. 2007. Adverse incorporation, social exclusion and chronic poverty, http://www.chronicpoverty.org/uploads/publication_files/WP81_Hickey_duToit.pdf (accessed May 29, 2013).

Humphrey, C. 2002. Subsistence farming and the peasantry as an idea in contemporary Russia. In *Post Socialist Peasant?*, eds. P. Leonard and D. Kaneff, 136–60. New York: Palgrave.

IndexMundi. 2014. Agricultural production by country, http://www.indexmundi.com/agriculture/?commodity=wheat&graph=production (accessed June 22, 2014).

Joseph, K.J. 2012. In search of spaces of social exclusion in innovation systems. The case of plantation agriculture in India. Paper presented at the first International Conference on Development and Innovation in the Emerging Economies. Punjabi University, Patiala.

Kay, S. 2012. *Positive investment alternatives to large-scale land acquisitions or leases*. Transnational Institute for Hands off the Land Alliance, Amsterdam.

Kobuta, I., O. Sikachyna, and V. Zhygadlo. 2012. Wheat export economy in Ukraine. FAO Policy studies on rural transition.

Koteneva, O. 2010. Land market: Salvation for black soil or a forthcoming tragedy? [in Russian], http://rescomzem.gov.ua/vse-novosti/stati,-intervyu/ryinok-zemli:-spasenie-dlya-chernozemov-ili-gibel.html (accessed September 19, 2012).

Kropivko, A. 2012. Farmers realities. [in Ukrainian] *Agrobusiness Journal* 9 (232) May, http://www.agro-business.com.ua/component/content/article/32-2011-05-11-22-31-13/1048-2012-05-18-14-59-07.html (accessed September 24, 2014).
Lapa, V., A. Lissitsa, and A. Tovstopyat. 2008. Super-large farms in Ukraine and land market. Paper presented at IAMO Forum 2008, Hulle.
Lerman, Z., S. Csaki, and G. Feder. 2004. Evolving farm structures and land use patterns in former socialist countries. *Quarterly Journal of International Agriculture* 43, no. 4: 309–35.
Lerman, Z., D. Sedik, N. Pugachev, and A. Goncharuk. 2006. Ukraine after 2000: A fundamental change in land and farm policy? Discussion Paper. Hebrew University of Jerusalem.
Lerman, Z., D. Sedik, N. Pugachov, and A. Goncharuk. 2007. *Rethinking agricultural reform in Ukraine*. Halle: IAMO publication.
Malienko, A. 2010. Problems of agricultural reforms in Ukraine. [in Ukrainian] *Zerkalo Nedeli*, http://gazeta.zn.ua/SOCIETY/problemy_agrarnyh_reform_v_ukraine.html (accessed June 22, 2014).
Mamonova, N. 2013. Defenders of the countryside: Focal outbreaks of civil protest. [in Russian], http://civilsolidarity.wordpress.com/2013/05/05/защитники-подмосковья-очаговые-вспы/ (accessed June 01, 2013).
Mamonova, N., and O. Visser. 2014. State marionettes, phantom organisations or genuine movements? The paradoxical emergence of rural social movements in post-socialist Russia. *Journal of Peasant Studies* 41, no. 4: 491–516.
Mathijs, E., and J. Swinnen. 1998. The economics of agricultural decollectivization in East Central Europe and the former Soviet Union. *Economic Development and Cultural Change* 47, no. 1: 1–26.
McCarthy, J.F. 2010. Processes of inclusion and adverse incorporation: Oil palm and agrarian change in Sumatra, Indonesia. *Journal of Peasant Studies* 37, no. 4: 821–50.
McMichael, P. 2006. Peasant prospects in the neoliberal age. *New Political Economy* 11, no. 3: 407–18.
Mintz, S., and R. Price. 1973. *An anthropological approach to the study of Afro-American history*. New Haven: Yale University.
Moroz, S. 2010. Changes in rural areas of Ukraine: Problems and opportunities. Paper presented at the 118th seminar of the EAAE, Ljubliana.
NAS survey. 2013. Land relations in Ukraine: Sociological portrait of the situation. The Centre of Social Expertise of the Institute of Sociology of NAS of Ukraine. [in Ukrainian] http://www.dazru.gov.ua/terra/control/uk/publish/article;jsessionid=4A3099EDFB03CBDA0B75C604240F01B2?art_id=144665&cat_id=130839 (accessed multiple times 2013–2014).
Nikulin, A. 2011. From post-kolkhoz to oligarkhoz. *Bulletin of the Russian Peoples' Friendship University*. Sociology, 2.
O'Brien, D.J., V.V. Patsiorkovski, and S.K. Wegren. 2004. Poverty and adaptation in rural Russia. *Journal of Peasant Studies* 31, no. 3–4: 457–88.
Paige, J. 1975. *A theory of rural class conflict, Agrarian revolution*. New York: The Free Press.
Petrick, M. and M.R. Carter. 2009. Critical masses in the decollectivisation of post-Soviet agriculture. *European Review of Agricultural Economics* 36, no. 2: 231–52.
Petrick, M., J. Wandel, and K. Karsten. 2013. Rediscovering the virgin lands: Agricultural investment and rural livelihoods in a Eurasian frontier area. *World Development* 43: 164–79.
Plank, C. 2013. Land grabs in the black earth: Ukrainian oligarchs and international investors, http://www.tni.org/sites/www.tni.org/files/download/land_in_europe_1.pdf (accessed June 23, 2013).
Prokopa, J., and E. Borodina. 2012. What model of the agricultural sector need Ukraine? [in Russian] *Mirror of the week*, 18 May, http://zn.ua/ECONOMICS/kakaya_model_agrosektora__nuzhna_ukraine-102318.html (accessed September 19, 2012).
Pye, O. 2010. The biofuel connection – transnational activism and the palm oil boom. *Journal of Peasant Studies* 37, no. 4: 851–74.
Quan, J. 2000. Land tenure, economic growth and poverty in Sub-Saharan Africa. In *Evolving land rights, policy and tenure in Africa*, ed. C. Toulmin and J. Quan, 197–206. London: IIED.
Rosset, M., B.M. Sosa, A.M. Jaime, and D.R. Lozano. 2011. The Campesinoto-campesino agroecology movement of ANAP in Cuba: Social process methodology in the construction of sustainable peasant agriculture and food sovereignty. *Journal of Peasant Studies* 38, no. 1: 161–91.
Rylko, D. 2009. New agricultural operators (agroholdings) in Russia and Black Sea FSU: Causes, current state, and future challenges. http://www.agribenchmark.org/fileadmin/Dateiablage/B-Cash-Crop/Conferences/2010/Presentations/a2-_agroholdings_in_Russia_Rylko.pdf (accessed September 29, 2014)

Schneider, A. 2011. What shall we do without our land? Land grabs and resistance in rural Cambodia. Paper presented at the International Conference on Global Land Grabbing, 6–8 April, in University of Sussex.
Scott, J.C. 1985. *Weapons of the weak: Everyday forms of peasant resistance*. New Haven: Yale University Press.
Silver, H. 1994. Social exclusion and social solidarity. *International Labour Review* 133, no. 5–6: 531–78.
Síocháin, S. 2003. Peasant Society. *The encyclopedia of Ireland*, 864–65. Dublin: Gill and Macmillan.
Skryzhevska, Y., and D. Karacsonyi. 2012. Rural population in Ukraine: Assessing the reality, looking for revitalisation. *Hungarian Geographical Bulletin* 61, no. 1: 49–76.
Smalley, R., and E. Corbera. 2012. Large-scale land deals from the inside out: Findings from Kenya's Tana Delta. *Journal of Peasant Studies* 39, no. 3–4: 1039–75.
Spoor, M., and O. Visser. 2004. Restructuring postponed? Russian large farm enterprises coping with the market. *Journal of Peasant Studies* 31, no. 3–4: 515–51.
Stoler, L. 1986. Plantation politics and protest on Sumatra's east coast. *Journal of Peasant Studies* 13, no. 2: 124–43.
Tarassevych, O. 2005. Ukraine dairy and products annual 2005, USDA Foreign Agricultural Service, GAIN Report.
Taubman, W. 2004. *Khrushchev: The Man and His Era*. New York: Norton&Co.
UkrStat. 1990–2013. Production of main agricultural products. Reports are available for 1990–2013, http://www.ukrstat.gov.ua/ (accessed December 22, 2014).
UkrStat. 2014. Reports, http://www.ukrstat.gov.ua/ (accessed multiple times 2013–2014).
Van der Ploeg, J.D. 2009. *The new peasantries: Struggles for autonomy and sustainability in an era of empire and globalization*. London: Routledge.
Viacampesina.org. 2013. Hundreds of actions around the world to celebrate the International Day of Peasant struggles. Press Release 17 April, http://viacampesina.org/en/index.php/actions-and-events-mainmenu-26/17-april–day-of-peasants-struggle-mainmenu-33/1397–17th-april-hundreds-of-actions-around-the-world-to-celebrate-the-international-day-of-peasants-struggles (accessed 25 September 2014).
Visser, O. 2010. Insecure land rights, obstacles to family farming, and the weakness of protest in rural Russia. *Laboratorium* 2: 275–95.
Visser, O., and N. Mamonova. 2011. Large-scale land acquisitions in the former Soviet Union. A study of rural social movements and land conflicts in Russia and Ukraine, http://www.landgovernance.org/system/files/LSLA_FormerSovietUnion.pdf (accessed September 01, 2012).
Visser, O., and M. Spoor. 2011. Land grabbing in Post-Soviet Eurasia. The world's largest land reserves at stake. *Journal of Peasant Studies* 38, no. 2: 299–324.
Visser, O., M. Spoor, and N. Mamonova. 2014. Is Russia the emerging global 'breadbasket'? Re-cultivation, agroholdings and grain production. *Europe-Asia Studies* 66, no. 10: 1589–1610.
Vlasenko, N.S. 2008. Rural poverty in Ukraine. *Problems of Economic Transition* 51, no. 7: 21–28.
Von Braun, J., and D. Lohlein. 2003. Policy options to overcome subsistence agriculture in the CEECS. In *Subsistence agriculture in Central and Eastern Europe: How to break the vicious circle?*, ed. S. Abele and K. Frohberg, 46–70. Halle: IAMO.
Wegren, S. 2005. From communism to capitalism? Russia's agrarian relations in the twentieth century and beyond. In *Rural adaptation in Russia*, ed. S. Wegren, 1–38. London: Routledge.
White, B., S.M. Borras, Jr, R. Hall, I. Scoones, and W. Wolford. 2012. The new enclosures: Critical perspectives on land grabbing. *Journal of Peasant Studies* 39, no. 3: 619–47.
Wilkinson, J., B. Reydon, and A. Di Sabbato. 2012. Concentration and foreign ownership of land in Brazil in the context of global land grabbing. *Canadian Journal of Development Studies* 33, no. 4: 417–38.
Witcher, S. 2003. Reviewing the terms of inclusion: Transactional processes, currencies and context. Research Paper, http://sticerd.lse.ac.uk/dps/case/cp/CASEpaper67.pdf (accessed May 20, 2013).
World Bank. 2010. *Rising global interest in farmland: Can it yield sustainable and equitable results?* Washington, DC: World Bank.
Yurchenko, A.D., and A. Miroshnichenko. 2006. Socio-economic and legal aspects of the moratorium on private farmland. [in Russian] *Bulletin of the Ministry of Justice* 12: 59–75.
Zemstov, I. 1991. *Entsiclopedia of Soviet life*. New Brunswick: Translation Publishers.

Politics from below? Small-, mid- and large-scale land dispossession in Teso, Uganda, and the relevance of scale

Matt Kandel

While processes of land dispossession – or 'land grabbing' – have garnered significant attention from researchers in recent years, local reactions to instances of land alienation have received insufficient scrutiny. This paper focuses on small-, mid- and large-scale land dispossession in the post-conflict Teso region in Uganda, and considers how people assert their agency when their tenure rights are infringed upon. I argue that those who lose tenure rights through small-scale land dispossession are primarily focused on reacquiring tenure rights and meeting the demands of their basic social reproduction. In these cases, there is little resistance that is definitively 'political'. In contrast, a 'politics from below' more clearly emerges in the cases of mid- and large-scale land alienation, which I attribute to particular structural conditions.

If there is anything that the topic of land grabbing is not lacking it is global publicity, and Sub-Saharan Africa has been at the epicenter of the attention. Since the 2007–2008 global commodities crisis, vast tracts of land have been acquired in the Global South as a reaction to a 'convergence of crises' that has centered on food, energy (especially demand for biofuel), the climate and finance (Borras and Franco 2010). However, over the last several years, academics have made a point to explicitly call for more nuanced critiques of land grabbing. As Peluso and Lund put it (2011), there is no 'one big land grab', and others have similarly underlined the preexisting social relations and processes in which new acquisitions are embedded (Cotula 2012; Pedersen et al. 2012; Borras and Franco 2013; Edelman and León 2013; Edelman, Oya, and Borras 2013). Scholars have also called for more nuanced conceptualizations of scale in processes of land dispossession (Cotula 2012; Edelman 2013). Global publicity has centered on the deals involving millions of hectares of land in countries as geographically disparate as Ghana, Ethiopia, Zambia and Madagascar. However, the intense fascination with the quantity of land in question can serve as a distraction from other components of scale that actually carry greater social importance. Moreover, as Cotula (2012) notes, the cumulative number of hectares involved in small-scale land acquisitions might be greater than the quantity of land in the largest commercial acquisitions (> 1000 hectares).

In rural Sub-Saharan Africa, one must also look on the village level in order to understand regimes of accumulation and factors of basic social reproduction. In many cases, land is acquired through a combination of predatory practices and legal mechanisms. Another common way in which land titles are transferred is through defaults or distress sales (Deininger 2003; Chimhowu and Woodhouse 2006; Colin and Woodhouse 2010).[1] Succinctly put, large-scale commercial acquisitions of land are far from the sole driving force behind dispossession in Sub-Saharan Africa. Scholars began noticing an increase in small-scale land dispossession across the continent well before the global commodities crisis of 2007–2008. They have emphasized the prevalence of village-level actors who attempt to expand their landholdings through extra-legal means (Downs and Reyna 1988; Van Donge and Pherani 1999; Fred-Mensah 1999; Berry 2002; Deininger and Castagnini 2006). Often, the land in question might not even amount to one hectare.[2]

One challenge for researchers is studying how people's reactions might differ when their tenure rights are infringed upon. Scholars have criticized the tendency in the land grab literature to presume that indigenous people are always displaced in cases of large-scale land acquisitions, and that they are necessarily opposed to the deals (Borras and Franco 2010). In point of fact, reactions to land grabs are heterogeneous in nature (Mamonova 2012; Smalley and Corbera 2012; Borras and Franco 2013). Further complicating matters is the fact that the non-governmental organizations (NGOs) and local civil society organizations (CSOs) that work with victimized populations often possess contrasting views from those they serve (Borras, Edelman, and Kay 2008; Pye 2010; Borras et al. 2011; Mamonova 2012).[3]

Critiquing 'politics from below' in cases of land dispossession also hinges on the conceptualization of resistance and politics. Many have argued that 'everyday forms of resistance' (exemplified by actions such as foot dragging, sabotage or privately cursing an employer) predominate in societies with high levels of political repression (Adas 1986; Scott and Kerkvliet 1986; Kerkvliet 2009; Adnan 2013). These 'covert' forms of resistance contrast resistance that is 'overt', which is generally defined as open dissent by an individual or group which takes public accountability for their actions (Adas 1986; Scott and Kerkvliet 1986; Adnan 2007; Walker 2008; Kerkvliet 2009). If we are to understand 'politics from below' as constituting actions that are performed in the public sphere with the intent of addressing an issue that affects a community, then not all resistance is political. Acts that are 'political' directly challenge perceived asymmetries in the control and distribution of power and resources in societies. In the case of Sub-Saharan Africa, most argue that resistance to land reform and land grabbing tends to fall under the 'everyday' form (Amanor 2005; Mbunda 2009; Greco 2010, 2012). It has been noted that, in general, there has been 'relatively weak transnational organized opposition to global land grabbing' (2011, 43).

---

[1]See e.g. Deininger and Mpuga (2004) and Place (2009) for a discussion of the increase of rental markets in Sub-Saharan Africa. Chimhowu and Woodhouse (2006) use the term 'vernacular markets' to underline the informal mechanisms undergirding these markets. Adoko and Levine (2007) discuss this specifically with respect to Teso.

[2]Throughout this work, I use terms such as 'land dispossession' or 'land expropriation' rather than 'land grabbing' in order to reserve the latter for describing large large-scale land acquisitions (> 1000 hectares). Except for two cases, every instance of land dispossession referred to here involves much smaller extensions of land. I use the term 'small-scale' to refer to land that amounts to less than 20 hectares, although the majority of cases of land dispossession in Teso involve much smaller extensions – typically less than 10 hectares.

[3]My distinction between CSOs and NGOs is based on differences in scale. I consider the former to constitute locally run organizations and the latter to denote national and/or international organizations. In Teso, CSOs typically rely on international financing (such as from private individuals or NGOs from Western countries) but they are generally locally managed and operated.

Any forms of resistance must be analyzed within a specific social context. In the case of this work, the context is Teso region in northeastern Uganda, which is where I conducted ethnographic research during 2012–2013. Like every region in Uganda – be it in rural, peri-urban or urban environments – there has been an explosion in land dispossession within the last several decades, and the problem is only worsening (Rugadya, Nsamba-Gayiiya, and Kamusiime 2008; Rugadya 2009). Compounding the situation is that Teso – similar to other regions in Northern Uganda – is in the early stages of recovering from three violent conflicts. As others have pointed out (Kibreab 2002; Richards et al. 2005; Bruce 2007; Alden-Wily 2008, 2009; Rugadya, Nsamba-Gayiiya, and Kamusiime 2008), tenure insecurity and rearrangements in property relations are prominent features of post-conflict environments. Ultimately, not all cases of land dispossession in Teso are identical in form, and the types of indigenous reactions differ as well.

During my research, I was based in Soroti Town in Soroti District. My data were generated through semi-structured interviews, unstructured interviews and participant observation techniques. I interviewed research participants in villages, trading centers, local government offices and CSO offices, and at CSO-organized workshops and conferences. A large number of research participants were professed victims of land expropriations. I also interviewed local government officials (at district, sub-county, parish and village levels), smallholder farmers, clan leaders, members of the security forces, small business owners, elders, central government officials, court officials and a wide array of civil society actors. One-on-one interviews lasted anywhere from 10 minutes to two hours. I conducted focus-group discussions in villages and trading centers, which involved anywhere from three to 20 people. I relied on an interpreter when the interviews were conducted in Ateso, Kumam, Luganda and Karamojong. While I conducted research in all eight districts of Teso, the majority of my research was carried out in the districts of Katakwi, Amuria, Bukedea, Kumi and Soroti. I also conducted research in the Karamoja districts of Moroto, Napak, and Abim (see Figure 1).

I will begin this paper by briefly summarizing the history of the violent conflicts in Teso, as well as the drivers of land dispossession. The third and fourth sections are organized around my typology of land dispossession in Teso. In the former, I focus on how people assert their agency in cases of small-scale land expropriations. The latter analyzes local reactions to one mid-scale and one large-scale case of land expropriation. I argue that while a discernible 'politics from below' does not emerge in cases of small-scale land dispossession, the mid- and large-scale cases provide the necessary conditions for political mobilization. I conclude the paper by arguing that even though large-scale land acquisitions generate the greatest publicity, it is in fact processes of small-scale land dispossession that pose the greatest long-term threat to stability both regionally and nationally in Uganda, and in Sub-Saharan Africa, in general.[4]

Teso: a history of violence, and the drivers of land dispossession

Teso is a semi-arid/arid region that consists of approximately 1.6 million people (Chapman and Kagaha 2009). It is comprised of the districts of Soroti, Ngora, Kumi and Bukedea in the south; Serere and Kabermaido in the southwest; and Amuria and Katakwi in the north. The Iteso – the dominant ethnic group in Teso – are part of the Nilotic ethnic cluster that

[4]Due to the political sensitivity of land-related issues in Uganda, a number of participants requested anonymity. Therefore, I have removed or changed some identifiers such as names and professions. However, the locations of sites (when specified) are all accurate.

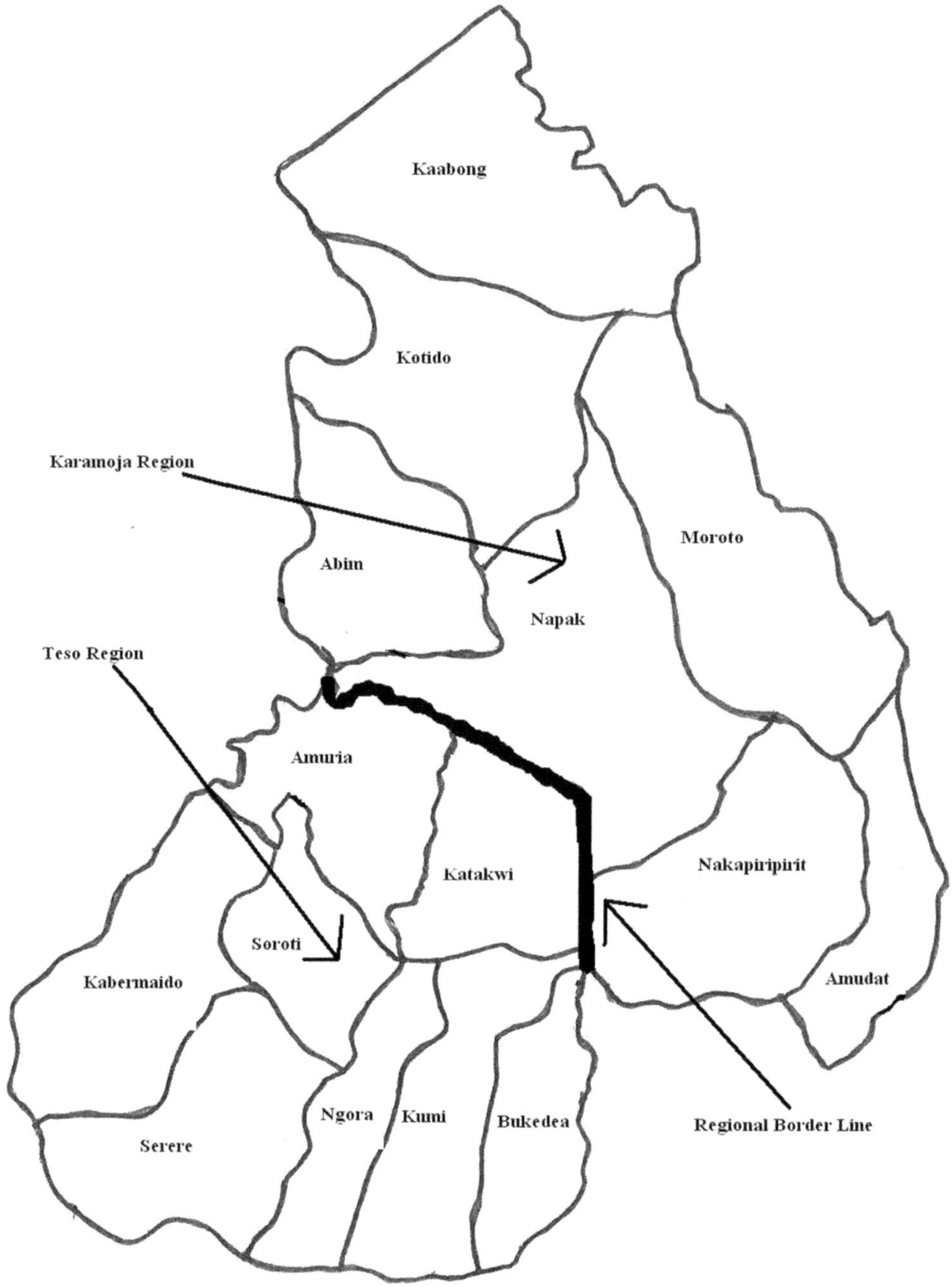

Figure 1. Map of Teso and Karamoja Regions (with districts) (approximate sketch by author).

populates much of the Ugandan North. The region is located within the historic Ugandan 'cattle corridor' – a crucial resource for the nation's pastoralists – which covers roughly a quarter of the country's total surface area, cutting diagonally from the northeast to the southwest (see Figure 2; Vincent 1982; Kisamba-Mugerwa 1997; Rugadya 2009). There

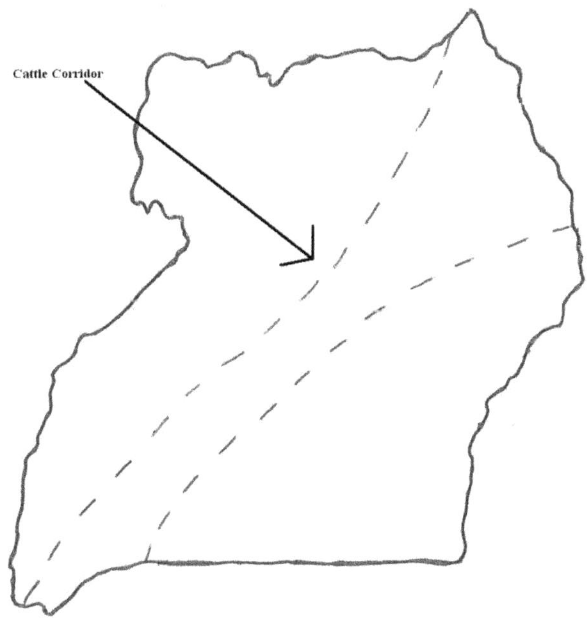

Figure 2. Map of cattle corridor in Uganda (approximate sketch by author).

are also a number of wetlands in Teso.[5] The Teso economy has historically revolved around peasant agriculture, pastoralism, fishing and hunting. This remains the case today, in addition to an upward trend in commercial agriculture and speculative land purchases. While Teso was once a major cotton-exporting region in the early twentieth century, exports dropped drastically during the presidency of Idi Amin from 1972 to 1979, and there is currently only very minimal cotton cultivation.

From the late 1980s to the mid 2000s, three violent conflicts further decimated the Teso economy. It has been estimated that virtually all livestock was lost during the peak years of the violence from the late 1980s to the early 1990s (Mkutu 2007; Jones 2009). Civil war between the National Resistance Army (NRA), the recent victors of a national civil war that stretched from 1981 to 1985, and the Uganda People's Army (UPA), a Teso-based insurgent group, lasted from 1987 to 1993. Overlapping with the civil war were large-scale cattle raids originating from Karamoja, a predominantly pastoralist region that borders Teso to the north. Large-scale cattle rustling – which first began in northern Teso in the mid 1960s – continued across the northern belt of Teso into the mid 2000s. While people were beginning to resettle southern Teso by the early 1990s, the Lord's Resistance Army (LRA), an insurgent group from Acholi region in the North, caused another bout of displacement when it infiltrated Amuria from the northwest in 2003, continuing south to Soroti and Kabermaido districts as well (Refugee Law Project 2008). The Ugandan People's Defence Force (UPDF), along with a Teso paramilitary group known as the Arrow Boys, successfully repelled LRA members from Teso by 2004. In addition to the scores of people who were killed during the violent conflicts, hundreds of thousands were displaced from their customary land into regional Internally Displaced Persons (IDP) camps or outside of Teso.

[5]Thirteen percent of the total surface area of Uganda is wetlands (Matete and BakaNume 2010).

The most impactful immediate driver to land dispossession in Teso is the mass displacement caused by the violent conflicts. I refer to this driver as the 'displacement–resettlement dynamic' in order to highlight the historical continuities between the conflict and post-conflict years. Processes of displacement and resettlement have functioned very fluidly, which is to say that they have unfolded cyclically and unevenly across the region since the mid 1960s. There are five other immediate drivers to land dispossession in Teso: (1) increasing population density (and especially an exploding youth population); (2) an inadequate system for land demarcation; (3) ineffective formal and informal justice systems; (4) opportunistic actors who seek to acquire land through dubious means; (5) ecological transformations. I classify these drivers as 'immediate' in order to differentiate them from the most structural impetus for regional land dispossession, specifically fundamental transformations in the Teso political economy.

Teso is undergoing a period of capital accumulation (albeit on a small scale) and social differentiation, which I mark as beginning in the early 1990s. This can be seen in the growth of a largely autochthonous accumulating group that is comprised of local government officials, civil servants, NGO workers and other professionals, all of whom are acquiring land locally for commercial agriculture and speculative purposes. It is also evidenced by a growing segment of the population that is at least partially dependent on performing agricultural wage labor for their social reproduction. Many in this group fall under Bernstein's category of 'classes of labor' (2007), since they are not fully dispossessed from their customary land, even if the remaining connection is a tenuous one. There is another section of this group that has been fully separated from their traditional land, and their social reproduction is premised on a combination of agricultural wage labor, cultivating informally borrowed land, and other economic activities. In my view, political economic transformations in Teso are interacting with the immediate drivers to create a very particular context of widespread land alienation. However, there are a variety of forms of land dispossession in the region, and these differences impact people's reactions.

Small-scale land dispossession: the imperatives of basic social reproduction and structural challenges

The vast majority of cases of land dispossession in Teso occur on a quantitatively small scale, and there is hardly a single village that has been unaffected. Far from being rooted in the demand for biofuels from Western countries or food crops from the Middle East, these instances of dispossession often involve only a single hectare of land. Disputes over property lines usually precede land expropriations, although not all disputes will result in dispossession. Those who are dispossessed of land will continuously struggle to regain their tenure rights. So, cases of dispossession should not be understood as single occurrences: they are ongoing affairs. There are specific segments of the population that are most commonly targeted for their customary land. This includes (with the potential for overlap) the elderly, widows, women, orphans, children and those who are ill. While traditional, clan-based justice systems were historically relied on for resolving land tenure disputes in Teso, they have become increasingly ineffective, especially as elders' political power has significantly waned. Unfortunately, the underresourced and corruption-prone formal justice system has been unable to fill the legal vacuum. It is not unusual for cases to pend for 15 or 20 years in the regional magistrates court. In an effort to reduce the burden on the formal courts, village-level Area Land Committees were created by the 1998 Land Act. However, they can only assist in resolving intra-clan land conflicts, and are commonly accused of being influenced by bribery. Poverty is a major obstacle for the most vulnerable groups in Teso. They frequently encounter difficulties in affording the necessary legal and extra-legal fees to maintain land tenure rights. Victims are also reticent to seek legal address against an encroacher who possesses firearms, out of fear of a violent attack.

There are five forms of small-scale land dispossession in Teso, although there is a high degree of overlap among the first four: (1) intra-family, (2) intra-clan, (3) inter-clan, (4) inter-ethnic and (5) freehold acquisitions. Intra-family (which is also necessarily intra-clan) and intra-clan land dispossession occur within the same village. Inter-clan expropriations typically involve land that borders two separate villages. A similar dynamic usually exists in inter-ethnic dispossession, although there are cases where separate ethnic groups inhabit the same village, and conflicts over land arise there as well. There is also inter-ethnic land dispossession along the regional borders of Teso and Karamoja, and Teso and Sebei. Most cases of small-scale land dispossession which fall under the first four categories involve an opportunistic individual – quite commonly a fellow clan member or in-law – who is seeking to expand his landholdings at the expense of another family. His actions can best be viewed as an attempt to hedge one's bets against a rising tide of land fragmentation and general productivity challenges to peasant farming. Land expropriations in this context commonly contain coercive and extra-judicial dimensions.

A typical example of an intra-family and intra-clan land expropriation involves the case of Atungo Monica in Asuret Sub-County, Soroti District. She and her husband – both of whom are elderly – bought a little over one hectare of customarily held land from a relative and fellow clan member in 2000. However, the seller almost immediately instructed his son to reclaim the land. Over this time period, she and her husband have been subjects of different forms of abuse. The encroachers have threatened to kill her if she does not leave the land, even once holding her at gunpoint. Her son was killed as a result of the dispute and her home was burnt down. While Mrs. Atungo has attempted to pursue justice through both the formal and traditional justice systems, her only victory was recouping 150,000 UGX for damages caused to her crops by the encroachers.[6]

A case of an intra-clan and inter-ethnic conflict over land that has not yet resulted in dispossession involves Osuban Andrew, a middle-aged teacher at the secondary level in Kabermaido District. While he possesses a freehold title to property on the outskirts of Kabermaido town, he still maintains customary tenure rights to more than five hectares of land in a village in Bululu Sub-County. While Kumam first settled in this part of Bululu, Bantu ethnic groups were permitted to settle here decades ago. Inter-ethnic settlement laid the grounds for intermarriage and Andrew is such an example. His father is of Bantu origin and his mother is Kumam. For several years, an uncle on his mother's side of the family has been attempting to dispossess him of his tenure rights to land in the village. His uncle has threatened to kill him, which has influenced Mr. Osuban's decision to live in town and rent plots of his land in the village to several different families. In his view, the civil war and cattle raids are to blame for Kumam who seek to dispossess Bantu of land. Prior to the violent conflicts, 'Bantu and Kumam coexisted peacefully and intermarried', but the mass displacement engendered a new social environment. He believes that current inter-ethnic tensions in the village are simply a manifestation of the deep social ruptures caused by the violent conflicts.

Small-scale land dispossession occurs not only through predatory means but through legal mechanisms as well. Or, quite frequently, the two are combined. In these cases, a

[6]2750 UGX is roughly equivalent to 1 USD.

freehold title (which bestows outright ownership) is acquired on land that was previously customarily held.[7] The high cost of acquiring a freehold title to land means this option is generally limited to members of the local accumulating group. Freehold-based land dispossession arises for three main reasons: (1) customary land is sold to someone outside of the seller's clan/ethnic group and the seller is intending to relocate to land that he was displaced to during the violent conflicts (and to which he acquired tenure rights). Such a transaction is viewed as deceitful by other members of his clan, since the seller is considered to have resettled his customary land only so that he could immediately sell it off to make a profit; (2) customary land is sold by someone who has been squatting on land that is customarily held by a family that has yet to resettle since their displacement; (3) customary land is acquired via freehold title on the basis that it is a 'free land', but it simply has yet to be resettled. Many of these purchases are speculative (and this is especially true in northern Teso where vast tracts of land have still not been resettled), although some are made for the purpose of developing small-scale commercial agricultural enterprises. Freehold-based acquisitions usually involve larger amounts of land than transfers of land that remain under customary tenure.

Similar to how the legacy of the violent conflicts profoundly influences the nature of small-scale land expropriations in Teso, it also exerts a powerful impact on opportunities for resistance. Many cases of dispossession involve widows (most of whom lost their husbands during the civil war or from cattle raids) who are attempting to resettle their traditional land, but are prevented from doing so by their in-laws. Young male adults who lost their fathers during the violence encounter a similar situation. Many of these young men (they are referred to as orphans in Teso) attempt to resettle their fathers' customary land, but since they grew up in IDP camps and do not know the plot boundaries, they are swindled out of tenure rights by other members in their clan. For both widows and orphans, their dispossession is directly tied to the years of violence. Their social position can be characterized as one of extreme powerlessness, and they allocate their energy and minimal resources to the imperatives of basic social reproduction. Other groups that are most vulnerable to land dispossession must also primarily address the demands of basic social reproduction. Even if they have not lost tenure rights as a direct result of the violent conflicts, many certainly lost capital (such as livestock) during the violent years, which has exacerbated their poverty. Those who are dispossessed entirely or partially from their customary land try to regain their tenure rights through both the traditional and formal justice systems, although they are encumbered by the higher costs of the latter. The majority of these people do not aspire to achieve political objectives in their pursuit of reacquiring access to cultivable land. While they recognize that many in their village and surrounding villages share a similar plight, this has not served as a basis for political mobilization.

A limitation to organized political mobilization in small-scale cases derives from the role of CSOs. Many people who are dispossessed of land or have their tenure rights challenged appeal to CSOs that are known to offer assistance to victims of land expropriation. They might also seek assistance from high-standing members of their communities such as parish councilors and religious leaders. Yet the main focus for those offering assistance is

[7]There are four forms of land tenure recognized by the 1995 Constitution and the 1998 Land Act: mailo, freehold, leasehold and customary (Coldham 2000; Hunt 2004; Rugadya 2009). Mailo tenure rights are found exclusively in the central region of Uganda. According to Land Office officials in Teso, 70 to 80 percent of land in the region is customarily held.

mediation of the conflict. For instance, a CSO might bring the two parties in disagreement to their office and employ a third-party mediator in an attempt to foster a resolution. Assistance also comes in the form of educating victims of their legal rights. For example, there are a number of CSO-affiliated women activists in Teso who specifically seek to inform women of their constitutionally protected rights to customary land. Therefore, the guiding policy framework for CSOs is based on conflict resolution rather than political advocacy. While Teso CSOs are certainly advocates for vulnerable social groups, they mainly assist people in meeting the day-to-day demands of social reproduction. Their strength lies in the support networks they can provide rather than political networks.

Nonetheless, this should not be construed as an indicator that CSOs lack the desire to achieve political objectives. CSO members are deeply attuned to how political, economic and social structures and networks can function exploitatively and illegitimately on both the regional and national levels. They are especially cognizant of how agents of political power such as local and central government officials abuse their office to illegally dispossess people of land. However, CSOs – in addition to NGOs – must cope with a difficult operating environment, for there is currently no issue more volatile in Uganda than conflicts over land. They are keenly aware of the potential problems they can encounter when protesting land dispossession, particularly when government or military officials are implicated. Victims are often too intimidated to publicly discuss a case that involves accusations against a political official or a member of the military.[8] In Soroti Town, organized protests against politically sensitive topics such as government corruption have been violently repressed by security forces. Organized meetings or rallies by oppositional political parties and figures are often met with violent repression as well. Most efforts to address small-scale land dispossession have come through less politically sensitive channels like CSO advocacy reports. This pragmatic or 'immediate needs-based' approach that has been adopted by CSOs is strongly influenced by political realities.

An important point to consider, however, is whether the dynamics underlying small-scale land dispossession even allow for contexts to emerge where reactions can constitute a 'politics from below'. The vast majority of cases retain a private dimension because immediate family members, clan mates and in-laws are the antagonists. The only time where a disagreement over tenure rights between two parties carries greater political overtones is when the encroacher is a member of the local government or UPDF. In these cases, the legitimacy of the state is necessarily called into question because the encroacher is considered to be taking advantage of his enhanced access to political power. Yet even in these instances the accuser and encroacher often live in the same village, or share a plot of land adjacent to their respective villages. Therefore, similar to how scale is crucial for understanding processes of land alienation, it is just as important for determining the nature of the reactions that emerge from below. Cases of small-scale land dispossession possess what I consider to be a very internal character; that is, they unfold on the village level and involve two parties that already maintain social ties to one another. They are most prominently local in nature. In contrast, there is a stronger external dynamic to processes of large-scale land alienation, as the orchestrating actors or institutions are at least several scales removed from village-level social relations. It is in these cases where a more clearly defined 'politics from below' emerges.

[8]A Human Rights Watch report (Burnett 2012) cites instances of NGO actors who have been arbitrarily detained by district security personnel for attempting to assist victims of land dispossession.

Expanding the scale: local resistance in the cases of Adukut and Amoding

There are a handful of cases in Teso where tenure rights to much larger amounts of land are at stake. I will concentrate on two such instances. The first site is in Kapelebyong Sub-County in Amuria District, and the second is in Malera Sub-County in Bukedea District. In both case studies, I draw on data that I generated through interviews and a focus-group discussion (in the case of the latter) near the sites of contestation, as well as from interviews of CSO actors, local and central government officials, and court officials in Soroti Town. One-on-one interviews in Kapelebyong and Malera included activists, clergy, local government officials, smallholder farmers and elders. The focus group discussion consisted of a mix of people from different backgrounds, including retired civil servants, CSO actors, elders and smallholder farmers. I traveled to Kapelebyong on two separate occasions, one time on a day trip and the other time staying for five days. I traveled to Malera sub-county, along with the sub-counties of Kolir and Bukedea (where I also conducted research on the Malera case) multiple times on day trips.

Both of these cases of land dispossession are not isolated to a single village or two villages, but rather involve entire parishes and sub-counties. They also feature institutional actors, specifically the local government, central government, UPDF and a private investment group (in the second case). The state – on both the local and central levels – already operates with a significant legitimacy deficit in Teso. Indeed, the main challenge for introducing any kind of development project in Teso is that people are intuitively skeptical. The prevailing assumption in Teso is that the government only harbors malicious intent towards the region, so the direct involvement of state actors in the alienation of land only further erodes state legitimacy.

The central government proposal to locate a new military barracks and livestock-breeding center in Kapelebyong Sub-County has been met with fierce opposition from the local population. This mid-scale land expropriation involves 120 hectares of land that is known as Adukut. It is located along the Teso-Karamoja border in Okunguru Parish. It is part of a long stretch of highly valued land along the border that is locally known as the 'green belt' due to its fertility (see Figure 3). The central government, the Member of Parliament (MP) from Kapelebyong, senior officials in Amuria district government and high-ranking political officials from the sub-county all support the proposal. They refer to Adukut as a 'free land'. They argue that these two projects will bring much-needed development to an extremely poor part of Amuria, including vital improvements to infrastructure. They also contend that the military barracks will provide security against the ongoing threat of cattle raids from Karamoja. The Resident District Commissioner has publically stated that Adukut is government-owned land, claiming it is part of the Upe-Pian game reserve that was established by the British colonial government in 1937 (Emwamu 2014).

Most Kapelebyong residents are in strong disagreement with government officials on the proper use of the land. First of all, many counter that families possess customary tenure rights to at least parts of Adukut, and the problem is that they had not yet resettled their land at the time of the government's proposal. Second, they reject the government's justification for the military barracks. While they acknowledge that for years they had repeatedly petitioned the government for a military presence along the border in Kapelebyong, their request was continually ignored. Due to tremendous improvements in inter-regional peace over the last five years (much of which is due to CSO-led Iteso–Karamojong reconciliation projects), they argue a military barracks in Kapelebyong is no longer needed. Communities feel it would send a wrong signal to the Karamojong and risk destabilizing the inter-regional peace. Many people – including some local government officials on the

Figure 3. Map indicating location of ‘green belt’ in Teso and Karamoja regions (approximate sketch by author).

village and parish levels – believe that the true intent of the government is to acquire rights over land which contains mineral deposits and possibly even gold. A popular theory amongst CSO actors, low-level local government officials and residents in districts along both sides of the Teso–Karamoja border is that there is a ‘gold belt’ that runs along the border and further west into Lango region. They point to the mining of gold, iron ore, bauxite and other minerals in Karamoja, and think Teso's comparable geological features indicate the presence of similar subterranean deposits.[9]

CSO actors, residents, and some current and former members of local government have led the opposition against the Adukut proposal. Dissent to the government plan has been expressed in a variety of ways. Kapelebyong women community activists have suggested that the land be used to resettle widows who have been dispossessed from their customary land. As one woman activist put it to me, the central problem for people in Kapelebyong is not threats to security, but 'landlessness'. Their counterproposal recommends dividing the 120 hectares into four-hectare plots which would then be allocated to widows in the community. Several Soroti Town-based CSOs have also rallied around the opposition to the Adukut proposal. During the sixth annual Peace Week in Kapelebyong in 2012, which is a week-long event that seeks to advance Iteso–Karamojong reconciliation efforts through a variety of activities, a memo was drafted and signed by participants that specifically rejected the rationale for the military barracks. Perhaps the most publicly visible opponent to the plan has been former Amuria District chairperson (2006–2011), Julius Ochen. On 16 February 2013, he led a 'bare-chested' protest at a local government-led community outreach meeting (Emwamu 2013). The protest featured dozens of shirtless men who displayed placards voicing their opposition to the proposal. The protesters also used song and prayer to express their dissent.

An example of large-scale land alienation in Teso (although as of 2013 it had not yet been formalized) involves the use of more than 2500 hectares of a wetland along the Teso–Karamoja and Teso–Bugisu regional borders. Residents from Malera Sub-County in Bukedea District – one of the potentially affected areas – refer to this stretch of land as Amoding. Wetlands are a highly valued resource in semi-arid/arid regions in Sub-Saharan Africa (Scoones 1991; Taylor, Howard, and Briggs 1995; Rebelo, McCartney, and Finlayson 2010), and the volatility of conflicts over tenure rights to wetlands has not gone unnoticed in the land-grab literature (Peters and Kambewa 2007; Duvail et al. 2012). The central government considers Amoding a 'free land', and in 2008 proposed using the location as a site for a commercial sugar plantation and an irrigation system. While the 1998 Land Act stipulates that all wetlands in Uganda are government owned (and the same holds for any land that contains underground natural resources), this has never been accepted by communities across Uganda. Despite opposition to the project by the Minister of Teso Affairs, support has been voiced by the Bukedea District Chairman and Malera MP. Both officials concur with the central government that the sugar plantation would provide an important alternative source of income for the local population. Local government officials who are supportive of the initiatives also note that the irrigation system would provide a stable, year-round supply of water to a drought- and flood-prone area of Teso.

Like the Adukut proposal, most residents are strongly opposed to the development project. They similarly claim that families possess customary tenure rights to some of the land but they have not yet resettled. Residents indicate that families began permanently settling Amoding in the mid 1950s, and that non-permanently settled sections have historically served as sites for hunting and fishing. Many emphasize the symbolic importance of Amoding in addition to the material value it holds. Those in opposition believe that the

[9]Twenty-five percent of Karamoja's total surface area (27,700 square kilometers) is licensed for mining (Rugadya, Kamusiime, and Nsamba-Gayiiya 2010).

construction of a commercial sugar plantation in Busoga region (in the Ugandan South) has worsened conditions for families that lost their customary tenure rights. They suspect that the government wants to dispossess them of their ancestral land for reasons that have gone publicly undeclared. Their suspicions are raised whenever a foreigner (especially someone who is assumed to be from a Western country or Asia) is seen in the area, as it is assumed that this person might be a private investor.

Resistance to the Amoding development project has so far proceeded in unstructured ways. Youth, in particular, have threatened violent retaliation against any government security forces that attempt to prevent them from accessing the wetland.[10] While they lack firearms, they have declared they will employ traditional weapons like machetes and spears. They have also threatened to burn the vehicles of any investors who come to Malera. The most vocal proclaim a steadfast willingness to die in order to preserve access to the wetland and their customary tenure rights. As is the case across Teso, young men are especially concerned with the issue of rising land scarcity because they know that they will inherit substantially less land than did their father or father's father. Perhaps unsurprisingly, there have already been several casualties due to the development proposal. In late 2010, the Bukedea District Speaker (a local government official who works under the District Chairman) and a town clerk were visited in their respective homes by residents offering them a mango. The mangos turned out to be poisoned, and the town clerk died as a result. The district speaker survived after several months of recuperation. Both men had become strongly identified with the Amoding initiative because they were spearheading local government efforts to build grassroots support for the project. Residents cite the highly opaque nature of the planning process as one of the main reasons why they are so steadfastly opposed to any development project and assume malicious intent on the part of the government.

In contrast to the Adukut initiative, those opposed to the Amoding development project have not yet mounted any organized resistance. This has been influenced by at least several factors: (1) it is in earlier stages of planning. In the case of Adukut, local and central government officials have already declared that it will proceed regardless of opposition; (2) complications stem from land-use patterns and overlapping tenure rights. While the 1998 Ugandan constitution protects communal tenure rights, these can be ignored by the government when wetlands are involved. The wetland is also shared with Karamojong and Bagisu, so competing inter-regional claims add another dynamic to the situation. Also, some Malera Sub-County residents (in violation of customary law) sold plots of land to Iteso from other districts when many families were still displaced. In other cases, Sabim from Sebei region and Nandi from eastern Kenya – all of whom settled in parts of Malera before customary rights holders had resettled – sold land to Iteso from outside the sub-county.

If the central government decides that there is too much dissent to proceed with the Amoding development project, this would not be the first time that resistance from communities has blocked such an initiative. Resistance also stymied the construction of a commercial sugar plantation on the Agu wetlands between Soroti and Ngora districts. Residents from the Agu area suggested that smallholder farmers be allowed to maintain their customary tenure rights and grow sugar as independent peasant producers for the Madhvani Group (one of Uganda's largest private corporations) rather than be converted to wage workers. However, not everyone in Malera opposes the development scheme – or at least not on

[10]In Teso, 'youth' generally refers to anyone under the age of 30.

principle. Some point out that smallholder farmers would greatly benefit from an irrigation system.

CSO actors and officials from district land offices largely attribute opposition to state development projects to the opaque planning process. Even opposition to public infrastructure projects such as the construction of roads – despite its presumable benefit to entire districts – is widespread. In general, people are extremely hesitant to relinquish tenure rights to their customary land in any situation. CSO members hypothesize that with a more 'bottom-up approach', which would involve the active participation of community members in decision-making, development projects could garner support. Adukut and Amoding, however, are both classic examples of a 'top-down' approach. The military component to Adukut further complicates the initiative, as distrust and fear of the UPDF is still high in Teso.

Conclusion

To adapt Peluso and Lund's point, there are in fact 'many land grabs' in Teso, and they are deeply embedded within very complex and particular socio-historical contexts. These contexts are not solely determined by changes in property relations, alterations to land-use patterns, or broader political economic shifts. Rather, other factors such as violent conflicts, an exploding youth population and ineffective legal (traditional and statutory) justice systems also shape the ways in which conflicts over tenure rights unfold. While a 'politics from below' has more clearly emerged in cases of mid-scale and large-scale land dispossession, it is mainly because the former creates better opportunities for organized opposition. It is easier for people to organize against one project that would affect scores of people as opposed to just one family. However, it should not simply be assumed that greater resistance to large-scale land acquisitions means that these phenomena exert the most destructive impact on societies. Indeed, one must consider whether the minimal attention to small-scale land dispossession is problematic. Cotula's (2012) point that the aggregate number of hectares involved in many small-scale commercial land acquisitions might outnumber those in large-scale land acquisitions should provoke serious thought, and other researchers have made a similar point (Hilhorst, Nelen, and Traoré 2011; Becker 2013; Baglioni and Gibbon 2013; Peters 2013).

While commercial acquisitions of land (as well as speculative purchases) are on the rise in Teso, the vast majority of cases of dispossession involve land which remains customarily held. In general, land expropriations tend to feature a combination of extra-judicial and coercive measures. The central antagonist here is not global capital, but national and local actors. As one scholar puts it, rising struggles over tenure rights have 'followed myriad social fault lines, pitting national and local elites against ordinary citizens, neighbor against neighbor, kinsman against kinsman, and husbands against wives' (Berry 2002, 639). Scholars have documented how the use of violence is increasingly common in these cases, and that it is often ethnically motivated (André and Platteau 1998; Chauveau 2000; Daudelin 2002; Addison and Laakso 2003; Peters 2009). Alden-Wily (2009) argues that conflicts over tenure rights are even more volatile in post-conflict societies, which she considers to be due to the misunderstanding and mismanaging of the shifting contexts of property relations. In her view, 'far too little attention is paid to the role of a mismanaged peace in distributing property relations in post-conflict states' (2009, 31). This point pertains especially to the Teso–Karamoja border, as it is only within the last five or six years that inter-ethnic violence has significantly decreased.

Researching how people assert their agency in cases of small-scale land dispossession is just as important as studying how communities might mobilize against large-scale acquisitions. Foreign investment groups that acquire tens of thousands of hectares of land can certainly destabilize communities. The investments can displace thousands of indigenous people, alter traditional forms of social reproduction and destroy the symbolic value of ancestral lands. Yet they are relatively isolated in number, and capital can be pulled out rather quickly if an investor becomes wary because of a military coup or the potential for civil war. This contrasts sharply from the abundance of small-scale land dispossessions that are spread out across rural, peri-urban and urban Sub-Saharan Africa. In Teso, the majority of these cases are very small scale – only one hectare might be at stake. Unlike the large-scale land acquisitions, they cannot simply be resolved by a suddenly wary foreign investor or change of government; they are deeply woven into national and local social structures and relations.

Multilateral organizations have begun directing their attention to improving the fairness of the contracts that govern global land deals. They have also pushed for the strengthening of land rights for local populations (Wolford et al. 2013). However, these efforts focus on large-scale, commercial land acquisitions. Improvements to global governance structures do not necessarily filter down to the widow who is being dispossessed of one hectare of land in a village by an in-law. In my view, small-scale land dispossessions carry greater potential for long-term negative impact in Sub-Saharan Africa than do large-scale commercial acquisitions. They are vastly more numerous and their deep embeddedness within local political economies makes them much more challenging to resolve. Any potential for short-term resolutions is all the more unlikely because of the wide variety of powerful local drivers. One way to conceptualize this point is that whereas large-scale land acquisitions are driven most prevalently by exogenous social forces, small-scale land dispossessions are more prominently endogenous developments, and they are tearing apart communities 'from within'.

Acknowledgements

I would like to thank the anonymous reviewers for their contributions to improving the quality of this paper.

References

Adas, M. 1986. From foot dragging to flight: The evasive history of peasant avoidance protest in south and South-East Asia. *Journal of Peasant Studies* 13, no. 2: 64–86.

Addison, T., and L. Laakso. 2003. The political economy of Zimbabwe's descent into conflict. *Journal of International Development* 15, no. 4: 457–70.

Adnan, S. 2007. Departures from everyday resistance and flexible strategies of domination: The making and unmaking of a poor peasant mobilization in Bangladesh. *Journal of Agrarian Change* 7, no. 2: 183–224.

Adnan, S. 2013. Land grabs and primitive accumulation in deltaic Bangladesh: Interactions between neoliberal globalization, state interventions, power relations and peasant resistance. *Journal of Peasant Studies* 40, no. 1: 87–128.

Adoko, J., and S. Levine. 2007. *A land market for poverty eradication? A case study of the impact of Uganda's Land Acts on policy hopes for development and poverty eradication.* Kampala: LEMU.

Alden-Wily, L. 2008. Whose land is it? Commons and conflict states. *Rights and Resources initiative.*

Alden-Wily, L. 2009. It's more than about going home … Tackling land tenure in the emergency to development transition in post-conflict states. In *Unchartered territory, land, conflict and humanitarian action*, ed. S. Pantuliano, 27–53. London: Humanitarian Policy Group, Overseas Development Institute.

Amanor, K.S. 2005. Night harvesters, forest hoods and saboteurs: Struggles over land expropriation in Ghana. In *Reclaiming the land: the resurgence of rural movements in Africa, Asia and Latin America*, ed. S. Moyo and P. Yeros, 102–18. New York: Zed Books.

André, C., and J.-P. Platteau. 1998. Land relations under unbearable stress: Rwanda caught in the Malthusian trap. *Journal of Economic Behavior & Organization* 34, no. 1: 1–47.

Baglioni, E., and P. Gibbon. 2013. Land Grabbing, Large- and Small-scale Farming: What can evidence and policy from 20th century Africa contribute to the debate? *Third World Quarterly* 34, no. 9: 1558–81.

Becker, L.C. 2013. Land sales and the transformation of social relations and landscape in peri-urban Mali. *Geoforum*, 46, 113–23.

Bernstein, H. 2007. Rural livelihoods in a globalizing world: Bringing class back in. In *Paper for conference on 'Policy Intervention and Rural Transformation: Towards a Comparative Sociology of Development'*, 10–6. Beijing: China Agricultural University.

Berry, S. 2002. Debating the land question in Africa. *Comparative Studies in Society and History* 44, no. 4: 638–68.

Borras, S.M. Jr., Edelman, M. and Kay, C. 2008. Transnational agrarian movements: origins and politics, campaigns and impact. In *Transnational agrarian movements confronting globalisation*, ed. S.M. Borras Jr., M. Edelman and C. Kay. Oxford: Wiley-Blackwell.

Borras, S.M., and J. Franco. 2010. Towards a broader view of the politics of global land grab: Rethinking land issues, reframing resistance. *Initiatives in Critical Agrarian Studies Working Paper Series*, 1.

Borras, S.M., and J.C. Franco. 2013. Global land grabbing and political reactions 'from below'. *Third World Quarterly* 34, no. 9: 1723–47.

Borras, S.M., R. Hall, I. Scoones, B. White, and W. Wolford. 2011. Towards a better understanding of global land grabbing: An editorial introduction. *Journal of Peasant Studies* 38, no. 2: 209–16.

Bruce, J.W. 2007. Drawing a line under crisis: Reconciling returnee land access and security of tenure in post-conflict Rwanda. *An HPG Background Paper, ODI, London.*

Burnett, M., and R.W. (Organization) Human. 2012. *Curtailing criticism: intimidation and obstruction of civil society in Uganda*. New York, NY: Human Rights Watch.

Chapman, C., and A. Kagaha. 2009. Resolving conflicts using traditional mechanisms in the Karamoja and Teso regions of Uganda. *Minority Rights Group International.* Available from: http://www.refworld.org/docid/4a97dc232.html (accessed August 18, 2014).

Chauveau, J.-P. 2000. The land question in Côte d'Ivoire: a lesson in history. *Issue Paper-Drylands Programme, International Institute for Environment and Development*, (95).

Chimhowu, A., and P. Woodhouse. 2006. Customary vs private property rights? Dynamics and trajectories of vernacular land markets in Sub-Saharan Africa. *Journal of Agrarian Change* 6, no. 3: 346–71.

Coldham, S. 2000. Land reform and customary rights. The case of Uganda. *Journal of African law* 44, no. 1: 65–77.

Colin, J.P., and P. Woodhouse. 2010. Introduction: Interpreting land markets in Africa. *Africa* 80, no. 1: 1–13.

Cotula, L. 2012. The international political economy of the global land rush: A critical appraisal of trends, scale, geography and drivers. *Journal of Peasant Studies* 39, no. 3–4: 649–80.

Daudelin, J. 2002. Agrarian structures, agrarian policies and violence in Central America and Southern Mexico. *unpublished paper for the North-South Institute.*

Deininger, K. 2003. Land markets in developing and transitioning economies: Impact of liberalization and implications for future reform. *American Journal of Agricultural Economics* 85, no. 5: 1217–22.

Deininger, K., and R. Castagnini. 2006. Incidence and impact of land conflict in Uganda. *Journal of Economic Behavior & Organization* 60, no. 3: 321–45.

Deininger, K.W., and P. Mpuga. 2004. *Does greater accountability improve the quality of delivery of public services?: Evidence from Uganda*. Washington, DC: World Bank Publications.

Downs, R.E., and S.P. Reyna. 1988. *Land and society in contemporary Africa*. Hanover: University of New Hampshire.

Duvail, S., C. Médard, O. Hamerlynck, and D. Wanja Nyingi. 2012. Land and water grabbing in an East African coastal wetland: The case of the tana delta. *Water Alternatives*, 5, no. 2.

Edelman, M. 2013. Messy hectares: Questions about the epistemology of land grabbing data. *Journal of Peasant Studies* 40, no. 3: 485–501.

Edelman, M., and A. León. 2013. Cycles of land grabbing in Central America: An argument for history and a case study in the Bajo Aguán, Honduras. *Third World Quarterly* 34, no. 9: 1697–722.

Edelman, M., C. Oya, and S.M. Borras. 2013. Global land grabs: Historical processes, theoretical and methodological implications and current trajectories. *Third World Quarterly* 34, no. 9: 1517–31.

Emwamu, S.P. 2013. Amuria residents protest over planned land takeover [online]. *The Daily Monitor*, 18 February. Available from: http://www.monitor.co.ug/News/National/Amuria-residents-protest-over-planned-land-takeover/-/688334/1697028/-/yodtlyz/-/index.html (accessed April 11, 2014).

Emwamu, S.P. 2014. Kapelebyong constructions to go on, says Amuria RDC [online]. *The Daily Monitor*, 4 February. Available from: http://www.monitor.co.ug/News/National/Kapelebyong-constructions-to-go-on-says-Amuria-RDC/-/688334/1683614/-/ojqnnez/-/index.html (accessed Apr 11, 2014).

Fred-Mensah, B.K. 1999. Capturing ambiguities: Communal conflict management alternative in Ghana. *World Development* 27, no. 6: 951–65.

Greco, E. 2010. The 'Brazilian model' in Africa: A view from Tanzania [online]. In *Conference on Agrarian reforms and Natural Resources Management in Africa and Latin America; University of Lleida, Spain. 2010.* Available from: https://www.escholar.manchester.ac.uk/uk-ac-man-scw:194370 (accessed Mar 24, 2014).

Greco, E. 2012. Struggles and resistance against land dispossession in Africa: An overview [online]. In *Handbook of land and water grabs in Africa*, ed. T. Allan et al. Routledge. Available from: https://www.escholar.manchester.ac.uk/uk-ac-man-scw:194365 (accessed Mar 24, 2014).

Hilhorst, T., J. Nelen, and N. Traoré. 2011. Agrarian change below the radar screen: Rising farmland acquisitions by domestic investors in West Africa. Results from a survey in Benin, Burkina Faso and Niger. *Unpublished paper by the Royal Tropical Institute and SNV.*

Hunt, D. 2004. Unintended consequences of land rights reform: The case of the 1998 Uganda land act. *Development Policy Review* 22, no. 2: 173–91.

Jones, B. 2009. *Beyond the state in rural Uganda*. Edinburgh: Edinburgh University Press.

Kerkvliet, B.J.T. 2009. Everyday politics in peasant societies (and ours). *Journal of Peasant Studies* 36, no. 1: 227–43.

Kibreab, G. 2002. When refugees come home: the relationship between stayees and returnees in post-conflict Eritrea. *Journal of Contemporary African Studies* 20, no. 1: 53–80.

Kisamba-Mugerwa, W. 1997. The impact of individualisation on common grazing land resources in Uganda/by Wilberforce Kisambe-Mugerwa.

Leff, J. 2009. Pastoralists at War: Violence and security in the Kenya-Sudan-Uganda border region. *International Journal of Conflict and Violence* 3, no. 2: 188–203.

Mamonova, N. 2012. Challenging the dominant assumptions about peasants' responses to land grabbing: A study of diverse political reactions from below on the example of Ukraine. In *International Conference on Global Land Grabbing II*. pp. 17–9.

Matete, N. and BakamaNume, B. 2010. Climate of Uganda. In *Contemporary Geography of Uganda*, ed. B. BakamaNume, 1–34. Dar Es Salaam: MKuku Na Nyota.

Mbunda, F.M. 2009. *Shadows from the abyss*. Bamenda: African Books Collective.

Mkutu, K.A. 2007. Small arms and light weapons among pastoral groups in the Kenya–Uganda border area. *African Affairs* 106, no. 422: 47–70.

Pedersen, R.H., Rachael Spichiger, Sarah Alobo, and Michael Kidoido. 2012. Land tenure and economic activities in Uganda: A review of the literature.

Peluso, N.L., and C. Lund. 2011. New frontiers of land control: Introduction. *Journal of Peasant Studies* 38, no. 4: 667–81.

Peters, P.E. 2009. Challenges in land tenure and land reform in Africa: Anthropological contributions. *World Development* 37, no. 8: 1317–25.

Peters, P.E. 2013. Land appropriation, surplus people and a battle over visions of agrarian futures in Africa. *Journal of Peasant Studies* 40, no. 3: 537–62.

Peters, P.E., and D. Kambewa. 2007. Whose security? Deepening social conflict over 'customary' land in the shadow of land tenure reform in Malawi.

Place, F. 2009. Land tenure and agricultural productivity in Africa: A comparative analysis of the economics literature and recent policy strategies and reforms. *World Development* 37, no. 8: 1326–36.

Pye, O. 2010. The biofuel connection – Transnational activism and the palm oil boom. *Journal of Peasant Studies* 37, no. 4: 851–74.

Rebelo, L.-M., M.P. McCartney, and C.M. Finlayson. 2010. Wetlands of Sub-Saharan Africa: Distribution and contribution of agriculture to livelihoods. *Wetlands Ecology and Management* 18, no. 5: 557–72.

Refugee Law Project. 2008. Conflict, justice and reconciliation in Teso: Obstacles and opportunities. Briefing Note No. 1. Kampala, Uganda: Makerere University, Faculty of Law. Available from: http://www.refugeelawproject.org/files/briefing_papers/RLP.BP0801.pdf (accessed February 1, 2015).

Richards, P., S. Archibald, B. Bruce, W. Modad, and E. Mulbah. 2005. Community cohesion in Liberia: A post-conflict rapid social assessment.

Rugadya, A.M. 2009. Escalating land conflicts in Uganda: A review of evidence from recent studies and surveys. Report to the International Republican Institute (IRI) and the Uganda Round Table Foundation. Kampala. Mimeo. Available from: http://www.mokoro.co.uk/files/13/file/lria/escalating_Uganda_landconflicts.pdf (accessed August 18, 2014).

Rugadya, A.M., E. Nsamba-Gayiiya, and H. Kamusiime. 2008. Analysis of post conflict land policy and land administration: A survey of IDP return and resettlement issues and lesson: Acholi and lango regions. *Northern Uganda land study*, 1–80. Available from: http://landcoalition.org/sites/default/files/publication/714/northern_uganda_land_study_acholi_lango.pdf

Rugadya, M.A., H. Kamusiime, and E. Nsamba-Gayiiya. 2010. Tenure in mystery: Status of land under wildlife, forestry, and mining concessions in karamoja region, Uganda. TROCAIRE.

Scott, J.C., and B.J. Kerkvliet. 1986. *Everyday forms of peasant resistance in South-East Asia*. London: Psychology Press.

Smalley, R., and E. Corbera. 2012. Large-scale land deals from the inside out: Findings from Kenya's Tana Delta. *Journal of Peasant Studies* 39, nos. 3–4: 1039–75.

Taylor, A.R.D., G.W. Howard, and G.W. Briggs. 1995. Developing wetland inventories in Southern Africa: A review. *Vegetatio* 118: 57–79.

Van Donge, J.K., and L. Pherani. 1999. Law and order as a development issue: Land conflicts and the creation of social order in Southern Malawi. *Journal of Development Studies* 36, no. 2: 48–70.

Vincent, J. 1982. *Teso in transformation: The political economy of peasant and class in Eastern Africa*. 1st Printing edition. Berkeley: Univ of California Pr.

Walker, K.L.M. 2008. From covert to overt: Everyday peasant politics in China and the implications for transnational agrarian movements. *Journal of Agrarian Change* 8, no. 2–3: 462–88.

Wolford, W., S.M. Borras, R. Hall, I. Scoones, and B. White. 2013. Governing global land deals: The role of the state in the rush for land. *Development and Change* 44, no. 2: 189–210.

Social struggles in Uganda's Acholiland: understanding responses and resistance to Amuru sugar works

Giuliano Martiniello

On Wednesday 18 April 2012, between 80 and 100 women from Amuru District in northern Uganda stripped naked in a protest to block their eviction from land they claim is rightfully theirs. They did this in front of representatives of the Local District Board and surveyors of the sugar company Madhvani Group, the firm seeking land in the area for sugarcane growing. By resisting dispossession and challenging state violence, small scale poor peasants reiterated the political salience of rural social struggles and highlighted the significance of land and agrarian questions. By placing social struggles over control, access and use of land and existing social relations – property and labour regimes – at the core of social analysis, this papers aims to contribute to further understanding both the character of contemporary land grabs and the nature of peasant resistance. It argues that escalating rural social protests manifested in both everyday, hidden practices of resistance and moments of open, militant contestation are aimed at (re)establishing and securing access to means of social reproduction. Yet these struggles cumulatively embody claims of land sovereignty and autonomy *vis-à-vis* capitalist markets and state.

Introduction

On Wednesday 18 April 2102, more than 100 people resisted eviction from land they claimed to be rightfully theirs in Amuru District in northern Uganda, close to the border with South Sudan. Women stripped naked before representatives of the Local District Board and surveyors of the Madhvani Group, the firm seeking 40,000 ha of land in the area for a new commercial sugarcane estate. By resisting dispossession and challenging state violence, poor rural communities in Uganda and elsewhere remind us of the political salience of rural social struggles. The event illuminates crucial aspects of peasants' agency, brings to the fore the present dynamics of national and global political economy and highlights the role of the state in current land acquisitions and agrarian transformation.

The Amuru Sugar Works project, initiated in 2007–2008 but stalled at inception, was planned to create employment for 7000–8000 people and additionally to provide livelihoods from sugarcane cultivation to 7000–10000 outgrower farmers, according to Madhvani (Madhvani 2012). The latter would be housed in labour camps with 10 ha each: 8 ha under sugarcane and 2 ha for food crops. The investor, Madhvani Group, which is a Ugandan company, would supply equipment to clear, plough and furrow the land as well as distribute treated cane seeds and give technical advice on agricultural matters. The proposed project would have displaced approximately 20,000 people (Penytoo, interview 16 May 2012), almost all family farmers, around the village of Lakang in this economically depressed region on the periphery, both politically and economically, of Uganda. The overwhelming majority of small-scale rural producers rejected the proposed enclosure of their land, and refused to be incorporated as either outgrower farmers or agricultural labourers.

Large-scale capitalist enclosures that activists labelled as 'land grabbing' (La Via Campesina 2011), and others see as a 'development opportunity' (FAO, IFAD, UNCATD and WB 2010), spread globally in the wake of the global commodities crisis of 2007–2008. As capital's response to declining profitability rates in the context of inextricably linked and mutually reinforcing food, financial, energy and ecological crises, vast tracts of land and other natural resources have been acquired in the global South through a variety of coercive mechanisms (Borras and Franco 2012). The African continent has been the geographical epicentre of these processes as an estimated 60 percent of total land acquisitions are located in Sub-Saharan Africa (White et al. 2012, 620). In the case of Uganda, large-scale commercial deals concluded between 2008 and 2010 represent 14.6 percent of the country's agricultural land (Friis and Reenberg 2010, 12). Here, the current wave of capitalist enclosures has taken multiple forms: land acquisitions for food and bio-fuel production for export by Trans-National Corporations (TNCs), ranching schemes set up by national capitalists, land enclosures driven by Reduction of Emissions from Deforestation and Degradation (REDD) carbon capture schemes and forestry creation, demarcations of conservation areas and game reserves for tourist purposes, and acquisitions especially in oil- and mineral-rich regions by high-ranking government and military officials.

The re-drawn geography of corporate-driven sugarcane production in Southern and Eastern Africa is developing to the detriment of locally oriented food production systems. The push for sugar, and related energy and biofuel production, seems to follow trends of oligopolistic control of agriculture and its enhanced interpenetration with finance capital (Hall 2011; Richardson 2010). The configuration of new sets of economic and political relationships appears to be also related to global contextual trends as the anticipation of food security and new forms of resource extraction for fuel security (Borras et al. 2011, 627–628). The increased corporate control of the international food regime and its approximation to a food-for-fuel regime (McMichael 2009) also represented major drivers of the consolidation of agri-business power in the region.

The emerging scholarship on land grabs paid only scant attention to the way politics from below is constituted by and in the agency of agrarian subjects and how it affects the trajectories of agrarian change (Clapp 2014; Fairbairn 2014; Zoomers 2010). Notwithstanding a rich tradition in peasant and agrarian studies (Brass 1991; Hobsbawm 1973; Isaacman 1990), the analysis of rural social protests and political reactions from below to land grabs has not undergone the same 'rush' and interest. Political repression by state apparatuses tends to silence instances of contestation, but the forms of resistance are also frequently difficult to apprehend, as the character of rural social struggles is sometimes subterranean (see Scott 1985). Furthermore, mainstream characterizations of African countrysides as *tabula rasa*, i.e. as empty spaces endowed with natural resources that need to be brought within the orbit of capitalist markets, reiterate a fictitious representation of peasants as simple commodity producers who are passive victims waiting to be rescued by philanthropic interventions and modernizing forces of the capitalist market (De Soto 2000; World Bank 2011).

Yet peasants have made their presence felt on the political scene by engaging in a multitude of different forms of struggle *vis-à-vis* externally posed threats and attempts at surplus extraction by state and accumulating classes (Scott 1975; Williams 1976). Social analyses from different disciplinary perspectives focused on rural politics explored the significance of peasant political actions in revolutionary struggles of the twentieth century (Shanin 1971; Wolf 1969) and national liberation anti-colonial movements in Africa (Davidson 1974; Fanon 1967). Other enquiries uncovered the relevance of the study of peasant consciousness in the study of peasant politics (Ranger 1985). Yet there is wide disagreement among scholars about the forms of resistance and political attitudes of peasants. To Fanon (1967), peasants represented the quintessence of the revolutionary subject. Scott (1975) defined their actions as mainly oriented to 'minimize risks'. The literature further bifurcates into those who became interested in the study of social revolts as moments that revealed the existence of a separate political domain which elite domination and hegemony have been unable to supersede or suppress (Arnold 1984; Guha 1983), and those who maintained that peasants' agency and dissent was largely manifest in low-intensity, everyday, hidden practices of resistance of a non-confrontational nature (Scott 1985). Land struggles are more likely to embody 'uneasy and erratic, contradictory and shifting alliances of different class elements and tendencies than to express the interests of some unambiguous and unitary class subject' (Bernstein 2009, 253). However, recent critical agrarian scholarship has returned to unpacking land struggles, motivated in part by the need to understand the stubborn persistence of peasants and small farmers in the face of a developmental model geared towards their extinction (Desmarais 2007, 195; Moyo 2008; Van der Ploeg 2008).

In order to explore these questions, I follow Kerkvliet's (2009) suggestion to move the perimeter of the study of politics beyond the institutional terrain of conventional politics towards everyday peasant politics, which is constituted at different multi-layered levels (household, community, village). If politics as he suggests is the terrain of struggle 'over norms and rules regarding authority over control, allocation, production and use of natural resources and the value and ideas underlying those activities', then every peasant politics incorporates the tensions deriving from people 'embracing, complying with or contesting them' (Kerkvliet 2009, 232). Drawing upon Isaacman (1990, 3), this paper focuses on the struggles over labour process and property regimes as key entry points to understanding how power is negotiated and executed in the countryside, and what avenues for social dissent exist.

This paper places social struggles over control, access and use of land and existing social relations – land property and labour regimes – at the core of its analysis, and aims to contribute to further understanding both of the character of contemporary land grabs and of the nature of resistance.

The paper explores the relation between land dispossession and rural social struggles, and the implications of these for the trajectories of agrarian change in Northern Uganda, by raising a set of interrelated research questions: how are enclosures implemented and resisted? How do they differentially affect social groups? Who are the agents of resistance? How do they organize their *praxis* of resistance? And how does all this affect trajectories of social change?

Understanding the constitutive processes of land dispossession, its discourses and practices, will help to display wider class conflicts manifested in political, economic and ideological forms. This is furthermore important in the context of post-conflict resettlement after 20 years of forced internment of almost the totality of the Acholi population in internally displaced people (IDP) camps. With the aim to contribute to re-politicizing existing debates over land, this paper argues that looking at the geo-politics of capital at the global scale is only one side of the coin that has to be supplemented with a simultaneous analysis of the social implications of land enclosures from the perspective of everyday peasant politics.

Genealogy of struggles for sovereignty and relative autonomy in Acholiland

Acholi peasants have a long history of interpenetration and relative autonomy *vis-à-vis* market and state forces, which precedes colonialism. Unravelling this history is essential to understanding the long-term practices that emerged as a sign of contestation or defiance of the established authority, and influenced the responses from below to contemporary land enclosures. Anthropological and linguistic studies support the idea that Acholi people are descendants of Nilotic-speaking ancestors and that their presence in today's northern Uganda is the outcome of a gradual but constant infiltration from Sudan starting around 1700 (Girlings 1960, 12–14). Explanations of the causes of what Girlings termed the 'Shilluk migration' have not been elaborated. A possible and suggestive hypothesis links the migration to profound changes in the systems of land tenure and growing appropriation of peasant surplus occurring in Northern Sudan, which fell under the Turco-Egyptian rule in 1821. The state initiated the control of large tracts of land previously held by peasants, imposed forced agricultural labour, established a new land tax policy and promoted private property in land (Zeleza 1997, 120). The growth of agricultural slavery and land confiscation was met by desertions and mass migrations by peasants who exerted their right to escape or exit adverse political conditions as a tactic to evade state control and rule (Zeleza 1997, 135).

The area today inhabited by Acholi people was at the crossroads of many distinguished political and economic influences in the mid-nineteenth century. From the North, there were the Arabic slave raiders and traders, who emanated from centralized state structures of the Sudanic states; from the South, there were the Swahili merchants who extended exchange networks from the Sultanate of Oman (Girlings 1960; Mamdani 1976; Mukherjee 1956). In response to politico-economic and ecological factors and to constant threats coming from outside, regular movement became a necessary aspect of production (Mamdani 1976, 20). Simple herding and shifting cultivation satisfied this necessity. Constant movement also led to the dispersal of families, resulting in decentralized and segmental social units. War and defence were at the core of the social organization of the village unit. Age classes of Acholi males from 15 years upwards formed the fighting organization of the people and were organized on a territorial basis (Girlings 1960, 75). Mukherjee termed them 'military democracies' in the light of the segmented and acephalous character of their political organization (1956, 77).

The practice of shifting cultivation, which is still predominant in Acholiland today, demanded mobility of populations. Any village had the liberty to occupy uncultivated land or land where cultivation had been abandoned. Security of tenure was therefore guaranteed by the permanent use of land. Such forms of occupation, however, did not imply permanent ownership but granted the usufruct for determinate periods (Parsons 1960, 13; Mafeje 2003). Through customary land tenure regimes, people also were guaranteed grazing rights, hunting rights, water rights and rights over ant-hills and shea butter-nut trees (Parsons 1960, 14). These complex and nested regimes of land rights combined and articulated both the individual and the collective rights in non-conflictual ways.

Colonial enterprise aimed to push peasants to produce cotton in order to pay taxes and other kind of fees, and afford the imported European consumer goods that penetrated the colonial economy. Yet Acholiland was marginal in many ways to the early British colonial rule in the late nineteenth century. As a dry, geographically remote and sparsely populated area located far to the north of the country, it seemed of little interest to the commercial appetites of the colony. The new colony became in fact structured upon the economic and political centrality of the Buganda kingdom in the South, which became the pivot of indirect rule and bifurcated despotism (Mamdani 1976, 1996). A nation of agriculturalists and stockbreeders, Acholi show propensity neither to cash-crop production nor to labour migration into the Southern region where economic activities were concentrated (Atkinson 2010, 5). In 1920–1921, 81,000 pounds of lint were produced in Uganda, of which 85 percent were grown in the Southern regions (Mamdani 1976, 47). Land availability and the absence of individualized land tenure gave comparative stability to the 'traditional' socio-economic order (Girlings 1960, 183).

Following Scott's characterization of forms of resistance in geographically remote peripheries, we interpret these localized, social, economic and cultural practices as deliberate efforts by people to withdraw from state control (2009, 51) and claim land sovereignty. The location of the Acholi at a distance from the control of more powerful and centralized kingdoms of Southern Uganda, living at the margins of trade routes, the simplification of social structure and means of subsistence, shifting cultivation and continuous mobility, far from being signs of primitivism or backwardness, can rather be interpreted as dynamic elements and adaptations to evade state capture (see Scott 2009, 30).

The Lamogi rebellion of 1911 is an instance of the 'art of not being governed'. Provoked by British colonial restrictions on the possession of firearms (Adimola 1954, 169) but in the context of resistance to the imposition of taxes, forced labour and land requisitions (Mamdani 1976; Tosh 1978; Vincent 1977), the event itself and subsequent repression are alive in the memory of Acholi people and their world-views. I interpret this as a moment in the more complex and long-term confrontation with external political and economic forces, to maintain political and economic sovereignty and autonomy over a specific geographical territory and social group. Similarly, the forced introduction of cotton into the area in the late 1930s by colonial authorities was met with substantial opposition (Leys 1967; Tosh 1978). Its net effect was the creation of a minority of 'progressive' medium- and large-scale commercial cotton farmers, often combining this with salaried employment. Yet commercial farming never took off in Acholiland (Leys 1967, 50; Mamdani 1976, 46), an area that colonial officials perceived as backward (Branch 2011, 50) and which successive governments after independence have continued to treat as peripheral to the national economy and polity, while also a terrain for extractive enterprises (Atkinson 2010; Branch 2011).

By replicating and widening the efforts of the colonial state, the post-colonial state developed means to extract surplus produce from peasants through taxes and the establishment of marketing boards, which monopolized the purchase of cash crops in the countryside (below market price) and their sale on international markets. Compounding this was the erosion of customary land tenure, consolidated with Idi Amin's Land Reform Act of 1975, which claimed all land to be state-owned and aimed to turn peasants into the state's tenants (Mamdani 1987). Initiated in the years of neoliberal restructuring of agriculture during the late 1980s, the state's efforts to increase the 'legibility'[1] (see Scott 1998) of the countryside were aimed at enhancing the registration and formalization of land, facilitating its titling and transfer, improving small-holders' integration in agricultural commodity chains and consolidating agri-business. State-led development projects promoted the standardization and simplification of rural spaces, facilitating their decryption and subsequent control. According to Mamdani (2012), the 1998 Land Act's aim of recognizing customary land tenure must be seen as the latest phase in the modern state's endeavour to colonize society. The identification and mapping of land under customary forms of

[1]The term refers to the quality of being clear enough to be read.

tenure through geographical information systems (GIS) and digitalized cadastral services is not aimed at protecting customary rights but at extending state control over people and territory, and eventually eliminating or converting these rights. As Mitchell (2007, 29) notes, the creation of formal legal title is a mechanism for transferring properties from poorer urban and rural classes to more affluent ones, and concentrating ownership in fewer hands. While just 17 percent of land in Uganda is held under freehold (World Bank 2012), the state is expanding its efforts to consolidate its fiscal basis, enhancing territorial control over reluctant northern populations and actively promoting the formation of a class of politically connected businessmen (Mamdani 2012). The imposition of a new definition of property formidably biased in favour of landowners, which was aimed at eradicating agrarian use rights not juridically defined, generated exclusive and individualized access to land undermining other communal/cooperative/collective forms of land tenure (see Thompson 1971). The reduction of international agricultural prices, and the progressive measures of liberalization and deregulation of the agricultural economy, spurred many small-scale peasants in Uganda and Tanzania to retreat into food crops for local exchange, like cow and pigeon peas, cassava, sorghum, legumes and sesame (Daviron and Gibbon 2002, 152).

Twenty years of war in the northern regions against the Lord's Resistance Army led by Joseph Kony and other insurgent groups of rebels (terminated in 2006) was characterized first by counter-insurgency military tactics, then by forced encampment of rural populations, displacement and dispossession and flows of food aid (see Branch 2011). During the same period, state violence ravaged the northern countryside, first by means of deportation and encampment of rural populations in IDP camps, then by means of unlawful land annexation of land by political and military elites. The new strategy by Museveni's government included sudden and violent forced displacement of the entire rural population of western Acholiland, estimated at approximately 2 million. In 1996, the government gave a 48-hour ultimatum to the population to abandon their homes and assemble at designated trading posts, after which the army began bombing villages, burning huts and granaries and killing civilians who refused to comply (Branch 2013, 3153). People in the camps were highly dependent on relief aid and suffered from severe lack of protection, being at the mercy of both government troops and rebels. The forced interruption of agricultural production created the basis for the development of a humanitarian industry: by 2003 over 100 relief organizations were working in northern Uganda, and by 2007 USD 200 million were annually spent in the camps (Branch 2013, 3156; UNOCHA 2005).

According to the United Nations High Commissioner for Refugees (UNHCR), by 2012 almost 95 percent of the camps' inhabitants had left (UNHCR 2012). Yet the long-term forced internment, dependence on food aid and extreme poverty generated by war created the pre-conditions for systematic land dispossession through both the state and market. On the one hand, individuals with political connections and enough wealth were able to manipulate state institutions and use state repressive power to dispossess peasants. Indeed, exploiting people's absence from their homes during the war, the government funded the formation of the Amuru District Commercial Farmers Association, led by a group of high-ranking military officials and Members of Parliament (MPs) who lobbied for the preferential allocation of 20,000 ha and huge sums of public funds (Atkinson 2008). On the other hand, there are those who are giving up land because of desperate poverty faced by much of the rural population. As a consequence, the wave of land enclosures that targeted the Amuru district is paving the way for the creation of a surplus population of the dispossessed (see Li 2010). The consequences of violent displacement affected Gulu's population, the closest town to the Amuru District, which dramatically increased from below 40,000 people in the early 1990s to over 150,000 in the last few years (Branch 2013, 3160). The proportion of people living below the poverty line in Gulu and surrounding environments increased to 69 percent in 2009/2010 (Gulu Municipal Council 2011).

Yet in Amuru, the majority of people access land through inheritance (87 percent) and hold it in customary tenure (98 percent), and certificates of customary ownership amount only to 1.4 percent and freehold property to 0.4 percent of property arrangements (Ravnborg et al. 2013, 18–22). Land and agricultural commercialization don't seem to be proceeding as in the rest of the country. Access to labour power is secured by household members (or through kin) and through *awak*[2] at times of clearance and harvest, and only very rarely through hiring within the community. Labour income is used mainly to satisfy the consumption and reproductive needs of the household, plus to fund *ceremonial* and *replacement* activities (see Wolf 1966). Acholi peasant households in Amuru tend to sell 10–20 percent of their agricultural production (Uganda Bureau of Statistics 2010) and use the remaining part for different forms of productive consumption at household and village levels. Small-scale cultivators in Kololo-Lakang take their produce by bicycle or motorbike to the nearest market in Amuru, 45 km away. Seeds are generally accessed thanks to the careful selection of women, who at harvest time dedicate knowledge and energy in order to clean and store them. After marriage, women bring with them seeds from the father's household to begin cultivation.

The degree of commercialization of agriculture and commodification of subsistence is very minimal. In Acholi, moreover, 80 percent of the population practices shifting cultivation (Atkinson 2012). With an average availability of 2 ha per household, peasant households manage the cycle of agricultural production according to social norms based in cultural repertoires and moral economies, by planting combinations of food crops such as finger millet, pigeon, cowpeas and chickpeas, sesame, sorghum and cassava. Conjunctly, rice and maize are grown with a commercial intent. Yet involvement within national markets in Amuru is among the lowest of the country. The low degree of monetization of economic relationships and the low mobility of factors of production provide a form of resistance to capitalist commoditization (Friedmann 1980). This does not mean that peasants can retreat in complete isolation from negative external pressures. The same notion of 'peasant' bears an understanding of embedded relations into powerful and exploitative political, social and economic networks. Peasants are still subject to the extractive mechanisms of uneven exchange with local merchants and middlemen and through very low farm-gate prices. However, they still maintain their sovereignty over the mobilization of labour and use of land, as well as deciding which channels to use to market their agricultural surplus. Informal markets, petty trade, simple commodity production, forms of bartering within the community, links of reciprocity and mutuality, and labour cooperation all represent obstacles to generalized commoditization of social reproduction (see Polanyi 1957).

Resistance to penetration of capitalist social relations therefore begins with the mechanisms used by households to pursue economic self-provisioning and relatively autonomous social reproduction. In a context of increasing marginality, dependence and subordination, it is at the core of the creation and development of a self-controlled and self-managed resource base. This in turn allows for forms of co-production of humanity and living nature to improve the process of co-production, enlarge autonomy and thus reduce dependency (Van der Ploeg 2008, 23). Village organization and cohesion, maintained through a set of rituals, customs, marriages and reciprocity with neighbours, and

[2]Community labour groups.

kinship groups, allowed for limited penetration of market imperatives, as social reproduction could be enhanced through non-market practices.

Land enclosures in Amuru: the power of state and capital

This paper analyses the recent attempt by the Ugandan state to alienate 40,000 ha of land in Acholiland for the establishment of a sugarcane plantation and processing factory run by the Madhvani Group, the largest sugar company in the country. The Madhvani Group has a long history of presence in the country since the 1930s when, after having obtained 800 ha of land from the Busoga kingdom and the colonial government, it established the Kakira Sugar Factory. The Indian elite with interests in commercial activities became a partner, together with the African petty bourgeoisie, of the colonial government in the enterprise of developing a cash-crop economy (Mamdani 1976). The Madhvani Group is today an empire in East Africa with interest in sugar, energy, insurance, floriculture and construction.

Empirical research in the area around the Kakira Sugar Factory highlighted the social implications of sugarcane cultivation especially in terms of food insecurity, indebtedness and land loss (see Kafuko 2005). Similarly in the Kigali District in Rwanda, where in 1997 the state leased 3100 ha to Madhvani Group, a study concluded that the majority of interviewed households experienced increasing rates of dependence on, and indebtedness to, Madhvani (Veldman and Lankhorst 2011). In both cases the company, with monopsonistic powers, was able to determine non-negotiable prices and decide when the cane is ripe, and prevented outgrowers from being present when the harvest was weighed (Veldman and Lankhorst 2011, 8; see also Tibakuno 2000). These developments in eastern Africa reiterate the question of adverse incorporation of small-scale petty commodity producers into vertically organized global commodity chains elsewhere on the continent (see Oya 2012; Little and Watts 1994).

The process of enclosure and the ongoing contestation it generated constitute an advantageous entry point for social enquiry of escalating processes of dispossession, commoditization and resistance. The case epitomizes the converging pressures and typical features of land grabs. Seen from the angle of global capital expansion (financial and agri-business) and penetration into previously un-captured resources, territories and populations, the deal follows a larger trend in the continent oriented towards reviving and expanding industrial agriculture in Africa. The pattern alters not only tenure relations but also patterns of land use, and is based on the conversion of large tracts of land, mostly peasant-owned, into large-scale, mono-crop, highly mechanized and chemically-intensive plantations, often in combination with outgrowers or contract schemes.

Behind the label 'private–public partnership', the state is profoundly involved and invested in the Amuru Sugar project. Not only did it deploy its usual arsenal of violence and bribery in an effort to evict local inhabitants and secure land for the company but, with promises of infrastructural development, wealth creation, rural employment, outgrower schemes and energy security, the Ugandan government actively promoted this and similar projects, propagating the view that 'every sugar plantation is an oil-field' (Child 2009, 249).

Amuru district, an area known for fertile and vast land, and low population density, has been the epicentre of land enclosures in the immediate aftermath of the war. In 2008, exploiting the absence of people who had been interned in IDP camps, the Land District Board fraudulently allocated 10,000 ha to the general Julius Oketta and 1,000 ha to Harriet Aber, the reputed girlfriend of Salim Saleh, president Yoweri Museveni's brother

(High Court of Uganda 2008). In Apaa village, in 2011–2012, the creation of a conservation area and game reserve for tourist purposes over an area of 20,000 ha took precedence over the rights of local populations (Lenhart 2013). In order to facilitate the flow of commodities and connect the area to regional markets, Uganda's government has invested in improved transport infrastructure to connect Gulu to Juba in South Sudan. In 2012 it granted a commission to China Henan Industrial Corporation Group, a large-scale parastatal enterprise, as part of the wider bilateral cooperation between the two countries (New Vision, 2012).

The origins of the story at the core of this paper started when the Madhvani Group of Companies applied for 40,000 ha of land in Amuru for a sugarcane plantation and factory during the eighth tenure of Uganda Parliament (2007–2008). The Madhvani Group has been an important funder of the electoral campaign of President Museveni. So the deal was part of a political exchange which consolidated the patronage networks of the existing regime and the politics of land capture. The plan aimed to provide employment to 7000–8000 outgrowers (and approximately 8000 agricultural labourers) and to boost Uganda's sugarcane production and foreign exchange earnings. The project presumed that Madhvani would supply equipment to clear, plough and furrow the land as well as distribute treated cane seeds and give technical advice on agricultural matters. Outgrowers would eventually pay unspecified rents on the 10 ha and housing costs. With an overall cost of USD 100 million, the plan, we are told by its promoters, will bring enormous development within 100 km of the factory and will improve the livelihood of individuals in Amuru (Wesonga 2015). The average salary proposed for people in charge of cane cutting is estimated at about 50,000–60,000 Ugandan shillings (USD 20–24; Komakech, interview May 16, 2012).

When the Madhvani application reached the Office of the erstwhile Chairperson of the District Land Board (DLB) in 2008, the latter decided to lease 10,000 ha of land in Lakang and Kololo villages in Amuru Sub-county, instead of 40,000 ha. Yet the land was customarily owned by the people of Lamogi. Therefore, in the same year, Amuru leaders (clan leaders and MPs) sought redress by taking the Amuru DLB to the Gulu High Court. They claimed that the land had been unlawfully allocated to Madhvani as it did not belong to the state. The first judgement in the High Court of Gulu in April 2008 declared the land to be customarily owned as hunting and growing grounds on the basis of archival research (High Court of Uganda 2008; Ojok, interview May 13, 2012). The legal avenue of contestation was initiated by more affluent people who insisted on negotiations with state authorities. Yet interviews with local residents showed that the majority of poor peasants mistrusted the legal avenue as it was expensive and it did not provide any guarantee that the state would respect that obligation. In late 2008, in the attempt to persuade local communities about the positive impacts of the project, politicians, elders and opinion leaders were taken to Kakira Sugar Works in Busoga (Serwajja 2014), the area that has the highest concentration of land under sugarcane cultivation in the country.

After the first legal victory by Lakang-Kololo communities, the state appealed the verdict. In the second round of judgment at the High Court of Gulu in February 2012, Judge Musane, who presided over the matter, ruled that the land in the Lakang-Kololo area was not held under customary tenure (High Court of Uganda 2008). According to the Hon. Gilbert Olanya, member of Parliament for Kilak County in Amuru district, after a quick site visit of the land that the Amuru DLB proposed to lease, the judge declared all the settlements to be relatively new, reiterating the idea that the land was not used for agricultural purposes and was therefore public land under the custody of the DLB (Olanya, interview 14 June 2012). Yet during my first visit to Lakang-Kololo communities in March 2012, I observed the existence of numerous huts and plots under cultivation.

Peasants interviewed on this subject considered the remaining part of the land as grazing and hunting grounds (though cattle had been massively stolen by the Ugandan army and rebel groups during the war), and to cater for the necessities of next generations (personal communication, 6 March 2012). In other words the judge's 'terra nullius' perspective failed to account for the context of post-conflict resettlement, while simultaneously missing the multiple patterns of land uses of Acholi peasant communities.

Local communities sought legal redress in the Court of Appeal, but the case has not been heard since then. In the light of mounting opposition to the deal, the government secured the support of key institutions which aligned with the state: the Resident District Commissioner as the head of security, Local Councils (LCV), District Land Board and MPs for Acholi (Ojok, interview 13 May 2012). Youth interviewed in the communities of Lakang further claimed that local council officials attempted to bribe the young members of the communities in an attempt to divide the cohesion of the community and implement the deal.

Contesting dispossession, resisting displacement

In the face of combined pressures from the state, foreign investors and accumulating classes, peasant populations in Amuru have responded in a variety of ways to threats of dispossession and displacement. These take many forms: small-scale (women) agricultural producers attacking the Amuru Sugar Works caravan of surveyors and technicians and Resident District Commissioner attempting to enter the area in Lakang; people in Paboo breaking down fences put down by the Uganda Police Defence Force; and persistent skirmishes with game wardens and rangers of the Uganda Wildlife Authority around conservation areas in Apaa (Serwajja 2014). Among the tactics aimed at defending or regaining access to land and other resources are cultivation of food crops inside protected areas, marginal or 'nomadic' agriculture, recalcitrant pastoralists' movements inside fenced areas and widespread contestation over enclosed *commons* such as water sources, ponds, wild fruits, medicinal herbs and plants. Beside covert and non-confrontational struggles, more militant forms of dissent took place in the case of neighbouring rural communities in Kololo and Lakang, which resurrected sustained forms of local organization, mobilization and inter-community solidarity (Community Meeting, 20 June 2012).

In order to prevent the initiation of surveying and registration works necessary for the instalment of the sugar plantation by Amuru Sugar Works, on 18 April 2012, local people organized a demonstration of non-violent protest, physically blockading the area to prevent Madhvani representatives and local councillors, escorted by soldiers, from entering the area designated for the sugar estate. Approximately 100 women took the lead of protest while men, mostly youths, occupied the second row with spears to avoid direct confrontation. Besides challenging the intruders, women undressed themselves as a sign of anger and displeasure but also an exhortation to respect moral obligations towards women in their reproductive and nurturing capacity. These acts of resistance manifested at interconnected levels, both material and symbolic. In particular, undressing themselves and showing their breasts in front of state officials and Madhvani representatives was meant to convey a very confrontational message: if you bring sugar here, our breasts will have no milk to feed ourselves. Women's practices in this sense brought to the fore the moral question through the mobilization of cultural symbolism.

In a focus group with women, shortly after the protest, one subsistence farmer said: 'We are determined to be killed for this land' (Women Focus Group, 2 May 2012). Another woman, a rice and maize farmer involved in petty commodity production, interviewed on this matter argued: 'the problem is the war still – the government kept us in the camps and now it wants to kick us off our ancestral land. Government has no place to put people' (Women Focus Group, 2 May 2012). Such discourses highlight the centrality of women in land struggles, especially in a context like northern Uganda where insecurity is the norm, and maintaining the possibility to access and use land can make a difference between life and death (see Federici 2004, 49).

The overall effect of the protest was to prevent the Resident District Commissioner and the Madhvani representatives from entering the area and initiating land surveying. Tensions mounted between the police and local residents but did not degenerate into open clashes. The convoy with the RDC and Madhvani officials left the area followed by screams of jubilation among the protesters (personal communication, 3 May 2012).

In order to overtake the impasse, the President himself travelled twice to Amuru in the aftermath of the protest and in May in order to convince the people about the portrayed benefits of the project using discourses of national development and modernization. Simultaneously, the state increased the militarization of social spaces by regularly patrolling the area, occupying the locally managed school, checking movements in and out of the area, and threatening interested journalists and sympathetic researchers (Lakang Primary School Teachers, interview 15 May 2012). Yet it continued to take local politicians, MPs, and clan and religious leaders to visit sites of alleged 'success' projects such as the Kalangala Palm Oil Project and Kakira Sugar Works (Serwajja 2014).

As an organized response to protracted state coercion which followed the protest, local communities of Lakang and Kololo held regular meetings on a monthly basis involving the participation of all social segments – elders, men, women and youth – as well as neighbouring communities and clans (Community Meeting, 20 June 2012). Organized by the local Rwot Kweri of Lakang, literally the chief of the hoe, collective assemblies, which I had the privilege to observe during one year of fieldwork in the area, represented in this context the political space *par excellence,* framed from below where claims of land sovereignty emerged. Meetings were held in Kololo, on the premises of the local market where women used to sell their agricultural produce. In these spaces both men and women, elders, and clan leaders – 'peasant intellectuals' to say it with Feierman (1990) – developed localized narratives of resistance, dealing with interpretations of actors and power dynamics involved, framing tactics of permanent watchfulness and alert, and considering constraints and opportunities of different forms of political contestation (Community Meeting, 18 May 2012). It is in this context that the decision to continue to contest and oppose the deal was taken, and where claims to land sovereignty were elaborated. The right to survival and to social reproduction were the key questions that concerned the participants in the assemblies. The overwhelming majority of Lakang villagers, however, opposed the idea of individually selling land, which is alien to the customary land-tenure system, and opted for a path of contestation (Community Meeting, 18 May 2012). According to the former district speaker of Amuru, a tiny minority of local residents who pushed for the option of selling or leasing the land to the investors took part in other meetings in Gulu at the instigation of Local District councillors and Members of Parliament, with the intent of promoting the project and explaining the benefits it would bring (Lakony, interview 14 May 2012). In fact, there existed a minority of the members of the Kololo and Lakang communities who paraded a win–win scenario. In other words the land deal ended up causing intra-family land wrangles due to alleged benefits from such investment (Opio, interview 12 February 2013). This portrait of rural social struggles exposes the fractures of competing social interests existing in rural communities, and their eventual re-composition or de-composition. Moreover, it highlights the uneven and differential impact of land deals upon different social groups.

Yet these kinds of struggles represented a qualitative leap from the mostly subterranean character of rural struggles as these intended to reach a wider audience, i.e. neighbouring communities, sympathetic non-governmental organizations (NGOs), engaged journalists and researchers, and other civil society organizations.

In one of these assemblies, a male peasant noted:

> Government says land does not belong to us after we came back from camps. They sent the army, the police, and game reserves rangers. They are fighting us. This has become the norm. They killed seven people in Apaa and arrested many more; they burned people's huts and destroyed crops in the gardens. We have not been treated as human beings but as animals (Community Meeting, 18 May 2012).

Another peasant at the meeting put this set of dominant forces in historical and political perspective:

> President Museveni allowed the interest of Madhvani and yet this is our ancestral land. Museveni took our cattle during the war and gave guns to the Karamojong. Now he wants our land. Where would we go? (Community Meeting, 18 May 2012).

These statements give a sense of both the extent of the protracted effort in capturing peasants' resources by the state and its permanent use of violence as a means of depredation and looting. These representations are furthermore useful to understand the effects of war on rural populations and its implications on the structure of control, access and use of land. Both war and post-conflict reconstruction have provided opportunities for the state and state-connected elite to expand their control of land and other natural resources (mainly oil) in Amuru. The expansion of state intervention and institutions in rural affairs further cemented the politics of land capture and the use of land for political patronage. Yet the overall effect of grassroots practices and forms of mobilization has been to impede the implementation of the project by delegitimising state-inspired development projects.

One of the immediate mobilizing factors that shaped responses and resistance in the Amuru Sugar case was the state's non-recognition of clan authority over land. Community members and clan leaders claimed since the beginning of debates on the deal not to have been informed of government's intention to allocate land to Madhvani, nor to have been invited to discuss the terms of the agreement (Penytoo, interview 16 May 2012). It is not surprising therefore that clan leaders are becoming catalysts for struggles of resistance and contestation as they are still widely considered the paramount authority in land matters. In this sense, traditional authorities on the ground in northern Uganda have become a vector of contestation of unrepresentative, 'invented' and co-opted paramount authorities. This is indicative of the multi-layered character of traditional authorities and the tensions that inhabit the 'customary' (Mamdani 1996).

Why was this instance of rural social protest successful in preventing land dispossession and displacement in Lakang and Kololo communities? I identify five reasons behind its success, albeit likely to be temporary. First is the capacity to maintain unity in the face of mounting pressures from within and without to fragment its constituent parts. In particular the ability of peasant intellectuals (Feierman 1990) to articulate views and narratives that framed a common platform of multi-class interests proved to be important. Second is the successful utilization of inter-elite rivalry and cleavages within structures of authority (state and traditional authorities) and the ability to reach the wider public arena and mobilize other sympathetic sections of civil society, exploiting the possibilities of the political opportunity framework (see Borras and Franco 2013). Third is the combined utilization of non-violent tactics (peaceful protests) and militant forms of struggle (permanent social mobilization of communities, high level of alert and protection of territories by preventing other investors from visiting the area). Fourth is the extent of rural protests throughout the country which challenged the legitimacy of state action. Fifth is the remoteness of the area which might have stimulated what Scott (1975) refers to as 'geographical resistance'– that is, remote locations represent areas which present problems of rule and control to the state.

Resistance was successful in delaying the project but state and capital have recently regrouped and are trying to revive the project through a new strategy. In fact, under pressure from Madhvani Group the state is trying once again to disrupt the cohesion of the community in an attempt to implement the project. In January 2015, the same clan leaders and MPs who during the tenure of the eighth parliament had sued the government were seen in Rakitura (President Museveni's countryside residence) for the signing of an agreement to avail 10,000 ha of land to the investor in return for compensation to all affected members (Atube, interview 14 January 2015).

Yet whereas an agreement has been signed between government and those who purport to be the trustees of the communities' land owners, the terms of the deed of settlement need to be communicated to the community members (Veremoi 2015). Moreover the mandate of the signatories is questionable as there is no evidence that the communities have delegated to the signatories the power to decide on these matters (Olanya, interview January 2015). It seems, therefore, that government carefully and cunningly selected the communities' representatives, excluding from the negotiation those leaders who opposed the deal. This sort of manipulation is a *dèja vu*: a continuation of the tactics of divide-and-rule and cooptation.

> Preparations are in high gear to get the work of the land valuer started. A decisive meeting is planned for late March 2015 which should bring together representatives of the Madhvani Group, central government officials and the rural communities, to negotiate and agree upon the terms of reference (scope of the lease offer, responsibility of the investor, responsibility of the beneficiary community, compensation and resettlement and priorities for corporate social responsibility). (Olanya, interview 16 January 2015)

These testimonies provide important insights in this case study. On the one hand, the state seems to have been pushed by local mobilizations to abandon the terrain of violence and coercion and initiate a path of negotiation and compromise. The question of compensation has been integrated in the negotiations for the first time, and this has to be seen as a success emerging from the protracted process of contestation. Whether or not the communities will accept the new terms of the deal or will initiate a new wave of struggles cannot be predicted. Far from being passive victims, peasants and their practices and agencies profoundly shaped the character of struggles over land and affected the spectrum of political possibilities and opportunities.

Conclusions

By analysing forms of rural social protest, and the motivations and rationales behind practices of resistance, this paper argues that persistent rural social struggles in Amuru district embody not only different elements of what Borras and Franco (2013) define as struggles against dispossession, exploitation, concentration and centralization, but also struggles for autonomy and sovereignty (Van der Ploeg 2008; Scott 2009). More open manifestations of dissent, although stimulated by the threat of dispossession or displacement, cannot in fact be mechanically related to it. The paper maintains instead that the current wave of local struggles against land dispossession and displacement is the culminating moment of the wider and longer praxis of everyday peasant resistance. It calls for a recuperation of historicity to unveil how everyday social practices and struggles shape, and are in turn shaped by, socio-historical dynamics of capital accumulation, dispossession and commoditization. Peasant everyday politics represents therefore a crucial domain of analysis for understanding the norms and practices that surround issues of control, access and use of land (Kerkvliet 2009).

These insights into the agricultural social reproduction strategies of Acholi peasants illuminate the dual character of contemporary social struggles, which manifest both political and socio-economic strategies. Though social struggles can be expressed through protests and land occupations, they are also manifest in the everyday efforts at the household level to ensure social reproduction and the improvement of available resources through constant adaptations in a context of increased politico-economic and ecological pressures. In between the two moments of resistance (protest and court case), other moments – hidden or open, daily or occasional – work as a continuum of social struggles whose form alters as conditions change.

As a result of war and land alienation, rural households in Amuru are under increased pressures for land privatization, agricultural commercialization and modernization. That the villagers in Kololo and Lakang took recourse to more manifest forms of militant or symbolic resistance signals that the largely subterranean forms of struggle, those located in the household reproductive strategies, are approaching a crisis point which does not allow them to be effective against new challenges that emerge. Such overt and collective acts of defiance normally come only after a protracted struggle on a different terrain or simultaneously. The revival of land struggles in Uganda at large brings to the fore the centrality of land and agrarian questions in the strategies of social reproduction of rural households. These localized struggles do not detract from the significance of broad-based transnational agrarian movements; rather they draw attention to the diverse geographies, patterns of commoditization and practices of resistance in processes of enclosure, and the necessary synergies between different *loci* of social struggles at both local and global levels.

Acknowledgements

I wish to thank Arthur Owor Spender and Dave-Ngendo Tshimba respectively for fieldwork and research assistance. My heartfelt thanks to Ruth Hall for her critical commentaries and editorial suggestions, and to Eria Serwajja for important details about the Amuru case, which greatly improved the quality and rigour of the manuscript. Last but not least, I need to thank the villagers of Kololo-Lakang communities who shared their time and knowledge. Without them this work would not have been possible. To them this work is dedicated.

References

Adimola, A.B. 1954. The Lamogi rebellion. *Uganda Journal* 18, no. 2: 166–77.

Arnold, D. 1984. Gramsci and peasant subalternity in India. *Journal of Peasant Studies* 11, no. 4: 155–77.

Atkinson, R. 2008. Land issues in Acholi in the transition from war to peace. *The Examiner* 4: 3–25.

Atkinson, R. 2010. *The roots of ethnicity: The origins of the Acholi of Uganda before 1800*. Kampala: Fountain Publishers.

Atkinson, R. 2012. Monitoring and mapping land disputes in the Acholi sub-region. Paper presented at the Conference *Perceptions of Peace-Building in Northern Uganda*, UN-Gulu University, 4–5 April.

Bernstein, H. 2009. Agrarian questions from transition to globalization. In *Peasants and globalization: Political economy, rural transformation and the agrarian question*, ed. A.H. Akram-Lodhi and C. Kay, 239–61. London and New York: Routledge.

Borras, J.S., and J. Franco. 2012. Global land grabbing and trajectories of agrarian change: A preliminary analysis. *Journal of Agrarian Change* 12, no. 1: 34–59.

Borras, J.S., and J. Franco. 2013. Global land grabbing and political responses 'from below'. *Third World Quarterly* 34, no. 9: 1723–47.

Borras, S., R. Hall, I. Scoones, B. White, and W. Wolford. 2011. Towards a better understanding of global land grabbing: an editorial introduction. *Journal of Peasant Studies* 38, no. 2: 209–16.

Branch, A. 2011. *Displacing human rights. War and intervention in Northern Uganda*. Oxford: Oxford University Press.

Branch, A. 2013. Gulu in war ... and peace? The Town as camp in northern Uganda. *Urban Studies* 50, no. 15: 3152–67.

Brass, T. 1991. Moral economists, subalterns, new social movements and the (Re-) emergence of a (Post) modernized middle peasant. *Journal of Peasant Studies* 1, no. 18: 173–205.

Child, K. 2009. Civil society in Uganda and the struggle to save the mabira forest. *Journal of Eastern African Studies* 3: 240–58.

Clapp, J. 2014. Financialization, distance and global food politics. *Journal of Peasant Studies, Special Issue: Global Agrarian Transformation Vol. 1: New Directions in Political Economy* 41, no. 5: 797–814.

Daviron, B., and P. Gibbon. 2002. Global commodity chains and African export agriculture. *Journal of Agrarian Change* 2, no. 2: 137–61.

Desmarais, A. 2007. *La Via Campesina. Globalization and the power of peasants*. London: Pluto Press.

De Soto, H. 2000. *The mystery of capital: Why capitalism triumph in the west and fails everywhere else*. London: Black Swan.

Davidson, B. 1974. African peasantries and revolution. *Journal of Peasant Studies* 1, no. 3: 269–90.

Fairbairn, M. 2014. Like gold with yield: evolving intersections between farmland and finance. *Journal of Peasant Studies, Special Issue: Global Agrarian Transformation Vol. 1: New Directions in Political Economy* 41, no. 5: 777–95.

Fanon, F. 1967. *The wretched of the earth*. London: Penguin Books.

FAO, IFAD, UNCTAD and World Bank. 2010. *Principles for responsible agricultural investments that respect rights, livelihoods and resources*. Washington, DC: World Bank.

Federici, S. 2004. Women, land struggles, and the reconstruction of the commons. *The Journal of Labour and Society* 14: 41–56.

Feierman, S. 1990. *Peasant intellectuals: Anthropology and history in Tanzania*. Madison: University of Wisconsin.

Friedmann, H. 1980. Household production and the national economy: Concepts for the analysis of agrarian formations. *Journal of Peasant Studies* 7, no. 2: 158–84.

Friis, C., and A. Reenberg. 2010. *Land grab in Africa: Emerging land system drivers in a teleconnected world*. GLP Report N. 1. Copenhagen: GLP-IPO.

Girlings, F. 1960. *The Acholi of Uganda*. London: Her Majesty Stationery Office.

Guha, R. 1983. *Elementary aspects of peasant insurgency in colonial India*. Delhi: Oxford University Press.

Gulu Municipal Council Local Government (GMCLG). 2011. *Five years development plan 2011/2012–2015/2016*. Gulu: Republic of Uganda.

Hall, R. 2011. Land grabbing in Southern Africa: The many faces of the investor rush. *Review of African Political Economy* 38, no. 128: 193–214.

High Court of Uganda. 2008. *N. 126 Judgement*. Gulu: Republic of Uganda.

Hobsbawm, E.J. 1973. Peasants and politics. *Journal of Peasant Studies* 1, no. 1: 3–22.

Isaacman, A. 1990. Peasants and rural protest in Africa. *Africa Studies Review* 33, no. 2: 1–120.

Kafuko, L.A. 2005. Impact of outgrowers scheme of Kakira Sugar Works on food security of smallholder farmers of Busede Subcounty, Jinja District. MSC Dissertation, Kampala: Makerere University.

Kerkvliet, B.J.T. 2009. Everyday politics in peasant societies (and ours). *Journal of Peasant Studies* 36, no. 1: 227–43.
La Via Campesina. 2011. Conference declaration: Stop land grab now. International Peasant Conference. Nyeleni, Mali, 17–19 November.
Lenhart, L. 2013. Alleged land grabs and governance: Exploring mistrust and trust in northern Uganda – The case of the Apaa land conflict. *Journal of Peace and Security Studies, Special Issue: Unfolding Land Conflicts in Northern Uganda* 1: 64–85.
Leys, C. 1967. *Politicians and Policies. An essay on politics in Acholi Uganda 1962–65*. Nairobi: East Africa Publishing House.
Li, T.M. 2010. To make live or let die? Rural dispossession and protection of surplus population. *Antipode* 41, no. 1: 66–93.
Little, P.D., and M. Watts. 1994. *Living under contract*. Madison: University of Wisconsin Press.
Mafeje, A. 2003. *The agrarian question, access to land, and peasant responses in sub-saharan Africa*. Geneva: United Nations Research Institute for Social Development.
Madhvani, M. 2012. Amuru Sugar project will bring development to northern Uganda. *Daily Monitor*, 9 February.
Mamdani, M. 1976. *Politics and Class formation in Uganda*. New York and London: Monthly Review Press.
Mamdani, M. 1987. Extreme but not exceptional: Towards an analysis of the agrarian question in Uganda. *Journal of Peasant Studies* 14, no. 2: 191–225.
Mamdani, M. 1996. *Citizen and subjects: Contemporary Africa and the legacy of late colonialism*. Princeton: Princeton University Press.
Mamdani, M. 2012. The contemporary Ugandan Discourse on Customary Tenure: some historical and theoretical considerations. Paper presented to the Workshop *The Land Question: Capitalism, Socialism and the Market*, Makerere Institute of Social Research, 9–10 August.
McMichael, P. 2009. Food sovereignty, social reproduction and the Agrarian question. In *Peasants and globalization: Political economy, rural transformation and the agrarian question*, ed. A. Akram-Lodhi and C. Kay, 288–312. London and New York: Routledge.
Mitchell, T. 2007. The properties of markets. In *Do economists make markets? On the performativity of economics*, ed. D. Mackenzie et al., 244–275. Princeton: Princeton University Press.
Moyo, S. 2008. *African land questions, Agrarian transitions and the state. Contradictions of neoliberal land reform*. Dakar: Codesria.
Mukherjee, R. 1956. *The problem of Uganda*. Berlin: Akademia-Verlag.
New Vision. 2012. Museveni launches Gulu-Juba road works, to cost Ush 89 billion. 10 May.
Oya, C. 2012. Contract farming in Sub-Saharan Africa: a survey of approaches, debates and issues. *Journal of Agrarian Change* 12, no. 1: 1–33.
Parsons, D.J. 1960. *The systems of agriculture practiced in Uganda: The northern systems*. Kampala: Department of Agriculture Uganda Protectorate.
Polanyi, K. 1957. *The great transformation: The political and economic origins of our times*. Boston: Beacon Press.
Ranger, T. 1985. *Peasant consciousness: Culture and conflict in zimbabwe*. Berkeley: University of California Press.
Ravnborg, H.M., B. Bashaasha, R.H. Pedersen, R. Spichiger, and Turinawe, A. 2013. *Land tenure under transition: Tenure security, land institutions and economic activity in Uganda*. Copenhagen: Danish Institute for International Studies.
Richardson, B. 2010. Big sugar in Southern Africa. *Journal of Peasant Studies* 37, no. 4: 917–38.
Scott, J.C. 1975. *The moral economy of the peasant*. New Haven, CT: Yale University Press.
Scott, J.C. 1985. *Weapons of the weak. everyday forms of peasant resistance*. New Heaven and London: Yale University Press.
Scott, J.C. 1998. *Seeing like a state: How certain schemes to improve human conditions have failed*. New haven and London: Yale University Press.
Scott, J. 2009. *The art of not being governed: An anarchist history of upland southeast Asia*. Yale: Yale University.
Serwajja, E. 2014. An investigation of land grabbing amidst resettlement in post-conflict amuru district, Northern Uganda. PhD Dissertation, Cape Town: University of Western Cape.
Shanin, T. 1971. The peasantry as a political factor. In *Peasants and peasant societies: Selected readings*, ed. T. Shanin, 238–63. London: Penguin Books.

Thompson, E.P. 1971. Mode de domination et revolution en Angleterre. *Actes de la Recerche en Sciences Sociales* 2, no. 2: 133–151.

Tibakuno, F. 2000. Kakira Sugar Works Outgrowers Scheme: an analysis of the costs and benefits of monopoly-monopsony. MA Dissertation, Kampala: Makerere University.

Tosh, J. 1978. Lango agriculture during the early colonial period: Land and labour in a cash-crop economy. *The Journal of African History* 19, no. 3: 415–39.

Uganda Bureau of Statistics. 2010a. *Uganda census of agriculture. Vol. III agricultural household and holding characteristics report*. Kampala: Ministry of Agriculture, Animal Industry and Fisheries.

UNOCHA (United Nations Office for the Coordination of Humanitarian Affairs). 2005. *Uganda 2005: Consolidated appeal process*. Geneva: UNOCHA.

UNHCR. 2012. UNHCR Global Trends 2012: Displacement, The New 21st Century Challenge. 19 June 2013, available at http://www.refworld.org/docid/51c169d84.html [accessed 10 January 2015]

Van der Ploeg, J.D. 2008. *The new peasantries: Struggles for autonomy and sustainability in an era of empire and globalization*. London: Earthscan.

Veldman, M., and M. Lankhorst. 2011. *Socio-economic impact of commercial exploitation of Rwanda marches: a case study of sugar cane production in rural Kigali*. Rome: International Land Coalition.

Veremoi, L. 2015. LRA's Maj. Gen. Ongwen and Madhvani land agreement could prove to be intolerable elephant tasks for Uganda. *Acholi Times*, 26 January.

Vincent, J. 1977. Colonial chiefs and the making of class: A case-study from Teso, Eastern Uganda. *Africa: Journal of the International African Institute* 47, no. 2: 140–59.

Wesonga, N. 2015. Amuru Sugar Works: What is in it for Uganda. *Daily Monitor*, 24 January.

White, B., S.M. Borras Jr, R. Hall, I. Scoones, & W. Wolford. 2012. The new enclosures: critical perspectives on corporate land deals. *Journal of Peasant Studies* 39, no. 3–4: 619–47.

William, G. 1976. Taking the part of peasants. In *The political economy of contemporary Africa*, ed. P.W. Gutkind and I. Wallerstein, 131–54. London: Sage Publications.

Wolf, E. 1966. *Peasants*. Englewoods Cliffs: Prentice-Hall.

Wolf, E. 1969. *Peasant war of the twentieth century*. New York, Evanston and London: Harper and Row Publishers.

World Bank. 2012. *Uganda: Promoting inclusive growth*. Washington, DC: World Bank.

World Bank. 2011. *Rising global interest in farmland: Can it yield sustainable and equitable benefits?* Washington: World Bank.

Zeleza, T.1997. *A modern history of Africa. Vol. I The nineteenth century*. Nairobi: East African Educational Publishers.

Zoomers, A. 2010. Globalization and foreignization of space: Seven processes driving the current global land grab. *Journal of Peasant Studies* 37, no. 2: 429–47.

Territorial restructuring and resistance in Argentina

Zoe W. Brent

This article argues that the logic of territory is particularly important for understanding the processes of capital accumulation and resistance in Latin America. The analysis focuses on Argentina, but draws on examples from throughout Latin America for a regional perspective and from the provinces of Jujuy, Cordoba and Santiago del Estero for subnational views. Section one describes the territorial restructuring of meaning, physical 'places' and politico-legal 'spaces', as it plays out at multiple scales to facilitate the investment in and sale and export of natural resource commodities. I argue that land grabs contribute to this process but are not solely responsible for it. Section two explores the territorial logic of resistance. In what might be understood as territorial restructuring from below, rural communities are finding their own ways of restructuring places, legal spaces and the meaning of resistance from a peasant struggle for land reform to a peasant–indigenous alliance in defense of territory. This emerging alliance is not only important for understanding the nature of reactions to land grabbing and land conflict today. Recognizing and navigating the differences between peasant and indigenous histories of collective action are also crucial for sustaining such alliances at the regional, national and subnational level.

Introduction

> It is no longer possible to address agrarian reform without bringing indigenous peoples into our struggle. They are the front lines of the battle to defend territory, and thus over time they have become the principal strategic member and ally of the struggle for a real genuine and integral agrarian reform. (Torrez 2013, 764)
>
> — Faustino Torrez, Peasant leader from La Vía Campesina, Nicaragua

A flurry of research and media attention on land grabbing[1] has put land and territory in the spotlight of development debates and signaled a renewed interest in investing in natural

[1]See GRAIN's 2008 report, 'Seized: The 2008 land grab for food and financial security' and their ongoing news and analysis at www.farmlandgrab.org. Also: *Third World Quarterly*, 34(9), Global Land Grabs (November 2013; eds: Marc Edelman, Carlos Oya & Saturnino M. Borras Jr.); *Journal of Peasant Studies*, 40(3) – Forum on Land Grabbing part 2 on methodologies, 2013; *Journal of Peasant Studies*, 40(5) – Debate on methodologies between Scoones et. al. and Rulli et al, 2013; *Journal of Peasant Studies,* special issue: *Green Grabbing* (April 2012; eds: James Fairhead, Melissa Leach & Ian Scoones); *Development & Change* special issue: *Land Grabbing and the State* (March 2013; eds: J. Borras, R. Hall, I. Scoones, B. White & W. Wolford); *Globalizations*

resources. A growing academic literature on land grabbing has helped reveal the dynamics of this trend, key actors and drivers; however, less research has been done on resistance to it.[2] I hope to contribute to this question in Latin America, with special emphasis on the Argentine case. However, I argue that neoliberal reforms in Argentina established a pattern of territorial restructuring that land grabs also reproduce, but are not solely responsible for. This process is facilitating the expansion of multiple industries, namely industrial soy production and mining, driving agrarian change and triggering resistance. Defense of territory in resistance discourse initially emerged in Latin America as an ethnic claim, linking land struggles to indigenous mobilizations, but the concept has also been increasingly incorporated into peasant movement discourse, signifying an important alliance.

Argentina's indigenous population identified by census data has traditionally represented a small fraction (roughly 1 percent) of the population (Van Cott 2007, 129), and thus it is more often than not left out of regional analyses of indigenous politics (Assies, van der Haar, and Hoekema 2000; Yashar 2005). Although the 2010 census shows an increase to 2.4 percent of the population registered as indigenous (a remarkable 60 percent rise; cited in Wald 2013, 603–04), this blind spot in the literature continues to further invisibilize a population whose role in agrarian change historically has been central and whose mobilizations today shape the agenda of resistance politics. Moreover, although much of the new literature on land grabs in South America focuses on Brazil (Oliveira 2013; Sullivan 2013), Argentina is also a country whose agrarian structure has been shaped by land conflict and land grabbing, but it has received less scholarly attention. It therefore offers an especially relevant context in which to explore the connections between land grabbing, land conflict and indigenous and peasant resistance.

In this paper, I argue that the logic of territory is particularly important for understanding the processes of capital accumulation *and* resistance in Latin America. For Arrighi (1994) and Harvey (2003), state making is based either on territorial power or capitalist power. Territorial power consists of control over places, people and socio-political spaces. In contrast, capitalist power is based on control over money and processes of accumulation. I highlight that the processes of capital accumulation themselves have taken on a notably territorial logic. In other words, the 'real' (territorial) and 'financial' (capitalist) sides of the economy have become increasingly interwoven. Alonso-Fradejas (2012, 512) offers valuable insights by highlighting the 'complementarity' of the territorial and capitalist logics of power that characterizes and makes unique what he calls 'land-control grabs'. Similarly, for Holt-Giménez, the fusion of these two logics in Guatemala is what drives processes of 'territorial restructuring' of the 'social and economic institutions in a country's hinterlands in favor of agribusiness, tourism, or extractive industries' (Holt-Giménez 2008, 5). This idea of territorial restructuring is useful in understanding the current character of the agrarian question in Latin America, which I elaborate in the next section. That is, how capital with the help of the state rearranges physical 'places' and socio-political 'spaces' (Holt-Giménez 2008, 6) in order to accumulate more capital – the logic of capital in combination with the logic of territory. Examining this process in Argentina reveals, however, that the complementarity of these two logics is indeed precarious at

journal: *Land Grabs and Global Governance*, (March 2013; eds: M. Margulis N. McKeon, S. Borras); *Water Alternatives* journal: *Water-Grabbing*, (2012; eds: L. Mehta, Jan Gert,v G., J. Franco); *Canadian Journal of Development Studies*: *Land Grabs in Latin America and the Caribbean* (December 2012; eds: J. Borras, C. Kay, S. Gomez and J. Wilkinson); two international conferences on land-grabbing (2011, 2012). For working paper series, see: www.iss.nl/ldpi

[2]Indeed, this collection is an exciting contribution to the gap.

times, as it causes tension within the state which seeks to facilitate capital accumulation and also maintain political legitimacy (Fox 1993). Building on Holt-Giménez's 'places' and 'spaces', I suggest a third dimension of territorial restructuring – broadly understood as political or ideological meaning. In this analysis, I highlight this dimension as expressed through political ideology and discursive framing. The restructuring of places, spaces and meaning plays out at multiple scales. To capture this, I anchor my analysis on Argentina, but draw on examples from throughout Latin America for a regional perspective, and from the provinces of Jujuy, Cordoba and Santiago del Estero for subnational views. This research is based on a review of secondary data and literature as well as participant observation and semi-structured interviews with social movement representatives, government researchers and policy makers, academics and farmers conducted throughout 2011 and 2012 in the Argentine provinces of Jujuy, Santiago del Estero, Cordoba and Buenos Aires.

The second section also critically engages with the land grabbing literature, exploring its relevance in Argentina, a country where land conflicts are not all linked to the convergence of food and financial crises that culminated in 2008, nor are they all large scale, as contemporary land grabs are commonly understood. Nonetheless, they contribute to broader processes of territorial restructuring and shed light on the current character of the agrarian question in this case. I argue that a process of territorial restructuring is happening at multiple scales in Latin America to facilitate the investment in, and sale and export of, natural resource commodities, a process in which the logics of territory and of capital are in large part complementary. Nonetheless, the Argentine case brings out a number of tensions that the state must negotiate.

In the third section, I suggest that we are also seeing an emergent territorial logic of resistance. In what might be understood as territorial restructuring from below, rural communities are exerting direct control over places through occupation, and legal spaces are being leveraged to politicize territorial rights for indigenous and subsequently peasant groups. Despite differences, there is evidence that the identity and discourse framing of some resistance movements involved in conflicts over land are changing from a peasant struggle for land reform to a peasant–indigenous alliance in defense of territory against the expansion of capital. It is important to note that here I use 'indigenous' to refer to an ethno-cultural identity, while I use 'peasant' as a reference to a particular class of rural people.[3] Class and ethnicity are interrelated but distinct concepts, the meaning of which is context specific (Van Den Berghe 1979, 254). Throughout the region many indigenous people are also peasants, and identification with one or the other or both can be motivated by political, economic, cultural or ethnic affiliations. But many peasant movements in Latin America have a Marxist legacy, mobilizing on the basis of class, while indigenous movements have largely made claims on the basis of shared ethnic identity. In many parts of Latin America, there has been a clear shift in recent decades towards ethnic recognition and thus political demands articulated on the basis of indigeneity. However, peasant movements grounded in class politics have not disappeared (Veltmeyer 1997; Wald 2013, 603; Fontana 2014, 297). This work explores the ways in which agrarian resistance movements today are attempting to integrate notions of class and ethnicity. Land claims by peasant and

[3]These are admittedly simplified uses of these concepts, used here in this way for analytical clarity and to highlight the dynamics between class and identity politics. For a deeper discussion of the definition of a peasant and its complexities see Edelman (2013), for elaboration on indigenous ethnicity as related to class see Van Den Berghe (1979) and for the intersection of the two in Argentina see Wald (2014).

indigenous movements throughout Latin America have mobilization trajectories that have been at times overlapping, complementary, contested and even conflicting. Therefore, this emerging alliance in defense of territory is not only important for understanding the nature of reactions to land grabbing and land conflict today. Recognizing and navigating the differences between histories of collective action is also crucial for sustaining such alliances at the regional, national and subnational level in order to resist the dispossession of peasant and indigenous communities.

Territorial restructuring and the expansion of capital

The high prices on international markets for Latin American commodities are and have been without a doubt an important draw for capital to the region. But these market-based explanations mask the details of the way capital penetrates and restructures agrarian production systems – today's agrarian question. To supply this demand, a complex process of territorial restructuring is underway. Initially, the so-called 'Washington Consensus' justified this change, and now, increasingly, the commodities boom or the 'Commodities Consensus' gives the persistence of this production model meaning. Landscapes throughout the region have been ripped open, re-planted and paved over to facilitate the movement of goods to the international market, and the expansion of capital into new territories. Importantly, particular political choices have been made that activate institutions, regulation and laws to privatize lands, displace peasants and indigenous peoples, and silence dissent – the restructuring of 'spaces'. While by and large this process has favored capital accumulation, in Argentina's 'post-neoliberal' political climate, it has also brought out some of the tensions between the logic of territory and the logic of capital.

Land grabbing

In the context of this wider panorama of territorial restructuring, I suggest that land grabbing contributes to it by also restructuring places, spaces and meaning, but is not solely responsible for it. To limit this analysis to resistance to land grabbing alone not only misses broader processes of agrarian change, it is also complicated by the fact that in Argentina (as in many places) the term 'land grabbing' gets used in widely different ways. For some, like Naharro and Álvarez (2011) in their research in Salta, land grabbing refers generally to acquisitions of indigenous lands by 'new owners' for soy production for export. The National Peasant and Indigenous Movement (MNCI) in Argentina uses the term in an article describing a violent eviction of family farmers in Esteban Echeverría, Buenos Aires province (UST-MNCI 2011), or, more generally, the 'offensive of industrial agriculture and agribusiness' (Prensa De Frente 2011).

A Food and Agriculture Organization (FAO) of the United Nations study (2011) of Latin America, defines a land grab as a phenomenon with three key characteristics: (1) recent large-scale land acquisitions, (2) transactions involving foreign governments and (3) negative impacts on food security in the host country. Of the 17 countries in the region examined, this study only found land grabbing present in Argentina and Brazil. In Argentina, transactions like the stalled deal for 320,000 ha with the Chinese company Beidahuang State Farms Business Trade Group Co., Ltd. in Rio Negro, or the 200,000 ha acquired by the Saudi Arabian Al-Khorayef Group in the province of Chaco in 2010, represent the restructuring of 'places' to produce commodities for export. These deals depend on negotiated agreements and access to political 'spaces', and have signaled that, no matter how limited the definition, land grabbing is not just an African phenomenon, and is indeed happening in Latin America. The 2012 data from GRAIN based on a similarly narrow definition of land grabbing[4] in Argentina suggest that a total of 961,552 ha have been grabbed, primarily for the production of soybeans and other grains (GRAIN 2012b). These definitions highlight compelling cases, but must be problematized in three key ways.

First, limiting the meaning of land grabbing to foreign investors as 'the grabbers' misses the role of domestic actors. Gras and Hernandez (2014) point out that not only have domestic agribusinesses been central in the development of soy in Argentina, they are diverse in size and structure themselves. Nonetheless, the Cristina Fernández de Kirchner government's institutional response to the issue has been largely directed at limiting foreign ownership of land. In 2011, Argentina passed a law to limit the total land area that can be foreign owned to 25 percent, which, according to Aranda (2011), was hailed by government-friendly media as if it were an agrarian reform, but ultimately made little difference to peasants and indigenous communities engaged in conflicts over land. Murmis and Murmis (2012) remind us that while much of the trade in commodities is dominated by multinational firms, control of land and resources to produce those commodities is exercised in a variety of ways, combining domestic and foreign capital, investment 'pools' and land leasing as well as outright purchase. In the words of Argentine journalist Darío Aranda, 'The main problem for peasants and indigenous peoples is not foreign ownership, [but] rather the dominant model of agricultural production'[5] (2011). Key actors advancing the dominant model of agricultural production are both foreign and domestic (Murmis and Murmis 2012) and they rely on political and institutional support, as the following sections describe.

Second, measuring land grabs by acreage, and focusing only on large-scale acquisitions, has been called into question by Borras et al. (2012) who note that other factors like the size of the capital involved, extraction of resources, land control transfer (rather than ownership) and changes in meaning and use of land are perhaps more relevant criteria for identifying land grabs. Using this broader lens, Borras et al. found land grabbing present in at least 10 countries in Latin America, as opposed to the two found in the FAO study. In Argentina, looking at acreage being grabbed is also misleading given the large number of conflicts over small pieces of land. According to a Ministry of Agriculture, Ranching and Fishing (MAGyP) study in 2013, there are 857 distinct conflicts over land, affecting 63,843 family farms, covering 9.3 million ha – 10 times the amount of land identified as having been 'grabbed' in the GRAIN study. Nationally, nearly a quarter of Argentina's farming families are engaged in some kind of dispute over their land. Forty-eight percent of the 857 cases identified are conflicts over parcels of 500 ha or less. The sources and types of conflict vary, including: incomplete or inexistent titles (18.25 percent); usurpation of peasant or indigenous lands (8.95 percent); dispossession (8.15 percent); demand for recognition of indigenous territory (7.89 percent); lack of land (6.57 percent); issues arising from public land management at the provincial level (6.39 percent); fraud (6.13 percent); lack of information (6.8 percent); and other (9.17 percent) (Bidaseca et al. 2013). Because of the broad range in the size of 'places' in dispute in Argentina, a large-scale lens does not capture the diversity of processes of agrarian conflict and dispossession happening today. The territorial restructuring framework, on the other hand, complicates this

[4]Deals that 'were initiated after 2006, have not been cancelled, are led by foreign investors, are for the production of food crops, and involve large areas of land' See: GRAIN (2012a)
[5]Translated by the author, as are all direct quotes of Spanish-language text cited in this paper.

picture by looking not just at the size of the place that is grabbed, but also at the political spaces and meanings that are restructured.

Finally, land grabbing is often linked to the convergence of food, energy and financial crises, as Borras et al. have done (2012, 851). Anchoring the land grab concept to these multiple crises prevents the term from being rendered irrelevant by applying it to too widely to large-scale transfers of land and resources throughout history. While I see this contextualization as key to maintaining the analytical utility of the concept, focusing so precisely, as GRAIN and FAO studies have, on land grabs in the post 2007–2008 crisis period also does not provide a full explanation of land struggles in the Argentine context. Processes of agrarian transformation have been exaggerated in recent years, but they build on patterns of accumulation that gained momentum in the neoliberal period in the 1990s. According to the MAGyP study, 64 percent of registered cases of land conflict began within the last 20 years. For this reason, as Borras et al. (2012) rightly point out, the land grabbing lens offers a useful but incomplete view of the dynamics of agrarian change, as the Argentine case affirms.

Meaning: from the 'Washington Consensus' to the 'Commodities Consensus'

Latin America has a long history of natural resource extraction and primary commodity production, but recent shifts in production patterns since the beginning of the neoliberal period have consistently deepened dependency on these sectors. What has not been consistent during that time is the way economic development strategies have been framed ideologically by governments and scholars throughout the region. When neoliberalism lost social legitimacy, the so-called 'Washington Consensus' shifted to the 'Commodities Consensus'.

A focus in the post-WWII years until the late 1970s on an import substitution industrialization model (ISI) of development emphasized diversified domestic production and state-led development of mainly industrial sectors. The neoliberal turn in response to the debt crisis in the 1980s reversed this logic, instead promoting an opening up and deregulating of national economies, lowering tariffs, rolling back the role of the state and pushing for outward-looking export-led development. This shift towards global markets favored specialization in export commodities and a complex process of 'reprimarization' of Latin American economies, away from manufacturing and increasingly geared towards production of low-value-added primary goods (Svampa 2013). The 1990s was a time of increasing protest and social struggle against these policies. Faced with this pressure, many Latin American governments saw sweeping changes in political discourse in rejection of neoliberalism – towards 'neostructuralism' (Leiva 2008) and a return of the state. This time, however, state-led development did not focus on industrial production as it had during ISI. The majority of South American nations doubled down on primary goods for export.

Now, booming international commodities markets, especially the sustained boom from 2001 to 2008, are framed as key drivers behind the expansion of natural resource frontiers. New technologies like lithium batteries and increased grain-fed meat consumption have created a high demand for Latin America's primary goods. An important factor in this boom is the growth of Chinese consumption, capturing an increasing share of exports (Sinnott, Nash, and de la Torre 2010, 9). Indeed, processes of productive change triggered by the neoliberal Washington Consensus continue today, but new ideological meaning and justification for this path have emerged. Led by the dynamism of Brazil's economy and a sense of post-hegemonic regionalism, a wave of leftist governments proposing a post-neoliberal agenda – most notably in Argentina, Bolivia, Ecuador and Venezuela – has grown.

Despite this ideological shift, the Washington Consensus has been replaced by what Svampa (2013) calls a 'Commodities Consensus'. Her term captures the tension between the political rejection of the neoliberal project and a renewed commitment to the model of agrarian production based on export of primary commodities, which that same neoliberal project established. As Fox (1993) points out, the need to facilitate capital accumulation *and* maintain social legitimacy is a tension embedded in the state, which the current commodities consensus is exacerbating in Argentina.

Places: 'mountains were moved and valleys obliterated'

Mining and industrial agriculture and transportation networks are re-drawing territories (places) to facilitate the sale of commodities on the global market. Mining has been present in the region for centuries, but technological developments deepened its impact on physical places. The emergence of open-pit mining in the 1960s transformed copper, iron and bauxite mining processes in particular, and dramatically increased production. Similarly, the introduction of cyanide leaching in gold mining in the 1990s made it more feasible and profitable to extract gold from low-grade ore deposits, but this has also come with increased environmental impacts per unit of gold (Urkidi and Walter 2011, 683). Thus, to expand mining, as Dore (2000) describes, 'Mountains *were* moved and valleys obliterated. Fertile soil that had supported plant and animal life was covered by toxic tailings' (16, emphasis in original). Large-scale industrial agriculture has also had serious impacts on South American landscapes, as commodity exports have grown. Most notably, deforestation has advanced at an alarming rate to clear new areas for extensive agriculture or for other activities displaced by it. The Intergovernmental Panel on Climate Change (IPCC) warns that 48.3 percent of Latin America's greenhouse gas (GHG) emissions are due to deforestation and land use change. Sadly, Latin America is unparalleled in this regard. Forests were converted to agriculture at a rate of 57,800 km^2 per year during the first half of the 1990s, accounting for the greatest percentage loss of forest cover of any region in the world (Carr, Bilborrow, and Barbieri 2003, 2).

In line with regional trends, by 2013, Argentina had 614 distinct mining projects (active mines, concessions or prospective mines), the bulk of which are open-pit, large-scale developments, producing silver, copper and gold, with growing interest in lithium (MICLA 2012). Deforestation has swept across the northwest to make way for genetically modified soy, which now covers over half (59 percent) of all cultivated land in the country (Aranda 2012). Argentina is the world's third largest producer of soy, 99 percent of which is transgenic and 95 percent is for export (Aranda 2010a).

These changes in cropping systems and land use have been paralleled by the development of massive infrastructure projects to facilitate the movement of primary goods (Svampa 2013, 35). In South America, under the banner of territorial ordering (*ordenamiento territorial*), the Initiative for the Integration of Regional Infrastructure in South America (IIRSA), a multi-country regional integration project established in 2000, aims to build and improve transportation lines, energy production and communications. In the first 10 years, 86 percent of the projects launched by this initiative were in the transport sector and 46 percent of them were roads (IIRSA CCT Secretariat 2011, 97). In other words, IIRSA is enabling commodities to move. And it has worked. Among the different regional development hubs delineated by IIRSA, the average increase in dollar value of exports eight years into the project was 248 percent (IIRSA CCT Secretariat 2011). All of the top five exports in every hub are primary goods (especially crude oil and soybeans) except in the Guianese Shield Hub where airplanes and other aircraft rank fifth. When examined by country, Argentina is home to the highest number of IIRSA projects in the region (IIRSA CCT Secretariat 2011).

Spaces: making way for soy and mining expansion

Changes in physical places are made possible by complex systems of socio-political relations and power dynamics that restructure political 'spaces' in order to take hold of physical 'places'. Here, I look at four key arenas, which are by no means exhaustive, but serve to illustrate the process of restructuring of socio-political spaces: state support for transgenic soy, investment incentives for mining, land titling, and dispossession and population control.

State support for transgenic soy

The introduction of genetically modified or GMO soy has played a central role in the rapid spread of industrial agriculture in the Southern Cone of Latin America and opened the door to powerful multinational companies. In Argentina, the benefits reaped from this expanding sector are highly concentrated in the hands of a few large companies. Six corporations (Cargill, Bunge, Dreyfus, AGD, Vicentín and Molinos Río de la Plata), for instance, control 89.34 percent of soy derivatives export (Teubal and Palmisano 2010, 207). This concentration has been largely made possible by the dominance of transgenic seed, which lends itself to large-scale production and grows in areas where non-GMO soy can't. Newell (2009) notes that Argentina has shown particular enthusiasm for biotechnology in agriculture. Here, control over institutional spaces 'derives from and is manifested in access to bureaucratic structures and decision-making procedures within the state institutions that have responsibility for governing agricultural biotechnology' (Newell 2009, 47). President Menem's (1989–1999) neoliberal reform of agricultural inputs sectors privatized and concentrated control of seed markets for maize and soy, selling national seed companies to multinational producers (Newell 2009, 33). These powerful industry players maintain access to government decision-making processes directly and through representative organizations like the *Asociación de Semilleros Argentinos* (ASA) and the *Foro Argentino de Biotecnología* (FAB). This preferential treatment has been criticized by Greenpeace as a revolving door of personnel, which ensures regular meetings between industry and government representatives every two to three weeks, depending on the issue (Newell 2009, 48).

The proximity of the biotech seed industry to policy making has been effective, and support from the federal government for soy production is clear. The National Agro-food Production Strategy, 2010–2016, proposes an expansion of soy production by 20 million tons, and by 2020 to reach a 160-million-ton harvest, an amount 60 percent higher than 2010 levels (Aranda 2011, 11). In response to this proposed increase, one of the main peasant and indigenous organizations in the country, the MNCI, has warned, 'there is no way to do this besides displacing peasant families' (cited in Aranda 2011). The 35 percent export tax on soy exports that President Kirchner collects is a key source of income for her government, which has greatly increased government spending on social policies (Richardson 2009). In other words, the way President Kirchner seems to be dealing with the tension between social legitimacy and capital accumulation is by tacitly allowing the expansion of soy to displace the rural poor, but using the tax revenues it generates to fund the public assistance programs that those displaced people then rely on.

Investment incentives for mining

Through Structural Adjustment Programs (SAPs), international finance institutions (IFIs) like the International Monetary Fund (IMF) played a key role in shaping political spaces in ways that encouraged the expansion of mining throughout Latin America throughout the 1980s and 1990s. But, increasingly, financing for extraction is coming from the private sector, while IFIs are focusing on integration projects like IIRSA to move goods (Hildyard 2008, cited in Bebbington 2009, 8). Although Latin America provides the natural resources, key actors profiting from their extraction are often foreign firms. For example, Canadian companies are not the only actors behind mining expansion, but they represent the majority. In 2012, there were 47 Canadian mining firms operating in Argentina, 37 in Brasil, 46 in Chile, 40 in Colombia, 169 in Mexico and 77 in Peru (Bebbington 2009, 8).

Without the pressure from IFIs to invest, Argentina has found facilitating capital accumulation and maintaining political legitimacy to be challenging. The Argentine government celebrates the fact that mining exports in Argentina increased by 434 percent between 2001 and 2011 (Minería Argentina: oportunidades de inversión 2011). However, its attempt to capture mining revenues from foreign firms to fund domestic needs has not been as effective as in the soy sector. Increasing taxes and regulations on remittances to headquarters combined with serious inflation and currency restrictions are all factors that have cut into perceived profits (Romig 2013). Additionally, President Kirchner's nationalization of Spanish oil company YPF with no compensation, in 2012, has investors nervous. In the words of one multimillion-dollar mining company president, 'The country of Argentina has consistently over the past 2 years introduced legislation and modified laws to "extract" more economic benefits for the country without thought or concern about the impact on long term resource development' (quoted in Wilson and Cervantes 2014, 65).

This highlights the contradictory nature of the anti-neoliberal platform that proposes to fund social programs with revenues from extractive industries, which leftist governments like Argentina have taken. As these industries expand, they face increasing social resistance from the very base that elected presidents like Kirchner. On the other hand, if they exert too much state power or lean too heavily on tax revenues from foreign corporations, companies will take their investments elsewhere.

Land titling

Another mechanism facilitating the entry of capital to a given territory is land privatization. In Scott's (1998) words, it makes space and nature 'legible' (and sellable). The institutions that grant land titles are key political spaces of contestation in the process of territorial restructuring. In Jujuy, increasing recognition of indigenous territorial rights appeases growing indigenous resistance movements, but it comes to a head with the demand for the incorporation of untitled lands into private and unfettered land markets, in order to facilitate the expansion of capital. Jujuy is the province with the third highest percentage[6] of its population identifying as indigenous in the nation (Instituto Nacional de Estadística y Censos (INDEC), cited in Lipcovich 2012) and indigenous land titles have been the source of debates throughout Jujuy's history since the

[6]According to the 2010 census, 7.8 percent of the population of Jujuy identifies as indigenous (Lipcovich 2012).

founding of the Republic. Though not in the heart of soy country, between 2005 and 2012, the area planted with soy in Jujuy still increased by 310.2 percent[7] and the province experienced a 1948 percent increase in mining investments since 2003 (El Libertario 2012). With nearly half of all farms lacking titles and clearly defined limits (INDEC 2008), these changes have reignited competing interests over land and the call for communal land titles, which reflect indigenous pastoral and collective land use practices. Collective titles can't be sold, and therefore disrupt the operation of private land markets.

In the 1990s, national government institutions began to see greater indigenous representation among staff; coupled with the rise of indigenous movements throughout the region, this resulted in more calls for communal land titles. In an agreement signed by the national government's Institute on Indigenous Affairs (INAI) and the provincial government, in 1997 the Program to Regularize and Allocate Lands to Jujuy's Indigenous Population (PRATPAJ) was launched, officially recognizing indigenous collective territorial rights as part of the province's land-titling program. In 2006, a push for communal titles appeared on the national agenda, with law No. 26.160. This law proposed to halt all evictions of indigenous communities that didn't have titles to their lands until every province carried out what's called the National Survey of Indigenous Territories Program (RETECI), which Jujuy had already begun with PRATPAJ. In Jujuy, relying on a number of institutions to survey, register and issue deeds, and, ultimately, executive approval from the governor to grant communal land titles, this process has been slow. In 2006, only seven of the communities demanding communal titles had received them (Borghini 2010, 146). By 2013, the Jujuy public notary claimed this number had gone up to a total of 44 titles, representing 30 percent of the public lands in the province (OEA 2013, 14). Meanwhile the Jujuy Institute of Colonization (IJC), formed in 1988, operates independently and continues to grant private titles.

The tension between the interests of capital and communal ownership is not lost on indigenous groups waiting for their collective titles. In 2003, 200 representatives of indigenous communities from Jujuy sent a letter to Alicia Kirchner, the Minister of Social Development of the Nation, stating, 'We think that the long delays [in granting communal titles] could have various causes, from simple inefficiency to racism masked by double speak' (ENDEPA 2003). The slow action by the state in the institutional spaces that handle matters of collective titles has allowed privatization to make new lands available to investors, rather than protecting indigenous communities who currently reside there.

Processes of land regularization are also shaped by the current territorial development model in Argentina, which was introduced to Argentina in 2004 (RIMISP 2004). This framework promotes decentralized governance (Schejtman and Berdegué 2004) and ultimately means implementation happens in provincial government 'spaces' where the interests of capital have proven dominant. Beginning with then president Perón's first attempt in 1947, each indigenous land titling program in Jujuy has followed a similar dynamic: indigenous land titles are promised by the national government, but efforts to grant them are undermined by the provincial government. While granting indigenous territorial rights remains slow, plans to expand soy and mining continue. The Provincial

[7]In 2005–2006, it covered 3970 ha, and in 2009–2010 it reached 16,285 ha (Proyecto Relevamiento del Noroeste de Argentina - Instituto Nacional de Tecnología Agropecuaria (ProReNOA - INTA) Salta, 2010, cited in Ministerio de Producción de Jujuy, 2011, 144).

Ministry of Production's Strategic Production Plan (PEP) proposes to expand and strengthen soy, mining *and* smallholder agricultural production. The authors of the plan admit that the challenge to the growth of this sector in Jujuy is 'the eventual conflicts with rural communities' (Díaz Benetti 2011, 350). On this point, the PEP explicitly offers no solution. Instead, the authors of the provincial government's development plan avoid the entire land issue by claiming it is a national matter, thus leaving the demands of peasants and indigenous communities unresolved. Despite the existence of legal frameworks to protect indigenous collective rights, the political spaces of implementation are shaped by the interests of capital. Allegiance to large-scale mining and agro-industrial development at both the federal and provincial levels has hampered the full expression of indigenous rights.

Dispossession and population control

Though titling programs are stalled, territorial restructuring continues to drive dispossession of peasants and indigenous communities, which in turn generates resistance. In this sense, taking hold of and maintaining control of spaces is also about the politics of population control. Despite a renewed focus on production in rural areas, increased mechanization of agriculture and open-pit mining practices require less labor. What is needed is not people, but land. While labor conditions in mining may have improved, now the problem is unemployment (Dore 2000, 21). Thus, the majority of Latin America's rural population has been converted into an impoverished semi-proletariat in a process of depeasantization (Veltmeyer 2007, 8). Although agrarian production expands, the rural population is dwindling, as Figure 1 demonstrates. The numbers for Argentina show similar trends but are even more exaggerated than the regional average, with the rural population in 2012 representing only 7.3 percent, while nearly 54 percent of the total land is used for agriculture (Figure 1).

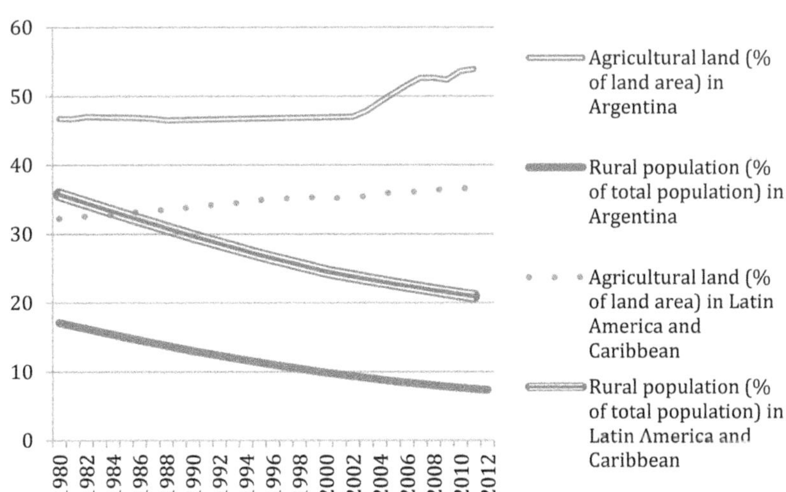

Figure 1. Agricultural land vs. rural population in Argentina and Latin American & Caribbean (LAC).
Source: Author's compilation of data from World Development Indicators, see: http://data.worldbank.org/indicator.

Peasant and indigenous organizations claim that, in order to free up new lands for soy, private security forces hired by new land claimants use violence to evict rural communities (FM Del Monte MOCASE-VC 2012). Between 2009 and 2012, 11 farmers and indigenous people died,[8] all of whom opposed the incursion of large-scale developments on their lands (Aranda 2013). Some were murdered in cold blood, while others died in mysterious traffic accidents that their families claim were also premeditated (Aranda 2013). Mining projects are upsetting neighboring communities as well. Lithium exploration in the Salinas Grandes salt flats on the border of Jujuy and Salta provinces, for example, has sparked a conflict with the indigenous inhabitants. They worry that the mining operation would rob them of the water they need to sustain their way of life based on the production of llamas and sheep, forcing them to migrate to precarious urban settlements (Comunidades de la Mesa de Pueblos Originarios de la Cuenca de Guayatayoc y Salinas Grandes 2012).

As resistance grows to the increasing levels of dispossession throughout the region, many countries have begun passing or reviving antiterrorism laws, which some activists and journalists warn provide a legal mechanism to criminalize protest. In Chile, indigenous Mapuche groups defending their territory have been disproportionately targeted by this law (EFE 2011). In Ecuador, the Confederation of Indigenous Nationalities claimed in 2011 that there were some 189 cases of people accused of terrorism or sabotage for protesting the privatization of natural resources (Picq 2011). Similar laws exist in most Latin American countries, including Argentina, which passed its own version in 2011. This has raised alarm among grassroots organizations and members of congress alike who warn that the law could be used against peasants and indigenous communities defending their right to land or communities protesting open-pit mining (cited in Valente 2011). While in the case of Argentina it is too early to assess the full impact of this legislation, these laws throughout Latin America provide a legal tool that can be and has been used for population control, as dispossession from the expansion of extractive industries sparks social unrest.

Resistance: reshaping territories from below

In this section I argue that we are seeing the emergence of a territorial logic in the context of resistance, which is characterized by the same three features of territorial restructuring as outlined in the second section: reshaping places, meaning and political spaces. In this case, however, change is coming 'from below'. The development of this territorial logic of resistance is uneven as different peasant and indigenous organizations navigate contextually specific and historically rooted divisions among and between them. The differences among peasant and indigenous movements have been especially shaped by the particular politico-legal opportunities for claim making and the types of political identities that are given the opportunity to express themselves – what Yashar calls a 'citizenship regime' (Yashar 2005). In Argentina's neoliberal period, state recognition on the basis of culture and identity has helped 'politicize ethnic cleavages' (Yashar 2005, 81), between peasants and indigenous groups and masked class-based commonality between them. As Brass has warned, this focus on identity over class can become 'politically problematic' (Brass 2003, 6). By looking at the three dimensions of territorial restructuring from below in this context, I explore how such tensions and commonalities between class and ethnicity are being negotiated by social movements at different levels.

[8]Javier Chocobar, Ely Sandra Juarez, Roberto Lopez, Mario Lopez, Mártires Lopez, Cristian Ferreyra, Miguel Galván, Celestina Jara, Lila Coyipé, Imer Flores and Juan Diaz Asijak.

The territorial turn in resistance: reclaiming rural places

As natural resources are ever more the target of capital expansion, for peasants and indigenous communities facing threats of displacement throughout the region, the defense of territory, especially rural 'places', has become central to resistance efforts. From their compilation of research from Africa, Asia and Latin America, Moyo and Paris (2005) conclude, 'rural movements today constitute the core nucleus of opposition to neoliberalism and the most important sources of democratic transformation in national and international politics' (6). This territorial turn in resistance represents a shift away from the wage wars and industrial conflicts spearheaded by labor unions that characterized the 1960s and 1970s in Latin America (Seoane, Taddei, and Algranati 2005, 115). While rural revolutionary guerilla movements and land reform efforts were also important at this time, according to Veltmeyer, they were often peasant-based, but not peasant-led (2005, 307). As neoliberal reforms changed the nature of production systems and 'reprimarized' regional and national economies, the nature of protest in turn has shifted towards a 'territorial basis' (Seoane, Taddei, and Algranati 2005, 115). Following the rise of indigenous movements in the 1970s and 1980s, Latin American peasants emerged as leaders of their own new movements as well.

Rural social movements in Latin America have sought to defend their territory through a variety of strategies, some of which rely on legal and political mechanisms and seek to reclaim socio-political spaces, but perhaps most notably, peasants and indigenous peoples are taking and maintaining control over land (places) by way of direct land occupation (Veltmeyer 2005, 308). The Landless Workers' Movement (MST) in Brazil has made famous this brand of 'land reform from below' (Langevin and Rosset 1997), and in so doing managed to reclaim lands for some 350,000 families who now have legal recognition, and another 90,000 still occupying disputed territory (Watts 2014).

This renewed focus on land among both indigenous movements and new peasant movements, indeed provides fertile ground for building shared territorial claims and unifying issues of concern to both rural peasants and indigenous communities. However, a close reading of the distinct social movement histories of indigenous peoples and peasants in Latin America reveals that while there has been overlap and complementarity, there has also been tension, especially in regards to control over land. In the 1960s and 1970s, indigenous communities began claiming their peasant or class-based identities rather than making ethnically based claims (Bengoa, cited in Soliz 2012, 128). State-led land reforms, for example in Mexico (1934), Bolivia (1953), Guatemala (the short-lived reform of 1952), Ecuador (1964 and 1973) and Peru (1968), targeted peasant communities and offered incentives for Indians to register with peasant organizations in order to gain access to land and the state (Yashar 2005, 61). Such complementary and fluid political identities have not always been the case. Argentina never had an agrarian reform, and it was immigrant peasant farmers, not indigenous peoples, who benefited from early titling programs in the transition from a Spanish colony to a new republic. In fact, the state effectively 'usurped' indigenous lands to give to European colonists (Giordano 2003, 2).

In this context, much of the mobilization by European settler farmers focused not on land control, but on the terms of incorporation. Most accounts of non-indigenous rural uprisings in Argentina begin with the famous *Grito de Alcorta* in 1912, and the formation of the Argentine Agrarian Federation (FAA) where primarily Italian immigrant farmers demanded better contracts (Solberg 1971, 24). This was a struggle over terms of incorporation, and the FAA has historically served as a conduit for the political interests of the Pampean (plains) farmers, who have traditionally been those most linked to export commodity production and carry significant political and social weight still to this day (Bidaseca 2010, 259). Peasant mobilization continued in the 1970s with the *Ligas Agrarias*, which mobilized primarily non-indigenous small-scale farmers throughout the northeast. In this case, demands centered again on terms of incorporation, specifically commercialization and control over distribution (Bartolomé 1982, 29). However, the brutal repression by provincial governments and the military dictatorship that ruled the country from 1976 to 1983 limited sustained rural or labor movements in those years.

In contrast, indigenous social movements in the country grew out of a deep history of cultural invisibilization and land loss that was part of the Argentine project of nation-building. Mobilization, as Gordillo and Hirsch argue, was fundamentally about not just becoming visible, but state recognition (2003, 5). The basis on which claims are made has evolved over time, but in large part has been distinct from peasant uprisings. In Jujuy, for example, the most famous uprising in an attempt to reclaim control of rural lands, in the highlands during the pre-sugar era in 1879, developed from an 'indigenous condition' (Karasik 2006, 292). One exception is the Malón de la Paz in 1946, where the farmer and the indigenous identities converged, but this convergence was not sustained (Karasik 2006, 292). In 1972, the formation of the First National Indigenous Parliament (*Futa Traum*) represented a high point in growing indigenous mobilization, which during that era was divided among those promoting ethnic-cultural demands and those pushing for political and economic recognition (Gordillo and Hirsch 2003, 17). Like peasant movements, severe repression during the dictatorship limited indigenous activism at that time. But with the founding of INAI in 1982, resurgent indigenous mobilization focused on a politics of participation and demands for cultural recognition. In turn, such recognition facilitated 'the reemergence of groups that had supposedly disappeared' (Gordillo and Hirsch 2003, 20).

Although race and ethnicity still shape land access, what once may have been clear ethnic divisions between European settlers and indigenous communities are no longer the primary factor upon which dispossession and land control is determined. As described in the first part of this paper, territorial restructuring has put new lands in the sights of soy and mining development, and the communities that are under increasing pressure of displacement are unified by their shared class as rural peasants, despite their diverse ethnic and cultural affiliations. Historically and today, land occupation is a common resistance strategy used by both peasant and indigenous rural social movements throughout Argentina. According to a pamphlet on land rights published by the La Red Puna in Jujuy, 'occupation has always been the best way to demonstrate that land is ours' (1998). Increasingly, there are new land occupations or squatter settlements in urban and peri-urban areas (El Libertario 2009). However, for groups like La Red Puna, and other members of the MNCI, the strategy is actually about gaining recognition for land on which they have historically lived. The national civil code establishes that legal possession may be granted to those without land titles, after 20 years of uninterrupted occupation with the 'intention of ownership' (Vélez Sársfield 1871). In many areas with incomplete or confusing land registries, direct occupation is the most secure way of controlling land. In fact, many rural communities have been 'occupying' their lands for generations. However, the title obtained through this process is a private land title that provides little protection from the economic pressures that can force peasants and indigenous communities to sell their land. For this reason, land occupation is complemented with other strategies of resistance.

The meaning of struggle: from land reform to defense of territory

In contrast to the discourse of the Washington Consensus, or the Commodities Consensus and post-neoliberalism, rural social movements frame current patterns of dispossession as inherent to neoliberalism, which, despite leftist governments' post-neoliberal discourse, continue today. In his discussion of the increasingly territorial perspective of land struggles adopted by Latin American peasant movements, Faustino Torrez, Nicaraguan peasant leader from La Vía Campesina, explains the motives for resistance:

> We are in a contradictory moment of both strong depeasantization, ever decreasing peasant agriculture in many places, displaced by the *territorial logic* of agribusiness, with repeasantization in other areas ... the neoliberal economic system has made peasant and family farm agriculture unviable. (Torrez 2013, 766, emphasis added)

As threats to peasant and indigenous livelihoods have broadened and grown, La Via Campesina 'has increasingly learned to think in terms of territory' (Rosset 2013, 726). Thinking in terms of territory has also shaped the discursive framing of the movement, increasingly expressed as an alliance between peasants and indigenous communities united by common threats to their territory from the expansion of agribusiness and mining in the context of neoliberal capitalism.

Defense of territory is proposed as a unifying theme that can help facilitate new alliances between peasant and indigenous groups. This discourse is especially notable at the international level and among movement leaders. In Latin America, the Latin American Coordination of Rural Organizations (CLOC) and, globally, La Via Campesina have facilitated these linkages as well as internal debate and exchange in order to strengthen the process of combining peasant and indigenous agendas in one movement. A key moment in the evolution of how land struggles are framed and resistance movements are composed in the region took place in March 2006 in Porto Alegre, Brazil, at the 'Land, territory and dignity' forum organized by La Via Campesina as a lead-up to the FAO International Conference on Agrarian Reform and Rural Development (ICARRD) (Rosset 2013, 724). This encounter was the first to bring together peasants with non-peasant allies from outside of La Via Campesina who are also threatened by enclosure in rural areas, including nomadic pastoralists, fisher folk and indigenous peoples. But the cross cultural conversations that had begun within the context of the International Planning Committee on Food Sovereignty provided the foundation of the alliances that were solidified at this event (Monsalve, personal communication, 2014). This conversation started within La Via Campesina at the meeting of the landless at the second World Social Forum in Porto Alegre in 2002, where indigenous leaders from member organizations challenged the Global Campaign for Agrarian Reform (GCAR) within the movement to rethink agrarian struggles in terms of the indigenous notion of territory, not just land. The continuation of this conversation in 2006 gave rise to a collective analysis that sought to reframe land reform from a territorial perspective so that it would not pit peasants against indigenous or pastoralist communities, as land reform programs in the past had done. Indeed, Borras notes, this process has unearthed tensions, as some within La Via Campesina have expressed that the organization 'feels like a peasant space, not an indigenous peoples' space' (2010, 791).

While the regional dynamics are important, Harvey's (1998) research on the way peasant, indigenous and student organizations converged in Zapatista rebellion in Chiapas, Mexico, serves as a reminder that much of the work of forming and sustaining such alliances happens at the national and local levels (also cited in Edelman 2001, 293). Examples from Bolivia and Argentina, for instance, show that this alliance is manifesting in different and uneven ways. In Bolivia, we see peasants linking up with indigenous groups, maintaining distinct identities, but working in collaboration. Fontana offers a helpful historical perspective on how the relationship between peasants and indigenous groups has evolved. She argues that the Morales government's attempt at uniting these groups in a broad alliance (Unity Pact) has fallen apart. As the chief of the Conciliation and Conflict Management Unit of the National Institute of Agrarian Reform (INRA) puts it, 'Nowadays, the greatest land conflicts in Bolivia are between native communities and syndical [peasant] organizations. These conflicts are more intense than the conflicts between communities and big landowners' (INRA 2010, cited in Fontana 2014, 303). These conflicts have been shaped by a politics of cultural recognition that has facilitated a shift from 'resource-based claims to ethno-identitarian issues' (Fontana 2014, 304). This so-called 'political ethincization' and its encouragement by international cooperation agencies, academics and Bolivian public officials has reshaped the way resistance is framed in a way that some groups claim discriminates against peasant organizations in favor of those that identify as indigenous (Fontana 2014, 306). The context of scarcity of land resources and differences among views about property relations (i.e. collective vs. private) have further compounded these identity-based tensions (Fontana 2014, 304).

In Argentina, on the other hand, Via Campesina member groups have focused on strengthening the peasant–indigenous alliance through coalition building and by reconnecting with the invisibilized indigenous roots of peasant organizations, thus cultivating a 'double consciousness' that links class and identity (Wald 2013). After 10 years of strengthening coalitions within Argentina, the MNCI was born in 2005 (Aranda 2010b, 138). The MNCI represents over 20,000 families in over 1000 peasant and indigenous grassroots organizations throughout nine provinces, and reflects increasingly territorial perspectives within the movement. Not only has this organization formed a coalition of peasant and indigenous rural organizations, it offers a unifying discourse by framing its diverse membership as threatened by the advance of the same neoliberal capitalist system. At one of the early founding meetings in 2006, the young organization drafted a collective declaration summing up its members' struggle: 'We struggle for land and territory, against injustice and a common enemy: capitalist values' (cited in Muñoz 2012, 17).

Although many of its members identify as indigenous, the indigenous movement history of Argentina was not well represented within the organization initially. How to resolve this omission was a deliberate debate that began before the MNCI was officially established and continues today. The topic was discussed at length in plenaries in Quimili, Santiago del Estero (November 2006) and Juella, Jujuy (February 2007). This led to the writing of an internal report on how to unite peasants and indigenous struggles via 'transformative opportunities and practices beginning at the territorial level, that construct a different reality in favor of the poor and the oppressed' (cited in Aranda 2010b, 138). One of the driving questions is 'How do we join our struggles and rebuild our territory?' (cited in Aranda 2010b, 138). This is an open-ended conversation that remains unresolved, and is being taken up to varying degrees by MNCI member groups.

In Santiago del Estero, for example, the oldest member group within MNCI, the Santiago del Estero Peasant Movement (MOCASE) first emerged in the 1990s as a peasant movement. But it has increasingly shifted internally to adopt a double consciousness among its members that highlights their peasant *and* indigenous identity. As Dominguez (2005) claims, in the context of land tenure insecurity, social mobilization first encouraged the process of 'repeasantization' that later led to a process of 'reindianization'. The birth of this movement was influenced by ideas from the peasant organization *Ligas Agrarias*, the Revolutionary Workers Party, young activists and agronomists working within the National

Institute of Agricultural Technology (INTA), and the ideas of liberation theology and Rodolfo Kusch that he and others studied together at the University of Cordoba (Guarnaccia and de la Calle 2012). Later, MOCASE began receiving student exchange groups initiated by the Argentine Federation of Agronomy Students (FAEA), but for peasant leader Diego Montón, alliances of all kinds have been crucial:

> This in reality is the strength of the movement, creating conditions for synthesis. We don't represent a kind of peasantry or indigeneity where no one else can contribute, nor is it academia that has come to teach the peasants, rather we try to achieve a synthesis between distinct histories, different knowledges and different origins. (quoted in Guarnaccia and de la Calle 2012)

As the organization has matured and opened up spaces of collective action and political expression, its members have begun to recuperate their indigenous origins, register with the INAI and reconstruct ancestral social norms and uses of plants. The expansion of networks also facilitated connections with other similar agrarian organizations that began to emerge in other parts of Argentina throughout the 1990s.

In contrast, rural mobilizations in Jujuy have not followed the same evolution. Unlike MOCASE, La Red Puna began as an indigenous organization, and Wald notes that despite increasing alliance with groups like MOCASE, its members tend not to describe themselves as peasants (2013, 600). It is important to note, however, that an analysis of the economic and material conditions their members face has been present since the founding of the organization in 1998, indicating that, while different from how it developed in Santiago del Estero, a form of double consciousness that links class and ethnicity also exists in Jujuy (Wald 2013, 607–08). Similarly, Hristov's discussion of the indigenous movement the Indigenous Regional Council of Cauca (CRIC), in Colombia, supports this strategy of double consciousness. She argues that, on one hand, 'It is undeniable that ethnicity/race is of significance in the organization of the CRIC', but, at the same time, 'those who ignore the mechanisms generating economic inequalities are in a very weak position to capture the forces that have kept most indigenous people in a subordinate position' (Hristov 2009, 59).

Legal spaces: politicizing territorial rights

The process of reshaping legal spaces in favor of territorial rights for peasants and indigenous communities has born a number of significant achievements, but also reveals some of the tensions within and among resistance movements. Throughout Latin America, the sort of multicultural citizenship reforms that have granted territorial rights to indigenous groups are serving as a model for other marginalized groups.

Indigenous territorial rights frameworks have been developed at the international and national levels. The 2007 United Nations Declaration on the Rights of Indigenous Peoples (UNDRIP) and the 1989 International Labor Organization (ILO) Convention 169 have served as guides for constitutional reform efforts and given backing to local indigenous land rights claims. In 1992, the Argentine government formally adopted ILO Convention 169 in the form of Law No. 24.071, which promotes respect for the cultural and spiritual relationships that indigenous communities have with land and territory.

La Via Campesina has spearheaded a process to approve a similar international declaration on the rights of peasants, which seeks to protect the rights of all marginalized rural communities, including indigenous peoples. In 2012, the United Nations (UN) Assembly of the Human Rights Council accepted the final text, and in July of 2014, the same body authorized the continuation of the negotiating process to draft a declaration (La Vía Campesina 2014). In this document, the authors seek to address the lack of an existing territorial rights framework for peasants by asserting their right to land and territory, owned collectively or individually, as has previously been articulated for indigenous communities in the UNDRIP.

Similarly, in Argentina, the MNCI has been pressuring executive and legislative bodies to support legal recognition of peasant territorial rights and collective titles also (Barbetta 2014, 9). This targeting of political actors rather than judges comes out of a frustration with the judicial system, and represents the politicization of legal spaces. Unlike indigenous communities that have seen greater institutionalization of their political agenda throughout the neoliberal period (namely via the INAI), small-scale peasant producers have not had the same degree of institutional representation at the national level in Argentina (Bidaseca 2010, 262). Development policy specifically targeted at rural areas didn't emerge until the 1980s, consisting mostly of social services for the poor (Manzanal 2008). At the same time, neoliberalism took hold and there was a rise of indigenous movements in Latin America, strengthened by international human rights frameworks (Van Cott 2005; Yashar 2005). As I have argued, the productive strategy pursued in this period – the expansion of export commodities – effectively excludes peasant farmers. Manzanal (2008) argues that what is called rural development in Argentina actually serves as a form of 'relief' for those marginalized by the country's 'economic policy' (7). Schwittay (2003) points out that Argentinian peasants historically received handouts or 'favors', while indigenous peoples now claim 'rights'. Increasingly, peasants are demanding rights also.

In collaboration with other peasant and indigenous groups throughout the country, the MNCI has proposed a peasant law (*Ley de Campesinos*), commonly referred to as Cristian Ferreyra's law in commemoration of his death while resisting eviction from his land to make way for soy plantations in 2011. This legislation would suspend all displacement of peasants in much the same way that law No. 26.160 does in relation to indigenous peoples, until a survey of all lands, not just indigenous territory, is completed. Like the declaration of peasants' rights at the international level, this proposed law is an attempt at the national level to politicize and strengthen territorial rights beyond indigenous peoples, to include peasants' rights also.

A similar dynamic is playing out in the province of Cordoba in the face of land conflict. In September of 2013, a historic court case finally laid the groundwork for non-indigenous peasants to assert collective territorial rights. The community of El Chacho has been engaged in a struggle over land for nine years with a businessman by the name of Martín Rodolfo Buttié, who charged community members with trespassing on land he claimed to own (Justicia ratifica posesión de tierras campesinas en El Chacho 2012). Upon appeal, the Superior Court of Justice of the province of Cordoba found no proof that Buttié was the legitimate owner of the disputed territory, and overturned the criminal charges against the eight families. Notably, the judge not only recognized the area in dispute as the ancestral land of the community, but also referred to their lands as 'communal property'. This set a new legal precedent for non-indigenous peasant farmers to gain collective land rights, representing an important victory for MNCI and rural communities not officially recognized as indigenous (Rumi 2013).

On one hand, peasant movements are emulating the way that indigenous movements have reshaped politico-legal spaces. On the other hand, the MNCI claims the institutional focus that indigenous movements have received throughout the neoliberal period from political parties and the state (via INAI) is set up 'to coopt the indigenous identity and quickly delineate its institutional and organizational space so that it conforms to the parameters of the system' (cited in Aranda 2010b, 138). As Claeys suggests, multicultural rights frameworks may also deepen the 'institutionalization of particularity' (Claeys 2013, 6) based on essentialized versions of historically fluid identity groups. Moreover, Hooker (2005) points out that throughout the region, rights and recognitions have not been granted in an equal way among ethnic subgroups. Afro-Latinos, for example, often get excluded from both peasant and indigenous rights regimes. Although notable afro-Latino peasant mobilizations exist (for example, the Quilombo groups in Brazil), they are often not well incorporated into other peasant or indigenous organizations. Hooker argues:

> 'it is easier for indians to win collective rights than blacks under Latin America's new multicultural citizenship regimes because such rights are awarded based on the perceived possession of a distinct cultural group identity, not a history of political exclusion or racial discrimination'. (Hooker 2005, 298).

In Colombia, the creation of peasant reserve zones (ZRCs) represents an attempt to claim autonomy based on a peasant identity, in much the same way that indigenous peoples have made ethnically based claims to territory. However, the very identity groupings supported by Colombia's multicultural reforms – peasants, indigenous peoples and afro-colombians – have also surfaced as the dividing lines between groups in conflict over land (see for example García 2009, 83 on the conflict in the Cauca region).

In many ways, the broadening of social movement coalitions through a shared territorial framing of land issues may be key to bridging peasant and indigenous struggles in the face of capital expansion and land grabbing. This strategy of alliance building in Latin America, while in practice challenging and imperfect, can be interpreted as a move to counter the cooptation and fragmentation noted throughout this section, and to build class-based mobilization rather than ethnically driven politics that 'delimits, and *produces* cultural difference rather than suppressing it' (Hale 2005, 13, emphasis in original). However, as Rosset (2013) rightly points out, this is an ongoing conversation that has had and no doubt will continue to have some sticking points. Does creating parallel but separate rights frameworks strengthen these movements, or divide and weaken them? Does merging peasant and indigenous movements mask histories of tension and conflict over lands? And to what extent is an alliance able to overcome the current realities of competition over finite land resources among different rural communities?

Conclusion

In this paper, I have set out to explore the dynamics of resistance to land grabbing in Argentina. I argue that while land grabbing helps us to understand the territorial logic behind recent patterns of capital expansion, a more robust understanding of the motives for resistance is captured by taking a longer view of patterns of dispossession, understanding them as part of a broader process of territorial restructuring. This framework helps to recast the agrarian question in the context of neoliberal reform in Latin America and its lasting impacts. In order to facilitate the expansion of capital and the export of primary commodities from the region, landscapes have been altered to move goods to international markets. Political spaces, institutions and regulation have shifted to promote investment in mining and expand transgenic soy cultivation. Land titling programs have facilitated privatization despite calls for collective titles; peasant and indigenous communities are being displaced; but new laws are in place to control social unrest. As the Argentine state struggles to sustain the tension between capital accumulation and social legitimacy in a post-neoliberal political climate, all of this is now understood as part of supplying the commodities boom. In this context, peasant movements have also adopted a territorial logic, combining forces with indigenous movements in defense of territories, physically occupying lands to hold on to their 'places', politicizing new legal 'spaces' and demanding territorial rights. These alliances are crucial to breaking out of identity categories that construct difference and de-emphasize class-based collective action. Nonetheless, overlapping and at times competing social movement histories require a careful reading of buried fault lines and potential tensions if such alliances are to be sustained.

Acknowledgements

I would like to thank the anonymous reviewers whose comments greatly improved this paper. Any remaining errors are my own. I would also like to thank Marcelo Saguier for his guidance from the very beginning, as well as Tanya Kerssen for her insightful feedback throughout my research and writing process. I am ever grateful to Jun Borras and Eric Holt-Giménez for their support. And most importantly, I am thankful to my colleagues and comrades in Argentina who have taken the time to help me learn, and whose work and struggle continue to inspire me.

References

Alonso-Fradejas, A. 2012. Land control-grabbing in Guatemala: the political economy of contemporary agrarian change. *Canadian Journal of Development Studies*, 33(4), 509–28.

Aranda, D. 2010a. Si hace BOOM, es soja. *Revista MU*, Año 4, no. 35: 12–13.

Aranda, D. 2010b. *Argentina Originaria; Genocidios, saqueos y resistencias*. Buenos Aires: La Vaca Editora.

Aranda, D. 2011. Tierra Adentro. *Revista MU*, Año 5, no. 46: 10–11.

Aranda, D. 2012. Patria Grande y Sojera. *Revista MU*. Aug. 6. Online article: http://www.lavaca.org/notas/patria-grande-y-sojera/ (accessed October 16, 2014).

Aranda, D. 2013. Argentina Profunda: Extractivism and Resistance. *Upsidedown World*, 19 Feb.

Arrighi, G. 1994. *The Long Twentieth Century; Money, Power, and the Origins of Our Times*. London and New York: Verso.

Assies, W., G. van der Haar, and A. Hoekema, eds. 2000. *The challenge of diversity; Indigenous peoples and Reform of the State in Latin America*. Amsterdam: Thela Thesis.

Barbetta, P. 2014. Aportes a la cuestión jurídica campesina en la Argentina del agronegocio. *Trabajo y sociedad* 22: 5–14.

Bartolomé, L.J. 1982. Base social e ideología en las movilizaciones agraristas en Misiones entre 1971 y 1975 Emergencia de un populismo agrario. *Desarrollo Económico* 22, no. 85: 25–56.

Bebbington, A. 2009. Latin America - Contesting extraction, producing geographies. *Signapore Journal of Tropical Geography* 30: 7–12.

Bidaseca, K. 2010. The peasants of El ceibal and access to justice. Land rights and precarious land tenure in Santiago del Estero, Argentina. *Laboratorium* 2, no. 3: 257–74.

Bidaseca, K., A. Gigena, F. Gómez, A.M. Weinstock, E. Oyharzábal, and D. Otal. 2013. *Relevamiento y sistematización de problemas de tierras de los agricultores familiares en Argentina*. Buenos Aires: Ministerio de la Agricultura, Ganadería y Pesca de la Nación.

Borghini, N. 2010. Tenencia precaria de la tierra y políticas públicas en Jujuy, Argentina. Un análisis de los vínculos entre provincia, nación y pueblos originarios. *Apuntes, Centro de Investigación de la Universidad del Pacifico*, 67, 129–55.

Borras, S.M., J. Franco, S. Góm, C. Kay, and M. Spoor. 2012. Land grabbing in Latin America and the Caribbean. *Journal of Peasant Studies* 39, no. 3–4: 845–72.

Borras, S.M., C. Kay, S. Gómez, and J. Wilkinson. 2012. Land grabbing and global capitalist accumulation: key features in Latin America. *Canadian Journal of Development Studies/Revue canadienne d'études du développement* 33, no. 4: 402–16.

Brass, T. 2003. Introduction: Latin American peasants-new paradigms for old? In T. Brass, ed. *Latin American peasants*, 1–42. London, Portland, OR: Frank Cass.

Carr, D.L., R.E. Bilborrow, and A. Barbieri. 2003. Population, agricultural land use and the environment in Latin America at the dawn of the 20th century: Evidence of change at the regional, national, and local scales. In *Open Meeting of the Human Dimensions of Global Environmental Change Research*. Montreal, Canada, p. 22.
Claeys, P. 2013. From food sovereignty to peasants' rights: An overview of via campesina's struggle for new human rights. In *La Via Campesina's open book: Celebrating 20 years of struggle and hope*, 1–10. Jakarta: Via Campesina.
Comunidades de la Mesa de Pueblos Originarios de la Cuenca de Guayatayoc y Salinas Grandes. 2012. *Press Conference*.
Díaz Benetti, W. 2011. *Plan Estratégico Productivo Jujuy, 2011–2020*. Jujuy, Argentina: Ministerio de Producción, Strategic Plan.
Domìnguez, D. 2005. Movimiento Campesino e Indigena en Argentina: Luchas contra el saqueo y colonialismo del siglo XXI. *La Otra Historia*. Available online: http://vivalatinoamerica-vivalatinoamerica.blogspot.nl/2008/11/movimiento-campesino-e-indigena-en.html (accessed February 16, 2015).
Dore, E. 2000. Environment and society: Long-term trends in Latin American mining. *Environment and History* 6, no. 1: 1–29.
Edelman, M. 2001. Social movements; Changing paradigms and forms of politics. *Annual Review of Anthropology* 30: 285–317.
Edelman, M. 2013. What is a peasant?. What are peasantries?. A briefing paper on issues of definition. *Intergovernmental Working Group on a United Nations Declaration on the*.
EFE. 2011. Número de mapuches presos o procesados pasa de 106 a 62 en un año. *elmostrador. mundo*, 23 Jun.
El Libertario. 2009. 5200 familias viven en asentamientos en la capital de Jujuy. *El Libertario Online*, 25 Jul.
El Libertario. 2012. Según la Secretaría de Minería hubo una histórica inversión de riesgo en 2011. *El Libertario Online*, 16 Jan.
ENDEPA. 2003. Indígenas de Jujuy denuncian al INAI por demoras en la entrega de tierras. *Indymedia*, 8 Oct.
FM Del Monte MOCASE-VC. 2012. Siguen amenazas y persecusión de paramilitares a camepsinos. *MOCASE VIA CAMPESINA*.
Fontana, L.B. 2014. Indigenous peoples vs peasant unions: Land conflicts and rural movements in plurinational Bolivia. *The Journal of Peasant Studies* 41, no. 3: 297–319.
Fox, J. 1993. *The politics of food in Mexico: State power and social mobilization*. Center for US-Mexican Studies.
García, J.J.R. 2009. Diversos y comunes: elementos constitutivos del conflicto entre comunidades indígenas, campesinas y afrocolombianas en el departamento del Cauca. *Analisis Politico* 22, no. 65: 53–93.
Giordano, M. 2003. Intrusos o propietarios. Argumentos y percepciones sobre el derecho a la propiedad de la tierra del indígena chaqueño. *Gazeta de Antropología* 19, no. 26: 1–16.
Gordillo, G., and S. Hirsch. 2003. Indigenous struggles and contested identities in Argentina histories of invisibilization and reemergence. *Journal of Latina American Anthropology* 8, no. 3: 4–30.
GRAIN. 2008. Seized! The 2008 land grab for food and financial security. *GRAIN Briefing*. Available online: http://www.grain.org/article/entries/93-seized-the-2008-landgrab-for-food-and-financial-security (accessed February 16, 2015).
GRAIN. 2012a. GRAIN releases data set with over 400 global land grabs. *GRAIN*. Available online: http://www.grain.org/article/entries/4479-grain-releases-data-set-with-over-400-global-land-grabs (accessed 17 February 2015).
GRAIN. 2012b. *Land grab deals. GRAIN*. Available online: http://www.grain.org/article/entries/4479-grain-releases-data-set-with-over-400-global-land-grabs (accessed February 16, 2015).
Gras, C., and V. Hernández. 2014. Agribusiness and large-scale farming: Capitalist globalisation in Argentine agriculture. *Canadian Journal of Development Studies / Revue canadienne d'études du développement* 35, no. 3: 339–57.
Guarnaccia, S., and E. de la Calle. 2012. Movimiento Nacional Campesino Indígena (MNCI): Origen, herencias, historia. *Agencia Paco Urondo*, 15 Aug.
Hale, C.R. 2005. Neoliberal multiculturalism: The remaking of cultural rights and racial dominance in central America. *PoLAR: Political and Legal Anthropology Review* 28, no. 1: 10–19.
Harvey, D. 2003. *The New Imperialism*. New York: Oxford University Press.

Harvey, N. 1998. *The chiapas rebellion; The struggle for land and democracy.* Durham and London: Duke University Press.
Hildyard, N. 2008. *A (crumbling) wall of money: financial bricolage, derivatives and power.* UK: The Corner House, Work in progress. Available online: http://www.thecornerhouse.org.uk/pdf/document/WallMoneyOct08.pdf (accessed February 16, 2015).
Holt-Giménez, E. 2008. *Territorial restructuring and the grounding of agrarian reform: Indigenous communities, gold mining and the World Bank.* Amsterdam: Transnational Institute (TNI). 11.11.11, No. 2.
Hooker, J. 2005. Indigenous inclusion/Black exclusion: race, ethnicity and multicultural citizenship in Latin America. *Journal of Latin American Studies* 37, no. 2: 285–310.
Hristov, J. 2009. Social class and ethnicity/Race in the dynamics of indigenous peasant movements: The case of the CRIC in Colombia. *Latin American Perspectives* 36, no. 4: 41–63.
IIRSA CCT Secretariat. 2011. *IIRSA 10 years later: Achievements and challenges.* Buenos Aires: BID-INTAL.
INDEC. 2008. *Censo Agropecuario, resultados provisorios.* Buenos Aires: Instituto Nacional de Estadística y Censos.
Justicia ratifica posesión de tierras campesinas en El Chacho. 2013. *CBA 24*, 4 Sep.
Karasik, G. 2006. Etnicidad, cultura y clases sociales. Procesos de formación histórica de la conciencia colectiva en Jujuy, 1985–2003. PhD, updated from original version (2005). Facultad de Filosofía y Letras de la Universidad Nacional de Tucumán.
Langevin, M.S., and P. Rosset. 1997. Land reform from below: The landless worker's movement in Brazil. *Institute for Food and Development Policy, Food First Backgrounder* 4, no. 3: 332–334.
La Red Puna. 1998. *Nuestra Tierra.* Pamphlet published with support of INAI (Instituto Nacional de Asuntos Indígenas). Jujuy, Argentina..
La Vía Campesina. 2014. A victory on our path to an international declaration on the rights of peasants. *Press Release*, 7 Jul.
Leiva, F.I. 2008. *Latin American neostructuralism.* Minneapolis, London: University of Minnesota Press.
Lipcovich, P. 2012. Lo que el Censo ayuda a visibilizar. *Pagina 12*, 30 Jun.
Manzanal, M. 2008. Rural development programs in argentina and its institutions (in the context of neoliberal macroeconomic adjustment). In A.V. Burlingham and W.N. Townsand, eds. *Rural Development Issues*, 137–56. New York: Nova Science Publishers Inc., pp. Ch. 5.
MICLA. 2012. Latin America: Mining in Conflict, an Interactive Map.
Minería Argentina: oportunidades de inversión. 2011. Argentina: Secretaría de Minería.
Moyo, S., and Y. Paris, eds. 2005. *Reclaiming the land: The resurgence of rural movements in Africa, Asia and Latin America.* London: Zed Books.
Muñoz, A.K.T. 2012. La emergencia del movimiento campesino en Argentina: de su invisibilización a la lucha política emancipadora. *Alba Sud; Investigación y comunicación para el desarrollo* 2: 1–41.
Murmis, M., and M.R. Murmis. 2012. Land concentration and foreign land ownership in Argentina in the context of global land grabbing. *Canadian Journal of Development Studies* 33, no. 4: 490–508.
Naharro, N., and A.L. Álvarez. 2011. *Acaparamiento de Tierras y Producción de Soja en Territorio Wichí, Salta – Argentina.* Germany and Argentina: Bread for the World & Asociana, Case Study.
Newell, P. 2009. Bio-hegemony: The political economy of agricultural biotechnology in Argentina. *Journal of Latin American Studies* 41: 27–57.
OEA. 2013. *Premio Interamericano a la Innovación para la Gestión Pública Efectiva 2013.* Organización de Estados Americanos, Secretaría de Asuntos Políticos (SAP)/Departamento para la Gestión Pública Efectiva (DGPE), Bases de Postulación.
Oliveira, G.de L.T. 2013. Land regularization in Brazil and the global land grab. *Development and Change* 44, no. 2: 261–83.
Picq, M. 2011. Indigenous resistance is the new 'terrorism'. *Aljizeera*, 10 Jul.
Prensa De Frente. 2011. Comunicado de prensa: Una ley contra los desalojos - un paso hacia la función social de la Tierra. *Seminario Alternativas*, No. 166. Available online: http://www.semanario-alternativas.info/archivos/2011/5%20-%20mayo/166/internacionales/paginas_%20internacional/argentina/articulos/EL%20MNCI.html (accessed February 16, 2015).
Richardson, N.P. 2009. Export-oriented populism: commodities and coalitions in Argentina. *Studies in Comparative International Development* 44, no. 3: 228–55.

RIMISP. 2004. Sintesis de las Ponencias y del Debate. In *Seminario-Taller*. Presented at the Transformación Productiva e Institucional del Mundo Rural de la Argentina, Buenos Aires.
Romig, S. 2013. Miners pull back from projects in Argentina. The Wall Street Journal, 21 May.
Rosset, P. 2013. Re-thinking agrarian reform, land and territory in La Via Campesina. *Journal of Peasant Studies* 40, no. 1: 721–75.
Rumi, M.J. 2013. Una batalla ganada para la tierra. Pagina 12, 5 Sep.
Schejtman, A., and J.A. Berdegué. 2004. *Desarrollo territorial*. Santiago de Chile: RIMISP, Centro Latinoamericano para el Desarrollo Rural, No. 1.
Schwittay, A.F. 2003. From peasant favors to indigenous rights; the articulation of an indigenous identity and land struggle in Northwestern Argentina. *The Journal of Latin American Anthropology* 8, no. 3: 127–54.
Scott, J.C. 1998. *Seeing like a state: How certain schemes to improve the human condition have failed*. New Haven: Yale University Press.
Seoane, J., E. Taddei, and C. Algranati. 2005. The new configurations of popular movements in Latin America. *BORON, A.; LECHINI, G.(Comp.). Politics and social movements in an hegemonic world. Buenos Aires: CLACSO.*
Sinnott, E., J. Nash, and A. de la Torre. 2010. *Natural resources in Latin America and the Caribbean; beyond booms and busts?* Washington, DC: The International Bank for Reconstruction and Development/The World Bank.
Solberg, C. 1971. Rural Unrest and Agrarian Policy in Argentina, 1912–1930. *Journal of Interamerican Studies and World Affairs* 13, no. 1: 18–52.
Soliz, C. 2012. El otro rostro de América Latina; En diálogo con La emergencia indígena en América Latina, de José Bengoa. *Nueva Sociedad* 238, (March-April): 126–137.
Sullivan, L. 2013. Identity, Territory and Land Conflict in Brazil. *Development and Change* 44, no. 2: 451–71.
Svampa, M. 2013. 'Consenso de los Commodities' y lenguajes de valoración en América Latina. *Nueva Sociedad* 244, (Marzo-Abril): 30–46.
Teubal, M., and T. Palmisano. 2010. El conflicto agrario: características y proyecciones. In *Del paro agrario a las elecciones de 2009: tramas, reflexiones y debates*, eds. N. Giarracca and M. Teubal, 193–252. Buenos Aires: Anthropofagia.
Torrez, F. 2013. Reflection: Our evolving collective vision of agrarian reform and the defense of land and territory. *Journal of Peasant Studies* 40, no. 4: 721–75.
Urkidi, L., and M. Walter. 2011. Dimensions of environmental justice in anti-gold mining movements in Latin America. *Geoforum* 42, no. 6: 683–95.
UST-MNCI. 2011. Violento acaparamiento de Tierras en Esteban Echeverría. *Unión de Trabajadores Rurales Sin Tierra de Cuyo*. UST-MNCI Blog: http://ust-mnci.blogspot.nl/2011/12/acaparamiento-de-tierras.html (accessed March 4, 2014).
Valente, M. 2011. ARGENTINA: Anti-Terrorism Law Upsets Harmony Between Government and Activists. *IPS, Inter Press Service News Agency*, 22 Dec.
Van Cott, D.L. 2005. *From movements to parties in Latin America; the evolution of Ethnic Politics*. New York, USA: Cambridge University Press.
Van Cott, D.L. 2007. Latin america's indigenous Peoples. *Journal of Democracy* 18, no. 4: 127–42.
Van Den Berghe, P.L. 1979. Ethnicity and class in Highland Peru. In *Peasants, primitives and proletariats; the struggle for identity in South America*, eds. D.L. Browman and R.A. Schwarz, 253–66. The Hague, Paris, New York: Mouton Publishers.
Vélez Sársfield, D. 1871. *Codigo Civil Argentino*.
Veltmeyer, H. 1997. New social movements in Latin America; The dynamics of class and identity. *Journal of Peasant Studies* 25, no. 1: 139–69.
Veltmeyer, H. 2005. The dynamics of land occupations in Latin America. In *Reclaiming the land: The Resurgence of rural movements in Africa, Asia and Latin America*, eds. S. Moyo and Y. Paris, 285–316. London: Zed Books.
Veltmeyer, H. 2007. *Peasants in an era of neoliberal globalization: Latin America on the move*. Brighton: Institute of Development Studies, University of Sussex: IDS.
Wald, N. 2013. Bridging identity divides in current rural social mobilisation. *Identities* 20, no. 5: 598–615.
Watts, J. 2014. Brazil's Landless Workers Movement renews protest on 30th anniversary. *The Guardian*, 13 Feb.

Wilson, A. and M. Cervantes. 2014. *Survey of mining companies 2013*. Vancouver, Canada: Fraser Institute.

Yashar, D.J. 2005. *Contesting citizenship in Latin America; The rise of indigenous movements and the postliberal challenge*. New York, USA: Cambridge University Press.

Networked, rooted and territorial: green grabbing and resistance in Chiapas

Dianne E. Rocheleau

Land grabbing has been characterized by large-scale commercial land deals or green grabs of large conservation tracts. In Chiapas, Mexico, green grabs employ a networked strategy across state, corporate and civil society lines to evict peasant and indigenous communities, and facilitate entry of extractive industries, plantations and industrial 'ecotourism'. The resistance is rooted in place(s) and in a coalition of civil society organizations and autonomous communities. Network illustrations and field reports show that several environmental organizations occupy pivotal positions in grabbing and/or resistance networks, with large powerful groups linked to state and corporate interests. The experience in Agua Azul, a key node in a planned tourism megaproject, illustrates the deployment of networked and dispersed power to unmake and remake territories across scales. Small purchased plots form nodes in far-flung circuits of ecotourism and archeological sites. The substantial resistance is likewise rhizomatic in character, reaching across archipelagos of forest and farming communities and distant allies, to reconstitute autonomous territories. Ongoing land struggles play out in networked spaces, with entire territories, and many lives, at stake. Emerging coalitions of human rights, indigenous, religious and environmental groups promise an expanding resistance to evictions and territorial green grabs in Chiapas and elsewhere.

Introduction

Land grabs by nation states, multinational corporations, investment firms and wealthy individuals have recently captured the attention of eager investors, as well as a diverse range of actors implicated in, or impacted by, this alarming global trend (Blas and Wallis 2009; De Shutter 2010; Borras et al. 2011a; Sassen 2013). In addition to global media, this issue has engaged United Nations (UN) agencies (Food and Agriculture Organization (FAO), International Labor Organization (ILO) and UN High Commission for Refugees (UNHCR)), as well as scholars, human rights groups, and food policy and farmers' organizations worldwide (Rosset 2011; Torrez 2011; Rosset and Martinez-Torres 2012; Martínez-Torres and Rosset 2014). Last but not least, land grabbing has affected and grievously harmed people who have been denied access to forest, rangeland, farmland and water resources, or have been uprooted from their homelands (Grajales 2011; Borras et al. 2011b).

The phenomenon is not new (Verma 2014), nor is it exclusive to a single region, yet the recent wave of land grabs has gained notoriety based on cases of direct sales and long-term leases of mega-parcels in Africa and the Middle East, ostensibly to produce food or energy crops (Blas and Wallis 2009). In other cases, vast tracts of land are the object of green grabbing for conservation, recreation and tourism (Fairhead, Leach, and Scoones 2012; Corson 2011; Corson 2012; Corson and MacDonald 2012; Ojeda 2012).

In contrast, this paper examines the use of *networked, distributed, rooted, and territorial power* by both land grabbers and resistance movements in Chiapas, Mexico (Rocheleau 2011a, 2011b, 2012a; Borras et al. 2011b). The focus on rainforest and archeological tourism, as well as biodiversity conservation, and the mobilization of *distributed networked power*, by both grabbers and resisters, provide a window on green grabs in general, especially in Latin America (see Wolford 2010).

The first section contrasts the current wave of large-scale land deals (especially in Africa), with networked, distributed green grabs in Mexico. A case study from Agua Azul in the municipality of Chilón in the state of Chiapas illustrates the nature, cost and effectiveness of equally networked resistance across dispersed locations in a larger, non-contiguous territory. The discussion and conclusion relate the case study to territorial green grabbing and resistance in Latin America more generally. They also signal the fluidity and potential for change in the constellations of networked actors among both grabbers and resisters.

The dominant model of land grabs by simple purchase

The new scramble for land in Africa has become the iconic example of the new wave of land grabbing through outright purchases of mega-parcels. Individual transactions range from tens of thousands to hundreds of thousands of hectares. This phenomenon has been discussed by international agencies largely in terms of corporate, state and individual actors as buyers, and as property owners. Rural people in the region, who are neither buyers nor sellers, are cast simply as those whose lives and livelihoods 'are affected' and who must give (or not) 'prior informed consent'. One takes away an impression of rural people suffering 'collateral damage' from business as usual. The theft of homelands, the destruction of livelihoods and the appropriation of entire ecosystems are normalized, ironically, as part of a process of 'land tenure reform' and 'free trade'. At best, we are led to expect more participatory 'negotiations' between rural communities, multi-national corporations and states.

The diagram of the dominant model of land grabs (Figure 1) presents what I take to be the view of the mainstream development agencies, and highlights some of the contradictions in that scenario. Investment capital and relationships between investors are hidden in a cloud, which obscures their workings and relationships from the gaze of the other actors. The UN system and related nongovernmental organizations (NGOs) provide advice on land deal policy and practice by state and private-sector actors, including contradictory advice to privatize land, to respect human rights and to secure free, prior and informed consent from owners and/or residents. Even when something called 'consent' is procured, and delivered back to the cloud of investors, the terms of such processes are murky and suspect (see helicopter in Figure 1).

The state is present, participating and complicit in a posture of passivity. This model links land grabbing to 'failed' or 'weak' states, with very low land prices, and assumes purchase or long-term lease of single large parcels of land. The land itself is treated as a single entity, a substrate, for 'development', though real people, other living beings and whole worlds are at stake. Land use conversion to industrial food and energy monocrops provides low wage or seasonal work on plantations for some. The destination of people expelled from the site of the land deal is pictured as a cloud of 'elsewhere', cloaking the various fates of displaced people.

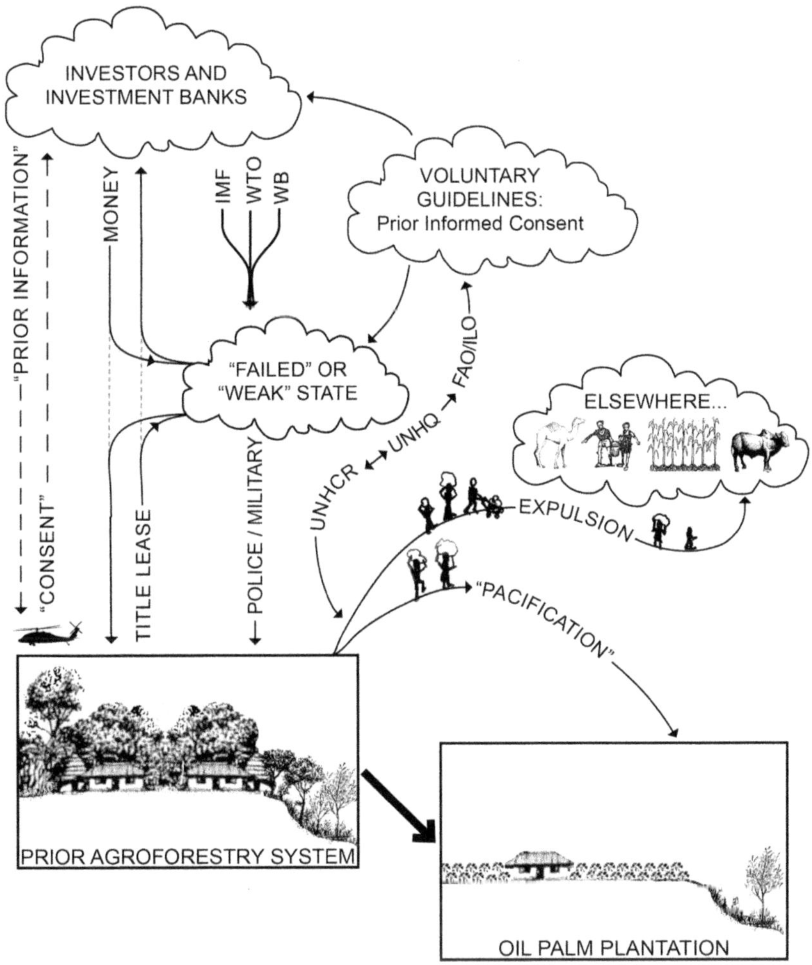

Figure 1. Land grabbing: the prevailing model.[1]

While it is likely that people resist these land deals in a variety of ways, there is little written as yet about that resistance in Africa. Many of the best known and publicized land deals have occurred in war-torn regions and conflict zones where the stakes of direct resistance are especially high. If and when it does occur, both resistance and its repression may also be rendered invisible within a broader tapestry of explicit and visible violence, as for example in Somalia or Southern Sudan. In other cases, with strong national states, swift and brutal repression may overwhelm resistance and both may go un- or under-reported. And as Borras and Franco (2013) point out, resistance is not always the main or the only response.

[1]Organizations noted in Figure 1: International Monetary Fund (IMF); World Trade Organization (WTO); World Bank (WB); United Nations High Commission for Refugees (UNHCR). United Nations Secretariat (UNHQ), UN Food and Agriculture Organization (FAO) and the International Labor Organization (ILO).

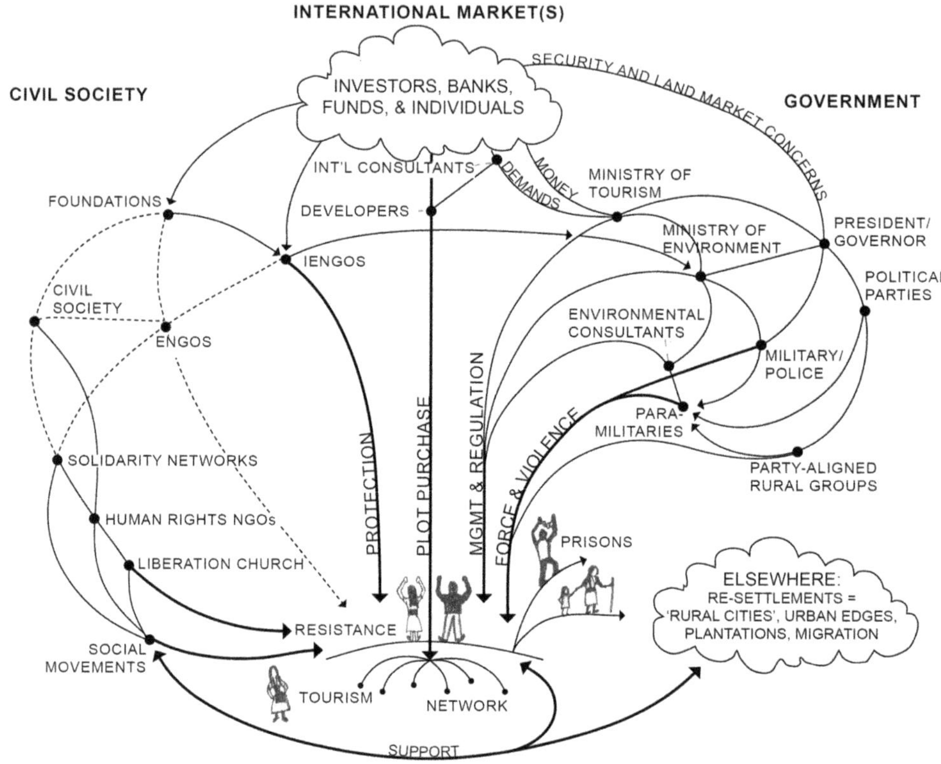

Figure 2. Rooted networks, green grabbing and resistance.[2]

Contrasting case of green grabs and resistance in Chiapas, Mexico

The state of Chiapas, in contrast, presents a complex case of networked, territorial green grabbing and equally networked, dispersed and persistent resistance (Figure 2). A strategy of multiple forces brought to bear by a diversity of actors in parallel land acquisition processes is exemplified by the last 20 years' experience in the state. Networked land grabbing processes driven by conservation and tourism interests, or the pretext of such, are less visible, more distributed and more complex than the large land deal form of grabbing, but no less significant, or violent. As Figure 2 suggests, there is a decidedly Foucauldian dimension of dispersed power at work here, a Latourian dimension of networked assemblages, and a rhizomic structure of relations among both grabbers and resisters (Deleuze and Guattari 1987; Foucault 1991; Latour 2007). Yet the Chiapas land grabbing process defies definition and explanation by any one of these, since what is most significantly at play, and at work, is a struggle between multiple, entangled and networked powers, with roots in distinct territories, even worlds, often overlapping in the same Cartesian space (see Rocheleau and Roth 2007; Escobar 2008; De La Cadena 2010; Blaser 2013).

[2]Key to abbreviations for organizations and groups: ENGOS, Environmental non-governmental organizations, local and national; IENGOS, International Environmental Non-governmental organizations; Ministry of tourism, Secretariat for tourism (SECTUR) and tourism development agency (FONATUR); Ministry of Environment, Secretariat of Environment and Natural Resources.

Histories of grabbing and resistance

Both land grabbers and resisters in Chiapas are also rooted in the very specific history of Mexican land law and agrarian culture, where the land is for the people who live and work on it, and care for it[3] (Conant 2010). The Mexican Revolution in the early twentieth century resulted in a sweeping land reform, though imperfect and unfinished (Esteva 1983). Under Article 27 of the 1917 constitution, the *ejido* system provided land for farmers to use, but not to buy and sell (Bartra 2004). It entitled community members to land allocations for residential and agricultural use, governed by local assemblies made up of the recognized community members (initially composed of all – and only – male heads of households). Some indigenous communities maintained '*communidades agrarias*' in a system roughly parallel to *ejidos*. In Chiapas, the revolutionary reforms came decades later, and many communities remained legally landless, as tenants of largeholder ranchers and farmers.

National counter-reforms were initiated in 1987 and implemented in 1992 to amend Article 27, followed by programs to survey and privatize individual parcels, to disband the existing *ejidos* and to end the process of forming new ones (de Ita 2006; Hernandez Espino 2007). This neo-liberal counter-reform of land law, and the North American Free Trade Agreement (NAFTA), paved the way for the current land grab and spawned a surge of political and cultural resistance by a broad base of social movements and civil society organizations (Collier 2005; Muñoz Ramírez et al. 2008). They were, in effect, engaging in preemptive resistance to land grabbing, based on analysis of the likely outcome of these policies. And they were right (Esteva 2013).

In 1994, a broad social movement coalesced around the struggle for land and territory, with the Zapatista Army of National Liberation, (henceforth EZLN, for *Ejército Zapatista de Liberación Nacional*) and the related autonomous civilian communities preeminent among them (Harvey 1994, 1996, 1998; Stephen 2002; Rosset 2009; Baschet 2013). The Zapatistas timed their catalytic uprising on 1 January 1994 in direct response to the implementation of NAFTA on that date, and the related assaults on agrarian communities and communal property. Other groups resisting the counter-reforms and supporting recuperation of peasant and indigenous lands included Christian ecclesiastical base communities, the pacifist Catholic communities of *Las Abejas*, and several other peasant and indigenous associations, rural artisans' unions and farmers' unions, some directly and others indirectly allied with the Zapatistas, and some not at all as noted by Miguel Angel Garcia Aguirre (pers. comm. August 2011) and Maderas del Pueblo del Sureste (2008). The Liberation Theology wing of the Catholic Church supported the land struggle with several thousand catechists who served as rural community organizers and human rights promoters. Bishop Samuel Ruiz of San Cristobal took a lead in convening peace negotiations between the government and the Zapatistas and in guaranteeing the safety of the latter.

A diverse array of national and international civil society organizations rapidly coalesced around these groups forming locally rooted and internationally networked solidarity movements, including religious, indigenous, peasant, feminist, human rights and, to some extent, environmental networks. While social theorists may debate whether such networked movements are best understood in Marxist (Harvey 2012), post Marxist (Hardt and Negri 2000, 2009), Foucauldian (Escobar 2011), feminist (Gibson-Graham 2006), regional and postcolonial (Escobar 2011; Escobar and Alvarez 1992), anarchist (Scott 2009; Baschet

[3]For an articulation of this at the international level, see Martínez-Torres and Rosset 2014 on similar framings by La Via Campesina.

2013), indigenous (Nash 2001; Marcos 2010) or decolonial (Sousa Santos 2006; Escobar 2008; Esteva 2013; Mignolo and Escobar 2013) terms, the people on the ground were busy taking pages from all of the above and orders from none. It seems clear that elements of several liberatory traditions as well as new creations were at work (See also Gutierrez Aguilar, 2014 on similar phenomena in Bolivia). The Zapatistas and their allies wrote more than a few pages of their own into the emergence of the alter-globalization and resurgent indigenous movements (Benjamin 1995; Marcos 1997, 2002, 2004, 2006, 2014; Marcos and Le Bot 1997; Baschet 2013).

The communities in resistance refused to accept landlessness, eviction, resettlement or even continued residence under new terms, without rights to farm, gather and graze their animals, manage and protect their forests, and govern themselves[4] (Marcos and Le Bot 1997; Baschet 2013). After the brief uprising and 2 years of negotiation, the Zapatistas and President Ernesto Zedillo signed the San Andres accords in 1996, which provided for recognition of indigenous territories nationwide, autonomy for self-governing indigenous communities and reversal of the constitutional changes threatening communal lands. The original San Andres Accords were not ratified by the Congress, which instead passed a more conservative and limited Indigenous Law in 2001.[5] However, Zapatista communities and many other indigenous and peasant groups continued to respect the San Andres Accords, based on the recognition and respect of indigenous territories, as opposed to individual or community property. This reflects a strong current of contemporary resistance thought in the region, based in legitimacy versus legality (Cideci Seminar 2013), and indigenous autonomy versus representation (Juntas de Buen Gobierno 2013a, 2013b, 2013c, 2013d).

From 2000 to 2006, the PROCEDE program[6] offered surveys to document and legalize individual holdings in ejido lands. They eventually also offered to legally register entire communal holdings as property. However, the land would still be eligible for sale, or as collateral for loans. Many indigenous and *campesino* organizations and civil society allies continued to oppose PROCEDE, including the communal option (Stephen 2002; Collier 2005) and insisted on the recognition of indigenous and campesino territories. Signs posted clearly at the entrance to Zapatista communities still proclaim the prohibition on trading in land:

> Esta usted entrando en territorio Zapatista. Aquí no se vende ni se compra la tierra ... Si a eso viene, usted no es bienvenido
>
> You are entering Zapatista Territory. Here we do not buy or sell land .... If that is your intention you are not welcome.
>
> (Author translation of signs observed in or near Zapatista communities from 2005 to 2013).

Twenty years on from the 1994 uprising, the Zapatistas and several other networks of communities are engaged in non-violent resistance to eviction, in the face of intimidation by a formidable group of armed forces arrayed against them (Rocheleau 2012b). These include: paramilitary-type organizations; local, state and national police forces; the military; private

[4]Scott (2009) has discussed the history of similar quests for autonomy, as opposed to taking of state power, among people in the mountain communities of Southeast Asia.

[5]The Indigenous Law passed by the congress lacked provisions for territorial rights and autonomous self-government that were key elements of the original accords.

[6]PROCEDE, the Certification of Ejido Rights Program, followed from the reform of Article 27 and the new Agrarian law.

security forces and federal security agencies (Centro de Derechos Humanos Fray Bartolomé de Las Casas 2012). They are also subject to fragmentation through non-military, government sponsored counter-insurgency measures and massive subsidy programs, as well as internal changes in alignment within movements.

They persist in the struggle to realize their collective visions of local livelihoods, culture and non-violent, self-governed communities joined in regional networks (Pérez Espinosa 2011; Juntas de Buen Gobierno 2013a, 2013b, 2013c, 2013d). The Zapatistas and their allies continue to build and maintain connections to national and international networks of people in solidarity with their struggle, aspirations and accomplishments (Conant 2010; Evans 2005).

Current green grabs in Chiapas: the Palenque tourism megaproject (CIPP)

The current green land grabs and the resistances in Chiapas (Figure 2) proceed against this historical backdrop, in stark contrast to the simple land purchase model (Figure 1). The Mexican federal state is not 'failed' or even 'weak'. The strong national state, with a diversified economy and high land values, facilitates the expropriation of land for exclusionary protection, or exploitation, of natural resources in Chiapas, characterized by an agricultural economy, low land values and low wages. In spite of extreme poverty and inequality, Chiapas is also one of the richest states in Mexico in terms of mineral, energy and forest resources, and scenic wonders, all now targets of the acquisitive powers of a host of actors from investors to conservation organizations, the tourism industry, mining interests, industrial agriculture giants (prominent among them, Monsanto[7]) and alternative energy developers (CAPISE 2002). The state was singled out by former Mexican President Felipe Calderon, and the former Governor, Juan Sabines, as the 'pilot project' for the regional development initiative formerly known as Plan Puebla Panama (PPP), now the MesoAmerica Project.[8] The multi-lateral 'regional integration' effort (conceived and promoted by the US), commits Mexico, Central America and Colombia to joint ventures by state and private capital, with major US participation. The initiative focuses on transportation and energy infrastructure, with much of the power destined for mining and manufacturing industries, as well as energy consumers in the US (Bartra 2001, 2004; Wilson 2008).

The most relevant element of this integrated plan, with respect to green grabs in Chiapas, is the Palenque Integrated Planned Center (hereafter CIPP), a combined conservation and tourism initiative originated in 2000 by President Vicente Fox. Although it could not be realized due to the 'inability to secure the needed territorial reserves for the project in 2004' (i.e. popular resistance) it surfaced again as a flagship project of both President Calderon and Governor Sabines (Wilson 2008; Maderas del Pueblo de Sureste 2008; Zunino 2010a, 2010b, 2010c; Pickard 2011). The CIPP was planned as a world-class inland tourism archipelago of archeological sites, pristine forest stands and scenic waterfalls and lakes, in a green sea of biodiversity conservation, carbon storage and 'environmental

[7]In fact, Monsanto is on Conservation International's 'Business and Sustainability Council' (Conservation International 2013).

[8]The inaugural projects of the PPP, particularly large dams, encountered stiff resistance throughout the country and especially in the states of Chiapas, Oaxaca and Guerrero. Renamed the MesoAmerica Project in 2008, it linked regional development plans to US and regional military, policing, Drug War and border control strategies (Zunino and Pickard 2008, 2009; Maderas del Pueblo del Sureste 2008; Wilson 2008).

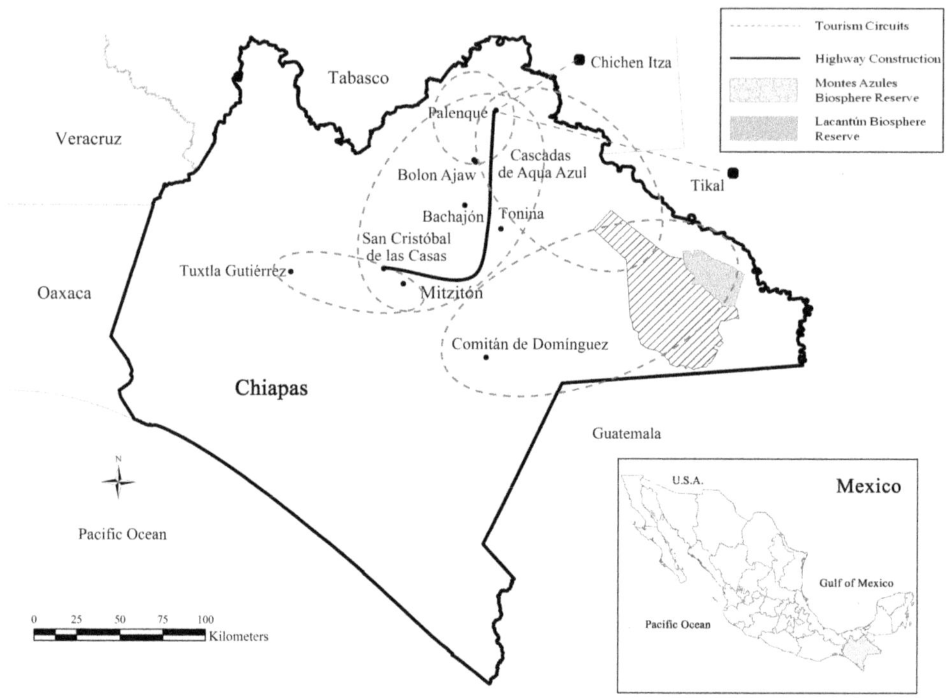

Figure 3. Planned tourism circuits in Chiapas.

services' (Figure 3). The plan also included several Chiapas hotspots of ecotourism and endangered ecosystems of the Meso-American Biological Corridor (a transcontinental ribbon of linked ecological reserves, public and private). Cultural tourism, featuring indigenous people as spectacle, was widely lauded as a potential engine of economic development linked to the CIPP (Gonzalez 2007; Bellinghausen 2008).

As a candidate for governor in 2006, Sabines explicitly promised 'Cancun in the Rainforest' and staked development and poverty alleviation in Chiapas on the tourism megaproject (Gonzalez 2007; Calvo 2008; Centro de Derechos Humanos Fray Bartolomé de Las Casas 2012). While the Palenque CIP, along with four others, did not come to fruition under the past two administrations, the Palenque project is back on the table as the only CIP proposed by the new administrations at federal and state level. A study commissioned by the Federal Tourism Promotion Agency (FONATUR) in March of 2014 placed it next in line (Ramírez 2014).

The necessary evictions and land grabs for the CIPP have not yet been realized, but several kinds of cartographic and discursive sleight of hand have been employed to develop multiple, distinct territories, most of them inherently incompatible with conservation and 'ecotourism', and unsustainable over the long term (see Balvé 2011 on Colombia, and Vandergeest and Peluso 2006; Peluso and Vandergeest 2001, 2006 on Southeast Asia). The Centro de Investigaciones Economicas y Politicas de Accion Comunitaria, henceforth referred to as CIEPAC (CIEPAC 2010) and Otros Mundos (2014a) have mapped sites of mineral and petroleum exploration permits near recently constructed, planned rural resettlement centers within these same circuits, and palm oil plantations have already been introduced into the region (García Aguirre 2011) While these multiple objectives and trajectories are not ultimately compatible, the channeling of different flows, movements and lines of sight can, for a time, protect the direct gaze of tourists from any unsightly views of mining, pipelines and plantations. Likewise, their gaze can be selectively focused on commercial spectacles and performances of ancient Mayan cultures, while removal of living indigenous peoples from their homelands remains invisible to the seemingly casual yet highly regimented touristic gaze (see Bellinghausen 2008).

The land grab within the area of the planned CIPP is both driven and further supported by the fog of greening generated by dominant paradigms of global environmental conservation, the related selective reclassification of people and their lands, and the smoke, mirrors and maps of global financial investment practices.

The fog of greening

Once we move beyond the simple purchase model of state, buyers, sellers and residents, a new set of key actors emerges. The 'fog of greening' is generated, unwittingly or intentionally, with the help of selected, powerful international and national environmental NGOs, and national and state agencies with mandates for environment, tourism and land reform. Federal, state, corporate and NGO actors employ a diverse portfolio of techniques in a layered process of succession, to facilitate or directly enforce the acquisition of locations desired for specific 'green' attributes (Zunino 2010a, 2010b, 2010c; Chapin 2004; and see Ojeda 2012, 2013 for similar cases in Colombia). Miguel Pickard (pers. comm October 2013) and Miguel Angel García Aguirre (pers. comm. August 2011) both cite multiple instances where federal and state environmental and tourism agencies, and environmental NGOs helped to secure state control of large tracts of reserve land, creating the matrix from which new territories are made. This coalition of actors employs meta-strategies to redefine the terms of connection between people and land, often trying to sever those connections for some, while facilitating them for others. New land tenure laws and land use rules (market-led agrarian reforms promoted by the International Monetary Fund (IMF), World Bank and some UN agencies) combine with green pretexts of ecotourism and conservation to legitimate new exclusive reserves and subsequent eviction of farming communities in the area (Figure 2).

The fog drifts from forest green to neon green as various federal and state officials invoke visions of 'Cancun in the rainforest' and 'Disneyland in the rainforest' (Gonzalez 2007; Bellinghausen 2008; Calvo 2008; Centro de Derechos Humanos Fray Bartolomé de Las Casas 2012). This process is also abetted, directly or indirectly, by programs of a handful of UN agencies (United Nations Environment Programme (UNEP), United Nations Educational, Scientific and Cultural Organization (UNESCO) and United National Human Settlements Programme (UN-Habitat)), the Meso-American Biological Corridor program, and environmental programs of development banks, bilateral funders (US, UK, EU), investors and philanthropic foundations. International and national tourism industry actors also play a major role: linking tourism to reserves, parks and greening; lobbying central governments and selected agencies to deploy police and military force to provide a greater sense of security for investors and tourists; and promoting the region as a vast untrammeled wilderness for eco-adventure, discovery and spectacular vistas.

Several international conservation organizations actively support the removal of rural communities from areas that have been reclassified as 'reserves' (Chapin 2004; Zunino and Pickard 2008, 2009; Pickard 2011). Some of these organizations have been linked to government cleansing of campesinos from the *campo* in the area of Las Cañadas, in the Montes Azules and Lacandon Biosphere Reserves, and across the border in Guatemala (CAPISE 2002; Choudry 2003; Grandia 2012). The World Wildlife Foundation (WWF)

(2013), The Carlos Slim Foundation,[9] The Nature Conservancy, Environmental Defense Fund and Conservation International are all engaged in the politics of reserves and/or in REDD+ carbon offset pilot efforts in Chiapas, both of which have impacted communities and rural livelihoods in Montes Azules and Lacantun Biosphere Reserves (Pskowski 2013; The REDD Desk 2013; Global Justice Ecology Project 2011; Comité de Derechos Humanos Fray Pedro Lorenzo de la Nada 2011; Bellinghausen 2014b). Most of the international conservation organizations active in Chiapas have remained silent in the face of violent repression and evictions, as well as the rapidly expanding and ecologically destructive 'development' outside of reserves and parks. Both occur at the expense of small farms with ecologically and nutritionally diverse cropping systems (García Aguirre 2011).

While the fog of greening can and does occur elsewhere, it is particularly important in Mexico, given its agrarian revolutionary history and culture, to legitimate eviction through environmental protection and public interest. The push to secure territorial reserves for the CIPP also facilitates the removal of oppositional communities from the vicinity of planned commercial and industrial development, under the twin pretexts of national and global nature conservation and tourism as a clean, green development mechanism.

The Cancun and Disney metaphors bandied about in 2006–2012 invoke visions of regional landscapes and economies transformed by the networked nodes of tourist destinations. The tourism industry already brings 4.25 million tourists annually to Chiapas. Tourism makes new territories and specific landscapes and ecologies through concrete practices that directly affect ecological structure and function, and regional landscape character, as well as economies and cultures. One might say that the industrial variant of 'eco' or nature-based tourism, more than any other enterprise of similar magnitude, destroys the basis of its own production/existence, also known as the second contradiction of capital (O'Connor 1988, 1991; Henderson 2009). Intrinsic territorial transformation and environmental degradation by large-scale tourism itself is further compounded by the instrumental use of green pretexts (see Ojeda 2012, 2013) to grab land for the other elements of the regional plan, from oil palm plantations and oil and gas fields to mines and pipelines.

Dispossession by delegitimation

Another obligatory prelude to dispossession is the reclassification of indigenous and campesino groups and specific communities to delegimitize them and justify deterritorialization. Various federal and state agencies, environmental NGOs and commercial interests, including mass media, collaborate directly and indirectly to recode the status of land and people and the identities of multiple, entangled territories. Modernist concepts of culture and nature are weaponized as discursive tools in campaigns of *dispossession by deligitimation*. Members of peasant and indigenous communities are cast as inefficient farmers who deforest the land, deplete soils, displace wildlife and live in misery. Alternatively, they may be branded as culturally inauthentic, or falsely accused as violent criminals (especially in the case of leaders). In Guatemala and Colombia (Sundberg 2003, 2004; Ojeda 2012, 2013), researchers have reported that states and international conservation NGOs have selected specific, often small indigenous or campesino groups as the 'authentic indigenous'

[9]Carlos Slim Helú, telecommunications magnate, and the world's second wealthiest billionaire, is also a major investor in mining (Berman 2013; Forbes 2013).

people of the zone. This is often accompanied by disparaging the legitimacy of other groups with equal or stronger claims to indigenous or traditional status.[10]

In Mexico, the Lacandones (some of whom live in Chiapas) have been celebrated in national commercial television ads (aired frequently on Televisa 2010, 2011), posters and magazine covers as the 'true guardians of the rainforest'. Yet their exclusive claims to reserves in southern Chiapas are not supported by history (de Vos 2002). The national advertisements, paid for by the state of Chiapas, served to delegitimize (through silence and absence) the place of other larger and less compliant indigenous and campesino groups in the rainforest (for a distinct and detailed analysis of the Lacandones see Calleros-Rodriguez 2014). Over 40 communities of other ethnicities have already been evicted on this pretext from the area of the Montes Azules and Lacantun Reserves, in recent decades.

Smoke, mirrors, maps and smoking guns

The networked strategy of shopping for pixels, purchasing polygons and making/taking territories is well adapted to the specific economic and investment conditions of the state. Chiapas land prices are low in the Mexico context, but high compared to other international 'investment opportunities'. Investors and developers engage in a strategic, selective approach, and purchase or lease relatively small land parcels. Developers focus on capital investments on site, the provision of contracts and jobs in the region, and promise 'trickle-out' benefits for local communities.

This strategy relies on massive state investments in transportation infrastructure and social re-engineering of territorial identity and extent, as well as the location, lives and livelihoods of indigenous and campesino communities. The federal and state plans for these takings and remakings of territory have been maintained as de facto state secrets, protected from scrutiny by indigenous, political, social and human rights organizations, a decision reported in a government document (FONATUR 2011).

State agencies, developers, banks, pension funds and speculators have been issuing contracts to geographic information system (GIS) firms and university researchers to identify pixels that meet specific lists of criteria. These may include: proximity to roads; proximity to airports, hotels and towns; presence of and proximity to scenic features, including waterfalls, rivers and lakes; presence of or access to 'good' water; soil types; carbon storage potential, land tenure, individual property tracts; demographic data; and political history, current configuration and disposition.[11]

The resulting maps of color-coded cells reflect the client's criteria and serve to identify blocks or patches of land with fixed boundaries (polygons) for potential purchase. The polygons may be as small as 4 hectares, as in a Lake Miramar community bordering the Montes Azules Reserve (Comité de Derechos Humanos Fray Pedro de la Nada 2011), or 600 hectares at Agua Azul in the CIPP circuit (Figure 3). Both sites are home (Henríquez 2011a) to people whose good fortune, their scenic water features and surrounding rainforests, have become liabilities as these features have lit up their home places on the map searches of developers.

What is less obvious, but crucial to green grabbing in Chiapas, is the investment climate for tourism and the inverse relationship of strong peasant social movements

[10]See also D. Hall, P. Hirsch and T. Li (2011) on indigenous status and land conflicts in southeast Asia.

[11]See Ramachandra and Shruthi (2007) for a detailed description of a similar process of remote exploration and technical identification of renewable energy sites in Karnataka state in India.

to security ratings for investment. The ratings rest in part on foreign analysts' perceptions of 'security' and 'political stability', and the *financial analysts' opinions about the perceptions of investors.* In the past, while money poured into regions of Mexico ravaged by drug war violence, some multi-national banking representatives made investment in Chiapas (one of the least affected areas) contingent on 'getting rid of the Zapatistas'.[12] State and corporate concerns about security, politics and the perceptions of financial investors continue to drive policy and practice. Human rights groups and journalists have documented provocations, threats, subversion and direct violence against Zapatista and other communities in resistance by federal and state police and/or allied paramilitary-type organizations, much of it concentrated in the area of the CIPP. It has resulted in loss of land, crops and livestock, as well as grievous personal injury and death (Centro de Derechos Humanos Fray Bartolomé de las Casas (FRAYBA) 2012; Bellinghausen 2014a).

Resistance to the CIPP

The CIPP has not proceeded unopposed. It has been met with distributed, coordinated, non-violent territorial resistance by indigenous and campesino communities, supported by continuing and resurgent social movements and civil society networks, and global solidarity initiatives (Maderas del Pueblo del Sureste 2008; Rocheleau 2012b; Bellinghausen 2014a). Since 2008, non-violent resisters have been hard at work defending a number of communities on the tourism circuits or in the (likely) path of the highway (Figure 3). The affected and mobilized communities stretch from the starting point of the expanded highway in Mitziton, at the edge of San Cristobal de las Casas (Figure 3), to the areas around San Sebastian Bachajon and Agua Azul, to Palenque.

Rural violence is fomented to make the state 'safe' for investment, by removing or silencing rural people opposed to eviction and/or development plans. Once violent attacks occur, or even peaceful meetings to resolve conflicts, state actors, political party operatives or their proxies may then deploy police, military and/or paramilitary forces to specific points of 'environmental' interest to 'restore order'. Conflict justifies removal of people, once they have been identified as inappropriate, out of place or criminal, in newly redefined territories of conservation and tourism development.

Where resistance flourishes, and persists, in spite of the fog of greening, and the smoke and mirrors of tourism development, it is met with dispersed, networked repression, including the smoking guns of targeted political assassinations. Leaders have faced prison, assault and death. Even negotiators working to address conflicts risk criminalization and arrest (Ruiz 2014). Recent assassination and violent attacks have led to accusations of federal, state and municipal government and /or party involvement in fomenting paramilitary violence against individuals and organizations opposed to the CIPP (Centro De Derechos Humanos Fray Bartolomé de las Casas 2012; Sociedad Civil Las Abejas de Acteal 2014).

After eviction of the delegitimized groups from the newly declared ecological reserves and integrated tourism development zones, reterritorialization can follow. The declaration of reserves excluding peasant communities enables the redistribution of land use rights and

[12] A message from a Chase-Manhattan Bank security consultant to the office of Mexican President Ernesto Zedillo in 1995 (Silverstein and Cockburn 1995) noted that it was the perception of investors that was at stake and not any real safety threat. This posture has remained more or less the same for the last 20 years.

authority by the state (through sale, lease or concession) and the capture of multiple revenue streams for state actors and allies. Ecotourism expands to include Cancun-like hubs and circuits of tourism (consumption of rainforest nature; Figure 3). Once states and commercial interests wrest control of new areas, they can stretch the idea of serving the public good to allow simultaneous creation of multiple territories of extraction (mining and drilling), industrial agriculture and industrial forest production. The remaining land can be committed to payment for environmental services (PES) and carbon credit contracts (pilot projects for REDD+)[13] (Gonzalez 2013). This is not a simple linear narrative of eviction of landless rural people by corporate and state interests. It is a carefully choreographed performance that simultaneously builds and obscures multiple overlapping territories, parallel worlds hidden from each other in plain sight.

Agua Azul: networked and rooted resistance to the CIPP

The specific, recent experience of communities near Agua Azul, in the heart of the CIPP, epitomizes, and illuminates, less visible territorial grabbing strategies, based on linked sequential and simultaneous actions by multiple state and corporate actors. Agua Azul (Blue Waters) is a popular tourist attraction on the existing San Cristobal-to-Palenque road (Figures 3). The site of a recently declared reserve, as well as a proposed luxury resort and further commercialization of the falls, it illustrates the combined local, regional and national strategy to wrest control of land and related resources from farming communities who neither accept government development plans for their area, nor agree to leave. It is also a major focus of ongoing struggle by communities and individual community members affiliated with the Other Campaign, and adherents of the Sixth Declaration of the Selva Lacandona[14] and other political and religious organizations in the vicinity.

The proposed tourism project would change the character of the site, the surrounding landscape and access to the river and pools, and nearby forests, fields and homes (Figure 4). The entire community of Bolom Ajaw would be evicted. The new Palenque-to-San Cristobal highway would dramatically affect several nearby towns, displacing homes, fields, businesses, churches, public buildings and plazas. State officials and developers have promised hotel and restaurant jobs, and payment for lands and buildings taken to support the planned development.

The actors involved in the struggle over Agua Azul include: the residents of the Agua Azul area and Bolom Ajaw; the small business owners, merchants and employees at Agua Azul Falls; the ejido authorities and members of San Sebastian Bachajon; the officials of the municipal government of Chilon; members of the Other Campaign and adherents of the Sixth Declaration within San Sebastián Bachajón, Bolom Ajaw and nearby communities; the Tzeltal Tourism Cooperative of Agua Azul; a local branch of OPPDIC (Organización Para la Defensa de los Derechos Indígenas y Campesinos, a state-aligned indigenous organization) and alleged 'renegade' members of same; municipal state and federal government officials including the Governor's office; municipal, state and federal police; employees and

[13]REDD+ refers to Reducing Emissions from Deforestation and Degradation, a UN carbon trade program to mitigate climate change through payments by carbon emitters in industrial countries, ostensibly to protect forests in the global south.

[14]The Other Campaign formed in 2006 as a national alternative to party affiliation and electoral participation, and an organizational alliance in solidarity with the Zapatistas. Adherents of the Sixth Declaration of the Selva Lacandona (EZLN 2005) constitute a national and international solidarity network supporting its principles.

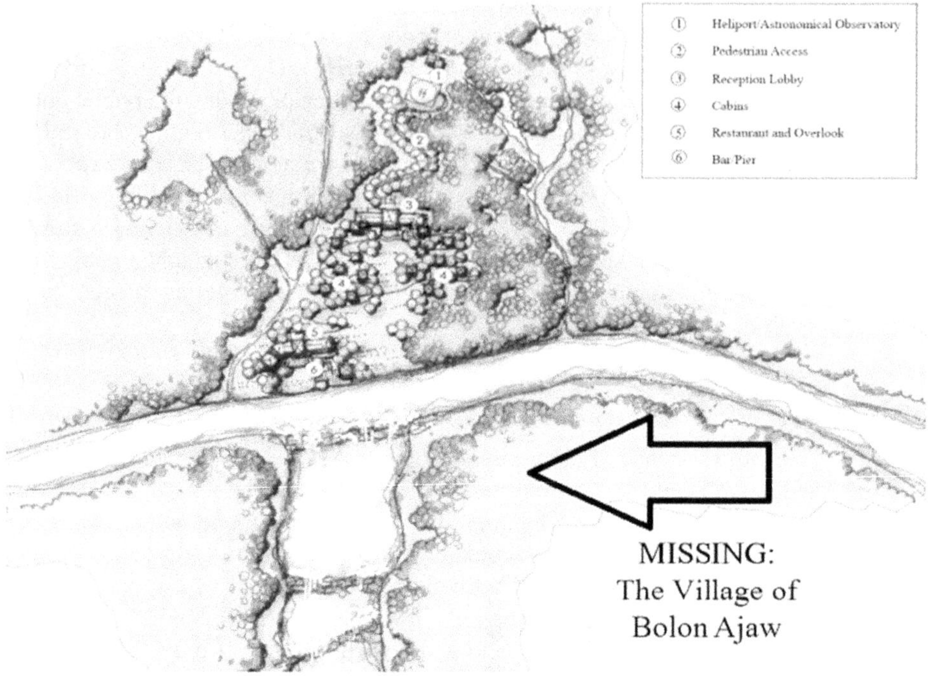

Figure 4. Planned rainforest resort at Agua Azul Falls.

officials of FONATUR, the Palenque CIPP, Comisión Nacional de Áreas Naturales Protegidas (CONANP) and Secretaría de Medio Ambiente y Recursos Naturales (SEMARNAT);[15] two international environmental planning consulting firms; an invisible network of unnamed investors and developers; pro-CIPP environmental NGOs (local to global); resistance-aligned environmental NGOs; Frayba and a network of national and international human rights organizations; and active, widely dispersed, international solidarity networks.

The community of Bolom Ajaw, the ejido of San Sebastián Bachajón and members of several other communities in the municipality of Chilón have waged a multi-year struggle to resist the selective eviction of their communities, the take-over of the waterfall site revenues by state officials and state-aligned residents, and the construction of a major commercial tourist resort as well as the new highway through the region, as illustrated in Figures 3 and 4 (Author’s field notes 2011; Centro de Derechos Humanos Fray Bartolomé de Las Casas 2012; FONATUR 2006, 2008, 2011; Comisión Nacional de Áreas Naturales Protegidas CONANP 2010; Davies 2010). People have organized at various times to take, to defend and, later, to restore the payment kiosk at the entrance to the tourist site, unarmed. They have also blocked the highway and have built and occupied roadside encampments near the entrance on several occasions.

State and federal authorities have portrayed this as an inter- or intra-community struggle between government-aligned community members (from OPDDIC) and those they refer to as ‘outsiders’ from the Other Campaign, or adherents of the Sixth Declaration (La Cronica

[15]Translations: Parks and Protected Area Commission and Secretariat of Environment and Natural Resources.

de Hoy 2011; Hernández Nava 2012). In February 2011, 117 residents were arrested and imprisoned after hundreds of police converged on the rural site of a peaceful meeting convened to discuss the conflicting views of various groups. The police selectively arrested affiliates of the Other Campaign (Centro de Derechos Humanos Fray Bartolomé de las Casas 2011). After a short time, all but five of those originally arrested were released (Henríquez 2011b). The Bachajón Five spent from several months to 2 years in prison on criminal charges, including murder, that were later dismissed.[16]

Criminalization of the movement continued in September 2011 when Miguel Vázquez Deara, a leader of the opposition to the resort project and the erasure of Bolom Ajaw, was arrested at his taxi service job in Palenque (Enlace Zapatista 2011). The man who accompanied the police and identified/accused him was the same one who had already issued death threats against him over his opposition to the CIPP. He was arrested, detained, tortured into confessing to theft, convicted, sentenced, imprisoned and later released in June 2013, after a long campaign for his freedom by Frayba and a diverse network of national and international organizations (Enlace Zapatista 2013a).

On the night of 24 April 2013, Juan Vázquez Guzmán, a previously detained and vocal leader of the Other Campaign in San Sebastián Bachajón, answered a knock at his door. He was shot six times point blank. The Other Campaign organized a national and international campaign for justice, and also called for the release of Miguel Demeza Jiménez and Antonio Estrada Estrada, who were imprisoned in 2010 and 2011, respectively (Gutiérrez Luna 2013; Bellinghausen 2013a; Enlace Zapatista 2013b, 2013c, 2013d).[17] Both were released in December of 2013 (Bellinghausen 2013b, 2013c). The murder of Vázquez Guzmán remains in impunity. The last reported assassination of a CIPP opposition leader occurred on the morning of 21 March 2014. Juan Carlos Gomez Silvano (22 years of age) was ambushed and shot 20 times by high-caliber gunfire as he drove home towards the autonomous community of the Virgen de Dolores (Virgin of Sorrows). He was the regional coordinator of the adherents of the Sixth Declaration in the ejido of San Sebastián Bachajón[18] (Enlace Zapatista 2014).

Other leaders and their communities continue to live under threat of bodily harm, disappearance, death and/or false arrest, as well as eviction from their homes and lands. The strategy of the resistance has been to publicly denounce and confront government officials and their practices from municipal to federal level, through unarmed resistance, and to avoid violent confrontation with other rural people, whether indigenous or campesino, and regardless of party, religious or other affiliations. This strategy has been met with continued violence from police and paramilitiary actions.

These are not simply localized actions; the scenario played out in Agua Azul is typical of several places in the Lacandon Rainforest of Chiapas, all of which are part of a larger scheme to take control of and redefine a territory of smallholder farmers, including the heartland of the Zapatista movement. The vision is to string together a series of sites that

[16]The last two prisoners were released in December 2013 after an intensive national and international solidarity campaign (Centro de Derechos Humanos Fray Bartolomé de las Casas 2012; Bellinghausen 2013b, 2013c).

[17]Additional detailed reports from communities in the Chilón Municipality and human rights organizations from 2011 through 2013 can be found at the Enlace Zapatista, the civil society communication hub of the EZLN at www.enlacezapatista.ezln.org.mx.

[18]I have revised this account twice to report the assassination of yet another leader opposed to the CIPP near Agua Azul. Several others have died at other sites over the last seven years, from Mitziton to Chinkultic (Centro de Derechos Humanos Fray Bartolomé de Las Casas 2012).

form nodes, in a network of rainforest and archeological wonders that cluster around Palenque as a major new tourist hub (Figure 3). The maps, drafted by state agencies and their consultants between 2006 and 2008 (FONATUR 2006, 2008, 2011) were released formally and informally through NGO networks in the interest of transparency and justice for the communities threatened by displacement.[19]

It is notable that each of the points along these elliptical tourist paths is slated to be joined by a new highway. Several communities along this path have been subjected to attack, threats and harassment by paramilitary-type organizations, as well as provocation of conflict within or between communities and suborning of local officials to support the CIPP. While they suspected a relationship, the people in the affected communities and their allies had no information about the path of the planned highway until they were 3 years into the campaigns of intimidation, threats and aggression by municipal, state and federal police forces and paramilitary-type organizations (Author' notes 2010, 2011). The latest version of the CIPP (Ramírez 2014) has been scaled back to focus on the main highway corridor with key nodes at Palenque, Agua Azul, San Cristobal de Las Casas and Chiapa de Corzo, confirming the central role of Agua Azul and the Palenque–San Cristobal highway within the CIPP.

The resistance has been predicated in part on the collection and sharing of information about the CIPP plan, from the highway route, to the ciruits of eco- and archeological sites, to the plans for individual reserves and resorts such as Agua Azul. In contrast to the outright purchase of vast tracts of land by outside investors, these tourism circuits nested in the green matrix of almost a third of the state's land area (Figure 3) involve extensive preliminary work by national and state governments. The slides shared by one NGO in March of 2011, based on 2006 and 2011 FONATUR documents, demonstrate that this is a buyer's market. The potential investors and developers in 'high-end' tourism demand, through the voices of consultants in the internal report, that, first, the region be cleansed of conflicting claims on land, and that all property be secured by proper title. This fails to recognize that most of the indigenous settlements in the region are based on indigenous territorial claims and/or lands reclaimed during the Zapatista uprising. While not currently honored by state and national governments, these lands are recognized under the San Andres Accords.

The exclusive Agua Azul camp will install a private heliport for travel from Palenque to the 'isolated' luxury camp, only a few kilometers off the main highway. The report stressed that hotel investors, developers, managers, employees and guests must be safe, and more importantly, they must *feel* secure at all times. Finally, the report specifically notes that nothing 'unnatural' can interfere with the panorama of the 'pristine' rainforest and waterfall setting, specifically as seen from the planned luxury hotel and camp. In the landscape architect's watercolor depiction of the future resort (see sketch version in Figure 4), the community of Bolom Ajaw has been removed. The erasure of Bolom Ajaw is a highly significant absence, that implies an explicit and violent process of rural cleansing, still being thwarted by non-violent resistance (FONATUR 2006, 2008, 2011, Comisión Nacional de Áreas Naturales Protegidas CONANP 2010, Davies 2010).

As illustrated by Figure 2, the imperatives from developers and investors to the state, via international consultants, are translated into action through attempted selective cleansing of

[19]Davies (2010) states: 'The sources of the report quoted are FONATUR, March 2008 and the Secretary of Tourism and International Relations of the Chiapas government. They have been made available in Spanish by Frayba. http://www.slideshare.net/pliegoelbuenas/100217-informe-bolom-ajaw-anexo-1-1-1-3218096'

peasant communities, based on complex combined ethnic and political criteria, with the aim of turning the region into *not* smallholder agrarian territory. The state 'brands' the new territory as the backdrop for the 'greater Palenque' rainforest and archeological circuit, with options for stops at one, a few or the whole package of sites (Figure 3). Land that forms the 'background' to these circuits can be earmarked for forests for carbon offset projects, 'productive reconversion' to commercial monocrop plantations, or other commercial uses.

As illustrated in Figure 2, some national and international environmental NGOs have played a major role in the politics of reserves and the promotion of ecotourism. The NGOs in favor of the Agua Azul reserve and the larger CIPP project have been conspicuous in their silence over the arrests, assassinations and repression of opposition leaders as well as the environmental impact of the planned highway and commercial developments in the area.

According to the project plan, once the cleansing is done, the ground is ready for sale and resort construction (Hernández Nava 2012). In Agua Azul, this has not yet been accomplished after 13 years of planning and 6 years of concerted efforts toward that end. It has been deterred by the tenacious, non-violent resistance by the community of Bolom Ajaw, members of the Otra Campana and adherents of the Sixth Declaration in nearby communities within the ejido of San Sebastián Bachajón, and allied individuals and communities in the region, all supported by regional, national and international solidarity networks and human rights groups (Centro de Derechos Humanos Fray Bartolomé de las Casas 2012; Bellinghausen 2014a). This process does not appear in the mainstream imaginary of land grabbing; however, resistance is active, effective and persistent in Chiapas (Davies 2013).

Convergence of broader networked resistance(s) across differences

Government, media and academic analysts have reported on the divisions and fragmentation within the peasant and indigenous organizations in Chiapas, yet there is also ample evidence of persistence and resolve among the communities in resistance. This is matched by a resurgence of religious, indigenous, human rights and other political solidarity networks, and an expansion of regional coalitions to resist local evictions and territorial land grabs. A few surprising developments warrant special mention.

New alliances in the Montes Azules and Lacantun reserves

In a surprising development, since 2010, the Lacandones of the Lacantun Biosphere Reserve (Figure 3) have negotiated an agreement to recognize three Tseltal communities in the reserve as legitimate occupants, after previously siding with the state and officially petitioning to oust them, and other communities already evicted. The three communities, Nuevo San Gregorio, Salvador Allende and Ranchería Corozal, are affiliated with the Asociacion Rural de Interes Colectivo (ARIC) Historico and ARIC Independiente, peasant organizations that continue to resist evictions of some indigenous communities in the region (see online illustration of the roots and shoots of resistance in Chiapas, Maderas del Pueblo del Sureste 2008). Representatives of both the Lacandon and Tseltal groups journeyed to Mexico City in 2011 to demand federal recognition of the Tseltal communities, but the federal authorities refused (Comité de Derechos Humanos Fray Pedro Lorenzo de la Nada personal communication 2011). Recent threats by national authorities (Mandujano 2014; Secretaría General de Gobierno del Estado de Chiapas 2014) to evict the three communities have been met by a campaign organized by the Mazules Environmental

Protection and Indigenous Rights Coalition. They demand an end to the evictions, and the recognition of Tseltal communities and others like them in the Montes Azules, Lacantun and other reserves in the region, including Agua Azul. Some of the groups previously evicted from the reserves also continue to seek restitution and to support other groups resisting eviction (Henríquez 2011c).

While one of the strongest movement-aligned environmental NGOs in Chiapas (CIEPAC) has dissolved, and another (Maderas del Puelo del Sureste) has relocated to Oaxaca, key actors from both continue to participate from other venues, and new groups such as Otros Mundos (Friends of the Earth, Mexico) have arisen. Together with the current Mazules Coalition campaign and the ongoing negotiations between Lacandon and other indigenous communities, this signals a diversification and expansion of the coalition against dispossession and environmental destruction in the rainforests of Chiapas (Abraca 2013).

Broad resistance to dissolution of ejido and community assemblies

After 15 years of land survey and privatization projects, a surprising resistance has emerged, across political lines. During this period, some people have left the struggle or specific organizations, some have maintained organized resistance and others have aligned with the government. Yet the strength of peoples' roots in community, and the rootedness of communities on land, and in place, have held fast, in what Miguel Angel García Aguirre (pers. comm. August 2011) calls an act of 'deep political intuition'. The relatively high rejection rates of PROCEDE in Chiapas demonstrate this political consciousness. When the program ended in 2006, 589, or 20 percent, of Chiapas' *nucleos agrarios* (either *ejidos* or communal lands) had rejected the program (Secretaria de la Reforma Agraria [SRA] 2006). This form of resistance has had significant results, as in 2006, Chiapas had more ejidos and agrarian communities (*nucleos agrarios*) than any other state, and these covered 61 percent of the state's land area (SRA 2006).

Even among communities that *did* accept PROCEDE, the overwhelming majority have maintained their ejido or community assemblies as the form of local government (Miguel Angel García Aguirre, personal communication, 2011). Yet the ability to buy, sell and mortgage land hinges on completing the last step of the privatization process, the dissolution of the community assembly, by a 75 percent majority vote of the ejido assembly members. Without that last step, land transactions still fall under ejido or agrarian communal law, not private land law. This is an example of subliminal struggle against land grabbing, based on a way of seeing the world, one's place in it and the territorial terms of connection, and it applies across the political spectrum. As a result, developers of tourism, agricultural and energy projects have had to negotiate long term leases with ejidos, rather than direct purchase, opening development plans to community scrutiny. Some ejidos have removed elected leaders who have entered into deals prejudicial to the community and its lands, and have refused to honor the deals, as in one community at Lake Miramar (Comité de Derechos Humanos Fray Pedro Lorenzo de la Nada 2011).

Resurgence of the national indigenous congress (CNI)

The Congreso Nacional Indígena (CNI), founded in 1996, came out of two national forums convened by the EZLN as part of the peace process and formulation of the San Andres Accords on Indigenous Rights and Culture. The CNI held regional forums leading up to the national forums, a practice which it has followed in subsequent years. It represents a departure from previous national organizations in the politics of land issues, compensation, integration and identity. The CNI has focused on territory and autonomy, not on land as property, and has insisted on respect for differences both between indigenous and non-indigenous people and among indigenous groups. Since 2012, CNI has proposed a new wave of activism in defense of territory and autonomy, grounded in ILO Convention 169 on the Rights of Indigenous and Tribal Peoples (ILO 1989), and has convened two national conferences with the EZLN, in August 2013 and August 2014. This resurgence derives in large part from the need to respond to widespread land grabbing, including green grabs, in indigenous lands across Mexico, and environmental destruction from large dams, other energy projects, timber and mining concessions, commercial tourism and luxury residential development.

The CNI stakes its claims on the legitimacy of territorial rights versus the narrower legal framing of property rights. While (non-exclusive) territorial rights are not recognized in all national legal systems, they are enshrined in the ILO Convention. They are also the basis on which billions of people in the world recognize connections to land, water, living beings, the Earth and each other. CNI conferences and press releases as well as social movement seminars in Chiapas highlight the mismatch of new land tenure and trade laws with the cultural, economic, ecological and political practices of the vast majority of rural people whose lands are targets of campaigns to acquire land for parks, reserves, tourism, carbon sinks, 'biofuels' and other forms of 'green' development by public and private actors (Congreso Nacional Indigena 2013; Cideci Weekly Seminar 2013). Fernando Hernandez Espino (pers. comm. September 2014) suggests that this is an 'ontological divide, a tale of two moral economies' (see also Wolford 2005). The CNI, including the EZLN as a member, has staked its campaigns for cultural and ecological justice, and against land grabbing, on the cultural and moral framing of territorial rights, both drawing from and supporting resistance to land grabbing in Chiapas (Congreso Nacional Indígena 2013).

Return of liberation theology and Catholic Church solidarity with land struggles

The consciousness of territory being made and broken is both strong and explicit among Catholic civil society organizations in Chiapas (Author's notes 2007, 2009, 2010, 2011, 2012, 2013). While it may come as no surprise to find land and territory on the lips of Zapatistas, recent developments in the ranks of Catholic groups in the Diocese of San Cristobal de Las Casas suggest a renewed and widespread sense of outrage about 'maldevelopment' (Shiva 1988) and a sense of hope based on the defense of '*tierra y territorio*' (land and territory; Henríquez 2011a).

On 24 November 2011, approximately 8000 Catholics from the 54 parishes of the diocese of San Cristóbal de Las Casas conducted a pilgrimage through the city streets, ending with a mass at the Cathedral plaza (Mandujano 2011; Henríquez 2011a). The Diocese had taken the Care of the Earth (*El Pastoral de la Tierra*) as one of its main annual themes, along with poverty and social justice. In reference to a biblical passage about Daniel in the lion's den, Bishop Felipe Arizmendi Esquivel said: 'The lions are the mining companies, the projects that seek to appropriate the lands of the campesinos, [and] the corrupt authorities who sell out and … dedicate themselves to the logging of forests'.

The pilgrimage was organized by the faithful (*Pueblo Creyente*) of the diocese, and the Ecclesiastical Base Communities, who issued a joint communiqué stating:

> We see with pain that in our state of Chiapas there is much poverty, migration … [and] looting of lands. We are witnesses to governmental programs [that] … .create dependencies and poverty, and … 'mega-projects' which originate in and respond to transnational interests

> [that] seek to appropriate and control the territory and natural resources of our state. In many communities, this dynamic provokes division and confrontation .... (derived from excerpts from the Communique by the Pueblo Creyente of San Cristobal de Las Casas and the Ecclesiastical Base Communities, published in Henríquez 2011a)

The phrase 'looting of lands' in the same document (above) as references to 'government-sponsored and corporate-led mega-projects', including tourism, constitutes a searing denunciation of current state and corporate initiatives, by the Catholic faithful of the diocese. Their annual march and communique was supported by the Bishop, who was originally expected to 'depoliticize' the diocese. Subsequent events and statements organized by the Catholic faithful of the diocese in 2012 and 2013 have reiterated these points and the Bishop recently (1 January 2014) went on record in an Associated Press (AP) interview in support of the Zapatistas, peasant political and social resistance, and the establishment of autonomous communities (AP News 2014).

More recently, the Diocese of San Cristobal and the Pueblo Creyente convened a pilgrimage of 15,400 people. The half-day pilgrimage entitled 'For peace, in defense of life, Mother Earth and our communities', took place simultaneously in several communities from San Cristobal to Palenque, on 19 July 2014 (Otros Mundos 2014b). The event focused on opposition to the Palenque–San Cristobal highway and the CIPP, with references to land grabbing, human rights, political violence and the imposition of development and conservation plans on indigenous and campesino communities (Rieublanc 2014; Otros Mundos 2014b). The networked, rooted and territorial nature of the event, and the larger movement, was unmistakable.

Conclusion

Perhaps the first and clearest conclusion to be drawn from the experience with green grabs to date in Chiapas is that Conservation and Ecotourism are the leading edge and the pioneer outposts of de- and reterritorialization in Chiapas. The green grab is not only for itself but, through the fog of greening, serves to open the land and the people to a variety of extractive and exploitative industrial developments. Disneyland in the forest, and Cancun in the forest, are prelude to pipelines in the forest, plantations in the forest, highways through the forest, cash crops in the forest, paradise for sale in the forest, and *despojo* and *desalojo* (dispossession and eviction) in the forest. This strategy requires a complex network of actors far larger than what is required for direct purchase of large single tracts of land[20] (Figure 2).

While we are newly accustomed to think of social movements as agile navigators of complex networks, across scales and within territories, between a diversity of types of actors, corporate and state actors are not far behind. The land grabbers in Chiapas, and beyond, are skilled at network navigation, in search of profit through accumulation by dispossession. In turn, dispossession is attempted through delegitimation of peoples' identities and their claims to belong to specific territories, as a prelude to forceful eviction. The resistance, with a long history of *rooted networks*, above and below ground, has built and maintained an agile, flexible and territorial response in defense of 'life, people and the Earth'. Based on the experience in Agua Azul and throughout Chiapas more broadly, land grabbing can be accomplished, or resisted, through territory-breaking and territory-making, through presence and practice on the part of multiple networked actors, acting simultaneously and in sequence.

[20]Note that even apparently simple grabs of large single parcels are rooted in complex histories and geographies of power, as in the long history of land grabs in Africa (Verma 2014).

Given the nature of this process, UN initiatives and related efforts to deal with land grabbing cannot rely on rules of engagement between buyers and sellers. Environmental justice with respect to land and territory requires that we consider more than just economic rights to land and legally recognized property. Land and environmental policy needs to recognize and respect networked cultures and ecologies and their construction of, and roots in, multiple territories.

The eviction of rural people under the fog of greening offers state and federal authorities the chance to shine at being green, to selectively remove 'inconvenient' political and social opposition, and to take and remake territories in a neo-liberal frame that will support their political objectives, and the progress of the MesoAmerica Project. As such, the real 'danger' to the state from the Zapatistas – and broader loose networks of communities in resistance – is not that they make the space violent or threaten the security of visitors and residents. They do not. Rather, the problem for the state and private tourism developers is that the resisters insist on dignity and justice and will not go quietly. They have their own agenda for rural livelihoods in forest and agrarian territories. They refuse to fade into an assimilated, landless and captive rural or urban labor force, while others sell an airbrushed history of their ancestors on their own stolen land. They publicly contest the prevailing assumptions about who threatens forests and biodiversity, and they challenge the illusion of compatibility and sustainability among the parallel universes of extractive industries, mega-infrastucture projects, high-profile new town settlements, industrial agriculture and 'pristine' sites of tourism and conservation. They insist on making audible and visible the violence that is being visited upon them and their lands by explicit participation of political parties and government agencies at local, state and national levels, supported by the complicity (willing or unwitting) of several international environmental and development agencies and NGOs, and an invisible network of financial investors and developers.

Recent developments bring the promise of a diversified and resurgent resistance with the renewal of national indigenous activism under the CNI, reintegration of more active Catholic Church participation and the formation of new environmental and human rights coalitions. This in turn begs the question of whether the large international and national environmental NGOs will remain allied with the land grabbers or whether they can find common cause with the resisters.[21]

[21]A set of corollary questions directed to state and NGO environmental and sustainable development organizations might include: Are they willing to reassess and reframe their perceptions, policies and practices as well as their alliances? Will they consider withdrawing their substantial support (direct or indirect) from the networked, violent campaign to take and remake roughly one third of the land of Chiapas into a multi-purpose territory, based on indigenous and peasant cleansing, shrouded in the fog of greening? The communities will not wait for answers to these questions and will continue to resist (Davies 2013; Bellinghausen 2014a). Yet the question remains, do these organizations plan to continue paying for new reserves and/or tourism development with the blood, sweat and tears of campesino and indigenous communities evicted (or worse) to serve an exclusionary 'land sparing' approach (Fischer et al. 2011) to conservation in Chiapas and elsewhere? And will they continue to look the other way as much of the land 'freed up' by conservation takings is chopped into concessions for commercial tourism development, mining, oil and gas drilling, and oil palm and timber plantations? And finally, would they consider reframing conservation and sustainable production within the context of matrix ecology (Vandermeer and Perfecto 2007; Perfecto, Vandermeer, and Wright 2009) with recognition of the legitimacy of forest communities as currently proposed in Chiapas by the Mazules Coalition of environmental and human rights groups and internationally by Via Campesina, Friends of the Earth International and many others?

Most importantly, the implication of the experience of Agua Azul and the larger circuits of the CIPP is that resistance costs, but it can work. It can slow or stop the progress of green grabs through widely networked efforts rooted in history, in place and on the ground, and carefully attuned to the actions and intents of the land grabbers. It has cost people their homes, livelihoods, lands, years in prison, and the lives of a long list of dead and disappeared persons, many of them promising leaders and all of them someone's friend, relative, spouse or teacher. There is also the sacrifice of time and energy diverted from building, raising crops and livestock, teaching and learning. The question remains as to whether rural communities in Chiapas will have to continue to pay such a high price to resist the vast, violent, networked green land grab.

Acknowledgements

I owe special thanks to Jun Borras and two anonymous reviewers for their patience, guidance and comments, and to Rosaluz Perez Espinosa, Katherine Foo, Fernando Hernandez Espino, Padini Nirmal, Martha Pskowski, Michelle Andrews, Miguel Pickard and Miguel Angel García Aguirre for insightful contributions. This paper also benefited from the seminars, conferences, workshops and publications of Centro de Investigaciones y Estudios Superiores en Antropología (CIESAS); Centro Indígena de Capacitación Integral (CIDECI); Centro de Estudios Superiores de México y Centro América (CESMECA); El Colegio de la Frontera Sur (ECOSUR); Universidad Autonoma de Chiapas (UNACH); Universidad Nacional Autonoma de México (UNAM); Centro de Investigaciones Económicas y Políticas de Acción Comunitaria (CIEPAC); Otros Mundos, Maderos del Pueblo and the Escuelita Zapatista.

References

Abraca, L., Moderador. 2013. La Voz de las Organizaciones Campesinas desde el Territorio con organizaciones campesinas e indígenas de Chiapas e invitados de Guatemala. Seminario Internacional Las Venas Abiertas de Chiapas Contemporáneo: Diálogos socio ambientales de actores de lo local a lo global. 25 October. Universidad Nacional Autonoma de Chiapas (UNACH). San Cristobal de las Casas, Chiapas, Mexico.

AP News. 2014. Mexico's Zapatista Rebel movement marks 20 years. *Town Hall.* 1 Jan. http://townhall.com/news/politics-elections/2014/01/01/mexicos-zapatista-rebel-movement-marks-20-years-n1770728/ (accessed March 10, 2014).

Balvé, T. 2011. Territory by dispossession: Decentralization, statehood, and the Narco Land Grab in Colombia. Presented at the American Association of Geographers (AAG) annual meeting in Seattle, Washington, DC. 12–16 April.

Bartra, A., ed. 2001. *Mesoamérica: Los ríos profundos*, ed. A. Bartra, México: El Atajo.

Bartra, A. 2004. The South: Mega-plans and utopias in Equatorial America, in *Profound rivers of mesoamerica: alternatives to Plan Puebla Panama*, ed. A. Bartra, 17–55. México City: Instituto Maya.

Baschet, J. 2013. *Haciendo otros mundos.* San Cristóbal de las Casas, Chiapas: Ediciones Cideci-Unitierra Chiapas.

Bellinghausen, H. 2008. Promotores del turismo en Chiapas ignoran a indígenas y sus tradiciones. *La Jornada*, 28 Sep. http://www.jornada.unam.mx/2008/09/29/index.php?section=politica&article=019n1pol/ (accessed September 6, 2013).

Bellinghausen, H. 2013a. Asesinan al dirigente de los ejidatarios pro zapatistas en Bachajón, Chiapas. *La Jornada*, 26 April. http://www.jornada.unam.mx/2013/04/26/politica/028n1pol/ (accessed September 6, 2013).

Bellinghausen, H. 2013b. Liberan a otro ejidatario de San Sebastián Bachajón en Chiapas. *La Jornada*, 24 Dec. http://www.jornada.unam.mx/ultimas/2013/12/24/liberan *a preso politico antonio estrada en Chiapas 5952.html/* (accessed February 20, 2014).

Bellinghausen, H. 2013c. Liberan en Chiapas a Miguel Demeza, adherente a la Sexta. *La Jornada*, 22 Dec. http://www.jornada.unam.mx/ultimas/2013/12/22/liberan *en chiapas a miguel demeza adherente a la sexta 6777.html/* (accessed February 20, 2014).

Bellinghausen, H. 2014a. Cinco presidentes de México han enfrentado la resistencia de las comunidades zapatistas. *Desinformemonos 131*, 10 Feb. http://desinformemonos.org/2014/02/agresiones-a-zapatistas-10-de-abril/ (accessed February 20, 2014).

Bellinghausen, H. 2014b. Advierten sobre privatización de tierras en el norte de la selva Lacandona. *La Jornada* 28 Jan. http://www.jornada.unam.mx/2014/01/28/politica/027n1pol/ (accessed February 20, 2014).

Benjamin, M. 1995. Interview: Subcomandante Marcos. In *First world, ha,ha,ha!: The Zapatista challenge*, ed. A. Katzenberger, 57–71. New York: City Lights Books.

Berman, J. 2013. Bill Gates surpasses Carlos Slim to become richest man In the world. 16 May. *Huffington Post.*

Blas, J., and W. Wallis. 2009. U.S. investor buys Sudanese warlord's land. *Financial Times*, 9 Jan. http://www.ft.com/cms/s/0/a4cbe81c-de84-11dd-9464–000077b07658.htm or http://www.jornada.unam.mx/2014/01/28/politica/027n1pol/ (accessed March 3, 2014).

Blaser, M. 2013. Ontological conflicts and the stories of peoples in spite of Europe. *Current Anthropology* 54, no. 5: 547–568.

Borras, S.M., and J.C. Franco. 2013. Global land grabbing and political reactions 'from below'. *Third World Quarterly* 34, no. 9: 1723–1747.

Borras, S.M., J.C. Franco, C. Kay, and M. Spoor. 2011a. El acaparamiento de tierras en Latino América y el Caribe visto desde una perspectiva internacional más amplia. Food and Agriculture Organization (FAO). http://www.tni.org/sites/www.tni.org/ *files/download/borras franco kay spoor lac land grabs spanish nov 2011.pdf/* (Acessed Sep 5, 2013).

Borras, S.M., Ruth Hall, Ian Scoones, Ben White, and Wendy Wolford. 2011b. Towards a better understanding of global land grabbing: An editorial introduction. *Journal of Peasant Studies* 38, no. 2: 209–216.

Calleros-Rodriguez, H. 2014. Land, conflict, and political process: The case of the Lacandon community, Chiapas, Mexico (1972–2012). *Journal of Peasant Studies* 41, no. 1: 127–155.

Calvo, C. 2008. Chiapas se perfila como el nuevo Cancún. *CNN Expansión*, 31 Jul. http://www.cnnexpansion.com/obras/pulso-de-la-construccion/chiapas-se-perfila-como-el-nuevo-cancun/ (accessed September 6, 2013).

CAPISE. 2002. Report: Conservation international, the Trojan Horse. San Cristobal de las Casas, Chiapas: CAPISE.

Centro de Derechos Humanos Fray Bartolomé de las Casas (FRAYBA). 2011. Privan arbitrariamente de la libertad a 117 ejidatarios de San Sebastian Bachajón. Boletín de prensa No. 03. http://www.frayba.org.mx/archivo/boletines/11020503 *detenciones bachajon.pdf/* (accessed September 5, 2013).

Centro de Derechos Humanos Fray Bartolomé de las Casas (FRAYBA). 2012. Entre la política sistémica y las alternativas de vida: Informe sobre la situación de los derechos humanos en Chiapas durante los gobiernos federal y estatal 2006–2012. http://www.frayba.org.mx/archivo/informes/130212 *informe frayba prov.pdf/* (accessed September 5, 2013).

Chapin, M. 2004. A challenge to conservationists. *World Watch* 176, Nov/Dec: 17–31.

Choudry, A. 2003. Conservation international: Privatizing nature, plundering biodiversity. *Seedling. http://www.grain.org/article/entries/406-conservation-international-privatizing-nature-plundering-biodiversity* (accessed September 9, 2013).

CIDECI Weekly Seminar. 2013. UniTierra. San Cristobal de las Casa.

CIEPAC. 2010. Peregrinación contra proyectos de muerte: Minas, represas, ciudades rurales. Youtube. http://www.youtube.com/watch?v=2EPba9He5us/ (accessed September 6, 2013).

Collier, G.A. 2005. *Basta! land and the Zapatista rebellion in Chiapas*. 3rd ed. New York: Food First Books.

Comisión Nacional de Áreas Naturales Protegidas Región Frontera Sur, Istmo, Pacifico Sur (CONANP). 2010. Oficio No. DIR/REG/RFSIPS/426/2010. http://www.conanp.gob.mx/contenido/pdf/1615100026010.pdf/ (accessed September 5, 2013).

Comité de Derechos Humanos Fray Pedro Lorenzo de la Nada. 2011. Interview with Exec. Committee, Ocosingo, Chiapas, Mexico. August.

Conant, J. 2010. *A poetics of resistance: The revolutionary public relations of the Zapatista insurgency*. Oakland: AK Press.

Congreso Nacional Indígena. 2013. Statement from the First Session of the Tata Juan Chavez Alonso Travelling Chair August 17–18. CIDECI (Indigenous Center for Integrative Training). San Cristóbal de Las Casas. http://enlacezapatista.ezln.org.mx/2013/08/23/statement-by-the-chair-tata-juan-chavez-alonso-cni/ (accessed August 12, 2014).

Conservation International. 2013. Monsanto. Webpage. http://www.conservation.org/how/partnership/corporate/Pages/monsanto.aspx/ (accessed September 9, 2013).

Corson, C. 2011. Territorialization, enclosure and neoliberalism: Non-state influence in struggles over Madagascar's forests. *Journal of Peasant Studies* 38, no. 4: 703–726.

Corson, C. 2012. From rhetoric to practice: How high-profile politics impeded community consultation in Madagascar's new protected areas. *Society & Natural Resources* 25, no. 4: 336–351.

Corson, C., and K.I. MacDonald. 2012. Enclosing the global commons: The convention on biological diversity and green grabbing. *Journal of Peasant Studies* 39, no. 2: 263–283.

Davies, J. 2010. The government's plans for tourism in Chiapas, and their implications for indigenous peoples and the environment. The Narcosphere. Posted February 26, 2010 at 10:26 am. http://narcosphere.narconews.com/notebook/jessica-davies/2010/02/governments-plans-tourism-chiapas/ (accessed October 10, 2013).

Davies, J. 2013. Mexico: San Sebastián Bachajón, Six Months after the assassination of Juan Vázquez Guzmán. *Upside down World* 23 Oct. *http://upsidedownworld.org/main/mexico-archives-79/4524-mexico-san-sebastian-bachajon-six-months-after-the-assassination-of-juan-vazquez-guzman/* (accessed February 20, 2014).

De la Cadena, M. 2010. Indigenous cosmopolitics in the Andes: Conceptual reflections beyond 'Politics'. *Cultural Anthropology* 25, no. 2: 334–370.

Deleuze, G., and F. Guattari. 1987. *A thousand plateaus: Capitalism and Schizophrenia.* Minneapolis: University of Minnesota Press.

De Shutter, O. 2010. Report of the special rapporteur on the right to food. http://www.srfood.org/images/stories/pdf/officialreports/20101021_access-to-land-report_en.pdf/ (accessed September 6, 2013).

Enlace Zapatista. 2011. Detención de un compañero y hostigamiento del mal gobierno. Denuncias de ejidatarios de San Sebastián Bachajón. 30 Sep. *http://enlacezapatista.ezln.org.mx/2011/09/30/detencion-de-un-companero-y-hostigamiento-del-mal-gobierno-denuncias-de-ejidatarios-de-san-sebastian-bachajon/* (accessed September 9, 2013).

Enlace Zapatista. 2013a. Frayba: Se repone el procedimiento a Miguel Vázquez, indígena tseltal por graves violaciones a los derechos humanos. 27 June. *http://enlacezapatista.ezln.org.mx/2013/06/26/frayba-se-repone-el-procedimiento-a-miguel-vazquez-indigena-tseltal-por-graves-violaciones-a-los-derechos-humanos/#libertadmiguelv/* (accessed September 9, 2013).

Enlace Zapatista. 2013b. Denuncia de adherentes a la sexta de San Sebastián Bachajón sobre el asesinato de Juan Vazquez. 27 April. *http://enlacezapatista.ezln.org.mx/2013/04/27/denuncia-de-adherentes-a-la-sexta-de-san-sebastian-bachajon-sobre-el-asesinato-de-juan-vazquez/* (accessed September 9, 2013).

Enlace Zapatista. 2013c. Denuncia del Ejido San Sebasián Bachajón, exigen la liberación de los presos políticos y justicia para Juan Vázquez. 26 June. *http://enlacezapatista.ezln.org.mx/2013/06/26/denuncia-del-ejido-san-sebasian-bachajon-exigen-la-liberacion-de-los-presos-politicos-y-justicia-para-juan-vazquez/* (accessed September 9, 2013).

Enlace Zapatista. 2013d. Comunicado Adherentes a la Sexta de San Sebastián Bachajón exigiendo justicia y libertad. 2 July. *http://enlacezapatista.ezln.org.mx/2013/07/02/comunicado-adherentes-a-la-sexta-de-san-sebastian-bachajon-exigiendo-justicia-y-libertad/* (accessed September 9, 2013).

Enlace Zapatista. 2014. El Ejido San Sebastián Bachajón, Adherente a la Sexta Declaración de la Selva Lacandona, denuncia el asesinato de Juan Carlos Gómez Silvano (The Ejido of San Sebastian Bachajon, Adherent of the Sixth Declaration of the Selva Lacandona, denounces the assassination of Juan Carlos Gomez Silvano. March 25th, 2014. *http://enlacezapatista.ezln.org.mx/2014/03/25/en-ejido-san-sebastian-bachajon-aderentes-a-la-sexta-declaracion-de-la-selva-lacandona-chiapas-mexico-a-23-de-marzo-de-2014/* (Acessed Junio 20, 2014).

Escobar, A. 2008. *Territories of difference: Place, movements, life, redes.* Durham: Duke University Press.

Escobar, A. 2010. Latin America at a crossroads: Alternative modernizations, post-liberalism, or post-development? *Cultural Studies* 24, no. 1: 1–65.

Escobar, A. 2011. *Encountering development: The making and unmaking of the Third World.* Princeton: Princeton University Press.

Escobar, A., and S. Alvarez. eds. 1992. *The making of social movements in Latin America: Identity, strategy and democracy.* Boulder: Westview Press.

Esteva, G. 1983. *The struggle for rural Mexico.* South Hadley, MA: Bergin & Garvey.

Esteva, G. 2013. Zapatista's Warning Over NAFTA Rings True 2 Decades Later. The Real News Network. 5 Jan 2014. http://therealnews.com/t2/index.php?option=com_content&task=view&id=31&Itemid=74&jumival=11281/ (accessed August 4, 2014).

Evans, P. 2005. Counter-hegemonic globalization: Transnational social movements in the contemporary global political economy. In *Handbook of political sociology*, eds. T. Janoski, A. M. Hicks, and M. Schwartz, 655–670. Cambridge: Cambridge University Press.

EZLN (Zapatista Army of National Liberation). 2005. The sixth declaration of the Selva Lacandona. http://www.amazon.com/Declaration-Lacandona-Zapatista-National-Liberation/dp/B004QQS4R0/ (accessed Junio 20, 2014).

Fairhead, J., M. Leach, and I. Scoones. 2012. Green grabbing: A new appropriation of nature? *The Journal of Peasant Studies* 39, no. 2: 237–261.

Fischer, J. et al. 2011. Conservation: Limits of land sparing. *Science* 4 Nov 334: 593.

FONATUR. 2006. Informe de Rendición de Cuentas de la Administración 2000–2006. http://www.fonatur.gob.mx/transparencia/abre_contenido_ind.asp?modulo=01-TRFON&cve_sec=1349&inciso=21&indice=3&subindice=&bases/ (Accessed September 6, 2013).

FONATUR. 2008. Análisis de la Estratégia de Desarrollo Palenque –Cascadas de Agua Azul, Chiapas, México. Preparado para FONATUR y el estado de Chiapas por Norton Consulting Inc. and EDSA. http://www.slideshare.net/pliegoelbuenas/100217-informe-bolom-ajaw-anexo-1-1-1-3218096 (accessed October. 2011 from slide share).

FONATUR. 2011. Acta de la Séptima Sesión Extraordinaria de 2011. 15 April. *http://www.fonatur.gob.mx/es/_soporte/abre_contenido_archivo.asp?modulo=01-TRFON&cve_sec=5824&inciso=17&indice=1&subindice=103&bases=undefined* (accessed February 20, 2014).

Forbes. 2013. *Carlos Slim Helu & family. Forbes*. http://www.forbes.com/profile/carlos-slim-helu/ (accessed March 5, 2013).

Foucault, M. 1991. *Discipline and Punish: The birth of a prison*. London: Penguin.

Garcia Aguirre, M.Á. 2011. Las plantaciones agrocombustibles en Chiapas, México. Maderas del Pueblo Sureste, A.C. http://www.ecologiaradical.com.mx/ *ARTAgrocombustiblesChiapas.pdf/* (accessed September 5, 2013).

Gibson-Graham, J.K. 2006. *The end of capitalism (as We Knew It): A Feminist Critique of Political Economy; with a New Introduction*. Minneapolis: U of Minnesota Press.

Global Justice Ecology Project. 2011. Action Alert and Video: Amador Hernandez, Chiapas- Starved of Medical Services for REDD+. *Climate Connections*, 26 July. *http://climate-connections.org/2011/07/26/action-alert-and-video amador-hernandez-chiapas-%E2%80%93-starved-of-medical-services-for-redd/* (accessed September 10, 2013).

Gonzalez, S. 2007. Quiere el gobierno de Chiapas usar zona arqueológica como centro turístico. *La Jornada*, 27 May. http://www.jornada.unam.mx/2007/05/27/ *index.php?section=economia&article=026n1eco* (accessed September 6, 2013).

Gonzalez, G. 2013. Chiapas state government says REDD is alive and well and far from 'cancelled'. *Ecosystem Marketplace*, 19 July. http://www.ecosystemmarketplace.com/pages/dynamic/article.page.php?page_id=9848 (accessed September 9, 2013).

Grajales, J. 2011. The rifle and the title: Paramilitary violence, land grab and land control in Colombia. *Journal of Peasant Studies* 38, no. 4: 771–792.

Grandia, L. 2012. *Conservation, cattle, and commerce among the Q'eqchi' Maya Lowlanders*. Seattle and London: University of Washington Press.

Gutierrez Aguilar, R. 2014. *Rhythms of the Pachakuti: Indigenous uprising and state power in Bolivia*. Translated by Stacey Alba D. Skar. London and Durham: Duke University Press.

Gutiérrez Luna, D. I. 2013. Lo más cabrón es cuando el mal gobierno no nos deja vivir tranquilos, así es más difícil construir el vivir digno: Juan Vázquez, prozapatista asesinado en Chiapas. *Desinformemonos*, 28 April. *http://desinformemonos.org/2013/04/lo-mas-cabron-es-cuando-el-mal-gobierno-no-nos-deja-vivir-tranquilos-asi-es-mas-dificil-construir-el-vivir-digno-juan-vazquez-prozapatista-asesinado-en-chiapas/* (accessed February 20, 2014).

Hall, D., P. Hirsch, and T. Li. 2011. *Powers of exclusion: Land Dilemmas in Southeast Asia*. Singapore and Honolulu: National University of Singapore Press/University of Hawaii Press.

Hardt, M., and A. Negri. 2000. *Empire*. Cambridge: Harvard University Press.

Hardt, M., and A. Negri. 2009. *Multitude: War and democracy in the age of empire*. New York: Penguin Books.

Harvey, N. 1994. Rebellion in Chiapas: Rural reforms, campesino radicalism, and the limits to salinismo. No. 5. Center for US-Mexican Studies.

Harvey, N. 1996. Rural reforms and the Zapatista rebellion: Chiapas, 1988–1995. *Neoliberalism Revisited: Economic Restructuring and Mexico's Political Future*. Boulder, CO: Westview Press.

Harvey, N. 1998. *The Chiapas Rebellion: The struggle for land and democracy*. London and Durham: Duke University Press.

Harvey, D. 2012. *Rebel cities: From the right to the city to the urban revolution*. New York: Verso.

Henderson, G. 2009. Marxist political economy and the environment. In *A Companion to Environmental Geography*, eds. N. Castree, D. Demeritt, D. Liverman, and B. Rhoads, 266–93. Oxford, UK: Wiley-Blackwell.

Henríquez, E. 2011a. Católicos marchan en Chiapas contra empresas mineras. *La Jornada*, 25 Nov. http://www.jornada.unam.mx/2011/11/25/estados/036n1est/ (accessed September 6, 2013).

Henríquez, E. 2011b. Liberan en Chiapas a 106 indígenas; otros 10 son acusados de varios delitos. *La Jornada*, 6 Feb. http://www.jornada.unam.mx/2011/02/06/index.php?section=politica&article=015n1pol (accessed September 5, 2013).

Henríquez, E. 2011c. Plantón de choles en San Cristóbal de las Casas. *La Jornada*, 13 July. http://www.jornada.unam.mx/2011/07/13/politica/021n2pol/ (accessed September 9, 2013).

Hernandez Espino, F. 2007. PROCEDE and its effects on rural livelihoods: The case of the ejido San Juanito Itzicuaro, Michoacan, Mexico. Master's Thesis. University of East Anglia. Norwich, United Kingdom.

Hernández Nava, J. 2012. Pueblos indígenas, la gestión del territorio y el estado de derecho en las áreas protegidas estudio de caso: área de protección de flora y fauna cascadas de Agua Azul, Chiapas, México. CONANP (Comision Nacional de Areas Nacionales Protegidas). http://congresomesoamericano.conanp.gob.mx/pdf/izamal1/S3_L_Jos%C3%A9%20Hern%C3%A1ndez%20N.pdf/ (accessed September 6, 2013).

International Labor Organization (ILO). 1989. Convention No. 169. http://www.ilo.org/indigenous/Conventions/no169/lang–en/index.htm/ (accessed July 1, 2014).

de Ita, A. 2006. Land concentration in Mexico after PROCEDE. In *Promised Land: competing visions of agrarian reform*, eds. P. Rosset, R. Patel, and M. Courville, 148–164. New York: Food First.

Juntas de Buen Gobierno Zapatistas. 2013a. Gobierno Autonomo I: Cuaderno de texto de primer grado del curso 'La Libertad Según l@s Zapatistas'. Chiapas, Mexico. http://anarquiacoronada.blogspot.mx/2013/09/primera-escuela-zapatista-descarga-sus.html/ (accessed February 20, 2014).

Juntas de Buen Gobierno Zapatistas. 2013b. Gobierno Autonomo II: Cuaderno de texto de primer grado del curso 'La Libertad Según l@s Zapatistas'. Chiapas, Mexico. http://anarquiacoronada.blogspot.mx/2013/09/primera-escuela-zapatista-descarga-sus.html (accessed February 20, 2014).

Juntas de Buen Gobierno Zapatistas. 2013c. Participación de las Mujeres en el Gobierno Autónomo: Cuaderno de texto de primer grado del curso 'La Libertad Según l@s Zapatistas'. Chiapas, Mexico. http://anarquiacoronada.blogspot.mx/2013/09/primera-escuela-zapatista-descarga-sus.html/ (accessed February 20, 2014).

Juntas de Buen Gobierno Zapatistas. 2013d. Resistencia Autónoma: Cuaderno de texto de primer grado del curso 'La Libertad Según l@s Zapatistas'. Chiapas, Mexico. http://anarquiacoronada.blogspot.mx/2013/09/primera-escuela-zapatista-descarga-sus.html (accessed February 20, 2014).

La Cronica de Hoy. 2011. CONANP administra desde hoy caseta única en 'Agua Azul'. *La Cronica de Hoy*, 11 April. http://www.cronica.com.mx/notas/2011/573834.html (accessed September 5, 2013).

Latour, B. 2007. *Reassembling the SOCIAL: An introduction to actor-network theory*. Oxford: Oxford University Press.

Maderas del Pueblo del Sureste, A. C. 2008. Historia reciente de la lucha por la defensa de los derechos de los Pueblos Indígenas sobre el territorio y el resguardo y control de los recursos naturales en la Selva Lacandona, Chiapas.' http://maderasdelpueblo.org.mx/archivos/pdf/HistLuchaSelvaLacandPortIndicRes.pdf/ (accessed February 20, 2014).

Mandujano, I. 2011. Miles de indígenas de Chiapas realizan peregrinación por la paz. *El Proceso*, 24 Nov. http://www.proceso.com.mx/?p=289185 (accessed September 6, 2013).

Mandujano, I. 2014. Desconocen acuerdo para regularizar asentamiento en la Reserva de la Biósfera Montes Azules. *Diario ContraPoder en Chiapas*. Miércoles, 14 Mayo 2014 01:50 http://www.diariocontrapoderenchiapas.com/2014/index.php/chiapas/1028-desconocen-acuerdo-para-regularizar-asentamiento-en-la-reserva-de-la-biosfera-montes-azules (accessed September 8, 2014).

Marcos, Silvia. 2010. Cruzando fronteras: Mujeres indígenas y feminismos abajo ya la izquierda. *México, CIDECI,* Centro Indígena de Capacitación Integral Fray Bartolomé de las Casas.

Marcos, Subcomandante. 1997. La quatrième guerre mondiale a commencè. *Le Monde Diplomatique* 521 (1997): 1–4.
Marcos, Subcomandante. 2002. *Our word is our weapon: selected writings*. New York: Seven Stories Press.
Marcos, Subcomandante. 2004. The Seven loose pieces of the global Jigsaw Puzzle (Neoliberalism as a Puzzle), in *Ya Basta! Ten Years Of The Zapatista Uprising—Writings Of Subcomandante Insurgente Marcos*, 257–78. Marcos: Oakland.
Marcos, Subcomandante. 2006. *The other campaign: The zapatista call for change from below*. San Francisco: City Lights.
Marcos, Subcomandante. 2014. Between light and shadow. Enlace Zapatista. Presented on 24 May 2014. Posted on 27 May 2014. http://enlacezapatista.ezln.org.mx/2014/05/27/between-light-and-shadow/ (accessed August 4, 2014).
Marcos, Subcomandante and Y. Le Bot. 1997. *El sueño zapatista*. Barcelona: Ed. Anagrama. Vol. 34.
Martínez-Torres, M.E., and P. Rosset. 2014. Diálogo de saberes in La Vía Campesina: food sovereignty and agroecology. *Journal of Peasant Studies* ahead-of-print: 1–19.
Mignolo, W.D., and A. Escobar, eds. 2013. *Globalization and the decolonial option*. New York and London: Routledge.
Muñoz Ramìrez, G. et al. 2008. *The fire and the word: A history of the Zapatista movement*. San Francisco: City Light Books.
Nash, J. 2001. *Mayan visions: The quest for autonomy in an age of globalization*. New York: Rutledge.
O'Connor, James. 1988. Capitalism, nature, socialism a theoretical introduction. *Capitalism, Nature, Socialism* 1, no. 1: 11–38.
O'Connor, James. 1991. On the two contradictions of capitalism. *Capitalism, Nature Socialism* 2, no. 3: 107–109.
Ojeda, D. 2012. Green pretexts: Ecotourism, neoliberal conservation and land grabbing in Tayrona National Natural Park, Colombia. *The Journal of Peasant Studies* 39, no. 2: 357–375.
Ojeda, D. 2013. War and tourism: The Banal geographies of security in Colombia's 'retaking'. *Geopolitics* 18, no. 4: 759–78.
Otros Mundos. 2014a. Mapas: Intereses Territoriales en Chiapas. http://otrosmundoschiapas.org/materiales/docs/pdf/lonas/lona_mapas_chiapas.pdf/. (accessed August 3, 2014).
Otros Mundos. 2014b. Porqué los pueblos originarios rechazan la autopista San Cristóbal de Las Casas - Palenque: *http://otrosmundoschiapas.org/index.php/temas-analisis/31–31-resistencias/1718-porque-los-pueblos-originarios-rechazan-la-autopista-san-cristobal-de-las-casas-palenque/* (Accessed August 3, 2014).
Peluso, N., and P. Vendergeest. 2001. Genealogies of the Political Forest and Customary Rights in Indonesia, Malaysia, and Thailand. *The Journal of Asian Studies* 60, no. 3: 761–812. http://www.jstor.org/stable/2700109/ (Accessed February 20, 2014).
Peluso, N.L., and P. Vandergeest. 2006. Empires of forestry: Professional forestry and state power in Southeast Asia, Part 1'. *Environment and History* 12, no. 1: 31–64.
Pérez Espinosa, R. 2011. *L'autonomie zapatiste 1995–2007: une fenêtre sur le possible. Fragments d'un témoignage, memoria del Diploma de la EHESS*. París: Editions de l'Ecole des hautes études en sciences sociales.
Perfecto, I., J. Vandermeer, and A. Wright. 2009. *Nature's matrix: Linking agriculture, conservation and food sovereignty*. London: Earthscan.
Pickard, M. 2011. Año 2011 en Chiapas: los gobiernos federal y estatal planean 'despejar' el camino de comunidades en resistencia a megaobras. CIEPAC. Published March 2, 2011. http://www.ciepac.org/documento.php?id=316 (accessed February 10, 2014).
Pskowski, M. 2013. Mother Earth is not for sale- love and defend her: Forest Carbon in Chiapas, Mexico. Honors Thesis for BA. Hampshire College, School of Critical Social Inquiry. Amherst, Massachusetts.
Ramachandra, T., and B. Shruthi. 2007. Spatial mapping of renewable energy potential. *Renewable and Sustainable Energy Reviews* 11, no. 7: 1460–1480.
Ramírez, E. 2014. Integran estudio para impulsar CIP de Palenque. *El Economista*, 13 March. http://eleconomista.com.mx/industrias/2014/03/13/integran-estudio-impulsar-cip-palenque (accessed June 18, 2014).
The REDD Desk. 2013. EDF-AMBIO pilot capacity building model for forest ejidos and communities. *The REDD Desk. http://www.theredddesk.org/activity/edf_ambio_pilot_capacity_building_model_for_forest_ejidos_and_communities/* (accessed September 10, 2013).

Rieublanc, M. 2014. Porqué los pueblos originarios rechazan la autopista San Cristóbal de Las Casas – Palenque. *http://otrosmundoschiapas.org/index.php/temas-analisis/31–31-resistencias/1718-porque-los-pueblos-originarios-rechazan-la-autopista-san-cristobal-de-las-casas-palenque*. (accessed August 2, 2014).

Rocheleau, D. 2011a. Dispossession by Green Deceit. Paper presented at International Conference on Global Land Grabbing at the Institute for Development Studies in Sussex, England. 6–8 April.

Rocheleau, D. 2011b. Networks, territories and distributed power in land grabs in Latin America. Plenary panel presentation: International Conference on Global Land Grabbing at the Institute for Development Studies in Sussex, England. 6–8 April. http://www.future-agricultures.org/panel-a-session-summaries/7569-plenary-panel (accessed March 9, 2014).

Rocheleau, D. 2012a. Resistance to Green Land Grabbing: New articulations within and between social movements in Chiapas, Mexico. Paper presented at the Academic Conference on Global Land Grabbing II, at Cornell University in Ithaca, NY. 17–19 October.

Rocheleau, D. 2012b. Field notes. Interview with the Council of Good Government (Junta de Buen Gobierno), Oventik, Chiapas, Mexico. August 2012.

Rocheleau, D., and R. Roth. 2007. Rooted networks, relational webs and powers of connection: Rethinking human and political ecologies. *Geoforum*, 38, 433–437.

Rosset, P. 2009. La Guerra por la tierra y el territorio. Págs. 159–175 en CIDECI-UNITIERRA (ed), Primer Coloquio Internacional In Memoriam Andrés Aubry: planeta tierra: movimientos antisistémicos. San Cristobal de las Casas: Cideci-Unitierra Ediciones.

Rosset, P. 2011. Food sovereignty and alternative paradigms to confront land grabbing and the food and climate crises. *Development* 54, no. 1: 21–30.

Rosset, P.M., and M.E. Martinez-Torres. 2012. Dialogo de saberes. Rural social movements and agroecology: Context, theory, and process. *Ecology & Society* 17, no. 3: 17.

Ruiz, M. 2014. Experiencia con la Detención por Negociación y Mediación. Presentación en Taller sobre mujeres y tenencia de tierras. Centro de Derechos Humanos de la Mujer. CIDECI San Cristobal de Las Casas.

Sassen, S. 2013. Land grabs today: Feeding the disassembling of national territory. *Globalizations* 10, no. 1: 25–46.

Scott, J. 2009. *The art of not being governed: An anarchist history of upland Southeast Asia.* New Haven: Yale University Press.

Secretaria de la Reforma Agraria (SRA). 2006. ACUERDO para el cierre operativo del Programa de Certificación de Derechos Ejidales y Titulación de Solares (PROCEDE). *Diario Oficial.* 18 Oct. http://www.ordenjuridico.gob.mx/Federal/PE/APF/APC/SRA/Acuerdos/2006/27012006%282%29.pdf (accessed September 11, 2013).

Secretaría General de Gobierno del Estado de Chiapas. 2014. Gobierno estatal y federal se pronuncian por la no regularización de asentamientos en Montes Azules. Official website of the state government of Chiapas, Mexico 13 May 2014. http://www.sgg.chiapas.gob.mx/may 13 de mayo. (accessed September 8, 2014).

Shiva, V. 1988. *Staying alive: Women, ecology and development.* London: Zed Books.

Silverstein, K., and A. Cockburn. 1995. Major U.S. Bank urges Zapatista wipe-out: A litmus test for Mexico's stability. *Counterpunch* 2, no. 3: 1–3.

Sociedad Civil Las Abejas de Acteal. 2014. Nuevo comunicado de la Sociedad Civil Las Abejas de Acteal del 22 julio 2014. SIPAZ, Chiapas. *http://sipaz.wordpress.com/2014/07/25/chiapas-nuevo-comunicado-de-la-sociedad-civil-las-abejas-de-acteal/.* (accessed July 30, 2014).

Sousa Santos, B. de. 2006. *The rise of the global left: The world social forum and beyond.* Zed Books: London.

Stephen, L. 2002. *Zapata lives! Histories and cultural politics in Southern Mexico.* Berkeley: University of California Press.

Sundberg, J. 2003. Conservation and democratization: Constituting citizenship in the Maya Biosphere Reserve, Guatemala. *Political Geography* 22, no. 7: 715–740.

Sundberg, J. 2004. Identities in the making: Conservation, gender and race in the Maya Biosphere Reserve, Guatemala. *Gender, Place and Culture: A Journal of Feminist Geography* 11, no. 1: 43–66.

Televisa. 2010. Stars of the Bicentennial Estrellas del Bicentenario CHIAPAS HD ®TELEVISA 3 mins. http://vimeo.com/15447923 Uploaded Oct. 1, 2010 (accessed March 3, 2014).

Televisa. 2011. Stars of the Bicentennial Estrellas del Bicentenario CHIAPAS HD ®TELEVISA. http://www.youtube.com/watch?v=8TjEJ3ySRJI (accessed March 3, 2014).

Torrez, F. 2011. La Via Campesina: Peasant-led agrarian reform and food sovereignty. *Development* 54, no. 1: 49–54.
Vandergeest, P., and N.L. Peluso. 2006. Empires of forestry: Professional forestry and state power in Southeast Asia, Part 2. *Environment and History* 12, 359–93.
Vandermeer, J., and I. Perfecto. 2007. The agricultural matrix and a future paradigm for conservation. *Conservation Biology* 21, 274–277.
Verma, R. 2014. Land grabs, power, and gender in east and Southern Africa: So, what's new? *Feminist Economics* 20, no. 1: 52–75.
de Vos, J. 2002. *Una Tierra Para Sembrar Sueños: Historia Reciente de la Selva Lacandona*. Mexico City: Centro de Investigaciones y Estudios Superiores en Antropología Social CIESAS.
Wilson, J. 2008. The New Phase of the Plan Puebla Panama in Chiapas. Bulletin 560. CIEPAC Centro de Investigaciones Económicas y Políticas de Acción Comunitaria. http://www.ciepac.org/boletines/chiapas_en.php?id=560 (accessed September 5, 2013).
Wolford, W. 2005. Agrarian moral economies and neo-liberalism in Brazil: Competing world-views and the state in the struggle for land. *Environment and Planning A* 37: 241–261.
Wolford, W. 2010. Contemporary Land Grabs in Latin America. Paper presented at the TNI-ICAS-FIAN Side Event to the 13th Session of the FAO World Food Security Council, October 2010, Rome. http://www.tni.org ('agrarian justice'). (accessed September 5, 2013).
World Wildlife Fund. 2013. Chiapas Selva Lacandona. http://www.wwf.org.mx/wwfmex/descargas/wwf-fcs/fs15-chiapas-lacandona.pdf (accessed September 10, 2013).
Zunino, M. 2010a. Integración para el despojo: el proyecto Mesoamérica, o la nueva escalada de apropiación del territorio (I/III). Boletín Chiapas al Día No. 583.CIEPAC, Chiapas Mexico (28 de mayo de 2010). http://site.adital.com.br/site/noticia.php?lang=ES&cod=48203&langref=ES& … (accessed February 10, 2014).
Zunino, M. 2010b. Integración para el despojo: el proyecto Mesoamérica, o la nueva escalada de apropiación del territorio (II/III). Boletín Chiapas al Día No. 584.CIEPAC, Chiapas Mexico. (8 de junio de 2010). http://site.adital.com.br/site/noticia.php?lang=ES&cod=48977&langref=ES& … (accessed February 10, 2014).
Zunino, M. 2010c. Integración para el despojo: el proyecto Mesoamérica, o la nueva escalada de apropiación del territorio (III/III). Boletín Chiapas al Día No. 585.CIEPAC, Chiapas Mexico (21 de junio de 2010). http://site.adital.com.br/site/noticia.php?lang=ES&cod=49023&langref=ES&… [Accessed 10 Feb 2014]. and from: http://www.gritomesoamerica.org/index.php/integracion-regional/35-integracion regional/74-boletin-qchiapas-al-diaq-no-585.html (accessed September 14, 2014).
Zunino, M., and M. Pickard. 2008. Rural Cities in Chiapas, Boletin Chiapas Al Dia Dec, 26, 2008. No. 571 CIEPAC, Chiapas Mexico. http://jeffconant.wordpress.com/2010/10/06/rural-cities-in-chiapas-government-plundering-the-peasantry/ (accessed September 14, 2014).
Zunino, M., and M. Pickard. 2009. Ciudades rurales en Chiapas: despojo gubernamental contra el campesinado; Ecoportal.net 20/01/09 http://www.ecoportal.net/Temas_Especiales/Economia/ciudades_rurales_en_chiapas_despojo_gubernamental_contra_el_campesinado (accessed September 10, 2013).

Guerrilla agriculture? A biopolitical guide to illicit cultivation within an IUCN Category II protected area

Connor Joseph Cavanagh and Tor A. Benjaminsen

Protected areas now encompass nearly 13 percent of Earth's terrestrial surface. Crucially, such protection often denotes exclusion – of farmers, of pastoralists and of forest-dwelling people. Engaging with the biopolitical implications of these displacements, this paper explores the emergence of an increasingly widespread type of resistance to conservation in the developing world: guerrilla agriculture, or the illicit cultivation of food within spaces zoned exclusively for the preservation of nonhuman life. In doing so, it undertakes a comparative analysis of three groups of farmers at Mount Elgon, Uganda, which support an overarching strategy of illegal cultivation with a variety of nonviolent, militant, discursive and formal-legal tactics. Far from passive victims of global economic and environmental change, we demonstrate how the struggles of farmers at Mount Elgon are frequently effective at carving out spaces of relative autonomy from both conservationists and the Ugandan state apparatus.

Introduction: the biopolitics of global biodiversity conservation

As measured by the United Nations Environment Programme's (UNEP) World Conservation Monitoring Centre (UNEP-WCMC 2012), protected areas (PAs) now encompass nearly 13 percent of the Earth's terrestrial surface, an area approximately equivalent in aggregate size to the continent of South America (Kareiva, Lalasz, and Marvier 2011). Yet conservationists argue that additional increases in PA coverage are necessary to prevent further species loss and ecosystem degradation, and thus actively campaign against 'protected area downgrading, downsizing, and degazettement' or PADDD (Mascia and Pailler 2011). Others promote expansion by emphasizing how forested PAs assist in global efforts to mitigate global environmental change by sequestering carbon and preventing emissions from deforestation (Adams 2008). Still others justify the extension of the existing PA network by noting how, in the context of the nascent 'green economy' and related initiatives to commodify ecosystem services, PAs may contribute to sustainable development through the local redistribution of revenue from both payment for ecosystem service (PES) schemes and ecotourism ventures (see Fairhead, Leach, and Scoones 2012 for a critique). Collectively, these arguments comprise an influential 'triple win' narrative, in which conservation ostensibly contributes to the simultaneous realization of positive outcomes for biodiversity protection, climate change mitigation and economic growth (Büscher et al. 2012).

Notwithstanding such enthusiasm, the delineation of PA boundaries is an inherently political act (Adams and Hutton 2007). Crucially, protection often denotes exclusion – of farmers, of pastoralists and of forest-dwelling people. Indeed, the (re)territorialization of both colonial and post-colonial PAs is increasingly integral to broader dynamics of land grabbing and 'green grabbing' (e.g. Zoomers 2010; Fairhead, Leach, and Scoones 2012) – as well as to processes of state formation and consolidation (Corson 2011; Cavanagh and Himmelfarb 2014) – wherein land and resources are removed from customary systems of tenure and use on environmentally justified grounds (Corson and MacDonald 2012). As Marx (1995 [1867], 501) famously notes in Part Eight of *Capital, Volume One*, such enclosures of common property constitute a form of 'primitive accumulation', or a 'process of divorcing the producer from the means of production', albeit one that 'forms the pre-history of capital'. As numerous scholars have rightfully noted, however, conservation is also intimately related to ongoing processes of primitive accumulation or 'accumulation by dispossession' (Harvey 2005; Kelly 2011), in which environmental rents and incomes are increasingly appropriated in addition to land and resources themselves (Benjaminsen and Bryceson 2012). Conversely, of course, there is no *necessary* reason why conservation and environmental change mitigation must entail accumulation by dispossession. Nevertheless, we highlight the incentives that states, donors and investors increasingly face for marginalizing customary forms of ownership and use, not least to further open 'nature' itself as a frontier for the reinvestment of surplus capital, and thus to stimulate ostensibly 'green' forms of economic growth (Harvey 2005, 148; see also Büscher et al. 2012; Fairhead, Leach, and Scoones 2012; Büscher and Fletcher 2014).

Further, a variety of empirical studies from East Africa demonstrate that when benefits from conservation actually do exist and are slated for redistribution, access to these is often highly asymmetrical and reproductive of existing socioeconomic inequalities (e.g. Tumusiime and Sjaastad 2014). Revenues from ecotourism and payments for ecosystem services (such as carbon offsets) can be usurped by the state, by private enterprises or by corrupt officials, with little 'trickling down' to the communities that bear the opportunity costs of conservation (Beymer-Farris and Bassett 2012; Benjaminsen et al. 2013; Cavanagh and Benjaminsen 2014). Consequently, when the expropriation of land or resource access rights remains uncompensated, and when indirect benefits remain inequitably shared or non-existent, rural populations arguably subsidize both the territorialization of individual PAs and global biodiversity conservation more broadly.

By implication, biodiversity conservation is now central not only to ongoing processes of accumulation by dispossession, but also to more-than-human forms of global biopolitics (Biermann and Mansfield 2014). In Foucault's (2003) terms, the concept of biopolitics encompasses the ways in which the classical sovereign power to 'take life or let live' gradually became complemented by mechanisms for 'making live or letting die' at the level of the population, as evidenced by the rise of disciplines and institutions of demography, public health, and humanitarian intervention (Duffield 2007). Today, however, contemporary biopower functions not only through the 'racist' (Foucault 2003, 254–55) categorization of human populations. Rather, biopolitics now also hinges on initiatives that select certain human populations and nonhuman species to prosper under rapidly changing political-economic and environmental conditions, whereas others are marginalized from access to the means of subsistence or 'let die' (Li 2010; Cavanagh 2014). Indeed, as Biermann and Mansfield (2014, 2) put it, 'modern conservation science is shaped by a biopolitical logic that emphasizes distinctions between biopolitical kinds and develops interventions based on these distinctions – a logic that also informs racial, biological distinctions among humans'.

Unwilling to accept the logic of environment and development projects that marginalize them, however, rural populations often dispute the legitimacy of conservation as an acceptable land use, and resist its implementation with a variety of both covert and overt tactics (Norgrove and Hulme 2006). Despite the widespread prevalence of these activities in case studies of conservation,[1] however, various researchers have questioned whether or not local people actually pose a substantive challenge to conservation governance. Indeed, as Brockington (2004) argues, researchers and activists often underestimate the state's capacity to firmly and decisively repress local resistance to PAs, implying that there is no necessary connection between local disenchantment and the efficacy of 'fortress conservation'.

Engaging these concerns, this paper conducts a comparative analysis of three groups of farmers that have chosen to openly resist conservation efforts at Mount Elgon National Park in Uganda. In doing so, we compare and contrast their strategic objectives, their tactics for achieving these and their probability of posing a substantive challenge to conservation efforts in the region. Of particular interest here is the salience of what we call 'guerrilla agriculture' or illegal food production strategies – defined as the means by which farmers circumvent state regulations and cultivate food within spaces zoned exclusively for the preservation of nonhuman life. Consequently, we conceptualize these actions not just as resistance to conservation, *per se*, but also as struggles against the broader processes of colonization, marketization and centralization of state control over natural resources that threaten to transform peasants into a 'surplus population' relative to the needs of capital (Marx 1995 [1867]; Li 2010; Cavanagh and Himmelfarb 2014). Viewed from this perspective, there is much more than mere resource access at stake for local farmers; indeed, struggles against conservation are also partly struggles against the biopolitical precarity that crises of global economic and environmental change entail for certain rural populations.

Accordingly, this contribution will proceed in four sections. First, we frame the biopolitics of resource conflicts between local populations and conservation at Mount Elgon by drawing on Nixon's (2011) notion of 'slow violence', as well as on studies of resistance from geography, anthropology and political ecology (e.g. Scott 1985, Ortner 1995; O'Brien 1996; Holmes 2007). Second, we provide an exposition of the ethnographic approach to fieldwork that was adopted, and discuss its advantages for critically examining the political-ecological milieu of farmer-activists in the Mount Elgon context. Third, we historically situate resistance strategies at Mount Elgon, before presenting findings on four empirically identified categories of tactics that local people used to support a broader strategy of guerrilla agriculture: (1) nonviolent, (2) militant, (3) discursive and (4) formal-legal. We conclude with a discussion of the implications of this strategy for environmental justice amidst the broader context of global economic and environmental change.

Situating guerrilla agriculture: slow violence, everyday resistance

The violence that has marked the worldwide dissemination of the PA model of biodiversity conservation – from only a few hundred PAs in 1925 to nearly 160,000 in 2011 (UNEP-WCMC 2012) – remains both absent from conventional histories and largely hidden from the international public sphere. Despite largely being non-democratically formulated at the supranational level by epistemic communities of elite conservation professionals (Corson and MacDonald 2012; MacDonald and Corson 2012), 'win–win' representations

[1]See, for example, Holmes' (2007) review of 34 case studies of resistance to conservation.

of PA management continue to dominate conventional academic, donor and policy-based discourses on the subject (Büscher 2014). Increasingly, conservation agencies and their financial supporters uphold win–win representations even when such portrayals contradict the findings of empirical researchers, who present evidence of 'conservation refugees' or conservation-displaced populations (Cernea and Schmidt-Soltau 2006; Dowie 2009) – as well as various forms of human rights abuse (e.g. Hurinet Uganda 2011; Beymer-Farris and Bassett 2012) – denoting that conservation initiatives tend to 'fail forward' (Fletcher 2013). In particular, such findings highlight the growing disconnect between discourse and practice in African conservation initiatives (Benjaminsen and Svarstad 2010), as the rapid proliferation of 'community-based', 'participatory' and 'collaborative' rhetoric since the 1980s has often not been accompanied by substantive changes to the deleterious consequences experienced by PA-adjacent populations (see also Dressler et al. 2010).

As such, the negative socioeconomic consequences of these organizations' actions reveal the relevance of 'slow violence' as an analytic perspective (Nixon 2011). As donors like USAID and nongovernmental organizations such as the World Wide Fund for Nature (WWF) frequently remind us, they do not directly advocate for the eviction or harm of indigenous populations during the implementation of conservation programmes.[2] Rather, conservationists usually construe such actions as unfortunate excesses involved in the operations of local government agencies, such as the Uganda Wildlife Authority (Norgrove and Hulme 2006) or Tanzania's Wildlife Division (Benjaminsen and Bryceson 2012; Benjaminsen et al. 2013). As a result, conservation-related evictions and violence appear as though disconnected from second-order policy decisions and the discursive battles fought to obfuscate such connections (Cavanagh and Benjaminsen 2014). Differently put, while conservation-related evictions and displacements are relatively easy to identify and challenge, the slow, 'everyday violence' of uncompensated crop and wildlife raiding, exclusion from common pool resources and routine abuse by conservation personnel remain artificially separated from decisions made by resource management professionals in international fora. Not least, these include the United Nations Convention on Biological Diversity and the International Union for the Conservation of Nature's (IUCN) World Conservation Congresses (Corson and MacDonald 2012), especially considering the former's admonition that member countries set aside 10 percent or more of their major biomes for conservation purposes (Corson 2011).

Of course, neither the direct nor the 'slow' violence of conservation remains unopposed, although such opposition often manifests in subtle ways. As Eric Hobsbawm (1973) famously remarked in the inaugural issue of this journal, the goal of resistance for subsistence agriculturalists is often to pursue strategies not for overthrowing some elite group or class, but for 'working the system […] to their minimum disadvantage'. Of course, James Scott (1985) later conceptualized these subtle tactics as 'the weapons of the weak': 'foot dragging, dissimulation, desertion, false compliance, pilfering, feigned ignorance, slander, arson, sabotage, and so on' (Scott 1985, xvi). In contexts where institutional change is unlikely, where collective mobilization is expensive and where formal or quasi-authorized practices of 'rightful resistance' (O'Brien 1996) seem infeasible or compromised by poor governance, such an approach often constitutes the most pragmatic option for resistance. Moreover, as Scott (2013, 5) notes in his most recent writing on the subject, peasants 'are particularly risk averse; they strive to minimize the danger of a

[2]See, for example, Beymer-Farris and Bassett (2012) and the response from WWF in *Global Environmental Change* (Burgess *et al.* 2013).

life-threatening economic failure. […] They are likely to plant several different crops in different fields to minimize the effects of the failure of one'. As we will see, such pragmatism certainly constitutes an integral component of farmers' resistance to conservation as a land use at Mount Elgon.

Indeed, one could argue that the weapons of the weak are of particular importance in relation to biodiversity conservation. In many cases, and across Sub-Saharan Africa in particular, the expansion and regulatory intensification of conservation is legal, often profitable and arguably warranted on purely environmental grounds. As such, groups seeking to openly resist these initiatives will likely face swift and heavy-handed repression from states, often with financial, in-kind or ideological support from investors, donors and pro-conservation organizations abroad (Fairhead, Leach, and Scoones 2012). For example, Holmes' (2007) meta-analysis demonstrates how PA neighbours implement these tactics in 34 case studies from across the developing world. Of particular interest here are the recurring patterns and similarities in tactics that rural populations utilize – in 27 of these case studies, the continuation of banned livelihood practices constitutes the main form of resistance. Other, more overt forms of resistance to conservation include the deliberate slaughter of wildlife or destruction of forest cover, as observed in selected cases from Uganda (Adams and Hulme 2001), Tanzania (Mariki, Svarstad, and Benjaminsen 2015) and Kenya (Western 1994). That said, in its most extreme incarnations, anti-conservation resistance can also take the form of threatened, attempted or actual assault, murder or torture of conservation personnel (Norgrove and Hulme 2006; Robbins et al. 2006).

What separates these acts from petty crime or mere opportunism are the 'hidden transcripts', laden with political meaning, which accompany them. As many critics of the literature on everyday resistance have argued, petty criminality perhaps remains correctly identified as such if the acts involved are not coupled with the *intention* to engage in resistance (see e.g. Fegan 1986). With the notion of 'hidden transcripts', however, we again draw upon Scott (1992) in referring to the narratives that subaltern individuals use to interpret their own experience of domination or oppression, to give meaning to their resistance and to frame alternatives. For Scott (1992, 27, emphasis original),

> the hidden transcript represents discourse – gesture, speech, and practices – that is ordinarily excluded from the public transcript of subordinates by the exercise of power. The practice of domination, then, creates the hidden transcript … [it], in turn, reacts back on the public transcript by engendering a subculture and by opposing its own variant form of social domination against that of the dominant elite.

Of course, as Mitchell (1990) argues in his influential critique of Scott's (1985) initial thesis, conceptualizing political relations in terms of such a public/hidden, domination/resistance binary potentially entails a number of conceptual limitations. Indeed, for Mitchell (1990, 545–46), Scott's (1985) conceptualization of resistance relegates the Gramscian notion of 'consent' to the realm of ideology, and identifies coercion solely with the material domain, allowing Scott to claim that the presence of the 'weapons of the weak' and accompanying hidden transcripts signifies the absence of hegemony. Unconvinced of this argument, Mitchell (1990, 571–72) instead proposes the concept of 'enframing' to encompass the ways in which hegemonic power influences perceived conditions of political and social possibility, thus manifesting itself in the various ways in which individuals engage in self-monitoring and self-regulation in accordance with prevailing institutions and norms.

While analytically impressive, we ultimately find Mitchell's (1990) critique to be overly dismissive of both the political agency of rural populations and the radical potential of their hidden transcripts. As Neumann (1998, 48) puts it, '[w]hile Scott may strain too hard to argue the lack of hegemony demonstrated by everyday forms of resistance, Mitchell goes too far in the other direction to discount the political importance of these acts'. Accordingly, we prefer to read Scott's (1992) work on hidden transcripts through the prism of Gramsci's (1971) notion of the 'organic intellectual', which usefully allows for a perception of rural and perhaps formally uneducated individuals as powerful and potentially transformative agents, fully capable of combining discourse and practice in the pursuit of progressive social change. For example, the most common 'hidden transcripts' articulated by such organic intellectuals at Mount Elgon refer to alternative constellations of interaction between humans and their 'natural' environment, which either condemn fortress conservation altogether, or (re)imagine it in ways that are radically inclusive of humans. Indeed, the environmentalism of farmers at Mount Elgon is one that could be described as valuing 'ecology without nature' (Morton 2007), in which local people have developed a nuanced critique of the complex intersection between PA governance, environmental change, state power and their own agrarian political economies. In other words, despite recurring admonitions from the Uganda Wildlife Authority that local communities must be 'sensitized' to the value of forest conservation (e.g. UWA 2009), these communities generally value their biophysical surroundings for practical, aesthetic and cultural reasons, but do not conceive of 'the environment' as an ontologically separate category from 'society'. Rather, farmers assert that they remain more than capable of both living within and sustainably managing forests at Mount Elgon, as their ancestors had done for generations prior to the advent of British colonialism. In this sense, farmers generally conceive of themselves as embedded *within* what conservationists refer to as 'nature', rather than alienated from or external to it, favouring stewardship as opposed to enclosure and subsequent 'fortress conservation' (Brockington 2002). In the following section, we provide an exposition of the methodology that was used to gain access to such insights, as well as an introduction to the geographical characteristics of the Mount Elgon study area.

Conservation and the politics of environmental science

Originally gazetted as a 'Crown Forest' by the colonial administration of the Uganda Protectorate under the Legal Notice No. 100 of 1938 (Cavanagh and Himmelfarb 2014), Mount Elgon is a 4321-metre-high extinct volcano. The mountain's forested slopes straddle the border between Uganda and Kenya, of which the Ugandan portion encompasses approximately 1145 km^2 of PA. Combined with the mountain's fertile volcanic soils, abundant rainfall guarantees that the region can support a diverse variety of crops – including Uganda's largest share of commercially valuable Arabica coffee – as well as one of the densest rural populations in East Africa (Bunker 1991).

Currently, eight districts border the circumference of the park, with most of these being recently created in accordance with ongoing processes of administrative decentralization (Francis and James 2003). A predominantly agriculturalist Bantu group, the Bagisu, populates the southern districts of Manafwa, Bududa, Mbale, Sironko and Bulambuli. Likewise, a Nilotic agro-pastoralist group, the Sabiny or Sebei, primarily inhabits the northern districts of Kapchorwa, Kween and Bukwo. Based on Uganda's 2002 census projections, population densities now range from more than 800/km^2 in the Bagisu region to approximately 130/km^2 in the Sabiny region (Uganda Bureau of Statistics 2002). Livelihood strategies and resource use patterns are broadly similar around the whole of the national park, although for cultural reasons the Sabiny rely more heavily on cattle and livestock husbandry than the Bagisu (Himmelfarb 2012). Consequently, for both groups, charcoal and fuelwood constitute the primary source of energy for domestic heating and cooking. Non-timber forest products are also used to supplement agricultural diets, and herbal medicines generally constitute the only affordable means of treating illnesses (see also Norgrove and Hulme 2006, 1101).

The first author conducted fieldwork during September–December 2009 and July–December 2011 with three purposively selected groups of Bagisu farmers that have chosen to openly oppose conservation at Mount Elgon National Park. Two of these groups are located in Manafwa district, whereas the third is located in Bulambuli. The district-level locations of these groups may be safely disclosed, as they are already well known to local authorities. Indeed, as part of their struggles, all three organizations have launched lawsuits against both the Uganda Wildlife Authority (UWA) and the Ugandan Attorney General, and have chosen to publicly disseminate this information. However, given that this paper discusses both formal-legal challenges and informal tactics (many of which are technically illegal), we will not refer to specific persons, nor will we attribute agency for certain resistance tactics to individual groups. Instead, when necessary to disaggregate the analysis between actors, we will anonymously refer to these as Resistance Group A (RG-A), Resistance Group B (RG-B) and Resistance Group C (RG-C), so as to avoid incriminating them.

Clearly, conducting fieldwork on everyday resistance presents a number of methodological and epistemological challenges. In the first instance, it must be emphasized that the communities living adjacent to Mount Elgon National Park are complex and internally differentiated in terms of their kinship, religious and ethnic ties; formal and informal political structures; and economic security in the form of land, livestock and other property holdings. Conflicts exist both within and among communities; these manifest most explicitly as ethnicity- or clan-based disputes over land, livestock and resources, but also more subtly as gender-based violence and other intra-household forms of abuse, which are often related to alcoholism (see, e.g., Heald 1986). Rural life in the area is far from idyllic; it is characterized by deep poverty, hard labour and recurring financial insecurity, conceptualized as the inability to obtain sufficient access to food, medication, education and other basic necessities.[3] Further, land conflicts with the national park are a recurring theme in the local politics of administrative decentralization (e.g. Francis and James 2003), with incumbent politicians often promising improved access to land and resources if re-elected. In this sense, both the negative and the (decidedly limited) positive externalities of conservation potentially articulate with these social and economic differentiations, at least theoretically suggesting the possibility of a variety of different responses 'from below' (Borras and Franco 2013). Accordingly, then, we must first echo both Ortner's (1995) and Agrawal and Gibson's (1999) warnings concerning researchers' tendency to treat rural communities as homogenous, undifferentiated collectives – at Mount Elgon, 'local communities' of course have both the means and the motive to engage in conflicts amongst themselves in relation to any combination of the factors identified above.

In this context, the sensitive character of the subject matter also denotes that standard approaches to structured and semi-structured interviewing are unlikely to be effective. Most informal resistance tactics are technically illegal and, if detected, would conceivably provoke UWA and law enforcement authorities to take action to further restrict resource access and shared benefit distributions in relevant communities. Further, as noted by

[3]See Norgrove (2002) for a detailed analysis of livelihoods in Mount Elgon National Park (MENP)-adjacent communities.

Gupta (2001), the empirical substance of 'everyday resistance' – sabotage, pilfering, vandalism and so on – is often exaggerated by elites to justify the 'routine repression' of various marginalized populations. This highlights the second-order risk that studies of 'resistance' might inadvertently bolster the very forms of domination that they seek to undermine, as they may unintentionally provide elites with evidence that ostensibly indicates the necessity of further coercion. Although the topic of such risks was raised with respondents, the opportunity to express a critical perspective on conservation in the region was always prioritized. That said, although community members were generally very enthusiastic about participating in interviews, they were notably also hesitant to provide information in the form of a structured or semi-structured interview. The following reaction from one of RG-B's leaders, delivered after consulting his colleagues about the prospect of allowing community members to participate in semi-structured interviews, is exemplary of a more widespread hesitation to engage in such structured interactions:

> We're sorry, but we can't answer your questions in that way [referring to a questionnaire presented to them]. In our grandfathers' time, a mzungu [white man] like you came here with those questions, and used them to take the mountain away from us. We are happy to discuss our problems with you, but we refuse to use those papers. (Interview, RG-B committee member, 2011)

At issue, here, was not the provision of information as such, but the form in which the information was conveyed. Indeed, these individuals were happy to engage in what one could describe as an 'unstructured interview', where respondents were not simply required to provide responses to pre-designed questions. In other words, RG-B was not concerned about providing information, but with providing enough information, which would adequately contextualize, justify and explain their decisions, so that their actions could not be extricated from the situational rationales that informed them. In this sense, these 'organic intellectuals' were making a point very similar to Sherry Ortner's (1995) concerning 'ethnographic refusal', or researchers' tendency to ignore the kinds of social 'thickness' that the respondents were here trying to communicate. Interestingly, it thus also appears that part of this group's resistance programme was also an opposition to the imposition of a pre-structured interview protocol and subsequently de-contextualized analysis by researchers and practitioners.

As a result, archival document analyses, unstructured in-depth interviews and ethnographic observation form the primary basis for this research. Intensive, recurring unstructured interviews were held with the leadership committees of each resistance group, their legal representation and the human rights-based NGOs that provided them with in-kind support. Simultaneously, these interactions were triangulated with five focus group discussions and 53 key informant interviews with 'ordinary' community members who did not hold leadership positions, local government officials, and UWA employees. Throughout, the first author also observed resource use and agricultural practices, as well as patterns of interaction between group members, government officials and conservation authorities. Oral and written histories delivered by both local people and conservation authorities were compared and contrasted with official documents contained in the library of the Faculty of Forestry and Nature Conservation at Makerere University in Kampala, as well as in the National Archives in Entebbe. Here, our hermeneutic approach to analyzing both texts and verbally delivered narratives was inspired by Nixon's (2011) conceptualization of 'slow', 'invisible' and other subtle forms of violence – an approach that decidedly renders visible the ways in which inherently biopolitical policy decisions translate into tangible, often detrimental effects in the lifeworlds of vulnerable communities.

In what follows, we first historically situate resistance to conservation at Mount Elgon with the findings of oral histories and content analyses, before providing an exposition of various tactics used to support a broader strategy of 'guerrilla agriculture'.

Colonists, foresters and kleptocrats: understanding resistance at Mount Elgon

In Uganda, the strife entailed by the post-independence regimes of Milton Obote (1962–1971), Idi Amin (1972–1979) and Milton Obote (again, 1980–1985) effectively neutralized one of the Bagisu's historically most potent resistance tactics. Previously, in the face of pressure from the colonial state to increase production for export markets, withdrawing into subsistence agriculture had constituted a form of veto or 'exit option' to protest undesirable policies or terms of trade (Hyden 1980, 32; Bunker 1991). Indeed, as Bunker (1983, 750) succinctly puts it, production for subsistence is not 'something the state can sell or tax'. Although purely subsistence agriculture entails a decline in living standards that accompanies the reversion to reliance on land and livestock, rather than on cash incomes, it simultaneously denotes a degree of autonomy from the potentially exploitative policies of governments.[4]

As Bunker (1985, 373) argues in his seminal work on agricultural practices in the Bugisu region of Mount Elgon, however, both corruption and Amin's depletion of Uganda's foreign reserves wreaked havoc on commodity exports, leading to 'the nearly complete abandonment of cotton production and to a steep decline in coffee production'. Given that a disproportionate amount of Uganda's coffee – and especially its high-quality Arabica coffee – is grown at Mount Elgon, the sudden loss of access to export markets placed significant pressure on farmers to secure their livelihoods through purely subsistence means, such as encroachment into forests. Under Amin, though, farmers' decision to do so was suddenly a matter of exigency rather than of strategy. While Amin's 1975 Land Reform Decree encouraged encroachment in order to 'double agricultural production' and reduce the rural population's dependence on the state's rapidly declining ability to facilitate export-oriented agriculture (Turyahabwe and Banana 2008, 650), the collapse of these exports made such encroachment a necessary condition for survival in many parts of the country.

Similarly, under Milton Obote's second regime and the civil war that followed it, economic dysfunction and the declining real value of public salaries provided conservation officials with incentives to facilitate encroachment by selling illicit resource and land-use permits to local farmers (Norgrove and Hulme 2006, 1098). As noted by the British colonial foresters Webster and Osmaston (2003, 167), 'inflation resulted in the purchasing power of the salary of a forest officer in 1988 being worth only 0.4 percent of what it was in 1962, enough to buy four loaves of bread a month'. Today, however, many farmers who perhaps unknowingly purchased these illicit permits – and their descendants – emphatically claim that they retain their validity. Indeed, ostensibly 'illicit' permits issued during this period for land within the Mount Elgon reserve's boundaries, which the first author examined during fieldwork, are often physically indistinguishable from their 'legitimate' counterparts.

Further, evidence suggests that corrupt officials may also have granted larger scale concessions. For example, one resistance group in Manafwa district (RG-C) claims that the Forest Department agreed to degazette approximately 1000 hectares of the reserve for

[4]For an extra-regional comparison, see also James Scott's (2009, especially 187–207) work on practices of state-evasion and 'escape agriculture' in upland southeast Asia.

the use of one of their clans in 1980, during Milton Obote's second regime. In a written statement of the RG-C's history that was prepared by the group's leadership committee, they claim that:

> Since the creation of the reserve's boundary in 1936/38, several excisions have been made under Mt. Elgon forest reserve to relief [sic] forest department and safely settle and incorporate families living in the forest reserve in their village communities. Notable among the excisions is part of the forest reserve was excised in favour of the [name withheld] family in [location of RG-C] in 1980. This explains clearly that the land we claim is our ancestral land. (Written historical statement, RG-C leadership committee, 2011)

Consequently, RG-C's leadership traces its claim to disputed land to managerial decisions allegedly taken by Forest Department officials during Obote's second regime. Unfortunately for these communities, however, contemporary government and conservation authorities do not consider such claims to be legitimate (e.g. UWA 2009, 48).

Indeed, it appears that the validity of many permits and excisions allegedly granted under Obote's regime did not survive the civil war that deposed his government. Shortly after Yoweri Museveni's National Resistance Movement (NRM) restored relative stability to Uganda in 1986, the new government launched a countrywide initiative to regain control over its PA estate and repair the ecological degradation that occurred during Uganda's tumultuous post-independence period. As part of this initiative, the government upgraded the Mount Elgon Forest Reserve to a Forest Park (1989) and later to National Park status (IUCN Category II) in 1993. These initiatives were financed by national-level forest conservation programmes from USAID and the European Community, as well as by a Norwegian Agency for Development Cooperation (NORAD)-financed and IUCN-implemented initiative known as the Mount Elgon Conservation and Development Project (MECDP). In addition, a Dutch NGO – the Forest Absorbing Carbon Emissions (FACE) Foundation – offered to finance the reforestation of Mount Elgon in exchange for the rights to the carbon stored in the new forest compartments (Cavanagh and Benjaminsen 2014).

In the process of upgrading the reserve to a national park, however, paramilitary conservation rangers and National Resistance Army personnel evicted local people from approximately 25,000 hectares of encroached parkland (Himmelfarb 2012). A written account provided by RG-B describes the evictions as follows:

> In 1992–3 a gang of soldiers of the then-National Resistance Army together with Uganda Wild Life Authority rangers armed with guns mounted [four villages, names withheld]. They carried out an illegal and massive eviction which left several homes homeless and many people landless. They burned and demolished houses, and looted property [...] Both cash crops and food crops were all destroyed causing irreparable suffering to the local peasants who after provoked to seek refuge in nearby trading centres. (Written historical statement, RG-B leadership committee, 2011)

Although official records were not kept regarding the number of people displaced by these evictions, Vangen (2009) roughly estimates that the overall figure could total more than 100,000 individuals. Given that the region immediately adjacent to MENP is one of the most densely populated areas in rural Uganda (Uganda Bureau of Statistics 2002), such estimates are plausible. In the present study alone, the three evicted groups of farmers that were studied collectively amount to 2923 households or approximately 14,900 individuals, assuming a regionally average household size of approximately 5.1 persons (Norgrove 2002, 87). By comparison, Himmelfarb (2012) found that approximately 6000 people had been evicted from 1500 hectares of land claimed by UWA in some of the least-densely populated districts to the north and west of Mount Elgon. Moreover, based on statistics kept by the Uganda Communications Commission (2010), the total MENP-adjacent population is approximately 1,592,400. To spatially contextualize this figure, the westernmost borders of park-adjacent districts in Bugisu region extend not farther than 30–40 km from the border of MENP.

Finally, the simultaneous existence of two park boundaries – one from 1993, and another stemming from a 'boundary correction' that was demarcated in the early 2000s – further complicates the land tenure situation at Mount Elgon (UWA 2010b, 5). Unfortunately for local communities, the enforcement of the more recent boundary was also characterized by violent evictions. Indeed, an account from RG-A highlights the similarity of the actions taken by UWA nearly 10 years after the original territorialization of the national park:

> In the year 2001, the servants/employees of Uganda Wild Life Authority and Attorney General of Uganda – UPDF [Uganda Peoples Defense Forces] soldiers dressed in combat uniforms armed with scaring guns jointly with game rangers armed with guns attacked our residents [...] They maliciously destroyed acres and acres of land covered with crops like coffee, banana plantations, beans, maize, cocoyams, passion fruits, tomatoes, cabbages, among others. They burnt down people's homes, demolished houses, and looted iron sheets and used roof timbers and wall poles for fire wood. They looted livestock of all classes [...] one person [name withheld] was killed in the incident. (Written historical account, RG-A leadership committee, 2011)

By contrast, UWA (2010a, 2010b) claims that corrupt surveyors compromised the 1993 demarcation exercise by allegedly accepting bribes from local communities in exchange for altering the boundary in their favour. As such, the agency commissioned a new survey, this time using global positioning system technology, which expanded the boundaries of MENP up to 1 km into community land in some locations (UWA 2010b, 5). Rather understandably, therefore, communities seek to counter these violent, recurring dispossessions with a range of tactics to maintain their agricultural livelihoods, as we examine in detail throughout the ensuing sections.

Guerrilla agriculture at Mount Elgon

Indeed, in the socioeconomic context of recurring dispossessions on Mount Elgon, it is unsurprising that the production of food constitutes the centrepiece of resistance to conservation. Here, we define 'guerrilla agriculture' as the range of tactics that rural communities use to circumvent laws and regulations that criminalize agricultural production, and to ensure their own food security. By their very nature, these tactics blur the contours between subsistence and 'improvement', or between economic opportunism and political grievance – not least because the overarching context of dire poverty renders the distinction rather narrow. As one local government official described the situation of his constituents who had been evicted from their homes within the national park:

> Things are not good. We are camped in disputed land. [...] Since there are many people here, we have no food, no education, no clothing, and high mortality. When we try to harvest, UWA harasses us. They destroy our coffee and *matooke* [plantain] plantations. Now, as many as five people per month are dying of famine. We will even bury one body today. (Key informant interview, local government, RG-C, 2009)

Hence, in the worst-affected MENP-adjacent communities, the practice of guerrilla agriculture is often synonymous with the assertion of a right to survival, or the rejection of the legitimacy of environmental conservation programmes that would otherwise see them 'let die' (Li 2010). Whereas farmers in Bugisu once sought to 'veto' unfavourable state policies by refusing to grow coffee and other cash crops for export, the Ugandan government's contemporary dependence on influxes of foreign aid and credit greatly reduces the impact of such resistance tactics (Bunker 1991), given that the enormity of these inflows renders the scale of a Bagisu coffee production boycott rather insignificant. In subsequent portions of this section, we thus further present four ideal types of tactics that farmers use to support this broader guerrilla agricultural strategy: (1) nonviolent, (2) militant, (3) discursive and (4) formal-legal.

Nonviolent tactics

Given that these tactics involve the smallest degree of risk, nonviolent resistance forms the core of farmers' opposition to conservation at Mount Elgon. Perhaps the most obvious of these, covert planting involves the cultivation of fast-yielding food crops in sections of the PA that local people believe to be neglected by ranger patrols. Typically, community members clear small portions of forest and plant crops within the park while they collect forest resources such as firewood or bamboo. In addition, both key informant interviews and UWA reports confirm that such planting increasingly occurs at night (Mafabi 2012). Moreover, due to the risk of illegally entering and exiting the park, most covertly planted crops lie only marginally within the reserve boundary.

Given the amount of time between planting and harvest, however, it is nearly impossible for even small gardens to remain completely hidden from park rangers. As a precaution, therefore, communities utilize many of the 'weapons of the weak' described in detail by Norgrove and Hulme (2006, 1102): bribery, park boundary manipulation, feigned ignorance, false compliance with orders to cease cultivation, and the obstruction of routes toward their illegal gardens. Building upon this contribution, however, we stress that these tactics have continued to evolve in the context of both local politics and national economic change. For example, although Norgrove and Hulme (2006) refer to the illicit exchange of money for access to resources as 'bribery', rangers also appear to market such transactions to communities in accordance with fluctuations in the real value of their salaries. As asserted by an employee of a human rights NGO in Mbale town,

> confusion is a large source of the conflict. Rangers make little money, so they often extort cash from community members in exchange for access and grazing. Only later, they [community members] become frustrated when they are evicted by the strict UWA officials. (Key informant interview, NGO Legal Officer, Mbale, 2009)

For example, between periods of fieldwork in 2009 and 2011, the value of the Ugandan shilling (UGX) fell from approximately 2100 to nearly 2900 per USD, following President Museveni's decision to massively deplete Uganda's reserves of foreign exchange by purchasing several Russian fighter jets (Barigaba 2011). To compensate, the prices of many goods and services rose accordingly. Yet, throughout this period, the average ranger's monthly remuneration remained static at approximately 200,000 UGX. This created great strain on rangers' capacity to both fulfill day-to-day needs and remit money to their families for health and educational purposes, such as for the omnipresent requirement to pay school fees. By contrast, farmers were relatively insulated from inflation as a result of the prevalence of subsistence cultivation, and could 'pay' rangers with food, village-brewed alcohol and other goods in exchange for access to protected forests. Consequently, worth noting here are the ways in which divergent commentators refer to the same activity as either 'bribery' (instigated by communities) or 'extortion' (instigated by UWA personnel). More realistically, similar to the conditions under which Forest Department officials sold illicit permits in the early 1980s, both local poverty and fluctuations in the real value of UWA salaries likely periodically create mutual incentives for trading in illegal access and use rights.

Despite the prevalence of these nonviolent tactics around the circumference of MENP, they are not always sufficient to prevent interference from UWA personnel. In such cases, communities thus sometimes resort to real or threatened violence to deter the enforcement of conservation regulations.

Militant tactics

Although the aforementioned forms of nonviolent resistance frequently assist in the maintenance of small gardens within the national park, UWA's practice of rotating park rangers between outposts often compromises mutually beneficial relationships. In other words, these rotations may lead to the sudden cessation of illicit agreements that enable access to land and resources, causing members of affected communities to attempt to violently 'discipline' UWA staff. When present, as observed in Heald's (1986) account of Bagisu 'vigilante groups', these tactics oddly resemble 'mafia-style' reprisals against informants. Shortly before fieldwork began in 2009, for example, two rangers who had allegedly reneged on illegal resource access arrangements were tortured before one was hacked to death with a machete (Key informant interview, legal NGO, 2009). Another two rangers were killed and a third injured at the same location in 2002 (Edyegu 2009). These events occurred in the immediate vicinity of RG-A's disputed territory, although it should be noted that no firm evidence exists to link individual members of the group to any of these assaults or killings.

Simultaneously, communities also employ violent tactics in reprisal for the human rights abuses allegedly perpetrated by UWA personnel. Also in 2009, for instance, community members burned down a local UWA outpost after a young woman was shot in the back of the head by a ranger (Hurinet Uganda 2011). Another outpost in Manafwa district was razed in 2010, following the slaying of a young boy (Kazungu 2010). Similarly, shortly after fieldwork ended in 2011, residents in nearby Bududa district burned down a third UWA outpost in reprisal for the killing of a local farmer (Ssalongo 2012). In a focus group discussion, one member of RG-B justified violence as a form of vigilante justice:

> What were we to do? These are crimes against humanity. The woman was shot dead, and 12 people have been killed since 2005. Just lately, there have been three cases of rape, and the rangers have also sodomized old men, just to humiliate them. They will not let us have peace. (Focus group discussion, RG-B members, 2009)

Despite their severity, community members have not presented most of these allegations to local police. In 2011, the first author questioned RG-B's leadership about why it had chosen not to pursue legal action against the individuals who allegedly committed these acts. In response, one of the group's leaders replied as follows:

> When we go to the police, they either ignore us or they intimidate us. I once filed a complaint of rape, but nothing happened. When I returned to the police station to follow up, I was told the

> file could not be found. Earlier this year, the same woman was again raped by rangers. Now you tell me, how much time should I waste? (Focus group discussion, RG-B committee member, 2011)

In another focus group discussion, an RG-C leader offered another reason why complaints cannot be brought to the police or government officials:

> UWA tries to say that we are rebels. They tell the UPDF [the Ugandan military] that we want to fight the government, but we do not. If we try to go to police they just say we are agitating and they intimidate us. (Focus group discussion, RG-C committee member, 2011)

As such, communities are drawn to violent tactics in response to both the direct violence suffered at the hands of UWA and security forces, as well as the intimidation that they face when attempting to rectify these injustices through law enforcement institutions. Consequently, these tactics serve the dual purpose of both maintaining illicit access to land and resources within the national park, and providing the threat of 'vigilante justice' as a deterrent for violent evictions perpetrated by security forces and UWA staff. Interestingly, although these communities are not involved in guerrilla activity in the conventional sense, the state itself appears to perceive illegal agricultural production as a threat not just to conservation, but also to its authority and power in the region. Indeed, a group known as the Sabaot Land Defence Forces (SLDF) launched a rebellion on the Kenyan side of Mount Elgon in 2007, resulting in hundreds of deaths and thousands of displaced people (Kenya National Commission on Human Rights 2008). Yet, in order to prevent their actions from being characterized as mere 'crime', or, alternatively, as an act of open rebellion against the state like the case of the SLDF, each of the three resistance groups on the Ugandan side of the mountain also engages in a variety of what we will term 'discursive' tactics.

Discursive tactics

Here, we refer to the attempts of communities to solicit political support from NGOs, media outlets, human rights groups, government agencies, researchers and local politicians. In short, their goal is to utilize normative pressure from sympathetic parties to prevent UWA from enforcing its own policies. As mentioned above, a second objective is also to publicly frame resistance tactics primarily as a livelihood strategy, rather than as criminal activity or open rebellion against state authority. For example, during fieldwork in 2011, the first author attended two workshops that brought together all three resistance groups, local politicians, journalists and community-based organizations. A prominent Ugandan NGO organized the first of these, whereas an international NGO organized the second. At these workshops, leaders from each group delivered well-rehearsed accounts, posed for pictures and conducted individual interviews with journalists from national newspapers and television stations.

In these and similar settings, discursive tactics involve the promulgation and distribution of narratives that justify the illegal agricultural use of land within Mount Elgon National Park. Typically, this is accomplished through the assertion of a combination of indigenous, ancestral, human and property rights to the PA. In an exemplary statement, one community elder asserted all of the above during a workshop group discussion:

> The park belongs to our ancestors, many of them are even buried here [ancestral claim] [...] In 1935, the British conserved the land, rangers were there, but we were allowed to cultivate

> because we are the indigenous people [indigenous claim] [...] Since 1993 and the national park, there are now too many boundaries, so they also take the land that we own [property rights claim] [...] Why should we go hungry on our fathers' land? [human rights/ancestral claim]. (Focus group discussion, RG-C members, 2011)

In some cases, this may also be coupled with selective allegations of human rights abuse, corruption or criminality directed against UWA personnel. As a member of RG-A emphatically stated:

> Since these UWA people grabbed our land in 2002, we have seen torture, killings, shootings, property grabbing, and burnt houses. They have looted our livestock and money. The government has never followed up the evictions, and the police ignore our complaints about the rangers. (Focus group discussion, RG-A members, 2011)

Once developed, local people disseminate such narratives to potential allies in the above-mentioned organizations, who are invited to pressure UWA to acquiesce to the community's demands. Occasionally, the mere threat of negative publicity may also be used as leverage, in an attempt to ensure such acquiescence. Here, the influence of the media should not be underestimated; for example, combined with numerous reports of conflicts between UWA and local communities, the killing of a Belgian tourist by alleged 'poachers' in 2008 prompted Canadian, American, British and Australian foreign services to issue travel advisories for the Ugandan side of Mount Elgon. Later, UWA officials came to attribute continually declining volumes of park visitors between 2008 and 2011 to both these decisions and associated press coverage (UWA 2009, Key informant interview, UWA tourism warden, 2011).

Further, given the novel pressures that neoliberal reforms and 'new public management' schemes are currently placing on Ugandan PAs to 'pay their own way' by securing revenues from ecotourism and various PES initiatives, conservation authorities are perhaps increasingly vulnerable to such widely disseminated activist campaigns (Cavanagh and Benjaminsen 2014). For example, although local revenues from ecotourism and PES schemes at MENP are currently marginal – amounting to only approximately USD 200,000 in the 2010–2011 financial year (see UWA 2010a) – and are thus generally overshadowed by incomes received from national-scale donor programmes and centralized state transfers, local conservation officials are nonetheless under intense pressure to increase local sources of revenue as a result of the aforementioned neoliberal reforms.

When combinations of the above tactics prove ineffective at intimidating conservation authorities, however, communities that are able to raise sufficient resources also seek to challenge the legitimacy of both conservation itself and the manner in which it is enforced through the Ugandan legal system.

Formal-legal tactics

This final category of resistance is extremely costly, and is infrequently pursued by most communities at Mount Elgon, as it involves navigating the Ugandan law enforcement and justice systems. That said, in an attempt to retain ownership rights to land that currently lies between the 1993 and 2002 park boundaries, all of the three resistance groups in this study have sued UWA and the Ugandan Attorney General through the High Court in Mbale town. In each case, communities have successfully obtained High Court injunctions, which theoretically allow for the continuation of cultivation while the court deliberates on the case. Since the main suit in these cases was filed between 7 and 10 years ago, one can perhaps see the attainment of injunctions as a valuable tactic in itself, irrespective of the final ruling. Further, a 2005 consent judgment delivered by the Mbale High Court recognized the Sabiny-Benet in Kapchorwa and Bukwo as the 'historical and indigenous' inhabitants of the Mount Elgon forest, and ordered the cessation of evictions by UWA (Himmelfarb 2012). Needless to say, this greatly encouraged each of the three resistance groups examined in this paper.

In order for formal-legal tactics to be feasible, however, substantial financial resources are required, as well as the ability to frequently travel to Mbale town for consultations with lawyers, hearings and other meetings. The costs for such activities alone, over the course of 10 years, are enormous for communities. Further, the need to procure cash to finance these lawsuits denotes that farmers must restructure their agricultural strategies in favour of producing substantial volumes of cash crops (such as coffee) instead of a wider variety of less valuable food crops for primarily subsistence purposes. That said, the groups examined in this study generally perceived the costs of maintaining a lengthy legal challenge as being lower than the costs of immediate eviction and its attendant processes of dispossession.

Additionally, despite some successes with the adoption of formal-legal tactics, all three groups have reported that UWA has periodically failed to respect the High Court injunctions that were obtained. Undoubtedly, the agency remains highly aware that these groups finance their legal campaigns by selling cash crops such as coffee and *matooke*, and has reportedly taken action to destroy portions of their respective harvests in order to disrupt this revenue stream. As a lawyer for RG-B noted:

> These people from UWA have taken a number of steps to frustrate us. When the rangers grow bold, they slash my clients' crops, frustrating their ability to pay for this case [...]. We have raised this issue with the court and police, but they do not seem to care. (Key informant interview, lawyer for RG-B, 2009)

Further, many group leaders suspect that UWA and the Ugandan government are deliberately prolonging these cases in order to sap their already meagre resources. Hence, although the participation of farmers in these judicial processes might be potentially seen as a form of 'rightful resistance' (O'Brien 1996) that is more or less authorized – if not particularly encouraged – by the state, the actual experiences of each resistance group appears to suggest otherwise. For example, when the first author concluded fieldwork in 2009, all three groups were confident that the High Court would soon reach a favourable decision. As 2011 drew to a close, however, and yet another hearing was scheduled for a date four months later, these perceptions began to change. In frustration, one of RG-A's leaders put it thusly:

> we travel here from [location of RG-A] for the hearings with the little means we have. Once or twice a year, the judge mysteriously does not appear for the hearings, so we must adjourn until a later date. It is like this for 10 years now. [...] When we return home, they threaten us, intimidate us, slash our crops [...] UWA or the court, it is all the government, and the government wants us finished. (Key informant interview, RG-A committee member, 2011)

As such, rather than accepted participants in an institutionalized and constitutionally sanctioned manifestation of rightful resistance, these communities are perhaps instead trapped at the intersection of both direct and other 'slow' forms of violence, in which the state is apparently able to exert its will through – or even *in spite of* – the judiciary and law enforcement agencies. Indeed, each of the three groups examined in this study simultaneously bears the indirect costs of PA-adjacent residency – such as damages from crop and wildlife raiding and restricted access to resources – in addition to the violence directly inflicted by the state and its agents. Conversely, the tactics employed in response – whether nonviolent, militant, discursive or formal-legal – yield some relief from these deleterious processes. Indeed, in conjunction with one another, these tactics enable communities to hold on to subsistence, however precariously, amidst a governance context in which they are being let – or sometimes even made – to die (Li 2010).

Conclusion

Amidst the overarching context of global economic and environmental change, rural populations find themselves increasingly trapped between conventional expropriations for extractive industry, export-oriented agriculture or large development projects, and new, 'green' enclosures for biodiversity conservation, carbon offset forestry or biofuel plantations (Fairhead, Leach, and Scoones 2012). Rather tragically, the latter type of 'green' enclosure now frequently displaces populations in an attempt to mitigate the deleterious environmental impacts of the former. In particular, as the scale of global biodiversity conservation increases in response to anthropogenically induced biodiversity decline, so too does the scale of human precarity that it engenders. Thus, similar to other cases from throughout the developing world (Holmes 2007; Benjaminsen and Bryceson 2012; Beymer-Farris and Bassett 2012; Benjaminsen et al. 2013), local people at Mount Elgon National Park endure the effects of both direct and indirect forms of violence as a result of these processes. In contrast to the simultaneous prevalence of direct violence such as evictions and human rights abuse, much of the latter is 'slow' in the sense that it arises from legislation and policies that were enacted years or even decades previously (Nixon 2011), and which obscures its own relationship to value-laden decisions made by individuals and organizations. Fieldwork conducted on the socioeconomic impacts of both direct and structural violence at Mount Elgon further reveals often-grim insight into the lifeworlds of individuals and communities who are, in a biopolitical sense, largely being 'let die' (Li 2010).

Too often, however, critiques of environment and development interventions that 'make live or let die' rob rural populations of their own agency. At Mount Elgon, local 'organic intellectuals' employ a variety of guerrilla agricultural tactics to maintain their livelihoods against the threat of both dispossession and policies that seek to subsidize the lifestyles and livelihoods of other populations at their expense. This paper found that these tactics broadly correspond to interrelated nonviolent, militant, discursive and formal-legal categories. Combined, these tactics support a broader strategy of 'guerrilla agriculture', which allows communities to illicitly cultivate food within spaces zoned exclusively for the preservation of nonhuman life, and thus to circumvent policies that bolster the global public good of biodiversity at the expense of local and traditional livelihoods. In this sense, rather than being passive victims of 'fortress conservation', farmers at Mount Elgon are frequently effective at carving out spaces of relative autonomy from both conservationists and the Ugandan state apparatus.

Consequently, further research is needed not only on the more-than-human biopolitics of global economic and environmental change, but also on potentially differentiated *responses* or reactions 'from below' (Borras and Franco 2013) to various types of imposed environmental governance. In other words, we might ask, how do communities resist various forms of 'naturalization by dispossession' (Cavanagh and Benjaminsen 2014), and how are these resistances differentiated according to – or articulated with – complex intersections of class, ethnicity, gender and other socioeconomic characteristics?

In what ways can vulnerable populations neutralize or negotiate with legislation and policy decisions that deprive them of the necessary preconditions for productive livelihoods, and especially when these are formulated supra-nationally and in nondemocratic fora? Not least, we contend, such inquiries may provide a fruitful basis for (re)invigorating the pursuit of global environmental justice in times of ecological, social and economic crisis.

Acknowledgements

Funding for this research was provided by the Norwegian Research Council through the Protected Areas and Poverty in Africa (PAPIA) project. The first author also gratefully acknowledges research funding from the Department of International Environment and Development Studies (Noragric) at the Norwegian University of Life Sciences, and thanks both Adrian Nel and Dave Himmelfarb for useful comments and discussions. Permissions for the PAPIA project were granted by the Uganda National Council for Science and Technology and the Uganda Wildlife Authority.

References

Adams, W.M. 2008. Conservation, carbon, and the transition to sustainability. *Oryx* 42, no. 4: 469–70.

Adams, W.M., and D. Hulme. 2001. If community conservation is the answer in Africa, what is the question? *Oryx* 35, no. 3: 193–200.

Adams, W.M., and J. Hutton. 2007. People, parks, and poverty: Political ecology and biodiversity conservation. *Conservation and Society* 5, no. 2: 147–83.

Agrawal, A., and C.C. Gibson. 1999. Enchantment and disenchantment: The role of community in natural resource conservation. *World Development* 27, no. 4: 629–49.

Barigaba, J. 2011. $740 m fighter jets scam sneaks under the radar. *The East African* (04.04.2011). http://www.theeastafrican.co.ke/news/+740%20m+fighter+jets+scam+sneaks+under+the+radar/-/2558/1137840/-/3kw0g3z/-/index.html (accessed 05.07.2014).

Benjaminsen, T.A., and I. Bryceson. 2012. Conservation, green/blue grabbing and accumulation by dispossession in Tanzania. *Journal of Peasant Studies* 39, no. 2: 335–55.

Benjaminsen, T.A., and H. Svarstad. 2010. The death of an elephant: Conservation discourses versus practices in Africa. *Forum for Development Studies* 37, no. 3: 385–408.

Benjaminsen, T.A., M.J. Goldman, M.Y. Minwary, and F.P. Maganga. 2013. Wildlife management in Tanzania: State control, rent seeking and community resistance. *Development and Change* 44, no. 5: 1087–109.

Beymer-Farris, B.A., and T.J. Bassett. 2012. The REDD menace: Resurgent protectionism in Tanzania's mangrove forests. *Global Environmental Change* 22, no. 2: 332–41.

Biermann, C., and B. Mansfield. 2014. Biodiversity, purity, and death: Conservation biology as biopolitics. *Environment and Planning D: Society and Space* 32: 257–73.

Borras, S.M., and J.C. Franco. 2013. Global land grabbing and political reactions "from below". *Third World Quarterly* 34, no. 9: 1723–47.

Brockington, D. 2002. *Fortress conservation: The preservation of the Mkomazi game reserve, Tanzania*. Oxford: James Currey.

Brockington, D. 2004. Community conservation, inequality, and injustice: Myths of power in protected area management. *Conservation and Society* 2, no. 2: 411–32.

Bunker, S.G. 1983. Center-local struggles for bureaucratic control in Bugisu, Uganda. *American Ethnologist* 10, no. 4: 749–69.

Bunker, S.G. 1985. Peasant responses to a dependent state: Uganda, 1983. *Canadian Journal of African Studies* 19, no. 2: 371–86.

Bunker, S.G. 1991. *Peasants against the state: The politics of market control in Bugisu, Uganda, 1900–1983*. Second edition. Chicago, IL: University of Chicago Press.

Burgess, N.D., S. Mwakalila, P. Munishi, M. Pfeifer, S. Willcock, D. Shirima, S. Hamidu, G.B. Bulenga, J. Rubens, H. Machano, and R. Marchant. 2013. REDD herrings or REDD menace: Response to Beymer-Farris and Bassett. *Global Environmental Change* 23, no. 5: 1349–54.

Büscher, B. 2014. Selling success: Constructing value in conservation and development. *World Development* 57: 79–90.

Büscher, B., and R. Fletcher. 2014. Accumulation by conservation. *New Political Economy*. doi:10.1080/13563467.2014.923824.
Büscher, B., S. Sullivan, K. Neves, J. Igoe, and D. Brockington. 2012. Towards a synthesized critique of neoliberal biodiversity conservation. *Capitalism Nature Socialism* 23, no. 2: 4–30.
Cavanagh, C. 2014. Biopolitics, environmental change, and development studies. *Forum for Development Studies* 41, no. 2: 273–94.
Cavanagh, C., and T.A. Benjaminsen. 2014. Virtual nature, violent accumulation: The "spectacular failure" of carbon offsetting at a Ugandan national park. *Geoforum* 56: 55–65.
Cavanagh, C., and D. Himmelfarb. 2014. "Much in blood and money": Necropolitical ecology on the margins of the Uganda Protectorate. *Antipode*. doi:10.1111/anti.12093.
Cernea, M.M., and K. Schmidt-Soltau. 2006. Poverty risks and national parks: Policy issues in conservation and resettlement. *World Development* 34, no. 10: 1808–30.
Corson, C. 2011. Territorialization, enclosure and neoliberalism: Non-state influence in struggles over Madagascar's forests. *Journal of Peasant Studies* 38, no. 4: 703–26.
Corson, C., and K.I. MacDonald. 2012. Enclosing the global commons: The convention on biological diversity and green grabbing. *Journal of Peasant Studies* 39, no. 2: 263–83.
Dowie, M. 2009. *Conservation refugees: The hundred-year conflict between global conservation and native peoples*. Cambridge, MA: MIT Press.
Dressler, W., B. Büscher, M. Schoon, D. Brockington, T. Hayes, C.A. Kull, J. McCarthy, and K. Shrestha. 2010. From hope to crisis and back again? A critical history of the global CBNRM narrative. *Environmental Conservation* 37, no. 1: 5–15.
Duffield, M. 2007. *Development, security, and unending war: Governing the world of peoples*. Cambridge: Polity.
Edyegu, D. 2009. Sironko mob kills forest ranger. *New Vision* (14 June 2009). http://www.newvision.co.ug/D/8/13/684748 (accessed February 16, 2014).
Fairhead, J., M. Leach, and I. Scoones. 2012. Green grabbing: A new appropriation of nature?. *Journal of Peasant Studies* 39, no. 2: 237–61.
Fegan, B. 1986. "Tenants" non-violent resistance to landowner claims in a central Luzon village. *Journal of Peasant Studies* 13, no. 2: 87–106.
Fletcher, R. 2013. How I learned to stop worrying and love the market: Virtualism, disavowal, and public secrecy in neoliberal environmental conservation. *Environment and Planning D: Society and Space* 31, no. 5: 796–812.
Foucault, M. 2003. *Society must be defended*. New York: Picador.
Francis, P., and R. James. 2003. Balancing rural poverty reduction and citizen participation: The contradictions of Uganda's decentralization program. *World Development* 31, no. 2: 325–37.
Gramsci, A. 1971. *Selections from the prison notebooks*. New York: International Publishers.
Gupta, D. 2001. Everyday resistance or routine repression? Exaggeration as a stratagem in agrarian conflict. *Journal of Peasant Studies* 29, no. 1: 89–108.
Harvey, D. 2005. *The new imperialism*. Oxford: Oxford University Press.
Heald, S. 1986. Mafias in Africa: The rise of drinking companies and vigilante groups in Bugisu District, Uganda. *Africa* 56, no. 4: 446–67.
Himmelfarb, D. 2012. In the aftermath of displacement: a political ecology of dispossession, transformation, and conflict on Mt. Elgon, Uganda. PhD diss., Athens: University of Georgia.
Hobsbawm, E. 1973. Peasants and politics. *Journal of Peasant Studies* 1, no. 1: 3–22.
Holmes, G. 2007. Protection, politics, and protest: Understanding resistance to conservation. *Conservation and Society* 5, no. 2: 184–201.
Human Rights Network (Hurinet) Uganda. 2011. *Resource based conflicts and human rights violations in Uganda: A case study of selected protected areas*. Kampala: Hurinet-Uganda/Diakonia-Sweden.
Hyden, G. 1980. *Beyond ujamaa in Tanzania: Underdevelopment and an uncaptured peasantry*. Berkeley, CA: University of California Press.
Kareiva, P., R. Lalasz, and M. Marvier. 2011. Conservation in the Anthropocene: Beyond solitude and fragility. *Breakthrough Journal* 2, http://thebreakthrough.org/index.php/journal/past-issues/issue-2/conservation-in-the-anthropocene (accessed February 16, 2014).
Kazungu, D. 2010. Residents destroy wildlife outpost. *Daily Monitor* (09 July 2010). http://www.monitor.co.ug/News/National/-/688334/954662/-/x21g7b/-/index.html (accessed February 16, 2014).

Kelly, A.B. 2011. Conservation practice as primitive accumulation. *Journal of Peasant Studies* 38, no. 4: 683–701.

Kenya National Commission on Human Rights. 2008. *Mountain of terror: A report on the investigations of torture by the military at Mount Elgon.* Nairobi: Kenya National Commission on Human Rights.

Li, T.M. 2010. To make live or let die? Rural dispossession and the protection of surplus populations. *Antipode* 41, no. s1: 66–93.

MacDonald, K.I., and C. Corson. 2012. "TEEB begins now": A virtual moment in the production of natural capital. *Development and Change* 43, no. 1: 159–84.

Mafabi, D. 2012. Elgon encroachers use new tricks. *Daily Monitor* (17 May 2012). http://www.monitor.co.ug/News/National/-/688334/1407378/-/ahw2d4z/-/ (accessed February 16, 2014).

Mariki, S.B., H. Svarstad, and T.A. Benjaminsen. 2015. Elephants over the cliff: Explaining wildlife killings in Tanzania. *Land Use Policy*. doi:10.1016/j.landusepol.2014.10.018

Marx, K. 1995 (1867). *Capital: A critique of political economy, volume one.* S. Moore and E. Aveling (Trans.); F. Engels (Ed.). Moscow: Progress Publishers. http://marxists.org/archive/marx/works/1867-c1/index.htm (accessed February 16, 2014).

Mascia, M.B., and S. Pailler. 2011. Protected area downgrading, downsizing, and degazettement (PADDD) and its conservation implications. *Conservation Letters* 4, no. 1: 9–20.

Mitchell, T. 1990. Everyday metaphors of power. *Theory and Society* 19, no. 5: 545–77.

Morton, T. 2007. *Ecology without nature: Rethinking environmental aesthetics.* Cambridge, MA: Harvard University Press.

Neumann, R. 1998. *Imposing wilderness: Struggles over livelihood and nature preservation in Africa.* Berkeley, CA: University of California Press.

Nixon, R. 2011. *Slow violence and the environmentalism of the poor.* Cambridge, MA: Harvard University Press.

Norgrove, L. 2002. Parking resistance and resisting the park: The theory and practice of national park management, a case study of Mount Elgon National Park, Uganda. Unpublished PhD dsis., Manchester, UK: University of Manchester.

Norgrove, L., and D. Hulme. 2006. Confronting conservation at Mount Elgon, Uganda. *Development and Change* 37, no. 5: 1093–116.

O'Brien, K.J. 1996. Rightful resistance. *World Politics* 49, no. 1: 31–55.

Ortner, S.B. 1995. Resistance and the problem of ethnographic refusal. *Comparative Studies in Society and History* 37, no. 1: 173–93.

Robbins, P., K. McSweeney, T. Waite, and J. Rice. 2006. Even conservation rules are made to be broken: Implications for biodiversity. *Environmental Management* 37, no. 2: 162–9.

Scott, J.C. 1985. *Weapons of the weak: Everyday forms of peasant resistance.* New Haven: Yale University Press.

Scott, J.C. 1992. *Domination and the arts of resistance: Hidden transcripts.* New Haven: Yale University Press.

Scott, J.C. 2009. *The art of not being governed: An anarchist history of upland southeast Asia.* New Haven: Yale University Press.

Scott, J.C. 2013. *Decoding subaltern politics: Ideology, disguise, and resistance in agrarian politics.* New York: Routledge.

Ssalongo, J.E. 2012. Mob burns down UWA outpost in Bududa. *Uganda Radio Network* (09 March 2012). http://ugandaradionetwork.com/a/story.php?s=40844 (accessed February 16, 2014).

Tumusiime, D.M., and E. Sjaastad. 2014. Conservation and development: Justice, inequality, and attitudes around Bwindi Impenetrable National Park. *Journal of Development Studies* 50, no. 2: 204–25.

Turyahabwe, N., and A.Y. Banana. 2008. An overview of history and development of forest policy and legislation in Uganda. *International Forestry Review* 10, no. 4: 641–56.

Uganda Bureau of Statistics (UBS). 2002. *Uganda population and housing census: Population size and distribution.* Analytical Report. Kampala, Uganda: UBS.

Uganda Communications Commission (UCC). 2010. *Rural communications development fund (RCDF): UCC support through the RCDF programme.* Kampala: UCC.

Uganda Wildlife Authority (UWA). 2009. *Mount Elgon National Park general management plan, 2009–2019.* Kampala: UWA.

Uganda Wildlife Authority (UWA). 2010a. *Budget for the financial year 2010/2011.* Kampala: UWA.

Uganda Wildlife Authority (UWA). 2010b. *UWA-FACE progressive forest restoration report, Jan 1994 – Oct 2010.* Kampala: UWA.

United Nations Environment Programme – World Conservation Monitoring Centre (UNEP-WCMC). 2012. *Biodiversity indicators partnership – coverage of protected areas.* Indicator Factsheet 1.3.1. http://www.wdpa.org/resources/statistics/2010BIP_Factsheet_Coverage_of_Protected_Areas.pdf (accessed February 16, 2014).

Vangen, C. 2009. Evicted in the name of nature: The process of eviction and its impact on local rural livelihoods in Mount Elgon, Uganda. MSc dsis. Ås: Norwegian University of Life Sciences.

Western, D. 1994. Ecosystem conservation and rural development: The case of Amboseli. In *Natural connections: Perspectives in community-based conservation*, ed. D. Western, R.M. Wright and S.C. Strum, 15–52. Washington, D.C.: Island Press.

Webster, G., and H. Osmaston. 2003. *A history of the Uganda forest department, 1951- 1965.* London: Commonwealth Secretariat.

Zoomers, A. 2010. Globalisation and the foreignisation of space: Seven processes driving the current global land grab. *Journal of Peasant Studies* 37, no. 2: 429–47.

Reclaiming the worker's property: control grabbing, farmworkers and the Las Tunas Accords in Nicaragua

Bradley R. Wilson

In this paper I explore a land grabbing resistance movement composed of unemployed coffee workers in Central Nicaragua. Between 1996 and 2000, a private agro-export conglomerate appropriated worker-owned coffee estates previously designated as the Area Propiedad del Los Trabajadores (APT), or the Worker's Property. Following mass protests between 2001 and 2004, worker representatives from the Asociación de Trabajadores del Campo (ATC) and government officials negotiated and signed the Las Tunas Accords which provided redistributed land from 18 of those coffee estates to 2500 families. Drawing on interviews with movement participants carried out between 2003 and 2012, I argue that the roots of the control grab and the resistance movement can be traced to the contradictions of the Sandinista National Liberation Front (FSLN)-led agrarian reform in the 1980s, the conflicts over property in the post-war period and the failed consensus on how rural labor should organize and be represented in the face of land re-concentration and capitalist consolidation.

On 11 September 2002, 3000 unemployed workers from coffee estates in Matagalpa, Nicaragua, formed a human roadblock near a little village called Las Tunas. Behind the barricades, farmworkers demanded emergency food and medical relief, short-term employment, and control over foreclosed, indebted and abandoned properties where they had previously lived and worked. Protesters had been living in makeshift encampments for more than a year after they were displaced from coffee estates following layoffs and farm foreclosures associated with the rapid decline in farm-gate coffee prices.[1] Hunger was widespread. Entire families including children and the elderly joined in the protest, mobilizing a powerful symbolic attack against the neoliberal state's indifference to the plight of the rural poor hardest hit by the economic crisis. With growing domestic and international media attention, government officials appointed a diplomatic team to review farmworker grievances and come to a resolution with the civil society organizations representing them. In a matter of days, negotiators hashed out an agreement, called the Las Tunas Accords. In the Accords, the State promised to redistribute land from 18 coffee estates to

[1]The encampments symbolized the Nicaraguan experience of the global coffee price crisis and illustrated the extreme vulnerability of landless workers whose livelihoods depended upon permanent or seasonal wage employment and housing in the coffee estates (Wilson 2013).

2500 families – the single most extensive pro-poor land reform since the end of the Contra war in 1990.

Taking the Las Tunas Accords as a point of departure, in this paper, I describe the political formation and the uneven outcomes of what has become known as the Las Tunas movement.[2] While the protests at Las Tunas took place in the context of a humanitarian disaster associated with the decline in coffee prices, the history of the farmworkers' movement that forced these agreements can be traced to an epic land control grab that occurred a decade prior to the road blockade (Wilson 2013). In the 1990s, an agro-industrial conglomerate made up of two enterprises Consorcio Nicaraguense Agropecuario and Agropecuaria Renacer de San Miguel (CONSAGRA-AGRESAMI hereafter) purchased and provided loans to distressed and cash-poor coffee estates managed by worker-owned enterprises, popularly called the Worker's Property (APT), which were established in the peace accords ending the Contra War. In just 6 years, the conglomerate gained control of an estimated 18,000 ha of land in coffee production, making it the largest financier, producer and exporter of coffee in the country by 2000 (Nitlapan-Envio 2000). CONSAGRA-AGRESAMI's speculation on land and agro-export commodity markets was a tremendous gamble for the conglomerate, the banks and the people employed. When coffee prices hit record lows in 2000, the conglomerate collapsed and thousands of workers abandoned the coffee estates and formed makeshift encampments (plantones) along the highway through the municipalities of San Ramon, El Tuma-La Dalia and Rancho Grande.[3] It was out of these encampments that farmworkers built the movement that marched on Las Tunas.

In many regards, the Las Tunas Accords represented a tremendous victory and an example of successful grassroots pressure to reclaim land for those who work it. All 18 coffee estates mentioned in the Accords were directly or indirectly tied to CONSAGRA-AGRESAMI. However, rather than celebrating the momentary success of the protest at Las Tunas in 2002, in this paper I describe the complicated history and protracted political struggle surrounding the Las Tunas Accords. Indeed, just 9 months after these negotiations, the agreements were abandoned by state officials, thus forcing farmworkers to return to the encampments once again. Farmworkers protested for 2 more years before the state finally fulfilled its promises to assign the land in the worker's names. However, during this 2-year

[2]The research for this paper was conducted over a total of 16 months in 2003 and 2005–2007, and in follow-up interviews conducted in 2012. I conducted 71 interviews and repeated field visits in 11 worker communities/estates that were active in the Las Tunas movement. Eight of these worker communities/estates were selected because they have been occupied by workers since at least 2002 and appear in the Las Tunas Accords documents as properties in worker possession. The other three communities/estates did not appear in the accords and movement participants in those sites remain landless and/or are reported to have not received benefits from their participation. In each community/estate, I completed at least three oral histories, in an effort to grasp the particularities of my informants' experiences as well as background on each location for the sake of comparison. To understand other institutional and political perspectives, I also conducted interviews with signatories of the Las Tunas Accords, including the mayors of San Ramon and La Dalia in 2002, FSLN party officials in Matagalpa, representatives from the Union of Farmers and Ranchers (UNAG), the Catholic Church and the directors of the Rural Workers Association (ATC) in Matagalpa. I have used pseudonyms throughout the paper to protect the anonymity of my informants.

[3]In addition to the thousands moving to roadside encampments, thousands more left the estates and sought refuge in the city of Matagalpa, Managua, or migrated abroad. The Red Cross in Matagalpa fashioned an encampment in a city park to treat some 850 people with health problems caused by malnutrition (Rocha 2001), and the regional campus of the National University created an encampment supported by donations from students, faculty and community members to help some 1200 people with no place to go. But many more stayed behind in the hinterlands.

period, farmworkers struggled to survive, let alone remain politically organized. Stifled by the volatile legacies of land grabbing in the region (Abu-Lughod 2000), the lengthy process of re-titling CONSAGRA-AGRESAMI properties ultimately led to attrition, manipulation and corruption of the movement by leaders and other opportunists. Indeed, only some 25 percent of those who marched on Las Tunas ultimately acquired land. As I show, even those farmworkers who were able to secure land continue to struggle for control over their properties due to historic land tenure insecurity, a problem throughout rural Nicaragua but particularly acute in the cattle ranching and coffee producing regions of Matagalpa (Broegaard 2005, 2009).

The paper is organized in five main sections. I begin by couching my work within a labor-centric analysis of land grabbing (Li 2011). Farmworkers provide a critical perspective on speculative agricultural investments, yet they have received less attention than peasant farmers in the contemporary land grabbing literature. Second, I introduce the history of land conflict surrounding the Nicaraguan agrarian reform and its uneven impacts and trajectories for farmworkers in the coffee sector (Abu-Lughod 2000; Everingham 2001; Jonakin 1996). In particular, I focus on the formation of worker-owned coffee enterprises called The Worker's Property, or APT, which were established in the peace accords following the civil war. Third, I explain the rise of CONSAGRA-AGRESAMI and how the conglomerate capitalized on the vulnerabilities of farmworkers within the APT enterprises to build their coffee empire. Fourth, I describe the formation of the Las Tunas movement after the collapse of CONSAGRA-AGRESAMI. Given farmers' past political experiences with the ATC and livelihood vulnerability on the estates, I show how the goals of the farmworkers coalesced around the distribution of individual land titles for subsistence production. These demands for individual titles, rather than collective titles like those previously held under the APT, served as a major point of contention between labor leaders and farmworkers in the negotiation of the Las Tunas Accords. Fourth, I draw upon my field research in the communities that participated in the movement to describe the aftermath and differential effects of the Las Tunas Accords on movement participants. While the movement won significant concessions on paper, ultimately large numbers of farmworkers were excluded because of the protracted struggle for material survival and the uneven resource allocations within worker communities. Furthermore, even those who did receive land struggle to gain, maintain and control access to the properties allocated to them.

The labor question in the land grab debate

In recent years, scholars have sought to document, analyze and unravel the implications of a new global rush for resources, particularly large-scale speculative land deals for agro-food and fuel production (Borras and Franco 2012; Pearce 2012; Peluso and Lund 2011; Sikor and Lund 2009; White et al. 2012; World Bank 2010; Zoomers 2010). Much of this work has focused on land deals that benefit transnational corporations and foreign states, and explores various capitalist ventures and commodity circuits and the social/environmental conflicts that they yield (Borras and Franco 2012). Victims of global land grabbing are often represented as landholding peasants and subsistence producers with a strong moral, political or legal claim to land or resources. When the land is needed but the labor is not, landholders are displaced by capital investors or state-supported projects who then institute a new commodity production scheme. Such landholder-centric analyses, however, tend to misrepresent the effects of land grabbing on differentiated rural classes, and reproduce an agrarian imaginary in which land grabbing by foreign and domestic states and multinational corporations is only accelerating the loss of peasant subsistence livelihoods (Borras and Franco 2012). Yet as numerous scholars in agrarian studies argue, this is only part of the land-grabbing story. As Borras and Franco (2012, 46) write,

> [i]t is not possible to fully understand the differential impact of land-use change on the 'rural poor' without deploying class analysis. For example, rich peasants renting out some parts of their lands under arrangements with estates, while farming the remainder themselves, are in a more advantageous position than cash-strapped poor farmers leasing out their entire plots and then seeking (part-time, precarious) employment as labourers on estates. Both are integrated into the emerging plantation enclaves, but on very different terms.

Frequently forgotten in accounts of land- and resource grabbing are agricultural laborers who may be incorporated into or employed in commodity production schemes facilitated by land grabbing. Rather than impediments to land deals or a problematic afterthought, landless or land-poor agricultural laborers incorporated into commodity production (in both plantation-based and contract-based production operations) are vital to the success of particular commodity production schemes on acquired lands. In many cases, land *and* labor are needed to fix capital investment in a place for a time.

Tania Li's (2011) effort to spotlight class inequalities and labor questions raised by land and resource grabbing therefore makes a critical intervention which I seek to extend. Li's commentary drew needed attention to the relationship between contemporary land grabbing and ongoing dispossession of the rural poor (see also Li 2009). Challenging a teleological reading of Marx's theory of primitive accumulation (Hart 2002; Perelman 2000; Read 2002), scholars employing the concept of ongoing dispossession hold that capitalist circuits are kept in constant motion through the displacement of laborers from land, their incorporation into commodity production schemes and, as I demonstrate, their expulsion from said production schemes when commodity booms go bust (Bair and Werner 2011a, 2011b; Glassman 2006; Wilson 2013). The conceptualization of dispossession as ongoing, rather than a single act of displacement rooted in the past, suggests that contemporary land grabbing is an integral part of an iterative, repeated and continuous process through which capitalist circuits are reproduced (Harvey 2003; Peluso and Lund 2011). Thinking about contemporary land grabbing as part of an ongoing process of dispossession calls attention not only to the initial displacement of surplus people from the land, but also to how they may be incorporated into and expelled from future commodity production schemes.

As Li argues, agricultural labor is often necessary to ensure that a successful control grab results in economic gain for the investors. Nevertheless, speculative agricultural investments also create tremendous vulnerability for rural peoples without access and control over land and resources. Moreover, even though speculative agricultural investments may promise jobs, agro-export production schemes that follow may or may not generate sufficient rural employment opportunities to ensure stable rural livelihoods (Araghi 2009; Li 2009). If no rural employment opportunities exist, it is also uncertain whether domestic labor markets sufficiently support pathways to employment for migrating workers (Araghi 2009; Li 2009). In effect, Li argued that the displacement of people and their limited incorporation into wage work or subsistence production caused by large-scale land acquisitions creates a surplus population for whom there 'is no pathway from country to city, agriculture to industry, or even a clear pathway into stable plantation work that pays a living wage' (Li, 2011, 296). Yet, as I demonstrate, even in circumstances where agricultural laborers are incorporated into commodity production schemes on grabbed lands, they still remain susceptible to a loss of livelihood should these speculative ventures fail.

As my work on the Las Tunas movement illustrates, agricultural laborers who are critical to commodity production schemes on grabbed lands as waged workers may also face the harsh reality that their labor and livelihoods are dispensable. In the face of the collapse of speculative agricultural investments, access and control of land may provide agricultural laborers with a means for survival. Indeed, for agricultural laborers without a recognized legal claim on the asset in question, access to that resource may be one of the only ways to ensure short- and long-term food security. As Li writes, a 'tiny patch of land' can be used as a safety net in future crises (Li 2011), or as a means of breaking out of the kind of wage labor dependence that marginalized farmworkers both politically and economically in the past (Wilson 2013). Looking forward, demands for land can be seen as a 'backstop' economic strategy (Li 2011) to resist being drowned, yet again, in a sea of dispossession. Yet, as Li writes, under conditions of ongoing dispossession, the demand for land is not a romantic struggle of the rural poor seeking to 'conserve an ancient way of life'. Rather, the persistence of struggles over land suggests that surplus people are unwilling to accept, wholesale, 'their de facto proletarian status'. Indeed, for many farmworkers, 'there is no sign that they can move into a proletarian future' (Li 2009).

As I demonstrate in the remaining sections of the paper, the situation of farmworkers in Matagalpa and the political demands of the Las Tunas movement reflect precisely the concerns regarding surplus people and large-scale land acquisitions. Because they were dependent on wage employment on the coffee estates, farmworkers in Matagalpa were extremely vulnerable to job loss and food insecurity when commodity prices fell (Wilson 2013). With little sign that the state would provide them a sufficient safety net in the face of economic crisis, and no promise that wage employment in the coffee estates would offer them long-term livelihood security, land became the central bargaining point. Yet, as the movement progressed, it became clear that the struggle for land was no panacea. As I illustrate in the next section, both CONSAGRA-AGRESAMI's control grab and the Las Tunas movement were deeply entangled in the political conflicts surrounding land control in the post-war period (Abu-Lughod 2000; Everingham 2001). As I demonstrate, the very agrarian reform history and land tenure insecurity that enabled CONSAGRA-AGRESAMI to perpetrate its control grab would also limit the possibility of equitable land distribution for farmworkers, thus rendering them vulnerable once more within a system of ongoing dispossession.

The workers' property: agrarian reform trajectories and the politics of land in Nicaragua

Contemporary land grabbing and resistance to land grabbing in Nicaragua must be understood in the context of a longer struggle over land and livelihood that stretches back in time (see Gould 1998). Untangling the history of agrarian reform in Nicaragua in particular is crucial to making sense of the rise of CONSAGRA-AGRESAMI. The popular revolution and agrarian reform led by the Sandinista National Liberation Front (FSLN) (1979–1990) was one of the most highly politicized, widely documented and thoroughly researched counter-enclosures in the world.[4] As a pro-poor control grab, the scale of land redistribution

[4]Since the nineteenth century, land grabbing by domestic and transnational investors has established massive inequalities in resource control, produced a class of landless laborers and created the conditions

was immense. By 1989, the revolutionary Nicaraguan state transferred more than 2.5 million ha of arable land from large-scale, elite-owned latifundios to farming collectives, individual peasant farmers and state-owned enterprises called Area Propiedad del Pueblo (the People's Property) (CIERA, 1989). In the decades since, a large literature has explored the effects of the agrarian reform on new landholder beneficiaries and agricultural cooperatives. Far less scholarly work has considered the agrarian trajectories of farmworkers employed on the state-owned enterprises (Abu-Lughod 2000).

The Area Propieded del Pueblo (APP) was a state managed agro-industrial complex made up of coffee, cattle, cotton and sugar estates controlled by state officials in close collaboration with the Rural Workers Association (ATC). In the coffee-producing region of Matagalpa and Jinotega, the focus of my research, the APP properties encompassed roughly 20,000 ha of coffee land and employed tens of thousands of rural workers (Rocha 2003). APP properties represented a central foreign revenue stream for the FSLN's revolutionary socialist project (Enriquez 1991). However, when the FSLN lost the presidential elections in 1990 to the United Nicaraguan Opposition (UNO) party, many of these properties were privatized and transferred to workers and ex-military through the *Concertacíon*, an agreement between the ATC, the Union of Farmers and Ranchers (UNAG) and the Chamorro administration that promised workers possession of an estimated 80 properties in a 20-year lease with a right to purchase (Everingham 2001; Gonzales 1994). Under this agreement, various state-owned properties would be renamed The Workers' Property, or APT, and beneficiaries would include rural workers, ex-military personnel and even some ex-Contra combatants. The APT is often represented as a hard-fought victory for the ATC to protect farmworker's claims to those lands in the face of privatizing counter-agrarian reform taking place under the neoliberal government (Abu-Lughod 2000). As Abu-Lughod argued, without pressure from the ATC, the Sandinista military and the Contra resistance, the transitional government may have taken an even harder line on property restitution to their ex-owners, a position strongly favored by the US government. ATC's intervention guaranteed, at least provisionally, that rural workers on the state-owned enterprises would benefit from the FSLN-led agrarian reform and win some small piece of land redistributed following the civil war. In total, the APT represented 33 agro-industrial enterprises with 10,000 worker shareholders (Rocha 2003). Nine of those enterprises were based in the coffee sector and encompassed some 17,000 ha of coffee orchards (Rocha 2003). The APT coffee enterprises were vertically integrated into one exporting company called AGROCAFE which had 2032 worker shareholders and produced roughly 7 percent of total exports in 1994 (Rocha 2003).

Unlike agrarian reform titles given to individual- or even collectively owned properties, land titles under the APT rested with jointly owned businesses (Rocha 2003). In these cases, worker shareholders in the businesses did not appear on the actual land titles for the APT coffee estates (Gonzales 1994; Nitlapan-Envio 2000; Rocha 2003). This created

of possibility for successive export booms. As Biderman explained, "the process of dispossession and 'commodification' of land which began in the coffee areas during the late nineteenth century was generalized and intensified after 1950, during the cotton and cattle booms. In addition to making land a commodity which was increasingly appropriated by larger capitalist producers, the dispossession of small food producers forced them to sell their labor power (at least on a seasonal basis) in order to survive. Though some proletarianization did occur, the expansion of coffee did not eliminate servile or precapitalist social relations, which continued to predominate … [yet] even this interpretation may exaggerate the extent to which there was a real evolution towards capitalist development (as opposed to continued primitive accumulation)" (Biderman 1983, 11).

considerable ambiguity over who actually owned the properties and who made decisions (Nitlapan-Envio 2000; Ramirez 2011). Ex-state officials and party leaders who negotiated the *Concertacíon* in 1991 maintained tremendous control over administering the properties and, in some cases, as Ramirez argues, even took ownership themselves through an extension of the infamous piñata (Ramirez 2011, see also Gonzales 1994; Rocha 2010). In sum, against the more romantic image of the APT promoting worker ownership, farmworkers claimed that while they held de jure control over the enterprises, it was really ATC leadership that retained de facto control over the estates and administrative control over all business decision-making (see also Abu-Lughod 2000).

These ambiguities and concerns about worker control created very complicated relations of trust between the rank and file of the ATC, the worker-owners of the APT and the leadership of the APT and ATC in the 1990s. As one informant, Rigoberto, described, 'First it was the people's property and then it was the workers' property'. Satirizing how the previous state officials and party leadership retained control over the APP properties, he continued to explain the APT's logic: 'We are handing over the property to you now and it is yours, but we still need to control it for a while since you can't do it yourselves' (Interview Rigoberto, 26 October 2006). These sentiments expressed by Rigoberto were shared by a majority of my informants and instilled a sense of skepticism about the goals of ATC leadership who resisted the individual parcelization of the estates for workers in favor of collective ownership – concerns later reinforced by the events surrounding the rise of CONSAGRA-AGRESAMI. As I describe in the next section, CONSAGRA-AGRESAMI, through investment, collusion and force, acquired many of the coffee estates held by the APT enterprises with little or no consultation with their worker-owners (Wilson 2013). As I demonstrate, this history of misrepresentation and lack of trust combined with the specific circumstances surrounding the collapse of CONSAGRA-AGRESAMI led rank-and-file farmworkers to demand individual titles for the worker's properties, thereby ensuring greater sovereignty over their own productive assets, instead of conceding that power to the ATC leadership.

The rise and fall of CONSAGRA-AGRESAMI in Matagalpa, Nicaragua

CONSAGRA-AGRESAMI's land acquisition focused almost exclusively on directly and indirectly accumulating previously state-owned and worker owned land assets. An estimated 80 percent of the coffee estates they acquired were APT properties (Interview, Enrique, 22 October 2006). CONSAGRA-AGRESAMI grew so large as a coffee enterprise that, according to a report by the rural development think-tank Nitlapan, based at the University of Central America, it was responsible for 40 percent of total exports in 1999 (Nitlapan-Envio 2000). But CONSAGRA-AGRESAMI was not just a coffee producer and exporter. In the same study conducted by researchers at Nitlapan, they showed evidence that the conglomerate leveraged their APT assets for further investments in sesame processing and export companies, a sugar refinery, shrimp enterprises and a cattle-breeding operation, all with links to other enterprises assigned to APT enterprises following the *Concertacíon* (Nitlapan-Envio 2000). The CONSAGRA-AGRESAMI consortium was seen as such an excellent speculation that investors with the second-largest private financial institution in Nicaragua, Banco Intercontinental S.A. (or INTERBANK), had bankrolled it to the tune of 52 million US dollars (NotiCen 2000). INTERBANK, formed with Sandinista capital in 1992, made CONSAGRA-AGRESAMI 40 percent of its entire loan portfolio (Nitlapan-Envio 2000).

The leadership of CONSAGRA-AGRESAMI capitalized on the ambiguities over land ownership generated through the transfer from APP to ATP and preyed upon the vulnerabilities of the worker-owners. The economic base of CONSAGRA-AGRESAMI's coffee empire was the coffee estates managed by five APT enterprises in Matagalpa and Jinotega: Juan de Dios Munoz, Jorge Vogl, Deniz Gutierrez, Chale Haslam and Alfonso Nunez (Interview, Enrique, 10/22/06). Each enterprise managed five to nine coffee estates. While the workers vis-à-vis the APT enterprises had won possession of these properties, they lacked working capital to manage them. With coffee prices at record lows in the early 1990s, CONSAGRA-AGRESAMI financed APT enterprises, taking farm leases as collateral for loans. As one of the only active lenders, CONSAGRA-AGRESAMI then provided credit to finance orchard maintenance and harvest costs (Interview, Enrique, 10/22/06). Although CONSAGRA-AGRESAMI did not appear on the legal title, they were able to gain de facto control over the land, labor and coffee production by taking over the leases. As early as 1998, CONSAGRA-AGRESAMI began to usurp APT properties for failing to deliver sufficient coffee to pay off debts.

Another reason that CONSAGRA-AGRESAMI was able to quickly gain control was that leaders of the organization effectively navigated the cultural, political and economic context of post-war Nicaragua (Abu-Lughod 2000). They possessed knowledge of lucrative properties and maintained relationships with state and economic institutions that were knowledgeable about the production potential and ability of the enterprises. CONSAGRA-AGRESAMI's holdings and financing of APT properties was far-reaching. In one of the few published revelations of their dealings with APT properties, La Prensa reported that CONSAGRA-AGRESAMI had mortgages on nine APT properties for nearly USD 6.5 million (Sánchez 2000). However, my informants claimed that these reported holdings represented just a small fraction of CONSAGRA-AGRESAMI's coffee estate assets and only a small portion of APT properties that were registered in their name.

The extent of the conglomerate's investments would not become clear until 2000. In 2000, coffee prices on the world market dropped to record lows, triggering a devastating domino effect in Nicaragua, throughout Central America and around the world. The drop in coffee prices blew down CONSAGRA-AGRESAMI's empire, which turned out to be a house of cards. To try to fend off a total collapse of their speculative agricultural investment, CONSAGRA-AGRESAMI cut their lending and stopped paying workers on the APT properties. In 2001, CONSAGRA-AGRESAMI suffered capital losses on their loans and supply losses from a lack of production. INTERBANK folded under the weight of these outstanding loans. In an investigation of INTERBANK's failure, state officials and journalists descended upon CONSAGRA-AGRESAMI's coffee warehouse in 2001 to find thousands of coffee bags filled with rice shells being used as collateral for short-term pre-export commercial loans to cover their operating expenses.

According to workers I interviewed, CONSAGRA-AGRESAMI cut wages and turned away seasonal harvesters on APT and other properties, starting as early as 1999. Worker households on APT and other properties struggled to meet household food needs, cutting meals and eating foraged bananas, citrus and wild game when available. As all of my informants remarked, hunger was widespread, with some families eating only one meal a day. In one example, an informant explained the traumatic the experience of hunger: 'We were all hungry. The children were starving. We did everything we could to find food. It was worse than anytime I can remember. It was worse than the [civil] war' (Interview, Maura, 26 October 2006).

Worker communities faced down the prospects of hunger-based migration, but lack of food wasn't the only problem. With the liquidation of CONSAGRA-AGRESAMI's assets and foreclosures on coffee estates throughout the region, many workers were also evicted from the land. Beginning in May 2001, workers began to abandon the coffee estates in search of food, work and shelter, forming makeshift encampments along the highway in the central Matagalpa Valley.

Convergence spaces: movement formation and the Las Tunas Accords

Even though the encampments were initially formed as centers for food aid and shelter, their function grew to encompass much more. They were small communities that enabled social movement formation. The proximity of so many workers in these 18 encampments provided a critical opportunity to organize and pressure the government to act on their grievances. The organizing experience of the workers inhabiting the encampments was tremendous. Some had been rural union organizers since the 1970s. Others had served in the military during the civil war. Building on the experience of guerrillas and military personnel, the encampments were also structured in a platoon style with appointed leadership, political orienteers to provide motivation, rationing of food and water and a range of camp maintenance duties for residents.

While the encampments were initially composed of and coordinated by men who were ex-military personnel, women with no military experience played an important role in the adoption of non-violent tactics that built broad-based legitimacy for their cause. Although the experience of many men in the encampments revolved around military service, many of the women drew upon shared experiences of a different kind. Their social networks were established through seasonal agricultural work, their household labor and their relations within churches. While men may have approached the coordination of the encampments like guerrilla columns, the presence of entire families and communities looked nothing like a military unit. Women brought a different perspective on the struggle and the strategy. Marta, a woman with four children, remarked, 'It was a battle, but we all weren't soldiers'. According to Marta, the women brought pragmatism and peace to the encampments: 'We were little communities and we had to account for everyone's needs and everyone's abilities. The strategy came from that' (Interview, Marta, 6 November 2006). Another union organizer, Tomasa, remarked that 'if we didn't agree with what the men were advising we would disagree. We outnumbered them so they'd listen. We said we were not going to take up arms. We had to protect the children and the elderly' (Interview, Tomasa, 6 November 2006). Dinora, an elderly woman, claimed that men thought they were in charge but that it was ultimately women who made many of the most important decisions: 'We cooked the food. We coordinated the encampments. When we marched we organized the provisions. Women and men shared responsibilities in the movement' (Interview, Dinora, 22 October 2006).

My informants suggested that the Las Tunas movement did not result in armed conflict or violence because of the involvement of large numbers of women as leaders and participants. In fact, the symbolism of women leading the movement, often with their children in tow, shaped public perceptions of their cause. As a result, the Las Tunas movement projected a very different image in the struggle for land than did past conflicts. Armed violence disappeared, and in its place emerged the image of a woman trying to protect her children. The non-violent tactics employed through the image of motherhood engendered strong sympathies. The presence of women and children in the encampments and the later marches gave the movement legitimacy and what Margarita, an organizer from El Tuma, called a kind of 'transcendent' quality: ' It was a transcendental cause. We had been abandoned to die, but we would not die. We had to fight' (Interview, Margarita, 12 November 2006).

The material reality of hungry children and hungry women struggling to feed them established some credibility of the movement within the media outlets and created a powerful symbol with which to shame the government. Such attention to the material situation of farmworkers and such a powerful symbolic narrative would have been impossible had the movement been led solely by ex-military combatants.

Women's leadership and participation in the movement also pressed concerns other than those related to land into discussion. While the movement focused almost exclusively on gaining control over land, women that I interviewed in the movement frequently contextualized access to land among a range of other demands that included permanent employment, just salaries and educational and health care access for themselves and their children. Yet for the majority of my informants, improving the conditions of wage work alone would never be sufficient. The decline in coffee prices had revealed that farmworkers in the Matagalpa Valley were expendable. Marta, a middle-aged woman with two young children, described why they organized the encampments:

> We wanted [the state and the landowners] to listen and to fulfill our demands. We no longer wanted to be forced to work on the estates. Many days and nights in this struggle I would cry for this little piece of land where our family could live in peace. (Interview, Marta, 6 November 2006)

Farmworkers' lack of control over land, as Marta's comments illustrate, reproduced the conditions of their exploitation in a property regime that 'forced' them to work for their own survival (Wilson 2013). The collapse of CONSAGRA-AGRESAMI and the need to form encampments merely spotlighted their lack of control over land for subsistence production and to gain some semblance of freedom and independence from the estates (Wilson 2013).

In each of my interviews, Las Tunas movement participants articulated a demand for individual property titles, effectively subdividing CONSAGRA-AGRESAMI properties and redistributing the land to each movement participant based on the estates they heralded from. The leadership of ATC, which negotiated on behalf of those in the encampments, however, steered the farmworkers toward a different goal: gaining control over CONSAGRA-AGRESAMI properties as collectively owned estates. Given the ATC leadership's knowledge of legal uncertainties and foreclosure proceedings surrounding the CONSAGRA-AGRESAMI landholding, they targeted the land for reclamation and demanded that the government create a land bank for landless coffee farmworkers in the region.

With 3000 farmworkers surrounding the secondary school in Las Tunas, on 13 September 2002, the farmworkers were represented by a negotiation team from the ATC and representatives from the UNAG, as well as FSLN party members and the mayors of San Ramon, El Tuma, La Dalia and Matagalpa. The government agreed to the demands set forth by the ATC. The agreement contained four major points. First, the parties agreed that 12 properties in possession of CONSAGRA-AGRESAMI were to be retitled under agrarian reform law in the names of workers occupying those properties under a 20-year lease. This was feasible since the bankruptcy of the company had left the fate of those lands to be negotiated by state officials. Second the parties agreed to a new 20-year lease and debt relief for six APT enterprises managed by the workers due to the coffee crisis and their manipulation by CONSAGRA-AGRESAMI. Third, government officials agreed to establish a land bank with its existing land assets and to construct new settlement projects to house workers in key locations within Matagalpa. Fourth, the parties agreed to an emergency employment fund to put 6000 workers in temporary jobs.

In the years following the Accords, movement participants claimed that the interests shaping the Las Tunas Accords continued to reflect those that led to the formation of the APT in the first place. At Las Tunas, FSLN leaders once again stepped into the foreground to represent the farmworkers. No rank-and-file member of the ATC participated directly in negotiations or signed the accords. Indeed, although the farmworkers had suffered in the encampments and articulated a diverse set of demands which included land for subsistence, their representatives seemed to be negotiating a very different kind of agreement – one which ensured that CONSAGRA-AGRESAMI assets would remain intact rather than falling into foreclosure or into the hands of individual farmworkers. This is not to say that the goal of gaining control over CONSAGRA-AGRESAMI properties was not shared among many farmworkers in the Las Tunas movement, especially those who worked or lived on those estates. However, what was absent in the Las Tunas Accords was a clear description of how the lands would be transferred in those estates, and how they would be divided and redistributed to workers in the movement – goals which more closely reflected the aspirations of the farmworkers.

Broken promises: afterlives of the Las Tunas Accords

To fully understand how the Las Tunas Accords diverged from the early goals of the farmworkers to transform the conditions of their marginality, it is necessary to understand their aftermath. Nearly one year after the Accords were signed in July 2003, I began my field research on the Las Tunas movement. In July, farmworkers took to the highway again to demand the fulfillment of the Las Tunas Accords. 'The March of the Hungry', as they named their protest, was not hyperbole. With coffee prices remaining at record lows, the populations living in the encampments in Matagalpa not only continued but also swelled from an estimated 5000–6000 people in 2002 to more than 7000 by 2003. Farmworkers who returned to the encampments struggled to organize politically while ensuring their material survival. It was already 9 months after signing the Accords, and state officials showed absolutely no signs of fulfilling their end of the bargain to redistribute land from the estates slated for reform in the Las Tunas Accords. Indeed, the Accords seemed to have been abandoned by state officials.

I first encountered the March of the Hungry on 30 July, as they were setting up camp for the night on a hillside pass called Cerro Largo (Long Hill), located halfway between the city of Matagalpa and Las Tunas. It was lunch-time and groups were eating around communal pots of donated rice. Entire families had been brought along, many with nowhere else to go. The heavy rain was unrelenting. Leaders had made the thoughtful decision to end the day's march at 12:00 p.m., following the death of an infant from a fever and an elderly man from dehydration and exhaustion that morning. It was a grim scene. The marchers were in mourning and visibly exhausted. All were concerned about the poor and deteriorating weather conditions. Throngs of people unprepared for the rain stretched from the foreground to the horizon. Crowds of people stood, sat and slept on the side of the road, still many kilometers away from their intended destination.

After speaking with ATC leaders, I began to circulate among the camps to distribute sheets of black plastic for pitching makeshift tents. As I walked among the crowd, I noticed a group of families who appeared to need more shelter. There I met Soledad, a mother of three teenage boys. I asked her why she had come to Cerro Largo; why she had joined the march. Her voice was soft but earnest: 'Because we exist', she said

(Interview, Soledad, 30 July, 2003). I squatted down to hear her more clearly. The cold rain began to pound harder against the tarp above our heads, nearly drowning out her voice.

> We have been abandoned, but we still exist. The workers, the campesinas, the people of the countryside. Where we live, it is just a little place, but there are many hungry people there. There are many communities just like ours where the children are malnourished, without homes and sick. We have been forgotten but we exist. So we have come here to the road to see that the government fulfills our demands. (Interview, Soledad, 30 July, 2003)

Over the next hour, Soledad explained her demands and the demands of others in the march. While Soledad called for the fulfillment of the Las Tunas Accords, she and 35 other families in her community specifically demanded legal possession and individual land titles for a 154-ha coffee estate called La Suana where they had worked and lived for more than 30 years. La Suana was acquired in the 1980s by the revolutionary state and was designated as part of the APP. In the early 1990s, La Suana was re-designated as part of the APT within the enterprise called Chale Haslam. CONSAGRA-AGRESAMI acquired the estate in a shady deal around 1996. Soledad did not know much about the firm or how CONSAGRA-AGRESAMI had acquired the property. But the consequences of the conglomerate's financial and legal maneuvering were all too clear in 2000, when the enterprise collapsed. Soledad and her husband helped organize the workers of the La Suana estate into an encampment and pressed for the estate to be included in the Las Tunas Accords. They had been successful in that regard, but they still had not received title to the property and still feared that their claims were insecure. Some 90 people from La Suana, including children and elderly, were marching again to Las Tunas to win that security. 'We will continue on', she said, 'with only God by our side' (Interview, Soledad, 30 July, 2003).

Soledad's existential claim – 'we exist' – captured the moral outrage of the other marchers that I interviewed as well as the desperate situation in which they had found themselves. After 3 years of struggle in the encampments, many of my informants still had not received land nor any of the other promised reforms. Life in the encampments was taking an intense physical and emotional toll. The sense of hope that animated the early movement had waned. None of the farmworkers knew whether all the suffering that the movement participants had endured would actually generate any results. Those who did remain involved held dearly to the possibility of breaking the cycle of vulnerability faced by generations of landless farmworkers. In an interview with Soledad in 2007, she reflected on the difficulties of 2003 and her hope that through her participation in the movement, her children and grandchildren would break the cycle of landlessness and insecurity that she lived through:

> We endured the hot sun and hunger, slept on the ground, and all with our children. All I wanted was for the state to fulfill the Accords and that they would turn over the land that I had struggled for so I could forget this situation and leave it behind. I told my husband that I hoped God would touch the hearts of these people, that they would give us the land so that my children and grandchildren would be able to stop running on this treadmill like my parents, like me; working from age 13 as a farmhand on the estates. (Interview, Soledad, 26 April, 2007)

Soledad's sentiments about the desire to break away from her dependence on unstable wage work were shared by other informants surveyed in 2006 and 2007 in the communities of La Pintada, San Jose and La Lucha. Marcos, a community leader from La Pintada, also traced this desire for land as the underlying promise of the peace accords in 1990 and the Sandinista Revolution before it. He explained, referencing the promise of agrarian reform:

> Land for those who work it. We fought for it in the 1970s and the 1980s. I have brothers that died for that land. The Las Tunas Accords must be fulfilled. They must fulfill a promise made to me and the workers so long ago. (Interview, Marcos, 15 December 2006)

In 2003, the March of the Hungry effectively brought state officials back to the table to negotiate the titling and transfer of the properties appearing in the 2002 accords. At that meeting, the Accords were revised to include more specific details on the CONSAGRA-AGRESAMI properties to be transferred, and details regarding the assignment of land in government-owned properties to farmworkers. Ultimately, while the March of the Hungry did raise national consciousness of the crisis faced by farmworkers, it did not achieve its intended goals quickly. In fact, it was not until 2004 that the state finally provided formal documentation to movement participants. By that time, many farmworkers had given up on the movement, leaving the region altogether to find food, work and shelter. As Marcos said, referencing attrition from the movement, ‘that was the saddest thing to see, people who had lost everything and struggled with us those years, but they just couldn’t continue. The struggle lasted too long’ (Interview, Marcos, 15 December 2006). Maura, an encampment leader from San Jose and mother of two teenage girls, explained the situation of attrition in the camp she helped organize:

> In 2002, the first time we went [to Las Tunas], there were 32 households with us. By 2004, it was just 14 heads of family. There were only a few of us who still believed we might still be able to win the land. By the end, people were just begging for employment again. (Interview, Maura, 26 October 2006)

Enrique, an ATC leader heavily involved in organizing the encampments, estimated that more than 2000 people who marched on Las Tunas in 2002 had left the movement by 2004 (Interview Enrique, 22 October 2006).

When the government finally provided legal documentation to the remaining farmworkers still engaged in the Las Tunas movement in 2004, it became apparent that the ATC leadership in Matagalpa intended to pursue collective worker-ownership and to consolidate the properties into a vertically integrated coffee producing cooperative – intentions that diverged from those expressed by the majority of landless farmworkers in the movement. In other words, ATC leadership in Matagalpa was interested not only in land reform but in enterprise development, effectively requiring that the coffee estates *not* be subdivided into individual parcels that corresponded to each movement participant. In sum, the ATC leadership demanded that the coffee estates remain much as they had under the APT. Although this was ideologically framed as an effort to promote worker-ownership and cooperativism, my informants from worker communities argued that this ideology had not originated in the bases of the movement. The concept of preserving the integrity of the estates through collective titles had been introduced from above by ATC leaders. Like the critique of the politics surrounding the APT properties (Abu-Lughod 2000; Everingham 2001), my members from the worker communities argued that the ATC leadership could continue to exercise de facto control over these prized assets created through the privatization of the state-run enterprises in 1991, a perceived agenda which has ultimately strained relations between the ATC and the movement base in the years since the Las Tunas Accords.

For farmworkers who persevered in the encampments until 2004, the state provided documents of possession with 20-year leases for land in 19 coffee estates composed of roughly 3000 ha. After some 4 years of organizing, roughly 600 farmworkers emerged from the long struggle with a claim on a piece of land. However, to my informants from La Suana, La Pintada and San Jose, even those documents remained suspect. The lease documents for each estate noted the names of individual farmworkers from that estate who participated in the movement. However, the legal ownership structure, as the ATC negotiated, had been written to reflect collective management of the estates as a whole. For instance, in the La Suana estate where Soledad lives, 55 names are represented on the land lease. Internal conflicts over how to distribute the land immediately emerged. All of the estates included more than 100 ha of cultivable land, in most cases more than 3 ha of area for subsistence plots per beneficiary. But there was no blueprint for distributing parcels. Moreover, all of the estates included more than 50 ha of coffee orchards which were in poor condition but nevertheless represented a valuable asset. As my informants explained, the distribution of land for subsistence tended to benefit men over women either in the size of the claims or the quality of the land. In La Lucha, women claimed that the men had usurped the 60 ha of coffee orchards for themselves and treated the women only as laborers. The uneven distribution of benefits created tremendous frustration in the communities, leading to strife among reform beneficiaries, particularly men and women.

Another problem confronted by beneficiaries in La Suana, La Pintada and La Lucha was the incursion of opportunitists claiming to own land within the existing estates or arriving with falsified documents and claiming to appear in the Las Tunas Accords. In La Suana, 35 claimants usurped a quarter of the estate and, according to Soledad and her husband, had acquired support from the ATC to settle on the property without the consent of the farmworkers who lived there. Within the year, Soledad explained, that group had sold the property to a foreign investor from El Salvador with property elsewhere in the region. A similar story was recounted by the leadership of the La Pintada community, where people arrived to the property with a previous land reform title to stake a claim on a small portion of the estate, only to sell it shortly thereafter. These opportunistic actions by outsiders not only upset and frustrated the reform beneficiaries but also threatened their fragile claims by challenging the legal integrity of their documents and the boundaries of their land claims. Indeed, as pieces of the properties were sold off – some through distress sales (Jonakin 1996; Broegaard 2005, 2009) – Las Tunas Accord beneficiaries who did not sell also feared that these new landowners might themselves begin to manipulate the land titles so that, in the future, they might try to displace the farmworkers once again. In La Suana and La Pintada, reform beneficiaries made accusations that this smaller scale land grabbing went so far as to even implicate leaders of the ATC.

Soledad's story, like many of those who received land following the Las Tunas Accords, offers a critical perspective on the continued vulnerability of the farmworkers who marched on Las Tunas. After ensuring that her name – as well as that of her husband, brother- and sister-in-law and three sons – appeared in the registry of the La Suana estate, by participating in 3 years of active protest, she was allotted 2 ha of coffee orchards and shared a 3-ha plot for subsistence production within a management plan established by the male leaders on the collectively held property document provided through the Las Tunas Accords. However, as early as 2006, she had already become entangled in a legal dispute over the coffee orchards apportioned to her. Coffee orchards in the La Suana estate were very valuable, and pressure on the Las Tunas beneficiaries to sell the property was particularly strong.

The La Suana estate was located at high altitude and close to paved transportation routes and the city of Matagalpa. By late 2006, half of the original farmworker claimants, including Soledad's brother-in-law, were in the process of selling small plots of land to various buyers. Soledad's coffee orchard was claimed by one of the opportunist landholders who had settled on the farm in 2004. With little money to pay legal expenses to fight the dispute, she went to the ATC leadership in Matagalpa to support her land claim. However, the ATC leadership would not intervene, claiming that it was an internal matter to be dealt with by the collective as a whole. When I visited Soledad in 2007, she explained that she had given up the case for her coffee orchard for lack of money and concerns that pursuing the case further may put her and her family in difficult position vis-à-vis other members of the collective and the ATC leadership. With tensions rising, she decided instead to work with her youngest son to cultivate the remaining 3 ha of land in corn, beans, squash and other vegetables allotted to her. She remained optimistic about retaining her subsistence plot. But when I returned again in 2012, she explained that over time it had become increasingly difficult for her to co-manage her plot with her son, who was beginning a family of his own. She was going to abandon her small subsistence plot and return to work at a neighboring estate to earn cash for herself and her household.

Conclusion

The history of the Las Tunas Accords and the farmworkers' movement that brought them about offer critical insights on resistance to control grabbing. As I have illustrated, large-scale land acquisitions like those achieved by CONSAGRA-AGRESAMI are entangled in historical geographies and embedded within much longer histories of land conflict and struggle that are still unsettled. Untangling the history of agrarian reform in Nicaragua, as I have demonstrated, was crucial to making sense of the rise of CONSAGRA-AGRESAMI as well as the particular political objectives of the rank and file of the Las Tunas movement. Out of the makeshift encampments of evicted and unemployed workers in Matagalpa, thousands of people pressed the state for more than 3 years to gain a little piece of land, a backstop against continued food insecurity.

At the root of the control grab and the resistance movement lay the contradictions of the FSLN-led agrarian reform in the 1980s, the conflicts over property in the post-war period and the failed consensus on how rural labor should organize and be represented in the face of land re-concentration and capitalist consolidation (Abu Lughod 2000; Rocha 2010). In the face of an unstable property regime, and experiencing the violent effects of a failed speculative investment, workers within the Las Tunas movement encampments articulated demands for individual land titles. These demands diverged sharply from the strategy of the ATC leadership, who wished to keep the foreclosed properties intact as they had under the banner of the APT. Although the ATC strategy ultimately achieved a significant victory by forcing a redistribution of 19 coffee estates to workers, in the end, some 75 percent of farmworkers behind the barricades in 2002 would never see the benefits of even a small piece of land for subsistence. For many who marched on Las Tunas, the struggle simply lasted too long. The time horizon to victory combined with the subsistence crisis and political repression in the encampments ultimately led to broken spirits and attrition. Even for beneficiaries of the Las Tunas Accords, many live in fear of losing the small gains they made over 3 years of protest.

The story of the Las Tunas movement demonstrates that resistance against control grabbing is not only about defending the land of the landed, but implicates the landless as well. A focus on farmworkers in land grabbing research can highlight the pernicious and violent environments produced by unstable property regimes, control grabs and the capitalist circuits that benefit from them. It is my hope that the story of CONSAGRA-AGRESAMI illustrates these implications of speculative investments and land control grabbing. The history of the Las Tunas Accords also demonstrates the aspirations, betrayals and hard struggle of farmworkers and other surplus people who fight for a land and livelihood in the face of repetitive and ongoing control grabbing (Gould 1998; Li 2009). Indeed, the difficulties confronted courageously by farmworkers like Soledad and the others who marched on Las Tunas are a testament to the struggle of precarious classes and surplus people struggling for land reform all over the world.

Acknowledgements

I would like to thank the Land Deal Politics Initiative (LDPI) organizing committee, Cynthia Gorman and three anonymous reviewers for their critical comments and encouragement. Most importantly, I would also like to recognize the farmworkers of Matagalpa and, specifically, participants in the Las Tunas movement whose testimonies form the basis for this work. Their daily struggles against injustice in the coffee lands are a constant reminder of the violence of dispossession perpetuated by land grabbing.

Funding

This research was made possible by funding from Fulbright, a small grant from the LDPI and a Faculty Development and International Travel grant from West Virginia University.

References

Abu-Lughod, D. 2000. Failed buyout: Land rights for contra veterans in postwar Nicaragua. *Latin American Perspectives* 27, no. 3: 32–62.

Araghi, F. 2009. The invisible hand and the visible foot: Peasants, dispossession and globalization. In *Peasants and globalization: Political economy, rural transformation, and the agrarian question*, eds. A.H. Akram-Lodhi and C. Kay, 111–47. London: Routledge.

Bair, J., and M. Werner. 2011a. Guest editorial. Commodity chains and the uneven geographies of global capitalism: A disarticulation perspective. *Environment and Planning A* 43: 988–97.

Bair, J., and M. Werner. 2011b. The place of disarticulations: Global commodity production in La Laguna, Mexico. *Environment and Planning A* 43: 988–1015.

Biderman, J. 1983. The development of capitalism in Nicaragua: a Political Economic History. *Latin American Perspectives* 10, no. 36: 7–32.

Borras, S.M. Jr, and J.C. Franco. 2012. Global land grabbing and trajectories of agrarian change: A preliminary analysis. *Journal of Agrarian Change* 12, no. 1: 34–59.

Broegaard, R. 2005. Land tenure insecurity and inequality in Nicaragua. *Development and Change* 36, no. 5: 845–64.

Broegaard, R. 2009. Land access and titling in Nicaragua. *Development and Change* 40, no. 1: 149–69.

CIERA (Centro de Investigaciones y Estudios de la Reforma Agraria). 1989. *La Reforma Agraria en Nicaragua 1979–1989.* 10 vols. Managua.

Enriquez, L. 1991. *Harvesting change: Labor and agrarian reform in Nicaragua, 1979–1990.* Chapel Hill, NC: University of North Carolina Press.

Everingham, M. 2001. Agricultural property rights and political change in Nicaragua. *Latin American Politics and Society* 43, no. 3: 61–93.

Glassman, J. 2006. Primitive accumulation, accumulation by dispossession, accumulation by 'extra-economic' means. *Progress in Human Geography* 30: 608–25.

Gonzales, M. 1994. APT: café dulce, café amargo. *Revista Envio*, 147 http://www.envio.org.ni/articulo/847

Gould, J. 1998. *To die in this way: Nicaraguan Indians and the Myth of Mestizaje, 1880–1965.* Durham, NC: Duke University Press.

Hart, G. 2002. *Disabling globalization: Places of power in post-apartheid South Africa*. Berkeley, CA: University of California Press.
Harvey, D. 2003. *The new imperialism*. Oxford: Oxford University Press.
Jonakin, J. 1996. The impact of structural adjustment and property rights conflicts on Nicaraguan agrarian reform beneficiaries. *World Development* 24, no. 7: 1179–91.
Li, T. 2009. To make live or let die? Rural dispossession and the protection of surplus populations. *Antipode* 41, no. 1: 66–93.
Li, T. 2011. Centering labor in the land grab debate. *Journal of Peasant Studies* 38, no. 2: 281–298.
Nitlapan-Envio. 2000. Interbank bankruptcy opens a Pandora's box. *Revista Envio*. Managua, Nicaragua. http://www.envio.org.ni/articulo/1444
NotiCen. 2000. *Nicaragua: Bank scandal prompts political fights and complicates debt reduction*. The Free Library. Latin American Data Base/Latin American Institute. Accessed December 22, 2014.
Pearce, F. 2012. *The land grabbers: The new fight over who owns the earth*. London: Transworld and Boston: Beacon Press.
Peluso, N.L., and C. Lund, eds. 2011. New frontiers of land control. *Journal of Peasant Studies* 38, no. 4: 667–81.
Perelman, M. 2000. *The invention of capitalism: Classical political economy and the secret history of primitive accumulation*. Durham, NC: Duke University Press.
Ramirez, S. 2011. *Adios Muchachos: A memoir of the sandinista revolution*. Durham, NC: Duke University Press.
Read, J. 2002. Primitive accumulation: The aleatory foundations of capitalism. *Rethinking Marxism* 14, no. 2: 24–49.
Rocha, J.L. 2001. The chronicle of coffee: History, responsibility and questions. *Revista Envio*. 241, Managua, Nicaragua. http://www.envio.org.ni/articulo/1523
Rocha, J.L. 2003. La Decada de los Años 80: Revolucion en Nicaragua, Revolucion en la Caficultura Nicaraguense. *Anuario de Estudios Centroamericanos* 29, nos. 1–2: 69–99.
Rocha, J.L. 2010. The contradictory legacy of the sandinista agrarian reform. *Revista Envio*. http://www.envio.org.ni/articulo/4212
Sánchez, M. 2000. Agresami hipoteca 9 fincas millonarias. *La Prensa Nicaragua*, August 16.
Sikor, T., and C. Lund. 2009. *The politics of possession: Property, authority, and access to natural resources*. London: Wiley-Blackwell.
White, B., Borras, S., Hall, D., Scoones, I., and Wolford, W. 2012. The new enclosures: Critical perspectives on corporate land deals. *Journal of Peasant Studies* 39, nos. 3–4: 619–47.
Wilson, B. 2013. Breaking the chains: Coffee, crisis and farmworker struggle in Nicaragua. *Environment and Planning A* 45: 2592–609.
World Bank. 2010. *Rising global interest in farmland: Can it yield sustainable and equitable results?* Washington, DC: World Bank.
Zoomers, A. 2010. *Globalisation and the foreignization of space: Seven processes driving the current global land grab*. *Journal of Peasant Studies* 37, no. 2: 429–44.

The 'Goan Impasse': land rights and resistance to SEZs in Goa, India

Preeti Sampat

Conflicts over land-grabs for industry, infrastructure and urbanization are on the rise in emerging economies. A slew of policy measures undergird such land deals in India but have encountered successful resistance from peasants and citizens groups. In Goa, resistance led to the revocation of the state's special economic zone (SEZ) policy and cancellation of all approved SEZs, many developed by prominent realty firms. As battle over three SEZs continues in the Supreme Court of India, there is hope that commons will be returned to local communities. There is, however, an impasse on the ground that begs resolution if the gains over SEZs are to be secured. The Goan Impasse can be resolved with egalitarian and ecologically appropriate rights to land- and resource-use for all that counter existing inequalities. This requires programmatic social movements reconstituting relationships around and to land and resources from below.

> If so many people come to this land it will be polluted and our environment destroyed .... We have small plots of land, if they get destroyed, where will we go? Put it up anywhere else, but not on our lands. Our cattle get fodder from that land. Where will we go if a project comes there? Night and day, we left our meals and affairs and took a lot of trouble to oppose the project. ... If we give up this land, where will we go?
>
> Chinu Gawde of Kerim, peasant in her seventies and veteran protestor in Nylon 6,6 and SEZ agitations in Goa, interview 5 July 2012; translated from Konkani

Land-grabbers don't always win. Sometimes resistance thwarts land-grabbing, rendering possible a fundamental reconstitution of relationships with land and resources. In the western Indian state of Goa (Figure 1), intense opposition by peasants' and citizens' groups[1] in 2007–2009 led to the cancellation of all approved special economic zones

---

[1]I use the term peasants' groups here to refer to small and marginal land-owning farmers with less than 10 and two acres of land respectively, landless agrarian workers, pastoralists, fisherfolk, forest dwellers and other petty commodity producers. In India, peasants are also further stratified along ethnicity, religion, caste and gender lines.

Citizens' groups here refer to coalitions of individuals, often concerned professionals and representatives of non-governmental organizations (NGOs) that coalesce around contentious issues. They are not NGOs in themselves, and often do not take institutional funds or salaries, but are rather concerned people working voluntarily for campaigns who raise resources through individual donations.

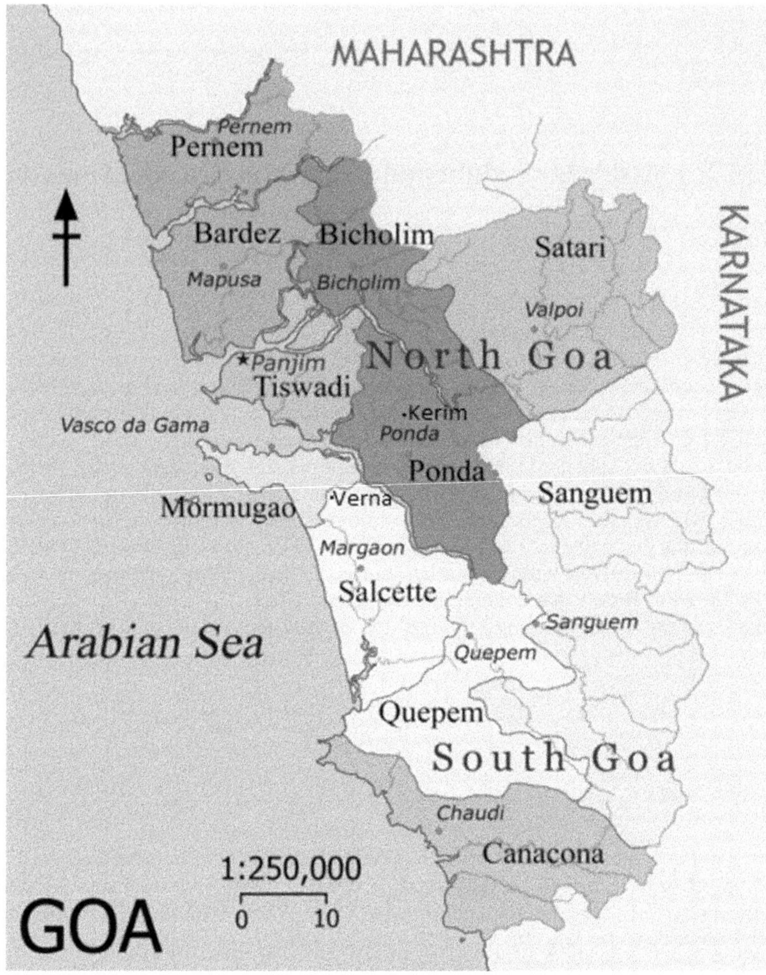

Figure 1. District and Taluka (administrative block of district) map of Goa.
Source: Map adapted from http://en.wikipedia.org/wiki/File:Goamap.png 126 × 158 mm (96×96 DPI).
Note: Names in Italics are major cities and towns or Taluka headquarters.

(SEZs), some with construction underway. The state government subsequently revoked its SEZ policy. As SEZ developers and agitators took matters to court, an 'impasse' emerged on the ground.

Indian SEZs were envisaged as comprehensive export-oriented enclaves for manufacturing, mining, agriculture and services, with considerable tax, environment and labor concessions under a 2005 national law. Goa's SEZ policy was drafted in 2006,[2] although some SEZs were approved in undue haste even before the policy was enacted. The extent of land allotted to Goan SEZs was relatively small (especially compared to other Indian states), totaling less than 4000 acres. There was also little fresh land acquisition for Goan SEZs, as most of the land allotted was already 'in possession'

[2]Several states enacted SEZ policies in consonance with the national law.

of the state government. By mid-2007, allegations of real estate scams and corruption catalyzed a Goa-wide anti-SEZ campaign, as a dynamic alliance of social forces drew on the state's living history of environmental activism, and assertions of 'Goan identity' (Figure 1).

Goa was not the only Indian state where SEZs became extremely controversial during this period, but it was the only state to officially revoke its policy and cancel all SEZs. How did this significant 'reversal of power' come about in Goa? What historical, political, economic and cultural specificities and strategies led to the success of Goa's anti-SEZ campaign? What are the implications of the 'Goan Impasse' for 'rights to land- and resource-use for all'[3] in Goa, and, by extension, in India? As 'capitalism-facilitating accumulation' (Adnan 2013, 123)[4] intensifies after over two decades of liberalization in India, investments in SEZs are crucial 'spatial fixes' (cf. Harvey 2001) for domestic and transnational capital. In what ways does resistance to dispossession, articulated through local histories, offer a counter to contemporary capitalist growth, and transformative potential for 'reconstitution from below' (cf. Barker et al. 2013)? The following account is organized around these questions.

The first section gives an overview of SEZs in India, locating them in contemporary global land-grabs; it introduces the resistance to SEZs in Goa and what I call the 'Goan Impasse', and contextualizes the emergence of Goa's anti-SEZ campaign in the state's vibrant history of environmental activism. The second section offers an account of the development of the anti-SEZ campaign, specifically by what came to be the SEZ Virodhi Manch (SVM; Anti-SEZ Front), an alliance across caste, class, gender and community difference that proved critical to the campaign. The third section analyzes the factors enabling the campaign's success. The final section discusses likely resolutions for the Goan Impasse; the possibilities for rights to land- and resource-use for all in its wake; and the relevance of such rights for Indian struggles against dispossession, and towards egalitarian reconstitution from below. The ethnographic account reveals the particularities that helped successfully reverse state policy, rare in the Indian context, and helps sift broader lessons for relationships to land and resources in the context of contemporary Indian land-grabs. The paper is based on fieldwork over five months between January 2012 and January 2013 in Kerim, Verna and Loutolim villages and Panjim (capital of Goa) and Margao cities in Goa.

---

[3]Albertina Almeida helped frame this as use-rights. In an earlier work I have used this phrase to refer to contextualized, ecologically appropriate and egalitarian land- and resource-use rights that counter prevailing caste, community, gender and class inequalities (see Sampat 2013; also Borras and Franco 2010 for pro-poor land reforms).

[4]Adnan (2013) offers this as a generic concept for transnational, domestic and local processes of primitive accumulation and accumulation by dispossession (distinguished as distinct phases) through direct and indirect mechanisms and institutions. Recent conceptual refinement has led some to describe land-grabs as only those land deals that are executed through 'extra-economic force' (see Levien 2012; Borras and Franco 2013; also Hall 2013 for an overview). My preference here is to go along with Adnan (2013) in contextualizing land-grabs within capitalist-facilitating accumulation that encompasses broader forces facilitating dispossession. I find the distinction between 'extra-economic' and 'economic' coercion unhelpful in the processes I describe below (there was little forcible acquisition in Goa), and prefer to think of coercion as the political aspect in political economy that may be deployed by 'the state' (and private actors) or 'the market'. The distinction between extra-economic and economic coercion then emerges from a forced distinction largely between the state and the market that under conditions of capitalism is only heuristic.

Contextualizing the conflict over SEZs

Land-grabs for industrialization, infrastructure and urbanization

In so-called emerging economies, land-grabs by domestic capital for industry, infrastructure and real estate form predominant capitalism-facilitating accumulation strategies. While recent land-grab literature focuses on acquisitions by global capital for agriculture (White et al. 2012; Margulis, McKeon, and Borras 2013; Borras, Franco, and Wang 2013), acquisitions by domestic capital (that may also be transnational[5]) for industrialization, infrastructure development and urbanization have received inadequate attention (see Walker 2006; Levien 2012 for exceptions).

In India, concerted policy emphasis aiding such accumulation is exemplified in the new land acquisition law[6] that deems investments in industry, infrastructure and urbanization 'public purpose', eligible for forcible land and resource acquisition. A slew of recent measures like the National Manufacturing Policy 2011, Public Private Partnerships Policy 2011, Petroleum Chemical and Petrochemical Investment Regions 2007 and the SEZ Act 2005 undergird this emphasis. Other market-led agrarian reforms (see Borras and Franco 2010) like the Land Titling Bill 2013 additionally promote regularization of land holdings to facilitate market transactions (Sampat 2013). Official data reveal that from 2007–2011, India's cultivable land area has shrunk by 790,000 hectares, largely due to diversion for construction, industries and other development activities (Mohan 2013).[7] Transfer of land and resources by force or market transactions towards industry, infrastructure and urbanization, with conflicts over such transfer, have consequently seen a phenomenal rise in recent years (see Banerjee-Guha 2008; Levien 2012; Chakravorty 2013; Podur 2013; Sampat 2013).

Indian SEZs, as comprehensive export-led enclaves with 'state-of-the-art' infrastructure and urban amenities, are at the same time not just another model of export-led 'exceptional' zones. In their scale and scope, and the broader field of policy contextualizing them, they represent a normative model of 'development' under liberalization that is increasingly conflated with 'economic growth', and the growth of (largely but not only) Indian capital. Expanding domestic capital has invested enthusiastically in Indian SEZs (see also Levien 2012). Thus, despite the 'global financial crisis'[8] between 2008 and 2011, the number of SEZs formally approved by the Government of India (GoI; federal) nearly doubled from 404 to 747 (GoI 2011a).[9]

Only 50 percent of SEZ land is legally restricted for economic activities;[10] the rest is dedicated for 'social infrastructure' like residential complexes, malls and golf courses.

---

[5]Land Matrix data show that 1,289,000 hectares have been acquired in 39 deals by Indian companies for agriculture in Africa and Asia (Rebello 2013; see also Grain 2008).

[6]The Right to Fair Compensation and Transparency in Land Acquisition and Rehabilitation and Resettlement Law 2013 was enacted in September 2013.

[7]A 2009 federal Committee on Land Reforms decried growing corporate investment in indigenous areas 'as the biggest land grab of tribal lands since Columbus' (GoI 2009, 160).

[8]The Indian economy was relatively insulated from the 'global crisis' in 2008–2011 by a combination of monetary policy, expanding domestic market and capital and a mixed bag of stimulus and welfare entitlements (see Subbarao 2009; UNDP 2011).

[9]This is not to imply that transnational capital of foreign origin has not invested in SEZs at all; Indonesian SALEM Group and South Korean POSCO are two examples of more controversial foreign investments in SEZs.

[10]Initially 25 percent, this limit was later raised on account of controversy.

Many SEZs have thus attracted developers who seek cheap land to 'develop' and sell at a high premium, especially in urban peripheries with real estate stakes. With their peculiar infrastructure–real estate configuration, Indian SEZs have thus formed significant avenues for the expansion of Indian capital, and have been roundly criticized as real estate grabs (see CPI (M) 2006; Basu 2007; Banerjee-Guha 2008; CAG 2008; Gopalakrishnan and Shrivastava 2008; Kale 2008; Sampat 2008, 2010; Levien 2012).

Peasants' and citizens' groups, on the other hand, have fiercely resisted SEZs, primarily (though not only) on account of land and resource transfers to SEZs.[11] In West Bengal, Maharashtra, Goa, Karnataka, Odisha and other states, the model attained notoriety within two years of legal enactment. As state governments responded variously with violent repression, tactical reversal and/or negotiations, the national SEZ policy framework underwent significant revision. In a letter to all states as early as April 2007,[12] for instance, the federal Board of Approval (BoA) for SEZs instructed that:

> The State Governments would not undertake any compulsory acquisition of land for setting up of the SEZs. BoA will not approve any SEZs where the State Governments have carried out or propose to carry out compulsory acquisition of land for such SEZs after 5th April 2007. (official copy obtained by author)[13]

This was a significant reversal, albeit little celebrated by peasants and citizens groups who in all likelihood were not even aware of it at the time.[14] The measure nonetheless reflects the vitiated national environment against SEZs and the scale of popular resistance that state and central governments faced. Resistance to land acquisition for SEZs became a major factor influencing the trajectory of the SEZ model and the national land acquisition law eventually enacted in 2013 after much unrest.

The Goan Impasse

On 31 December 2007, then-Chief Minister (CM) of the state Digambar Kamat buckled under pressure and announced 'a new year's gift to the people of Goa', scrapping all approved SEZs. The federal government declined to honor the decision for three SEZs that were already 'notified' (given final approval),[15] and Kamat declared that SEZ developers in Goa could 'go ahead at their own risk'. Soon after, the Goa government issued show-cause notices to SEZ developers for land allotment cancellation. Five developers

[11]Under the Indian Constitution, land comes under the jurisdiction of state governments. Acquisition for SEZs was thus initially undertaken by state governments through national or state-level acquisition laws, and state governments consequently bore the frontal brunt of anti-SEZ oppositions.
[12]The letter was backed by a circular to all states in October 2009.
[13]The provisions of India's Right to Information (RTI) Act 2005 significantly enabled research and I obtained copies of relevant public documents including this letter through its provisions. This law has been extensively used to obtain information, catalyze resistance and challenge SEZs in Goa and elsewhere in India.
[14]The onus for ensuring that no forcible acquisition was undertaken was left to the state governments, however, with no clear procedure for penalizing violations.
[15]SEZs are given final approval by an inter-ministerial BoA presided over by the federal Ministry of Commerce and Industry. Final notification is given when all land has been acquired by the developer and the SEZ is ready to start operations.

Table 1. Overview of Goa's special economic zones (SEZs).

Government of Goa approved SEZs		No.	
Total SEZs with government of Goa approvals		15	
Area allotted for 15 SEZs		1510.83 acres	
Projected investment		USD 2012.41 million[a]	
Projected employment		599,500 jobs	
Formally Approved SEZs (2nd stage of approval)	**No.**	**Location**	**Area (in acres)**
Total formally approved SEZs	7	Verna Industrial Estate	498.95 (4 SEZs)
		Sancoale Industrial Estate	50.31 (1 SEZ)
Employment expected (in five years)	312,000	Bhutkhamb Plateau	304.43 (1 SEZ)
		Soccor	45.71 (1 SEZ)
		Total	899.40
Notified SEZs (3rd stage of approval)	**No.**	**Developer**	**Area (in acres)**
Total Notified SEZs	3	K. Raheja SEZ in Verna Industrial Estate	261.70
Employment expected (in five years)	175,000	Peninsula Pharma SEZ in Sancoale Industrial Estate	50.31
		Meditab SEZ in Bhutkhamb	304.43
		Total	616.44

Source: Compiled by the author from GoG (2007).
Note: [a]At then prevailing rate of Rs. 43 = USD 1.

challenged the state government's decision in the High Court of Bombay at Goa,[16] as anti-SEZ campaigners appealed for accountability (punitive action) for irregularities in the SEZ approval and land-allotment processes. The court upheld the government's decision and took note of procedural irregularities, but stopped short of punishing responsible officials. The developers then challenged the ruling in the Supreme Court (SC) of India, while anti-SEZ campaigners simultaneously appealed to the higher court for accountability. The matter is currently under litigation, the legal status of the five SEZs and lands allotted to them unresolved. Until such time as the SC pronounces its verdict, an 'impasse' issues on the ground.

Politicians, bureaucrats and citizens' groups openly acknowledge, however, that this impasse is more in the nature of legal procedure, as politically it seems unlikely that SEZs will be reestablished in the state. De facto, the lands are under the watch and use of local communities since 2007. Even before the CM's announcement scrapping SEZs, villagers had thrown out construction crews in two SEZs where construction had begun, and would not let company personnel enter the premises. In Kerim village at the time of fieldwork in 2012–2013, *dhangars* (members of a pastoral nomadic community) freely grazed their cattle on 'SEZ lands'.

Of the 15 Goan SEZs given 'in-principle approval' (first stage of approval) in 2006–2007, seven received the federal government's 'formal approval' (second stage of approval) by 2007 (see Table 1 below). A total of 1510.83 acres were approved for 15 SEZs,

[16]Goa has a dedicated bench of the High Court of Bombay.

combining commons previously acquired by the Goa Industrial Development Corporation (GIDC) from *Comunidades*[17] and land claimed to be directly owned by developers. As such, they would not directly displace people and villages. While an additional 1548.44 acres was to be freshly acquired for four SEZs, final allotments for them never took place (Da Silva 2014). Towards the end of 2007, three of the seven formally approved SEZs were notified by the federal government: K. Raheja SEZ, Peninsula Pharma SEZ (both realty firms); and Meditab SEZ.[18] Construction had begun on two, K. Raheja and Meditab.

The anti-SEZ agitation was overwhelmingly a response to land- and resource (largely water)-grabbing for real estate and industry. While the scale of SEZ lands was small, Goa's relatively small size and existing burdens on land and resources made these transfers controversial. The state government was seen as *arbitrarily* and *illegally* handing over local land and resources to developers for profit from industry and residential colonies for rich metropolitans. It was not just the 'terms of inclusion' or exclusion (cf. White et al. 2012) of the people impacted by the SEZs that constituted the heart of contention; SEZs were perceived as adversely impacting existing local livelihoods and relationships with land and resources. The anti-SEZ agitation was principally against the use that the land was being put to, and against *anticipated dispossession* in the backdrop of accumulation processes already underway. The agitation quickly gained momentum, sundering the state–capital alliance over SEZs and reshaping the 'rule of law' in its ferment of dissent.

The 'Goan Impasse' over SEZs, however, is not just an impasse for capital, domestic or otherwise, nor is it only an impasse for state policy promoting capital. The Goan Impasse represents a deeper historical impasse – over 'rights to land- and resource-use for all' – confronting peasants' and citizens' groups resisting dispossession in Goa, and elsewhere. It establishes the role of 'the state' as contested space working on behalf of particular social forces at specific conjunctures (cf. Abrams 1982). A closer reading of the ethnographic material suggests that its resolution requires a renewed political commitment to locally ecologically appropriate, egalitarian and democratically determined development processes. This requires an alliance of social forces that can *oblige the state* to secure rights to land- and resource-use for all. In successfully pressuring the state to revoke the SEZ policy, the Goan Impasse renders possible fundamental reconstitution of relations

[17]Traditionally, *gaonkars* were considered the original inhabitants of a village, with collective ownership of land and resources leased for cultivation to 'users' through auctions. The income from auctions was equitably distributed among the *gaonkari* and the land could not be sold or converted for non-agricultural purposes. A share-holding system incorporated non-*gaonkars*. The *gaonkari* assigned fishing and market zones to fisherfolk; land to washers, barbers and gravediggers; land for crematoriums, housing and agriculture; and were responsible for the protection of fields, bunds, sluice-gates and other structures; and building and maintaining village temples and, later, churches. The Portuguese retained and legally codified this system as *Comunidades*. Anti-caste activists point out that Dalits, so-called 'lower' caste and indigenous communities and women, were not members of *Comunidades*, and whether traditional *gaonkari*s were more egalitarian is disputed. At present, *Comunidades* are present in every village and, in some villages like Loutolim and Verna, Scheduled Tribe members and women have shares in *Comunidades* depending on their economic capacity to buy shares. *Comunidade* areas have reduced considerably since 1961, with growing private fields, forests and orchards. The British colonial legacy of eminent domain supersedes *Comunidades* with land acquisition for 'public purpose', including industrial estates (see Sridhar 2010).

[18]K. Raheja and Peninsula have realty projects in several Indian cities. CIPLA's company profile describes it as one of the largest Indian exporters of pharmaceutical products with 'a strong presence' in over 170 countries and 'strategic arrangements' in the U.S. and Europe (see K. Raheja Corp 2012; Peninsula Land 2012; CIPLA 2012).

with land and resources from below, and indicates the significance of such reconstitution in other areas of land-grab in India.

This significance was driven home to me one overcast monsoon afternoon in 2012 near Bhutkhamb. I had joined artist and activist Dilesh Hazare, whose lush watercolors evoke his verdant Western Ghat[19] surroundings in Kerim village, on a tour of historical, religious and spiritual places of significance around the plateau. It was early evening when we reached the entrance of the Meditab SEZ (currently under litigation), fenced with over 10-foot-high barbed wire, cut wide in several places. We saw cattle grazing on the fenced-in land. As I stopped to click photographs, a woman carrying a headload of fuelwood made her way out from the 'SEZ land' through a cut in the fence, with her herd of about 40 goats. I called out a greeting to find out more. During the course of our conversation, Salu Kodekar, in her mid-fifties, revealed that she grazed her cattle on the plateau every day. When I asked her about the SEZ, she added:

> ... I have goats and cows, we have taken our animals to the plateau for grazing from the beginning ... we will only allow a factory to come up on the land if it gives something to us, gives us jobs, I don't have any other land to take the animals ... my knees hurt but this is my livelihood, I have to take the animals to graze for my stomach .... (Interview 7 July 2012; translated from Konkani)

About 50 meters from where we talked, just across the road from the SEZ entrance, lay the *samadhi* (a square stone memorial typically six feet across) dedicated to Nilesh Naik, Scheduled Tribe (ST; indigenous)[20] youth from Kerim 'martyred' in a police confrontation over the Nylon 6,6 agitation in 1995 for the same plateau, against a project of the transnational Du Pont. In Goa, as elsewhere, STs are predominantly peasants and among the state's poorest communities. The settlement around the *samadhi* where Kodekar lives is a *dhangar* settlement. Given their pastoral origins, *dhangars* are not originally from Goa, but some families settled here in the 1960s. *Dhangars* are typically not land owners and have no shares in *Comunidades*, generally subsisting as peasants and workers. Calls for a 'Goan identity'[21] may or may not resonate with equal valence for them as for others with deeper ancestral roots in the area. But they, along with other local communities, have a clear stake in the local commons and political economy.

Salu Kodekar and Nilesh Naik are at the crux of the Goan Impasse, mediated as it is by caste, community, gender and class inequalities. What happens to the SEZ lands once the SC verdict is out – to what end these lands and water resources are used and controlled and by whom – will reveal possibilities of the gains made over SEZs. Can the anti-SEZ agitation facilitate programmatic social movements with ecologically appropriate egalitarian

[19]Geographically, Goa lies between the Western Ghats mountain range and the Arabian Sea (see also Figure 1).

[20]Scheduled Tribes (STs) are indigenous communities noted in the Indian Constitution and historically oppressed by dominant Hindu upper-caste and other communities.

[21]A discussion of the frame of 'Goan identity' in the anti-SEZ agitation is taken up later in the paper. Goa was a Portuguese colony for 451 years, and its accession into India by the Indian military (that then ruled the state for six months) was controversial, with allegations of Indian imperialism. In 1967, an opinion poll was conducted by the GoI on Goa's merger with Maharashtra. A majority of Goans voted against the merger, consolidating Goa's status as a distinct political entity, albeit within the Indian union. Debates around the opinion poll articulated and mobilized a distinct 'Goan identity' and brought together the Hindus and Catholics threatened by a merger with Maharashtra (Rubinoff 1992).

agendas that actively counter existing inequalities? Unless this deeper resolution is attained, the conflict over SEZs may return in another form, pitting the forces of capital, state and peasants' and citizens' groups in standoff yet again. That evening, as Hazare and I turned a bend a few hundred meters from Bhutkhamb, in the valley to our right lay a massive mound of upturned loose black earth, waste from iron ore mines dumped unceremoniously, bearing witness to the implications of another resolution of the Goan Impasse.

A living history of environmental activism

Goa has a tropical moist climate and is marked by three broad types of physical divisions: the Western Ghats mountain range, the midland plateaus and the coastal areas. Nine river systems flow through the state, of which the river Sal originates in the Verna plateau. Each physical area has its own ecological and cultural characteristics impacting local political economies.

Extensive laterization with rich iron oxides that give Goan soil its deep red color have turned the state's mountainous region into a controversial mining belt. Rampant illegal and ecologically destructive mining has destroyed many water sources and adversely impacted agriculture. Diligent litigation by environmental activists, reports of judicial commissions and inquiries, however, have resulted in suspending all mining operations in Goa since 2012, pending comprehensive investigation.

Along the coast, tourism has been the economic mainstay. Policy frequently reflects the interests of pressure groups, with government machinery rewarded for non-enforcement or misinterpretation of rules (Alvares 2002). Violations of regulations for coastal zones, building height, untreated sewage release in the sea and extraction of groundwater causing salinization of aquifers are frequent. With returns from tourism, sand dunes are denuded or razed for unhindered views; *khazan* lands (low-lying coastal lands collectively used for salt pans, rice cultivation and prawn farms)[22] neglected; and land increasingly converted for beachfront hotels, beach shacks, restaurants and other entertainment activities (Alvares 2002; Kazi and Siqueira 2006).

The midland plateaus are traditionally used as grazing lands and form rich catchment areas for water, their laterite caps acting like sponges to store water and forming abundant sources for agriculture in the valleys and plains around them. The state's 21 industrial estates are atop and around several of these officially 'barren' plateaus acquired by the GIDC from *Comunidades*, and have been the source of much grievance and agitation.

Traditionally, Goan villages have congregated in the plains, the undersides of plateaus, or the coastal stretches, with no settlements atop the plateaus and sparse settlements in the mountainous Ghats (Alvares 2002). Goa's history of environmental activism has consequently unfolded along the plains, plateaus and coastal stretches. Earlier major agitations coalesced around Zuari Agro Chemicals in Sancoale in the 1980s; the Konkan Railway along coastal areas from the late 1980s – early 1990s; the Nylon 6,6 Du Pont plant in Bhutkhamb plateau from the late 1980s – early 1990s; the Meta-Strips plant in the late 1990s near Verna Plateau; and the state-wide Regional Plan (RP) 2011 in 2006. Numerous smaller local actions and legal activism by concerned individuals and citizens' groups in villages are also common. I briefly discuss below the agitations against Nylon 6,6, Meta-strips and the RP-2011, as these have closer bearing on the anti-SEZ agitation.

[22] *Khazans* are reclaimed from marshy mangroves by constructing dykes and sluice-gates.

Nylon 6,6

Bhutkhamb plateau near Kerim village (also the site of Meditab SEZ) is traditionally used for grazing and has religious significance for local communities with designated worship areas. The plateau serves as a water catchment area for the groves and farms around it. In the late 1980s, the GIDC acquired land on Bhutkhamb for Nylon 6,6 production by (transnational) Du Pont in collaboration with (Indian) Thapars. Despite using two highly hazardous chemicals (adipic acid and hexamythelenediamine), Nylon 6,6 was officially declared pollution free. As residents discovered environmental hazards, a long, drawn-out, state-wide agitation spanning several years was catalyzed. In a final showdown in 1995, the police opened fired at protesters, killing one, Nilesh Naik from Kerim (whose *samadhi* lies across Bhutkhamb today). In retaliation, protestors beat up the police, stripping some and chasing others into the woods, proceeding to the company's office in nearby Ponda town and burning everything they could find there, including cash. Thapar–Du Pont found no relief even in the court, which refused to extend police protection or issue restraint orders against protesters on account of the industry's pollution-generating potential. The company eventually shut shop and relocated to Tamil Nadu (see Alvares 2002; Sadhle 2000). This living history has significantly shaped local relationships with the plateau. While a largely younger generation spearheaded the anti-SEZ agitation, several veteran protestors from the Du Pont agitation supported their efforts.

Meta-Strips

The Meta-Strips agitation of the late 1990s unfolded around the Sancoale plateau (the site of Peninsula SEZ). Meta-Strips was to import and process scrap from Europe, sending valuable metals back and disposing of the waste in Goa. The project got the Government of Goa (GoG)'s clearance in 1996 in a record six days. An environmental impact assessment was conducted to preempt opposition, but it obfuscated potential hazards of the industry, that included unacceptable levels of toxic and carcinogenic metal fumes and groundwater pollution (Alvares 2002). Residents from surrounding villages, including the Verna plateau area (Sancoale and Verna are 10 kilometers apart), organized a campaign with road blockades and sit-ins facing severe police repression that resulted in serious injuries, and the death of a policeman. Meta-Strips retaliated by booking cases against activists in different states to harass them. By May 2000, with intense agitation on the streets, and the company's electricity and water supply cut, the High Court refused to entertain the company's applications for continued electricity and water supply citing environmental concerns. The state government finally ordered the plant shut and created an 'expert committee'. The committee confirmed the project's environmental hazards but did not recommend closure, recommending instead costly investment in pollution control. The plant operates today but its production is drastically reduced and it has had to invest heavily in pollution control technology (Alvares 2002).

Regional plan 2011[23]

The more recent state-wide anti-RP-2011 agitation in 2006 was spearheaded by the Goa Bachao Abhiyan (GBA; Save Goa Campaign) and foregrounded growing real estate pressures. Tourism and migration (both intra- and inter-state, given Goa's high human

[23]This account is largely constructed from interviews with Goa Bachao Abhiyan (GBA) activists (also Savegoa 2012).

development indicators; see PTI 2011) have put Goa on the real estate map and are exerting a pull on agricultural land, commons and forests. The phenomenon of 'second homes' or 'holiday homes' for rich metropolitans vacationing in Goa and keeping properties locked for most of the year is seen to drive property prices beyond local affordability.[24]

In 2006, when a resident of the popular tourist village Baga noticed construction on a local hill and made inquiries, he discovered that the entire hill was demarcated as 'settlement' area (with permission for real estate development) in the RP-2011 released earlier that year, whereas it was in reality a 'green' area (forest, agriculture or otherwise non-settlement). As he studied the plan with an architect, they discovered that large swathes of green areas were shown as settlement. They began sharing this information widely. News regarding the 'conversions' spread, and concerned residents of various villages undertook studies that disclosed that many mangrove forests, coastal regulation zones and fields were demarcated as settlements in the RP. After an initial meeting of a heterogeneous group of professionals, non-profits and interested persons, the GBA took shape and organized several public meetings. These culminated in a huge meeting in Panjim of about 10,000 people, and a subsequent protest at Margao demanding the cancellation of RP-2011. On Republic Day in January 2007, several *gram sabhas* (village assemblies) then took resolutions to scrap the RP-2011. The Goa government, under considerable public pressure with elections later that year, gave in and withdrew the RP-2011 by February 2007.

Reelected to power that year, the Congress government constituted a 'task force' with representatives from the RP agitation to design a methodology for drafting a new RP, subsequently changing its mandate to drafting the RP-2021. Resident committees from various villages undertook detailed physical and demographic mapping exercises for a locally appropriate RP-2021, but their submissions were disregarded, fueling controversy yet again. For a combination of reasons including the SEZ agitation, the opposition Hindu-right Bhartiya Janata Party (BJP) subsequently came to power in 2012, promising a review of the RP process in its election manifesto. The RP was set aside, however, as controversy over rampant 'illegal' mining absorbed state affairs from September 2012.

A mixed social base of caste, class, gender and community identities has been a historical feature of environmental struggles in Goa, and defies their categorization as 'environmentalism of the poor' (Guha and Martinez-Alier 1997, 3).[25] Agitations have comprised men and women; professionals and peasants;[26] educated, semi-literate and nonliterate people; Catholics from Scheduled Tribes, mixed-caste or Brahmin communities;[27] Hindus from various castes; and unconverted STs. Livelihood concerns flowing from environmental and infrastructure stresses are significant. Identities and

[24]A recent report puts the number of such houses at 21.8 percent of Goa's total houses (Firstpost 2013).

[25]This is not to 'exonerate' hierarchies within social movements, or to diminish the extremely necessary and important work of gender-, caste- and other community-based mobilizations for equity and justice.

[26]Peasants from ST and Scheduled Caste (so-called 'untouchable') communities often tend the lands of upper caste Catholics and Hindus and/or have small holdings. Depending on their class status in some villages, they may purchase *Comunidade* shares to cultivate rice, tend coconut and betel-nut groves, grow fruits and vegetables, produce coconut oil and farm prawns and other shellfish.

[27]Depending on a Catholic person's locality of origin, their 'original' caste can be determined and often, though not always, corresponds with their socio-economic status; Brahmin and 'upper-caste' Christians are generally better off than SC and ST Christians.

relationships around land and resources additionally form important refrains for mobilization. These struggles have also largely emerged in the more populated hence electorally significant plateau and coastal regions, enabling often-successful negotiations with the state. They have uncovered official disregard of environmental destruction and traditional livelihood bases in favor of capital, and a corrupt system enabling state and private actors to violate laws. *Land and resource grabs for capitalism-facilitating accumulation thus form a historical trajectory of development and resistance in Goa post 1961*,[28] and have had an abiding if implicit impact on the SEZ agitation. It is pertinent that the Congress Party came back to power in 2007 with the fresh experience of the state-wide RP-2011 agitation. By the time the SEZ agitation coalesced later that same year, the party was likely not in a position to politically withstand another state-wide agitation.

Amka Naka SEZ! Amka Zai PEZ! The anti-SEZ agitation

We don't want SEZ! We want PEZ![29]

> We had planned to take … ordinary dharna [sit-in] outside the police station. Means assemble at Azad Maidan [public park in Panjim]. We had a crowd which came from everywhere. Kerim was very supportive, Verna, Sancoale also, Loutolim … We made placards … We were supposed to have a silent march … We came out from the Azad Maidan, we crossed the street, we came to the police headquarters and we were supposed to stand out and you know, put those placards … Then, we just started moving … We just walked towards the gate, the gate was open, we expected them to close or come and stop us … Nothing happened, we just proceeded … We walked inside, the crowd followed. Inside we are scared and we were worried something may happen to us … They might lathi-charge [baton-charge] or something … But the crowd just moved in … 100–150 people … They wanted to arrest us … But we put the ladies in front, the Kerim ladies in front and the way they shouted … I'm sorry to say we abused the Goa police over there … We shouted … Goa police chor hai! [Goa police are thieves!] … We went to that extent, in the police headquarters, and the first time in the history of Goa … Next day it was headlines … . (Charles Fernandes, SVM Convener and small-scale businessman from Loutolim, interview 22 June 22 2012)[30]

The following account of the anti-SEZ campaign in Goa is predominantly from the perspective of SVM members.[31] Initial citizens' efforts around SEZs included a communication in 2005 about possible SEZs in Goa, between John Pereira from the Sancoale area to then Industries Minister (who claimed that no SEZs were planned in Goa); a symposium on SEZs by the Council for Social Justice and Peace (CSJP; the social work wing of the Archdiocese of Goa) in 2005 in which the Secretary, Industries Department, responded to questions raised by the women's non-profit Bailancho Saad; a Roundtable on SEZs by newly formed SEZ Watch in 2006 that resolved to track SEZ developments and contact affected villages; and a *gram sabha* resolution opposing SEZs in Verna initiated by Peter Gama in

[28]See Raghuraman (2013) for a discussion of the predominantly mercantile capital interests during and soon after Portuguese rule in Goa and Newman (1984) for an account of Goa's transformation into a bourgeois capitalist society post-1961.

[29]Pez is rice gruel in Konkani but as an acronym here also doubles as People's Economic Zones.

[30]I have deliberately avoided using the indicator 'sic' to resist privileging standardized English over local parlance.

[31]The caste and community affiliations of the individuals mentioned in this narrative are not explicitly disclosed given cultural sensitivities, but, needless to say, form major axes of inequality.

January 2007, after then CM Rane inaugurated the K. Raheja SEZ. It was not until after Monteiro stumbled upon information regarding SEZs however, that a concerted campaign effort coalesced.

The notified K. Raheja and Peninsula SEZs were located in Salcete *taluka* (administrative block of district) of South Goa district, with the largest Christian population (57.4 percent, GoI 2001a). The notified Meditab SEZ was in Ponda *taluka* of North Goa district, with a high Hindu population (84.9 percent, GoI 2001a). Consequently, the cultural idioms and repertoires of activists from the two *talukas* differed. I use the terms protesters, campaigners and local residents interchangeably in the narrative, but reserve the term activist for key organizers, although many local residents became politicized and evolved into key activists over the course of the agitation.

People's movement against SEZs

In the spring of 2007, Franky Monteiro, a small-scale builder from Loutolim village near Verna plateau, got wind of a Twenty-point Program (TPP)[32] approved by the GIDC on land acquired from Loutolim and Verna *Comunidades*. A response to his RTI application (see note 12) turned up inadequate information, and he requested an inspection of relevant documents. It was during the inspection that, he says:

> ... I found this minutes of the 287 meeting of the [GIDC] board of 19th April [2006] which showed land being given for SEZ companies to the tune of around 22 lakhs of sq. mts., four companies, and it said it was for SEZs. Now to me at that time, SEZ, I did not even know what was SEZs ... It seemed to be a very nice word, like special economic zones. So ... then I said let's just find out what is SEZ .... (Interview 5 January 2012).

Monteiro first obtained relevant information, 'which company had asked [for] what, what was the date of the minutes, everything'. Figuring project details, he was shaken:

> ... I saw that they were supposed to be declared as autonomous bodies, out of the control of the local bodies as well as the state government. There were ... no revenue for the local government where it was all supposed to be export-oriented ... and they were supposed to be given uninterrupted water ... and power supply, they were supposed to be having their own law and order ... I said ... this cannot happen here. I thought like if five SEZs means there will be five enclosures doing whatever they want in there ... and then ... SEZs included commercial units, recreational centers, hotels, resorts everything. So I said this cannot be ....

Monteiro, with his neighbor and later Convener of the SVM Charles Fernandes, the village *Sarpanch* (elected head) Sejo Fernandes and several others, began sharing this information with residents of Loutolim, Verna and other neighboring villages. Seven SEZs had been allotted land in April 2006, before the state's SEZ policy was even enacted. Meditab at Kerim and Peninsula at Sancoale were notified by mid-2007, but K. Raheja, notified only in November 2007, illegally initiated construction at Verna before its notification. Internet research by activists revealed that K. Raheja's SEZ was being promoted as a comprehensive

[32]The TPP is a contentious poverty alleviation scheme that has typically allotted *Comunidade* lands for housing low-wage migrant workers in slum-like conditions near industrial estates. These workers often form captive 'vote-banks' for political patrons in return for favors like housing, access to water, electricity, etc. While class-bias is a likely factor in the opposition to TPPs, SEZs were to attract white-collar immigrants, indicating an underlying issue of overburdened local resources and infrastructure.

township of 275 acres called 'Mindspace' on the company's website.[33] Local residents were already facing the brunt of the Verna Industrial Estate (VIE) and felt alarmed at the implications of the residential project for water, agriculture and infrastructure like transport and garbage disposal. In July 2007, residents from villages around the SEZ sites near the Verna and Sancoale plateaus met and subsequently formed the People's Movement Against SEZs (PMAS).

In Kerim near Bhutkhamb, a politically active schoolteacher, Ramakrishna Zalmi, had read a news report about SEZs in 2005. A Goa University seminar on SEZs soon after piqued his interest, and he sought more information. When the non-profit Jagrut Goem organized a meeting on SEZs in Panjim in 2006 with members from PMAS, Zalmi and others from Kerim participated. They sensed that the land lying 'unused' since the Nylon 6,6 agitation might be allotted for a SEZ. The pharmaceutical CIPLA had been active in the vicinity since 2006. At an initial meeting organized by the company, a local youth group, Abhiyan, had challenged its claims regarding local employment generation. Meditab SEZ, eventually allotted land on Bhutkhamb, turned out to be a CIPLA subsidiary.

An informal group of concerned residents in Kerim initially organized meetings with screenings of an anti-SEZ documentary film from Maharashtra, made available by SEZ Watch. In the local village elections, a dentist from this informal group, Dr. Videsh Zalmi, won a seat and was subsequently appointed the village *Sarpanch*. The informal group next formed the Kerim Kriti Nagrik Samiti (Kerim Citizens Action Committee; KKNS or Kerim Samiti) with about 80 registered members, and strategically appointed Dr. Zalmi its president. When the KKNS stepped up advocacy efforts, however, a local politician who was the Member of the Legislative Assembly (MLA) from the Maharashtrawadi Gomantak Party (MGP), whose trucks had been contracted for SEZ construction, allegedly sent people, sometimes drunk, to disrupt KKNS meetings.

Soon, local water tables began declining with illegal bore-wells pumping water for SEZ construction, which created unrest among villagers. When Kerim Samiti members tried to investigate the premises, the private security refused to allow them into the premises. Kerim Samiti then invited the MLA for a joint inspection for illegal bore-wells. On the appointed day the politician went about the premises in his car, while Samiti members on foot took the opportunity to chase construction workers away.[34] Construction soon resumed, and Kerim Samiti now organized a big public meeting in Kerim with support from PMAS, GBA and Jagrut Goem activists. Subsequent meetings were held in surrounding villages and were joined by veteran protesters from the Nylon 6,6 agitation.

As PMAS (now including the Kerim Samiti members) stepped up its agitation, the Goa Movement Against SEZs (GMAS), an outfit enjoying the tacit support of the BJP, now declared opposition to SEZs. PMAS constituents wished to maintain a clear

[33]After anti-SEZ campaigners cried foul over a real estate scam, the Mindspace SEZ advertisement disappeared from the company's website. Campaigners, however, had taken its printouts and subsequently furnished them as court evidence. The company's website still advertises several Mindspace SEZs in different Indian cities. Fieldtrips to the Verna plateau reveal an area ideal for a premium realty project given its location atop the plateau, with sea breezes, pristine views of the Zuari river, proximity to the airport, the Verna Industrial Estate (VIE) and Margao and Panjim cities, and abundant groundwater and natural springs.

[34]Construction workers across India are generally extremely poor and vulnerable immigrants from other states dependent on contractors and local residents for livelihoods and stay. In Goa, they are generally from rural Bihar, Jharkhand and Karnataka.

distance from GMAS, partly because of BJP's religion-based sectarian politics and partly to keep at bay partisan political interests. Late in October 2007, a meeting was held in Panjim with a pan-Goa presence from all SEZ-affected villages and activist groups like the GBA, Jagrut Goem, SEZ Watch, and the CSJP. SEZ Virodhi Manch (SVM; Anti-SEZ Front) now emerged as the new pan-Goa formation of the anti-SEZ campaign.

SEZ Virodhi Manch

From November 2007 to January 2008, the Manch stepped up its agitation, organizing relentless protest actions and public meetings with regular press releases and media reports. In early November, around 200 Manch supporters stormed the K. Raheja SEZ, chanting slogans, demanding construction halt immediately and chasing out the construction crew. Construction resumed and, to SVM's ire, the SEZ was officially notified three days later. Not only was the construction undertaken thus far illegal, the Congress Party had promised a comprehensive review of SEZs. Protest rallies followed. CM Kamat finally formed a Ministerial Committee to review SEZs, and directed the RP-2021 Task Force to prepare a report, as the Congress Party appointed a panel to study SEZs.

In the wee hours of 7 December, as Kerim residents were returning home from a ritual ceremony, they saw a construction truck from the SEZ accidentally ram into an electricity pole. Simmering frustration from having been unable to stop construction sparked a spontaneous decision, to immediately halt construction once and for all. Overnight, Kerim Samiti mobilized surrounding villages and state-wide supporters. Early that morning another minor accident, as a car struck the stationary truck, added to the already agitated atmosphere. Other Manch members, journalists and lawyers arrived by late morning, followed by police platoons. Zalmi recounts:

> We chased all the workers away. It was spontaneous as after the accident we got a chance to chase them. We went to Anna's [local spice plantation owner] and planned for arrests etc. We called four advocates beforehand. Here people are disciplined and don't get out of hand. The agitation was mature. We told the police we'll set fire to the machines. Poornima [from Kerim] threatened to set fire to herself. The police did not touch us. They knew Goa would burn. (interview with Ramkrishna Zalmi, schoolteacher and cultivator from Kerim, 5 July 2012)

The atmosphere remained charged but the police exercised restraint; no violence was reportedly used by either side. Activists warned the police to stay away, claiming SEZs were outside police jurisdiction since they were 'foreign territories'.[35] By evening, all construction workers were rounded up and, in a sympathetic gesture of solidarity for their wage-loss and obvious poverty, transported to the nearest bus terminal by the protesters at their own cost. Machines were brought out of the premises and their owner was warned to take them by the next day, or face damages. Construction never resumed on Bhutkhamb.

Energized by their success in Kerim, Manch members once again stormed the K. Raheja site in Verna on 11 December and chased the construction crew away. The police response was again restrained. In interviews with activists and residents, two likely possibilities emerge for the relatively soft response of the police – that Nylon 6,6 and Meta-Strips agitations had created political apprehensions over the use of violence, and that CM Kamat may have asked the police to go 'soft' to avoid political escalation (see discussion below).

[35]By law, SEZs are deemed foreign territories for all commercial purposes.

A massive public meeting in Margao city three days later gave a major signal of opposition, as about 10,000 people from across the state participated.[36] By 29 December, the Congress Party officially declared SEZs unviable. On the same day, the Ministerial Committee's White Paper echoed this sentiment, but recommended six SEZs. The following day, the RP Task Force concluded that SEZs were detrimental for Goa. That day, about 1000 people from villages around Verna and Sancoale walked in a 10-km rally to the house of the local Legislative Assembly member and then-Industries Minister, Alexio Sequeira, handing him a memorandum opposing SEZs. Sequeira, an ardent supporter of SEZs, was also the GIDC chair when the SEZs were approved and allotted lands. The rally was greeted by a large police contingent but, again, no physical violence was used.

On 31 December, then, Kamat announced his 'New Year's gift' and scrapped all approved SEZs. In early January 2008, SVM next organized a demonstration at the Panjim police station (see quote earlier), since it repeatedly refused to register cases against the Industrial Corporation and SEZ developers. Two days later, the state government issued stop-work orders to all notified SEZs.

By April, the federal SEZ Board conceded to the withdrawal of all approved SEZs, except the three notified at Verna, Sancoale and Bhutkhamb. They urged the state government to come to an amicable settlement with the developers. That same month, the developers and SVM approached the courts. In August 2008, despite the ongoing court case and stop-work order, the Manch members noticed construction activity in the K. Raheja SEZ. This time they stormed the premises and used physical intimidation to stop construction. No construction has taken place on the premises since. The Goa government formally withdrew its SEZ policy in June 2009.

Court proceedings

The first court petition was filed by Pereira and later clubbed with public interest petitions filed by SEZ Virodhi Manch members (with support from a legal aid non-profit), against irregularities in due process. Five developers, including the three notified SEZs, challenged the revocation of the SEZ policy and the issue of show-cause notices for land allotments. Each hearing was attended by 50–200 SEZ-affected residents to demonstrate continued opposition.

The court gave its final verdict in November 2010, and upheld the state government's prerogative to withdraw approvals and revoke the SEZ policy. The court reserved comment on the question of denotification as this was not specifically challenged by the petitioners. Acknowledging gross irregularities, it noted:

> The allotment of lands to the companies has been made in undue haste and without proper scrutiny of their applications. The allotment of lands has been made arbitrarily. Procedure adopted in the allotment is not fair and transparent. The allotments made by the GIDC do not stand the test of reasonableness. (Franky Monteiro and four others vs. State of Goa and six others 2010, 192)

Disappointingly for the anti-SEZ activists, however, no punitive action was taken against responsible officials. All parties subsequently appealed the judgment in the Supreme Court of India, where the case is currently under litigation.

---

[36]Soon after, at the peak of the Christmas–New Year tourist season, the GMAS announced that tourists should leave as a 'Nandigram-like situation' was developing in Goa (see discussion of other mobilizations below).

The professional class of activists from all caste and religious backgrounds bore responsibility for most monetary expenses (institutional donations were refused to retain independence) during the agitation and court proceedings, and for RTI, media and legal tasks. Peasants formed the backbone of public meetings, protest demonstrations and presence at the court hearings. Activists reported receiving 'offers' and indirect messages for peaceful settlement through 'well-wishers', as well as threatening phone calls. Fernandes' two dogs were mysteriously poisoned and killed one night. Faleiro and Monteiro faced bureaucratic delays and rejections for work-related applications. Solidarity, conviction and an abiding sense of ethics and responsibility were cited as sources of strength by activists in continuing the agitation.

Analyzing the success of the anti-SEZ agitation

An alliance of forces: resources, livelihoods, migration and the 'Goan Identity'

The Verna Industrial Estate has been a constant source of grievance for surrounding villages. Industries on the plateau pump ground water to meet their needs, impacting water levels in the area; a Coca-Cola plant is particularly notorious (the company's 2013 avowal respecting community resources notwithstanding; see Coca-Cola 2013). Waste from the industrial area finds its way into fields around the plateaus through canals. Many natural springs in the region, some said to be medicinal, have dried up. The source of the river Sal in the plateau has also been adversely affected, in turn affecting the fields along its banks. Activist Peter Gama of Verna, a civil contractor and *Comunidade* shareholder key to peasant mobilization in the area, points out:

> Sometimes people [would] grow three crops … [on] both the banks of river Sal. During my childhood, Utorda, Majorda [villages] was a famous place for watermelon; that time watermelons are not coming from outside Goa. Now due to scarcity of water this river Sal just dries up in … April … . (Interview, 19 July 2012)

Gawde echoes for the Bhutkhamb area: 'we harvest arecanut [betel-nut] and coconut in our orchard, but when they put a bore well and pumped ground water, we could not grow anything as water dried up … ' (Interview 5 July 2012; translated from Konkani).

SEZs in Goa promised the creation of 599,500 jobs, whereas the state's official unemployment estimate is 80,000. The anti-SEZ agitators were not explicitly against industrialization. In Gama's words, again:

> … Industry means they always promise 80% jobs to locals, but frankly speaking, or in practical, locals peoples does not even get 10% jobs in this industrial belt or area. And that's why we say … migrants, workers are coming from neighboring states, even from Jharkhand and UP [Uttar Pradesh], not only Karnataka and Maharashtra. So my point is this … why they're bringing more factories on this plateau? Instead of bringing factories or industries in this plateau or area, they have to give it to them … Karnataka or Jharkhand … .

Gawde argues:

> if they put up factories they will need technical expertise and such jobs are of no use to us … Using the land for cultivation will give us all work … Here we don't have a hospital or facilities … There is no old age home. That will be of use to us … . (interview, 5 July 2012; translated from Konkani)

Several bureaucrats, developers, activists and others I interviewed claimed that the native Goan population has grown by zero percent in recent decades. Population increases are perceived as resulting from migration. In 2001, immigrants in Goa were about 15 percent of the population, but in 2011 they were reportedly at over 30 percent of the state's 1.5-million population[37] (GoI 2001b, 2011b; TNN 2012). A 2013 government report raises apprehensions that by 2021 the Goan population will be outnumbered by migrants, and a delegation by CM Parrikar to the Prime Minister requested a 'special status' for Goa to prevent sale of land to non-Goans (Firstpost 2013). Shifting demographics have caused insecurity among some, exacerbated by growing resource constraints and rising property prices. Working-class migrants may be vilified as 'criminals' and 'drunks', and white-collar migrants resented with fears in some quarters assuming xenophobic and nativist overtones. SEZs were seen as promoting white-collar immigration to a scale that would destroy or threaten existing livelihoods, resources and infrastructure, raise real estate prices beyond local affordability and threaten local relationships with land and resources. In combination with the historical relationship of Goa to India (see note 21), these concerns fueled the perception and framing of the threat to the 'Goan identity' that SEZs posed.

'Our God was with us ... and God means nature'

A constant refrain among campaign activists, Catholic, Hindu or indigenous, when talking about the campaign's success was: 'our God was with us '. In Kerim, with a high indigenous population, this was almost always followed by 'and God means nature'. Activists from Kerim recounted how they first took the blessing of the village-God *Betal devta* through ritual practice, seeking divine will by the mediation of a priest, using flower petals as means of communication. The local campaign was initiated only after the divination. Borkar (2006) discusses natural worship practices in Goa that have helped conserve its rich biodiversity. Given that plateaus are the main source of water for orchards around them, it is possible that religious significance and 'sacred presence' was historically ascribed to Bhutkhamb for preservation. Residents of all communities recounted going to the plateau to offer prayers on special occasions and claimed that a project would prevent access to worship areas.

The Church is similarly significant to the Goan Christians, with parish sermons every morning and Sunday sermons in the main village churches that families diligently attend. Campaign members in Loutolim and Verna describe themselves as devout Catholics. Post-sermon exchanges helped them share and update information daily during the campaign. In Verna, Loutolim and Sancoale, parish priests also played key roles in mobilizing support against the SEZs. Fr. Jose Dias, a Sancoale priest in 2007 with a personal history of environmental activism from the Konkan railway agitation, and Fr. Eremit Rebello, mobilized support around Sancoale and Verna. Fr. Dias notes a growing awareness of 'environmental protection from destructive development' in the church (interview with Fr. Dias, 27 June 2012). The CSJP's participation and Fr. Maverick's participation were key to the SVM. Local religious values informing and drawing from environmental preservation practices thus added a complementary frame to the anti-SEZ campaign.

[37]The latest census figures for migration had not been officially released as of January 2014, and were unavailable online until September 2014. This estimate is based on a newspaper account of CM Parrikar's speech.

Evidence of irregularities

The GIDC was established to encourage small- and medium-scale industry. Export-oriented large enclaves violated its policy. Documents obtained through RTI applications revealed that not only was land for seven SEZs allotted (and fresh acquisition for one approved) before the state SEZ policy was enacted, all seven applications were incomplete when land was allotted, some missing their company seals. The GIDC approved two of these applications within a day, four within a week and one in 12 days. The land was allotted at discounted rates of approximately USD 14 per square meter[38] in Verna, USD 1.9 in Bhutkhamb and USD 6.3 in Sancoale, on account of a lack of infrastructure (see Da Silva 2014). GIDC's rules mandated individual plots for industrial units, whereas SEZs required contiguous large areas. Open spaces and roads were subsequently allotted to SEZs (initially for free but, after protests, at discounted rate) to help fulfill contiguity requirements. K. Raheja SEZ's status was changed from 'multi-purpose' to 'service sector' SEZ on its lease agreement to fulfill land criteria. Moreover, the GIDC's approval for four additional SEZs (1548.44 hectares) was greater than the total land acquired by it in five years!

According to Goa's Comptroller and Accountant General (CAG), the loss to the exchequer over SEZ land deals was over USD 20 million. The GIDC additionally took upon itself the responsibility to provide water, drainage and roads to SEZs. Rent concessions were also given with fixed rates for 30-year leases. The Town and Country Planning Department was further requested to increase the floor area ratio for new construction from 100 to 150 percent for information technology and other specified buildings, amounting to additional concessions. All of this information was used extensively by the campaigners in their advocacy, negotiations with the state and court arguments. (Da Silva 2014; Franky Monteiro, and others vs. State of Goa and others 2010; CAG 2008; GoG 2007).

Other anti-SEZ mobilizations

The Goa Movement Against SEZs, led by late activist and United Goan Democratic Party (UGDP) politician Mathany Saldanha, shared its platform with Hindu-right political parties like the BJP and the Shiv Sena, and was able to draw upon their network in all 40 state constituencies (Da Silva 2014). During the October 2007 bye-elections in South Goa, the BJP made SEZs a state-wide issue and helped pressure the Congress for a policy review. Initially, the GMAS and the BJP were both in favor of scrapping all except the three notified SEZs, but by November 2007, their demand was for wholesale scrapping of all SEZs. In December, the GMAS held a massive public meeting in Panjim, issuing deadlines to the government and warning of a 'Nandigram-like situation.'[39] On Christmas Eve, at the height of the tourist season, GMAS declared that all tourists should leave the state by 28 December, as the agitation could take an 'ugly turn'. However, while both the GMAS and the BJP helped catalyze a state-wide campaign until December 2007, SVM activists point out that both refrained from taking the issue to the courts, revealing, especially for the BJP, its politically motivated opposition to SEZs.

---

[38]Dollar figures are calculated at the 2006 prevailing rate of approximately USD 1 to Rs. 43.

[39]Nandigram, in West Bengal, was the site of the Indonesian Salim group SEZ that witnessed mass violence through 2007 as local farmers, residents and opposition political parties resisted land acquisition by the state government, with violence peaking in November 2007.

Electoral imperatives and police restraint

Goa has 40 elected representatives in its Legislative Assembly. A simple majority of over 50 percent requires 21 MLAs. Opportunist defections among the Congress, the BJP, the MGP, the UGDP, the Save Goa Front (SGF) or the Nationalist Congress Party (NCP) are common and, especially since the 1990s, the cause of much political instability (cf. Rubinoff 1992). It is very easy for a ruling party to lose its majority as allegiance from coalition partners or ministers from within the party shifts and they (threaten to) defect. Insecurity over electoral outcomes has made parties more receptive to popular pressures in Goa.[40] During and after the 2007 bye-elections, the Congress Party coalition partners had begun voicing opposition to SEZs (Da Silva 2014). As the SEZ agitation came on the back of the RP-2011 agitation, the Congress was unlikely to politically withstand another hostile state-wide agitation.

Internal divisions within the Congress were reflected in senior politicians' views. SEZs were promoted by the previous Congress CM Rane, and it is possible that CM Kamat was more receptive to popular pressure as he did not have a personal stake in them. In his interview, Kamat claimed:

> SEZs in Goa were scrapped because the people of Goa did not want any SEZs. Although one SEZ could have been tried, but it became a serious political problem with 10,000 people on the street and work being stopped so that even under police protection work could not continue. (interview, 20 July 2012)

Rane, on the other hand, favored one or two SEZs for the 'good of the state's economy' and argued that the agitators were parochial, withdrawing into regionalism, and needed to have a broader view, not a 'village mentality' (interview, 20 July 2012). Another senior Congress politician who requested anonymity but was an ardent promoter of SEZs called Kamat a 'weak' CM who should have '*lathi*-charged (baton-charged) the agitators to teach them a lesson' and implement the SEZs.

That the police did not unleash violence despite demonstrations, storming of SEZ premises, chasing of construction crews and even a siege on the police-station, is significant. The historically frequent and often successful negotiations by activists with the state may have impacted police response in the face of massive public protest. The Goan state's 'repertoires of repression' (Edelman and Leon 2013, 19) were blunted by historical 'repertoires of protest' (Tilly 1978, 1986) and electoral political contingencies.[41]

Small state and sympathetic media

The small size of the state worked to the advantage of the campaigners and helped focus media attention relatively quickly. People could congregate in meetings at short notice.

[40]See Heller (2005) for an account of such political pressures in Kerala.

[41]These 'viewings of the state' (Bedi 2013, 41) under CM Kamat's leadership may have enabled the anti-SEZ campaign's success, given the proximity with state actors in Goa and the 'receptivity' of CM Kamat. However, the role of Goa's vibrant history of environmental activism (that is checkered with violence) cannot be discounted in blunting the state's repertoires of repression. At the same time, anti-SEZ oppositions elsewhere have successfully mobilized despite violent repression, such as in Nandigram in West Bengal and Raigand in Maharashtra. In many of these areas and arguably in Goa, peasants' and citizens' groups risked their lives and livelihoods irrespective of state receptivity, to assert rights over land and resources.

As social distance is not acute, people often personally know politicians and bureaucrats and enjoy greater degrees of interaction with them. Frequent communication with government representatives facilitated receptivity to campaign demands. As the agitation intensified, sympathetic media representatives also ensured prompt coverage of events and press releases. Local journalists from Loutolim, Verna and Kerim helped sustain attention on the issue and were reportedly even present during the storming of SEZ sites.

A combination of contextual and contingent factors rooted in the historically interrelated fields of capitalism-facilitating accumulation, environmental activism, religious practices and repertoires of protest and repression contributed to the success of the anti-SEZ campaign in Goa. Such state-level policy reversal is rare, and was aided by the vitiated atmosphere around SEZs across India. How these gains over capital might be further consolidated, and their broader lessons for struggles against dispossession, is the discussion I turn to below.

Resolving the impasse: land rights and democracy

A representative of the K. Raheja SEZ I interviewed indicated unwillingness to give up 'sunk' investment. If lands are returned to SEZs by the Court, however, activists may intensify the agitation again and this time it could assume a very different form from the previously non-violent one. If they are returned to the state's Industrial Corporation, their fate will depend on the next project sanctioned on them. Having fought long and hard, local residents and activists are unlikely to give up easily. At the same time, the irregularities in the approvals and land allotment processes render both outcomes unlikely. How the Court deals with the 'sunk investment' argument remains to be seen, but there is precedent to assume that it may not be favorably disposed. For instance, in Jagpal Singh vs. the State of Punjab and Others (2011, 3), the Supreme Court noted that village commons have been

> grabbed by unscrupulous persons using muscle power, money power or political clout, and in many States now there is not an inch of such land left for the common use of the people of the village, though it may exist on paper .... This was done with active connivance of the State authorities and local powerful vested interests and goondas [thugs].

Dismissing acquisition in the particular instance, the Court further directed all state governments to evict 'illegal/unauthorized occupants of *Gram sabha*/Panchayat [village-level administrative unit]/Poramboke [grazing lands]/Shamlat [common] land' and restore these lands

> to the *Gram sabha*/Gram Panchayat for the common use of villagers .... Long duration of such illegal occupation or huge expenditure in making constructions thereon or political connections must not be treated as a justification for condoning this illegal act or for regularizing the illegal possession. (Jagpal Singh vs. the State of Punjab and Others (2011, 11–12)

The SVM activists have appealed for the land to be reverted to the original owners, the village *Comunidades*. However, there is a difference in local perceptions with regard to *Comunidades*. Verna and Loutolim village *Comunidades* have a mixed membership from communities, with women also holding shares, and are perceived as conducting their affairs transparently. In Kerim, the *Comunidade* is under the control of two Brahmin families who are not from the village and do not enjoy a relationship of trust with local residents. Activists from Kerim prefer that the land be brought under the control of the village *Panchayat*, circumventing the *Comunidade* altogether.[42]

Monteiro argues that combined control by the *Comunidade* and the required *gram sabha* quorum for decision-making, rather than a reversion to the village *Panchayat* or *Comunidade* exclusively is ideal, as the decisions taken by the *gram sabha* are more transparent and hence accountable to local residents. Nevertheless, the fundamental questions of egalitarian access to land and resources and the need for any development project to redress local caste, class, gender and community inequalities remain central to locally appropriate development needs.

Campaign activists have several suggestions for locally appropriate projects that will help conserve the environment and provide jobs to local youth, from agro-processing cooperatives to educational hubs. Existing and potential initiatives include farmers' cooperatives, land rights for Dalit and ST communities and PEZs. A consolidation of the gains made over SEZs, indeed made historically over capital in Goa, requires a renewed political commitment among social forces engaged in struggle, including the SVM. It requires a fundamental *reconstitution from below* of relationships around and to land and resources.

In this regard, a distinction needs to be made between *issue-based campaigns* and *programmatic social movements* with explicit agendas for democratically determined egalitarian and ecologically appropriate development. While SVM was successful as a broad-based campaign against SEZs, a fundamental reconstitution of relationships with land and resources requires focusing on existing and contentious inequalities, also rooted in and limited by *historically instituted social relations of power* (cf. Verdery 2003), such as unsuccessful pro-poor land reforms.

How relevant are the questions of egalitarian organization that the Goan Impasse poses to struggles against dispossession in other states of India? While the specificities of Goa's history and its small size have shaped the success of Goa's anti-SEZ campaign and are difficult to replicate, anti-SEZ agitations in other states have also similarly forged broad alliances of peasants' and citizens' groups, used a diversity of self-reliant mobilization based on voluntary contributions, and successfully blunted the state's repertoires of repression. Electoral implications of popular protests against SEZs have riven the political consensus over SEZs in other states as well. West Bengal is emblematic, where resistance to land acquisition in Nandigram and Singur villages (the latter for an automobile factory, not a SEZ) became a catalytic force in routing the Communist Party of India (Marxist) after nearly 35 years of rule in 2009. While other states where SEZs became controversial may not have revoked SEZ policies or canceled all SEZs, nor indeed witnessed concerted state-wide campaigns, several large SEZs have taken a beating across the country, and the model stands considerably derailed.[43] The question of democratically determined egalitarian and ecologically

[42]*Comunidade* properties have considerably reduced post 1961, and while many villages still have functioning *Comunidades*, these are collective but private bodies. The political and administrative unit at the village level is the *Panchayat*, that in Goan villages may (or may not) have acquired other commons under its jurisdiction since 1961. The *Panchayat* is the official representative body for the entire village.

[43]Recent rescinding of tax benefits by the Finance Ministry, and the global economic slowdown, have served more blows (see Mohanty 2010; Indian Express 2012, 2013; ET 2013). The number of formally approved SEZs was reduced to 576 by mid-2014 (GoI 2014), and a scrutiny of the minutes of recent SEZ board meetings shows growing requests by developers for project withdrawals or extension of approval periods as they fail to acquire desired land.

appropriate rights to land- and resource-use for all, that the Goan Impasse pries open, finds resonance in other areas of land-grabs in India.

The Goan Impasse demonstrates that 'the state', despite interests within it working actively in aid of capital, is not immune to popular pressure (even as 'land broker'; see Levien 2012, 945). This learning has also emerged in the course of successful resistance to SEZs in other areas, such as the Mumbai SEZ in Maharashtra or the Mangalore SEZ in Karnataka. The broad alliance of social forces that came to oppose SEZs in Goa (and elsewhere) underlines how few have stood to gain and many to lose from the model. If democracy remains quintessentially a class compromise (cf. Sandbrook et al. 2007), the Goan Impasse uncovers possibilities to push back the capitalist offensive. As the Indian economy and capital poise for 'growth' through investments in industry, infrastructure and urbanization, the ethnographic material here indicates that a deeper alliance of social forces intent on dis-embedding existing inequalities, and pushing the state toward egalitarian, ecologically appropriate and democratic rights to land- and resource-use for all, is critical. If the spirit of Goa's anti-SEZ campaigners walking through the gates of the police headquarters or grazing their cattle through the 'SEZ fence' daily stands witness, the possibility of walking through this impasse also beckons.

Abbreviations

BJP	Bhartiya Janata Party
BoA	Board of Approval
CM	Chief Minister
CSJP	Council for Social Justice and Peace
GBA	Goa Bachao Abhiyan
GIDC	Goa Industrial Development Corporation
GMAS	Goa Movement Against SEZs
GoG	Government of Goa
GoI	Government of India
GPCC	Goa State Congress Committee
KKNS	Kerim Kriti Nagrik Samiti
MGP	Maharashtrawadi Gomantak Party
MLA	Member of the Legislative Assembly
NCP	Nationalist Congress Party
PMAS	People's Movement Against SEZs
RP	Regional Plan
SC	Supreme Court
SEZs	special economic zones
SGF	Save Goa Front
SIE	Sancoale Industrial Estate
STs	Scheduled Tribes
SVM	SEZ Virodhi Manch
TPP	Twenty-point Program
UGDP	United Goan Democratic Party
VIE	Verna Industrial Estate

Acknowledgements

This study would not have been possible without the gracious support and invaluable advice of Pravin Sabnis, Albertina Almeida, Franky Monteiro, Charles Fernandes, Agnel and Mariya 'Emy' Fernandes, Peter and Luizinha Gama, Swati Kerkar, Ramkrishna Zalmi and Solano Da Silva. Many others in Goa also generously gave me their time and shared precious insights and experiences. Thanks are due to Solano Da Silva for generously sharing drafts of his chapter, and to Albertina Almeida for a careful reading of an earlier draft. My dissertation group helped rescue protagonists' voices from drowning in empirical details. Marc Edelman, David Harvey, Donald Robotham and Jeff Maskovsky shared insightful comments and suggestions on earlier drafts, as did the Land Deals Politics Initiative Collective. Thanks are due to two anonymous reviewers and the editors of *JPS*.

Funding

This study was supported by the National Science Foundation, the Wenner-Gren Foundation and the Land Deals Politics Initiative.

References

Abrams, P. 1982. *Historical Sociology*. Ithaca: Cornell University Press.

Adnan, S. 2013. Land Grabs and Primitive Accumulation in Deltaic Bangladesh: Interactions Between Neoliberal Globalization, State Interventions, Power Relations and Peasant Resistance. *The Journal of Peasant Studies* 40, no. 1: 87–128.

Alvares, C., ed. 2002. *Fish Curry and Rice*. Mapusa: The Goa Foundation.

Banerjee-Guha, S. 2008. Space Relations of Capital. *Economic and Political Weekly* 43, no. 47: 51–59.

Barker, C., L. Cox, J. Krinsky, and A. Nilsen. 2013. *Marxism and Social Movements*. Boston: Brill.

Basu, P. 2007. Political Economy of Land-grab. *Economic and Political Weekly* 42, no. 14: 1281–1287.

Bedi, H. 2013. Special Economic Zones: national land challenges, localized protest. *Contemporary South Asia* 21, no. 1: 38–51.

Borkar, M. 2006. Sacred yet scientific; eco-theological basis of biodiversity conservation in Goa. In *Multiple Dimensions of Global Environmental Change*, ed. S. Sonak, 182–194. New Delhi: TERI.

Borras, S. M., and J. C. Franco. 2010. Contemporary Discourses and Contestations around Pro-Poor Land Policies and Land Governance. *Journal of Agrarian Change* 10, no. 1: 1–32.

Borras, S. M., and J. C. Franco. 2013. Global Land Grabbing and Political Reactions 'From Below. Third World Quarterly 34, no. 9: 1723–1747.

Borras, S. M., J. C. Franco, and C. Wang. 2013. The Challenge of Global Governance of Land Grabbing: Changing International Agricultural Context and Competing Political Views and Strategies. *Globalizations* 10, no. 1: 161–179.

CAG. 2008. *Union Audit Reports (Central Excise, Service Tax & Customs)(Indirect Taxes - Report No. 6 of 2008) Performance Audit: 2006–2007* http://www.cag.gov.in/html/reports/indir_taxes/2008_6PA/contents.htm (accessed April 1, 2009).

CIPLA. 2012. http://www.cipla.com/ (accessed September 10, 2012).

Chakravorty, S. 2013. *The Price of Land: Acquisition Conflict Consequence*. New Delhi: Oxford University Press.

Coca Cola. 2013. *The Coca-Cola Company Commitment: Land Rights and Sugar*. http://assets.coca-colacompany.com/6b/65/7f0d386040fcb4872fa136f05c5c/proposal-to-oxfam-on-land-tenure-and-sugar.pdf (accessed September 13, 2014).

CPI (M). 2006. Press Release. Note on Special Economic Zones. New Delhi: CPI (M).

Da Silva, S. 2014. Goa: The Dynamics of Reversal. In *The Politics of India's SEZs*, ed. R. Jenkins, L. Kennedy, and P. Mukhopadyay, 108–136. New Delhi: Oxford University Press.

Edelman, M. 1999. *Peasants Against Globalization: Rural Social Movements in Costa Rica*. Stanford: Stanford University Press.

ET. 2013. Uttam Galva Steel surrenders its two SEZs in Maharashtra. *The Economic Times*, September 13.

Firstpost. 2013. Parrikar invokes Nehru to seek special status for Goa. *Firstpost*, June 13.

Franky Monteiro and others vs State of Goa and others. 2010, November 26. Judgment Pronounced in Writ Petitions 263, 310, 314, 316, 349, 380, 436, 438, 501, 507 of 2008 and 391 of 2009. http://www.hcbombayatgoa.nic.in/ (accessed Febryary 12, 2011).

GoG. 2007. White Paper on Special Economic Zones in Goa State. Panjim: GoG.

GoI. 2001a. *Population by Religious Communities*. New Delhi: GoI. http://censusindia.gov.in/Census_Data_2001/Census_data_finder/C_Series/Population_by_religious_communities.htm (accessed September 29, 2012).

GoI. 2001b. *Census of India 2001*. New Delhi: GoI. http://www.censusindia.gov.in (accessed May 11, 2014).

GoI. 2009. Committee on State Agrarian Relations and Unfinished Task of Land Reforms Vol. 1. New Delhi: GoI.

GoI. 2011a. http://sezindia.nic.in/ (accessed July 17, 2011).

GoI. 2011b. Census of India 2011: Provisional Population Totals Goa. New Delhi: GoI.

GoI. 2014. List of Formal Approvals Granted Under the SEZ Act 2005. http://sezindia.nic.in/ (accessed May 21, 2014).

Gopalakrishnan, S., and A. Shrivastava. 2008. 'SEZs have nothing to do with land acquisition.' *Seminar*, 582. http://www.india-seminar.com/semframe.html (accessed March 21, 2007).

Grain Briefing. 2008. Seize! The 2008 Land Grab for Food and Financial Security. http://www.grain.org/briefings_files/landgrab-2008-en.pdf (last accessed August 10, 2010).

Guha, R., and J. Martinez-Alier. 1997. *Varieties of Environmentalism: Essays North and South*. London: Earthscan.

Hall, D. 2013. Primitive Accumulation, Accumulation by Dispossession and the Global Land Grab. *Third World Quarterly* 34, no. 9: 1582–1604.

Harvey, D. 2001. *Spaces of Capital: Towards a Critical Geography*. New York: Routledge.

Heller, P. 2005. Reinventing Public Power in the Age of Globalization: Decentralization and the Transformation of Movement Politics in Kerala. In *Social Movements in India*, ed. R. Ray and M. Katzenstein, 79–106. New York: Rowman and Littlefield.

Indian Express. 2012. Maharashtra govt cancels 4 SEZs over land acquisition. *Indian Express*, July 31.

Indian Express. 2013. Govt gives in to farmers, withdraws 36 villages from Mandal-Becharaji SIR. *Indian Express*, August 15.

JAGPAL SINGH VS. THE STATE OF PUNJAB AND OTHERS AIR. 2011. SC. http://JUDIS.NIC.IN (accessed August 1, 2011).

K. Raheja Corp. 2012. http://www.cipla.com/ (accessed September 10, 2012).

Kale, S. 2008. *Anti SEZ Struggle: A Victory for Farmers and Workers*. Pune: NCAS.

Kazi, S., and A. Siqueira. 2006. Bridging local and global concerns: a study on globalized tourism and its implications on land-use and land-cover. In *Multiple Dimensions of Global Environmental Change*, ed. S. Sonak, 62–82. New Delhi: TERI.

Levien, M. 2012. The Land Question: Special Economic Zones and the Political Economy of Dispossession in India. *The Journal of Peasant Studies* 39, no. 3–4: 933–969.

Margulis, M. E., N. McKeon, and S. M. Borras. 2013. Land Grabbing and Global Governance: Critical Perspectives. *Globalizations* 10, no. 1: 1–23.

Mohan, V. 2013. Cultivable Land continues to Shrink. *The Economic Times*, August 16.

Mohanty, H. 2010. Tata Steel to resume work after notification of Gopalpur SEZ. *Business Standard*, April 13.

Newman, R. 1984. Goa; The transformation of an Indian Region. *Pacific Affairs* 57, no. 3: 429–449.

Peninsula Land. 2012. http://www.peninsula.co.in/ (accessed September 10, 2012).

Podur, J. 2013. The Bastar Land Grab in India: An Interview with Sudha Bharadwaj. *The Bullet: Socialist Project* 808.

PTI. 2011. Goa's per capita highest in India. *Goa News*. http://www.goanews.com/news_disp.php?newsid=1359 (accessed October 15, 2012).

Raghuraman, T. 2013. *Refiguring Goa: From Trading Post to Tourism Destination*. Saligao: Goa 1556.

Rebello, S. 2013. India buys land 9 times Delhi's size abroad. *The Hindustan Times*. October 19.

Rubinoff, A. 1992. Goa's Attainment of Statehood. *Asian Survey* 32, no. 5: 471–487.

Sadhle, K. 2000. *Bhutkhambcha Lokaladha*. Ponda: Nirmal Vishva Prakashan.

Sampat, P. 2008. Special Economic Zones in India. *Economic and Political Weekly* 43, no. 28: 25–29.

Sampat, P. 2010. Special Economic Zones in India: Reconfiguring Displacement in a Neoliberal Order? *City and Society* 22, no. 2: 166–182.

Sampat, P. 2013. Limits to Absolute Power: Eminent Domain and the Right to Land in India. *Economic and Political Weekly* XLVIII, no. 19: 40–52.

Sandbrook, R., M. Edelman, P. Heller, and J. Teichman. 2007. *Social Democracy in the Global Periphery*. New York: Cambridge University Press.

Sridhar, A. 2010. Eminent domain, absolute doubt: Crusade for Goa's comunidades. *Infochange*. http://infochangeindia.org/environment/coastal-commons/eminent-domain-absolute-doubt-crusade-for-goa-s-comunidades.html (accessed October 10, 2012).

Savegoa. 2012. http://savegoa.com (accessed September 12, 2012).
Subbarao, D. 2009, February 18. Impact of the Global Financial Crisis in India: Collateral Damage and Response. Speech by Duvvuri Subbarao, Governor of the Reserve Bank of India, delivered at the Symposium on *The Global Economic Crisis and Challenges for the Asian Economy in a Changing World*. Organized by the Institute for International Monetary Affairs, Tokyo. http://www.bis.org/review/r090223b.pdf (accessed March 15, 2014).
Tilly, C. 1978. *From Mobilization to Revolution*. Reading: Addison-Wesley.
Tilly, C. 1986. *The Contentious French: Four Centuries of Popular Struggle*. Cambridge: Harvard University Press.
TNN. 2012. Chief minister Manohar Parrikar: Policy to regulate flow of migrants. *The Times of India*. September 3.
UNDP. 2011. India's Job Guarantee Act Emerging as a Ray of Hope in Global Meltdown. http://www.undp.org/content/support/en/home/test_area/ourwork/democraticgovernance/successstories/india_s_job_guaranteeactemergingasrayofhopeinglobalmeltdown/ (accessed March 15, 2014).
Verdery, K. 2003. *The Vanishing Hectare: Property and Value in Postsocialist Transylvania*. Ithaca: Cornell University Press.
Walker, K. L. M. 2006. Gangster Capitalism' and Peasant Protest in China: The Last Twenty Years. *The Journal of Peasant Studies* 33, no. 1: 1–33.
White, B., S. M. Borras, R. Hall, I. Scoones, and W. Wolford. 2012. The new enclosures: Critical Perspectives on Corporate Land Deals. *The Journal of Peasant Studies* 39, no. 3–4: 619–647.

Oil palm expansion without enclosure: smallholders and environmental narratives

Antonio Castellanos-Navarrete and Kees Jansen

Recent debates on land grabbing and biofuels tend to link oil palm expansion to rural dispossession, environmental degradation and rural resistance. In this paper, we examine to what extent 'enclosure', a central concept in two critiques – 'environmentalism of the poor' and 'green grabbing' – is intrinsically linked to oil palm expansion. We argue that where enclosure is absent, poor peasants may seek greater market integration over resistance to modernisation processes. We analyse how and why peasants engage in oil palm cultivation and how their involvement undermines green efforts to curb its expansion in Chiapas, Mexico. Our analysis suggests that an exclusive focus on enclosure as the main driving force behind contestation and agrarian social relationships is unable to explain agrarian dynamics and the multiple uses to which environmental narratives are put.

Introduction

The rise in the price of palm oil by 412 percent between 2000 and 2011 (Index Mundi 2014) made oil palm cultivation highly profitable and encouraged its expansion. According to large environmental organisations, such growth comes at a cost, as seen in the following statement of Greenpeace (2013): 'this phenomenal growth of the palm oil industry spells disaster for local communities, biodiversity, and climate change as palm plantations encroach further and further into forested areas'. For Greenpeace, the appropriation of forests and lands for oil palm production endangers wildlife as well as the livelihoods of local communities. In the narratives of environmental organisations, oil palm expansion figures as a modernisation process that goes against the social and economic interests of family farmers, and only benefits transnational capital. Accordingly, one would expect smallholders to oppose oil palm expansion, as shown, for instance, by Gerber (2011) and Alonso-Fradejas (2012). Yet this is not always the case. In Chiapas, state programmes in support of palm oil have gained widespread acceptance amongst smallholders and rainforest settlers, including indigenous people. Support for such programmes, which also promote biofuels, is particularly striking in a region known for its peasant uprisings against the government (García de León 1997), particularly by the *Zapatistas* in the mid 1990s (Harvey 1998). The question then is why this is so.

The literature on oil palm cultivation confirms to some extent the environmental narrative of oil palm expansion as endangering both the environment and local communities. The expansion of large-scale plantations in Indonesia has resulted in extensive deforestation (Carlson et al. 2012; Lee et al. 2014; Obidzinski et al. 2012) and very significant greenhouse gas emissions (Fargione et al. 2008). Research has also shown how rapid expansion can lead to the loss of land and forest resources by local communities (Maher 2014; Schoneveld, German, and Nukator 2011; Yengoh and Armah 2014), a phenomenon particularly frequent in regions with weak land-tenure regimes (Hall 2011). Outcomes for smallholders who participate in oil palm cultivation are less clear. On the one hand, agrarian studies stress processes of social differentiation (Cramb and Sujang 2013; Koczberski and Curry 2004) in which poor farmers, indigenous producers or women are sometimes unable to reap the benefits (Julia and White 2012; McCarthy 2010). On the other hand, some researchers point to the high returns obtained from oil palm cultivation (Feintrenie, Chong, and Levang 2010a; Rist et al. 2010), leading even smallholders to disregard the environment (Feintrenie, Schwarze, and Levang 2010b). The study of smallholders in oil palm cultivation is particularly problematic for the popular environmental narrative. Despite critiques, smallholders continue to engage in oil palm production and even drive its expansion (Hall 2011). To be convincing, the narrative informing much environmental activism against palm oil needs to address the following questions: Why do smallholders participate in oil palm expansion? And why do actors involved in this expansion adopt different environmental narratives? This paper aims to answer these questions by taking the case of oil palm expansion in Chiapas.

The narratives deployed by environmental organisations against palm oil find echo in two predominant critical theses on the relationships between capital and environmentalism in the scientific literature. The first, known as 'environmentalism of the poor', focuses on how rural people resist the appropriation of their resources (e.g. Guha 1993; Martinez-Alier 2002). Enclosure in the form of grabbing of forests, water and land by investors, often aided by the state, has a detrimental impact on the livelihoods of the poor who depend on access to such productive resources. On occasion, this has led to popular protests often framed in environmental terms and sometimes undertaken in coalition with environmental organisations (Guha and Martinez-Alier 1997) as seen, for instance, in rural mobilisations against large-scale dam projects in India. The second perspective is 'green grabbing' (Fairhead, Leach, and Scoones 2012): investors, corporations or the state transform use values of nature into new exchange values (e.g. carbon markets) or appropriate resources on environmental grounds (e.g. claiming 'marginal' land for more sustainable biofuel production; e.g. Kelly 2011; McAfee 1999; Osborne 2011). The two positions assign a different role to environmentalists. The first thesis emphasises environmental non-governmental organisations (NGOs) struggling alongside rural communities against dispossession (Stonich and Bailey 2000; Veuthey and Gerber 2012). The second thesis usually critically deconstructs top-down environmental policies, often carried out with the support of 'environmentalists within the state', viewing green discourses as a 'Foucauldian' tool for disciplining, governing and justifying enclosure (Agrawal 2005; Luke 1997).[1] Enclosure here refers to the exclusion of people from access to the means of production. More descriptively, the term 'dispossession' is also in use. Both in theory and in popular environmental narratives, enclosure is often considered to be the main mechanism explaining the relationship between the environment and capital accumulation.

Enclosure is closely related to the concept of 'accumulation by dispossession', indicating that enclosure is not just 'primitive' or initial accumulation, as in Marx's work, but a key

[1]In addition to the environmentalism of the poor and green grabbing theses, there are other analyses of the relationship between accumulation and environmentalism, such as the role of environmental certification (e.g. Jansen 2004), but this paper focuses on the first two.

mechanism in contemporary capitalism (Harvey 2005). Resources commonly grabbed include common lands, forests, genes or even knowledge (Deibel 2013; Kloppenburg 2010; Toleubayev, Jansen, and van Huis 2010). Accumulation by dispossession is seen as a recurrent process whereby capitalists open up new profitable frontiers by appropriating common or key resources from the poor. Enclosure as land grabbing is the classic example in which peasants become proletarians, losing their lands to corporations and thereby being forced to sell their labour to make a living. Political responses to enclosure have often been conceptualised in terms of resistance (see Borras and Franco 2013 for a critique). Enclosure has been studied within the 'agrarian question' framework in political economy, with a focus on capitalism as a process of structuring relations between agrarian classes, the state and other economic sectors (Brenner 1986; Lenin 1967; Kautsky 1988). Recently, the commodification of nature, environmental destruction and associated social struggles have been recognised as key elements of the contemporary agrarian question (Akram-Lodhi and Kay 2010; Barraza et al. 2013; Gerber and Veuthey 2010; Jansen 1998). From this literature, we derive the need to analyse environmental narratives not just as discursive entities in themselves but also in relation to concrete processes of agrarian change.

The next section describes the two regions in our case study and the methodology employed. The third section discusses the role of the state and shows the uses made of, and the disparity between, an 'oil palm cultivation for biofuel' narrative and a modernisation practice in which oil palm is planted for conventional purposes. The subsequent section examines the impact of oil palm expansion on land tenure relationships. The fifth section argues that the state favoured rural organisations in the oil palm expansion for political reasons, leading rural organisations to adhere pragmatically to this modernisation project. We then examine how environmental NGOs opposed oil palm expansion but had little success in changing practices given the close relationship, and in part a shared environmental narrative, between small farmer organisations and the state. Where land grabbing is absent and conditions are favourable, small and medium farmers and their organisations may opt to actively engage in oil palm expansion rather than resist, despite critical environmentalist views on the crop. In the conclusion, we argue that neither the 'environmentalism of the poor' nor the 'green grabbing' thesis can explain why small farmers engage in oil palm expansion, and that we need to develop a complementary view on the greening of the agrarian question in situations without enclosure.

Study region and methods

This study examines two cases of recent agrarian change involving rapid oil palm expansion in Chiapas: the southern Lacandon rainforest and the coastal Soconusco (Figure 1). The southern Lacandon region, situated in the Marqués de Comillas and Benemérito de las Américas municipalities, is characterised by shrinking tall and medium evergreen rainforests on the edge of the *Montes Azules* Biosphere Reserve. In Soconusco, which stretches from Mapastepec to Suchiate municipalities, we focused on Huixtla and Villa Comaltitlán municipalities. Soconusco is characterised by mangroves and herbaceous marshes, which have been protected since 1995 by the *Encrucijada* Biosphere Reserve. Both regions have been colonised in the past but at different times and for different purposes. In Soconusco in the early nineteenth century, the state provided incentives for national and foreign capital to introduce large-scale modern capitalist agriculture (García de León 1997). By contrast, in the Lacandon rainforest, land was distributed in the early 1970s to landless families as a way of easing agrarian tensions elsewhere (De Vos 2002). While Soconusco is now characterised by commercial agriculture and the presence of large landed private

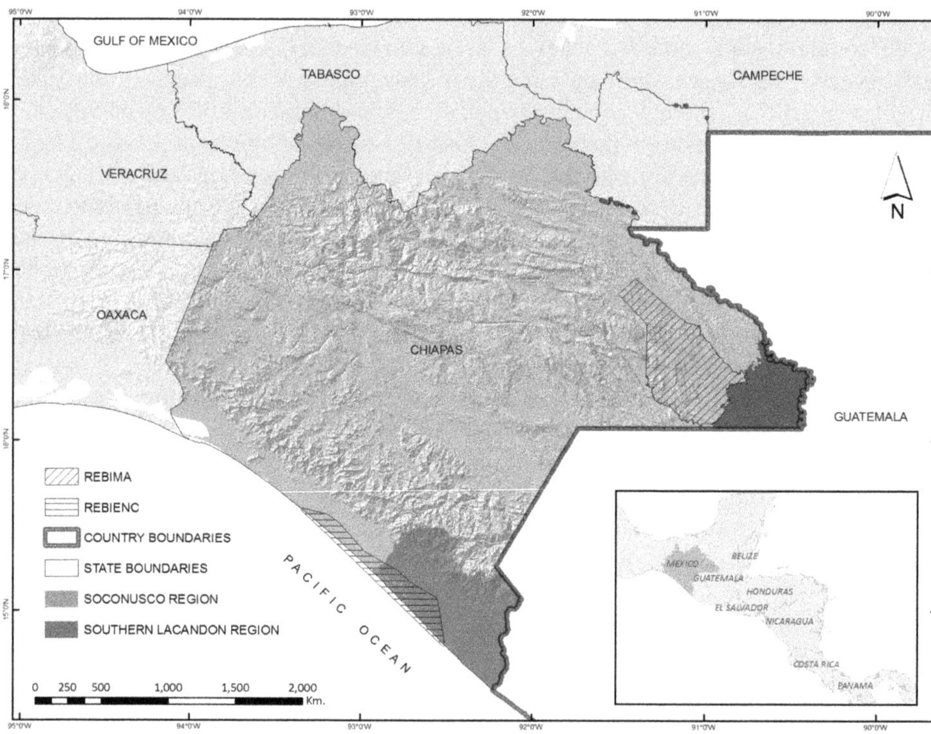

Figure 1. Selected study regions in Chiapas constituted by Soconusco and the southern Lacandon region. Note: REBIMA stands for the Montes Azules Biopshere Reserve, and REBIENC for the La Encrucijada Biosphere Reserve.

property, the southern Lacandon region is mainly constituted by *ejidos*, often indigenous, living from extensive cattle production (Table 1). *Ejidos* in Mexico are a land tenure form in which farmers are granted parcels and usufruct rights to common lands with restrictions on the right to sell and rent. People living in *ejidos* are often referred to as the 'social sector'. By including two regions in the study, we aimed to widen our understanding of the multiple processes shaping processes of agrarian change in the oil palm sector in Chiapas.

The southern Lacandon rainforest was first populated in the 1970s by peasants from central and southern Mexico. Later, in the 1980s, landless indigenous peasants from Chiapas moved in. Land grants in *ejidos* ranged from 20 to 50 hectares per adult. Peasant families obtained the legal title to their lands within a few years and received some government support, a fact that may have deterred their participation in the 1994 *Zapatista* uprising. Early stratification of this group, resulting in some cases from cross-border smuggling of cattle or drugs, made a small number of settlers particularly wealthy, with access to between 150 and 200 hectares. These larger farmers specialised in cattle, often entering into cattle raising arrangements with other farmers who lacked capital. Poor farmers, often indigenous, kept few cattle and cultivated a small proportion of their land, sometimes as little as two out of 20 hectares. When oil palm cultivation was introduced in 2005, it attracted both middle farmers, who grew this 'luxury crop' on relatively large plots (10 hectares on average), and smallholders, who planted the crop on smaller plots (eight hectares on average; Table 2). Several farmers sold cattle to invest in oil palm cultivation, whereas government subsidies and family labour investments

Table 1. Characterisation of study regions.

				Land access			Land uses[b]					
				Land tenure								
	People living in poverty[a]	Households relying on agriculture	Farms managed by indigenous producers	*Ejido* land tenure	Private property	Landless adults in *ejidos*	Pastures	Oil palm[c]	Coffee	Sugarcane	Maize	Other crops
	(% population)	(%)	(%)	(%)	(%)	(%)	(%)	(%)	(%)	(%)	(%)	(%)
Soconusco												
Huixtla	66	91	1	61	39	38	29	1	23	36	7	4
Villa Comaltitlán	83	96	1	62	38	37	41	15	24	7	7	6
Southern Lacandon rainforest												
Benemérito de las Américas	88	87	42	100	0	52	47	24	0	0	13	16
Marqués de Comillas	92	79	51	93	7	17	60	4	0	0	21	15

Sources: Data from CONEVAL (2010); INEGI (2007a, 2007b); SIAP-SAGARPA (2013).
Notes: [a]Multidimensional poverty index according to indicators presented in CONEVAL (2010).
[b]Approximate percentages as derived from INEGI (2007a) and SIAP-SAGARPA (2013).
[c]Total oil palm owned by farmers in our sample was greater than the official estimation reported for oil palm in Huixtla.

Table 2. Class conditions of surveyed oil palm growers in Soconusco and the southern Lacandon rainforest.

	Farmers	Average farm size	Average oil palm area	Family labour	Hired labour	Average cattle heads	Main income source: Oil palm	Cattle	Other cash crops	Wage labour	Off-farm income[a]
	(no.)	(ha)	(ha)	(no.)	(no.)	(no.)	(% farms)	(% farms)	(% farms)	(% farms)	(% farms)
Soconusco											
Social sector											
Poor	55	4.7	3.5	1	1	0	75	0	7	11	7
Middle-income	37	10.0	5.9	1	1	2	70	3	11	3	14
Wealthy	27	20.8	9.1	1	2	4	63	0	33	0	4
Private sector[b]	6	486.3	436.0	0	9	350	50	17	17	0	17
Southern Lacandon region											
Social sector											
Poor	47	18.7	8.1	2	1	1	85	0	6	6	2
Middle-income	36	28.7	10.2	2	2	3	92	0	0	0	8
Wealthy	38	85.9	24.4	1	4	21	79	11	8	0	3
Private sector	4	272.4	116.8	1	13	250	50	25	0	0	25

Source: Survey of 250 oil palm growers in the two study regions.
Notes: [a]Off-farm income refers to income derived from non-agricultural income sources (i.e. other jobs, business and remittances).
[b]The private sector comprises both oil palm companies and investors planting in *ejido* land or on private property. Investors also included individuals living in *ejidos* but who arrived there with the sole purpose of planting oil palm.

were more important for poorer peasants. Land availability also attracted several investors who set up much larger areas under oil palm (117 hectares on average).

In Soconusco, wealthy families or entrepreneurs established *fincas* or large landed properties in the *Sierra Madre*, where they cultivated coffee, and on the coastal plains, where they produced bananas or raised large cattle herds. Railways connected this region to distant markets, thereby favouring widespread cash crop cultivation. While landless peasants successfully struggled for land throughout the twentieth century (Reyes Ramos 2002), over time population growth and land subdivision left peasants in *ejidos* with smaller plots and increased the number of *avencidados* (*ejido* members with no land). The first oil palm plantation in Soconusco was established around 1952, by Johann Bernstoff, a German coffee landowner (interview, 24 May 2013, Finca La Lima). Farmers in *ejidos* started to plant oil palm in the mid 1980s with state support. The crop spread more widely in the 2000s when the Chiapas government intermittently prioritised this crop in the region. A final boost for oil palm expansion occurred in 2007, linked to biofuel production. Poor peasants planted oil palm on medium- to small-sized plots (four hectares on average). A few private-sector companies established large areas under oil palm on private land (436 hectares on average).

The organisation of oil palm processing differed between the regions. In the Lacandon rainforest, two private-sector mills in Palenque (240 km away) competed for the oil palm produced by family farmers. One mill ensured supply by entering into a commercial agreement with a large producer organisation with a network of collection sites. The rival mill, which concentrated on individual medium producers and a few large producers, paid slightly higher prices, provided technical assistance and arranged farm-gate collection. In Soconusco, processing relied on three types of mills. First, the Bernstoff family established a small processing plant in about 1958, followed by a second one in 1991. These mills were supplied mainly from their own plantations. Second, in 2000 and 2002, the private sector established two much bigger processing facilities, which were supplied mainly by family farmers, and a few privately owned or leased large *fincas*. And, third, three mills were managed by the social sector. One set up in the mid 1980s has since closed down, followed by two others in 1996 (Wolff 1999) and in 2012.

The fieldwork was carried out in three periods (October to December 2011, March to November 2012 and May to July 2013) in both regions as well as in major cities including the state capital – Tuxtla Gutiérrez. In total, we conducted 60 in-depth interviews with private-sector managers, technicians, producers, workers and environmentalists from NGOs and from the state. Questions focused on the biofuel chain, land-use changes, production, farmer incorporation (state programmes, innovation and credit), the organisation of labour, conflicts arising from oil palm expansion and actors' views on environmental issues, agrarian change and oil palm politics following a political ecology approach. Interviews were first organised by type of respondent and codified according to the key themes which emerged; coded fragments were then compared and analysed per type of respondent (Saldaña 2012). We also randomly surveyed 250 oil palm growers in Marqués de Comillas and Benemérito de las Américas municipalities (southern Lacandon region) as well as in Huixtla and Villa Comaltitlán municipalities (Soconusco). We supplemented this data collection with fieldwork observations and the collection of relevant documents and statistical data.

Biofuels and oil palm expansion in Chiapas: a contradictory state project

The recent oil palm expansion in Chiapas can only be explained by the strong intervention of the state. This intervention was characterised by inconsistent or even contradictory narratives. In some government communications palm oil was depicted as a green fuel, and even as a non-food (Gobierno del Estado 2010a). In others, government officials stressed the use of palm oil for food purposes (Gobierno del Estado 2010b). Such contradictions raise questions about the state's promotion of oil palm and the role of environmental discourses.

The recent promotion of oil palm in Chiapas was linked to two state projects. The first formed part of the Mesoamerica Project[2] in which oil palm cultivation was promoted as part of the expansion of biofuels. In April 2007, Colombia, the only country in the Mesoamerica initiative at that time with significant biofuel production, suggested developing biofuel production in the region. This proposal led to the Mesoamerican Biofuel Programme (MBP), with the aim of setting up both biodiesel processing plants and a research network. With funding from the Inter-American Development Bank and recipient countries, Colombia established biodiesel processing plants in El Salvador, Honduras and Chiapas in Mexico. The state-owned MBP biodiesel processing plant in Chiapas was officially opened in November 2010. The Mexican government also invested heavily in oil palm promotion: from 2007 to 2012, over 80 press releases were issued by the Chiapas government on both oil palm cultivation and biofuels. Government bulletins on using palm oil for biofuel production were picked up by the local media, resulting in a series of newspaper reports praising green plantations and the new green economy. Media coverage and prolific public advertising on sustainable biofuels constructed Chiapas as an environmental vanguard. To this we have to add a second state project derived from national policies.

Oil palm cultivation was promoted as part of the so-called 'productive reconversion' initiative, a label derived from the National Development Strategy (Gobierno de los Estados Unidos Mexicanos 2007) which explicitly aimed to deter deforestation through payments for environmental services (PES), for reforestation and for the establishment of commercial tree plantations. The assumption underlying the National Development Plan was clearly stated by the Chiapas governor in 2012: 'poverty also has lots to do with environmental deterioration' (public speech, 25 September 2012, San Cristóbal de Las Casas). Increased market involvement by rural people and natural resource valuation were the proposed solutions for halting deforestation. This neoliberal recipe fit well with recent global policy measures (e.g. the REDD+[3] mechanism) and with some green economy postulates fighting climate change. In this context, the oil palm expansion project was shaped by neoliberal ideology and focused on achieving greater integration of farmers into markets (Fletes-Ocón and Bonnano 2013). In Chiapas, the 'productive reconversion' strategy was proposed for all regions, with or without rainforests. Both the MBP and the 'productive reconversion' project presented oil palm cultivation as the remedy for exhausted soils, burnt forests or climate change.

The formal Chiapas state discourse was heavily environmental: oil palm expansion was held to serve green ends and was linked to sustainability in both state projects. Firstly, palm oil was regarded as a source of 'clean' fuel with biofuels from the MBP biodiesel plant as the political flagship. The biodiesel it produced provided fuel for public buses in two major cities, a fact seized on in public advertising campaigns. And, secondly, oil palm was presented as deterring the practice of shifting cultivation. Long-standing environmental concerns over slash-and-burn helped to frame this new permanent crop as 'sustainable'. A

---

[2]This project was previously known as the Puebla-Panamá Plan and aimed to encourage the economic integration of Mesoamerica.
[3]Reducing Emissions from Deforestation and Forest Degradation.

selective appeal was also made to science. Concepts such as 'soil cover loss' and 'degraded lands' were typically drawn on to refer to the consequences of burning rainforest for maize cultivation, whereas oil palm cultivation was depicted as environmentally friendly. However, economic developments gave rise to environmental contradictions.

While palm oil was considered to be a potential feedstock in 2007, by 2011 this option was no longer feasible. Global biofuel production consists of cheap ethanol and expensive biodiesel (Doering III and Tyner 2009; Lamers et al. 2011). Low maize prices in the US, and especially cheap sugar in Brazil, favoured increased ethanol production. In 2009, this accounted for 73 percent of all biofuels produced (Lamers et al. 2011). Sugar-processing plants in Brazil can flexibly shift between sugar and ethanol production according to changes in market price (Novo et al. 2010). Costly food oils needed for biodiesel production cannot compete with cheap maize or sugar, so biodiesel processing requires favourable policies. In 2003, EU mandatory biodiesel quotas on fuel combined with subsidies and tax exemptions in Germany made it possible to use rapeseed as a feedstock. Later, the withdrawal of German subsidies in 2007 opened up the market for biodiesel imports. While palm oil then appeared to be the ideal biodiesel source, being the cheapest food oil, heavily subsidised soybean took the lead, limiting palm oil imports into the EU to 11 percent (Lamers et al. 2011). At the end of the 2000s, rising palm oil prices made biodiesel production increasingly unprofitable (Mekhilef, Siga, and Saidur 2011; Sheng Goh and Teong Lee 2010). Mexico was not an exception.

Initial state plans in Chiapas relied on crude palm oil as a biofuel feedstock. However, high palm oil prices during 2011 discouraged Chiapas state purchases (interview with processing mill manager, 28 November 2011, Cantón Santa Elena) and resulted in a shift to waste restaurant oils for biofuel processing (interview with Chiapas government official, 1 February 2012, Tuxtla Gutiérrez). Collection of used cooking oil was expensive and its supply insufficient, leading to the failure of the biofuel project. The success of biodiesel production normally requires state subsidies for processing to keep costs down, or the implementation of a biofuel mandatory percentage of fuel to ensure demand. In Mexico, neither of these conditions was met (SAGARPA 2009)[4], stifling incipient biodiesel investments. By 2012, two private biodiesel processing plants in Mexico, located in the centre and north of the country, had closed down (interview with processing mill manager, 9 November 2011, Acapetahua; Torres 2011). Existing state incentives were directed towards increasing oil palm cultivation rather than its conversion to biofuel. According to a private-sector mill manager, the Secretary of Agriculture (SAGARPA in its Spanish acronym) agreed in the 1990s with the food industry that oil palm fruit bunches would be priced at 12.5 percent of the crude palm oil price to favour oil palm cultivation (interview, 21 October 2011, Palenque). To this we have to add the support given by the Chiapas administration to oil palm cultivation through the 'productive reconversion' strategy. In this politico-economic context, oil palm has not been used on a large scale for biofuel production, although cultivation has expanded because of state support. This has important implications.

In their communications and actions, the Chiapas administration associated oil palm expansion with sustainability and related green discourses. This was possible by linking oil palm to specific environmental rationales associated with biofuels on the one hand and the 'productive reconversion' strategy on the other. As pointed out by the 'green grabbing' thesis, environmental discourses are often used to gain legitimacy and justify

[4]In Mexico, it was mandatory to blend ethanol in fuel in only three urban regions.

interventions (Cárdenas 2012; Fairhead, Leach, and Scoones 2012). However we have to be careful not to conflate economic, political and environmental interests. For instance, adverse economic circumstances in Chiapas resulted in the failure of the biofuel initiative. Such failure led to inconsistent government narratives on the use of palm oil. Economic circumstances damaged the public perception of the Chiapas government, which was increasingly seen as promoting a scam (i.e. public money invested in biofuels without results). This points to some key contradictions that can arise from the employment of environmental narratives.

Oil palm expansion and dispossession: changes in access to land

The Chiapas government initiated a massive oil palm planting campaign in 2007, combining extensive advertising with the introduction of improved varieties and free distribution of seedlings to anyone interested. Varieties originating from Guatemala, Honduras and Colombia were made available to regional nurseries. The Institute for Productive Reconversion and Bioenergetics (IRBIO in its Spanish acronym) gave farmers a one-off land-clearing subsidy of 1000 pesos[5] per hectare along with the plant material. Farmers received about four million oil palm plants in just four years (interview with IRBIO staff, 4 November 2012, Tuxtla Gutiérrez). This resulted in a rapid pace of oil palm expansion (Figure 2). Oil palm cultivation was concentrated in the northern and southern Lacandon rainforest lowlands, and in coastal Soconusco. While in many countries landed elites (Marin-Burgos 2014) or transnationals (Borras, McMichael, and Scoones 2010) have controlled oil palm expansion, in Chiapas poor and middle-income farmers were significant actors. Government subsidies facilitated the participation of the social sector in oil palm cultivation, although initial support did not fully cover the costs.

Additional support to farmers was available through the Humid Tropic programme, created by the Secretary of Agriculture in 2009. This programme, with a special focus on Mexican humid tropical lands, granted subsidies to farmers with approved credit requests. Subsidies were proportional to credit size. In this way, state support further deepened producers' integration into the market. Farmers requesting these subsidies had to employ SAGARPA-approved rural agencies for the paperwork, to enter agreements with certified finance suppliers and to pay interest on credit to the order of 12–13 percent. Both credit and the subsidies from the Humid Tropic programme were key economic sources enabling many poor families to engage in oil palm production. Financial mechanisms such as credit have typically been associated with loss of land by peasant families, but this was not the case in rural Mexico.

Institutions providing credit to rural families in Mexico have few opportunities to recover their investment should farmers default. Land in *ejidos* cannot be legally seized. Credit institutions only have the right to use *ejido* lands to recover their investment. Under these conditions, the private sector rarely supplies credit to *ejido* members. Most credit associated with the Humid Tropic Programme was provided by the 'Fideicomisos Instituidos en Relación con la Agricultura' (FIRA), a group of public trusts linked to the Secretary of Finance and Public Credit and the Bank of Mexico. Unlike countries such as Guatemala or India, credit and land in Mexico are not as yet linked when it comes to *ejido* land. While subject to increasing pressure, oil palm growers in Mexico saw credit as a relatively risk free strategy to access capital. Risk for producers was also reduced by

[5]Equivalent to USD 97 in June 2008.

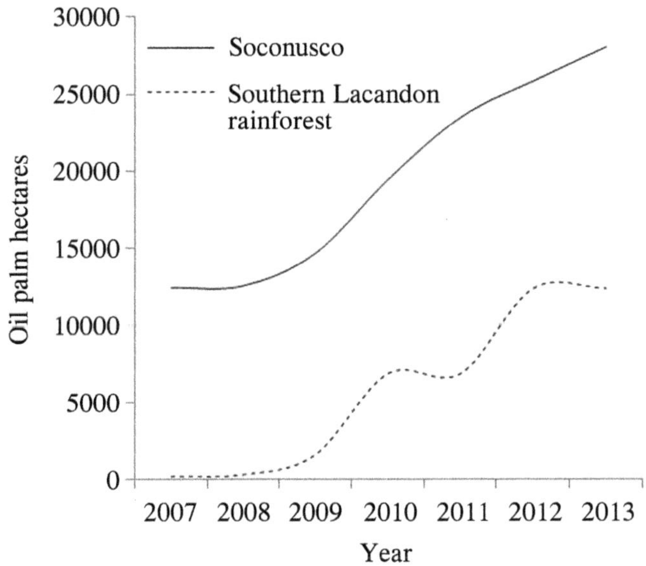

Figure 2. Oil palm hectares in Soconusco and southern Lacandon regions, 2007 to 2013.
Source: Based on data from SIAP-SAGARPA (2013).

collective requests of credit in which the group, and not the individual, was liable. Some small creditors even offered credit only for the period required to secure the Humid Tropic funds. Under these conditions, the increase of credit associated with oil palm hardly leads to loss of land. A related issue is to what extent the land tenure regime in Mexico prevents dispossession.

In the southern Lacandon region, rural lands are mostly held as *ejido*, a social tenure regime arising from the 1910 revolution in which land was owned collectively and members were legally banned from hiring labour. Tenure changed in 1992 when lands could be owned individually and land transactions were permitted for the first time (Assies 2007; Pérez Castañeda 2002). Land transactions are, however, often dependent on the approval of the *ejido* assembly, a form of collective decision-making. This has as yet partly prevented land grabbing in this area of Mexico. Some communities blocked land purchases for oil palm cultivation as, for instance, in López Mateos[6] where selling was permitted to 'peasants, like us' (interview with *ejido* authorities, 29 August 2012), but not to investors.[7] Such agreements were absent in large *ejidos* in the southern Lacandon rainforest where land transactions, such as in Benemérito de Las Américas, were considered more of a private affair. In any case, peasant families tended to double or triple land prices for outsiders, discouraging their establishment to some extent. To this must be added the common risk of extortion and kidnapping faced by investors in a region where a drugs

[6]Some *ejidos* such as Flor de Marqués blocked oil palm cultivation *per se* while other *ejidos* agreed on banning land transactions with oil palm investors.
[7]The 1992 land tenure reform certainly left *ejidos* more vulnerable to processes of land concentration. The importance of the *ejido* tenure is, however, evident when compared to rural communities with private property titles, as in Rio Salinas in the southern Lacandon rainforest where an investor bought about one third of all community lands (informal conversation with local investment manager, 24 August 2012).

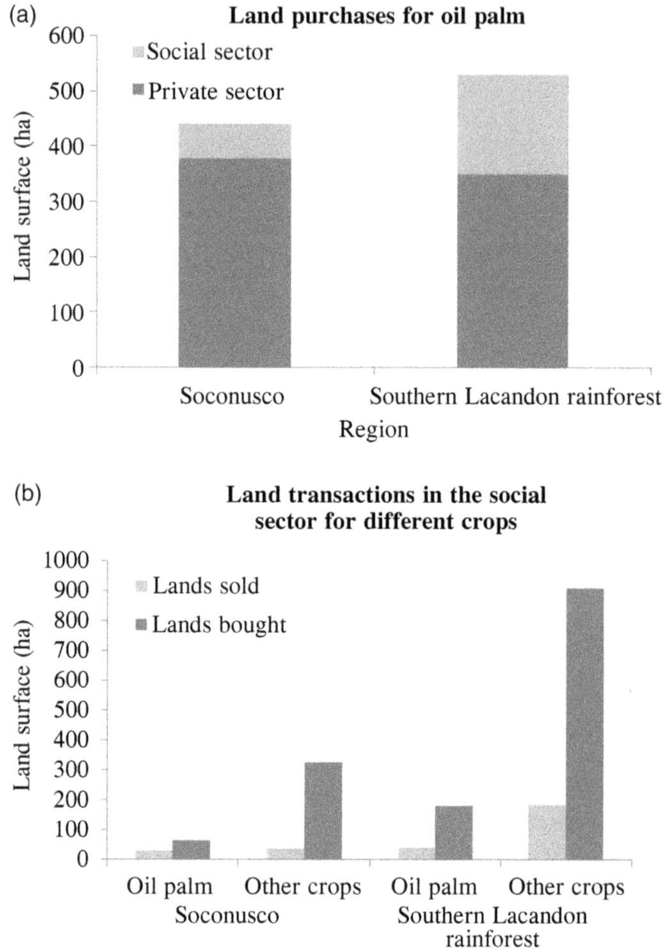

Figure 3. Land transactions in each study region.
Source: Survey of 250 oil palm growers in the two study regions.
Note: Land purchases for oil palm cultivation by the social and private sectors per region (a) and land sold and bought by social sector producers (b) per land use in the last 30 years.

economy has been in operation since the 1970s.[8] All these mechanisms limited land purchases by the private sector in the southern Lacandon rainforest (Figure 3). Moreover, and somewhat surprisingly, there also were obstacles to the expansion of companies on private lands, as seen in the Soconusco region.

Unlike the Lacandon region where 97 percent is held as *ejido* land (cf. Table 1), Soconusco had lands held as private property as well as *ejidos*. In Huixtla and Villa Comaltilán municipalities, private property averaged 39 percent of the total, compared to 61 percent under *ejido* tenure. Theoretically, this should have allowed the private sector to expand much more in Soconusco than in the southern Lacandon rainforest. Companies willing to purchase land in this region had, however, limited opportunities for expansion. Agrarian law in Mexico

[8]For instance, an agronomist working in a large private-sector oil palm plantation was kidnapped and murdered in 2013.

stipulates a maximum legal limit of 300 hectares for oil palm plantations held by individuals and 7500 hectares for limited companies.[9] In addition to this, banana companies and the sugar cane mill in Huixtla already occupied a significant portion of private land in the region. Furthermore, not all landowners had an interest in selling or even leasing land.

In Soconusco, private-sector land was often in the hands of cattle owners who rarely joined in the oil palm expansion. Cattle ranchers, while wealthy, probably lacked the capital to convert their medium-sized properties into intensive oil palm production. Thus, cattle ranchers received offers to either lease or sell their lands. Neither alternative was attractive enough to a sector which, despite being diversified and often urban-based, still had a strong economic and symbolic attachment to land. When asked about leasing, one cattle rancher responded in disbelief: 'How can I let another guy cultivate my land?' (interview, 12 November 2011, Tapachula). The loss of control over production was simply unacceptable to him. Oil palm cultivation offered few gains to cattle ranchers, who became increasingly concerned. An opposition, even framed in environmental terms, emerged. For instance, in a newspaper article, the president of the Tapachula cattle association denounced the loss of support for cattle and held the expansion of oil palm to be environmentally destructive. The article specifically stated that '[The cattle ranchers] are aware of the damages to the land that continuously expand [because of oil palm] and which leave in a situation of vulnerability the people in communities that were previously dependent on cattle' (Cuarto Poder 2013). A private-sector manager confirmed to us that many cattle ranchers rejected lease agreements, often on environmental grounds (interview, 3 August 2013, Villa Comaltitlán). At the time of writing, oil palm has not led to drastic modifications in land access.

At this point, we can conclude that enclosure was not the prime mechanism for oil palm expansion. We now ask to what extent social differentiation relates to land concentration. In the southern Lacandon region, oil palm growers and high-income producers in particular bought on average more land than they sold, pointing to an incipient land-based social differentiation process (cf. Figure 3). But it is important to note that in 2013, land in this region was still an abundant and cheap resource, as it had only recently been opened up to agriculture. The availability of land is illustrated by the significant number of rural families moving to the southern Lacandon rainforest, particularly from Soconusco. They initially moved to engage in cattle production, and only recently to cultivate oil palm. In contrast to the southern Lacandon rainforest, there are few opportunities to purchase *ejido* land in Soconusco, where the average size of plots purchased was 5.5 hectares compared to an average of 24.6 hectares in the southern Lacandon rainforest. Land is a vital asset in Soconusco, so that oil palm growers in economic difficulties avoid having to sell by occasionally leasing out their productive oil palm plots to others for harvesting. Owners retain access to land in this way. Oil palm cultivation in Soconusco was also undertaken by poor *ejido* farmers who sometimes crop as little as one hectare, whereas in the southern Lacandon rainforest local leaders who promoted oil palm cultivation required association members to plant a minimum of five hectares.[10] Since wealth is related not

[9]By law, any increase in plantation size of 300 hectares requires the participation of an additional partner to the company. A large-scale producer in Soconusco explained the implications of such a law: 'It is difficult to go against that law, the Agrarian Law, it is very difficult. I am outside of that [the law]; I know I am in danger, right? But as I have it [the property] divided in names [front men] is okay; but that also creates an internal problem, right? It is not that easy to handle' (interview, 22 July 2013, Tapachula). As evident in this interview, the risks associated with using front men as a way of legally owning a large area posed an obstacle to the growth of plantations.

[10]This minimum was not always strictly enforced.

only to land access but also to the amount of land a family can cultivate, this ruling excluded those households with little available capital or labour.

This section has explored the possible relationship between land concentration through enclosure and oil palm expansion, a topic discussed elsewhere (e.g. Alonso-Fradejas 2012; Cramb and Sujang 2013). In Chiapas, oil palm has not led to a significant loss of land by poor peasant families. In the southern Lacandon rainforest, investors purchased large plots mainly from high-income families in large *ejidos* with access to more land. In Soconusco, oil palm companies were set up on privately owned land, leaving most *ejidos* intact. Surprisingly, cattle owners perceived oil palm as a threat and resisted its expansion. Changes in land access were related more to processes of social differentiation. Purchase of land for oil palm cultivation by high-income farmers points to an incipient process of land concentration. It is, however, important to note that most land purchases by oil palm growers were concentrated in the southern Lacandon rainforest. As yet, oil palm cultivation has not led to a loss of land by poor and middle-income producers, even where they requested credit. Changes in land access in the two study regions are explained by the specific land tenure regime in Mexico, the resistance to a process of enclosure by some *ejidos* and by cattle ranchers, and by longer term processes of agrarian change that explain, for instance, the greater availability of land in the southern Lacandon rainforest.

Rural politics and local environmental narratives on oil palm

Since the 1994 *Zapatista* uprising, accounts of rural resistance in Chiapas have focused on struggles for autonomy (Nash 2001) by independent organisations (Harvey 1998). These studies have sometimes tackled tensions and conflicts with pro-government factions (Leyva Solano and Burguete 2007) and directed attention to those resisting government interventions. In this section, we identify a different relationship between rural people and the government, one in which farmers negotiate, push for and consent to state intervention. We analyse its importance for understanding agrarian change, in this case the success of the oil palm project in Chiapas. We argue that oil palm interventions by the state are a new and weaker form of the earlier clientelist politics. In this new form, the once-dominant National Peasant Confederation (CNC in its Spanish acronym) has lost its central position in the rural political landscape. The CNC dominated rural politics at a time when the single official party, the PRI (Institutional Revolutionary Party), exerted political control through affiliated or closely related mass organisations. One community leader expressed this phenomenon in typical fashion as follows: '[CNC] was the organisation allied with the PRI. It was like a power formula to win presidential and municipal elections, all those big slices [of pie]', (interview, 8 May 2013, Xochicalco Nuevo). The CNC concentrated political power by channelling government support to rural areas and presenting peasant demands as part of clientelist relations. Since the 1970s, changing state policies and mobilisations by independent organisations gradually displaced the CNC, opening up alternative and multiple channels (Harvey 1990), including cooperatives and other economic organisations, in some instances state designed.

In this context, oil palm organisations rapidly sprang up after the state's oil palm programme started. In the southern Lacandon, oil palm growers were organised in cooperatives and grouped together in a second-tier association. Peasants were aware that the government routinely privileged economic organisations, as under the former pattern of clientelist relations. Most support to rural producers was channelled through these organisations.

While, theoretically, any producer was eligible for oil palm seedlings, in practice farmers had to join an organisation to receive them:

> In the Soconusco area we have about 35 cooperatives that form the Soconusco Regional Committee. When we have the palm, we already know how big the cake is, how much each organisation gets. […] There is lots of demand, and if you are not organised, the truth is that it is very hard. (interview with private sector manager, 9 November 2011, Villa Comaltitlán)

Such emphasis on organisations favoured the incorporation of middle-income and poor peasants, sometimes to the detriment of private-sector producers, who were not often permitted to join.

The private sector realised that state support targeted other agrarian classes. In Soconusco, cattle ranchers were caught by surprise as smallholders were quick to press for oil palm expansion. A talkative *ranchero*, president of a cattle association, commented sarcastically: 'we will just be left to witness the winners passing by' (interview, 27 November 2011, Villa Comaltitlán). He saw the increasing number of palm growers favoured by government subsidies as being in stark contrast to their decaying cattle association. He painted a gloomy scenario: associations closing down, stricter enforcement of existing cattle regulations while cattle were constantly smuggled from Guatemala, and cattle ranchers giving up cattle production. Those with wealth, it seems, are not always favoured by government. 'I am not bitter with the government anymore', said Fernando, a northern blue-eyed farmer living in Tapachula who, along with some other large-scale producers, established 840 hectares of oil palm plantation in 1992. The Chiapas governor at the time had 'insisted and insisted' on their taking up oil palm cultivation, but their promises of support had not materialised. 'They offered us credit but it was never given, they offered us a processing mill, but it was never built', added Fernando (interview, 12 November 2011, Tapachula). They all suffered losses, with two farmers even going bankrupt. While some profited, state support for oil palm cultivation in Chiapas was not specifically intended to benefit the rich. The focus of the state's programme meant that oil palm cultivation was taken up by the social sector, and the emphasis on organised farmers ensured widespread expansion of the crop.

Government support to social organisations had a double rationality: from a technical and managerial perspective, the inclusion of the social sector ensured that a significant area was planted with oil palm, an important measure of success in the predominantly quantitative government evaluations; from a political perspective, embracing farmers from the social sector enhanced popular electoral support. Scale was in fact a recurrent topic in negotiations between organisations and the technical agency:

> We wanted to establish 1000 hectares and then IRBIO's director said that we should aim for 2000 hectares. At the end IRBIO said 1000 hectares was OK, but they left us a nursery of about 5000 hectares. He got me into a hell of a mess. (interview with organisation leader, 18 October 2011, Zamora Pico de Oro)

Negotiations between the Chiapas state and rural organisations over the number of hectares to be planted also took place for other 'biofuel' crops, in particular *Jatropha curcas*. The indigenous leader of a Jatropha producer organisation told us how their first proposal was rejected and the area doubled by government officials. He then consulted the participating rural communities, leading to yet another increase in size.

The oil palm programme, and biofuel interventions in general, also had political goals. Given their influence over the social masses, the state regards leaders of organisations as desirable allies both for political ends and for implementing programmes. The government often turns leaders into state supporters by making special concessions to them and their organisations. 'The government craves you when you are organised because you are united', explained a local leader in Soconusco (interview, 8 November 11, La Alianza). In a context of multiple organisations and competing political parties, this strategy is, however, far less efficient than in the past. As a leader from the southern Lacandon region put it:

> In the first election I said I had 800 [supporters], but in reality they were a maximum of 400, 250 for certain. Leaders from productive organisations sell votes, but nowadays people do not follow them much. People already know that the vote is free and secret. They take whatever is handed to them and then vote for another candidate. (interview, 7 March 2013, Huixtla)

In this new political context, the government in Chiapas was less able to reap the benefits from supporting organisations. Clientelist actions under these new corporative forms bear higher costs than in the past. An IRBIO official stated cautiously: 'They [the peasants] are more organised, but they demand more' (interview, 4 November 2011, Tuxtla Gutiérrez).

The rapid build-up of organisational capacity in the southern Lacandon region allowed farmers to negotiate better terms with both the government and the banks. For instance, leaders could avoid the need for members to provide collateral for credit by securing public and even private-sector funding. Organisations are indeed not passive in the political game, as shown at election time by an organisation managing state projects in the northern Lacandon region. 'We do not support any party, it depends on how good the rooster [candidate] is', explained one of its local leaders, 'But when there is an assembly we decide what is good for us'. He then explained how a candidate for governor had offered them four undersecretaries at the Chiapas agriculture secretary:

> We [the leaders of the organisation] would give the money to [the organisation] so that support would reach the people. Not like the PRI that gives nothing. We would deliver to gain social capital. I explained this to the organisation leaders, and I told them we could get our people in as deputies, municipal presidents and even senators. (interview, 1 November 2012, Ocosingo)

The PRI party in Mexico was well known for its concessions to leaders, often in the form of offering public offices in exchange for the political support of their organisation. This leader refers to such a mechanism for obtaining political power but argues that, in addition, leaders now struggle to obtain support for their members. Who is manipulating who, as Scott (1987) asked, is not a simple question. While co-optation is part of political practice, the rank-and-file are able to exert pressure. Some oil palm organisations are certainly hierarchical, oblivious to democratic procedures and lacking in cohesion. Leaders also reproduce relations of domination. But the leaders' political power ultimately rests on their members. Farmers continually charge leaders with corruption, though members accept that leaders make a living as 'managers' and support them so long as they continue to deliver projects. In other words, rank-and-file concede power to others, including the Chiapas administration, but place social limits on its abuse. Consent is accompanied by social pressure.

Political dynamics also explain the different forms of using environmental jargon. In both study regions, middle-income and poor farmers engaged in palm oil in the face of heavy environmental criticism from both wealthy cattle ranchers and non-participating poor peasants. Oil palm cultivation, they said, degraded lands and dried rivers. One dramatic claim, that the roots of the palm spread for several hundred metres or even kilometres, could generate tensions between neighbours who feared that their land might be degraded by adjacent oil palm plots. This kind of environmentalism came from several sources: internet sites, particularly those of the alternative media, and critiques by conservationists as well as by Catholic activists, including church sermons. The Catholic Church also organised meetings in some indigenous communities. For instance, in La Nueva Unión in the southern Lacandon rainforest, the Church invited a group of European activists who argued that oil palm cultivation was a source of poverty and land degradation. Their critiques discouraged quite a number of farmers from planting oil palm. Once oil palm cultivation proved profitable and the lands were not degraded, an indigenous oil palm grower stated:

> people [in the community] said: Maybe these people [the European activists] were sent by their governments, so that people, people here do not work, so that people here become consumers, … so people consume in order that they [people from other countries] benefit because they now sell their product. (interview, 1 September 2012)

The fact that the assertions of the European activists proved false demonstrated to this indigenous producer that environmental arguments could disguise economic motivations. More generally, environmental positions were recognised locally as being loaded with political and economic interests. This was evident in López Mateos in the southern Lacandon region, where the *ejido* assembly banned the sale of land for oil palm production for environmental reasons but allowed land sales for cattle pastures, even where the land being used was forested. This inconsistency in the way environmental arguments were translated into local land-use politics seemed linked to economic concerns. Accumulation in this *ejido* depended heavily on cattle production, and oil palm cultivation was perceived as an economic and environmental threat by key *ejido* leaders. While the data presented do not allow us to draw conclusions about the motives underlying the use of environmental critiques, they do reveal a locally shared sense of unease with the economic changes brought about by oil palm expansion. Hence, different local interpretations of these changes co-exist, depending on how production relations are understood.

Rural organisations echoed to some extent the government narratives on the beneficial environmental effects of oil palm cultivation. As a permanent crop, oil palm was presented as an alternative to shifting cultivation (the latter seen as synonymous with deforestation and burning). Interestingly, many farmers used similar perspectives themselves when interviewed. During our fieldwork, many farmers referred to oil palm cultivation as 'reforestation' and spoke of how oil palm 'kicks out oxygen' or 'captures water'. As oil palm was planted on pasture land, this reinforced environmental narratives, which depicted oil palm as resembling forests. This was particularly the case for the southern Lacandon region, historically subjected to intensive environmental pressure[11] by government agencies. Some oil palm growers expressed concern about environmental degradation and the changes in the region brought about by agriculture. Other oil palm growers, however, seemingly used environmentalist narratives to protect their moral standing in the face of environmental criticisms. And, finally, some seemed to copy official discourses on the beneficial environmental impact of biofuel crops for political convenience. For

[11]Environmental pressure dates back to the period immediately after land distribution. For instance, in 1989, the Chiapas governor, Patrocinio González, introduced a deforestation ban. State interventions also often prioritised productive activities considered compatible with rainforest conservation, such as cocoa or vanilla production.

instance, in Tulijá, an indigenous community in northeast Chiapas, the governor received a signed community agreement in which peasants promised to change their crop from maize to oil palm. 'We are convinced of taking care of nature, as our forefathers did', argued the community leaders (Gobierno del Estado 2009). Environmental discourses were indeed strongly shaped by political practices.

Rural politics and the relationship with the government explain the significant rural support for oil palm expansion. Rural organisations have been the preferred partner of the Mexican state for resource redistribution (Mackinlay and Otero 2004). While changes disquieted some who resisted planting oil palm because of environmental degradation, large numbers in communities enrolled in oil palm cultivation. Beyond resistance, we also found a pragmatic adherence to the government's oil palm modernisation project that was also justified by a green narrative. The relation with the state shaped local environmental narratives (Trench 2008). By omitting to consider the specific role played by the state, the 'green grabbing' and 'environmentalism of the poor' theses fail to grasp the complexity of peasant–state relations and how these may influence environmentalism. Rural people can be perceived neither as easily dominated, ruled by an inescapable environmentality, nor as actors always defending their sustainable livelihoods vis-à-vis the state. While environmental discourses were dominant, and shared by all actors (Cano Castellanos 2014), they were accommodated to different purposes, concerns and political practices. This brings us to the question of how global environmental narratives have been adapted to fit more specific local political contexts.

The wide gap between environmental NGOs and peasants

Environmentalists attempt to shape resource use by contesting existing perceptions of nature or by pressing to ban or change certain practices. This section explores how the interventions of environmental NGOs in Chiapas and of environmentalists within the state interacted with the objectives of rural organisations. The two most outspoken, though small, environmental NGOs were *Maderas del Pueblo del Sureste* and *Otros Mundos Chiapas*.[12] *Maderas* and *Otros Mundos* shared a common anti-capitalist stance according to which peasant dependence on markets and transnational companies results in impoverishment, environmental degradation and dispossession. Both contested, albeit in different languages, the way the Chiapas government conceived nature. *Otros Mundos* drew on a scientific narrative (e.g. carbon dioxide (CO_2) emissions, water pollution, etc.) to distance oil palm from nature (Castro-Soto 2009), whereas *Maderas* relied more on a political economy discourse.

In 2009, *Maderas del Pueblo* published a leaflet in everyday language pointing out the dangers of oil palm production (García 2009a). The text is quite subtle when describing the local situation but superficial when describing the wider context. The first part of the leaflet pits maize against oil palm production and includes a conversation between a young coastal farmer who is enthusiastic about oil palm, a curious indigenous woman and a sceptical old man. The young farmer casually rejects maize, arguing that palm oil is such a '*negociazo*'

[12]*Otros Mundos Chiapas* and *Maderas del Pueblo del Sureste* are two small Chiapas-based NGOs, which often rely on European funding. While *Otros Mundos* is part of Friends of the Earth, *Maderas del Pueblo del Sureste* arose from the division of a larger organisation due to internal conflicts. There are many other environmental NGOs active in Chiapas, but most did not lobby against oil palm or intervene in any way to modify the process of oil palm expansion.

(sweet deal). He represents the desire for material gain, depicted as the concern of many young people. This view is carefully balanced against that of the old farmer who conceives of modernity and development as destructive for nature and profitable only for the rich. To temper the youngster's excitement, the old man recalls the coffee crisis. The leaflet captures quite well the tensions and conflicts created by oil palm modernisation programmes, pitting traditional agriculture, including indigenous, against modernity. Herbicides are presented as both destructive and labour saving. When turning to address wider issues, however, the language becomes more simplistic, raising rhetorical questions that equate oil palm with deforestation, poverty, human rights abuses and land grabbing. These questions originate from an earlier lengthy report on biofuels that reflects *Maderas*'s position (Arellano Nucamendi and García 2009). This 2009 report conceptualises oil palm expansion and agrofuels as yet another capitalist project leading to land privatisation, pollution and poverty (see also García 2009b). It emphasises how traditional knowledge can hamper such developments. The report insists on self-sufficient communities and refers to concepts such as food sovereignty, which circulate in the international arena amongst transnational agrarian organisations such as *Via Campesina*. How does the general picture, which imagines rural people as mere victims of an external world, relate to farmers' views and activities?

A closer look at why farmers do what they do shows that there is often a wide ideological gap between rural people and green activists. Oil palm changed to some extent the livelihood opportunities of poor farmers. Emilio, an indigenous peasant in La Nueva Unión, explained the change:

> I want clothes, shoes and education for my son; but there is no way of getting it because maize and beans do not have a [market] price. To eat yes, but in the economy it does not work. Therefore we planted rubber and oil palm, to change [our situation]. And yes, something is gained, you can dominate the [economic] need. (interview, 5 September 2012, La Nueva Unión)

Given high returns per hectare in 2012, oil palm cultivation benefited those smallholders who took it up. In coastal Chiapas, some farmers planted oil palms within the protected mangroves of the *Encrucijada* Biosphere Reserve, not as a survival strategy but because it had the best soil: 'there is the mangrove, and in the middle there is the island; in between we plant. The advantage is that the soil is black and it holds the moisture for at least three months after the rains stop' (interview with smallholder farmer, 9 November 2011, Palmarcito). According to a government official, unpermitted planting in both buffer and nucleus regions amounted to 263 hectares (interview CONANP[13] official, 9 November 2011, Acapetahua). Oil palm cultivation opened up opportunities for farmers, as well as for the private sector, during seasonal floods, as the crop thrives in humid soils. Interviews with oil palm farmers showed their demands to be more mundane than resisting capitalism: technical support, subsidies, higher prices and better commercial agreements. Peasants were willing partners in state modernisation programmes, thereby widening the gap between them and environmental NGOs.

In Soconusco, the *Centro de Agroecología San Francisco de Asís* (CASFA in its Spanish acronym), an organisation focused on agroforestry and organic production, preferred to work with 'old-fashioned' farmers who did not participate in oil palm expansion. They did so because the level of economic support they provided could not compete with government programmes (interview, 11 November 2011, Tapachula). A troubled environmentalist from

[13]National Comission for Natural Protected Areas (CONANP in its Spanish acronym).

Otros Mundos highlighted the dominance of the government's environmental productivist discourse, recalling a meeting with agrarian organisations in the Lacandon heartlands:

> The people at the meeting were against mining, they had learnt the discourse well, and when we spoke about palm it ended up that some organisations copied the governor's discourse, the productive reconversion, the green alternative .... I think it is a lack of information. Also, in many cases it is about patronage relationships with the government in which the leader of the organisation goes to CDI [National Commission for Indigenous Rights, in its Spanish acronym] or to another position in the government. Finally, they receive lots of projects, and well, you don't bite the hand that feeds you. (interview, 3 October 2011, San Cristóbal de Las Casas)

The political system in place, with its close relationship between rural organisations and the state, leaves environmental NGOs with little room for manoeuvre. Without rural allies, these organisations cannot succeed in advancing their claims and views. Yet the demands of the environmental NGOs have little overlap with the demands and strategies pursued by many peasants and farmers' organisations. However, the ideological gap between farmer organisations and most environmentalists does not necessarily preclude alliances (see, for example, Conklin and Graham 1995; Doane 2008). In this context, environmentalists within the government were in a better position to advance environmental concerns.

'Environmentalists within the government' refers in particular to those officials active in the Mesoamerican Biological Corridor – Mexico (CBMM)[14] belonging to the federal government. Their intervention was uneven. While both Soconusco and the southern Lacandon region are priority regions for the Secretary of the Environment (SEMARNAT in its Spanish acronym), in practice CBMM and other environmentalists have targeted the Lacandon rainforest. Large rainforest areas still exist, as the area was only recently colonised at a time when environmental concerns first entered public policy debates. Continuous media attention and the emergence of agro-ecological discourses following the *Zapatista* uprising have constituted the region as the last Mexican paradise to be preserved. This environmental concern for the Lacandon region contrasts with the scant attention paid to the Chiapas coastal wetlands. It is in this context that CBMM concentrated on the southern Lacandon region where opportunities for environmental conservation were greater.

CBMM, originally the product of conservationists, was instrumental in shifting the focus from protected areas for nature conservation to a territorial approach that considers multiple land uses, including agriculture. While the emphasis on agricultural production was at odds with the views of some important conservationists, CBMM staff justified their position as follows:

> The question is to recognise that there are needs in the territory. This is, for instance, the case with cattle. We as conservationists cannot deny these needs. It happened that with cattle, there was neither support nor regulation. But everybody went for it, as it was the only thing that made [money]. (interview, 4 October 2011, San Cristóbal de Las Casas)

CBMM explicitly attempted to modify resource use in agriculture, considering agro-ecology to be the key tool. They did this by securing the position of 'technical agent' for

[14]While CBMM emerged as part of the Puebla–Panama plan, it was later incorporated as the General Coordination for Corridors and Biological Resources into the National Commission for Biodiversity Knowledge and Use (CONABIO in its Spanish acronym). Full disclosure: Antonio Castellanos-Navarrete was funded by CONABIO on a project to establish the impacts of oil palm in the southern Lacandon rainforest and to propose strategies to reduce them (see Castellanos-Navarrete 2013).

both agriculture and forestry secretaries (SAGARPA and CONAFOR, respectively) and thus being responsible for the distribution of state resources. They then requested groups interested in receiving SAGARPA support to sign agreements on zero deforestation, reduced burning and reduced agrochemical usage. This, and the reduction of agrochemical inputs in particular which many farmers benefiting from CBMM support regarded as unfeasible, inevitably created tensions (interviews with farmers, July–August 2012, southern Lacandon region). Oil palm growers were, however, unaffected, as they received state support directly from SAGARPA. In this context, CBMM staff could not shape resource use within oil palm production but could exert a degree of control over it at the political level. The CBMM mandate for biodiversity conservation granted them some power over other institutions active in the region. For instance, SAGARPA sought environmental approval for their Humid Tropic Programme from CBMM and SEMARNAT, who both ignored the request. This granted what CBMM staff called 'a little power'. 'If CONABIO [i.e. CBMM] says that they [farmers] are deforesting, that oil palm is destroying biodiversity, then SAGARPA has a problem' (interview with a CBMM staff member, 22 August 2012, San Cristóbal de Las Casas). Such soft power enabled environmentalists within the government to exert some pressure on government agencies promoting oil palm and indirectly shape its expansion to some extent.[15]

In short, environmentalists within the state were found to be important but not in the sense predicted by the green grabbing thesis (i.e. founding environmental governance on neoliberal market mechanisms; Fairhead, Leach, and Scoones 2012). They intervened in ways that sometimes went against accumulation, as when advocating agro-ecological practices or indirectly constraining support for oil palm planting. Personnel in CBMM considered oil palm cultivation as an environmental threat and reiterated views that held this crop responsible for deforestation and land degradation. However, they recognised the need to adapt to some extent to ongoing accumulation processes that were driving farmers' decisions on land-use change in the region. By contrast, more radical green organisations, such as *Maderas* and *Otros Mundos*, were unable to form coalitions at the local level, with the result that their critical environmental narratives, which are similar to those of large environmental organisations, found little local resonance. As shown in the previous section, the success of certain environmental discourses is related to the effectiveness of political practices.

Conclusions

Rural interventions in support of smallholders in oil palm production appear paradoxical. Environmental organisations and other civil society actors often hold oil palm cultivation in particular and biofuels in general as responsible for rural dispossession and environmental destruction. Involving smallholders in the expansion of this crop would thereby seem to go against their interest. We studied this issue in Chiapas, where a state programme for oil palm planting has left land ownership largely intact, although it has deepened

[15]An example is a small farmer group pioneering oil palm cultivation in the region: 'There were lots of obstacles. At slash and burning time, the [Chiapas] government did not want to approve the project because the forest would be devastated', explained a leader of this oil palm organisation (interview, 18 October 2011, Playón de la Gloria). In the absence of regulation over land use but under environmental pressure, the organisation self-regulated land use by limiting planting to degraded pastures and secondary vegetation patches. Government agencies accepted this as a *de facto* rule. As a result, the organisation was finally able to access Chiapas government support for oil palm.

farmers' integration into markets, especially through credit. We showed how in the absence of dispossession, poor and middle-income farmers supported an oil palm programme that was perceived to be economically beneficial to them rather than to wealthy private sector producers. Smallholders' access to land remained relatively secure, for three reasons. First, state support was biased in favour of social-sector producers through the preferential distribution of free oil palm seedlings and economic support. Second, the existence of *ejido* land tenure constrained dispossession by capital and ensured favourable conditions for smallholder participation in the oil palm boom. And, third, the rejection of and disaffection with oil palm by cattle ranchers, a key economic power group in Chiapas, limited the emergence of large-scale plantations on private land. In the absence of enclosure and land concentration, farmers pressed for improved terms of participation in oil palm expansion rather than resistance. Small farmers considered oil palm cultivation as the road to betterment compared to the meagre benefits offered by previous production systems, and willingly participated despite their awareness of environmental critiques. Our analysis suggests that a green agrarian question that focuses exclusively on enclosure as the main driving force behind agrarian social relationships is unable to explain agrarian dynamics. This may have consequences for interpretations of contestation and the multiple uses of environmental narratives.

Dispossession remains central to environmental and social critiques of oil palm cultivation as well as to such influential theses as 'environmentalism of the poor' and 'green grabbing'. This focus, in our opinion, limits our understanding of environmental conflicts. The 'environmentalism of the poor' thesis assigns a central role to the local formulation of environmentalist narratives in building resistance to enclosure. In the 'green grabbing' thesis, the focus is on the use made of environmental discourses by powerful actors to justify dispossession. These perspectives have certainly extended our understanding of the role of environmental politics in resource access. The arguments, however, lose force where enclosure does not take place. In the absence of land grabbing, farmers and their organisations may opt to engage in oil palm expansion rather than resist it. This has important theoretical implications. In the absence of enclosure, the articulation of environmentalisms is more complex, as processes other than resource access become significant. This is well illustrated by the cacophony of environmentalist voices arising from oil palm expansion in Chiapas: government officials, technicians, NGO workers and farmers adopted green vocabularies for multiple reasons. For instance, critical green narratives were drawn on not only by poor indigenous farmers, as would be expected by the 'environmentalism of the poor' thesis, but also, unexpectedly, by wealthy cattle ranchers and even high-input sugarcane producers on the Chiapas coast. Differently from the 'green grabbing' thesis, we found 'environmentalists within the state' aiming to curb the environmental degradation associated with oil palm expansion without dispossessing peasants. It is not dispossession but the particular role of the state, the social relations of production and wider market changes which are more important for understanding the variety of environmental discourses in play as a result of oil palm expansion in Chiapas. Only by developing this perspective is it possible to understand why specific actors employ a particular form of environmentalism.

Large environmental organisations have been extremely effective in stirring up a debate on the environmental impacts of oil palm cultivation (Gilbert 2012; Koh and Wilcove 2007). Oil palm has become synonymous with deforestation, poverty and even labour abuse, particularly in Southeast Asia. Their campaigns have forced companies purchasing palm oil to monitor their suppliers, often through certification (Pye 2010). This popular environmental narrative, however, largely portrays smallholders as victims. Such a view, which implicitly links smallholders with sustainability, cannot explain, for instance, rural mobilisation in favour of cheaper pesticides (Bernstein 2010) or indigenous communities bidding for nuclear dumping sites (Ishiyama 2003). These cases indicate a greater complexity in rural engagements with capitalism and the environment. The overemphasis on dispossession in both theory and in environmental campaigns against the spread of palm oil limits our understanding of the material and political responses of vast numbers of peasants to new green interventions. The neglect of the significant role played by smallholders also weakens attempts to reduce the environmental impacts of oil palm cultivation.

Acknowledgements

We would like to thank Abril Aidee Ruiz Medina, Henk van Rikxoort and Carlos Miguel López Sierra for research assistance. This contribution benefited from comments made in seminars at Wageningen University and Chapingo University. We also thank all interviewees for their time. Finally we thank the Land Deal Politics Initiative (LDPI) and the Mexican Council for Science and Technology (CONACYT in its Spanish acronym) for funding this research.

References

Agrawal, A. 2005. *Environmentality: Technologies of government and the making of subjects*. Durham: Duke University Press.

Akram-Lodhi, A.H., and C. Kay. 2010. Surveying the agrarian question (part 2): Current debates and beyond. *The Journal of Peasant Studies* 37, no. 2: 255–284.

Alonso-Fradejas, A. 2012. Land control-grabbing in Guatemala: The political economy of contemporary agrarian change. *Canadian Journal of Development Studies/Revue canadienne d'études du développement* 33, no. 4: 509–528.

Arellano Nucamendi, M., and M.A. García. 2009. *Agrocombustibles y palma africana: Peligros sobre nuestras comunidades y sobre la Madre Tierra*. San Cristóbal de Las Casas: Maderas del Pueblo del Sureste, A.C.

Assies, W. 2007. Land tenure and tenure regimes in Mexico: An overview. *Journal of Agrarian Change* 8, no. 1: 33–63.

Barraza, D., K. Jansen, B. van Wendel de Joode, and C. Wesseling. 2013. Social movements and risk perception: Unions, churches, pesticides and bananas in Costa Rica. *International Journal of Occupational and Environmental Health* 19, no. 1: 11–21.

Bernstein, H. 2010. *Class dynamics of agrarian change*. Black Point: Fernwood Publishing.

Borras, S.M., Jr., and J.C. Franco. 2013. Global land grabbing and political reactions 'from below'. *Third World Quarterly* 34, no. 9: 1723–1747.

Borras, S.M., Jr., P. McMichael, and I. Scoones. 2010. The politics of biofuels, land and agrarian change: Editors' introduction. *The Journal of Peasant Studies* 37, no. 4: 575–592.

Brenner, R. 1986. The social basis of economic development. In *Analytical Marxism*, ed. J. Roemer, 23–53. Cambridge: Cambridge University Press.

Cano Castellanos, I. 2014. Entre sueños agrarios y discurso ecologista. Las encrucijadas contemporáneas de la colonización de la Selva Lacandona (Chiapas, México). *Entre Diversidades*, primavera-verano 2014.

Cárdenas, R. 2012. Green multiculturalism: Articulations of ethnic and environmental politics in a Colombian 'black community'. *The Journal of Peasant Studies* 39, no. 2: 309–333.

Carlson, K.M., L.M. Curran, D. Ratnasari, A.M. Pittman, B.S. Soares-Filho, G.P. Asner, S.N. Trigg, D.A. Gaveau, D. Lawrence, and H.O. Rodrigues. 2012. Committed carbon emissions, deforestation, and community land conversion from oil palm plantation expansion in West Kalimantan, Indonesia. *Proceedings of the National Academy of Sciences* 109: 7559–7564.

Castellanos-Navarrete, A. 2013. *Elaboración de criterios de certificación para el desarrollo de plantaciones agroindustriales: Certificación del cultivo de palma africana en Marqués de Comillas (Chiapas)*. Reporte para la Comisión Nacional para el Conocimiento y Uso de la Biodiversidad (CONABIO). México, D.F.

Castro-Soto, G. 2009. *Monocultivos desastrosos: La producción de aceite de palma en Chiapas*. San Cristóbal de Las Casas: Otros Mundos, A.C.

CONEVAL. 2010. *Medición de la pobreza, Estados Unidos Mexicanos. Indicadores de pobreza, por municipio*. México, D.F.: Consejo Nacional de Evaluación de la Política de Desarrollo Social.

Conklin, B.A., and L.R. Graham. 1995. The shifting middle ground: Amazonian Indians and eco-politics. *American Anthropologist* 97, no. 4: 695–710.

Cramb, R.A., and P.S. Sujang. 2013. The mouse deer and the crocodile: oil palm smallholders and livelihood strategies in Sarawak, Malaysia. *The Journal of Peasant Studies* 40, no. 1: 129–154.

Cuarto Poder. (2013). Siembra de palma africana afectó ganadería, *Cuarto Poder*, October 13 2013.

Deibel, E. 2013. Open variety rights: Rethinking the commodification of plants. *Journal of Agrarian Change* 13, no. 2: 282–309.

De Vos, J. 2002. *Una tierra para sembrar sueños: Historia reciente de la Selva Lacandona 1950–2000*. México, D.F.: CIESAS, FCE.

Doane, M. 2008. The political economy of the ecological native. *American Anthropologist* 109, no. 3: 452–462.

Doering III, O.C., and W.E. Tyner. 2009. US and international policies affecting liquid biofuels' expansion and profitability. *International Journal of Biotechnology* 11, no. 1: 150–167.

Fairhead, J., M. Leach, and I. Scoones. 2012. Green grabbing: A new appropriation of nature? *The Journal of Peasant Studies* 39, no. 2: 237–261.

Fargione, J., J. Hill, D. Tilman, S. Polasky, and P. Hawthorne. 2008. Land clearing and the biofuel carbon debt. *Science* 319, no. 5867: 1235–1238.

Feintrenie, L., W.K. Chong, and P. Levang. 2010a. Why do farmers prefer oil palm? Lessons learnt from Bungo District, Indonesia. *Small-scale forestry* 9: 379–396.

Feintrenie, L., S. Schwarze, and P. Levang, 2010b. Are local people conservationists? Analysis of transition dynamics from agroforests to monoculture plantations in Indonesia. *Ecology and Society* 15, no. 4: 37.

Fletes-Ocón, H.B., and A. Bonanno. 2013. Responses to the crisis of neo-liberal globalization: State intervention in palm oil production in Chiapas, Mexico. *International Journal of Sociology of Agriculture and Food* 20, no. 3: 313–334.

García, M.A. 2009a. *¿¿¡¡¡Órale!!! ¡¡Ya vieron que rete chulas palmitas pusieron nuestros vecinos!!??* San Cristóbal de Las Casas: Maderas del Pueblo del Sureste, A.C.

García, M.A. 2009b. *¿¿Quésque en vez de tortillas, el maíz se hará gasolina??* San Cristóbal de Las Casas: Maderas del Pueblo del Sureste, A.C.

García de León, A. 1997. *Resistencia y utopía: Memorial de agravios y crónicas de revueltas y profecías acaecidas en la Provincia de Chiapas durante los últimos quinientos años de su historia*. México, D.F.: Ediciones ERA.

Gerber, J.F. 2011. Conflicts over industrial tree plantations in the South: Who, how and why? *Global Environmental Change* 21, no. 1: 165–176.

Gerber, J.F., and S. Veuthey. 2010. Plantations, resistance and the greening of the agrarian question in coastal Ecuador. *Journal of Agrarian Change* 10, no. 4: 455–481.

Gilbert, N. 2012. Palm-oil boom raises conservation concerns. *Nature* 487: 14–15.

Gobierno del Estado. 2009. *Mil 300 hectáreas de palma en 2009; en los últimos 10 años, 900 has, Boletín 1739, 19 de agosto del 2009*. Tuxtla Gutiérrez: Gobierno del Estado de Chiapas.

Gobierno del Estado. 2010a. *Chiapas: hacia la producción de más de 30,000 litros diarios de biodiesel, Boletín 0833, 24 de Marzo del 2010*. Tuxtla Gutiérrez: Gobierno del Estado de Chiapas.

Gobierno del Estado. 2010b. *Buenas expectativas para la palma de aceite en la región del Soconusco, Boletín 1124, 28 de Abril del 2010*. Tuxtla Gutiérrez: Gobierno del Estado de Chiapas.

Gobierno de los Estados Unidos Mexicanos. 2007. *Plan de Desarrollo Nacional 2007–2012: Poder Ejecutivo Federal*. México, D.F.: Presidencia de la República (Gobierno de los Estados Unidos Mexicanos).

Greenpeace. 2013. Palm oil. http://www.greenpeace.org.uk/forests/palm-oil (accessed December 19, 2014).

Guha, R. 1993. The malign encounter: The Chipko movement and competing visions of nature. In *Who Will save the forests? Knowledge, power and environmental destruction*, ed. T. Banuri and F. Apffel Marglin, 80–113. London: Zed Books.

Guha, R., and J. Martinez-Alier. 1997. *Varieties of environmentalism: Essays North and South*. London: Earthscan Publications.

Hall, D. 2011. Land grabs, land control, and Southeast Asian crop booms. *The Journal of Peasant Studies* 38, no. 4: 837–857.

Harvey, N. 1990. Peasant strategies and corporatism in Chiapas. In *Popular movements and political change in Mexico*, ed. J. Foweraker and A.L. Craig, 183–198. Boulder: Lynne Rienner Publishers.
Harvey, N. 1998. *The Chiapas rebellion: The struggle for land and democracy*. Durham: Duke University Press.
Harvey, D. 2005. *The new imperialism*. London: Oxford University Press.
Index Mundi. 2014. Palm oil and nitrogen fertiliser prices between the year 2000 and the year 2011. http://www.indexmundi (accessed date December 19, 2014).
INEGI. 2007a. *Censo agrícola, ganadero y forestal 2007*. Aguascalientes: Instituto Nacional de Estadística y Geografía.
INEGI. 2007b. *Censo ejidal*. Aguascalientes: Instituto Nacional de Estadística y Geografía.
Ishiyama, N. 2003. Environmental justice and American Indian tribal sovereignty: Case study of a land–use conflict in Skull Valley, Utah. *Antipode* 35, no. 1: 119–139.
Jansen, K. 1998. *Political ecology, mountain agriculture, and knowledge in Honduras*. Amsterdam: Thela Publishers.
Jansen, K. 2004. Greening bananas and institutionalizing environmentalism: Self-regulation by fruit corporations. In *Agribusiness and society: Corporate responses to environmentalism, market opportunities and public regulation*, ed. K. Jansen and S. Vellema, 145–175. London: Zed.
Julia and B. White. 2012. Gendered experiences of dispossession: Oil palm expansion in a Dayak Hibun community in West Kalimantan. *The Journal of Peasant Studies* 39, no. 3&4: 995–1016.
Kautsky, K. 1988. *The agrarian question*. London: Zwan Publications. First published in 1899.
Kelly, A.B. 2011. Conservation practice as primitive accumulation. *The Journal of Peasant Studies* 38, no. 4: 683–701.
Kloppenburg, J. 2010. Impeding dispossession, enabling repossession: Biological open source and the recovery of seeds sovereignty. *Journal of Agrarian Change* 10, no. 3: 367–388.
Koczberski, G., and G.N. Curry. 2004. Divided communities and contested landscapes: Mobility, development and shifting identities in migrant destination sites in Papua New Guinea. *Asia Pacific Viewpoint* 45, no. 3: 357–371.
Koh, L.P., and D.S. Wilcove. 2007. Cashing in palm oil for conservation. *Nature* 448: 993–994.
Lamers, P., C. Hamelinck, M. Junginger, and A. Faaij. 2011. International bioenergy trade – A review of past developments in the liquid biofuel market. *Renewable and Sustainable Energy Reviews* 15, no. 6: 2655–2676.
Lee, J.S.H., S. Abood, J. Ghazoul, B. Barus, K. Obidzinski, and K.P. Koh. 2014. Environmental impacts of large-scale oil palm enterprises exceed that of smallholdings in Indonesia. *Conservation Letters* 7, no. 1: 25 33.
Lenin, V.I. 1967. *The development of capitalism in Russia*. Moscow: Progress Publishers. First published in 1899.
Leyva Solano, X., and A. Burguete Cal y Mayor. 2007. *La remunicipalización de Chiapas: Lo político y la política en tiempos de contrainsurgencia*. México, D.F.: CIESAS, Miguel Ángel Porrua.
Luke, T.W. 1997. *Ecocritique: Contesting the politics of nature, economy, and culture*. Minneapolis: University of Minnesota Press.
Mackinlay, H., and G. Otero. 2004. State corporatism and peasant organizations: Towards new institutional arrangements. In *Mexico in transition: Neoliberal globalism, the state and civil society*, ed. G. Otero, 72–88. London: Zed.
Maher, D. 2014. Rooted in violence: Civil war, international trade and the expansion of palm oil in Colombia. *New Political Economy* 20, no. 2: 299–330.
Marin-Burgos, V. 2014. *Access, power and justice in commodity frontiers: The political ecology of access to land and palm oil expansion in Colombia*. PhD diss., University of Twente.
Martinez-Alier, J. 2002. *The environmentalism of the poor: A study of ecological conflicts and valuation*. Cheltenham: Edward Elgar Publishing.
McAfee, K. 1999. Selling nature to save it? Biodiversity and green developmentalism. *Environment and Planning D: Society and Space* 17: 133–154.
McCarthy, J.F. 2010. Processes of inclusion and adverse incorporation: Oil palm and agrarian change in Sumatra, Indonesia. *The Journal of Peasant Studies* 37, no. 4: 821–850.
Mekhilef, S., S. Siga, and R. Saidur. 2011. A review on palm oil biodiesel as a source of renewable fuel. *Renewable and Sustainable Energy Reviews* 15, no. 4: 1937–1949.
Nash, J. 2001. *Mayan visions: The quest for autonomy in an age of globalization*. New York: Routledge.
Novo, A., K. Jansen, M. Slingerland and K. Giller. 2010. Biofuel, dairy production and beef in Brazil: Competing claims on land use in São Paulo State. *The Journal of Peasant Studies* 37, no. 4: 769–92.

Obidzinski, K., R. Andriani, H. Komarudin, and A. Andrianto. 2012. Environmental and social impacts of oil palm plantations and their implications for biofuel production in Indonesia. *Ecology and Society* 17, no. 1: 25.

Osborne, T.M. 2011. Carbon forestry and agrarian change: Access and land control in a Mexican rainforest. *The Journal of Peasant Studies* 38, no. 4: 859–883.

Pérez Castañeda, J.C. 2002. *El nuevo sistema de propiedad agrarian en México*. México, D.F.: Textos y Contextos.

Pye, O. 2010. The biofuel connection – transnational activism and the palm oil boom. *The Journal of Peasant Studies* 37, no. 4: 851–874.

Reyes Ramos, M.E. 2002. *Conflicto agrario en Chiapas: 1934–1964*. Tuxtla Gutiérrez: CONECULTA.

Rist, L., L. Feintrenie, and P. Levang. 2010. The livelihood impacts of oil palm: Smallholders in Indonesia. *Biodiversity and Conservation* 19, no. 4: 1009–1024.

SAGARPA. 2009. *Programa de producción sustentable de insumos para bioenergéticos y desarrollo científico y tecnológico*. México, D.F.: Secretaría de Agricultura, Ganadería, Desarrollo Rural, Pesca y Alimentación (SAGARPA).

Saldaña, J. 2012. *The coding manual for qualitative researchers*. Sage: London.

Schoneveld, G.C., L.A. German, and E. Nukator. 2011. Land-based investments for rural development? A grounded analysis of the local impacts of biofuel feedstock plantations in Ghana. *Ecology and Society* 16, no. 4: 10.

Scott, J.C. 1987. *Weapons of the weak: Everyday forms of peasant resistance*. New Haven: Yale University Press.

Sheng Goh, C., and K. Teong Lee. 2010. Will biofuel projects in Southeast Asia become white elephants? *Energy Policy* 38, no. 8: 3847–3848.

SIAP-SAGARPA. 2013. *Oil palm surfaces for the period between 2007 and 2013*. México, D.F.: Servicio de Información Agroalimentaria y Pesquera (SIAP) de la Secretaría de Agricultura, Ganadería, Desarrollo Rural, Pesca y Alimentación (SAGARPA).

Stonich, S.C., and C. Bailey. 2000. Resisting the blue revolution: Contending coalitions surrounding industrial shrimp farming. *Human Organization* 59, no. 1: 23–36.

Toleubayev, K., K. Jansen, and A. van Huis. 2010. Knowledge and agrarian de-collectivisation in Kazakhstan. *The Journal of Peasant Studies* 37, no. 2: 353–377.

Torres, A. 2011. Fracasa proyecto de biodiesel. *El Economista*, 18 Julio.

Trench, T. 2008. From "orphans of the state" to the comunidad conservacionista institucional: The case of the Lacandón Community, Chiapas. *Identities* 15, no. 5: 607–634.

Veuthey, S., and J.F. Gerber. 2012. Accumulation by dispossession in coastal Ecuador: Shrimp farming, local resistance and the gender structure of mobilizations. *Global Environmental Change* 22, no. 3: 611–622.

Wolff, C. 1999. *The economics of oil palm production in Chiapas, Mexico*. Working Paper 99–09, Department of Agricultural Resource, and Managerial Economics. Ithaca: Cornell University.

Yengoh, G.T., and F.A. Armah. 2014. Land access constraints for communities affected by large-scale land acquisition in Southern Sierra Leone. *GeoJournal*, November 2014.

Rubber, rights and resistance: the evolution of local struggles against a Chinese rubber concession in Northern Laos

Karen E. McAllister

Over the past 10 years, transnational land grabs for rubber tree plantations have proliferated across Laos. Plantation concessions are being established on village lands that are represented as 'degraded' and legally classified as 'state forests', expropriated by government officials in the name of poverty alleviation with promises that plantations will provide new wage labour opportunities for those dispossessed. This contribution examines the evolution of various forms of resistance by a small, ethnic-minority Khmu community against a Chinese-owned rubber concession awarded on over half of their territory. Villagers combined different tactics of resistance to undermine the concession, including anonymous acts of sabotage, refusal to work for the company, identification of powerful allies in the government and civil society, and recourse to law and state institutions. They also appropriated the dominant state development ideology as a strategic representation to assert their territorial claims. By working within state structures rather than by open confrontation, the Khmu have stalled the establishment of the plantation on their lands. Khmu resistance to the concession evolved in response to shifting experiences of injustice and perceptions of risk and opportunity, and is one of many examples of resistance that are erupting in response to land deals across Laos.

Over the past decade, the area planted with rubber trees in Laos has expanded rapidly from approximately 900 ha in 2003 to 28,574 ha in 2007 (Douangsavang, Thammavong, and Noble 2008), and reaching an estimated 261,000 ha in 2014 (Vientiane Times 2014). In Northern Laos, Chinese companies are the main investors and are establishing monoculture rubber plantations in contract farming and concession-like arrangements (Alton, Bluhm, and Sananikone 2005; Manivong and Cramb 2008; Shi 2008; Thongmanivong et al. 2009). Chinese investment in rubber increased rapidly from the mid-2000s as part of a wider phenomenon of transnational enclosure motivated by Chinese international development policy which encourages overseas investment, trade and migration ('*zou chu qu*' – 'to go out') (Shi 2008; Cohen 2009). At this time, the demand for natural rubber to fuel national industrialisation had increased, while the production of rubber within China had stagnated and was constrained by limited land resources (Alton, Bluhm, and Sananikone 2005; Shi 2008; Cohen 2009). Global prices for natural rubber were rising and were predicted to continue to increase over the next decade (Vongkhamor et al. 2007; Manivong and Cramb 2008; Douangsavang,

Thammavong, and Noble 2008). In addition, in 2004 the Chinese government linked opium replacement projects with its international development policy. Chinese rubber plantations in Laos are promoted as development projects and opium replacement strategies targeting sources of illegal drugs into China (Shi 2008; Cohen 2009). Chinese companies are therefore subsidised with loans and tariff exemptions by the Chinese government.

Chinese commercial interests in developing rubber concessions in Laos intersect with Lao government policies to use natural resources in order to fuel national development and to encourage foreign direct investment (FDI). Rubber trees are planted mainly on 'mountainous' lands legally designated as 'state forests' but which are inhabited and farmed under various forms of customary tenure. State policies for developing these highland areas promote commercialised agriculture and the eradication of traditional subsistence-oriented shifting cultivation, which is perceived as 'backwards', wasteful and a cause of poverty and forest destruction (Minister of Agriculture and Forestry 1999; Government of Lao PDR 2005; Rigg 2005). Rubber trees are seen as a promising option to help meet these objectives as well as to alleviate poverty by providing wage labour opportunities for highland communities. Because tree plantations are classified as a type of forest in Lao law, rubber concessions are sometimes promoted as supporting national environmental goals for reforestation (Government of Lao PDR 2005). Transnational rubber concessions are also facilitated by the concurrent implementation of policies to resettle remote highland villages to roadsides, to zone forest lands for different purposes, and to allocate village usufruct rights within limited areas within 'state forests' (Vandergeest 2003). These policies can be (mis)applied to appropriate village territories for lease to companies. Ethnic minorities, who account for approximately 50 percent of Laos' 6.8 million people, have been disproportionately affected by rubber concessions and contract farming arrangements because many live in remote villages in 'state forests' and practice various forms of shifting cultivation, and therefore their lands are often targeted. Furthermore, most rubber is being planted in the north and south of the country where the populations of ethnic minorities are comparatively high.[1]

This contribution focuses on the evolution of local resistance against transnational land acquisitions for rubber plantations in Laos. The study is based on ethnographic fieldwork conducted in villages in Pak Ou District, Luang Prabang Province, northern Laos, between 2006 and 2007 with a follow-up research trip in 2012. The research coincided with the introduction of commercial rubber trees from China into the district. Taking the

[1]Data detailing how different ethnic groups are affected by land deals in Laos is incomplete and often not available. The most comprehensive and reliable study on land deals (Schönweger et al. 2012) suggests that the Lao-Tai (the dominant and most populous ethnic group) are the most affected by all types of land deals. However, the study indicates that rubber plantations affect Mon-Khmer ethnic minorities disproportionately relative to their population. This is likely because most rubber 'concessions' are granted in the South of Laos where the Mon Khmer represent a greater percentage of the population and because they tend to live in coveted forest lands, rather than because they are specifically targeted because of their minority status. Even so, the data likely underestimate the percentage of minority groups affected by rubber investments. Almost half of the land deals identified by the study lacked spatial information and so were excluded from this analysis. Furthermore, over 50 percent of rubber in Laos is planted in the Northern provinces, where ethnic minorities make up a very high percentage of the population. Most land deals in northern Laos are classified as contract farming arrangements, even though many are concession-like in their impacts on local land and labour relations. Contract farming arrangements were excluded from the study. Therefore, the proportion of ethnic minorities affected by rubber deals is likely much higher than reliable data suggest.

case of Ban Samsum,[2] a small ethnic-minority Khmu[3] village facing territorial dispossession by a Chinese-owned rubber concession, I outline official justifications for expropriating village lands, and the evolution of various forms of resistance by which villagers attempted both to defend their land rights and to negotiate better conditions of employment with the company. Khmu resistance to the concession evolved in response to shifting experiences of injustice and perceptions of risk and opportunity, and is one of many examples of rural resistance that are erupting in response to land deals across Laos.

Resistance against dispossession is simultaneously a claim to possession and is part of a broader struggle over land rights waged between rural villages and the Lao state. Hall, Hirsch, and Li (2011) identify four 'powers' that influence exclusion from land: (1) regulation (formal and informal laws, land zoning, rules of land access and use); (2) force (violence and the threat of violence); (3) the market (prices and incentives for commercial land transactions and for individualised land rights); and (4) legitimation (moral discourses, narratives and counter-narratives justifying competing claims). These are deployed by powerful and less powerful actors alike in struggles for land control in the context of land deals. Khmu villagers combined various tactics of resistance and 'legitimating narratives' to maintain their land and to seek better terms of employment with the company. They pursued 'rightful resistance' (O'Brien and Li 2006), and used regulation, formal laws and official channels to support their claims, seeking assistance from concerned state and elite actors. They also engaged in disorganised, covert and anonymous 'everyday forms of resistance' as are commonly enacted by marginal groups in situations where outright confrontation is risky (Scott 1986, 1990). Villages are divided by different interests and different groups are affected differently by land deals (Bernstein 2010; Borras and Franco 2013), and therefore the emergence of collective resistance by the Khmu against the concession is not a given and needs to be explained.

Faced with territorial dispossession, communities often unite around an ideological discourse and forge a collective 'resistance identity' as a political positioning to strengthen their claims to land (Hall 1996; Li 2000). Many autochthonous peoples such as the Khmu organise around the trope of 'indigeneity' in order to ally with environmental and indigenous rights activists 'against' the state. However, because of their specific political situation, the Khmu framed their resistance 'within' state ideologies and institutions rather than against them. The following case study describes the processes through which the rubber concession was established in Ban Samsum, and the evolution of different forms of individual and collective local resistance against the project. I outline how district government officials justified the expropriation of Khmu land in the face of local opposition, and explore how the Khmu strategically applied 'public transcripts' (Scott 1990) – the legitimating discourses and ideologies used by the state to justify authority – as resistance against perceived injustice in an attempt to hold those in power to the 'meaning' of their own rhetoric.

Introduction of rubber into Pak Ou District

According to provincial government officials interviewed in 2006, Chinese companies had plans to establish 20,000 ha of rubber in Luang Prabang province as plantation concessions

[2]The names of all villages described in the paper have been changed.

[3]The Khmu are classified as a 'Mon Khmer' ethnic group and are included in the Lao government category '*Lao Theung*' (midland Lao).

and contract farming arrangements, targeting the neighbouring districts of Pak Ou and Nambak. Rubber trees were introduced into Nambak district in 2003, and the area planted with rubber in the province expanded from approximately 300 ha to 2500 ha between 2005 and 2006 (Vongkhamor et al. 2007). In March 2005, the Division of State Assets under the Provincial Finance Office, with the approval of the provincial governor, signed a contract with the Chinese owned Sino-Lao Jinrun Development Company and their Lao subsidiary company, granting joint-venture concession rights in Nambak and Pak Ou Districts (Vongkhamor et al. 2007). That year, the Governor of Pak Ou District approved a 40-year lease of 7000 ha of 'state forest land' to the 'Sino' company for the development of a rubber plantation. The concession encompassed the territories of five neighbouring ethnic minority Khmu villages, all of which were located in the mountains and inaccessible by road. The area covered stretched to the border of Nambak district, enabling the establishment of a contiguous 14,000-ha plantation comprised of 7000 ha of land in each district.

Ban Samsum, a small Khmu village of 54 households located a two-hour hike from the main road, was chosen as the pilot site for the plantation. The Khmu are widely considered to be the most impoverished ethnic minority in Luang Prabang province, and Ban Samsum was one of the poorest villages in the district. Class and wealth differences within Ban Samsum, while they existed, were less significant than the differences between the Khmu and the neighbouring Lao and Lue communities along the road. Village livelihoods were primarily subsistence-based, organised around shifting cultivation for upland rice and some cash crops like sesame, paper mulberry (*posa*) and Job's tears. The majority of villagers were rice short every year, balancing precarious yields by selling labour to better-off neighbouring ethnic groups, by hunting and gathering for subsistence and sale, by selling *posa* bark and cash crops, and by keeping small livestock in the forest-fallow. Villagers often referred to themselves as '*ban nok*', which holds a negative connotation of backwardness similar to 'hillbilly', and expressed desires to become 'up to date'. As a poor, small and remote village, Ban Samsum was a prime candidate for the state resettlement policy that had forced the relocation of many neighbouring communities to overcrowded areas along the road. Villagers were acutely aware of their vulnerability to various state development policies.

In early 2006, Lao district officials and Chinese company representatives held a meeting in Ban Samsum to promote the establishment of a rubber plantation on village land. The plantation was advocated as a new opportunity for wage labour and cash cropping. Some villagers initially misunderstood that they would be entering into contract farming arrangements and were interested in cooperating with the company. However, when it became clear that the company would take their land and own the trees, most villagers opposed the concession. Three meetings were held in the village to gain local consent, and village leaders repeatedly rejected the proposal because they did not want to give away their land to the company. Eventually, the District Deputy Governor went himself to Ban Samsum and, according to villagers, 'slapped the table' telling them 'if you don't agree to let the Chinese plant rubber here, then you will always be poor'. Village leaders feared resettlement and felt they could not say no to the government, so the rubber plantation was approved with 'official' local consent. The most fertile half of the village territory was allocated to the company, and many households lost most or all of the fields to which they held customary cultivation rights.

Villages are divided by different interests related to class, wealth, ethnicity, gender, livelihood and so on, and different groups are affected differently by agrarian change (Bernstein 2010). In the context of land deals, some groups resist dispossession while others seek better terms of inclusion – better wages, employment conditions and compensation (Borras and Franco 2013). In Ban Samsum, men were initially divided about whether or not to support the concession. Shifting cultivation is arduous work and increased land pressure had contributed to declining rice yields. Some men were interested in the new opportunity for wage labour and supported the project, intending to clear new land farther from the hamlet if they lost their fields to the company. The Khmu have long worked as agricultural labourers for neighbouring communities, and wage labour was not a new concept. The headman himself thought that the plantation could be beneficial if the wages provided greater livelihood security:

> When I am working for myself, in some years I have a good yield or a bad yield and I get a good or a bad income. However, if you work for a company, then you can get money for a long time. I am happy that there will be ways for people in the village to earn money by weeding, planting, etc. If you work for yourself, then some years you get a lot, and some years you don't get anything. When you don't get anything, then you are short of rice, sometimes from early in the year. Every year some households in Ban Samsum are short of rice.

In contrast to the men, women were unanimously against the concession. However, village decisions in Ban Samsum are made by men, and most women were not present at the meetings. Women's interests are represented by the head of the village women's union (an official government post), who explained:

> The village headman's word was not for the women. The women did not want the rubber. The men decide on what we are doing – the men. Sometimes women have to deny them. The Chinese rubber – we denied that this should happen because this is a Khmu village and we don't have lowland rice paddies. We are worried about the future and where we will plant rice. The women do not want to plant rubber. Some men wanted it, some did not. Those who thought about the future did not want the rubber. However, they could say no to the Chinese, but not to the government.

Women's collective opposition to the concession may be related to the gendered division of labour, and their role in subsistence production. Khmu women are primarily responsible for weeding and maintaining crops once they are planted. The concession would enclose the most fertile fields close to the village and create new land constraints, resulting in shorter fallow periods and increased weed infestation. This, combined with longer travel time if villagers were forced to clear swidden fields farther from the hamlet, would increase women's workload specifically. Although they could potentially earn an income from weeding the rubber area, women's objection to the concession highlights the priority they placed on subsistence rice production.

Many villagers who had not attended the meeting blamed the headman for agreeing to the concession, accusing him of being paid to let the company take the land. However, village leaders repeatedly emphasized that they had no choice. All were concerned about future livelihood insecurity once their access to land was restricted, lamenting that there would be 'no land to eat' (*bo mee din kin*). Some Khmu were considering leaving the village.

State justifications for land grabbing

Confronted with local resistance, officials from the District Agriculture and Forestry Office (DAFO), who were tasked with establishing the concession once the agreement had been approved, used various narratives and legal arguments to legitimise the expropriation of village territory. They emphasised that the Khmu were short of rice every year and that the rubber plantation would alleviate poverty by providing new wage-labour opportunities. The legal status of Ban Samsum territory as 'state forest' was also given as a justification for choosing the village as the pilot site for the plantation. Beginning in the 1990s, a national Land and Forest Allocation Policy (LFAP) was initiated across Laos to demarcate village territorial boundaries, zone village lands and forests for specific uses, and institute more privatised forms of land tenure within village boundaries. The final step of this policy involves allocating usufruct rights to three land parcels of approximately one ha each per household labourer (often interpreted in practice as three plots per household) within village territory zoned as 'degraded forest'.[4] The goals of the LFAP are to formalise customary claims and to provide secure private rights to a limited number of fields. This is intended to motivate farmers to grow cash crops and to confine highland villages within specific territorial boundaries in order to restrict (and eventually eliminate) shifting cultivation, enabling the remaining 'forest land' to be protected or used for commercial production by the state. In Pak Ou District, DAFO officials began implementing the LFAP in 2000. By 2005, the process had been completed in roadside villages. However, in remote villages such as Ban Samsum, only village territorial boundaries had been demarcated. The headman had been instructed to allocate three land parcels per household, but land within village territory continued to be used under customary tenure. District officials argued that because the LFAP had not been fully completed, Ban Samsum's land still belonged to the state. Ignoring customary claims to specific fields, they deployed the final stage of the LFAP to redefine village boundaries by allocating private household rights within only half of village territory, thereby legally freeing up the most fertile village land for lease to the company. As one district official explained:

> It was the governor who gave the Chinese permission to plant rubber in these villages. These five villages haven't had land allocation yet, so it is still the government's land. We asked the farmers first [for consent for the plantation], but there's no land allocation yet. So we will make land allocation first, then what is left over, the governor will give to the Chinese company to rent for rubber. If the area where the rubber will be planted has lowland rice, fish ponds, or gardens, then we won't take this. We will only take the places where there are no permanent crops or teak. In places where there is upland rice or fallow, then the government will take the land and give it to the Chinese. [In villages where] there has already been land allocation and the farmers want to plant rubber, then the farmers will make contracts directly with the Chinese .... The target of the government for land allocation is that villagers have three more years during which they can plant rice, and after this, then the land should become a garden (*suan*) [i.e. a permanent crop]. If they keep planting upland rice after three years and they haven't yet made a garden, then the government will take back the land, because the government wants farmers to stop growing upland rice.

This statement illustrates how the implementation of the LFAP combined with national policies to eliminate swidden rice cultivation and encourage cash crops in the uplands are implicated in the appropriation of village territories for rubber concessions (see also Barney 2008). Titling programmes advocated to improve tenure security, to motivate more 'productive' and 'sustainable' land use, and to provide secure assets to enable access to formal credit also open up new processes of land accumulation and dispossession. Market processes and pricing may displace the poor, land grabbing occurs during programme implementation, and political decisions about what types of land are eligible or

[4]Two parcels of one ha each are allocated to households that own paddy rice fields.

not eligible for formal title influence whose rights are made secure and whose are undermined (Bruce 1993; Zoomers 2010; Hirsch 2011; Adnan 2013). The application of the final stage of the LFAP constituted a land grab on behalf of both the district and the plantation company. However, the openness of this district cadre complicates a simplistic analysis that positions him as legitimating state land appropriation at the expense of local people. Rather, it illustrates the pragmatic practice of bureaucracy in compliance with national policy, told with assurance that the process was a legitimate development intervention. District officials are under pressure to comply with national mandates to eradicate shifting cultivation and to develop cash cropping systems in the uplands. Rubber trees were seen as a promising solution to help villagers comply with state policies, and would also enable district officials to meet their obligations. According to the official, the plantation would not only provide wage labour for impoverished villagers but would also be a model that the Khmu could emulate to modernise their own agricultural system. The facts that the company had enclosed the most fertile half of village land, and that the Khmu had neither access to credit nor capital to invest in rubber on their own, were overlooked. In villages in the district where the LFAP had been fully completed, land rights were respected and villagers were encouraged to voluntarily enter into contract farming arrangements with Chinese companies. Thus, the policy was implicated in creating both security and insecurity of local land rights, depending on how it was interpreted and implemented locally.

DAFO is responsible for allocating land to highland farmers, for encouraging cash cropping and for finding land to lease for plantations. State officials responsible for implementing the LFAP are often the same individuals in charge of securing land for plantation companies. Therefore, these two policies are integrally implicated in processes of 'frontier capitalism' (Barney 2009) through which lands that are deemed 'empty' or 'degraded' are emptied of their original inhabitants and granted to lucrative business ventures. This process of dispossession is given legal legitimacy in the 1996 Lao Forest Law which was the framework for forest management at the time, which stipulates that forest land 'is owned by the state, however if an individual or organisation (with permission from the state) invests capital in the land in order to reforest it, then they can gain rights to the land' (Lao Forest Law 1996, Article 5). Lao legislation stipulates that concessions should be granted only for land classified as 'degraded' or 'barren' production forestland – the same type of 'forestland' to which villagers are granted usufruct rights[5] (Lao Forestry Law 2007; Government of Lao PDR 2009). The negative legal classification of village swidden land as 'degraded forest'[6] also obscures its importance for local livelihoods and helps justify its reallocation for tree plantations which can be portrayed as economic and environmental improvements (see also Barney 2008). An important modification in the 2007 Lao Forestry Law is that plantations are defined as a legitimate type of forest,

[5]A study of concessions across Laos indicated that one third of all the land area granted for all types of land deals was legally designated as 'forest land'. Although, legally, plantations are supposed to be established in 'production forest', the study found that 23 percent of all types of land deals were established in areas categorised as 'protection forest' (Schönweger et al. 2012).

[6]The 1996 Forest Law distinguishes between five different types of forests: 'production forests' (for timber and other forest products), 'conservation forests' (for conserving plant and animal species), 'protection forests' (to protect watersheds and prevent soil erosion), 'regeneration forests' (young fallow areas which should be left to regenerate into mature forests, and 'degraded forests' (areas deemed heavily damaged, to be allocated to villagers and organisations for agriculture, livestock grazing and tree plantations). These categories have been merged into three categories ('production', 'protection' and 'conservation' forest) in the more recent 2007 Forest Law, but the concept of 'degraded' forest remains the same.

while shifting cultivation is categorised alongside illegal logging as a culprit of forest destruction, and is being made illegal.

Everyday forms of village resistance

Following their unsuccessful attempts to formally reject the concession, villagers in Ban Samsum enacted various forms of resistance in an attempt to undermine the plantation. Villagers were instructed to clear and cultivate adjacent swidden plots within the concession area that year, and company representatives were to come later to teach them how to prepare their fields for rubber trees. During the first year, the trees would be intercropped with upland rice, but subsequently villagers would not be able to use the land for grazing livestock or for cultivation. Both men and women were paid for clearing the land, and most villagers intentionally chose to plant that year's rice crop within the concession area in order to earn money. Although villagers had started to refer to the area as 'Chinese land', in choosing where to clear and plant rice that year, customary tenure rights prevailed and villagers generally were paid for clearing those plots to which they had claims. Some villagers intentionally cleared away from the other fields hoping to prevent their land from being taken, while others did not realise their land was in the concession area and would have chosen to clear elsewhere had they understood that they would lose their land. Villagers who owned fields that were considered too steep for rubber trees but were within the concession area were disappointed because they were not paid for clearing the land, but would still lose rights to cultivate their fields once the rubber was established. Wages for clearing the land were low, ranging between 2 and 400,000 kip[7] (USD 20–40) per hectare depending on the type of tree cover, and were calculated for the area cleared rather than per labourer, and therefore had to be shared. In some parts of Ban Samsum, primary forests were cut down to make way for rubber.

Wage labour, presented by officials as the primary benefit (and justification) of the plantation, became a source of intense conflict and an avenue of local resistance. Rubber needs to be planted on level soils for tapping, so once land is cleared, bench terraces need to be constructed along the contours of sloping land (Alton, Bluhm, and Sananikone 2005). After this, holes must be dug and refilled with softer soils immediately prior to planting. The villagers initially waited for the company to return to teach them how to construct terraces before they planted their rice. However, the company arrived later than expected, by which time the fields had already been planted and the Khmu refused to uproot their crops. Withholding labour was an attempt to protect their crops, to negotiate for better wages and to resist the company appropriating their land. Faced with an uncooperative labour force, company representatives brought in Lue labourers from Nambak district to construct terraces through the cropped fields. Ban Samsum villagers protested openly and convinced the labourers not to destroy their rice crop because it was a 'sin'. This was a potent argument because in local cosmologies rice is believed to have 'souls' similar to people (Tambiah 1970; Simana and Preisig 1997; Évrard 2006). Caring for the souls of rice and people is considered important so that the souls don't leave their hosts, which would cause poor yields in rice and illness in people. In protesting the destruction of their rice crop, Ban Samsum villagers drew on spiritual understandings of reciprocal obligations between people and rice, in addition to local notions of moral justness. Their arguments were persuasive, and the labourers built terraces around the rice and refused to

[7]The US dollar values are estimated according to the exchange rate at the time of the research.

destroy the crops. Frustrated, company representatives returned with a new group of Lue labourers, and eventually about one third of Ban Samsum's crops were destroyed to make way for rubber. No compensation was given and villagers were concerned that they would not be able to meet their subsistence needs that year. An older Khmu couple described what happened when the second group of labourers destroyed the crops to build the rubber terraces:

> Woman: When the Chinese arrived the rice had grown about knee-height. Then they took it off. I was very angry. My husband didn't let me see because he was afraid that the Chinese would tie me up because I was very angry. A lot of people were very angry – men and women were angry. The headman and his wife were also very angry. Everyone was crying. People here scolded the Chinese, but they didn't listen. We tried to stop them, but they didn't stop .... I am upset that people took my rice off, because I had planted already .... I tried to stop them. I said 'Oh, we are very old. We are short of energy. We will be short of rice, and you will have sin'. But the Chinese, they didn't listen. They paid us for digging the rice off and clearing the fields. But this was not enough to replace the rice lost.

> Man: I spoke with other people and talked with the headman. The headman tried to stop them, but they didn't listen. The headman tried to stop them from cutting rice in every field. The Chinese only planted on the side with the rice fields. He asked them to plant on the other side. Not many people plant on the other side, only on this side. I went to the meeting. We didn't want the rubber, but we had no choice. We had no choice. Our land, they will take it, and next year we will be short of rice again. Because the government agreed with this, so we couldn't say no. This is state land, so we have to 'sell' it to the Chinese. We knew it was state land before the Chinese came. We knew it was state land because the government came and told us then. After we cleared the fields, they came and told us. If I had known they would take that piece of land, I would not have cleared land on this side, but on the other side. Next year I will plant on the other side, but only 2–3 *kalong* [not much land]. I have land on that side, but a lot of the villages use that area. It's good land, but not as good as on this side.

These narratives are representative of villagers' accounts of resisting the destruction of their crops. Some villagers, like the woman above, also emphasised their particular vulnerability to food insecurity in seeking to protect their particular field. One widow asked the labourers to spare her crops and to only take land 'where there was both a husband and a wife'. Villagers were primarily concerned with their inability to meet their subsistence needs that year.

After the bench terraces had been constructed and the crops had already been destroyed, some village men consented to dig holes for the company since they were short of rice and were losing an opportunity to earn wages to labourers from outside of the community. The local wages were 2500 kip/hole (USD 0.25) for digging the holes and 250/hole (USD 0.025) for filling them. At the time, the average wage for agricultural work on rice fields in the area (for planting, weeding, etc.) was between 10,000 and 15,000 kip/day (USD 1–1.50/day) depending on the task and on whether the employer provided food for lunch. The wages provided by the company were considered to be poor and were lower than what was originally promised and written in the official contracts. It is likely that some of the wages were appropriated by a middle man, since the wages paid by the same company to villagers in Nambak district were apparently slightly higher and concurred with the contracts. Before submitting to work for the company, the men tried unsuccessfully to negotiate for higher wages, demanding 4000 kip/hole (USD 0.40). Villagers also disliked working for the company because the managers yelled at them, did not allow them to take breaks to smoke and did not provide lunch as is customary for local agricultural labour. Furthermore, the company withheld wages until the entire job was finished, which caused anger because rice supplies were low and the Khmu were accustomed to being paid daily in order to buy food. Many villagers waited for payment for clearing land that had been completed 1–2 months earlier. By the time the company returned to the village to pay the wages and plant the rubber, the entire village was short of rice, and hostile. In protest to their poor treatment, some villagers and labourers from Nambak who were employed as porters to carry sacks of rubber saplings from the road to the village secretly dropped some into the streams or hid them in the forest *en route*. Saplings were planted upside-down when managers were not paying attention and those growing along paths were kicked, anonymously trampled or uprooted over time.

The ability of villagers to withhold labour as a means of resistance against dispossession and/or poor labour conditions is contingent on the ease with which companies can bring in labour from elsewhere, and on whether locals have been left with sufficient land to meet their livelihood needs. Unlike concessions elsewhere in Laos where villagers have been left with so little land that they are forced into wage labour in order to reproduce their households (Baird 2011; Kenney-Lazar 2012), villagers in Ban Samsum maintained enough land to survive without working for the company. Villagers who are not dependent on wages from plantations are difficult to control and are often depicted as 'lazy' by companies (Li 2011). By representing local people as unskilled or lazy, and by selecting areas with low population density, plantation companies are able to justify importing 'hardworking and skilled' labour from elsewhere (Li 2011). Vietnamese and Chinese plantation companies in Laos would prefer to hire labourers from their own countries who are perceived to work harder for lower wages (Vientiane Times 2011; Baird 2010, 2011). However, the Lao Labour Law (2004, Article 7) dictates that companies can only hire foreign labourers if there are no appropriately qualified Lao, while the Law on the Promotion of Foreign Investment (1994) stipulates that Lao workers must be given priority and restricts the number of foreign labourers to 10 percent of the workforce. DAFO officials in Pak Ou were aware of these regulations and had prevented the company from bringing in labourers from China. However, these laws are not always followed, and what counts as 'appropriately qualified' is open to interpretation. According to the *Vientiane Times*, there are approximately 200,000 illegal foreign workers in Laos, mainly from China, Thailand and Vietnam. The government has difficulty controlling illegal immigration because of concern for maintaining cordial relations with neighbouring countries. This, combined with pressure from companies to be allowed to import labour, has prompted the Lao government to consider providing permits to illegal workers in the country (Vientiane Times 2012a). Furthermore, these laws do not regulate movement of labour from elsewhere *within* the country, which may undermine wages and jobs for those displaced by concessions if other groups are considered to be better qualified or more disciplined. This has particular implications for the Khmu, who during my interviews with state officials and other ethnic groups were regularly derided as 'lazy', backward, dishonest and dirty, and were often blamed for their poverty. Furthermore, although rubber requires a relatively large amount of labour compared with other tree crops,[8] once it is planted little labour is required for maintaining the trees. Jobs do not materialise until 7–8 years after planting when the trees are mature enough to tap for latex, so villagers need to be able to survive in the meantime. This is a concern for contract farming arrangements, since farmers who are not left with enough

[8]Baird (2010) estimates that the amount of labour for tapping rubber trees ranges between 150 and 200 days/ha/year.

land to meet their subsistence and cash needs while the rubber matures are unlikely to be able to maintain ownership of their trees.

The imposition of the concession, the dispossession of the villagers from their best land, the inability to negotiate for fair wages, the delay in payment and the destruction of their crops combined to threaten the subsistence security of the Khmu and united the village in collective hostility against the concession. This merged with frustration with other government actions that were negatively affecting local livelihoods. One major concern was the policy to eliminate shifting cultivation for upland rice. District officials keen on complying with national policy were attempting to force the transition from subsistence to market production by requiring villagers to sign 'formal' contracts in which they agreed to stop planting rice by a specific year. These contracts were a district adaptation to enforce agricultural commercialisation and were not advocated by higher levels of government. The Khmu were concerned that their rice crops would be destroyed if they did not meet their contract obligations, because officials had destroyed opium poppy fields several years earlier. The mounting frustration against the combination of state interventions that threatened local food security was expressed well by one Khmu farmer:

> The government asked us to stop growing rice, and to grow pineapples, paper mulberry, sesame, or Job's tears instead ... I am afraid that the government will come and cut down the rice like they cut down the opium crop. Then what will we eat? If the government people come and cut down the rice crop, maybe I will shoot them. If the government people come to cut my rice field, I will just sit quietly in the field and wait for them. I will talk to them nicely in a quiet voice, and then when they start cutting the rice, I will shoot them with my gun and take the rice stalks that they've cut and stuff them in their mouths.
>
> We signed a contract with the government that we would stop growing upland rice by the year 2005, but the government didn't stop us because they didn't give us any alternatives. Then we had to sign a contract again – this time to stop planting upland rice by the year 2010 .... This time the government will say that they have given us an alternative with rubber. They will say that we can work on rubber and get wages from the Chinese instead of growing rice. But if we work for the Chinese, we will be poor and we still won't have enough rice to eat. The Chinese came with a bag of money and said they would give us the money if we worked for them. And at first, they gave us the money. But then, they said that they would come back to plant rubber in 10 days after the people had dug and filled the holes, but they haven't come back yet. The Chinese owe us a lot of money, but they haven't paid yet, and now we are short of rice. Working with the Chinese, we will be poor and still short of rice. But we won't be able to grow upland rice anyhow, because our land has been given to the Chinese.

While this narrative seems to invoke violence against the state, it should be interpreted as an expression of bravado and frustration against the injustice of state policies rather than an actual plan of action (see Scott 1990, on the use of narrative by subaltern groups as an expression of resistance). Villagers were very concerned about maintaining good relations with the government, which was seen as a source of 'protection' and services as well as a 'threat'.

Local counter-claims and the construction of resistance identities

Everyday forms of resistance such as those enacted by the Khmu are often considered to be non-threatening to the status quo. However, more overt resistance in Laos is risky (Stuart-Fox 2004; Barney 2008; Baird 2011). How can vulnerable groups such as the Khmu challenge powerful state claimants to their lands and resist displacements that are legitimised in the name of their own development? In some parts of the world, local counter-claims to territory against state and commercial interests have been framed through specific representations of 'indigeneity'. These 'counter-narratives' link indigenous identity with a specific territory, with place-based ecological knowledge (or wisdom), and with an ethic of environmental conservation (Tsing 1993, 1999; Brosius 1997; Li 2000, 2002; Peluso and Harwell 2001). Such essentialised representations of 'indigenous people' are often constructed in collaboration with outsiders, mirroring romanticised western imaginings reminiscent of the 'noble savage' that are advocated by international indigenous rights and environmental movements (Brosius 1997). This has facilitated collaboration between marginalised peoples and transnational environmentalists, providing both groups with political power to act while obscuring different and sometimes-conflicting goals. Such fragile alliances create new possibilities for social resistance and have been described as the 'hopeful edge of a political project' (Tsing 1999:162).

In Laos, as in much of Southeast Asia, 'indigeneity' is an ill-fitting construct. Different ethnic groups have long lived intermingled or in close proximity, ethnic boundaries are permeable, there has been a long history of mobility and all groups can arguably be considered indigenous. In such situations, 'indigenous' identities are sometimes constructed strategically in response to struggles over resources (Li 2000), and can be seen as 'resistance' identities formed as part of a legitimating narrative to assert preferential claims to resources and to resist dispossession. However, the use of 'indigeneity' as a basis for territorial claims implies that villagers have been exposed to these international discourses and are able to articulate their identity in a way that is recognisable and usable by their advocates (Li 2000). This is not the case for all marginal groups, many of whom, like the Khmu, live in remote areas and/or struggle with piecemeal territorial displacements on a daily basis that do not attract international attention, and who do not necessarily form a 'collective consciousness' of resistance based on ethnicity (Li 2000). Furthermore, unlike in some parts of Southeast Asia, Laos does not have a history of legal pluralism which grants certain ethnic groups special autonomous 'native rights' based on customary law – rights that are distinct from the legal rights of other citizens (see for example Cramb 2007; Davidson and Henley 2007; Potter 2009). Some ethnic minorities have successfully linked 'native rights' to discourses of indigeneity in their struggles for territorial claims (Li 2007).

The Lao government voted in favour of the United Nations International Declaration on the Rights of Indigenous Peoples in 2007; however, it does not recognise any one ethnic group as more indigenous than another. Imaginings of 'indigenous peoples' who have a special long-standing attachment to place and an ethic of environmental conservation are not part of popular discourse. This identity would be complicated as a basis for territorial claims in any case, given the continued mobility of the population and the relatively recent displacement of people during the Second Indochina war. Since taking control in 1975, the communist Pathet Lao government has been preoccupied with a nationalising agenda that incorporates ethnic minorities into the country as 'equal citizens' (Lao Front for National Construction (LFNC) 2005), and has followed a policy of assimilation that holds the politically dominant Lao-Tai as the standard. The 49 recognised ethnic groups are classified into three nationalising identities based on stereotypes about livelihood and topographical location: the *Lao Loum* (lowland Lao, including the politically dominant Lao-Tai), the *Lao Theung* (midland Lao including the Khmu), and the *Lao Sung* (upland Lao including the Hmong). Although given equal status in law, ethnic minorities living in mountainous areas are marginalised by state policies because their livelihoods do not fit the increasingly hegemonic image of what it means to be a modern Lao citizen.

Government ideologies of development are promoted to rural communities through policies designed to reshape local livelihoods, and through roadside billboards, local media, political speeches, and agricultural and health extension services. Road signs draw attention to 'modern sanitary villages' located near the road, which have a village water pump. In roadside 'model ethnic villages', villagers practice lowland rice cultivation and sell 'ethnic' handicrafts. 'Model farmers' and 'model villages' have abandoned swidden rice cultivation for cash crops. Field trips are organised to bring farmers from other areas to visit these model villagers, encouraging them to follow their lead. Such models impart not only development lessons for how to improve livelihoods but also ideas about how to be a better 'Lao'. To be a good rural Lao citizen in a model Lao village is to live near the road, to plant paddy rice in the lowlands and cash crops in the uplands, and to have water pumps and a school. Ethnic minorities practicing shifting cultivation for upland rice find themselves positioned outside of this ideal.

The Khmu are widely acknowledged as the 'original owners of the land', and to have special authority over territorial spirits (Aijmer 1979; Holt 2009). Although this could support a group representation of 'indigeniety' (regardless of histories of mobility), the 'resistance identity' that has been constructed by villagers in Ban Samsum in their struggle against the concession has taken on a different character. The axis of difference that frames their 'political' identity is the divide between the uplands/shifting cultivation/backwardness and lowlands/sedentary farming/modernity. Because the policies promoting resettlement and the rubber plantations that threaten to displace them are being deployed in the name of their own development, Ban Samsum villagers have framed their counter-claims to land by representing themselves as 'good', 'deserving' and adequately 'developed' Lao citizens, mirroring various state ideologies and values for modernity.

Khmu leaders emphasised that the state had officially recognised their territorial claims when the community boundaries were demarcated by the LFAP in 2003, and stressed that households paid taxes on three private land parcels as evidence of compliance with the final phase of the policy. They further highlighted that villagers had adopted cash crops such as teak, pineapples and paper mulberry trees that had been introduced by a government-run project several years earlier, and were now being asked to remove these because they were planted within the concession area.

> We didn't have paper mulberry (*posa*), and the governor told us to plant this. Then when we have *posa*, the governor tells us to cut it. I will go to the governor about the *posa*. I want to keep my *posa* garden.

Village leaders visited various district government offices to protest their rice being uprooted, to complain about low wages and to negotiate to keep land within the concession zone on which they had planted tree and cash crops in compliance with government policy. Some teak trees had been planted in cooperation with a businessman from the town, who had supplied capital while villagers had provided land and labour, with the intention that the profits would be shared. By appealing for his support, villagers had stalled the removal of teak trees growing within the concession area. Although DAFO officials stated that permanent crops such as teak would not be taken by the concession, when villagers sent a delegation to the district governor's office to protect their trees, they were told that any in the concession needed to be cut down. It was not clear whether or not compensation would be paid.

In order to give the village a more legitimate presence in the eyes of the state, the village headman had initiated a policy of accepting new immigrants into the community with the intention of increasing the population of the 54-household village in order to encourage state investment in infrastructure and to make the village less of a target for the resettlement programme. This programme, aimed at consolidating and relocating remote villages of less than 50 households to roadsides, was justified as providing villagers with better access to services such as schools and health clinics. The headman had welcomed more than 10 new households into the village within the previous two years, and was actively encouraging more immigration. The acceptance of new families created conflicts within the village since some households were expected to cede their customary land rights; however, the intension was to increase the security of the territorial claims of the village as a whole.

To solidify the presence of Ban Samsum, village leaders also petitioned to improve the schoolhouse and attempted to arrange a formal contract with a businessman to build water pumps and a road to the village in exchange for some valuable hardwood trees. The contract needed to be approved by the district government, and, when it was rejected, villagers accused authorities of wanting to benefit from the timber themselves. In summary, rather than emphasising their indigenous rights to place, Khmu counter-claims to territory and resistance to displacement took the form of fast-tracking the markers of development that were locally recognised as symbolic of a ‘model’ Lao village. They strategically appropriated state ideologies deployed to justify their dispossession into a discourse to secure their territorial claims. ‘Being developed’ therefore took on a dual meaning, both as a desired right to be claimed of the state (as the legitimate entitlement of a good Lao citizen) and as a ‘resistance identity’ through which to strengthen claims against the state in the face of resettlement or displacement from resources in the name of development (as ‘adequately developed’ good Lao citizens).

Emergence of rightful resistance

I returned to Ban Samsum in June 2012, anticipating finding an impoverished village relying on inadequate wage labour and an expanded rubber plantation encompassing four adjacent Khmu villages. However, the proletarianisation which has occurred in other parts of the country (Baird 2011; Kenney-Lazar 2012) had not transpired. Villagers continued to resist the plantation by withholding labour, working for the company only when convenient. They could do this because they had retained enough land to cultivate their own crops and to gather forest products for sale, and could continue to sell their labour locally. Villagers were able to earn better incomes from other local activities and from new wage opportunities in the town. In 2008, Ban Samsum was granted official permission to use some of their valuable hardwood trees to pay a private company to construct a road and several water pumps. The new dirt road had an enormous impact on village prosperity. Traders could enter the village with trucks, creating more competition and better prices for village produce. Some Khmu had become traders themselves. The road also facilitated trade in valuable timber. The increased income resulting from these various activities had enabled many households to convert their small bamboo huts into concrete houses with tin roofs, and to purchase motorbikes, satellite dishes and televisions powered by small hydroelectric generators in the stream. This had the side effect of giving the village more permanence, since concrete houses cannot be easily dismantled like their traditional woven bamboo counterparts.

Villagers’ ongoing resistance by anonymous sabotage and withholding labour had undermined the success of the rubber plantation, which had not expanded beyond the initial 93 ha. The company occasionally brought in outside labourers but, possibly because of lack of regular maintenance, the rubber trees in the concession area were small, skinny and neglected, and many had died. This contrasted with rubber trees owned by the eight village households who had planted rubber themselves, which were growing well. Although the land was still legally leased to the company, villagers had effectively reclaimed it and were using it for swidden rice cultivation.

Resistance to the plantation had also begun to take more active forms. When fire accidently spread into the rubber plantation while villagers were burning weeds along the road, they did nothing to prevent it from destroying some of the trees, as they would have done if the rubber was owned by a local farmer. Under customary rules, farmers who set fire to someone else's crop or whose animals destroy a crop are responsible to pay compensation. However, villagers refused to pay the compensation demanded by the company, arguing that it was an accident. Following this incident, a Chinese company representative was stationed in the village in order to better manage the rubber plantation and to deal with some of the local conflicts. While villagers accepted him, they continued to resent the plantation itself.

The company had also attempted to expand the plantation into the neighbouring Khmu community Ban Theung, which was also part of the concession. Like Ban Samsum, these villagers had rejected the concession, hoping instead to engage in contract farming arrangements. As one villager explained, 'I didn't want to sell labour for 40 years because I would be a slave to the Chinese for a long time'. Seeing what had happened in Ban Samsum, these villagers refused to allow the rubber to be planted, claiming that their land had not been properly surveyed as is required by law. Representatives from both villages met with a newly appointed district governor to negotiate getting their lands back from the company. Villagers felt that the previous governor had been paid to allow the plantation, although there is no evidence that this occurred. Furthermore, villagers maintained that the contract required the company to plant 1000 ha of rubber before the end of 2012 or the land would have to be returned to the original owners. If the company wanted to keep the land, they would need to revise the contract officially. Their argument had a legal basis since Lao legislation stipulates that concession contracts are cancelled and assets are reclaimed by the state if the 'industrial farm' is not completed within seven years (Government of Lao PDR 2009). The new governor acted in support of local claims and wrote a letter to the National Assembly on behalf of the villagers, arguing that the concession had not gone through the proper channels. Similar to accounts of 'rightful resistance' by Chinese villagers (O'Brien and Li 2006), the Khmu had identified potential allies within the state and had started to deploy legal narratives and official channels to resist the concession and reclaim their land. I do not know whether they learned about their legal rights from their interactions with the new governor, from popular radio broadcasts, from word of mouth with other communities facing similar problems or from elsewhere.

Opposition to concessions in Laos

The evolving conflict in Ban Samsum is one of many local land disputes resulting from transnational concessions that have been presented to the National Assembly (NA) over the past several years.[9] Dispossession, illegal encroachment, inadequate compensation,

[9]Baird (2011) documents an early case of local resistance in Champassak in 1992 against a Thai tree plantation which had enclosed the territories of 19 'ethnic minority' villages, preventing their access to grazing and forest resources. Villagers set fire to some of the trees. The Ministry of Agriculture and Forestry intervened and retracted 4000 ha of concession land, but instead of returning the land to the locals, conceded it to a different company. The plantation eventually failed because of the Asian Financial crisis in the late 1990s.

unfulfilled promises of local benefits and employment, and exploitative labour conditions are common grievances (Vaenkeo 2012). Companies have fined villagers when their water buffalos destroyed rubber trees planted on traditional grazing lands (Phouthonesy 2006a, 2006b). Village lands have been illegally appropriated without consent and their crops, forests, graveyards and shrines have been destroyed (Smith 2012a, 2012b). Companies have brought in foreign or outside labourers (Shi 2008; Sengdara 2010) and have used herbicides for weed control instead of providing promised jobs (Sengdara 2010). In resistance, villagers from across the country have written letters and/or travelled to Vientiane to present their grievances to the National Assembly (Vaenkeo 2012). They have organised petitions against concession companies (Phouthonesy 2006a, 2006b), withheld their labour (Shi 2008), prevented land surveys, threatened company bulldozers with their hunting rifles, enforced fines when companies broke the law, and spread rumours of violence against foreign workers (Baird 2010; Kenney-Lazar 2012). Some villagers aired their complaints on a national talk-in radio programme, which was shortly thereafter taken off the air (Smith 2012c). In one reported case, villagers were detained in their province to prevent them from presenting their grievances to the NA (Radio Free Asia 2012). Unlike in Ban Samsum where the Khmu have thus far been able to stall the expansion of the plantation on their lands, protests by villagers elsewhere in the country have not resolved land conflicts in their favour. However, it seems that villagers across Laos are becoming aware of the national laws and institutions that protect their rights, and are articulating their claims in legal terms and contesting injustices through formal channels, bringing their cases to the attention of the central government. International and recently formed Lao non-governmental organisations (NGOs; known as Lao non-profit organisations or NPAs) are beginning to work with villagers to teach them about the law (Baird 2010). It is possible that villagers are forming a collective resistance identity, demanding their recognition as Lao citizens with legal rights.

The mounting pressure of these isolated local protests, combined with national and international criticism of the unregulated allocation of concessions, has influenced national policy, prompting the beginnings of a Polanyi-type 'double movement' to protect the 'nature' and 'people' of Laos from exploitative market processes (Polanyi [1944] 2001). Since the mid-2000s, the legal and policy framework for foreign land acquisition in Laos has been continually readapted both to promote concessions and to constrain (or at least keep up with) their unregulated allocation by the provinces and districts. In 2008, provincial authorities in Luang Namtha banned large-scale rubber concessions in favour of contract farming arrangements that seemed more beneficial for farmers, although many of these devolve into concession-like arrangements over time (Shi 2008). Since May 2007, the President of Laos has announced a series of moratoriums and decrees intended to increase central government control and limit the authority and size of land concessions granted by the provinces and districts (Vientiane Times 2007, 2009b, 2009a; Government of Lao PDR 2009). Although these have not been very effective, they illustrate the government's desire to better regulate the situation. The most recent moratorium was announced in June 2012 and is to be maintained until December 2015 (Vaenkeo 2012; Vientiane Times 2012b).

Conclusion

Since 2000, land deals across all sectors of the Lao economy have increased by 50-fold, and are conservatively estimated to cover more than 1.1 million ha, or 5 percent of Lao territory[10] (Schönweger et al. 2012). In spite of a comprehensive legal and policy framework, the practice of granting concessions is not transparent and involves various departments and levels of government that do not necessarily communicate with each other. Local officials do not always understand or implement the laws in which they operate, laws are manipulated to empty land of its rightful owners, concession projects do not always comply with legislation, terms of contract are violated, there have been accusations of corruption and land under local or other legal claims has sometimes been conceded concurrently to more than one company for different purposes (Nanthavong et al. 2009; Vaenkeo 2012; Smith 2012a, 2012b). Some concessions are cover-ups for logging (Barney 2008; Vientiane Times 2012c, 2011). These 'land grabs' are promoted in the name of poverty alleviation but are having devastating effects on villagers. They are being driven by the intersection between transnational commercial interests and national economic development policies.

The case of Ban Samsum illustrates how politically marginalised ethnic-minority villagers attempted to resist dispossessions undertaken in the name of their own development, in the face of highly unequal power relations and in a political context in which open resistance is risky and unlikely to be successful. Khmu villagers combined various tactics of resistance to undermine the concession, including anonymous acts of sabotage, foot-dragging and refusal to work for the company, appropriation of the dominant state development ideology as a strategic representation to assert territorial claims, identification of powerful allies in the government and civil society, and recourse to law and state institutions. By working within state structures rather than by open confrontation or acts of violence, the Khmu have thus far been able to stall the establishment of the plantation on their lands. Such hidden resistances are likely occurring across Laos, unnoticed and unrecorded because they transpire in remote areas and/or don't appear as resistance and therefore don't attract public attention.

Although debates about land conflicts were becoming more open at the time of this research, the serious risks of advocating for villagers' rights and promoting an alternative approach to development were tragically brought to the world's attention with the abduction of Lao NGO leader Sombath Somphone in Vientiane in December 2012. This generated fear and effectively silenced many Lao village rights advocates. The question of how to assist marginal groups such as the Khmu and their Lao supporters in their struggles against injustices related to land deals is becoming increasingly important. Although claiming recognition as an 'indigenous people' could potentially provide a platform for an ethnic minority like the Khmu to advocate for their land rights by providing alliances with international actors, this would require state recognition of their distinct 'indigenous' status relative to other ethnic groups, and could potentially disadvantage ethnic minorities who were later migrants and who could be represented as 'less indigenous', such as the Hmong. Furthermore, such an identity would not assist the many marginal *Lao Loum* villagers that are also affected by land deals. The cases of village resistance that are erupting across the country indicate that villagers of all ethnic groups are beginning to use legal discourses and are seeking support from within (rather than against) the state to frame their claims to justice. The state is both the problem and the solution. It is perhaps by providing support for sympathetic Lao

[10]This estimate is based on verifiable spatial data and excludes the many deals which are not well documented, and does not include concessions for mining exploration which account for another 1 million ha, hydropower projects or contract farming arrangements.

officials, development workers and researchers to provide legal education to villagers and to advocate for the territorial and social rights of all ethnic groups as 'constitutionally' equal Lao citizens that the international community can best assist groups such as the Khmu.

Acknowledgements

I am extremely grateful for the helpful advice and comments of Jun Borras and the Land Deals Politics Initiative (LDPI) team, of John Galaty at McGill University who reviewed much earlier drafts of this work, and of the editors and anonymous reviewers of this journal collection. I am especially thankful to my Lao research assistant and to the villagers and concerned officials without whose assistance I could not have done this study.

Disclosure statement

No potential conflict of interest was reported by the author.

Funding

This research was supported with grants from the Social Science and Humanities Research Council of Canada (SSHRC), the International Development Research Centre (IDRC) and the Land Deals Politics Initiative (LDPI).

References

Adnan, S. 2013. Land grabs and primitive accumulation in deltaic Bangladesh: Interactions between neoliberal globalization, state interventions, power relations and peasant resistance. *Journal of Peasant Studies* 40, no. 1: 87–128.

Aijmer, G. 1979. Reconciling power with authority: An aspect of statecraft in traditional Laos. *Man* 14, no. 4: 734–49.

Alton, C., D. Bluhm, and S. Sananikone. 2005. *Para rubber study, Hevea brasiliensis, Lao P.D.R.* Vientiane, Lao PDR: German Organisation for Technical Assistance and Cooperation (GTZ), Lao-German Program Rural Development in Mountainous Areas of Northern Lao PDR.

Baird, I.G. 2010. Land, rubber and people: rapid agrarian changes and responses in southern Laos. *The Journal of Lao Studies* 1, no. 1: 1–47.

Baird, I.G. 2011. Turning land into capital, turning people into labour: primitive accumulation and the arrival of large-scale economic land concessions in the Lao People's Democratic Republic. *New Proposals: Journal of Marxism and Interdisciplinary Inquiry* 5, no. 1: 10–26.

Barney, K. 2008. China and the production of forestlands in Lao PDR: a political ecology of transnational enclosure. In *Taking Southeast Asia to market: commodities, nature, and people in the neoliberal age*, ed. J. Nevins and N.L. Peluso, 91–107. Ithaca: Cornell University Press.

Barney, K. 2009. Laos and the making of a 'relational' resource frontier. *The Geographical Journal* 175, no. 2: 146–59.

Bernstein, H. 2010. *Class dynamics of agrarian change*. Halifax: Fernwood Press.

Borras, S. Jr., and J.C. Franco. 2013. Global land grabbing and political reactions 'from below'. *Third World Quarterly* 34, no. 9: 1723–47.

Brosius, J.P. 1997. Endangered forest, endangered people: environmentalist representations of indigenous knowledge. *Human Ecology* 25, no. 1: 47–69.

Bruce, J. 1993. Do indigenous tenure systems constrain agricultural development? In *Land in African agrarian systems*, ed. T.J. Bassett and D.E. Crummey, 25–56. Wisconsin: University of Wisconsin Press.

Cohen, P.T. 2009. The post-opium scenario and rubber in northern Laos: alternative western and Chinese models of development. *International Journal of Drug Policy*. 20, no. 5: 424–430.

Cramb, R.A. 2007. *Land and longhouse: agrarian transformation in the uplands of Sarawak*. Copenhagen: Nordic Institute of Asian Studies (NIAS).

Davidson, J.S., and D. Henley. eds. 2007. *The revival of tradition in Indonesian politics: the deployment of adat from colonialism to indigenism*. London and New York: Routledge.

Douangsavang, L., B. Thammavong, and A. Noble. 2008. *Meeting regional and global demands for rubber: a key to poverty alleviation in Lao PDR?* Bangkok: Sustainable Mekong Research Network (Sumernet). http://lad.nafri.org.la/fulltext/2023-0.pdf (accessed March 11, 2015).

Évrard, O. 2006. *Chroniques des cendres: Anthropologie des sociétés khmou et des dynamiques interethniques du Nord-Laos*. Paris: Institut de Recherche pour le Development (IRD) Éditions.

Government of Lao PDR. 2005. *Forestry strategy to the year 2020 of the Lao PDR*.

Government of Lao PDR. 2009. *Prime Minister's decree on state lease or concession. No. 135/PM, 25/05/2009*.

Hall, D., P. Hirsch, and T.M. Li. 2011. *Powers of exclusion: land dilemmas in Southeast Asia*. Honolulu: University of Hawaii Press.

Hall, S. 1996. On postmodernism and articulation: an interview with Stuart Hall. In *Stuart Hall: Critical dialogues in cultural studies*, ed. L. Grossberg, D. Morley and K-H Chen, 131–50. London: Routledge. (Reprinted from *Journal of Communication Inquiry* (1986) 10(2):45–60).

Hirsch, P. 2011. Titling against grabbing? Critiques and conundrums around land formalisation in Southeast Asia. Paper presented at the International Conference on Global land Grabbing, 6–8 April 2011. Institute of Development Studies, University of Sussex. http://www.iss.nl/fileadmin/ASSETS/iss/Documents/Conference_papers/LDPI/34_Philip_Hirsch.pdf (accessed March 11, 2015).

Holt, J.C. 2009. *Spirits of the place: Buddhism and Lao religious culture*. Honolulu: University of Hawai'i Press.

Kenney-Lazar, M. 2012. Plantation rubber, land grabbing and social-property transformation in southern Laos. *Journal of Peasant Studies* 39, no. 3–4: 1017–37.

Lao Forest Law. 1996. [English translation]. Vientiane: Government of Lao PDR.

Lao Forestry Law. 2007. [Unofficial English translation]. Vientiane: Government of Lao PDR.

Lao Front for National Construction (LFNC). 2005. *The Ethnic Groups of Lao PDR*. Vientiane: Department of Ethnic Groups Lao Front for National Construction (LFNC), Government of Lao PDR.

Lao Labour Law. 2004. [English translation] Vientiane: Government of Lao PDR.

Lao Law on the Promotion of Foreign Investment. 1994. [English translation]. Vientiane: Government of Lao PDR.

Li, T.M. 2000. Articulating indigenous identity in Indonesia: resource politics and the tribal slot. *Comparative studies in society and history* 42, no. 1: 149–79.

Li, T.M. 2002. Ethnic cleansing, recursive knowledge, and the dilemmas of sedentarism. *International Social Science Journal* 173: 362–71.

Li, T.M. 2007. Adat in central Sulawesi: contemporary deployment. In *The revival of tradition in Indonesian politics: the deployment of adat from colonialism to indigenism*, ed. J.S. Davidson and D. Henley, 337–70. London and New York: Routledge.

Li, T.M. 2011. Centering labor in the land grab debate. *The Journal of Peasant Studies* 38, no. 2: 281–98.

Manivong, V., and R.A. Cramb. 2008. Economics of smallholder rubber expansion in Northern Laos. *Agroforestry Systems* 74: 113–25.

Minister of Agriculture and Forestry. 1999. *The government's strategic vision for the agricultural sector: a discussion paper prepared for the donor round table conference*. Vientiane: Minister of Agriculture and Forestry, Government of Lao PDR.

Nanthavong, V., O. Schoenweger, V. Anouvong, C. Khiamsombath, L. Thiangthammavong, and S. Lathasavong. 2009. *Findings of the state land concession and lease inventory project in the pilot of Vientiane Province Phase II*. Vientiane: National Land Management Authority, Land and Natural Resources Reseach and Information Centre, Lao-German Land Management and Registration Project (LMRP), German Technical Cooperation (GTZ).

O'Brien, K.J., and L. Li. 2006. *Rightful resistance in rural China*. New York: Cambridge University Press.

Peluso, N.L., and E. Harwell. 2001. Territory, custom, and the cultural politics of ethnic war in West Kalimantan, Indonesia. In *Violent environments*, ed. N.L. Peluso and M. Watts, 83–116. Ithaca: Cornell University Press.

Phouthonesy, E. 2006a. Petition for fences, buffalo grazing space: villagers need help from local authority, rubber plantations lack fences, roaming buffaloes cause damage. *Vientiane Times*. 14 August.

Phouthonesy, E. 2006b. Farmers cannot live without buffaloes. *Vientiane Times*. 11 September.

Polanyi, K. [1944] 2001. *The great transformation: The political and economic origins of our time*. Boston: Beacon Press.

Potter, L. 2009. Oil palm and resistance in West Kalimantan, Indonesia. In *Agrarian angst and rural resistance in contemporary Southeast Asia*, ed. D. Caouette and S. Turner, 105–34. London and New York: Routledge.

Radio Free Asia. 2012. Land Dispute Villagers Released. 29 June. http://www.rfa.org/english/news/laos/land-concessions-06282012173323.html (accessed March 11, 2015).

Rigg, J. 2005. *Living with transition in Laos: Market integration in Southeast Asia*. London and New York: Routledge.

Schönweger, O., A. Heinimann, M. Epprecht, J. Lu, and P. Thalongsengchanh. 2012. *Concessions and leases in the Lao PDR: Taking stock of land investments*. Vientiane: Lao Minister of Natural Resources and the Environment (MoNRE), University of Bern, Swiss Agency for Development and Cooperation (SDC), and German Cooperation. http://www.laolandissues.org/wp-content/uploads/2012/03/Concessions-Leases-Lao-PDR-2012-Eng.pdf (accessed March 11, 2015).

Scott, J.C. 1986. Everyday forms of peasant resistance. In *Everyday forms of peasant resistance in South-east Asia*, ed. J.C. Scott and B.J.T. Kerkvliet, 5–35. London and New York: Routledge.

Scott, J.C. 1990. *Domination and the arts of resistance: Hidden transcripts*. New Haven and London: Yale University Press.

Sengdara, S. 2010. Govt called to help locals swindled by foreign investors. *Vientiane Times,* 17 July.

Shi, W. 2008. *Rubber boom in Luang Namtha: A transnational perspective*. Vientiane: Deutsche Gesellschaft für Technische Zusammenarbeit (GTZ). http://www2.gtz.de/wbf/4tDx9kw63gma/ShiW_Rubber_Luang_Namtha_0802_final.pdf (accessed March 11, 2015).

Simana, S. and E. Preisig. 1997. *Kmhmu' livelihood: Farming the forest*. Vientiane, Lao PDR: Ministry for Information and Culture, Institute for Cultural Research.

Smith, B. 2012a. Coffee colonialism in Laos. *Asia Times Online*. 12 June. http://www.atimes.com/atimes/Southeast_Asia/NF20Ae01.html (accessed March 11, 2015).

Smith, B. 2012b. Coffee colonialism: Olam plantation displaces Lao farmers. *CorpWatch*. 4 June. http://www.corpwatch.org/article.php?id=15736 (accessed March 11, 2015).

Smith, B. 2012c. Off the air in Laos. *Asia Times Online*. 22 February. http://www.atimes.com/atimes/Southeast_Asia/NB22Ae01.html (accessed March 11, 2015).

Stuart-Fox, M. 2004. Politics and reform in the Lao People's Democratic Republic. *Political economy of development. Political economy of development Working Paper No. 1*. Williamsburg, Virginia: Program of Civil Society and Government, The College of William and Mary.

Tambiah, S.J. 1970. *Buddhism and the spirit cults in North-East Thailand*. Cambridge: Cambridge University Press.

Thongmanivong, S., Y. Fujita, K. Phanvilay, and T. Vongvisouk. 2009. Agrarian Land Use Transformation in Northern Laos: From Swidden to Rubber. *Southeast Asian Studies* 47, no. 3: 330–47.

Tsing, A.L. 1993. *In the realm of the diamond queen: Marginality in an out-of-the-way place*. Princeton: Princeton University Press.

Tsing, A.L. 1999. Becoming a tribal elder, and other green development fantasies. In *Transforming the Indonesian uplands*, ed. T.M. Li, 159–202. Amsterdam: Harwood Academic Publishers.

Vaenkeo, S. 2012. When can the poor take a rest. *Vientiane Times*. 27 July.

Vandergeest, P. 2003. Land to some tillers: Development-induced displacement in Laos. *International Social Science Journal* 55, no. 1: 47–56.

Vientiane Times. 2007. Govt suspends land concessions. 9 May.

Vientiane Times. 2009a. Govt resumes land concessions. 16 June.

Vientiane Times. 2009b. Govt again suspends land concessions. 2 July.

Vientiane Times. 2011. Limits set on future rubber plantations in Laos. 16 September.

Vientiane Times. 2012a. Govt to legalize undocumented foreign workers. 26 March.
Vientiane Times. 2012b. Govt halts new mining projects, land concessions for tree farms. 26 June.
Vientiane Times. 2012c. Forestry management practices need to be toughened up. 14 August.
Vientiane Times. 2014. Rubber becomes top export earner. 9 October.
Vongkhamor, S., K. Phimmasen, B. Silapeth, B. Xayxomphou, and E. Petterson. 2007. *Key issues in smallholder rubber planting in Oudomxay and Luang Prabang Provinces, Lao PDR*. Vientiane, Lao PDR: Upland Research and Capacity Development Programme, National Agriculture and Forestry Research Institute (NAFRI). http://lad.nafri.org.la/fulltext/LAD010320071379.pdf (accessed March 11, 2015).
Zoomers, A. 2010. Globalisation and the foreignisation of space: Seven processes driving the current land grab. *The Journal of Peasant Studies* 37, no. 2: 429–47.

Space for pluralism? Examining the Malibya land grab

Nicolette Larder

Recent years have seen a flood of pseudo-facts and falsely precise data on land deals. This has led some to call for a more careful approach to the study of land deals that moves away from the current hectare-centric focus towards a grounded case-study methodology. Heeding such calls, this contribution draws on fieldwork undertaken in Mali during 2011 to examine a well-known land deal, the Malibya project, which involved a contract for the transfer of control of 100,000 hectares of land within the *Office du Niger*. Locally and globally, the deal was denounced following the destruction of homes and gardens as a result of a canal development associated with project. In contrast, the Malian government has argued such projects are vital for expanded irrigation infrastructure and thus securing food self-sufficiency for Mali. Somewhere in between are the farmers of the *Office du Niger*, some of whom argue for the cessation of the project and others of whom argue the expansion of irrigation in the zone could benefit farmers, particularly those without sufficient access to land. This paper explores the differing viewpoints of the actors involved and the role the land-grabbing frame has played in mobilising these different responses.

1. Introduction

A significant number of contributions published in the pages of this journal have examined the recent global rush on agricultural land, the drivers of which have been located in the convergence of multiple food, fuel, climate and finance crises (Cotula 2012; McMichael 2012). The growing literature on land grabbing has examined the phenomenon from a variety of perspectives and drawn on case studies of land grabbing from a range of geographical locations. It is now established that the land-grabbing term, in its contemporary usage, began with the release of Barcelona-based non-governmental organisation (NGO) GRAIN's publication of the 2008 report *SEIZED* (GRAIN 2008). The subsequent take-up and reproduction of the land-grabbing terminology in both public discourse and academic publications was swift. Prior to 2009 there were only a few sporadic references to 'land grabbing' in academic journals, but by 2013 numerous special journal issues had appeared, hundreds of working and peer-reviewed papers had been published, and at least two well-attended global conferences had taken place. In public discourse, land grabbing seemed to emerge from nowhere to suddenly become the most pressing issue facing agrarian society globally: major media publications such as the *New York Times* and the *Guardian* ran stories on 'the great land rush', international civil society organisations with both environmental and social orientations started campaigns against land grabbing and national governments announced plans for registers of foreign-owned land and changes to rules about foreign ownership of land.

As a propaganda tool, the term 'land grabbing' has been successful in raising awareness around the potential negative impacts of increased flows of finance capital into land. Although it is difficult to quantify the extent of the frame's success, one need only reflect on the pervasiveness of the term to get an idea of its importance for problematising the post-2008 land-control shifts. The point of departure for this paper are the recent calls for greater scrutiny of issues of land grabbing, in recognition that 'competing definitions of land grabbing reveal and obscure aspects of the phenomenon, and serve different ends' (Margulis, McKeon, and Borras 2013, 15).

This contribution examines one of the early, and now iconic, cases used to underscore the land-grabbing narrative, the Malibya Project. Malibya, the lexical compounding of Mali and Libya, is the operating name of a company set up under the auspices of the Libya Sovereign Wealth fund.[1] Building on previous studies of land deals in Mali, this paper is devoted to an exploration of the politics of land access, agricultural investment and local responses to the Malibya project. My findings in part contest assumptions and claims made by organised ranks of civil society movements that are part of the broader (international) land-grabbing resistance movement about the nature of 'local' responses to land grabbing. Based on fieldwork undertaken in Mali in 2011, I argue that the current construction of the Malibya project has obscured local responses to the project, and that such local responses do not actually neatly fit within the dominant civil-society framing of land grabbing. Such a finding supports Borras and Franco's (2013) argument that local people do not respond to land grabbing uniformly and that diverse localised responses to land deals, including calls for incorporation, 'are probably more common than the popular literature would acknowledge' (Borras and Franco 2013, 1730).

At the same time, this paper suggests the land-grabbing frame has opened space for articulation of a variety of responses to the Malibya project. While these responses may not necessarily be represented within the simplified version of land grabbing, the frame has nevertheless created political space on a number of fronts including calls for inclusion by subsections of the smallholder farmer population. As a result, this paper argues that despite its somewhat oversimplified framing, as a political tool land grabbing matters, although in sometimes-unpredictable ways.

This essay first gives an overview of the Malibya case. This is followed by an exploration of the political character of the Malian-based response to the Malibya project. It demonstrates that peasants have responded to the Malibya project with both calls against their expulsion from their land and, at the same time, calls for inclusion into the project. This paper suggests the land-grabbing frame has created space for smallholders to articulate different and sometimes-competing claims related to the Malibya project. As a result, land grabbing emerges as a dynamic collective-action frame whose efficacy is evident in the opportunities it has created in the political structure for smallholders to voice their concerns and responses to land deals. The hope is that this will help inform further political strategising of social movements struggling for social justice.

[1]Malibya is an operating company of the Libyan African Investment Portfolio, an asset of the Libyan Investment Authority (LIA), Libya's sovereign wealth fund. The LIA was created by Safi Gaddafi in 2006 to invest the country's oil wealth and, although the fund was reported to have lost USD 1billion following the global financial crisis, the fund is currently valued at around USD 65 billion (Okpamen 2014).

2. Plurality in peasant responses

Sociological scholarship on social movements suggests movements employ various political tools when seeking to elicit change. Significant among these tools is the collective action frame. Framing theory emerged following the cultural turn when studies of movement's actions shifted somewhat away from networks, structures, resources and organisations towards aspects of culture, meanings, narratives and symbols (Friedland and Mohr 2004; Johnston and Klandermans 2003). Goffman (1974) first theorised frames as a set of basic, social frameworks, which groups use collectively to make sense of the world. Like the media and the state, social movement organisations play a key role in the construction of frames through the active production of new meaning, and the structuring and interpretation of existing meanings (Snow and Benford 1988, 198). Through the process of framing, social movement organisations occupy a key role as signifying agents that concentrate meaning for movement participants, antagonists and observers (Snow and Benford 1988).

It is possible to identify a number of broad frames that have collectively developed in response to recent shifts in land control. These include the 'win–win' frame of land deals embraced by proponents of large-scale corporatised agriculture (see for example Deininger et al. 2011) and the radical critique of land deals evident within the land-grabbing narrative. Embedded in both frames are a range of assumptions and particular ideological positions. Scholars have highlighted the usefulness of land grabbing because it emphasises unjust power relations (Margulis, McKeon, and Borras 2013). However, like all broad frames, it also has the power to obscure aspects of the problem. Scholars have long recognised social movements represent diverse interests and invariably exclude the concerns of portions of the group they purport to represent. A case in point was the calls to recognise gender-based difference within agrarian reform and sustainable agriculture movements (see for example Chiappe and Butler Flora 1998; Deere 2003; Sachs 1992).

The land-grabbing narrative is rooted in a critical stance against corporatisation and industrialisation of the food system and puts forward a solution in the form of food sovereignty and the rights of 'local' people (McMichael forthcoming). Implicit in the land-grabbing narrative is the idea that local people, wherever they are, struggle against and oppose land grabbing on the grounds that it displaces people from their communities, threatens cultures and destroys local economies. On the surface, responses to land grabbing appear uniform, largely in line with what the popular media reports, which tends to be similar to claims by civil society organisations. However, embedded in this consistent response is an assumption that 'local' people harbour identical aspirations and goals for the future. This conceals the heterogeneity of perceptions and experiences of shifting land control. Such differences are 'based on a whole range of variable and relative economic, political, social and cultural factors, conditions and calculations that are often not well understood and in any case would require much deeper inquiry than is often given' (Borras and Franco 2013, 1724).

In a timely reminder about the nature of responses to land grabbing, Borras and Franco (2013, 1730) suggested 'there are at least three intersections of political contestations within and between the state and social forces around current land grabbing … poor people versus corporate actors, poor people versus the state, and poor people versus poor people'. As a cursory review of documentation will attest, in the majority, the response to land grabbing has been dominated by agendas against those purchasing and leasing lands and against states accused of facilitating land grabs, through either adherence to a developmentalist agenda or weak governance. This tendency to overlook certain responses may be the result, as Friedmann and McNair (2008, 409–10) explain, of agrarian scholarship focusing on resistance to displacement over and above the 'concrete actions and feasible projects' peasants take to protect their farming cultures. Also at play here is the process of social movement framing, which by its very nature simplifies and codes aspects of the world in order to effect some change (Snow and Benford 1992). In other words, frames necessarily omit some truths in order to increase their efficacy. In the case of Mali, arguably missing from the land-grabbing frame are intra- and inter-class contestations occurring at the local level (Bernstein 2010), and articulations of pre-existing land access problems (Grigsby 2004). While these political differences may not meet the framing and agenda-setting needs of international civil society organisations, they nevertheless remain important for engaged scholarship that seeks to understand the nature of response to shifting land and labour control.

A second and perhaps more pertinent theoretical insight for this paper is the question of efficacy of social movement framing. Efficacy has been theorised in various stages: getting issues on the agenda, gaining discursive commitments from policy actors and states, causing procedural change at domestic and international levels, affecting policy and influencing behaviour change in target groups (Keck and Sikkink 1998). Many theories of success focus on variations of these stages (see for example Moyer 1987; Starr 2010).

Central to the success of social movement frames, political opportunity structures are the 'consistent but not necessarily formal or permanent dimensions of the political environment that provides incentives for people to undertake collective action by affecting their expectations for success or failure' (Tarrow in Meyer and Minkoff 2004, 1459). Operationalisations of the political opportunity structure theory differ substantially (Meyer and Minkoff 2004). This work draws on Schurman and Munro's (2009) theorisation that the external openings and closures actors face and construct in mobilisation are political and cultural; in other words, opportunities for success include those provided through exploitation of standard political opportunities and in the characteristics of and relationships between actors involved, including the state and those outside it. In short, movement success is judged on the basis of 'how the movement matters' in setting in motion processes of change.

3. The Malibya project

In late 2008, civil society organisations began to report on the marked increase of large-scale leases of agricultural land in the *Office du Niger*. The *Office du Niger* is the governing body of an irrigated rice-growing zone in the Ségou region of central Mali (Figure 1). The zone, which draws water from the Niger River, was set up by the French in the 1930s and came under the control of the Malian government after independence in 1960. Information on *Office* land under contract to foreign entities is not systematically recorded by the Malian government, but external reports estimated between 162,000 and 871,000 hectares of land in the zone was leased between 2005 and 2011 (Diallo and Mushinzimana 2009; Djiré, Keita, and Diawara 2012; Oakland Institute 2011). One of the most heavily interrogated deals was the 2008 agreement between the Malian and Libyan governments.

Under this project, the Malian government leased 100,000 hectares of land to the Malibya development company.[2] The contract, signed by both parties, provides the official

[2]Malibya is an operating company of the Libyan African Investment Portfolio, an asset of the the Libyan Investment Authority (LIA), Libya's sovereign wealth fund. The LIA was created by Safi Gaddafi in 2006 to invest the country's oil wealth and, although the fund was reported to have lost US$1billion following the global financial crisis, the fund is currently valued at around US$65 billion (Okpamen 2014).

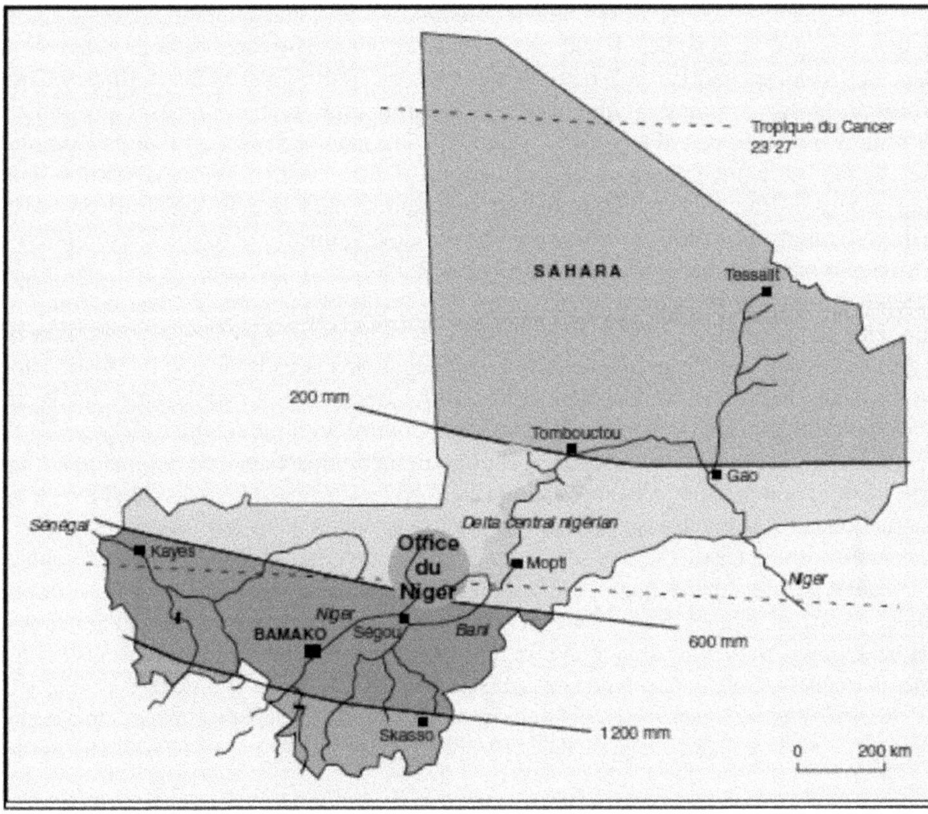

Figure 1. Location of the *Office du Niger*, Mali.
Source: Coulibaly et al. (2006).

view of the project's goals and details. The stated principle objective for use of the land is to be agriculture, herding and the transformation of agricultural products. The area of land designated to Malibya was not specified in the contract and gave the company rights to a site or sites of its choosing in the delta region of the Niger River. Under the contract, any pre-existing rights to control of land were invalidated. Rights to water use were also granted upon payment of an annual fee per hectare of irrigated land. The original contract made no mention of critical issues such as landholders' existing rights to land or future employment opportunities.

Land within the *Office du Niger* can not be owned and is leased to users based on one of five types of leasehold permit through which land tenure in the zone is administered: annual contract; farm permit; lease for a house plot; ordinary lease (30 years); and long lease (50 years) (Kater, Dembélé, and Dicko 2000). Annual contracts are normally applied for by family farmers, who lease irrigated land for the period of one year, renewable upon the lessor meeting the conditions of the lease. Under the annual lease agreement, the contract may be terminated by either party at the end of the season, but the contract will be terminated if the lessor either fails to maintain the irrigation channels or fails to pay the lease fee for the land/water (Republic of Mali 2010). The 100,000 hectares of land was leased to Malibya at no cost for a term of 50 years, the maximum lease term available in the *Office du Niger*, and renewable upon agreement of both parties. The first stage of the

Malibya project involved the development of a 40-km-long canal and bitumen road, neither of which are specific designated land uses within the zone. The canal extends between the villages of Kolongo and Boky-Wèrè and was built in 2008 by the Malibya-funded China Geo-Engineering Corporation International, a corporation of the Chinese government. The canal was developed along a *fala*, a pre-existing natural waterway that had supplied water to market garden lands along the length of the canal. Some smallholder farms living alongside the *fala* suffered loss of productive land due to construction of the canal, particularly in Kolongo, where the canal's development led to the subsumption of the village's main market garden lands (Figures 2 and 3). In addition, around 150 households were forced to relocate from Kolongo as a result of the canal's construction, only some with compensation.

Access to, and use of, land as set out in legal contracts is underpinned by various non-paper, socially based mechanisms (Benjamin 2006; Benjaminsen and Sjaastad 2003), and one of the critical norms governing land use and control within the *Office du Niger* is the historical notion of undesignated land. Although in theory leases can be applied to all land in the zone, in practice they have been reserved to govern irrigated land and land for village construction, and, as in the case of Malibya, to provide secure long-term access to large leaseholders in certain cases. As a result, there are large areas of land within the zone outside the irrigated portions and villages that are under the ultimate control of the *Office*, but are without governance mechanisms for legal use rights. 'Undesignated' is the official view of such lands and is somewhat akin to the 'vacant' lands rhetoric used by governments in other contexts to justify transfers of land control (see for example Ariza-Montobbio et al. 2010). The *Office du Niger* suggests it is this undesignated land that has been allocated to Malibya (Figure 4). In the official view of the *Office du Niger*, this section of land was always

Figure 2. Main area of market gardening in Kolongo, 2006.
Source: Google Earth (2012a).

Figure 3. Main area of market gardening in Kolongo, 2010.
Source: Google Earth (2012b).

planned for irrigated production and any use of this land for purposes other than irrigation is 'illegal'. For example, when asked about the customary rights governing market gardens destroyed in the development of the Malibya canal, both a key staff member from the *Office du Niger* and the Chief of Kolongo village claimed land holders had been warned that the land around the *fala* was designated for development, that they were using it without permission and that it could be resumed at any time.

As the case of the market garden land in Kolongo illustrates, undesignated does not mean unproductive or unused. The view of such lands as undesignated has its roots in the historical development of land policy within Mali and the *Office du Niger*. At the time of colonisation in Mali, the French recognised customary land as having use rights only, applying the concept of vacant and ownerless lands to indigenous-owned land under Article 539 of the French civil code of 1804 (Benjaminsen and Sjaastad 2003; Djiré 2007). This conceptual view of national land ownership continued after independence (Becker 2001). While systems were put in place gradually to record customary rights through various orders and decrees (Djiré 2007, 1), in contemporary Mali, secure access to land is gained primarily through a system of land registration and titling (although it is in peri-urban areas around the capital Bamako that registration is most likely to occur; Djiré 2007, 1). The state is still able to expropriate such lands, although this is more problematic than if they were not registered (Benjaminsen 2008, 30). The process of registration and titling is by no means unproblematic given the highly prohibitive costs associated with registering land, the fact that the majority of land title owners are absentee land owners and urban elites, and the corruption surrounding the practice of registering lands (Benjaminsen 2008; Benjaminsen and Sjaastad 2003; Djiré 2007).

Figure 4. The 'undesignated' block of land allocated to Malibya is at the top right of the image picture.
Source: Photo by the author.

Notions of vacant and ownerless lands were also applied to the land that became part of the zone of the *Office du Niger*. Today, all land within the zone is legally owned by the *Office*, which, technically, has recourse alone to legal decisions about how land is used. Unlike the rest of Mali, farmers in the zone are not able to register lands with the state, and officials continue to employ phrases such as 'we install farmers on newly irrigated lands', which serve to further emphasise the state's power over land in the zone. This material fact is reproduced in the discourse employed by farmers living in the zone, who were noted to make comments such as:

> these lands still belong to the government so to the *Office du Niger*. If there is a public need they will use it without problem. But when you want the owner of this land now, it's my father. Maybe after it can be the *Office* or the government … We hope this does not happen but …

The attitude of the *Office du Niger* towards land holders contrasts strongly with provisions set out in the country's agricultural law, the *Loi Orientation d'Agricole* (LOA 2006). The LOA, which set out the vision for Mali's agricultural future, has been seen by civil society and peasants' rights organisations both in Mali and internationally as a major step forward for the rights of smallholder farmers in Mali, due to two inclusions. First is the recognition given to family farmers in the document, particularly the requirement for a national land policy that recognises customary land rights. The groundwork for the development of this policy was being undertaken at the time of this research in 2011 by the Malian-based *Institut de Recherche et de Promotion des Alternatives de Développement en*

Afrique. However, discussions with experts and state officials in Mali raise questions about how the registration of customary title within the *Office du Niger* will work. For example, a land expert in Mali suggested the *Office du Niger* will likely be exempt from the land registration process because of its special legal status as a 'state within the state'. If registration of customary lands does not go ahead within the zone, the LOA will provide little security of tenure for farmers in the zone.

The second important inclusion within the LOA was the concept of food sovereignty. Food sovereignty was given a central place in the document, with the law stating that 'the aim [of the LOA] is to guarantee food sovereignty ... ' (Article 3) and devoting one chapter to setting out the path to food sovereignty in the Malian context. The legal recognition of food sovereignty was seen as a significant step forward for agrarian reform. Potentially problematic for the shift towards food sovereignty were findings from discussions with Malian government officials, who were often noted to conflate food sovereignty with food self-sufficiency, a long-time goal of the Malian government, rather than recognising the radical food sovereignty project put forward by peasants' rights organisations.

4. Responding to Malibya

Within Mali, the main opposition to the Malibya project has come from the Malian-based peasants' rights group *Coordination Nationale des Organisation Paysannes de Mali* (CNOP), which has been central in the construction and spread of the politicised land-grabbing frame within the country. Formed in 2003, CNOP's agenda lies in the defence of peasants' interests, and the organisation represents 11 regional farming groups from around Mali. In turn, CNOP is affiliated in West Africa with the *Réseau des organisations paysannes and de producteurs de l'Afrique du l'Ouest* (ROPPA), and internationally with La Via Campesina. In response to the Malibya project, CNOP have undertaken a number of actions including hosting national and international anti-land-grabbing events and conducting and publishing research findings on the impacts of development associated with land deals. In the case of Malibya, CNOP linked Libya's involvement in agriculture to the country's dependence on food imports, arguing Libya was following other Arab countries in seeking to overcome dependence on global rice markets by implementing a food security strategy using extraterritorial lands (Coulibaly and Monjane 2009). The group problematised land grabbing on the basis that it results in foreign control of sovereign land, competition for water and loss of seed diversity through the importation of hybrid rice varieties and genetically modified organism (GMO) rice. In a report published by CNOP, the impacts of land grabbing at the local level were used to contextualise these broader implications of shifting land control by drawing on first-hand observations of localised impacts, including: lack of an environmental and social impact analysis; lack of clear information for those affected; obstruction of livestock routes; creation of localised pollution; and destruction of houses, villages, orchards, market gardens and cemeteries, without full compensation. The response by peasants' rights groups to land grabs like Malibya is summarised in a declaration by the Global Alliance Against Land Grabbing, which said:

> In Mali, the government has a policy of promoting private investments in agriculture and it has transferred close to 800,000 hectares of land to private investors. The land belongs to communities that have been living on it for generations, if not centuries, whereas the Malian state was only created in the 1960s. The same situation can be found in many other countries that do not recognize customary law. To dispossess communities of their land is a violation of both their

> customary and historical rights. To be able to benefit from a safe access to land and to have control over land and natural resources are rights that are inextricably linked to the rights recognized by the Universal Declaration of Human Rights as well as many other regional and international conventions on human rights, such as, for instance, the right to self-determination, the right to an adequate standard of living, or the right to housing, food, health, culture, property and participation. We note with grave concern that states are not respecting their rights in this regard and that they consider the interests of the business world as more important that the rights of people. (La Vía Campesina 2012, 18)

This response is typical of the way the land-grabbing frame has developed in Mali, and reflects the kind of statements made in publications by civil society organisations and other peasants' rights groups within the broader anti-land-grabbing movement (see for example FIAN 2010; GRAIN 2008).

5. Rationalising Malibya

As evidenced in other African nations, claims of land grabbing have been strongly refuted by the state (see Lavers' 2012 findings in Ethiopia). Instead, the Malian government has welcomed the rejuvenation of investment interest in the *Office du Niger* zone. Discussions with key government officials in the agricultural sector in Mali and documentation produced by the *Office du Niger* and the government more generally suggest the Malian government has adopted an almost totalising discourse of investment as not only positive, but necessary for the *Office du Niger*. Moreover, the Malibya deal was seen by many in Mali as a positive strengthening of ties between Gaddafi's Libya and the country, and many Malians I spoke with were supportive of the flow of money from Libya for such infrastructure projects. This idea of mutual benefit for both countries was outlined in the contract signed for the Malibya project, which stated: 'In the framework of reinforcing the economic integration between Mali and Libya for the realisation of strategic projects that are in the common interest of the two countries, they are agreed on the necessity of an agricultural investment project ... ' (La Grande Jamahiriya arabe Libyenne populaire et socialiste and La République du Mali 2008).

Discussions with Malian government officials indicate they perceive the project as the coming together of long-term plans for the *Office du Niger*. The irrigated portions of the *Office du Niger* zone have grown in fits and starts over time. Throughout its history, those in charge of the *Office*, first the French and then the Malians, have sought to expand the superficies of the *Office* to reach the maximum capacity its original architects proposed it could cover: 960,000 hectares. That Libya is planning to irrigate 100,000 hectares fits with the consistent view within the Malian government of the *Office du Niger* as having great, but unrealised, potential. As an official in the *Office du Niger* said:

> The Libyans, they are redeveloping 100,000 hectares. Since 1932, the *Office* ... at 80 years old next year ... from 1932 until today, the agency has not set up 100,000 hectares. The State of Mali – it has not developed 100,000 hectares. Because to develop one hectare it takes four million [CFA].[3] One hectare, four million. The Libyans, they are trying to develop 100,000 hectares! What we could not do for 80 years, they are trying to do.

The official here refers to the fact that at present, less than 100,000 hectares of land has been irrigated in the zone since its creation in the 1930s. Libya's commitment to irrigating

[3]Approximately USD 6800.

100,000 hectares would therefore increase by more than 100 percent the land under irrigation. The proposal by the Libyans to develop and irrigate this amount of land was seen as a significant coup for the zone and the country more broadly and fits with the perception government officials hold that the Malian state is incapable of increasing the irrigated superficies in the zone due to lack of finances.

Much of the early planning and groundwork to install irrigation in the zone of the *Office du Niger* was conducted by the French, who planned to irrigate an area in the order of 960,000 hectares. Initially, plans were for the production of cotton, although this was later extended to rice and, in spite of the initial plan, by the time of independence total irrigated surfaces were less than 20,000 hectares. Following the drought from 1972 to 1974 and in continued pursuit of food self-sufficiency plans, by the late 1970s, the government of Mali began to solicit foreign donors to fund the rehabilitation of degraded lands and canals in the *Office du Niger* zone (Aw and Diemer 2005; Dougnon and Coulibaly 2007). Ongoing inter-regional and international policies for development fed the reinvigoration for expansion and improvement in the zone. Both the French and Dutch governments, along with the World Bank, funded the majority of repair and expansion work in the zone from the early 1980s until the mid-1990s, although the German, American and Malian governments also contributed financially (World Bank 1999). Financial assistance was guaranteed on condition of deep institutional and economic reform. In the decades following these reforms, the *Office du Niger* was hailed a 'success', and many saw these reforms as having been central in this regard (see for example Diarra, Staatz, and Dembélé 2000; IPRTID 2003; Plusquellec 2002). Success here was described mainly as a measure of increased yields, but also related to the opening up of the zone to a 'buoyant' private sector, population growth, diversification and intensification (Aw and Diemer 2005; Gabre-Madhin and Haggblade 2004).

Despite the apparent success of these structural reforms through the 1980s, calls for ongoing reform continued into the 1990s. This time, reform was seen as necessary for poverty reduction: in a country where the primary sector was the major contributor to gross domestic product (GDP), increased production was necessary for economic growth, and growth had become central to poverty reduction. As a result of this focus on poverty, in 1999 the International Monetary Fund (IMF) necessitated all loan recipients (of which Mali was one) put in place a Poverty Reduction Strategy Paper (PRSP). By early 2012, over 150 countries had PRSPs in place (IMF 2012a). The PRSPs were closely linked to the United Nations (UN)'s Millennium Development Goals (MDGs). One of the focal points of the two-pillar strategy adopted by the international community for the achievement of the MDGs was policy change in low-income countries, and the poverty reduction strategies, instituted as they were by the IMF with its agenda for structural reform, were closely aligned to the PRSPs (IMF 2012b). In Mali, the result of the PRSP process was the development of the Growth and Poverty Reduction Strategy Paper, published in 2002, which provided the basis for assistance from technical and financial partners, as well as debt relief (IMF 2008, 13). The overall goal of the plan was twofold: boosting the productive sector and consolidating public-sector reforms, both underpinned by 13 'priority areas of intervention', the first of which was food security and rural development (IMF 2008). As a result of this need to grow agriculture, the Malian government has engaged in a number of additional policy development actions. For example, Mali developed several strategies for increasing national rice production in the late 2000s, including *Operation Riz* in 2008 and the *National Strategy for the Development of Rice Growing* in 2009 (Republic of Mali 2009). Under these plans, the government hopes to double or even triple the amount of rice produced nationally, with the aim of turning Mali into a major exporter of rice. The strategies focus mainly on increasing high-yield production systems, which involves widespread deployment of New Rice for Africa (NERICA) seed, annual extension of land under irrigated rice cultivation and improvement in post-harvest techniques.

In the last two decades, modernisation has increasingly been facilitated through investment by the private sector in the form of foreign direct investment. In Mali, the desire for foreign investment has seen the government take steps aimed at improving the legal context within which foreign investment in the agricultural sector occurs. The first of these was the creation of the *Code des Investissements*, passed in 1991 (amended in 2005), which sets out the tax benefits, guarantees and conditions for approval of foreign investment in the country (Republic of Mali 1991). International financial institutions saw this code as central to facilitating a positive climate for foreign private investment (UNCTAD, ITE, and IIA 2006). More recently, the *Centre Nationale pour Promotion des Investissments* was replaced, on advice from the World Bank, with the *Agence pour la Promotion des Investissements au Mali* (API). As its name suggests, the purpose of the agency is to promote investment in four opportunity-sectors which fit with Mali's comparative advantages: agriculture, livestock, mining and tourism.

More specific to agriculture, the LOA includes provisions for easing costs and simplifying procedures for national and foreign actors wishing to invest in agricultural development in Mali to obtain land titles and leases, 'in the framework of investment promotion, of capitalization and growth in agricultural production' (Republic of Mali 2006, Article 82). A key government official charged with administering the LOA confirmed that the law had been developed to 'help secure and provide assurance to investors'.

These kinds of policy and political shifts have translated into a frame employed by Malian government agencies and their staff reflective of the policy changes. For example, the need to increase agricultural production to grow the economy was evidenced in interviews with officials in various government ministries. When asked why there is a need for foreign investment in the agricultural sector in Mali, an official in the Ministry of Agriculture responded:

> ... because we are, the country, we are classed in the less-developed countries and our primary sector in the last year contributed much to the GDP, roughly 40 percent ... agriculture is the backbone of our economy and agriculture it has, until now, been uncertain. That is to say, it suffers a lot, particularly related to climate and the percentages of irrigated lands are very low, so there is close to almost no gain ... so we need investors ... anything that improves GDP.

As seen in this statement, the perceived need for investment is closely linked to the ability to farm on irrigated lands. This is particularly true for the *Office du Niger* zone. While the major gains in yield returns following the reforms of the 1980s and 1990s, as outlined above, were cause for success, the leveling-off of yields along with an increasing population (both from in-migration and from natural population growth) led to increased pressure on irrigated land.

Current estimates of the total population of the zone and size of the irrigated rice-producing portions of the land vary between 350,000 to 400,000 people living in around 200 villages, and from 80,000 hectares up to 130,000 hectares (Diawara 2011; Dougnon and Coulibaly 2007; Kater, Dembélé, and Dicko 2000). Following the major gains in yield returns following the reforms of the 1980s and 1990s, the leveling-off of yields, along with population growth associated with in-migration following the drought of the 1970s, has increased pressure for access to irrigated land in the zone in recent decades (Coulibaly, Bélières, and Yénizié

2006). The amount of irrigated land has not kept pace with population growth, leading families to subdivide plots such that the number of plots grew from 12,900 in 1999 to 35,000 in 2011. Currently, each family has on average access to 3.7 hectares of irrigated land, although some families farm on as little as 0.25 hectares (Monimart and Tan 2011).

These pressures have led to calls for further extension of the irrigated surfaces of the zone, which translated into a plan adopted by the *Office du Niger* in 2008 to irrigate 200,000 hectares of land in the zone by 2020 (equal to a 200 percent increase on 2008 irrigated surfaces; Coulibaly, Bélières, and Yénizié 2006). The extension of irrigated surfaces remains of paramount concern for government officials. Such plans link to those outlined earlier to significantly increase rice production to make Mali a rice-exporting nation. Officials interviewed as part of this research argued for investment on the grounds that the government does not have the financial means necessary to expand irrigation infrastructure within the zone.

The state's cultural construction of its inability to 'do agriculture' has had a profound effect on its response to the charge of land grabbing. While the movement against land grabbing seeks to promote peasants' rights to land and the value of agrarianism, the state follows the somewhat typical narrative of a need for investment based on underdeveloped and non-industrialised farming systems. In effect, these are the kinds of arguments embedded in the 'win–win' frame of 'agricultural investment' already critiqued in the academic literature (Borras and Franco 2012; Da Vià 2011).

Outside of arguments around the logic used to promote expansion of industrial agriculture, the Malian government's response is perhaps telling of the kinds of openings and closures facing the anti-land-grabbing movement in Mali. While the movement has had some success in getting issues on the agenda, there has been little movement in terms of commitments to or follow-through on procedural and policy change. At the same time, the actions of the movement have exposed the flaws and inconsistencies in the country's preeminent agricultural law, particularly related to inclusions of provisions for easing foreign investment in agriculture alongside the overarching goal of food sovereignty.

6. Capitalising 'land grabbing': differentiated responses to Malibya

The previous section suggested the Malian government has justified projects like Malibya on the grounds that the state is unable to perform agriculture adequately without investment into irrigation infrastructure within the *Office du Niger*. Interestingly, these calls for expansion of the irrigated superficies have been echoed within the *Office du Niger*, suggesting some potentially uncomfortable overlap between the positions of the state and smallholder farmers when it comes to land deals. This is particularly the case for social movement organisations who critique the state's open stance to investment but support the rights of smallholder farmers. One clear point of tension evident in local characteristics of response to Malibya is the call for (partial) incorporation into the Malibya project made by the *Office du Niger* rice farmers union, *Syndicat des exploitants de l'Office du Niger* (SEXAGON). SEXAGON emerged as a rice farmers' union in the zone in the late 1990s out of land conflicts with the *Office du Niger*. They now represent around 12,500 rice farmers in the zone (approximately 13 percent of rice farmers). According to SEXAGON representatives, the union maintains an ongoing agenda to secure more irrigated land for its members, a task they have been engaged in since the union began in 1997.

Senior members within SEXAGON suggested the organisation had secured a discursive commitment from the *Office du Niger* for access to a portion of the irrigated lands once completed under the Malibya project. One member of SEXAGON's senior leadership went so far to say: 'we don't mind the land is being irrigated, we just want our fair share' (Niono, February 2011). The likelihood of SEXAGON's members gaining secure access to this land is unclear. The *Office du Niger* claim the Malibya canal can be used to irrigate areas above and beyond the 100,000 hectares allocated to Malibya; one senior *Office du Niger* staff member in particular was at pains to map for me just where and how the canal would benefit farmers in the zone. While SEXAGON's main office is located in Niono, some distance from the canal, the group's members are spread throughout the zone, and there is the question of how SEXAGON's geographically diverse membership will gain access to the irrigated plots under question.

If SEXAGON are successful in gaining access to land, there remains the problem of equity around access to lands associated with the Malibya project. Calls for inclusion into the Malibya Project were not uncommon among rice farmers I interviewed, who persistently lamented the problem of insufficient irrigated land on which to grow rice, and expressed sentiments of hope that the project would provide newly irrigated lands for local farmers. If some farmers do gain access to irrigated lands from this project, there seems no doubt others stand to lose as a result. It is not clear yet which lands Malibya will irrigate, nor what will happen to existing land users on these lands. If the initial development of the canal is indicative of the project's development modus operandi, lands will be usurped without consideration for existing land users. In such circumstances, the losers are likely to be those who farm crops other than rice on 'undesignated' lands; as already alluded to, irrigated land within the *Office du Niger* is both highly prized and in short supply, meaning such lands will likely be preserved. Those sections of the population who use undesignated lands, typically herders and women and the other landless, may find themselves further excluded.

Significant within the broader debate around land grabbing is the issue of how we are to understand the privileging of calls against expulsion over those for inclusion, which thereby privilege struggles against expulsion and downplay struggles over the terms of incorporation. In dominant representations the Malibya case has exemplified the 'roll-back' tendency identified by Borras, Franco and Wang (2013): local people are struggling against expulsion from land (see for example Oakland Institute 2011). Certainly there has been a vocal proportion of the population in the *Office du Niger* who support this position, as evidenced through initial protests against Malibya in Kolongo, the testimonies of farmers delivered at a number of forums and conferences in Mali, and interviews with farmers. Situating reactions within the broader politics of response to land grabbing, SEXAGON seem to have adopted a tactical response to mitigate the negative impacts and maximise the opportunities presented by the Malibya project. SEXAGON's position could be seen as an argument for corporatised agriculture with the same political tendencies as neoliberalism, albeit with an increased role for (some) peasants in food production. But the actual politics requires more nuance. Had famers been faced with a choice between secure access to irrigated land through a state-sponsored rice farming development or uncertain and potentially non-forthcoming access through incorporation into Malibya, we can almost certainly say they would have chosen the former.

More concretely, the radical response to the Malibya project shaped and moulded the political environment to create a number of openings within the political structure for smallholders to make claims on the state. These openings in the political opportunity structure were two-fold. First was the opening that allowed smallholders to call for compensation for loss of land associated with the development of the canal. The alignment between the relatively localised responses to loss of houses and market garden lands in Kolongo, and extra-local actors in the form of CNOP, La Via Campesina and others, meant the Malibya case was elevated to the international stage. As a result, those affected by the Malibya canal were presented with access to influential voices and thus a more powerful position from which to call for compensation for their losses. While the potential to call for compensation arguably always existed, by virtue of their case aligning with the global narrative emerging around land deals, people in Kolongo were afforded the ability to apply more pressure to the Malian state than would have otherwise been possible without external support.

At the same time, the radical response for calls to roll back land grabbing in the *Office du Niger* provided a platform for SEXAGON to open discussions with the state over their potential incorporation into the deal. Discussions with SEXAGON staff suggest it was only after the Kolongo forum (organised by CNOP to protest against land grabbing) that the *Office du Niger* verbally agreed to SEXAGON's demands for inclusion into the Malibya project. SEXAGON's success at securing a discursive commitment is perhaps an uncomfortable measure of efficacy for the radical movement who generally oppose any attempts to mitigate negative impacts and maximise opportunities in favour of stopping land grabbing (Borras et al. 2012). From the perspective of social movement studies, however, through their actions to get the issue of land grabbing on the agenda in Mali, the radical movement 'matters' because it cleaved multiple political opportunities for farmers in the *Office du Niger* to have their claims heard. Affected land holders were able to argue more strongly for their pre-existing rights to land, despite the fact these rights were not previously recognised by the state. At the same time, existing land holders who had not been affected by the development of the Malibya project were provided an opportunity to put forward their conditions of incorporation into the land deal.

7. The future for Malibya and farmers in the *Office du Niger*

The Malibya project stalled following unrest in Libya in early 2011 and, in light of ongoing conflict in both Libya and Mali, at the time of writing of this paper (early 2015), the future of the project is unclear. While Libya's commitment to the project is unclear, the already-developed canal sits as a visible reminder of the irrigable potential of the zone. As the Libyan Investment Authority clears the decks of its management structure and re-evaluates its investment portfolio, the future use of the 40-km-long canal it built in 2008 will likely become clearer. The LIA's funds were frozen in 2011 by the UN and remain so at the request of the LIA (Wright 2014). In 2014, the LIA undertook major actions to improve its investment operations, suing Goldman Sachs and Société Générale SA (GLE) for USD 2.5 billion over failed investments, hiring external accounting firm Deloitte to undertake an investigation into internal corruption, and undertaking a wholesale change of senior management (Chellel 2014; Wright 2014). These actions are, according to the LIA, in preparation for the fund to 'come back to the international fold' (Chellel 2014). What this means for the Malibya project is uncertain. Given the fund's attempts to recoup its losses suffered after the 2011 coup, and the significant investment already made in the project, it seems unlikely the LIA will walk away from Malibya. Even if that does come to pass, there is the possibility that the Chinese company Yuan Longping High Tech, who were suggested to hold a silent 30 percent share in Malibya and a contract to provide seeds and expertise, will continue with the project (Brautigam 2012). Either way, continuation of the project will require vast human and financial capital to bring the full 100,000 hectares into cultivation and, as Edelman (2013) explained, diseconomies of scale are likely to operate for single entities, such as Malibya, producing food at such a scale. Moreover, as the case of Qatar's Hassad Food has shown, sovereign wealth funds engaged in extra-territorial food production can face significant backlash (Sippel forthcoming).

8. Conclusions

It is not entirely clear why Malibya became an iconic case; perhaps in a climate where supposedly done deals are often cancelled, delayed or modified, and data sets are riddled with inaccuracies (Edelman 2013), the materiality of Malibya's canal and sheer scale made it impossible to ignore. Regardless, from conception to (partial) actualisation, the Malibya project has manifested concerns about injustices, lack of transparency and failure to follow due process, and many of these claims are well founded: the deal was conducted within the context of a Malian food self-sufficiency project but the project has, to a degree, weakened local food security through displacement of small-scale farmers, and dozens of families lost their homes in the first stage of the project. Critics argue the Malian government has sold out their population by signing up to the Malibya contract. While the state has, in various ways, been implicated as facilitating land grabbing at the expense of its population (Wolford et al. 2013), in the case of Malibya I suggest this is true, but only to a degree. It is easy to write off as flawed constructions the government's claims over lack of funding for expanding irrigation infrastructure. However, there is likely some partial truth to them: as the French discovered a century ago, irrigating land in the *Office du Niger* is difficult and expensive. While it seems Mali's goal of doubling the irrigated surfaces in the *Office du Niger* by 2020 is the result of an IMF-inspired economic growth agenda, the need for expansion of irrigated lands within the *Office du Niger* is also being argued from the ground up. Just how capable the Malian government is of delivering on this necessary infrastructure without foreign assistance is unclear.

Perhaps more clear is that the local response in Mali to the signing of the Malibya contract has been more nuanced than public discourse has acknowledged. This contribution has highlighted some of the heterogeneity evident in localised responses to land grabs in Mali. There is a proportion who have argued for the roll-back of projects like Malibya and, conversely, those who have sought to make deals for inclusion into such projects. Contrary to the dominant assumptions and claims embedded in the land-grabbing narrative, the majority of farmers in the *Office du Niger* have not been expelled or displaced (yet) by land deals, and some may even stand to benefit from such projects if they are incorporated. This is, of course, in a relative context where no other viable alternatives exist for such farmers. The outcomes of incorporation will depend in large part on the modalities through which the rice farmers are incorporated: as out-grower contract labour, as individuals farming on self-titled land or excluded altogether in favour of external labour. How and to what extent these benefits will reach incorporated households remains to be seen. Equally important to observe as this project moves forward is how the already marginalised – women and the other landless, herders and youths – will be impacted by land deals in the zone. Empirical research in this area into the future will be important for answering such questions.

For the movement against land grabbing, this case illustrates the sometimes-unpredictable effects framing can have. Within Mali, the movement faces a relatively closed standard political opportunity structure with the state seemingly holding firmly to the narrative that it is unable to 'do' agriculture without external investment. However, as successes such as winning compensation for those affected by the canal and gaining a discursive commitment for incorporation show, even within a closed structure there remain points of tension that can be exploited. At the same time, the latter may be something of an uncomfortable success for some in the movement, especially those who argue for the complete roll-back of land grabbing and against any kind of mitigation of the problem. Unfortunately for smallholders in the *Office du Niger*, the future looks precarious if uncertain incorporation into land deals is the best of limited options. The challenge remains to augment the efforts to protect farming cultures while meeting the real challenges of increasing access to land.

Acknowledgements

This paper draws on findings from my PhD thesis, and I thank my supervisors Kristen Lyons and Geoffrey Lawrence for their intellectual contributions to this material. Much gratitude to those who provided varying levels of feedback on drafts of this paper, including Jun Borras, Marc Edelman, Shona Hawkes, Amy McMahon and the three anonymous reviewers.

References

Ariza-Montobbio, P., S. Lele, G. Kallis, and J. Martínez-Alier. 2010. The political ecology of *Jatropha* plantations for biodiesel in Tamil Nadu, India. *Journal of Peasant Studies* 37, no. 4: 875–97.

Aw, D., and G. Diemer. 2005. *Making a large irrigation scheme work: A case study from Mali.* Washington, D.C.: World Bank.

Becker, L.C. 2001. Seeing green in Mali's woods: Colonial legacy, forest use, and local control. *Annals of the Association of American Geographers* 91, no. 3: 504–26.

Benjamin, C. 2006. Decentralization and livelihoods in the Malian Sahel: Challenges of legal pluralism in decentralized natural resource management. Paper presented at the 11th Conference of the International Association for the Study of Common Property, June 19–23, in Bali, Indonesia.

Benjaminsen, T.A. 2008. Does supply-induced scarcity drive violent conflicts in the African Sahel? The case of the Tuareg rebellion in northern Mali. *Journal of Peace Research* 45, no. 6: 819–36.

Benjaminsen, T.A., and E. Sjaastad. 2003. Race for the prize: Land transactions and rent appropriation in the Malian cotton zone. In *Securing land rights in Africa*, ed. T.A. Benjaminsen and C. Lund, 129–52. London: Frank Cass.

Bernstein, H. 2010. *Class dynamics of agrarian change.* Black Point and Sterling, VA: Fernwood and Kumarian Press.

Borras, S.M., and J.C. Franco. 2012. Global land grabbing and trajectories of agrarian change: A preliminary analysis. *Journal of Agrarian Change* 12, no. 1: 34–59.

Borras, S.M. and J.C. Franco. 2013. Global land grabbing and political reactions 'from below'. *Third World Quarterly* 34, no. 9: 1723–47.

Borras, S.M., J.C. Franco, S. Gomez, C. Kay, and M. Spoor. 2012. Land grabbing in Latin America and the Caribbean. *Journal of Peasant Studies* 39, no. 3–4: 845–72.

Borras, S.M., J.C. Franco, and C. Wang. 2013. The challenge of global governance of land grabbing: Changing international agricultural context and competing political views and strategies. *Globalizations* 10, no. 1: 161–179.

Brautigam, D. 2012. Whatever happened to these Chinese agricultural investments? http://www.chinaafricarealstory.com/2012/11/whatever-happend-to-these-chinese.html.

Chellel, K. 2014. Libya wealth fund to entrust $11 billion to fund managers. *Bloomberg*, April 18. http://www.bloomberg.com/news/2014–04–17/libya-wealth-fund-to-entrust-11-billion-to-fund-managers.htm

Chiappe, M.B., and C. Butler Flora. 1998. Gendered elements of the alternative agriculture paradigm. *Rural Sociology* 63, no. 3: 372–93.

Cotula, L. 2012. The international political economy of the global land rush: A critical appraisal of trends, scale, geography and drivers. *Journal of Peasant Studies* 39, no. 3–4: 649–80.

Coulibaly, L., and B. Monjane. 2009. Libyan land grab of Mali's rice-producing land. http://viacampesina.org/en/index.php?option=com_contentandview=articleandid=785:libyan-land-grab-of-malis-rice-producing-landandcatid=23:agrarian-reformandItemid=36

Coulibaly, Y.M., J-F. Bélières, and K. Yénizié. 2006. Les exploitations agricoles familiales du périmètre irrigué de l'*Office du Niger* au Mali: Évolutions et perspectives. *Cahiers Agricultures* 15, no. 6: 562–69.

Da Vià, E. 2011. The politics of 'win-win' narratives: Land grabs as development opportunity? Paper presented at the International Conference on Global Land Grabbing, 6–8 April, IDS, University of Sussex.

Deere, C.D. 2003. Women's land rights and rural social movements in the Brazilian agrarian reform. *Journal of Agrarian Change* 3, no. 1 and 2: 257–88.

Deininger, K., D. Byerlee, J. Lindsay, H. Selod, and M. Stickler. 2011. Rising global interest in farmland: Can it yield sustainable and equitable benefits? http://siteresources.worldbank.org/DEC/Resources/Rising-Global-Interest-in-Farmland.pdf

Diallo, A., and G. Mushinzimana. 2009. *Foreign direct investment (FDI) in land in Mali*. Eschborn: Deutsche Gesellshaft für Technishe Zusammenarbeit.

Diarra, S.B., J.M. Staatz, and N.N. Dembélé. 2000. The reform of rice milling and marketing in the Office du Niger: Catalysts for an agricultural success story in Mali. In *Development and democracy in Mali*, eds. R.J. Bingen, D. Robinson and J.M. Staaz, 169–88. East Lansing: Michigan State University Press.

Diawara, M. 2011. Development and administrative norms: The *Office du Niger* and decentralization in French Sudan and Mali. *Africa: The Journal of the International African Institute* 81, no. 3: 434–54.

Djiré, M. 2007. Land registration in Mali: No land ownership for farmers? Observations from peri-urban Bamako. *IIED Issues Paper no. 144*. Nottingham: IIED.

Djiré, M., A. Keita, and A. Diawara. 2012. *Agricultural investments and land acquisitions in Mali: Contexts, trends and case studies*. London/Bamako: IIED/GERSDA.

Dougnon, I. and L.B. Coulibaly. 2007. Institutional architecture and pro-poor growth in the *Office du Niger*: Responses from farmer organizations: A pilot study. Discussion Paper Series No. 14. Manchester: IPPG/Department for International Development UK.

Edelman, M. 2013. Messy hectares: Questions about the epistemology of land grabbing data. *Journal of Peasant Studies* 40, no. 3: 485–501.

FIAN. 2010. *Land grabbing in Kenya and Mozambique: A report on two research missons – and a human rights analysis of land grabbing*. Heidleberg: FIAN International Secretariat.

Friedland, R., and J. Mohr. 2004. The cultural turn in American sociology. In *Matters of culture: Cultural sociology in practice*, ed. R. Friedland and J. Mohr, 1–70. Cambridge: Cambridge University Press.

Friedmann, H., and A. McNair. 2008. Whose rules rule? Contested projects to certify 'local production for distant consumers'. *Journal of Agrarian Change* 8, no. 2–3: 408–34.

Gabre-Madhin, E.Z., and S. Haggblade. 2004. Successes in African agriculture: Results of an expert survey. *World Development* 32, no. 5: 745–66.

Goffman, E. 1974. *Frame analysis: An essay on the organization of experience*. London: Harper and Row.

Google Earth. 2012a. 13°52"33.86"N, 5°40'56.26" W, elevation 281M, April 2006. GeoEye. https://www.google.com/earth/

Google Earth. 2012b. 13°52"33.86"N, 5°40'56.26" W, elevation 281M, November 2010. GeoEye. https://www.google.com/earth/

GRAIN. 2008. *SEIZED: The 2008 land grab for food and financial security*. Barcelona: GRAIN.

Grigsby, W.J. 2004. The gendered nature of subsistence and its effects on customary land tenure. *Society and Nature* 17, no. 3: 207–22.

IMF. 2008. Mali: Poverty reduction strategy paper *IMF Country Reports No. 08/121*: International Monetary Fund.

IMF. 2012a. Fact sheet: Poverty reduction strategy papers (PRSP). http://www.imf.org/external/np/exr/facts/prsp.htm

IMF. 2012b. Fact sheet: The IMF and the millennium development goals. http://www.imf.org/external/np/exr/facts/mdg.htm

IPRTID. 2003. The irrigation challenge: Increasing irrigation contribution to food security through higher water productivity from canal irrigation systems. Issue Paper 4. Rome: International Programme for Technology and Research in Irrigation and Drainage/Food and Agriculture Organization.

Johnston, H., and B. Klandermans. 2003. The cultural analysis of social movements. In *Social movements and culture*, ed. H. Johnston and B. Klandermans, 3–24. London and New York: Routledge.

Kater, L., I. Dembélé, and I. Dicko. 2000. The dynamics of irrigated rice farming in Mali. Managing Africa's Soils No. 12. Edinburgh: IIED.

Keck, M.E., and K. Sikkink. 1998. *Activists beyond borders: Advocacy networks in international politics*. Ithaca and London: Cornell University Press.

Lavers, T. 2012. 'Land grab' as development strategy? The political economy of agricultural investment in Ethiopia. *Journal of Peasant Studies* 39, no. 1: 105–32.

La Grande Jamahiriya arabe Libyenne populaire et socialiste and La République du Mali. 2008. *Convention d’investissement dans Ie Domaine agricole entre La République du Mali et La Grande Jamahiriya arabe Libyenne populaire et socialiste*. May 2008.
La Vía Campesina. 2012. International conference of peasants and farmers: Stop land grabbing! Report and Conclusions of the Conference. Mali, 17 to 19 November 2011, Jakarta: La Vía Campesina.
Margulis, M.E., N. McKeon, and S.M. Borras. 2013. Land grabbing and global governance: Critical perspectives. *Globalizations* 10, no. 1: 1–23.
McMichael, P. 2012. The land grab and corporate food regime restructuring. *Journal of Peasant Studies* 39, no. 3–4: 681–701.
McMichael, P. Forthcoming. The land question in the food sovereignty project. *Globalizations*, 1–18.
Meyer, D.S., and D.C. Minkoff. 2004. Conceptualizing political opportunity. *Social Forces* 82, no. 4: 1457–1492.
Monimart, M., and S. F. Tan. 2011. *Gender and access to land and natural resources in Mali and Niger. Making gender and generation matter for sustainable development*. London: IIED.
Moyer, B. 1987. The movement action plan: A strategic framework describing the eight stages of successful social movements. Online: The Change Agency.
Oakland Institute. 2011. *Understanding land investment deals in Africa: Country report: Mali*. Oakland: Oakland Institute.
Okpamen, E. 2014. Libya’s sovereign wealth fund sues Goldman Sachs. *Ventures Africa*, February 3. http://www.ventures-africa.com/2014/02/libyas-sovereign-wealth-fund-sues-goldman-sachs/
Plusquellec, H. 2002. *How design, management and policy affect the performance of irrigation projects*. Bangkok, Thailand: FAO.
Republic of Mali. 1991. Code des investissements, Amended by Law No. 05–050 of 19 August 2005 C.F.R.
Republic of Mali. 2006. Loi d’orientation agricole (LOA), Loi No. 06–045 5 September 2006 C.F.R.
Republic of Mali. 2009. National strategy for the development of rice growing Bamako.
Republic of Mali. 2010. Les procédures d’attribution des terres à l’Office du Niger: Extrait du cahier des charge du système d’information global (signo). Ségou: Secrétariat d’Etat Auprès du Premier Ministre Charge Du Développement Intègre de la Zone Office du Niger/Office du Niger Service Conseil Rural.
Sachs, C. 1992. Reconsidering diversity in agriculture and food systems: An ecofeminist approach. *Agriculture and Human Values* 9, no. 3: 4–10.
Schurman, R., and W. Munro. 2009. Targeting capital: a cultural economy approach to understanding the efficacy of two anti-genetic engineering movements. *American Journal of Sociology* 115, no. 1: 155–202.
Sippel, S. Forthcoming. Food security or commercial business? Gulf State investments in Australian agriculture. *Journal of Peasant Studies*. DOI: 10.1080/03066150.2014.990448.
Snow, D.A., and R.D. Benford. 1988. Ideology, frame resonance, and participant mobilization. *International Social Movement Research* 1: 197–217.
Snow, D.A., and R.D. Benford. 1992. Master frames and cycles of protest. In *Frontiers of social movement theory*, ed. A.D. Morris and C. McClurg Mueller, 133–155. New Haven: Yale University Press.
Starr, A. 2010. Local food: A social movement? *Cultural Studies/Critical Methodologies* 10, no. 6: 479–90.
UNCTAD, ITE, & IIA. 2006. *An investment guide to Mali: Opportunities and conditions: October 2006*. New York and Geneva: United Nations.
Wolford, W., S.M. Borras, R. Hall, I. Scoones, and B. White. 2013. Governing global land deals: The role of the state in the rush for land. *Development and Change* 44, no. 2: 189–210.
World Bank. 1999. *Implementation completion report: Republic of Mali: Office du Niger consolidation project*. Rural Development III, Country Department 15, Africa Region. Report No. 19424.
Wright, C. 2014. Libya vs Goldman Sachs - the secret memo, Euromoney, April 30. http://www.euromoney.com/Article/3336411/Libya-vs-Goldman-Sachsthe-secret-memo.html?single=true

The right to resist: disciplining civil society at Rio+20

Catherine Corson, Bridget Brady, Ahdi Zuber, Julianna Lord and Angela Kim

Drawing on a collaborative ethnographic study of the United Nations (UN) Conference on Sustainable Development (Rio+20) and its preparatory meetings, we examine how the official UN 'participatory' process for engaging civil society in Rio+20 negotiations simultaneously enabled and disciplined contestation through processes such as seeking consensus around a common statement, professionalizing civil society representatives and controlling protests in order to protect broad access to negotiations. We document how, in doing so, the official participatory process undermined the right to voice diverse positions. We also find that Southern access to negotiations was limited by lack of funding, human resources, location and language. Finally, we illustrate how a group of non-governmental organizations based primarily in the Global South utilized the official UN Major Groups 'participatory process' to build alliances to protect resource rights language in the negotiating text. Ultimately, we argue that, through the struggle to build alliances, activists critical of the green economy became enlisted in reproducing its hegemony.

In the wake of the triple financial, food and fuel crisis in 2008–2009, the United Nations Environment Programme (UNEP) released its proposal for a 'Global Green New Deal' to stimulate global economic recovery (Barbier 2009). Its subsequent Green Economy Initiative laid out sector-specific ideas for a green economic system (UNEP 2011). In December of 2009, the United Nations (UN) officially endorsed 'the green economy' as a central theme for the June 2012 UN Conference on Sustainable Development (Rio +20), held in Rio de Janeiro on the twentieth anniversary of the 1992 Earth Summit. In anticipation of the meeting, non-governmental organizations (NGOs), businesses and governments, such as the Republic of Korea and Brazil, began re-framing their strategic plans, shifting funding priorities and re-drafting their explanatory rhetoric around the green economy (e.g., Huberman 2010; Federal Democratic Republic of Ethiopia 2011; Webb and Esakin 2011). Other states and civil society[1] organizations – from the Bolivarian Alliance for the Peoples of Our America (ALBA) countries[2] to the People's Summit for Social

[1]Recognizing the problematic nature of the term 'civil society', we follow the UN Major Groups practice and use the term to refer to non-national state actors, including business and local government. We use the term 'NGO' when we are specifically referring to non-profit organizations.
[2]The ALBA nations include Cuba, Bolivia, Ecuador, Nicaragua, San Vincent and The Grenadines, Antigua and Barbuda, and Venezuela.

and Environmental Justice – condemned it (e.g., Climate and Capitalism 2011; Cúpula dos Povos 2012).

With its promises to reduce carbon dependency, promote resource and energy efficiency and lessen environmental degradation (UNEP 2011, 16), the green economy comprises a successful political strategy to engage economists, finance ministers and financial investors in environmental politics. Yet it also moves beyond 'selling nature to save it' (McAfee 1999) to advocate selling nature to save the economy. With its narratives of crisis and scarcity, constructs of nature as capital, novel privatizations of rights to nature, and creation of new speculative frontiers, it has created the conditions for contemporary 'green grabbing' or 'the appropriation of land and resources for environmental ends' (Fairhead, Leach, and Scoones 2012, 238). The green economy has become a key discursive framework through which struggles over land and resource rights and access around the world take place. It has become intertwined with the expansion of global land grabs (for more on global land grabs, see Borras et al. 2011; Borras and Franco 2013; Borras, Franco, and Wang 2013; Margulis, McKeon, and Borras 2013; Wolford et al. 2013).

Because of its timing and UN efforts to solicit civil society input, Rio+20 and its lead-up meetings offered an ideal arena in which to observe struggles over the green economy unfolding. Drawing on a collaborative event ethnography (CEE)[3] of the Rio+20 conference and associated preparatory meetings held at the UN headquarters in New York City (NYC) between December 2011 and June 2012,[4] we examine how the official UN 'participatory' process for engaging civil society in Rio+20 negotiations shaped NGO efforts to contest the green economy. Then, we focus on the ways in which a group of NGOs based primarily in the Global South used the official participatory process to mobilize a movement, which they titled 'Rights-at-risk', in order to preserve language in the final conference document that protected equity in resource rights.

We argue that while the formal UN structure designed to facilitate civil society participation in UN negotiations opened up access for marginalized groups and offered a platform for organizing, it also disciplined activists into manageable subjects through processes such as seeking consensus around a common statement, professionalizing civil society representatives and controlling protests in order to protect broad access. These disciplining processes, we contend, suppressed the fundamental democratic right to voice a diversity of positions. In addition, we found that Southern access was limited by lack of funding, human resources, location and language. Finally, the designation of the green economy as the focus of the Rio+20 conference created an institutional context in which activists and proponents alike felt that they had to frame their agendas through the green economy in order to be heard, and, through their dynamic struggle to define and reshape the green economy, reinforced its discursive hegemony.

We begin with a discussion of the rise of the green economy discourse and associated shifts in public–private–non-profit relations in global environmental governance. We review academic debates about participatory process and rights-based resistance movements in order to provide the institutional and ideological context for our observations.

[3]CEE entails an innovative method that combines collaborative 'rapid or time-constrained ethnographic assessment […] with institutional and organizational ethnography' in order to 'capture engagements between scientific experts, decision-makers, and private sector and NGO actors in the context of a time-condensed meeting' (Brosius and Campbell 2010, 248; see also Campbell et al. 2014; Corson et al. 2014).

[4]The preparatory meetings began in December 2010, but we only conducted research at those between December 2011 and June 2012.

We then present our rationale for studying the negotiation of these processes at international conferences and we summarize our methodology. Our findings explore how civil society access and participation have expanded between the first Earth Summit and Rio+20, albeit disproportionately for Northern and Southern actors, while their political influence has declined. We then analyze the ways in which resistance to the green economy is disciplined and ultimately co-opted to reproduce its hegemony.[5] To illustrate these core arguments, we trace how the alliance of predominately Southern activists utilized the formal participatory process, alongside other tactics, to protect the inclusion of basic human rights in the negotiated text. Finally, we discuss the implications of our findings for both democratic processes and the hegemony of the green economy discourse.

The green economy and neoliberal environmental governance

The green economy's ascendance reflects the culmination of a 20-year process of transformation. Guided by Keynesian principles, 1970s environmentalism hinged on a confidence in state regulation and social protection, a belief in natural resource limits to economic growth and a commitment to redressing the negative environmental effects of growth (Meadows et al. 1972; UN 1972; McCarthy and Prudham 2004). By the 1980s, however, neoliberalism – with its worship of the market, antipathy toward state regulation and associated privatization of state services – had penetrated environmental politics. The 1987 *Brundtland report*, through the concept of sustainable development, institutionalized the idea that economic growth and environmental conservation were compatible (UN 1987). By the 1990s, aided by the rise of global environmental institutions, environmental degradation was increasingly framed as the result of market failure and best addressed through market-based mechanisms, such as payment for ecosystem services, biodiversity offsets and carbon trading (Igoe, Sullivan, and Brockington 2009; Brockington and Duffy 2010; Arsel and Büscher 2012; Büscher et al. 2012; Roth and Dressler 2012). Recently, the growing financialization of markets has led to rising speculation on land, carbon and wildlife. As these initiatives promote the privatization of new rights to nature, the creation of new commodities and the establishment of new markets for their exchange, they enclose formerly common resources, draw nature into financialized markets and offer investment opportunities for over-accumulated private capital (Harvey 2003; Bracking 2012; Corson and MacDonald 2012; Sullivan 2013).

Intertwined with the rise of market-based environmentalism has been a transformation in relations of governance, as the privatization of state services and withdrawal from social protection measures has paved the way for increased participation by private and non-profit organizations in public policy (Keck and Sikkink 1998; Mohan and Stokke 2000; Hart 2001; Ferguson and Gupta 2002; McKeon 2009). This rising prominence of non-state actors in global environmental governance was both reflected and reinforced at the 1992 Earth Summit conference. After hundreds of 'civil society' organizations, from indigenous groups to trade organizations, registered for access to the Earth Summit, held in Rio de Janeiro, Brazil, the UN established a formal 'Major Groups' (MGs) structure to facilitate

[5]In using the term 'resistance', we refer to a diversity of forms of 'pushing back', or the multitude of ways in which diverse sets of actors use conferences to contest or reshape hegemonic discourse. Following Hollander and Einwohner (2004), we understand resistance as relational and socially constructed, entailing both action and opposition, and not always overt or recognized. Furthermore, in emphasizing the complexities of social interactions, we hope to avoid any tendency toward a binary between resistance and domination (Brown 1996) or the romance of resistance (Sparke 2008).

participation in the post-1992 process (Chatterjee and Finger 1994). It divided civil society into nine MGs, the eclectic nature of which reflected the most vocal and influential groups at the time: Women, NGOs, Children and Youth, Business and Industry, Workers and Trade Unions, Local Authorities, Farmers, Indigenous Peoples, and the Scientific and Technological Community. In doing so, it embraced a broad definition of 'civil society': these groups included government officials, as well as business and industry representatives, who also lobbied separately through organizations such as the World Business Council on Sustainable Development and the International Chamber of Commerce.

However, even as participatory structures like the MGs have become more established in the past 20 years, they have often masked power dynamics behind the rhetoric and techniques of participation. They have co-opted activist agendas, exacerbated power differentials, legitimized hegemonic discourse and policy and ultimately further disempowered already-marginalized populations (Edwards and Hulme 1996; Young 1999; Mohan and Stokke 2000; Cooke and Kothari 2001; Ford 2003). McKeon (2009, 2) argues that, despite UN efforts to expand civil society involvement since the early 1990s, 'it has failed thus far to move from generic and often episodic participation to meaningful incorporation of these actors into global political process'.

In addition, the concurrent increase in corporate influence has complicated power dynamics within these participatory structures. By the 2002 Johannesburg World Summit on Sustainable Development, the idea that sustainable development was best pursued through public–private–non-profit partnerships was well entrenched (Scherr and Gregg 2006). As many environmental NGOs that had historically operated as external agents of change sought to attract greater financial and political attention to the biodiversity cause, they partnered not just with governments, but also with multinational corporations, the financial sector and the entertainment industry (Chapin 2004; Dowie 2005; Duffy 2006). Concurrently, however, globalization and technological advancement have enabled activists to transcend geographic boundaries in new ways, developing virtual transnational networks, and linking international and domestic movements as they endeavour to counter these changes (Keck and Sikkink 1998; Tarrow 2005). The combined result of these transformations is that contemporary forms of global environmental governance are increasingly cultivated through transnational and dynamic networks of public, private and non-profit organizations that blur boundaries among the market, state and civil society (Lemos and Agrawal 2006; Corson, MacDonald, and Neimark 2013).

Globalizing politics from 'below'

Among these new transnational social movements are a growing cadre of movements that link environment, livelihoods and political rights in battles against the dismantling of state protection and regulation. Many of these movements are articulating rights to land and resources as basic human rights, and, in doing so, they offer potential Polanyian counter movements to land and resource privatization and commodification (Cotula 2013).

Rights framings have been particularly effective in the UN, where activists can appeal to the 1948 UN Universal Declaration of Human Rights, as well as to the more recent 1986 Declaration on the Right to Development and the 2007 Declaration on the Rights of Indigenous Peoples, and the UN Human Rights Council resolutions on human rights and the environment. Like indigenous groups (Doolittle 2010; Kashwan 2013), agrarian movements are increasingly articulating their agendas in terms of human rights and using the UN to legitimate their claims (Edelman and James 2011; Suárez 2013). Of particular note are the 2012 inclusion of the right to food in the Voluntary Guidelines on the

Responsible Governance of Land, Fisheries and Forests at the Committee on World Food Security (Golay and Biglino 2013; McKeon 2013) and the push for a UN Declaration on the Right of Peasants (Edelman and James 2011). Often, the process of fighting for rights can be as important as the attainment of those rights. Rights-based movements bring attention to the ethical dimensions of the commodification and privatization of nature, and they emphasize government responsibility for these rights (Anand 2007). In doing so, they shift the terrain of global environmental policy-making, introducing new narratives and aligning new relationships that can open up unforeseen opportunities for progress.

Critical scholars continue to debate the effectiveness of using rights-based discourses to contest the privatization and commodification of nature. The framing of resource rights as basic human rights often constitutes an effective means of countering hegemonic powers (Mirosa and Harris 2012; Cotula 2013; Franco, Mehta, and Veldwisch 2013; Künnemann and Suárez 2013). In fact, writing about the 1980s and 1990s growth of transnational social movements, Keck and Sikkink (1998, 121) argue that it was precisely because 1990s environmental activists did *not* frame their arguments in terms of rights that they had 'a harder time giving their campaigns a human face'. However, the protection of rights does not necessarily ensure access to resources (Ribot and Peluso 2003) or offer a secure challenge to their privatization (Bakker 2007), and formalizing rights can undermine customary forms of resource access (Franco, Mehta, and Veldwisch 2013).

Capturing 'politics from below' across sites and scales

Despite the expanding literature in agrarian studies and political ecology that critiques green capitalism and analyzes rights-based social movements against land grabs, less attention has been paid to how transnational movements that strive to build resistance to global land and resource grabs operate within formal UN participatory processes (cf. McKeon 2009, 2013; Edelman and James 2011; Golay and Biglino 2013). By focusing on negotiations around the green economy discourse at Rio+20, we respond to calls by Borras et al. (2011) for research on how land deals are discursively justified and legitimized, as well as challenged and opposed. We build on scholars who argue that land grabs and green grabs come about through 'changing contexts, emergent process and forces and contestations' (Peluso and Lund 2011, 669) and that the confluence of processes, people and relationships entailed therein are best analyzed through place-specific ethnography (Wolford et al. 2013). However, we contend that such studies should not be restricted to 'local sites'. The material and meaningful struggles that are central to land grabbing span locales from villages to the halls of international conferences, and it is paramount to examine 'politics from below' (Borras and Franco 2013) across these sites and scales.

International conferences offer critical sites in which actors who are normally dispersed in time and space – including representatives from NGOs, indigenous communities, the private sector, trade associations, universities and research organizations – come together to negotiate policy, organize resistance and promote particular agendas. They are important not only for the official agreements and statements that are negotiated at them, but also for the public–private–non-profit relationships that they align around sanctioned concepts, such as the green economy (MacDonald and Corson 2012; Suarez and Corson 2013). Even as they may fail to extract binding commitments from Parties, the informal relationships developed, narratives solidified and ideas circulated at these events shift the terrain on which hegemonic environmental discourse is crafted. Furthermore, they serve as focal points for activists to lobby and organize transnational resistance to officially sanctioned agendas (Tarrow 2005; Death 2010). Thus, conferences comprise critical terrain on which struggles over hegemonic discourses are fought and critical sites for the manufacture of civil society's consent (Gramsci 2010 [1971]). Importantly, they are also sites in which these struggles become visible to researchers (Corson, MacDonald, and Campbell 2014).

Just as the 1992 Earth Summit launched sustainable development into mainstream discourse, the 2012 Rio+20 conference constituted a critical moment in the green economy's rise, and it offered a unique opportunity to study how the green economy emerged and became hegemonic in a time-condensed setting. Despite the debates about it, the green economy remained a core theme of Rio+20 and the framework through which most state, private and non-profit organizations articulated their positions. The result was that, even though the Rio+20 conference failed to agree to any binding targets, in what *Guardian* columnist George Monbiot (2012) called 'the greatest failure of collective leadership since the first world war', the conference still became a pivotal moment in manufacturing the green economy as a new global environmental paradigm.

Collaborative ethnography methods

The Rio+20 conference brought together some 50,000 people over the course of 14 days in Rio de Janeiro, Brazil, to finalize and adopt the official conference outcome document, *The future we want* (UN 2012b). However, the bulk of negotiations over a fittingly titled 'zero draft', took place in preparatory meetings at the UN Headquarters in NYC. For these meetings, staff from UN Department of Economic and Social Affairs (UNDESA) served as advisory and logistics liaisons between the MGs and the UN. Appointed, or self-nominated, Organizing Partners (OPs) for each group were responsible for coordinating input from their members and for liaising with the Communication and Outreach Branch of UNDESA. UNDESA also contracted the Stakeholder Forum, an international organization that facilitates the engagement of non-state stakeholders in global policy development and advocacy, to assist with outreach and to offer capacity-building workshops for new civil society representatives. The UN Non-Governmental Liaison Service provided some funding, particularly for representatives from the global South, to attend meetings. Finally, during preparatory meetings and the final conference, two OPs co-chaired the MGs' morning meetings, at which representatives summarized the previous day's negotiations, provided important logistical information and made announcements.

Between December 2011 and June 2012, we – as a team of six researchers[6] – carried out ethnographic research on the involvement of civil society in five of the Rio+20 preparatory meetings, as well as at the Rio+20 conference itself. At these events, we observed negotiations, press briefings, coffee and lunch hours, protests, receptions, morning civil society organizing and debriefing meetings, capacity-building workshops and side events (thematic presentations and panels organized by delegates and/or civil society groups in order to circulate information and ideas). While we focused on the official UN process, we also attended rights-based and other discussions at the June 2012 alternative People's Summit, held in Flamengo Park, about 50 miles from Riocentro, the main venue. Many activists moved between Riocentro and the People's Summit, as they invoked 'inside' and 'outside' strategies. Secondly, we conducted 34 semi-structured interviews with individuals identified through stratified and snowball sampling, including the OPs for all of the

[6]The team was comprised of a professor and five undergraduate students, and we worked as part of a larger 'umbrella' team that included four other professors and three graduate students (Campbell et al. 2013; Wilshusen and MacDonald in prep.).

MGs, state delegates, UN officials and civil society liaisons, and representatives from think tanks, NGOs, private companies and other organizations.[7]

Our findings show that while the MG structure opened up access for marginalized groups and offered a platform for organizing, it also disciplined their positions through processes such as seeking consensus around a common statement, professionalizing civil society representatives and controlling protests in order to protect broad civil society access. In this way, the participatory process diminished civil society's democratic right to voice a diversity of positions. Ultimately, we became interested in how a group of actors, representing organizations ranging from NGOs to trade unions to women's groups, worked both inside and outside the MG structure to contest the bracketing – or proposed deletion – of rights-based language from the draft negotiating text. We argue that, by aligning with advocates who endorsed a 'human rights-based approach to the green economy' in order to build alliances to protect this language, they became enlisted in reproducing the green economy's hegemony.

Institutionalizing participation in a changing political landscape

Civil society representatives and state delegates who had been at the first Earth Summit repeatedly underscored the exceptional access to state negotiations that non-state actors had in 2012 compared to 1992. During most of the preparatory meetings for Rio+20 and the conference itself, any organization affiliated with an MG and accredited by the UN could observe plenary and small 'contact group' negotiations. One interviewee highlighted the importance of the UN decision to open contact groups to civil society: 'I can tell you all these stories because we are in the room … in 20 years, step by step, we have been able to be in there a lot more'.[8] MGs were also invited to submit suggested text for the original zero draft,[9] and a UN-civil society liaison reflected on the invitation: 'This is the first time the UN [has done] that, and also for the first time ever, Major Groups were able to sit in the room for the negotiation and say, "on paragraph 45 we think that you should add that"'.[10] This latter statement referred to the invitation for selected representatives from each of the MGs to deliver end-of-day 2–3-minute interventions to delegates. Finally, formally scheduled 'discussions' between members of the Bureau and civil society, as well as UN-sanctioned press conferences, offered members additional opportunities to present their positions.

Many MG members stressed that this formal access was critical for developing relationships with delegates, especially for those who could not approach their governments at home '[because of] the lack of representation structures in the other [arenas]'.[11] They also acknowledged that financial and logistical support and training sessions enabled them to make effective use of that access. Once accredited, activists could also work outside of the formal consultative processes to lobby delegates or build alliances. As an NGO representative observed, 'A lot of the UN negotiation never really happens on the

[7]In order to protect confidentiality, we refer to interviewees by general position, rather than by name.
[8]Interview with an NGO representative, 20 June 2012.
[9]UNDESA compiled the initial zero draft from 677 submissions received from political groups, member states, UN organizations, intergovernmental organizations and civil society. The majority of the submissions, 493 (or 73 percent) were from civil society. The Bureau then created a massive compilation document, which was released in January, 2012 (UN 2012a).
[10]UN–civil society liaison, MGs Training Session, 12 June 2012.
[11]Interview with an OP, 22 June 2012.

floor; it always happens in the corridors .... So we sit one on one... catch them when they're going to the toilet, or when they're walking to coffee'.[12] Another interviewee summarized the diverse tactics s/he used to influence the negotiations, once in the door: 'You can divide it into participating through the NGO MG process ..., doing direct bilateral [lobbying of] agencies and governments [and] having autonomous, thematic-based initiatives, working with other civil society organizations not necessarily within the frame of the MG process'.[13] Here, s/he refers to how MG members organized themselves around thematic clusters, or voluntary associations, to develop common policy positions and lobbying strategies with respect to specific issues.

Declining and unequal influence over negotiations

Even as they pointed to increased access, however, MG members also expressed concern about their limited influence over negotiations. Some cited the contemporary absence of the energy, mobilization and ideas that had characterized civil society organizing at the 1992 Earth Summit:

> [In 1992], there was a serious amount of deliberation .... Every evening we would come together and strategize for the next day. I don't see that any more. It's just about people announcing ... what happened [in the negotiations]. I don't see any kind of emotions in that room.[14]

Others underscored that the targets of environmental activism have become more difficult to pinpoint:

> We need to look, not only at the fragmentation and incoherence in governance at the global level, but also at the national level [where] we are finding domination by the financial sector.... We're not quite sure, now, where we go to do business, because the rules of the game that the UN used to represent – a fair arena – are being undermined by the G20 [Group of Twenty major economies] and by a variety of [other] arenas.[15]

In short, broader global political economic transformations have underpinned the rising role of the financial sector in international politics and weakened states' ability to regulate the private sector. As a result, the multinational companies that many activists seek to challenge have become stronger. McKeon (2009, 2) reflects, 'the geopolitical and economic powers that have underwritten the neoliberal agenda that these civil society actors contest are more determined than ever to defend their interests'. An activist similarly observed, 'The "Spirit of Rio," remains more of a spirit ... the 1992 Rio agreements ... suffered from being overwritten by the globalization agreements, particularly the WTO [World Trade Organization] and later on the Free Trade Agreements'.[16]

In this context, the MG process ultimately reflected and reinforced, rather than confronted, the inequalities entailed in global power structures, and our findings echo those of Duffy (2013, 222) that 'the inclusion of non-state actors [in international negotiations] can serve to reinforce and deepen existing global inequalities'. Northern and transnationally

[12]Interview with an NGO representative, 22 March 2012.
[13]Interview with an NGO representative, 4 May 2012.
[14]Interview with an NGO representative, 21 March 2012.
[15]NGO representative, Side Event, 'Towards the People's Summit at Rio+20: alternative civil society perspectives on the zero draft', 23 March 2012.
[16]Side Event, 'What Rio+20 must do to achieve the future we want', 13 June 2012.

operating actors often have more ability to influence negotiations. Civil society access to UN negotiations has been limited to a 'fairly exclusive club', in which more radical groups have been marginalized (Ford 2003, 123), and national and regional NGOs have only been permitted to apply for UN Economic and Social Council accreditation since 1996 (McKeon 2009). The UN trust fund, which supports travel and lodging costs for participants from the Global South, depends on member country support and has limited funds. Thus, the location of most of the preparatory meetings in NYC gave US- and European-based groups an advantage. Furthermore, the reliance on English as a negotiating language limited participation by non-native English speakers.[17] The result, as an interviewee underscored, was that Northern-based groups – whose interests 'are not necessarily concomitant with those of the Southern NGOs' – dominated the MG process. This asymmetry in access was reinforced by the fact that many activists from the global South are often stretched thinly:

> The reason why sometimes you don't have the strong voices with the movements [here] is because many of our [groups] are dealing with frontline issues .... You don't have capacity to engage at this level because it requires resources. You need the funding and we don't always have that.[18]

Rectifying this imbalance, the first interviewee summarized, 'boils down to the question of funding and resources for Southern NGOs'.[19] We argue that, while protecting legal *rights* among Northern and Southern NGOs to negotiations is important, so too is ensuring equivalent *access*, and Southern access was limited by lack of funding, human resources, location and language, among other factors.

Disciplining resistance through formal participation

Many people we interviewed were also frustrated by the orchestration of formal mechanisms for civil society input, such as the end-of-day, 2–3-minute interventions on the negotiating floor and formal discussions with Bureau members. They argued against the rigidity of these orchestrated performances and the conservative approach of their facilitators: 'Our 2-minute statement is, in my view, killing imagination .... I think that [we can] push boundaries a little bit every time'.[20] These structured encounters gave an appearance of influence, but limited input to short, formal statements that elided the complexities of underlying concerns.

Interviewees also expressed concern about the associated disciplining of radical views in order to maintain civil society access and the fact that to present a unified front, the MG process discouraged radical action. At capacity-building workshops, in addition to providing logistical updates and information, organizers discussed topics such as formal dress, appropriate positions to raise and how to approach and lobby delegates. They constantly reiterated the importance of not losing hard-won access: 'Of course we should lobby, but lobby right ... being allowed to sit in the chair, inside the plenary and speak [is] the least

[17]As is normal in UN negotiations, simultaneous translation into all of the official UN languages was available to delegates, but text negotiation was conducted exclusively in English. While diplomats usually have language training and/or translators readily available to them, members of civil society who do not speak English find it challenging to participate in the process.
[18]Interview with an NGO representative, 3 May 2012.
[19]Interview with an NGO representative, 22 March 2012.
[20]Interview with an OP, 22 June 2012.

important point for lobbying; it's engaging the delegates here [that's important]'.[21] In sum, the push for professional activism – carried out through appropriate dress, language and moderation in advocacy – protected access, but also disciplined activists into manageable subjects.

This disciplining was most overt during the conference itself where all protests were to be registered 24 hours in advance and approved by conference organizers. During the daily morning debriefing sessions, attended by a few hundred civil society organizations, UN staff underscored that accredited members should behave so as to not threaten others' access:

> This is the most participatory conference the UN has ever had. We're going to reach 10,000 people registered today.... It's only by working together and following the rules without pushing the envelope from the outside that we're going to get more participation.[22]

A panel speaker reminded attendees during an MG meeting in Rio that the UN had removed accreditation from NGOs who participated in unapproved protests at the climate change negotiations in Copenhagen.[23] Another reinforced this claim:

> Your outside strategy needs to stay outside. When you bring your outside strategy inside, it compromises the access that so many of us have worked for and compromises the real good work that all of us are doing deep inside.[24]

Finally, attempts to develop common positions within and across the nine MGs funnelled diverse voices into one, watering down the more radical positions. Several MG representatives emphasized that private-sector actors within the groups often overpowered their voices. For example, the internal cohesion of the farmers' group, which encompassed members ranging from Via Campesina to multinational agribusiness, broke down over the attempt to develop a unified position on the promotion of private investment and market access in the negotiating text. This subordination of radical views also appeared in an effort during the final preparatory days to develop a Common Statement, in response to a UN request, which detailed a single 'civil society' position, including its red-lines, or positions on which civil society was unwilling to compromise. The task was enormous: as one OP reflected, 'We can't even have a common statement among NGOs, let alone among all the different groups, including industry'.[25]

Ironically, the result was the exclusion of controversial subjects. A UN-civil society liaison summarized: 'Some of the things that business and industries would reserve on, about the role of the private sector, were purposely left out'.[26] Four of the nine groups refused to sign a statement that stated anything less than their red-lines, and some of the NGOs from the Global South refused to sign onto a common statement that endorsed the green economy. One OP retorted, 'I am not going to water down my red-lines .... I am not going to communicate to governments that I am ready to accept less'.[27] S/he added,

---

[21]UN–civil society liaison, MG Training Session, 19 March 2012.
[22]UN–civil society liaison, MG Morning Meeting, 22 June 2012.
[23]UN–civil society liaison, MG Morning Meeting, 18 June 2012.
[24]UN–civil society liaison, MG Morning Meeting, 16 June 2012.
[25]Interview with an NGO representative, 20 June 2012.
[26]Interview with a UN–civil society liaison, 2 June 2012.
[27]Interview with an OP, 22 June 2012.

> This idea that if we come together that makes us stronger is true only if we are saying more than what we would say alone. We should not be coming together to say the minimum. We should come together to pull us up and not down.[28]

Ultimately, the nine MGs agreed to a statement with an uncontroversial chapeau that emphasized the need to protect civil society access in the structures that emerged from Rio+20, together with a compilation of separate groups' statements of red-lines.[29] In doing so, however, civil society relinquished one of its foremost democratic rights – the right to a diversity of opinions – in exchange for access and formal participation. While state delegates presented and defended their polarizing opinions during negotiations, civil society – representing some of the most disparate groups imaginable – were expected to come to a consensus outside of this arena. Rather than the rich and creative result of democratic debate, the MGs had to embrace the least common denominator, which diluted the diversity of positions within the MGs, as well as avoided advocating for more radical agendas.

Reproducing the green economy's hegemony

The UN designation of the green economy as the focus of the Rio+20 conference created the context in which delegates and activists alike felt that they had to engage with the concept in order to 'be heard'.[30] A UN–civil society liaison argued that they needed to use the green economy language in order to influence negotiations:

> How do you speak to negotiators if you're not speaking their language?.... Do you make up some random term [that] confuses people when they try to read it and they say, well how does this relate to the green economy? Or do you use their language and accept the failings of that as an intellectual concept, but accept it for the purposes of actually achieving a dialogue?[31]

Other liaisons pushed MG members to try to reshape, rather than to reject, the green economy discourse, arguing that, 'The role of civil society … is to help build into the negotiations criteria that establish what a truly green economy should be, so that corporations, governments and communities can be held to a certain standard'.[32] In short, the embrace of the green economy as the starting point for negotiation, and the time-pressure posed by the impending Rio+20 conference, limited the ability to challenge it. A Brazilian activist complained, 'We want a democratic green economy, but we don't have time to do this. It was just put from the top into our hands'.[33]

Furthermore, like sustainable development, the ambiguity about the green economy's definition was critical to its success. A Southern NGO leader retorted,

> They're even avoiding … defining what the green economy is. And this is deliberate, I think, because by keeping the definition open and vague, you can promote bio-fuels, nuclear energy,

[28]Interview with an OP, 22 June 2012.
[29]Interview with a UN–civil society liaison, 2 June 2012; MGs – Rio+20 common statement discussion paper, Final, endorsed version, 19 June 2012.
[30]UN–civil society liaison, MGs Training Session, 19 March 2012.
[31]Interview with a UN–civil society liaison, 2 June 2012.
[32]UN–civil society liaison, MGs Training Session, 19 March 2012.
[33]Brazilian civil society facilitator for Rio+20, Side Event, 'Towards the People's Summit at Rio+20: alternative civil society perspectives on the zero draft', 23 March 2012.

> carbon trading, the financialization of natural resource, geo-engineering, etc. as being part of green economy.[34]

As both delegates and civil society debated at length what the green economy actually was, they reinforced its hegemony and dispersed the energy against it. An observer summarized: 'For the last 2 years, most of the energy of this conference [went] into defining what is the green economy, what it is not ... and this has sucked away most of the energy of the conference'.[35] As those against the green economy sought to use it to push their own agendas, radical critiques against it were transformed in efforts to reshape it. Fractured by diverse and complicated positions, spanning advocates such as South Korea and India and critics such as Venezuela and Bolivia, the UN Group of 77 Developing Nations (G77) pushed to use the terminology 'green economies' to represent the multiple pathways to a green economy, as well as to demand the provision of technology transfer and foreign aid to help developing countries realize green economies. In turn, many organizations pushed for an 'inclusive' green economy that would protect social welfare. Finally, more moderate delegates and civil society organizations simply sought to differentiate it from 'green growth'.[36] Through their dynamic struggles to reshape the green economy discourse, all of these actors – whether advocating for the green economy or contesting it – helped to reproduce its discursive hegemony.

Rights-at-risk in the green economy

Intrigued by their effort to use official MG processes to build a movement that was critical of the green economy, we traced how a group of activists from mostly Southern-based organizations strategically utilized side events, morning meetings, thematic clusters, letters, petitions and protests as means to organize a movement to protect rights language in the zero draft. This movement, which we refer to as the 'Rights-at-risk' movement, appealed to a broad constituency by framing its agenda around the protection of a diversity of basic human rights and the preservation of the Rio Principles from the 1992 Earth Summit. In pre-Rio events, it attracted more than 500 participants, 80 percent of whom were from the Global South (Rights for Sustainability 2012, 2). Even as they used official participatory structures, its leaders also abandoned the MGs structure, as necessary, to take more critical actions, such as holding unapproved protests at the conference itself.

Early documents by the Rights for Sustainability (R4S) initiative, which led the Rights-at-risk movement, condemned the green economy as: promising growth, but not poverty eradiation; favouring big business; extending the life of the brown economy; not sufficiently addressing the climate crisis; favouring the privatization and enclosure of nature; and further constraining the ability of developing countries to balance environment and development (Verzola and Paul Quintos 2011). One of its leaders summarized their concerns:

> For us – many civil society organizations, particularly those from the global South ... we remain deeply uncomfortable with the green economy concept as it's being elaborated .... [There is] a great reluctance on the part of governments to make concrete commitments to

---

[34]NGO representative, Side Event, 'Towards the People;s Summit at Rio+20: alternative civil society perspectives on the zero draft', 23 March 2012.
[35]NGO representative, Side Event, 'What Rio+20 must do to achieve the future we want', 13 June 2012.
[36]UN–civil society liaison, MG Morning Meeting, 19 March 2012.

> do anything ambitious in terms of achieving sustainable development [and] there is a lot of emphasis now on the role of the private sector in promoting sustainable development [and] in implementing the green economy agenda.[37]

The initiative also endorsed regional civil society declarations opposing the green economy, such as the 'Position of Civil Society in Latin America and the Caribbean on Rio+20 and the Green Economy', the Nairobi Declaration on 'Reclaiming Rights at Rio: Civil Society Consultation to the African Agenda in the Rio+20 Summit' and the 'Asia Pacific People's Declaration on Rio+20'.

The Rights-at-risk movement advocated for the protection of a range of rights – from indigenous rights to the rights of Mother Earth to rights to water – in the negotiating text. It organized around a 'basic message... that, when states and member states make commitments at the Rio conference, they do so [by] respecting and certainly not undermining human rights obligations'.[38] As one of the organizers of the Rights-at-risk movement recounted:

> [W]e did not start with a human rights agenda looking at Rio, rather we started by studying the green economy proposal and becoming very, very worried .... We thought, 'should we try to advocate for a peoples' green economy?' Looking at the geopolitics of the negotiations upcoming, we realized that that's not the way to go. The way to go was to work on human rights .... And so we embarked on a campaign for rights for sustainability, which was meant to coordinate civil society organizations, not to be fragmented, but to convince them that the human rights agenda is the best way to go to strengthen the social pillar in Rio. On the other hand, outward, outside, we embarked on a strong no to corporate green economy agenda.[39]

Referring to a letter described below, an organizer for the movement reflected on the choice to mobilize resistance to the green economy around human rights within the UN: 'The rights advocacy of course has a universal resonance among civil society, so that's why when we raise alarm on Rights-at-risk, within 24 hours we had over 300 signatures'.[40] The Rights-at-risk metaphor allowed the movement to reach out to those concerned about bracketing of the rights to food, water, development and land, as well as the rights of women, indigenous peoples, workers and nature. It also enabled them to connect to an organized movement for democratic rights, encompassed in the Access Initiative, which has sought to promote Principle 10 of the Rio Declaration, or 'the right and ability of people to influence decisions that affect their lives and the resources they depend on'[41] (see also Banisar et al. 2012).

Protecting the Rio Principles

The Rights-at-risk movement gained substantial momentum in March 2012, when it utilized side events and roundtable discussions to draw attention to proposed deletions of references to particular resource rights in the zero draft. An organizer of one event summarized,

[37]NGO MG representative, Green Economy Press Conference, 4 May 2012.
[38]Representative from the Office of High Commissioner on Human Rights, Side Event, 'Roundtable discussion on rights at risk in the Green Economy', 24 April 2012.
[39]NGO representative, Press Conference, 'No sustainable development without human rights – honoring Principle One', 19 June 2012.
[40]Interview with an NGO representative, 4 May 2012.
[41]Interview with an NGO representative, 22 March 2012.

> There was concern that [the] human right to water might be an issue, but we also know there have been attacks on other rights and again, all the other Rio Principles. So, I think that we have to keep organizing. Part of this is a roundtable discussion on... strategies for how we can work together.[42]

On 26 March, an open letter entitled 'Rights-at-Risk' was circulated to the Secretary General of Rio+20, expressing concern about the attempted removal by some Parties of 'nearly all references to human rights obligations and equity principles in the text' (Ibon International et al. 2012). The accompanying petition gained 1000 signatures in just a few weeks. A March speech by one of the movement's organizers, called 'Deleting our rights, bracketing our future: why we need a Peoples' Summit' (Quintos 2012), called for a social movement organized around protecting the Rio Principles:

> We have been witnessing the systematic attempt by some powerful states to weaken, bracket or outright eliminate nearly all references to human rights obligations and equity principles in the text [for] Rio +20.... We must call on governments to alter the direction of negotiations at the moment, stand for rights, stand for Rio Principles in '92... calling on them not to backtrack on the human rights [or] obligations [in the] Rio Principles.[43]

In this manner, the protection of the Rio Principles became the red-line for the Rights-at-risk movement. As a panellist in a side event stated,

> If you go by the baseline of the origin of the Earth Summit [which] is grounded in human rights – this is precisely the baseline [that] we cannot allow Rio+20 to fall under. We cannot allow any regression on these principles or these rights.[44]

By linking the rights-based discourse with the protection of the Rio 92 principles, the Rights-at-risk movement mobilized a large constituency and raised larger questions about global inequality and transnational corporate influence.

Framing the resistance movement around Rights-at-risk and protecting the Rio Principles also allowed the activists to engage the UN Human Rights Commissioner. In March 2012, the High Commissioner for Human Rights, Navi Pillay, sent an open letter to all Permanent Missions in Geneva and NYC, arguing that 'The [1992] Rio Declaration was celebrated by the international community [because] it was thoroughly infused with human rights considerations essential to sustainable development' (Pillay 2012). A number of Special UN Rapporteurs sent other open letters to state negotiators regarding the outcome document for Rio+20. These interventions proved critical in convincing delegates to back down on the proposed deletions.

A human rights-based approach to the green economy

However, while the engagement of the UN High Commissioner for Human Rights was pivotal in reinstating rights in the text, the Commissioner's letter reframed the protection

---

[42]NGO representative, Side Event, 'Round table discussion on rights at risk in the Green Economy', 24 April 2012.
[43]NGO representative, Side Event, 'Towards the People's Summit at Rio+20: alternative civil society perspectives on the zero draft', 23 March 2012.
[44]NGO representative, Side Event, 'The need for a rights-based approach to sustainable development', 14 June 2012.

of rights not as opposition to the green economy, but as the *means* to it. The letter argued, 'At Rio, Member States should commit to ensuring full coherence between efforts to advance the green economy, on the one hand, and their solemn human rights obligations on the other', producing '*a human rights-based approach to the green economy*... to pursue a model of economic growth that is socially and environmentally sustainable, just and equitable, and respectful of all human rights' (Pillay 2012, emphasis added). So, despite the movement's 'outside strategy' condemning the green economy, its 'inside strategy' appeared to condone it by association.

Moreover, rather than pushing for radical change, its strategic goal – to preserve the Rio Principles – was to protect the status quo. As civil society groups and developing countries called for the reaffirmation of common but differentiated responsibility, precautionary principles, equity and human rights, all of which were emphasized in the Rio Principles, the ambition for Rio+20 became simply not to regress at the conference itself, and to turn instead to the post-Rio+20 process to push for more radical change:

> So we've come to this – our expectations are: please, reaffirm the Rio Principles and especially common [but] differentiated responsibility.... Please renew your pledge on finance and technology, even if you don't quite mean it.... These are all steps backwards. If we prevent these backwards steps, we at least reaffirm what it was 20 years ago, and if we take measures to save it after the conference ... although it may not sound very fantastic, it may, in realistic terms, start processes that may be more durable and long lasting than what Rio was 20 years ago.[45]

By the June 2012 preparatory meeting and conference, previously bracketed rights language was back in the zero draft, and it remained in the final Brazilian proposed text, which was presented to the heads of state on 20 June. However, while effective at mobilizing a successful social movement and engaging high-level political figures, the framing of resistance around rights elided larger challenges to the commodification of nature and the privatization of resource rights, as well as the structural reforms needed to reshape the new green economy, which were highlighted in early publications by R4S. Ultimately, it focused radical attention on protecting the status quo.

Conclusion

As one of the more radical and active movements within the Rio+20 official preparatory process, the Rights-at-risk movement used side events, UN officials, protests, letters and other means to successfully mobilize a movement to preserve rights-based language in the text. However, as it attracted a broad constituency by articulating the movement's mission as protecting the Rio Principles, its goal became to maintain the status quo, rather than to advance beyond it. By linking with authorities such as the UN High Commissioner for Human Rights, who endorsed the green economy, its message became protecting rights as a means of *achieving* the green economy, rather than the means to *protest* it. Through this struggle to build critical alliances, activists who had used rights to contest the green economy appeared to support it.

The struggle over the green economy at Rio+20 illustrates how international conferences, in bringing together and aligning actors around officially sanctioned agendas, and

[45]NGO representative, Side Event, 'What Rio+20 must do to achieve the future we want', 13 June 2012.

in enabling activists to organize resistance to these same agendas, become critical sites in the production of hegemonic environmental discourses. The designation of the green economy as the focus of the Rio+20 conference created a context in which there appeared to be no alternative but to embrace the green economy in order to be heard. It became the framework through which material and discursive struggles over land and resource rights were fought. In building common positions, UN–civil society liaisons encouraged activists to reshape, rather than reject, the green economy, and radical critiques of global structures of inequality and green capitalism in the G77 gave way to alliances for human rights-based, inclusive green economy or green economies. Rather than challenging the overarching framework of the conference, critics became enlisted in reshaping provisions in the negotiating text. Ultimately, through the dynamic struggles to reshape the green economy, proponents and opponents collectively reproduced its discursive hegemony.

In these struggles, while the MG structure provided activists with important access to delegates and a platform for organizing resistance, it also disciplined them in the name of protecting broad-based civil society influence. Likewise, insufficient funds to bring in delegates from the global South and the presence of business actors within the civil society group reinforced, rather than confronted, global power inequalities. Finally, processes such as seeking consensus around a common statement, professionalizing civil society representatives and controlling protests muted radical agendas. In this manner, civil society was expected to speak as one 'voice', even as governmental negotiations broke down over a lack of consensus. Here, a significant 'right-at-risk' in the participatory process was the loss of civil society's democratic right to voice diverse and radical positions.

As Rio closed, many activists conveyed a mixture of satisfaction and discontent with the text's outcome as language that each had been concerned about ultimately ended up in the text, yet the document as a whole fell short of original aspirations for the second Earth Summit. Since the failings of Rio+20 to produce an ambitious agenda for global sustainable development, civil society has turned to two post-2015 processes – an intergovernmental Open Working Group on Sustainable Development Goals that will succeed the Millennium Development Goals and an intergovernmental High-Level Political Forum, which replaced the Commission on Sustainable Development – in efforts to ensure ongoing multi-stakeholder engagement. But in focusing on preserving access, will these efforts also lose sight of the importance of voicing diverse views, whether Northern or Southern, mainstream or radical?

The maintenance of hegemony requires constant work, and it is within the constant struggle to contest it that we find the moments for transformative action. Fifteen years ago, Fisher (1997, 458) argued that 'The transformative potential of the NGO sector may emerge less from ordered and controlled participation than from relatively chaotic sets of multiple opportunities and interdependencies'. We agree that it is not always through the official structures of participation or orchestrated resistance that progressive action takes place, but often through the unforeseen moments of opportunity that such structures and movements enable. The ultimate goal must be not only to build systems that create these moments, but also to use them to advocate for a robust democracy – one that relies on the constant negotiation of diverse positions in order to reach meaningful and representative compromise. We conclude with a quote from an NGO leader: '[We need] to make sure we don't leave this Rio process up to our leaders. We need to assert and claim our rights in order to defend them'.[46] One of the rights that should be continually asserted and defended

[46]NGO MGs Representative, Women, NGO, and Indigenous Peoples Major Group Press Conference, 4 May 2012.

is the right to voice diverse positions, even in protest, in order to challenge hegemonic paradigms and to shift the terrain of negotiation, lest activists continue to find themselves enlisted in defending the status quo.

Acknowledgements

We would like to thank private donor Ron Oehl, the Mount Holyoke College Dean of Faculty and the Miller Worley Center for the Environment for their generous support of our research, Emma Puka-Beals for her assistance with data collection, and Eskedar Gessesse, Iman Abubaker and Shreeya Joshi for their help in data analysis and editing. We also thank two anonymous reviewers for their helpful suggestions. Finally, we extend our appreciation to the numerous people who shared their time and insights with us during our research. Their dedication and willingness to put in long hours in order to improve global environmental governance is inspiring.

References

Anand, P. 2007. Right to water and access to water: an assessment. *Journal of International Development* 19, no. 4: 511–526.

Arsel, M., and B. Büscher. 2012. Nature Inc.: changes and continuities in neoliberal conservation and market-based environmental policy. *Development and Change* 43, no. 1: 53–78.

Bakker, K. 2007. The 'commons' versus the 'commodity': alter-globalization, anti-privatization and the human right to water in the global south. *Antipode* 39, no. 3: 430–455.

Banisar, D., S. Parmar, L. de Silva, and C. Excell. 2012. Moving from principles to rights: Rio 2012 and access to information, public participation, and justice. *Sustainable Development Law and Policy* 12, no. 3: 8–66.

Barbier, E.B. 2009. Rethinking the economic recovery: a global green new deal. Report prepared for the Economics and Trade Branch in the Division of Technology Industry and Economics of the United Nations Environment Programme. Geneva: United Nations Environment Programme.

Borras, S.M., and J.C. Franco. 2013. Global land grabbing and political reaction 'from below'. *Third World Quarterly* 34, no. 9: 1723–1747.

Borras, S.M., J.C. Franco, and C. Wang. 2013. The challenge of global governance of land grabbing: changing international agricultural context and competing political views and strategies. *Globalizations* 10, no. 1: 161–179.

Borras, S.M., R. Hall, I. Scoones, B. White, and W. Wolford. 2011. Towards a better understanding of global land grabbing: an editorial introduction. *The Journal of Peasant Studies* 38, no. 2: 209–216.

Bracking, S. 2012. How do investors value environmental harm/care? Private equity funds, development finance institutions and the partial financialization of nature-based industries. *Development and Change* 43, no. 1: 271–293.

Brockington, D., and R. Duffy. 2010. Capitalism and conservation: the production and reproduction of biodiversity conservation. *Antipode* 42, no. 3: 469–484.

Brosius, J.P., and L.M. Campbell. 2010. Collaborative event ethnography: conservation and development trade-offs at the Fourth World Conservation Congress. *Conservation and Society* 8, no. 4: 245–255.

Brown, M.F. 1996. On resisting resistance. *American Anthropologist* 98, no. 4: 729–735.

Büscher, B., S. Sullivan, K. Neves, J. Igoe, and D. Brockington. 2012. Towards a synthesized critique of neoliberal biodiversity conservation. *Capitalism, Nature, Socialism* 23, no. 2: 4–30.

Campbell, L.M., C. Corson, N.J. Gray, K.I. MacDonald, and J.P. Brosius. 2014. Collaborative event ethnography at the 10th conference of the parties to the Convention on Biological Diversity. *Global Environmental Politics* 14, no. 3: 1–20.

Campbell, L.M., N.J. Gray, L.W. Fairbanks, J.J. Silver, and R.L. Gruby. 2013. Oceans at Rio+20. *Conservation Letters* 6, no. 6: 439–447.

Chapin, M. 2004. A challenge to conservationists. *World Watch* 17, no. 6: 17–30.

Chatterjee, P., and M. Finger. 1994. *The earth brokers: power, politics and world development.* New York, NY: Routledge.

Climate and Capitalism. 2011. *Alba nations declare: nature has no price!* [Accessed June 28 2013]. http://climateandcapitalism.com/2010/11/15/alba-nations-declare-nature-has-no-price/
Cooke, B., and U. Kothari, eds. 2001. *Participation: The new tyranny?* London: Zed Books.
Corson, C., and K.I. MacDonald. 2012. Enclosing the global commons: The Convention on Biological Diversity and green grabbing. *Journal of Peasant Studies* 39, no. 2: 263–283.
Corson, C., K.I. MacDonald, and L.M. Campbell. 2014. Capturing the personal in politics: ethnographies of global environmental governance. *Global Environmental Politics* 14, no. 3: 21–40.
Corson, C., K.I. MacDonald, and B. Neimark. 2013. Grabbing 'green:' markets, environmental governance and the materialization of natural capital. *Human Geography* 6, no. 1: 1–15.
Cotula, L. 2013. The new enclosures? Polanyi, international investment law and the global land rush. *Third World Quarterly* 34, no. 9: 1605–1629.
Cúpula dos Povos. 2012. *The People's Summit: what is it?* http://cupuladospovos.org.br/en/what-is-it/ (Accessed December 12, 2013).
Death, C. 2010. *Governing sustainable development: partnerships, protests and power at the world summit.* Oxon: Routledge.
Doolittle, A.A. 2010. The politics of indigeneity: indigenous strategies for inclusion in climate change negotiations. *Conservation and Society* 8, no. 4: 286–291.
Dowie, M. 2005. Conservation refugees: when protecting nature means kicking people out. *Orion* November/December: 16–27.
Duffy, R. 2006. Non-governmental organisations and governance states: the impact of transnational environmental management networks in Madagascar. *Environmental Politics* 15, no. 5: 731–749.
Duffy, R. 2013. Global environmental governance and north-south dynamics: the case of the CITES. *Environment and Planning C: Government and Policy* 31, no. 2: 222–239.
Edelman, M., and C. James. 2011. Peasants' rights and the UN system: Quixotic struggle? Or emancipatory idea whose time has come? *The Journal of Peasant Studies* 38, no. 1: 81–108.
Edwards, M., and D. Hulme. 1996. Too close for comfort? The impact of official aid on nongovernmental organizations. *World Development* 24, no. 6: 961–973.
Fairhead, J., M. Leach, and I. Scoones. 2012. Green grabbing: a new appropriation of nature? *Journal of Peasant Studies* 39, no. 2: 237–261.
Federal Democratic Republic of Ethiopia. 2011. *Ethiopia's climate-resilient green economy: green economy strategy.* Addis Ababa, Ethiopia: Environmental Protection Authority.
Ferguson, J., and A. Gupta. 2002. Spatializing states: toward an ethnography of neoliberal governmentality. *American Ethnologist* 29, no. 4, 981–1002.
Fisher, W.F. 1997. Doing good? The politics and antipolitics of NGO practices. *Annual Review of Anthropology* 26: 439–464.
Ford, L.H. 2003. Challenging global environmental governance: social movement agency and global civil society. *Global Environmental Politics* 3, no. 2: 120–134.
Franco, J.C., L. Mehta, and G.J. Veldwisch. 2013. The global politics of water grabbing. *Third World Quarterly* 34, no. 9: 1651–1675.
Golay, C., and I. Biglino. 2013. Human rights responses to land grabbing: a right to food perspective. *Third World Quarterly* 34, no. 9: 1630–1650.
Gramsci, A. 2010 [1971]. *Selections from the prison notebooks.* Translation by Q. Hoare and G.N. Smith. New York: International Publishers.
Hart, G. 2001. Progress reports - Development critiques in the 1990s: culs de sac and promising paths. *Progress in Human Geography* 25, no. 4: 649–658.
Harvey, D. 2003. *The new imperialism.* Oxford: Oxford University Press.
Hollander, J.A., and R.L. Einwohner. 2004. Conceptualizing resistance. *Sociological Forum* 19, no. 4: 533–554.
Huberman, D. 2010. *A guidebook for IUCN's thematic programme area on greening the world economy.* Gland, Switzerland: IUCN.
Ibon International, Vitae Civilis Institute, Stakeholder Forum, Council of Canadians, Consumers International, Sustainlabour, International Trade Union Confederation, CIVICUS, Women in Europe for a Common Future, Ecoropa, Global Ecovillage Network, World Transforming Initiatives, and World Alliance to Transform the United Nations. 2012. *Rights at risk at the United Nations.* http://rio20.net/en/iniciativas/rights-at-risk-at-the-united-nations/ (Accessed May 9, 2013).

Igoe, J., S. Sullivan, and D. Brockington. 2009. Problematising neoliberal biodiversity conservation: displaced and disobedient knowledge. *Current Conservation* 3, no. 3: 4–7.
Kashwan, P. 2013. The politics of rights-based approaches in conservation. *Land Use Policy* 31: 613–626.
Keck, M.E., and K. Sikkink. 1998. *Activists beyond borders: advocacy networks in international politics*. Ithaca, NY: Cornell University Press.
Künnemann, R., and S.M. Suárez. 2013. International human rights and governing land grabbing: a view from global civil society. *Globalizations* 10, no. 1: 123–139.
Lemos, M.C., and A. Agrawal. 2006. Environmental governance. *Annual Review of Environment and Resources* 31, no. 1: 297–325.
MacDonald, K.I., and C. Corson. 2012. 'TEEB begins now': a virtual moment in the production of natural capital. *Development and Change* 43, no. 1: 159–184.
Margulis, M.E., N. McKeon, and S.M. Borras. 2013. Land grabbing and global governance: critical perspectives. *Globalizations* 10, no. 1: 1–23.
McAfee, K. 1999. Selling nature to save it? Biodiversity and green developmentalism. *Environment and Planning D: Society and Space* 17, no. 2: 133–154.
McCarthy, J., and S. Prudham. 2004. Neoliberal nature and the nature of neoliberalism. *Geoforum* 35, no. 3: 275–283.
McKeon, N. 2009. *The United Nations and civil society: legitimating global governance – whose voice?* London, UK: Zed Books.
McKeon, N. 2013. 'One does not sell the land upon which the people walk': land grabbing, transnational rural social movements, and global governance. *Globalizations* 10, no. 1: 105–122.
Meadows, D.H., D.L. Meadows, J. Randers, and W.W. Behrens III. 1972. Limits to growth. A report for the Club of Rome's Project on the Predicament of Mankind. New York.
Mirosa, O., and L.M. Harris. 2012. Human right to water: contemporary challenges and contours of a global debate. *Antipode* 44, no. 3: 932–949.
Mohan, G., and K. Stokke. 2000. Participatory development and empowerment: the dangers of localism. *Third World Quarterly* 21, no. 2: 247–268.
Monbiot, G. 2012. After Rio, we know. Governments have given up on the planet. *The Guardian* 25 June.
Peluso, N.L., and C. Lund. 2011. New frontiers of land control: introduction. *Journal of Peasant Studies* 38, no. 4: 667–681.
Pillay, N. 2012. Open letter from the UN High Commissioner for Human Rights, to all the permanent missions in New York and Geneva.
Quintos, P. *Deleting our rights, bracketing our future: why we need a people's summit at Rio+20*, 2012 [Accessed 14 May 2013]. http://iboninternational.org/page/whats_new/138.
Ribot, J.C., and N.L. Peluso. 2003. A theory of access. *Rural Sociology* 68, no. 2: 153–181.
Rights for Sustainability. 2012. *Reclaiming peoples' rights for a transformative agenda at Rio+20 and beyond* Political Report, January to October 2012 [Accessed 17 June 2013]. http://peoplesgoals.org/download/policy_positions/Reclaiming%20Peoples%20Rights%20for%20a%20Transformative%20Agenda%20at%20Rio20%20and%20Beyond.pdf.
Roth, R.J., and W. Dressler. 2012. Market-oriented conservation governance: the particularities of place. *Geoforum* 43, no. 3: 363–366.
Scherr, S.J., and R.J. Gregg. 2006. Johannesburg and beyond: the 2002 World Summit on Sustainable Development and the rise of partnerships. *Georgetown International Environmental Law Review* 18: 425–490.
Sparke, M. 2008. Political geography – political geographies of globalization III: resistance. *Progress in Human Geography* 32, no. 3: 423–440.
Suarez, D., and C. Corson. 2013. Seizing center stage: ecosystem services, live, at the Convention on Biological Diversity! *Human Geography* 6, no. 1: 64–79.
Suárez, S.M. 2013. The human rights framework in contemporary agrarian struggles. *Journal of Peasant Studies* 40, no. 1: 239–290.
Sullivan, S. 2013. Banking nature? The spectacular financialisation of environmental conservation. *Antipode* 45, no. 1: 198–217.
Tarrow, S. 2005. *The new transnational activism*. Cambridge, UK: Cambridge University Press.
UN. 1972. Report of the United Nations Conference on the Human Environment, 5–16 June, Stockholm.

UN. 1987. *Our common future*. Report of the Brundtland Commission, A/42/427, General Assembly, Development and International Co-operation: Environment.
UN. 2012a. Compilation document for the zero-draft of the Rio+20 outcome document. Compiled by the Secretariat of Rio+20. January 10. http://www.uncsd2012.org/compdocument.html (Accessed January 13, 2015).
UN. 2012b. The future we want. Resolution adopted by the General Assembly on 27 July. A/RES/66/288.
UNEP. 2011. *Towards a green economy: pathways to sustainable development and poverty eradication – a synthesis for policy makers (advanced copy online release).* Nairobi, Kenya: United Nations Environment Programme. http://www.unep.org/GreenEconomy/Portals/93/documents/Full_GER_screen.pdf (Accessed June 28, 2011).
Verzola, P.J., and Paul Quintos. 2011. Green economy: gain or pain for the earth's poor? Policy Brief. Quezon City, Philippines: IBON International.
Webb, C., and T.C. Esakin. 2011. *A green economy for Canada: consulting with Canadians*. Toronto, ON, Canada: Canadian Institute for Environmental Law and Policy.
Wilshusen, P., and K.I. MacDonald. in prep. Fields of green: Corporate sustainability and the production of reform at Rio+20 and beyond.
Wolford, W., S.M. Borras Jr., R. Hall, I. Scoones, and B. White. 2013. Governing global land deals: the role of the state in the rush for land. *Development and Change* 44, no. 2: 189–210.
Young, Z. 1999. NGOs and the Global Environmental Facility: friendly foes? *Environmental Politics* 8, no. 1: 243–267.

Index

For Product Safety Concerns and Information please contact our EU
representative GPSR@taylorandfrancis.com
Taylor & Francis Verlag GmbH, Kaufingerstraße 24, 80331 München, Germany

www.ingramcontent.com/pod-product-compliance
Ingram Content Group UK Ltd.
Pitfield, Milton Keynes, MK11 3LW, UK
UKHW050053200926
475702UK00019B/2812
9780367234928